HOUGHTON MIFFLIN

Spelling and Vocabulary

A Resource for Teaching and Planning

WITHDRAWN

Senior Author
Shane Templeton

Consultant
Donald R. Bear

Consultant
Rosa Maria Peña

HOUGHTON MIFFLIN

BOSTON

Program Reviewers

Dear Teacher and Supervisors,

Knowledge of spelling and vocabulary underlies the efficiency with which students write and read. As students develop spelling knowledge, they are able to expand their vocabulary and improve their reading and communication skills.

In our book, *Words Their Way*, we describe the important research that has documented the developmental nature of word knowledge and the importance of organizing and sequencing instruction based on recognizable developmental phases. We describe a plan and activities for word study based on this research.

Houghton Mifflin Spelling and Vocabulary is based on the findings of this same research. The program provides sustained and systematic instruction and practice that follow the research-based phases of development and our recommendations in *Words Their Way*. Words familiar in reading that are also high-frequency words for writing are grouped into lists that focus on basic spelling principles. Students are guided to an understanding of the regularity in the spelling system at the levels of sound, pattern, and meaning. Recognizing this regularity will help students apply this knowledge to a large number of words rather than try to learn to spell the language one word at a time.

We believe that the instruction and practice with phonics, spelling, vocabulary, and writing in *Houghton Mifflin Spelling and Vocabulary* will foster the skills important for success in all areas of the language arts.

Best wishes for productive and enjoyable word study!

Shane Templeton
Donald R. Bear

ISBN: 0-618-31174-2

12345678910-B-11 10 09 08 07 06 05 04 03 02

Introducing

Houghton Mifflin Spelling and Vocabulary by Shane Templeton

Shane Templeton

Foundation Professor of Curriculum and Instruction; Program Coordinator, Undergraduate and Graduate Program in Literacy Studies; and Associate Director of the Center for Learning and Literacy at the University of Nevada, Reno

The spelling system of English represents sound *and* meaning. Students' spelling knowledge — understanding *how* and *why* letters represent sound and meaning — is a critical part of their overall word knowledge. Recent research has revealed that spelling knowledge is not only a powerful tool for writing — it also plays an important role in students' vocabulary development, reading comprehension, and reading rate and fluency.

Effective spelling instruction addresses three objectives:

- Students learn the major principles and patterns of English spelling.
- Students learn reliable spelling strategies that they can apply to both familiar and unfamiliar words.
- Students become aware of the rich network of spelling-meaning relationships that can significantly extend their vocabulary.

Developmental Phases of Spelling Knowledge

Studies of students' writing and word knowledge reveal that spelling knowledge develops according to the following developmental sequence.

Emergent phase: Students make scribbles on a page, eventually stringing consonants together to represent beginning and ending sounds.

Alphabetic phase: Students match letters with sounds in a left-to-right fashion, as in *BOT* for *boat*.

Within-word pattern phase: Students explore spelling patterns in single-syllable words — for example, the vowel/consonant/silent *e* pattern in *lake, rope,* and *bike.* Students begin to learn about inflectional endings (*-ed* and *-ing* added to single-syllable words) and spelling-meaning relationships as expressed through homophones.

Syllables and affixes phase: Students apply familiar syllable patterns to polysyllabic words; for example, *pillow* (VCCV) vs. *pilot* (VCV). Students explore the effects of combining base words with prefixes and suffixes.

Derivational patterns phase: Students explore the full range of spelling-meaning relationships, including the ways in which word families are derived *(compete/competition/competitive)* and the role of Latin and Greek word parts.

Developmental Phases of Spelling Knowledge

Grade 1	Grade 2	Grade 3	Grade 4	Grade 5	Grade 6	Grade 7	Grade 8
Alphabetic •••••••▶							
	Within-Word Pattern •••▶						
	Syllables and Affixes •••▶						
				Derivational Pattern (Greek and Latin Roots) ••••▶			

The Research Base for Spelling Instruction

Houghton Mifflin Spelling and Vocabulary, a systematic, developmentally appropriate word-study resource, has been created in response to the most current and important research findings.

Because learning to spell is a developmental process, students can learn the regularities of English spelling if instruction is paced to their development: students should move from what they know to what they are developmentally ready to learn. Emphasis should be placed on learning principles and patterns rather than on simply learning individual words — it's important for words that are already known in reading to be grouped together according to a common feature, such as

- *sound*
- *spelling pattern*
- *syllable pattern*
- *word part (base, prefix, suffix)*

Unless words are grouped at appropriate developmental levels according to common features, students are left to memorize the spelling of the entire language — *one word at a time.*

High-frequency words that do not follow predictable principles but that are important for writing should be included for study as well, though these words should not be the sole focus of spelling instruction. It is also helpful for students to add self-selected words that they wish to master, typically words that they have consistently been misspelling in their writing.

In addition, teachers can model for students how to develop strategies for applying spelling knowledge and for extending word knowledge — how to think about spelling during drafting and editing in writing and during reading when figuring out an unfamiliar word.

If I'm unsure how to spell a word, I will try to think of…

- Another word that is similar in sound — I can think of *picture* when I am trying to spell the second syllable of *nature.*
- A word that is related in meaning — I can think of *compose* if I'm uncertain about how to spell the vowel sound in the second syllable of *composition.*

Research strongly supports the notion that words should be examined from a variety of perspectives: Words should be compared and contrasted through

categorization activities, explorations of synonyms and antonyms, analogies, their use in context, and their origins. There should be a variety of opportunities for word play — enjoyable but meaningful explorations of the patterns and meanings of words.

At the intermediate grades and beyond, considerable emphasis should be placed on the exploration of spelling-meaning relationships. Research has shown that many words related in meaning are also related in spelling, despite changes in sound. For example: *sign/signal, please/pleasant, music/musician, impose/imposition.* These spelling-meaning relationships often explain spellings that may seem irrational at first glance.

What does research say about how teachers should integrate spelling and vocabulary instruction?

Understanding these relationships provides students with a powerful source of word knowledge that they can use in their reading and writing. This understanding also lays the groundwork for students' understanding of Greek and Latin word parts — their contribution to the meaning of words, how they combine to form words, and how an understanding of them supports spelling and vocabulary development.

Assessment of Students' Spelling Knowledge

Assessing Spelling Instructional Level

Although each level of *Houghton Mifflin Spelling and Vocabulary* accommodates a range of spelling abilities, it is helpful to determine each student's instructional level.

Prebook Assessment Teachers can duplicate the Prebook Test in the *Teacher's Resource Book* for their grade level and administer it in the multiple-choice format; alternatively, students can write the words as teachers dictate them. Students are at their instructional level for that book if they score between 40% and 90% on the Prebook Test. If any students score below or above those percentages, administer the Prebook Test for the preceding or succeeding levels respectively until the appropriate book for instruction is determined.

Qualitative Inventory of Spelling Knowledge Teachers can use the inventory on page xvi of this **Teacher's Edition** and the Qualitative Spelling Inventory Checklist (available as a blackline master at the back of this TE and also on the enclosed **Teacher's Resources CD-ROM**) to gather more information about where each student falls within a particular developmental level.

The inventory and the checklist will help teachers identify what students have learned, what they are still "using but confusing" and therefore need to study, and what is beyond their present level. The inventory can be given at the beginning, middle, and end of the school year.

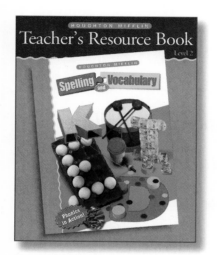

See pages 3–4 for the Prebook Test.

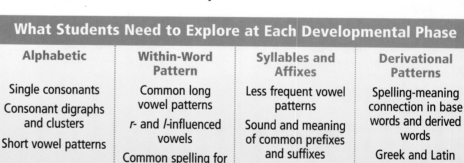

What Students Need to Explore at Each Developmental Phase

Alphabetic	Within-Word Pattern	Syllables and Affixes	Derivational Patterns
Single consonants	Common long vowel patterns	Less frequent vowel patterns	Spelling-meaning connection in base words and derived words
Consonant digraphs and clusters	*r*- and *l*-influenced vowels	Sound and meaning of common prefixes and suffixes	Greek and Latin word parts
Short vowel patterns	Common spelling for diphthongs |ou|, |oi|	Common syllable patterns examined	Absorbed prefixes
	Compound words	More complex prefixes and suffixes	
	Homophones		
	Common inflections		

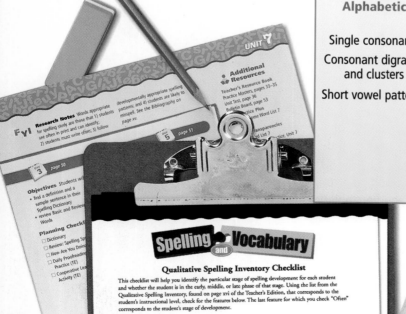

Ongoing Assessment and Weekly Assessment

A periodic assessment on a weekly basis together with a review every few weeks helps to ensure that students retain and apply what they have learned.

Pre-assessment/Self-assessment Weekly assessment begins on Monday with a pre-assessment (pretest) of the words to be studied during the week. The teacher can dictate the pretest to the class, or students can take the pretest independently, using the audiotape.

It is important that students check their own papers. They should first star any words they believe they have misspelled. Then they will compare every word on their list with the correctly spelled words. For any incorrect words, students should follow these steps.

- Look at the correct spelling, write the correct spelling on the same line as the misspelled word, and then check the spelling.

- Write the word a second time. Check this spelling. Then turn the paper over and write the word from memory.

A midweek assessment, often administered in a "buddy" system with students working in pairs, can help students monitor their improvement and focus their study.

Post-assessment At the end of the week, administer a post-assessment with small groups or use the audiotape or the buddy system. Peer or partner review, again, can be powerful, especially when combined with student self-correction. Periodic review of the list words is also important — usually every six weeks.

Assessing Spelling Knowledge in Students' Writing Analyzing students' writing is one of the best ways to gather information about their spelling knowledge and to determine instruction, review, or further study.

There may be several reasons why students misspell words in their writing.

- They may need to develop a "spelling conscience"—that is, learn how to proofread more carefully.

- They may not have completely learned some spelling principles and therefore need additional study.

- They may be "using but confusing" principles they have learned when they apply the principles to new words. This kind of error reveals that students are increasing their word knowledge but need more study or experience with those principles.

- They may be working beyond their spelling instructional level and should be placed at an easier level.

How can teachers conduct this kind of analysis? Here are some suggestions.

1. Periodically assess a writing sample from each student.
2. Circle each misspelled word. Note the type of error.
3. Identify what types of mistakes or spelling principles the student is having difficulty with. Do the mistakes reflect carelessness? an inability to apply learned principles or remember words studied for spelling? confusion about how to apply a principle?
4. Also note words that the student spells correctly to help understand the student's overall word knowledge and phase of development.

Look at the misspelled words in the two writing samples.

Sample A The misspellings in this sample are words that contain elements of words taught in the Within-Word Pattern phase, such as the double consonant in *summer*, the *ie* spelling for the short *e* sound in *friends*, the *igh* spelling for the long *i* sound in *highest*, the closed compound *homemade*, and the *ck* consonant digraph in *tricks*, that would not be studied until grades 2 and 3.

An indicator that this student is grasping the important principles taught at this level are the correctly spelled words with the vowel-consonant-*e* pattern. The correct spellings *show* and *cookies* suggest that this student is looking closely at words and has learned these vowel patterns independently.

Sample B Although the grade 2 writer has made a number of spelling errors, not all of them are a concern at this level. Misspellings such as *Frist, trun, yor,* and *showr* reflect unfamiliarity with patterns that spell *r*-controlled vowel sounds, which is not unexpected at this grade. These patterns are taught later in the Within-Word Pattern phase. The same is true for the final schwa + *l* sounds, as in *little*. The use of the final *e* with a word with the short vowel sound, *rinse,* is another pattern most grade 2 students would not know.

Misspellings of the words *sav* and *tak,* however, are of more concern. They reveal that this student has not learned the pattern vowel-consonant-*e* for these familiar words. Depending on the time of the school year, many students would also have mastered the spellings of the high-frequency words *should, off, when, use,* and *water.* This student would benefit from word sorts focusing on spelling patterns and words that the student has learned and should study the Review Words as well as the Basic Words in each unit.

Standardized/Formal Assessment Standardized or formal assessments of spelling are not as reliable for placement or for determining instructional levels. Students will perform better on these assessments if they have had sustained and systematic spelling instruction in the context of meaningful reading and writing and are familiar with the test formats. *Houghton Mifflin Spelling and Vocabulary* provides experience with formats in pupil book proofreading exercises and tests in the *Teacher's Resource Book*.

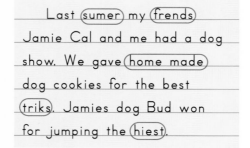

Student Writing Sample A: Grade 1

Student Writing Sample B: Grade 2

Day by Day

Systematic Instruction

Day 1 introduces Basic Words not only in a list but also in complete context sentences. Teaching art reinforces the spelling principle.

Day 2 reinforces the unit Spelling Strategy and provides meaning-based practice.

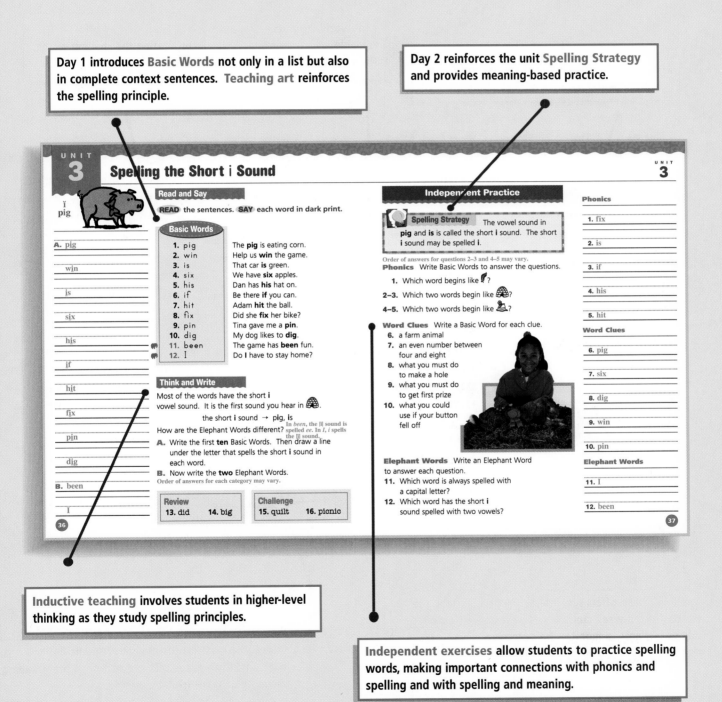

Inductive teaching involves students in higher-level thinking as they study spelling principles.

Independent exercises allow students to practice spelling words, making important connections with phonics and spelling and with spelling and meaning.

Day by Day

Systematic Instruction

Dictionary lessons boost students' proficiency in literacy skills.

Real-world formats — letters, posters, signs, etc. — offer valuable proofreading practice incorporating the spelling words. The unit word list appears again for easy reference.

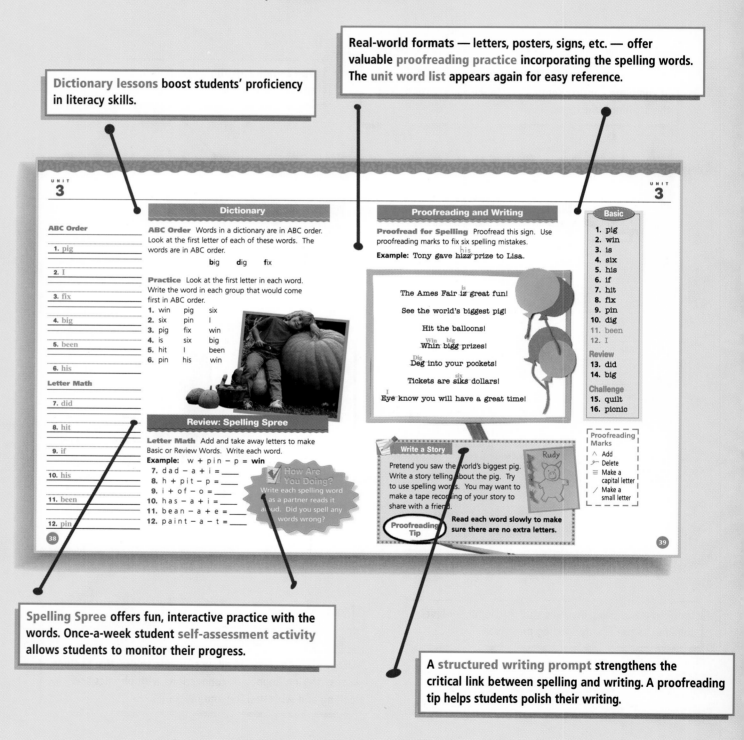

UNIT 3

Dictionary

ABC Order

1. pig
2. I
3. fix
4. big
5. been
6. his

Letter Math

7. did
8. hit
9. if
10. his
11. been
12. pin

ABC Order Words in a dictionary are in ABC order. Look at the first letter of each of these words. The words are in ABC order.

big dig fix

Practice Look at the first letter in each word. Write the word in each group that would come first in ABC order.

1. win pig six
2. six pin I
3. pig fix win
4. is six big
5. hit I been
6. pin his win

Review: Spelling Spree

Letter Math Add and take away letters to make Basic or Review Words. Write each word.

Example: w + pin − p = **win**

7. d a d − a + i = ____
8. h + p i t − p = ____
9. i + o f − o = ____
10. h a s − a + i = ____
11. b e a n − a + e = ____
12. p a i n t − a − t = ____

How Are You Doing?
Write each spelling word as a partner reads it aloud. Did you spell any words wrong?

38

Proofreading and Writing

Proofread for Spelling Proofread this sign. Use proofreading marks to fix six spelling mistakes.

Example: Tony gave hizz prize to Lisa. *(his)*

The Ames Fair iz great fun! *(is)*

See the world's biggest pig!

Hit the balloons!

Whin bigg prizes! *(Win big)*

Deg into your pockets! *(Dig)*

Tickets are siks dollars! *(six)*

Eye know you will have a great time! *(I)*

Write a Story

Pretend you saw the world's biggest pig. Write a story telling about the pig. Try to use spelling words. You may want to make a tape recording of your story to share with a friend.

Rudy

Proofreading Tip Read each word slowly to make sure there are no extra letters.

UNIT 3

Basic

1. pig
2. win
3. is
4. six
5. his
6. if
7. hit
8. fix
9. pin
10. dig
11. been
12. I

Review

13. did
14. big

Challenge

15. quilt
16. picnic

Proofreading Marks

∧ Add
⤻ Delete
≡ Make a capital letter
/ Make a small letter

39

Spelling Spree offers fun, interactive practice with the words. Once-a-week student self-assessment activity allows students to monitor their progress.

A structured writing prompt strengthens the critical link between spelling and writing. A proofreading tip helps students polish their writing.

Bonus Pages

Houghton Mifflin Spelling . . . *and Vocabulary!*
Two Bonus Pages for every lesson expand and enrich students' vocabulary.

Phonics and Spelling activities help students explore letter-sound relationships. **Vocabulary Enrichment activities** increase word power and language development.

Letters, newspapers, journals, and other real-world formats provide practice with high-utility content area vocabulary.

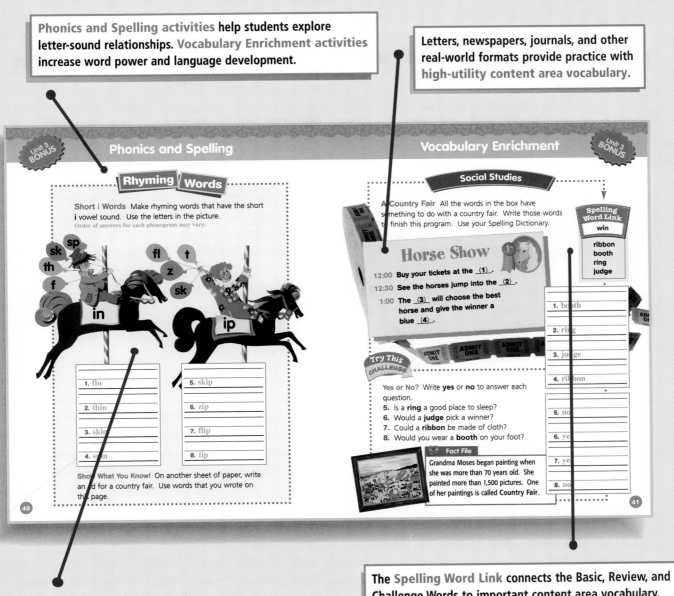

Word-building activities and interactive illustrations engage students in hands-on practice.

The **Spelling Word Link** connects the Basic, Review, and Challenge Words to important content area vocabulary.

Review Units

Spelling words from the Basic Units are reviewed every sixth unit.

Spelling-Meaning Strategy pages help students become familiar with word-family relationships.

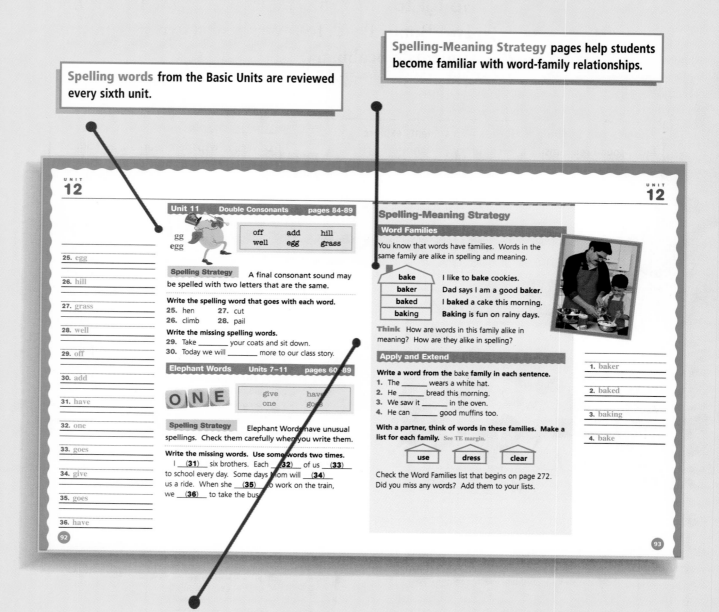

UNIT
12

UNIT
12

Unit 11   Double Consonants   pages 84-89

gg
egg

off	add	hill
well	egg	grass

Spelling Strategy   A final consonant sound may be spelled with two letters that are the same.

Write the spelling word that goes with each word.
25. hen   27. cut
26. climb   28. pail

Write the missing spelling words.
29. Take _____ your coats and sit down.
30. Today we will _____ more to our class story.

Elephant Words   Units 7–11   pages 60–89

ONE

give	have
one	goes

Spelling Strategy   Elephant Words have unusual spellings. Check them carefully when you write them.

Write the missing words. Use some words two times.
I __(31)__ six brothers. Each __(32)__ of us __(33)__ to school every day. Some days Mom will __(34)__ us a ride. When she __(35)__ to work on the train, we __(36)__ to take the bus.

25. egg
26. hill
27. grass
28. well
29. off
30. add
31. have
32. one
33. goes
34. give
35. goes
36. have

92

Spelling-Meaning Strategy
Word Families

You know that words have families. Words in the same family are alike in spelling and meaning.

bake	I like to **bake** cookies.
baker	Dad says I am a good **baker**.
baked	I **baked** a cake this morning.
baking	**Baking** is fun on rainy days.

Think   How are words in this family alike in meaning? How are they alike in spelling?

Apply and Extend

Write a word from the bake family in each sentence.
1. The _____ wears a white hat.
2. He _____ bread this morning.
3. We saw it _____ in the oven.
4. He can _____ good muffins too.

With a partner, think of words in these families. Make a list for each family. See TE margin.

| use | dress | clear |

Check the Word Families list that begins on page 272. Did you miss any words? Add them to your lists.

1. baker
2. baked
3. baking
4. bake

93

Students use higher-order thinking skills to apply what they have learned about spelling and meaning.

Literature and Writing

Mode-specific Writing Process guidelines help students write, evaluate, and revise their compositions.

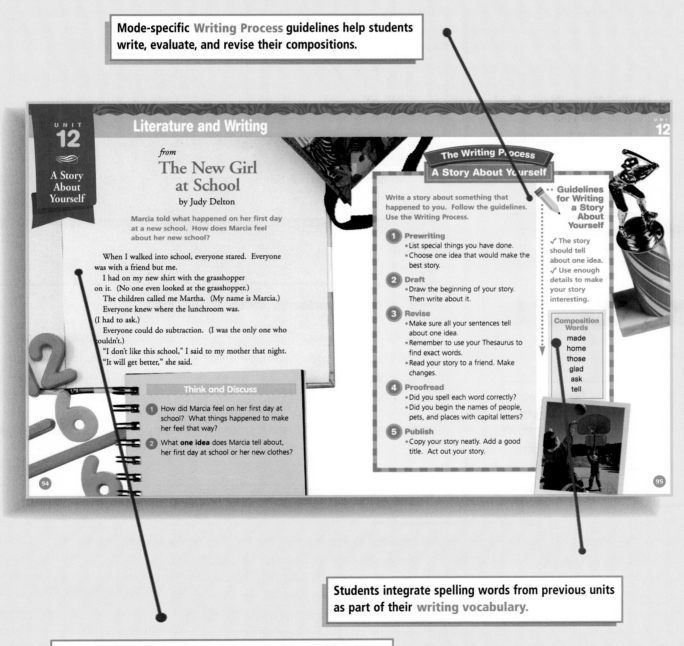

UNIT 12

A Story About Yourself

Literature and Writing

from

The New Girl at School
by Judy Delton

Marcia told what happened on her first day at a new school. How does Marcia feel about her new school?

When I walked into school, everyone stared. Everyone was with a friend but me.

I had on my new shirt with the grasshopper on it. (No one even looked at the grasshopper.)

The children called me Martha. (My name is Marcia.)

Everyone knew where the lunchroom was. (I had to ask.)

Everyone could do subtraction. (I was the only one who couldn't.)

"I don't like this school," I said to my mother that night. "It will get better," she said.

Think and Discuss

1 How did Marcia feel on her first day at school? What things happened to make her feel that way?

2 What **one idea** does Marcia tell about, her first day at school or her new clothes?

The Writing Process
A Story About Yourself

Write a story about something that happened to you. Follow the guidelines. Use the Writing Process.

1 **Prewriting**
• List special things you have done.
• Choose one idea that would make the best story.

2 **Draft**
• Draw the beginning of your story. Then write about it.

3 **Revise**
• Make sure all your sentences tell about one idea.
• Remember to use your Thesaurus to find exact words.
• Read your story to a friend. Make changes.

4 **Proofread**
• Did you spell each word correctly?
• Did you begin the names of people, pets, and places with capital letters?

5 **Publish**
• Copy your story neatly. Add a good title. Act out your story.

Guidelines for Writing a Story About Yourself

✓ The story should tell about one idea.
✓ Use enough details to make your story interesting.

Composition Words
made
home
those
glad
ask
tell

94

95

Students integrate spelling words from previous units as part of their writing vocabulary.

Selections from literature model good writing and inspire students to develop and publish their own compositions using the Writing Process.

Accommodates Individuals Differences

with Resources That Support and Challenge

Personalizing Word Lists

The **test-study-test** method enables both you and your students to personalize the word lists. Select from the Basic, Review, and Challenge Word lists to meet individual needs.

Test
↓
Study
↓
Test

Number of Words Misspelled	Assign
More than 6	first six Basic Words
2–6	all Basic Words
0–1	Challenge Words

For the Basic Units, the Teacher's Book provides additional Basic, Review, and Challenge Words to meet individual needs. Words Often Misspelled are also provided for each unit.

For Students Who Need Extra Support

In the Student Book
- Review Units
- Extra Practice and Review

In the Teacher's Book
- Meeting Individual Needs, Students Acquiring English Activities

In the Teacher's Resource Book
- Practice A and B pages

For Students Who Need Challenge

In the Student Book
- Challenge Words Activities

In the Teacher's Book
- Challenge Words Practice

In the Teacher's Resource Book
- Practice C pages

For Cooperative Learning

In the Student Book
- Phonics and Spelling/ Vocabulary Enrichment pages: Work Together
- Spelling-Meaning Strategy minilessons

In the Teacher's Book
- Cooperative Learning Activities

In the Teacher's Resource Book
- Spelling Games
- Bulletin Board ideas

Teaching Plan

This suggested Teaching Plan shows how the Basic Unit fits into a five-day schedule. Note that the Phonics and Spelling and the Vocabulary Enrichment Bonus Pages are optional and can be used on any day of the week. Use this plan or adapt it to fit your schedule.

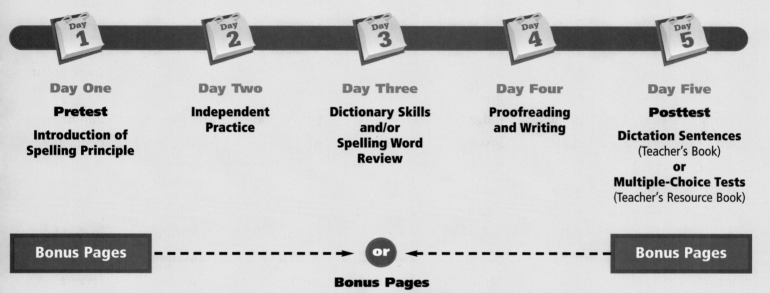

Day One
Pretest
Introduction of Spelling Principle

Day Two
Independent Practice

Day Three
Dictionary Skills and/or Spelling Word Review

Day Four
Proofreading and Writing

Day Five
Posttest
Dictation Sentences (Teacher's Book)
or
Multiple-Choice Tests (Teacher's Resource Book)

Bonus Pages ------> or <------ **Bonus Pages**

Bonus Pages
Use Bonus Pages any day of the week or in conjunction with the Posttest on Day 5.

Selected Bibliography

Gill, J. T. (1992). Focus on research: Development of word knowledge as it relates to reading, spelling, and instruction. *Language Arts, 69*, 444–453.

Invernizzi, M., Abouzeid, M., & Gill, T. (1994). Using students' invented spelling as a guide for spelling instruction that emphasizes word study. *Elementary School Journal,* 95, 155–167.

Read, C., & Hodges, R. (1982). Spelling. In H. Mitzel (ed.), *Encyclopedia of Educational Research.* New York: Macmillan.

Templeton, S. (1991). Teaching and learning the English spelling system: Reconceptualizing method and purpose. *Elementary School Journal,* 92, 185–201.

Templeton, S., & Bear, D.R. (Eds.) (1992). *Development of orthographic knowledge and the foundations of literacy: A memorial Festschrift for Edmund H. Henderson.* Hillsdale, NJ: Lawrence Erlbaum Associates.

Word Lists for Qualitative Spelling Inventory

LEVEL I (Grade 1)	LEVEL II (Grade 2)	LEVEL III (Grade 3)	LEVEL IV (Grade 4)	LEVEL V (Grade 5)	LEVEL VI (Grade 6)	LEVEL VII (Grade 7)	LEVEL VIII (Grade 8)
bump	batted	find	square	enclosed	absence	illiteracy	meddle
not	such	paint	hockey	piece	civilize	communicate	posture
with	once	crawl	helmet	novel	accomplish	irresponsible	knuckle
trap	chop	dollar	allow	lecture	prohibition	succeed	succumb
chin	milk	knife	skipping	pillar	pledge	patience	newsstand
bell	funny	mouth	ugly	confession	sensibility	confident	permissible
shade	start	fought	hurry	aware	official	analyze	transparent
pig	glasses	comb	bounce	loneliest	inspire	tomatoes	assumption
drum	hugging	useful	lodge	service	permission	necessary	impurities
hid	named	circle	fossil	loyal	irrelevant	beret	pennant
father	pool	early	traced	expansion	conclusion	unbearable	boutique
track	stick	letter	lumber	production	invisible	hasten	wooden
pink	when	weigh	middle	deposited	democratic	aluminum	warrant
drip	easy	real	striped	revenge	responsible	miserable	probable
brave	make	tight	bacon	awaiting	accidental	subscription	respiration
job	went	sock	capture	unskilled	composition	exhibition	reverse
sister	shell	voice	damage	installment	relying	device	olympic
slide	pinned	campfire	nickel	horrible	changeable	regretted	gaseous
box	class	keeper	barber	relate	amusement	arisen	subtle
white	boat	throat	curve	earl	conference	miniature	bookkeeping
	story	waving	statement	uniform	advertise	monopoly	fictional
	plain	carried	collar	rifle	opposition	dissolve	overrate
	smoke	scratch	parading	correction	community	equipped	granular
	size	tripping	sailor	discovering	advantage	solemn	endorse
	sleep	nurse	wrinkle	retirement	cooperation	correspond	insistent
			dinner	salute	spacious	emphasize	snorkel
			medal	treasure	carriage	scoundrel	personality
			tanner	homemade	presumption	cubic	prosperous
			dimmed	conviction	appearance	flexible	
			careful	creature	description	arctic	

See the **Teacher's Resource Disk** for information on administering the Qualitative Spelling Inventory.

Source: E. H. Henderson and M. Invernizzi, "Qualitative Inventory of Word Knowledge." McGuffey Reading Center, University of Virginia. Used with permission.

HOUGHTON MIFFLIN

Spelling and Vocabulary

Senior Author
Shane Templeton

Consultants
Donald R. Bear
Rosa Maria Peña

HOUGHTON MIFFLIN   BOSTON

Acknowledgments

For each of the selections listed below, grateful acknowledgment is made for permission to excerpt and/or reprint original or copyrighted material as follows:

SCRABBLE® and BOGGLE® are registered trademarks of Hasbro Inc. Used by permission of Hasbro Inc. All rights reserved.

Select definitions in the Spelling Dictionary are adapted and reprinted by permission from the following Houghton Mifflin Company publications. Copyright © 1994 THE AMERICAN HERITAGE FIRST DICTIONARY. Copyright © 1994 THE AMERICAN HERITAGE CHILDREN'S DICTIONARY. Copyright © 1994 THE AMERICAN HERITAGE STUDENT DICTIONARY.

Excerpt from *The Book of Giant Stories,* by David L. Harrison. Text copyright © 1972 by David L. Harrison. Reprinted by permission of the author.

Excerpt from *The New Girl at School,* by Judy Delton. Text copyright © 1979 by Judy Delton. Adapted and reprinted by permission of the publisher, Dutton Children's Books, a division of Penguin Books USA Inc.

Excerpt from *A Thousand Pails of Water,* by Ronald Roy. Copyright © 1978 by Ronald Roy. Reprinted by permission of Alfred A. Knopf, Inc.

ISBN: 0-618-31155-6

1 2 3 4 5 6 7 8 9 10-B-11 10 09 08 07 06 05 04 03 02

Contents

Contents

Contents

Contents

Contents

Contents

Contents

9

Picture Clues

Consonant Sounds and Letters

Bb
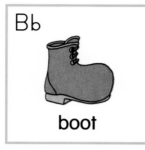
boot

Cc

cat

Dd

duck

Ff

feather

Gg

ghost

Hh

hat

Jj

jack-in-the-box

Kk

kite

Ll

lamp

Mm

monster

Picture Clues

Consonant Sounds and Letters

Nn

nest

Pp
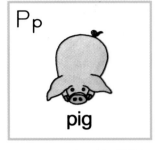
pig

Qq

quarter

Rr

rabbit

Ss

sock

Tt

tiger

Vv

vest

Ww

worm

Yy

yo-yo

Zz

zipper

11

Picture Clues (continued)

Vowel Sounds and Letters

A a

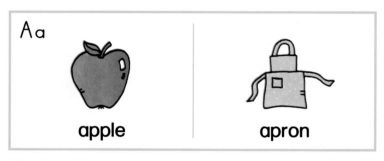

apple   apron

E e

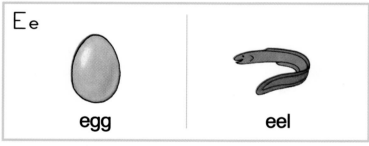

egg   eel

I i

igloo   ice

U u

umbrella

unicorn

O o

octopus   ocean

Phonics

Objectives *Children will*

■ study a photograph

■ identify details in a photograph

Using This Page

- Ask children to describe what the two children in the picture are **doing.** *(getting ready to spell some words)*

- Have children guess which words the children in the picture are going to spell. Write their responses on chart paper. Tell children that they will find out if their guesses are right when they begin the next section.

- Ask children to see how many words they can spell, using the letters in the picture.

About This Section

Phonics is a six-page introductory section. It allows children to experience success in working with words and sounds before they begin their spelling and vocabulary study in the next section, the Word Lists Units.

All the exercises in this section begin with a familiar picture. From a variety of visual clues, children associate a sound and a letter with a given picture and picture name.

Phonics includes three lessons:

- Picture Clue Review
- Consonants in Words
- Short Vowels in Words

These lessons, which are intended for the typical second-grade child during the first few weeks of the school year, provide a transition from the Level 1 book. In addition to reviewing all the Picture Clues presented in Level 1, each lesson focuses on either initial consonants, initial vowels, final consonants, or medial vowels.

Picture Clue Review

Objectives *Children will*

- ■ identify each Picture Clue
- ■ identify the letter that begins each Picture Clue name

Building Background

- Before children begin the exercises in Lesson 1, use pages 10–12 to review the Picture Clue names with children. For selected Picture Clues, ask children to suggest another word that begins with the same sound.

- Alternatively, use tongue twisters to review initial sounds. For example, for the pig Picture Clue, recite this model for children: *Peter Piper picked a peck of pickled peppers.* Ask for a volunteer to repeat your tongue twister.

- Then have volunteers invent tongue-twister sentences for other Picture Clues and letters.

Reviewing Picture Clues

Read the lesson title and the directions aloud to children. Explain that they will write one letter for each Picture Clue. Point out that they will write vowel letters twice (once for the short vowel sound and once for the long).

1   Picture Clue Review

Write the letter that begins each picture clue name.
If you need help, look at pages 10, 11, and 12.

1. g
2. s
3. d
4. a
5. i
6. v
7. n
8. l
9. f
10. e
11. y
12. b
13. u
14. c
15. m
16. o

14

1 Picture Clue Review

PHONICS

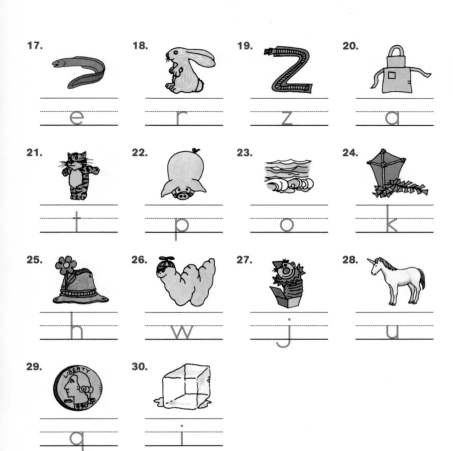

17. ___e___

18. ___r___

19. ___z___

20. ___a___

21. ___t___

22. ___p___

23. ___o___

24. ___k___

25. ___h___

26. ___w___

27. ___j___

28. ___u___

29. ___q___

30. ___i___

15

Consonants in Words

Objectives *Children will*

- identify picture names
- identify and write the initial consonant missing from picture names

Building Background

- Into a plain brown bag, put a pen, a sock, a leaf, and a small book. Explain to children that there are four things in the bag. The name for each thing begins with a different sound.

- Tell children that they will be playing a name game. Ask a volunteer to reach into the bag and identify one object without looking at it. The volunteer guesses the name of the object and then takes it out of the bag to see if the guess is correct.

- Ask children to tell what sound they hear first in the object's name. Have a volunteer say the letter that makes that sound.

- Continue the guessing game until all four objects in the bag have been identified correctly.

Reviewing Consonants

Read the title of Lesson 2 and the directions on page 16 aloud to children. Explain that they will write the letter that spells the first sound they hear in each picture name. Refer children to pages 10–11 if they need help forming the letters.

(continued)

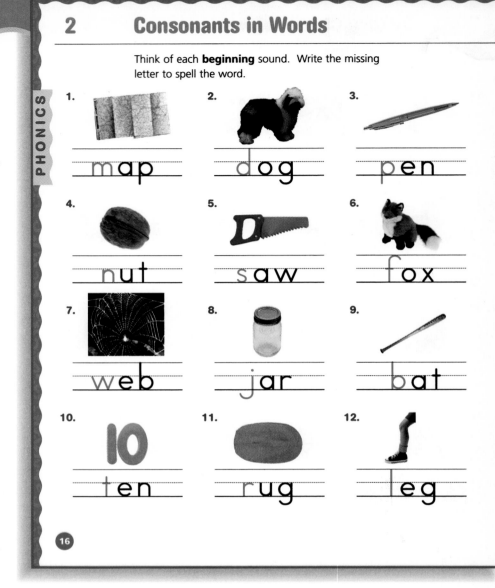

2 Consonants in Words

Think of each **beginning** sound. Write the missing letter to spell the word.

PHONICS

1. map
2. dog
3. pen
4. nut
5. saw
6. fox
7. web
8. jar
9. bat
10. ten
11. rug
12. leg

16

2 Consonants in Words

Think of each **ending** sound. Write the missing letter to spell the word.

1.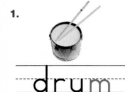
drum

2.
nail

3.
bed

4.
top

5.
pan

6.
bus

7.
six

8.
bag

9.
leaf

10.
tub

11.
cot

12.
car

17

PHONICS

Consonants in Words (continued)

Objectives *Children will*
- identify objects in given picture names
- identify and write the final consonant missing from picture names

Building Background

- Draw a dog on the chalkboard, or show a picture of a dog. Pronounce *dog*. Ask children what consonant sound they hear at the beginning of the word. *(the d sound)*

- Label the drawing *do__*. Say *dog* again. Have a volunteer identify the consonant sound at the end of *dog*. *(the letter g)* Have a volunteer go to the chalkboard and write the letter *g* in the blank.

Reviewing Consonants

Read the directions on page 17 aloud to children. Explain that they will write the letter that spells the last sound they hear in each picture name. Refer children to pages 10–11 if they need help forming the letters.

Short Vowels in Words

Objectives *Children will*

■ identify picture names

■ identify and write the vowel missing from the middle of picture names

Building Background

- Draw a drum on the chalkboard or show a picture of a drum. Pronounce *drum*. Ask children what consonant sound they hear at the end of the word. *(the* m *sound)*

- Label the drawing *dr __ m*. Say *drum* again. Ask children to turn to page 12. Have a volunteer identify the vowel sound in the middle of *drum*. *(the umbrella sound)* Ask children to name the letter that makes the vowel sound they hear in the middle of *drum*. *(the letter* u*)*

- Have a volunteer go to the chalkboard and write the letter *u* in the blank. Repeat this procedure with the words *hat, chin, dot,* and *pen*.

Reviewing Short Vowels

Read the lesson title and the directions aloud. Explain to children that all of the sounds in Lesson 3 are vowel sounds. Tell them that they will write one vowel to complete each picture name.

Point out that in this lesson, the missing letter is in the middle of the word. Refer children to page 12 if they need help forming the letters.

PHONICS

3   Short Vowels in Words

Think of each **middle** sound. Write a, e, i, o, or u to spell the word.

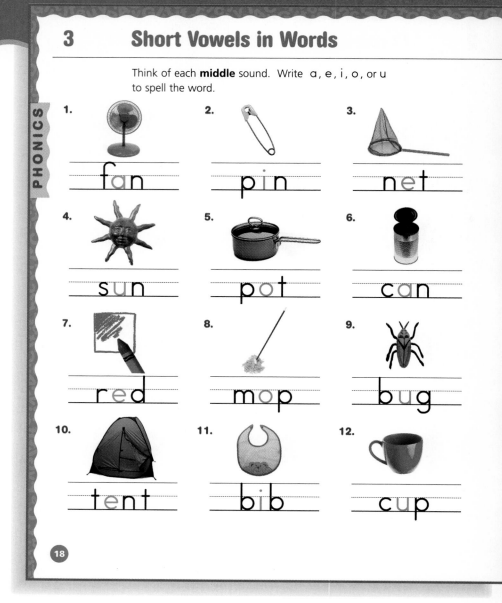

1. fan
2. pin
3. net
4. sun
5. pot
6. can
7. red
8. mop
9. bug
10. tent
11. bib
12. cup

18

3   Short Vowels in Words

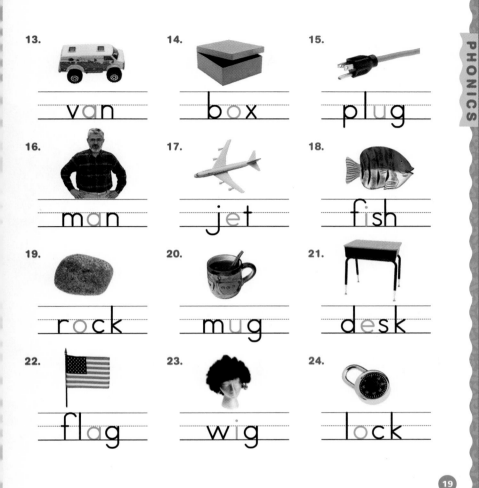

13. van

14. box

15. plug

16. man

17. jet

18. fish

19. rock

20. mug

21. desk

22. flag

23. wig

24. lock

Objectives *Children will*

▨ study a photograph

▨ identify details in a photograph

Using This Page

- Have children look at the picture. Elicit that the two children in the picture are the same ones who appear at the beginning of the Phonics section, page 13.

- Ask children to describe what is happening in the picture. *(The children are spelling words.)* Have a volunteer read each word aloud. Then have children compare these words with their "guess" list. (Refer children to the list they made on page 13.)

Word List Units

About This Section

This section includes thirty-six units, divided into six cycles. Each cycle begins with five Basic Units and ends with a Review Unit.

Basic Units

There are six pages in every Basic Unit. The first four pages focus not only on the list words and the unit principle but also on phonics, thinking skills, vocabulary, proofreading, language arts, dictionary, and writing.

The last two pages of each Basic Unit are **Bonus** pages. Children may choose or be assigned one or both of these pages at any time during the unit.

Review Units

On the first three pages of every Review Unit, there is practice on selected words from the five previous units. The next page, the Spelling-Meaning Strategy, concentrates on word families. The last two pages focus on a particular type of writing, such as a letter.

How to Study a Word

1 Look at the word.

- What letters are in the word?
- What does the word mean? Does it have more than one meaning?

2 Say the word.

- What are the consonant sounds?
- What are the vowel sounds?

3 Think about the word.

- How is each sound spelled?
- What other words have the same spelling pattern?

4 Write the word.

- Think about the sounds and the letters.
- Form the letters correctly.

5 Check the spelling.

- Did you spell the word the same way it is spelled in your word list?
- Do you need to write the word again?

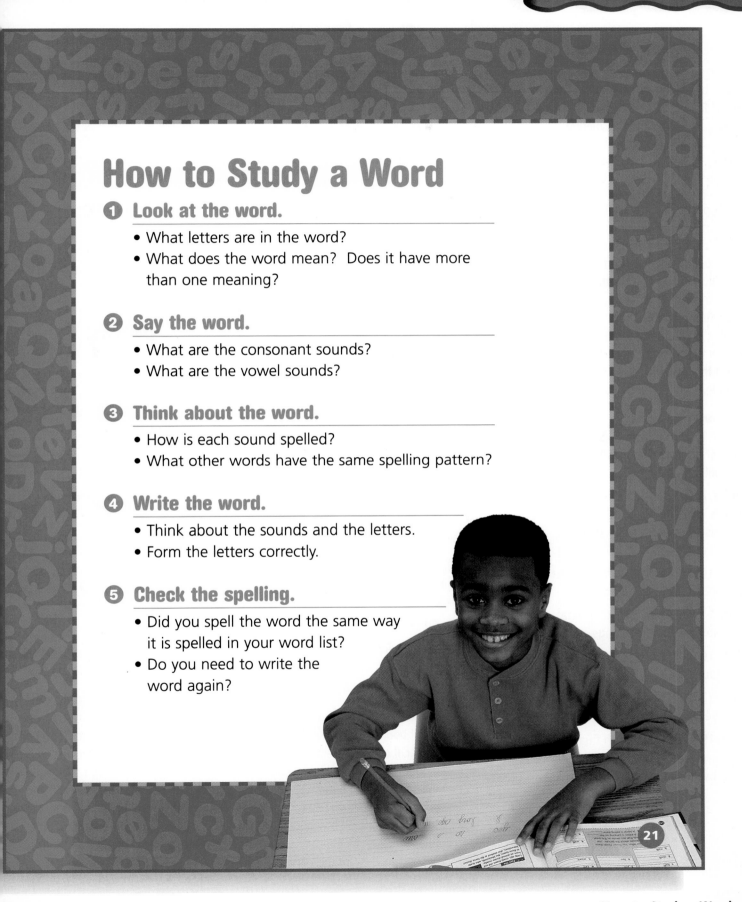

Using These Pages

These pages suggest activities and a game that can be used throughout the year to help children learn their Spelling Words and increase their word knowledge.

Word Sorts

Word sorting activities help children differentiate and remember sounds and spelling patterns. Early in the year, you may want to provide specific sorting criteria for children to use. After they gain more experience with word sorting activities, children may choose their own criteria. You can have them work only with the spelling principle they are currently studying, or you can provide criteria that will help them compare and contrast those principles with ones taught earlier. Some ideas are given below.

Ideas for Word Sorts

- **Units 1, 2, 3, 4, and 5** Sort words with short vowel sounds by sound and by spelling pattern.

- **Units 7, 8, 13, 14, 21, and 25** Sort words with the |ā|, |ī|, |ō|, |yo͞o|, and |ē| sounds by sound and by spelling pattern.

- **Unit 10** Sort words with different spellings for the |k| sound.

- **Unit 11** Sort words by their final double consonant spellings.

- **Unit 16** Sort words with the |sh| and |ch| sounds.

- **Unit 17** Sort words with the *th* and *wh* spelling patterns.

- **Unit 19** Sort words with final |nd|, |ng|, and |nk| sounds by sound and then by spelling pattern.

Activities and Games

Word Sorts

1. For each idea, make 10 word cards. Write a Spelling Word on each card. The words can come from different units.
2. Give your cards to a partner. Tell the ways the words should be sorted. Have your partner sort the words.
3. Check the sort with your partner.

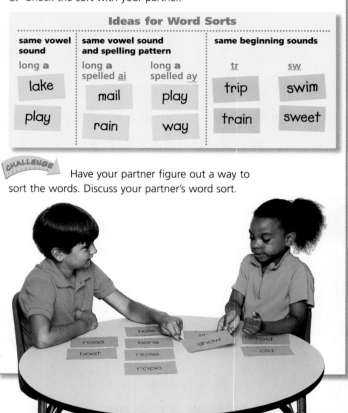

Ideas for Word Sorts

same vowel sound	same vowel sound and spelling pattern		same beginning sounds	
long **a**	long **a** spelled <u>ai</u>	long **a** spelled <u>ay</u>	<u>tr</u>	<u>sw</u>
lake	mail	play	trip	swim
play	rain	way	train	sweet

CHALLENGE Have your partner figure out a way to sort the words. Discuss your partner's word sort.

OPTIONS

Word Study Notebook

Have children divide a notebook into two parts—one part for spelling and one part for vocabulary.

Children can use either a 60-page spiral-bound notebook or a loose-leaf binder. If children use a loose-leaf binder, have them add new pages for the sound(s) and pattern(s) taught in each unit as they go along. If children use a spiral-bound notebook, tell them to use the last 14 pages (7 sheets of paper, 14 sides) for the Vocabulary section and to save the other pages for writing their Spelling Words.

Spelling As children study each unit, have them make at least one page for that unit in their notebook. Write on the chalkboard the sound(s) and the pattern(s) that they should include in their notebook for that unit. If several principles, sounds, or patterns are covered in one unit, more than one page may be necessary so that there is a separate

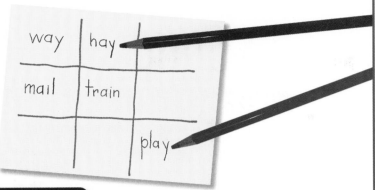

Ticktacktoe

Players: 2 and one caller
You need: paper, 2 pencils of different colors, Spelling Word lists

How to Play

1. One player draws ticktacktoe squares. Players choose who goes first. Each player chooses a pencil.
2. The caller reads a Spelling Word to Player 1. Player 1 spells the word aloud. If correct, Player 1 writes the word in any one of the ticktacktoe squares. If not correct, Player 1 does not write the word.
3. The caller reads a different Spelling Word to Player 2. Player 2 tries to spell the word aloud. If correct, Player 2 writes the word in any open ticktacktoe square. If not correct, Player 2 does not write the word.
4. Players take turns spelling and writing different Spelling Words. The first player who writes three words in a row in any direction wins. The winner becomes the next caller.

Go to www.eduplace.com/kids for more spelling activities. 23

Ideas for Word Sorts (cont.)
- **Unit 20** Sort plural words by whether they add -s or -es.
- **Unit 22** Sort words with the |o͝o| and the |o͞o| sounds.
- **Unit 26** Sort words with the y spelling for the final |ē| sound.
- **Unit 27** Sort words with the |ō| sound by the sound and by the ow and ou spelling patterns.
- **Units 31 and 32** Sort words with the |âr| and the |ôr| sounds by spelling pattern.

Ticktacktoe

Be sure everyone in the class understands how to play ticktacktoe. Explain and demonstrate the game with one child, if necessary. Show children that they can write three words across in one row, three words down in one column, or three words diagonally (left bottom to top right or top left to bottom right) to make a ticktacktoe.

You could also have children play the game with partners. Pairing a stronger speller with one who has difficulty, or with a child who is learning English, would be a good way to help children who need extra practice. Partners could help each other spell the word aloud correctly and take turns writing the correctly spelled word.

 INTERNET CONNECTION See **www.eduplace.com/rdg/hmsv** for printable pages with additional spelling activities and resource materials.

Word Study Notebook (cont.)

part of a page for each principle, sound, or pattern.

For example, for Unit 1, children would have only one section for words with the short **a** sound. For Unit 9, however, they would have two sections: one for words that begin with consonant clusters and one for words that end with consonant clusters.

Have children then sort the Spelling Words by writing each word in the appropriate section. Encourage children to add other words with the same sounds and spelling patterns that they find in their reading materials to the appropriate section in their Word Study Notebook.

Vocabulary Have children write new words that they find in their reading. Tell children to list together words that begin with the same letter. Allow a half page for each letter of the alphabet.

Spelling the Short *a* Sound

WORD LISTS

Spelling

Basic

1. hat
2. bag
3. as
4. am
5. has
6. sad
7. bat
8. ran
9. sat
10. bad
11. was
12. want

Review

13. a
14. can

Challenge

15. mask
16. fabric

Vocabulary

Art: Costumes

cape

gown

vest

crown

Introducing the Lesson

Read Aloud

Write the Basic Words on the board.

Making a Mask

Have you ever said, "I **am** bored. I have nothing to do?" **Was** it a rainy day? Maybe you **sat** and watched the rain **as** it **ran** down the window. When the weather is **bad**, you can pass the time by making a mask.

Take a large paper **bag**, and cut out a half-circle on each side so the **bag** will fit on your shoulders. Make sure your mask **has** two holes cut out for the eyes. Make a **hat**, some hair, a nose, and a happy or **sad** mouth. Glue them to the mask. If you **want** to make ears, glue these two pieces on the top. Add whiskers to make a cat mask, or glue wings on the back to make your mask look like a **bat**. Then color or paint your mask.

Responding Ask children what costume they learned about. (*paper bag mask*) Then ask what spelling word names something worn on the head. (*hat*) Have children name different types of hats.

Day 1 *page 24*

Objectives *Children will*

- take the pretest
- pronounce the list words
- learn about the spelling principle
- analyze words by their short vowel pattern

Planning Checklist

☑ Pretest (TE)

☑ Spelling principle/word list

☐ Review/Challenge Words

☐ Teaching the Principle (TE)

☐ Enrichment (TE)

☐ Additional Spelling Words (TE)

Assessment

Pretest

1. Tim is wearing a <u>hat</u>.
2. I have a pen in my <u>bag</u>.
3. We clap <u>as</u> we play.
4. I <u>am</u> big.
5. She <u>has</u> a new doll.
6. Why is Kim <u>sad</u> today?
7. I have a <u>bat</u> and a ball.
8. Ping <u>ran</u> fast.
9. We <u>sat</u> in our seats.
10. He had a <u>bad</u> day.
11. Rob <u>was</u> reading.
12. The cats <u>want</u> to nap.

Day 2 *page 25*

Objectives *Children will*

- practice spelling list words
- apply spelling strategies
- identify synonyms
- supply missing vowels in Elephant Words

Planning Checklist

☑ Spelling Strategy

☑ Independent Practice

☐ Daily Proofreading Practice (TE)

☐ Informal Assessment (TE)

☐ Extra Support (TE)

☐ Applying Spelling Strategies (TE)

Research Notes When we engage children in meaningful activities involving the careful examination of the spelling of words, we contribute to their ability to perceive and process words during reading. This, in turn, contributes to increasing reading rate and fluency. *See the Bibliography on page xv.*

 Day 3 *page 26*

 Day 4 *page 27*

Day 5 *page 27*

Objectives *Children will*
- learn that a dictionary has words in ABC order
- identify missing letters in alphabetical sequences
- review Basic and Review Words

Planning Checklist
☐ Dictionary
☐ Review: Spelling Spree
☐ How Are You Doing?
☐ Daily Proofreading Practice (TE)
☐ Cooperative Learning Activity (TE)

Objectives *Children will*
- proofread for spelling
- write and proofread an original composition

Planning Checklist
☐ Proofread for Spelling
☐ Write an Invitation
☐ Daily Proofreading Practice (TE)
☐ Challenge Words Practice (TE)
☐ Another Writing Idea (TE)

Objective *Children will*
- take the posttest

Assessment
☐ **Posttest** (TE) *See Day 5*
☐ Unit 1 Test

Additional Resources

Teacher's Resource Book
Prebook Test, pages 3–4
Practice Masters, pages 5–7
Unit Test, page 8
Bulletin Board, page 25

 Practice Plus
Take-Home Word List 1
Games

Spelling Transparencies
Spelling Word List 1
Daily Proofreading Practice, Unit 1
Graphic Organizers

Teacher's Resource Disk
Macintosh® or Windows® software.
Houghton Mifflin

Spelling CD-ROM
Macintosh® or Windows® software.
Houghton Mifflin

Internet
http://www.eduplace.com

Phonics Practice
Houghton Mifflin Phonics
The Listening Corner
Phonics Home Connection

 Meeting Individual Needs
Students Acquiring English

Spanish There is no |ă| sound in Spanish. The letter a in Spanish stands for a sound similar to the |ä| sound in *father*.
Activity Write Basic Words 1–10 on the chalkboard, leaving a blank for the letter a. Say each word, asking children to repeat after you. Have volunteers write in the missing vowels.
Asian Some Asian languages use characters rather than letters, and some of these languages are written differently, such as from right to left.
Activity Help children learn the alphabet by pointing to each letter on letter cards as you sing the ABC song.

Other Activities for Any Day
- Bonus activities from pages 28–29
- Practice Masters (easy, average, challenging)
  Teacher's Resource Book, pages 5–7
- Take-Home Word List 1
  Practice Plus

Day 1

Objectives *Children will*

- take the pretest
- pronounce the list words
- learn about the spelling principle
- analyze words by their short vowel pattern

Teaching the Principle

This lesson teaches the short vowel pattern for the |ă| sound (*a* followed by a consonant sound). Children learn the strategy of thinking of this pattern when they hear the short *a* sound.

To sum up the lesson, ask:

- What kind of letter follows the vowel in each word? (*a consonant*)

Explain that according to legend, elephants never forget. The elephant symbol next to *was* and *want*, therefore, reminds children to pay special attention to the spelling of the Elephant Words because these words do not follow the spelling pattern taught in the unit.

Enrichment

Vocabulary: Multiple Meanings
Have children use a dictionary to look up *bat*, *ran*, and *bad*. Discuss the meanings.

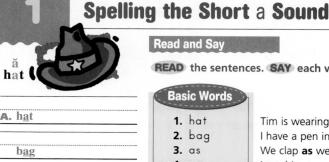

UNIT 1

Spelling the Short *a* Sound

ă
hat

Read and Say

READ the sentences. **SAY** each word in dark print.

Basic Words

1.	hat	Tim is wearing a **hat**.
2.	bag	I have a pen in my **bag**.
3.	as	We clap **as** we play.
4.	am	I **am** big.
5.	has	She **has** a new doll.
6.	sad	Why is Kim **sad** today?
7.	bat	I have a **bat** and a ball.
8.	ran	Ping **ran** fast.
9.	sat	We **sat** in our seats.
10.	bad	He had a **bad** day.
11.	was	Rob **was** reading.
12.	want	The cats **want** to nap.

A. h<u>a</u>t

b<u>a</u>g

<u>a</u>s

<u>a</u>m

h<u>a</u>s

s<u>a</u>d

b<u>a</u>t

r<u>a</u>n

s<u>a</u>t

b<u>a</u>d

B. was

want

24

Think and Write

Most of the words have the short **a** vowel sound. It is the first sound you hear in 🍎.

the short **a** sound → h**a**t, **a**s

How are the Elephant Words different?

The vowel a does not spell the |ă| sound in was and want.

A. Write the first **ten** Basic Words. Then draw a line under the letter that spells the short **a** sound in each word.

B. Now write the **two** Elephant Words.

Order of answers for each category may vary.

Review		Challenge	
13. a	14. can	15. mask	16. fabric

TEACHING OPTIONS

Meeting Individual Needs
Word Lists

You may want to assign Basic Words 1–5, the Elephant Words, and the Review Words to children who misspelled more than five words on the pretest. Assign the Challenge Words as appropriate. (You may want to have children write sentences, using the Challenge Words.)

Additional Spelling Words

Basic	Challenge	Words Often Misspelled
jam	apple	you
cab	rabbit	your
lap	plant	
ant	swam	
gas	patch	
	panda	

Home/School Involvement
Take-Home Word List • Goal-Setting

Have children set goals for the week on Take-Home Word List 1.

TRB Practice Master: easy   5

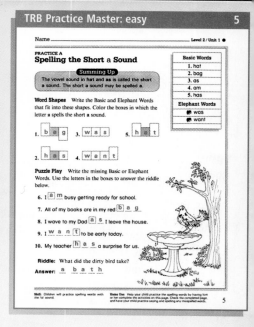

Independent Practice

Spelling Strategy The vowel sound in **hat** and **as** is called the short **a** sound. The short **a** sound may be spelled **a**.

Order of answers for each question may vary.

Phonics Write Basic Words to answer the questions.

1–2. Which two words begin like ?

3–5. Which three words rhyme with ? cat

Word Meaning Write the Basic Word that means the same or almost the same as each word below.

6. owns
7. unhappy
8. awful
9. raced
10. sack

Elephant Words Think of the missing letter in each Elephant Word. Write each word.

11. w __ nt **12.** w __ s

Phonics

1. as

2. am

3. hat

4. bat

5. sat

Word Meaning

6. has

7. sad

8. bad

9. ran

10. bag

Elephant Words

11. want

12. was

25

Objectives *Children will*

- practice spelling list words
- apply spelling strategies
- identify synonyms
- supply missing vowels in Elephant Words

Daily Proofreading Practice

I **im** going to the park. (*am*)

Where **wuz** Frank hiding? (*was*)

Meeting Individual Needs

visual/oral/auditory

Extra Support Check Independent Practice to determine who needs extra support. Write *set/sat, hat/hot, bug/bag,* and *ran/run* on individual word cards. Say each pair, asking children to clap when they hear the |ă| sound. Then post the cards. As you say each word, volunteers take turns finding the correct card, then reading and spelling the word aloud.

Name _____   Level 2 / Unit 1 ▲

Basic Words
1. hat
2. bag
3. as
4. am
5. has
6. sad
7. bat
8. ran
9. sat
10. bad

Elephant Words
was
want

PRACTICE B
Spelling the Short a Sound

Stairway to the Stars Write the Basic or Elephant Word for each clue.

1. → rested
2. ↓ a cap
3. → owns
4. ↓ used to be
5. → to wish
6. ↓ a wooden stick
7. → awful
8. ↓ unhappy

What Word Am I? Write the letter for each clue to find a Basic Word. Then write the Basic Words.

9. My first letter is in **bed**, but not in **led**.
My second letter is in **cat**, but not in **cut**.
My third letter is in **peg**, but not in **pet**.

9. ____bag____

10. My first letter is in **at**, but not in **it**.
My second letter is in **him**, but not in **hid**.

10. ____am____

11. My first letter is in **an**, but not in **on**.
My second letter is in **is**, but not in **it**.

11. ____as____

12. My first letter is in **red**, but not in **bed**.
My second letter is in **tan**, but not in **ten**.
My third letter is in **sun**, but not in **sum**.

12. ____ran____

b
a
g

a
m

a
s

r
a
n

Skill: Children will practice spelling words with the |ă| sound.

Home Use: Help your child practice the spelling words by having him or her complete the activities on this page. Check the completed page, and have your child practice saying and spelling any misspelled words.

6

Applying Spelling Strategies
To Spell New Words

- Read aloud: **The hot wax dripped down the candle.**
- Have children attempt to spell *wax* on their Have-a-Go charts.

- Model the following strategies as children try to spell *wax*.

> I hear the sound for *w* that I hear at the beginning of *worm*.

> The |ks| sound could be spelled *ks* or *x*. I'll have to check a dictionary.

wax

> This word has the short *a* sound. The short *a* sound is probably spelled *a*.

Day 3

Objectives *Children will*

- learn that a dictionary has words in ABC order
- identify missing letters in alpha-betical sequences
- review Basic and Review Words

Daily Proofreading Practice

We **satt** on the grass. (*sat*)
My mom **haz** a new job. (*has*)

UNIT 1

Dictionary

ABC Order The letters of the alphabet are in **ABC order**. You use ABC order to find words in a dictionary.

a b c d e f g h i j k l m
n o p q r s t u v w x y z

Practice Write the missing letters. Use ABC order.

1. o p __q__   **3.** f __g__ h   **5.** __t__ u v

2. d e __f__   **4.** v __w__ x   **6.** __k__ l m

Review: Spelling Spree

Vowel Swap Change the vowel in each word to make a Basic Word. Write each word.

7. bug   **10.** sit   **13.** went
8. is   **11.** bed   **14.** his
9. but   **12.** run

Vowel Swap

7. bag
8. as
9. bat
10. sat
11. bad
12. ran
13. want
14. has

26

How Are You Doing? Write the spelling words in ABC order. Practice with a partner any words you spelled wrong.

TEACHING **OPTIONS**

Cooperative Learning Activity
Word Sort
visual/oral/kinesthetic

Have partners write their spelling words and other short *a* words they know on word cards. Partners can then sort the words into groups, using categories that they determine. For example, children might sort the words by the number of letters, the beginning or ending sounds, the part of speech, or the meaning of the word. After completing one sort, have partners read the words in each group. Then suggest they try to sort the words another way, using different categories.

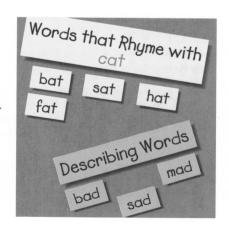

Words that Rhyme with *cat*
bat sat hat fat

Describing Words
bad sad mad

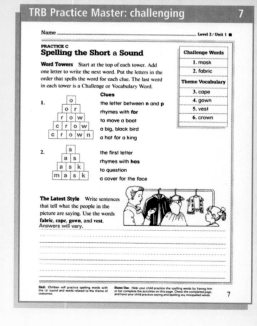

Name _____   Level 2 / Unit 1

PRACTICE C
Spelling the Short a Sound

Word Towers Start at the top of each tower. Add one letter to write the next word. Put the letters in the order that spells the word for each clue. The last word in each tower is a Challenge or Vocabulary Word.

Challenge Words
1. mask
2. fabric

Theme Vocabulary
3. cape
4. gown
5. vest
6. crown

Clues

1.
o
o r
r o w
c r o w
c r o w n

the letter between n and p
rhymes with **for**
to move a boat
a big, black bird
a hat for a king

2.
a
a s
a s k
m a s k

the first letter
rhymes with **has**
to question
a cover for the face

The Latest Style Write sentences that tell what the people in the picture are saying. Use the words **fabric**, **cape**, **gown**, and **vest**.
Answers will vary.

Skill Children will practice spelling words with the /a/ sound and words related to the theme of costumes.   **Home Use:** Help your child practice the spelling words by having him or her complete the activities on this page. Check the completed page, and have your child practice saying and spelling his misspelled words.

7

Proofreading and Writing

Proofread for Spelling Proofread this play that Alexis wrote. Use proofreading marks to fix six spelling mistakes.

Example: Hilda haz̶ a funny hat.
    has

HILDA'S FLAT HAT

Hilda: Oh, I em̶ so sadė!
              am   *sad*

Henry: I kaṅ tell. What happened?
              can

Hilda: I sat down in uḣ chair.
                           a

Henry: Is that so bad?

Hilda: My bag wuz̶ on the chair!
                    was

Henry: It could be worse.

Hilda: It is! My heṫ was in the bag!
                    hat

Write an Invitation

Write an invitation to a costume party. Tell the day, the time, and the place. Try to use spelling words. Draw a picture to go with your invitation.

Proofreading Tip

Remember to read your writing again one line at a time.

27

Basic

1. hat
2. bag
3. as
4. am
5. has
6. sad
7. bat
8. ran
9. sat
10. bad
11. was
12. want

Review

13. a
14. can

Challenge

15. mask
16. fabric

Proofreading Marks

∧ Add
ℐ Delete
≡ Make a capital letter
/ Make a small letter

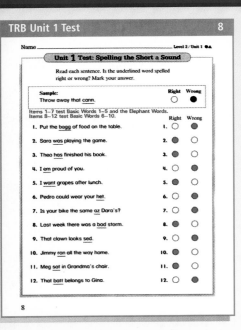

Meeting Individual Needs

Challenge Words Practice
Children can make a concept web for each Challenge Word, writing a Challenge Word in the center of each web and related words in the outer circles. Encourage them to write sentences using words from their webs.

Another Writing Idea Have children draw and write about a costume they would like to wear. Encourage them to use spelling words.

Day 4

Objectives *Children will*
■ proofread for spelling
■ write and proofread an original composition

Daily Proofreading Practice
They **wont** to play at the beach. (*want*)
Lucy put the toys in a **bagg**. (*bag*)

Day 5 Posttest

Sentences 1–5 test the first five Basic Words. Sentences 6–10 test the next five Basic Words. Sentences 11–12 test the Elephant Words.

Basic Words
1. She <u>has</u> a sled.
2. Jim likes the <u>hat</u>.
3. I <u>am</u> in the play.
4. We will get the <u>bag</u>.
5. I clap <u>as</u> you ride.
6. Pam <u>ran</u> with us.
7. My <u>bat</u> is red.
8. They <u>sat</u> by me.
9. He is a <u>sad</u> man.
10. The game is not <u>bad</u>.
11. It <u>was</u> not his.
12. I <u>want</u> the toy.

Review Words
13. Do you have <u>a</u> kite?
14. They <u>can</u> play with us.

Challenge Words
15. Her dress was made from red <u>fabric</u>.
16. The clown wore a funny <u>mask</u>.

These pages can be used at any time during the study of this unit.

Objectives *Children will*

- build words with short *a* phonograms
- identify rhyming words

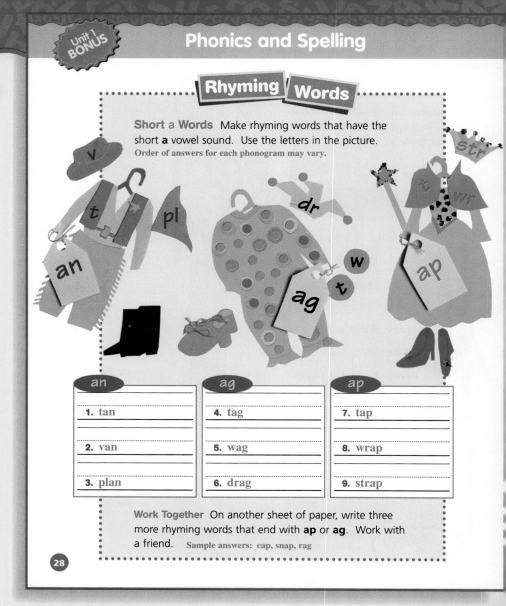

Rhyming Words

Short a Words Make rhyming words that have the short **a** vowel sound. Use the letters in the picture.
Order of answers for each phonogram may vary.

an	ag	ap
1. tan	4. tag	7. tap
2. van	5. wag	8. wrap
3. plan	6. drag	9. strap

Work Together On another sheet of paper, write three more rhyming words that end with **ap** or **ag**. Work with a friend. Sample answers: cap, snap, rag

28

EXTENSION OPTIONS

Learning Center Activity

visual/oral/kinesthetic

More Rhyming Words Have partners use letter cards or letter tiles to build more words that end with the phonogram *-ap*. Suggest they begin with the word *tap*, changing the initial consonant to make new words. Have partners record the words they make in a list then read their list aloud.

More -ap Words		
cap	map	scrap
chap	nap	slap
clap	rap	snap
flap	sap	trap
gap		

Vocabulary Enrichment

Art

Costumes All the words in the box have something to do with costumes. Write those words to finish this diary entry. Use your Spelling Dictionary.

Spelling Word Link

hat

cape
gown
vest
crown

June 4

I went to Sam's costume party dressed as a queen. I had a __(1)__ on my head. My long blue __(2)__ was made of silk. A warm __(3)__ covered my shoulders. My __(4)__ had no sleeves.

1. crown

2. gown

3. cape

4. vest

Try This CHALLENGE

Yes or No? Is the word in dark print used correctly? Write **yes** or **no**.
5. The princess wore a **gown** to the ball.
6. The actor's **vest** kept his arms warm.
7. She wore a **cape** on her feet.
8. The king's **crown** was made of gold.

5. yes

6. no

7. no

8. yes

Fact File

Long ago in Greece, actors wore big masks made of heavy cloth. The masks told the people watching the play if the actors were feeling happy or sad.

29

Objectives *Children will*
- expand their vocabulary by using words related to costumes
- show their understanding of the vocabulary words by completing context activities

Day by Day Planner

Vocabulary Checkup

Have children use the vocabulary words in sentences or match the words to the definitions below.

1. a head covering often made of gold and jewels *crown*
2. a sleeveless jacket worn over a shirt *vest*
3. a warm coat for wearing over the shoulders *cape*
4. a long, fancy dress worn by a woman *gown*

Fact File

Greek Masks

Point out Greece on a world map. Explain that in ancient Greece all the actors were men. Masks allowed each actor to play many roles, including female ones. Masks were first made of cloth or linen. Later, they were made of cork, leather, or papier-mâché.

Integrating Literature

Easy	Average	Challenging
The Best Bug to Be *by Dolores Johnson* Kelly gets a part as a bumblebee in the school play.	**Arthur's Halloween Costume** *by Lillian Hoban* Arthur can't decide what to be for Halloween.	**Dazzling Disguises and Clever Costumes** *by Angela Wilkes* A costume how-to guide.
Carnival *by Robin Ballard* Didi's friend Emma dresses as a butterfly for the carnival parade.	**Amazing Grace** *by Mary Hoffman* Grace wants to be Peter Pan in the school play.	**Sam Sunday and the Mystery at the Ocean Beach Hotel** *by Robin Supraner* Sam's friends wear disguises to surprise him.

Spelling the Short *e* Sound

WORD LISTS

Spelling

Basic

1. pet
2. leg
3. ten
4. yes
5. bed
6. help
7. set
8. went
9. pen
10. wet
11. any
12. said

Review

13. get
14. red

Challenge

15. elk
16. penguin

Vocabulary

Science: Unusual Pets

snail
parrot
hamster
lizard

Introducing the Lesson

Read Aloud

Write the Basic Words on the board.

Hedgehogs

Have you ever had a hedgehog as a **pet**? If you **said yes**, you know hedgehogs are easy to tame. Some live to be **ten** years old. A hedgehog is covered with needle-like points called "spines." When frightened, it curls itself into a spiny ball, with not even a **leg** showing.

Hedgehogs like to search for slugs in **wet** gardens. A hedgehog may be kept in a large **pen**, where it will dig a hole for its **bed**. To **help** it get used to you, **set** a dish of food in its **pen** and feed your **pet** by hand. **Any** snail or insect will do. Once it was tamed, even if your hedgehog **went** away, it would surely be home by dinner!

Responding Ask children what facts they remember about the hedgehog. Then reread the selection aloud, having children raise their hands when they hear a Basic Word.

Day 1 *page 30*

Objectives *Children will*

- take the pretest
- pronounce the list words
- learn about the spelling principle
- analyze words by their short vowel pattern

Planning Checklist

☑ Pretest (TE)
☑ Spelling principle/word list
☐ Review/Challenge Words
☐ Teaching the Principle (TE)
☐ Enrichment (TE)
☐ Additional Spelling Words (TE)

Assessment

Pretest

1. My pet dog likes to run.
2. He has a cut on his leg.
3. Ben has ten books.
4. Did she say yes?
5. The cat is on my bed.
6. Who will help me?
7. Luis set the pot down.
8. We went for a ride.
9. He has my pen.
10. Did the man get wet?
11. Do you have any games?
12. I said no.

Day 2 *page 31*

Objectives *Children will*

- practice spelling list words
- apply spelling strategies
- complete analogies
- supply missing vowels in Elephant Words

Planning Checklist

☑ Spelling Strategy
☑ Independent Practice
☐ Daily Proofreading Practice (TE)
☐ Informal Assessment (TE)
☐ Extra Support (TE)
☐ Applying Spelling Strategies (TE)

Management Tip You may want to introduce the Bonus pages to children on Day 1 or Day 2, and then have children work on these pages during their spelling time throughout the week.

 Day 3 *page 32*

 Day 4 *page 33*

 Day 5 *page 33*

Objective *Children will*
- review Basic and Review Words

Planning Checklist
☐ Review: Spelling Spree
☐ How Are You Doing?
☐ Daily Proofreading Practice (TE)
☐ Ongoing Assessment (TE)

Objectives *Children will*
- proofread for spelling, capitalization, and end marks
- write and proofread an original composition

Planning Checklist
☐ Proofread: Spelling and Telling Sentences
☐ Write a Description
☐ Daily Proofreading Practice (TE)
☐ Challenge Words Practice (TE)
☐ Another Writing Idea (TE)

Objective *Children will*
- take the posttest

Assessment
☐ **Posttest** (TE) *See Day 5*
☐ Unit 2 Test

 **Additional Resources**

Teacher's Resource Book
Practice Masters, pages 9–11
Unit Test, page 12
Bulletin Board, page 25

Practice Plus
Take-Home Word List 2
Games

Spelling Transparencies
Spelling Word List 2
Daily Proofreading Practice, Unit 2
Graphic Organizers

Teacher's Resource Disk
Macintosh® or Windows® software. Houghton Mifflin

Spelling CD-ROM
Macintosh® or Windows® software. Houghton Mifflin

Internet
http://www.eduplace.com

Phonics Practice
Houghton Mifflin Phonics
The Listening Corner
Phonics Home Connection

Meeting Individual Needs
Students Acquiring English

Spanish There is no |ĕ| sound in Spanish. Spanish-speaking children may substitute the |ā| sound and spell it e or ae. **Activity** Say *bed, red, met, let, men,* and *hen.* Ask how the words sound alike. Have children say the words with you.

Asian Some children may not know the alphabet. **Activity** Display alphabet cards with upper and lower case letters (*Aa, Bb,* and so on). Have children take turns picking a card and saying the name of the letter on the card.

Other Activities for Any Day

- Bonus activities from pages 34–35
- Practice Masters (easy, average, challenging)
  Teacher's Resource Book, pages 9–11
- Take-Home Word List 2
  Practice Plus

Day 1

Objectives *Children will*

- take the pretest
- pronounce the list words
- learn about the spelling principle
- analyze words by their short vowel pattern

Teaching the Principle

This lesson teaches the short vowel pattern for the |ĕ| sound (e followed by a consonant or a consonant cluster). Children learn the strategy of thinking of this pattern when they hear the short e sound.

To sum up the lesson, ask:

- What vowel spells the short e sound in each word? *(the vowel e)*
- What follows the vowel e in each word? *(a consonant or a consonant cluster)*

Enrichment

Vocabulary: Multiple Meanings

Have children use a dictionary to look up *pet, leg, set,* and *pen*. Discuss the different meanings.

UNIT 2 Spelling the Short e Sound

Read and Say

READ the sentences. **SAY** each word in dark print.

Basic Words

1.	pet	My **pet** dog likes to run.
2.	leg	He has a cut on his **leg**.
3.	ten	Ben has **ten** books.
4.	yes	Did she say **yes**?
5.	bed	The cat is on my **bed**.
6.	help	Who will **help** me?
7.	set	Luis **set** the pot down.
8.	went	We **went** for a ride.
9.	pen	He has my **pen**.
10.	wet	Did the man get **wet**?
🐘 11.	any	Do you have **any** games?
🐘 12.	said	I **said** no.

A. pet
_____
leg
_____
ten
_____
yes
_____
bed
_____
help
_____
set
_____
went
_____
pen
_____
wet
_____
B. any
_____
said
_____

30

Think and Write

Each word has the short **e** vowel sound. It is the first sound you hear in ⬭.

the short **e** sound → pet, leg

How are the Elephant Words different? *The |ĕ| sound is spelled a in any and ai in said.*

A. Write the first **ten** Basic Words. Then draw a line under the letter that spells the short **e** sound in each word.

B. Now write the **two** Elephant Words.

Order of answers for each category may vary.

Review	Challenge
13. get 14. red	15. elk 16. penguin

TEACHING OPTIONS

Meeting Individual Needs
Word Lists

You may want to assign Basic Words 1–5, the Elephant Words, and the Review Words to children who misspelled more than five words on the pretest. Assign the Challenge Words as appropriate. (You may want to have children write sentences, using the Challenge Words.)

Additional Spelling Words

Basic	Challenge	Words Often Misspelled
jet	penny	are
web	fence	girl
sled	seven	
left	every	
rest	pencil	
	present	

Home/School Involvement
Take-Home Word List • Goal-Setting

Have children set goals for the week on Take-Home Word List 2.

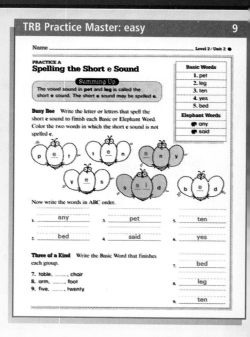

Independent Practice

Spelling Strategy
The vowel sound in **pet** and **leg** is called the short **e** sound. The short **e** sound may be spelled **e**.

Order of answers for questions 2–3 and 4–6 may vary.

Phonics Write Basic Words to answer the questions.

1. Which word begins like ?
2–3. Which two words end with two consonant sounds?
4–6. Which three words rhyme with **get**?

Word Pairs Write a Basic Word to finish the second sentence in each pair.

7. Your **hand** is at the end of your **arm**.
   Your **foot** is at the end of your _____.
8. A **bird** sleeps in a **nest**.
   A **person** sleeps in a _____.
9. You **draw** with a **crayon**.
   You **write** with a _____.
10. **Two** comes after **one**.
    Eleven comes after _____.

Elephant Words Think of the missing letter or letters in each Elephant Word. Write each word.

11. __ ny
12. s __ __ d

Phonics

1. yes

2. help

3. went

4. pet

5. set

6. wet

Word Pairs

7. leg

8. bed

9. pen

10. ten

Elephant Words

11. any

12. said

31

Objectives *Children will*

- practice spelling list words
- apply spelling strategies
- complete analogies
- supply missing vowels in Elephant Words

Daily Proofreading Practice
Do you know **eny** good jokes? (any)
Tina hopped on one **legg**. (leg)

Meeting Individual Needs
visual/auditory

Extra Support Check Independent Practice to determine who needs extra support. Give each child a card with the letter *e* on it. Say simple words with a variety of short vowel sounds. Children hold up their card each time they hear a word with the |ĕ| sound.

Applying Spelling Strategies
To Read New Words

- Write this sentence on the chalkboard:
  Ted kept his pet lizard in his room.
- Have children read the sentence silently.

- Model the following strategies as children try to decode *kept*.

I know that the letter *k* makes the sound I hear at the beginning of *king*.

This looks like a consonant cluster. I'll blend the sounds for *p* and *t* together.

kept

I see that the letter *e* is followed by two consonants. I think this is the short *e* vowel pattern.

K-e-pt. Kept. The word *kept* makes sense in the sentence.

Day 3

Objective *Children will*
■ review Basic and Review Words

Daily Proofreading Practice
Please **cet** the table. (*set*)
We all **wint** to the park. (*went*)

Silly Rhymes

1. red

2. bed

3. pen

4. went

Hidden Words

5. any

6. said

7. help

Code Breaker

8. set

9. leg

10. yes

11. pet

12. ten

(32)

Review: Spelling Spree

Silly Rhymes Finish these silly sentences. Write a Basic or Review Word to rhyme with the word in dark print.
1. That seal's **sled** is green and _____.
2. Lazy hippos are often **fed** in _____.
3. The smart **hen** writes with a _____.
4. The elephant _____ into the **tent**.

Hidden Words Find the hidden Basic Word in each box. Write the word.
5. eglkanpany   6. aisaidedin   7. ushelpper

Code Breaker Use ABC order to write the letter that comes between the letters in each pair. Use new letters to make Basic Words.

         p   e   n
Example: o q + d f + m o = **pen**

8. r t + d f + s u = _____
9. k m + d f + f h = _____
10. x z + d f + r t = _____
11. o q + d f + s u = _____
12. s u + d f + m o = _____

How Are You Doing?
Write the spelling words that are still hard for you. Practice them with a family member.

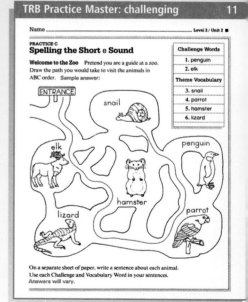

TEACHING OPTIONS

Ongoing Assessment

Omitting *m* and *n*

At the beginning of second grade, many children may still omit the letters *m* and *n* before other consonants. For example, *went* may be spelled WET and *lamp* may be spelled LAP. As children learn about vowel patterns in this unit and those that follow, they will begin to include these letters. It's important to remember that this misspelling does not occur because children don't hear the *m* or the *n* sound—they do!

TRB Practice Master: challenging   11

Name _____   Level 2 / Unit 2 ■

PRACTICE C
Spelling the Short e Sound

Welcome to the Zoo Pretend you are a guide at a zoo. Draw the path you would take to visit the animals in ABC order. Sample answer:

Challenge Words
1. penguin
2. elk

Theme Vocabulary
3. snail
4. parrot
5. hamster
6. lizard

ENTRANCE

On a separate sheet of paper, write a sentence about each animal. Use each Challenge and Vocabulary Word in your sentences.
Answers will vary.

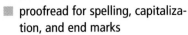

Proofreading and Writing

Proofread: Spelling and Telling Sentences

A **telling sentence** begins with a capital letter and ends with a period.

The pet store sells many animals.

Proofread this letter. Use proofreading marks to fix four spelling mistakes, two missing capital letters, and two missing end marks.

Example: i went to the pet store last week.

March 18, 1998

Dear Pat,

My pet fish is blue and redd. it lives in a bowl
by my bed. sometimes it splashes and I git wet!
Mom sed I could take Gil to school next week.

Love,

Max

Write a Description

Pretend that you are a frog. Write two or three sentences about yourself. Try to use spelling words. Share your description.

Proofreading Tip

Check that you began each telling sentence with a capital letter and ended with a period.

33

Basic

1. pet
2. leg
3. ten
4. yes
5. bed
6. help
7. set
8. went
9. pen
10. wet
11. any
12. said

Review

13. get
14. red

Challenge

15. elk
16. penguin

Proofreading Marks

∧ Add
⌒ Delete
≡ Make a capital letter
/ Make a small letter

Meeting Individual Needs

Challenge Words Practice
Have children write riddles for the Challenge Words and other animals they know something about. Partners can exchange riddles and write the answers.

Another Writing Idea Ask children to write an ad for a pet they would like to have or for one they need to give away. Encourage them to use spelling words.

Objectives Children will

■ proofread for spelling, capitalization, and end marks

■ write and proofread an original composition

Day 4

Daily Proofreading Practice
Who is sleeping in my **bedd**? (bed)
Will you **halp** me wash the dog? (help)

Day 5   **Posttest**

Sentences 1–5 test the first five Basic Words. Sentences 6–10 test the next five Basic Words. Sentences 11–12 test the Elephant Words.

Basic Words
1. This is my bed.
2. Your pet is here.
3. The ten men will go.
4. Dot cut her leg.
5. I will say yes.
6. She went out.
7. We will help her.
8. I set the table.
9. My pen is in the box.
10. The kite is wet.
11. He said we may go.
12. Do you see any cats?

Review Words
13. I have a red bike.
14. Did you get there on time?

Challenge Words
15. We saw some elk at the zoo.
16. A penguin is a bird that cannot fly.

Unit 2
BONUS

These pages can be used at any time during the study of this unit.

Day by Day Planner

Objectives *Children will*

- build words with short *e* phonograms
- identify rhyming words
- write original sentences

Rhyming Words

Short e Words Make rhyming words that have the short **e** vowel sound. Use the letters in the pictures.
Order of answers for each phonogram may vary.

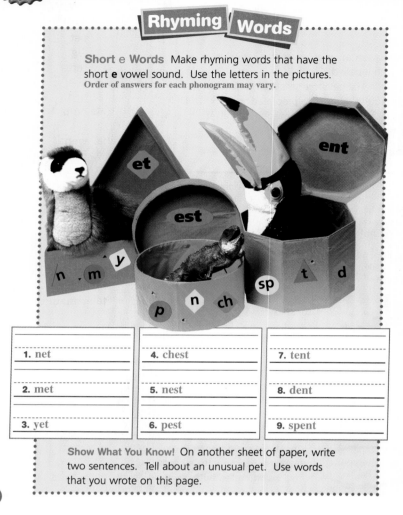

1. net	4. chest	7. tent
2. met	5. nest	8. dent
3. yet	6. pest	9. spent

Show What You Know! On another sheet of paper, write two sentences. Tell about an unusual pet. Use words that you wrote on this page.

34

EXTENSION OPTIONS

Learning Center Activity

visual/kinesthetic

Animal Pairs Ask partners to brainstorm and write words that end with the phonogram *-ent*. After making their list, have children look at each initial consonant and think of an unusual animal that begins with that letter.

On one set of cards, children draw each animal and its beginning letter. On a second set of cards, they write the letters *ent*. Children then play concentration with the cards, turning over pairs to make *-ent* words.

More *-ent* Words		
bent	rent	sent
cent	scent	vent
lent		

Vocabulary Enrichment

Unit 2 BONUS

Science

Unusual Pets All the words in the box have something to do with unusual pets. Write those words to finish this page from a book about animal facts. Use your Spelling Dictionary.

Spelling Word Link
pet

snail
parrot
hamster
lizard

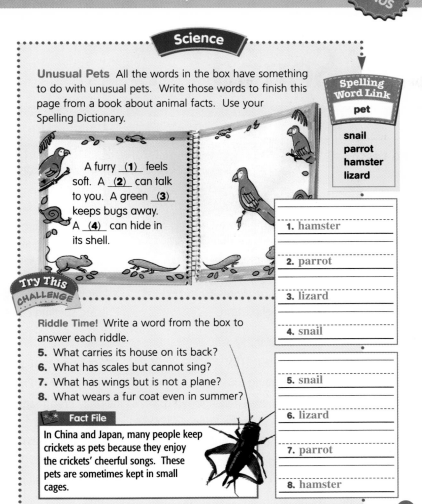

A furry **(1)** feels soft. A **(2)** can talk to you. A green **(3)** keeps bugs away. A **(4)** can hide in its shell.

1. hamster

2. parrot

3. lizard

4. snail

Try This CHALLENGE

Riddle Time! Write a word from the box to answer each riddle.

5. What carries its house on its back?
6. What has scales but cannot sing?
7. What has wings but is not a plane?
8. What wears a fur coat even in summer?

5. snail

6. lizard

7. parrot

8. hamster

Fact File

In China and Japan, many people keep crickets as pets because they enjoy the crickets' cheerful songs. These pets are sometimes kept in small cages.

35

Objectives *Children will*

- expand their vocabulary by using words related to unusual pets
- show their understanding of the vocabulary words by completing context and writing activities

Vocabulary Checkup

Have children use the vocabulary words in sentences or match the words to the definitions below.

1. a small furry animal with large cheeks and a short tail *hamster*
2. an animal with scales on its skin, four legs, and a long tail *lizard*
3. a land or water animal with a soft body and a hard shell *snail*
4. a bird with brightly colored feathers *parrot*

Fact File

Crickets

Different kinds of crickets produce different songs, usually trills or a series of chirps. Most crickets chirp by rubbing their front wings together. Most cricket songs are produced by the males.

Integrating Literature

Easy	Average	Challenging
I Love My Buzzard *by Tres Seymour* A boy's strange pets drive his mother out of the house.	**Rotten Ralph's Rotten Romance** *by Jack Gantos* Sarah's cat Rotten Ralph makes mischief at a party.	**Mrs. Merriwether's Musical Cat** *by Carol Purdy* A cat has a remarkable effect on some piano students.
Whistling Dixie *by Marcia Vaughan* Dixie comes home with a parade of preposterous pets.	**Hooray! A Piñata** *by Elisa Kleven* A girl treats her birthday piñata like a real dog.	**Martha Blah Blah** *by Susan Meddaugh* Martha the dog starts to speak gibberish.

[handwritten note: X-want help / last word / pin ~~pleasure~~]

Spelling the Short *i* Sound

WORD LISTS

Spelling

Basic

1. pig
2. win
3. is
4. six
5. his
6. if
7. hit
8. fix
9. pin
10. dig
11. been
12. I

Review

13. did
14. big

Challenge

15. quilt
16. picnic

Vocabulary

Social Studies: A Country Fair

ribbon
booth
ring
judge

Introducing the Lesson

Read Aloud

Write the Basic Words on the board.

A Prize-Winning Pig

A country fair **is** exciting! Bert hopes that **his pig** Petunia will do well in the show. Before the judge can pick a winner, workers have to **fix** a ramp that broke under another very large **pig**! Meanwhile, Bert has **been** playing games. He **hit** a target **six** times with a ball and won a prize. Bert can **win** another prize **if** he guesses how many marbles are in a jar. "Just let me **dig** inside and count them!" he jokes. Then Bert hears a voice announcing the prize-winning **pig**. "Who **is** the proud owner of Petunia?" the judge asks. "**I** am!" shouts Bert, and he beams as the judge bends over to **pin** a blue ribbon on him.

Responding Ask children what Bert and Petunia won and what it stands for. *(a blue ribbon; first place in a competition)* **Then have them listen for a Basic Word as you reread the first sentence of the selection. Ask a child to say the word and another Basic Word that rhymes with it.** *(is/his)* **Repeat with other words.**

Day 1 *page 36*

Objectives *Children will*

- take the pretest
- pronounce the list words
- learn about the spelling principle
- analyze words by their short vowel pattern

Planning Checklist

- ☑ Pretest (TE)
- ☑ Spelling principle/word list
- ☐ Review/Challenge Words
- ☐ Teaching the Principle (TE)
- ☐ Enrichment (TE)
- ☐ Additional Spelling Words (TE)

Assessment

Pretest

1. The pig is eating corn.
2. Help us win the game.
3. That car is green.
4. We have six apples.
5. Dan has his hat on.
6. Be there if you can.
7. Adam hit the ball.
8. Did she fix her bike?
9. Tina gave me a pin.
10. My dog likes to dig.
11. The game has been fun.
12. Do I have to stay home?

Day 2 *page 37*

Objectives *Children will*

- practice spelling list words
- apply spelling strategies
- identify Basic Words by using meaning clues
- identify Elephant Words by using spelling clues

Planning Checklist

- ☑ Spelling Strategy
- ☑ Independent Practice
- ☐ Daily Proofreading Practice (TE)
- ☐ Informal Assessment (TE)
- ☐ Extra Support (TE)
- ☐ Applying Spelling Strategies (TE)

 Day 3 *page 38*   **Day 4** *page 39*   **Day 5** *page 39*

Objectives *Children will*
- alphabetize groups of words to the first letter
- review Basic and Review Words

Planning Checklist
- ☐ Dictionary
- ☐ Review: Spelling Spree
- ☐ How Are You Doing?
- ☐ Daily Proofreading Practice (TE)
- ☐ Cooperative Learning Activity (TE)

Objectives *Children will*
- proofread for spelling
- write and proofread an original composition

Planning Checklist
- ☐ Proofread for Spelling
- ☐ Write a Story
- ☐ Daily Proofreading Practice (TE)
- ☐ Challenge Words Practice (TE)
- ☐ Another Writing Idea (TE)

Objective *Children will*
- take the posttest

Assessment
- ☐ **Posttest** (TE) *See Day 5*
- ☐ Unit 3 Test

● **Additional Resources**

Teacher's Resource Book
Practice Masters, pages 13–15
Unit Test, page 16
Bulletin Board, page 25

Practice Plus
Take-Home Word List 3
Games

Spelling Transparencies
Spelling Word List 3
Daily Proofreading Practice, Unit 3
Graphic Organizers

Teacher's Resource Disk
Macintosh® or Windows® software. Houghton Mifflin

Spelling CD-ROM
Macintosh® or Windows® software. Houghton Mifflin

Internet
http://www.eduplace.com

Phonics Practice
Houghton Mifflin Phonics
The Listening Corner
Phonics Home Connection

 Meeting Individual Needs
Students Acquiring English

Spanish There is no |ĭ| sound in Spanish. Spanish-speaking children may substitute the |ē| sound.
Activity List these word pairs: *it/eat, deep/dip, hit/heat, lid/lead, sheep/ship,* and *leap/lip.* Say each pair. Have children repeat. Ask volunteers to underline the word in each pair with the |ĭ| sound. Have children say and copy the word.
Asian For some children the |ks| sound is especially difficult.
Activity Have children match word and picture cards for short *i* words such as *pig, six,* and *pin.* Ask children to repeat the words after you.

Other Activities for Any Day

- Bonus activities from pages 40–41
- Practice Masters (easy, average, challenging)
  Teacher's Resource Book, pages 13–15
- Take-Home Word List 3
  Practice Plus

Objectives *Children will*

■ take the pretest

■ pronounce the list words

■ learn about the spelling principle

■ analyze words by their short vowel pattern

Teaching the Principle

This lesson teaches the short vowel pattern for the |ĭ| sound (*i* followed by a consonant sound). Children learn the strategy of thinking of this pattern when they hear the short *i* sound.

To sum up the lesson, ask:

• What vowel spells the short *i* sound in each word? *(the vowel i)*

• What kind of letter follows the vowel *i* in each word? *(a consonant)*

Enrichment

Vocabulary: Multiple Meanings

Have children use a dictionary to look up *hit*, *fix*, and *pin*. Discuss the different meanings.

Spelling the Short i Sound

ĭ
pig

A. p<u>i</u>g

w<u>i</u>n

<u>i</u>s

s<u>i</u>x

h<u>i</u>s

<u>i</u>f

h<u>i</u>t

f<u>i</u>x

p<u>i</u>n

d<u>i</u>g

B. been

I

36

Read and Say

READ the sentences. **SAY** each word in dark print.

Basic Words

1.	pig	The **pig** is eating corn.
2.	win	Help us **win** the game.
3.	is	That car **is** green.
4.	six	We have **six** apples.
5.	his	Dan has **his** hat on.
6.	if	Be there **if** you can.
7.	hit	Adam **hit** the ball.
8.	fix	Did she **fix** her bike?
9.	pin	Tina gave me a **pin**.
10.	dig	My dog likes to **dig**.
🐘 11.	been	The game has **been** fun.
🐘 12.	I	Do **I** have to stay home?

Think and Write

Most of the words have the short **i** vowel sound. It is the first sound you hear in .

the short **i** sound → **pig, is**

How are the Elephant Words different?

A. Write the first **ten** Basic Words. Then draw a line under the letter that spells the short **i** sound in each word.

B. Now write the **two** Elephant Words.

In been, the |ĭ| sound is spelled ee. In I, i spells the |ĭ| sound.

Order of answers for each category may vary.

Review	Challenge
13. did 14. big	15. quilt 16. picnic

TEACHING OPTIONS

Meeting Individual Needs
Word Lists

You may want to assign Basic Words 1–5, the Elephant Words, and the Review Words to children who misspelled more than five words on the pretest. Assign the Challenge Words as appropriate. (You may want to have children write sentences, using the Challenge Words.)

Additional Spelling Words

Basic	Challenge	Words Often Misspelled
him	mitten	how
milk	visit	now
drip	cricket	
hid	twins	
slid	nickel	
	inch	

Home/School Involvement
Take-Home Word List • Goal-Setting

Have children set goals for the week on Take-Home Word List 3.

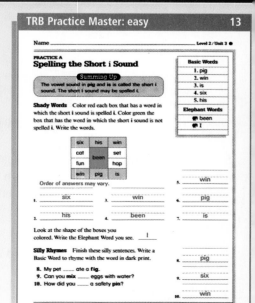

TRB Practice Master: easy   13

Name _____   Level 2 / Unit 3

PRACTICE A
Spelling the Short i Sound

Summing Up
The vowel sound in pig and is is called the short i sound. The short i sound may be spelled i.

Shady Words Color red each box that has a word in which the short i sound is spelled i. Color green the box that has the word in which the short i sound is not spelled i. Write the words.

six	his	win
cat	been	set
fun		hop
win	pig	is

Order of answers may vary.

1. ___six___   3. ___win___

2. ___his___   4. ___been___

5. ___win___

6. ___pig___

7. ___is___

Look at the shape of the boxes you colored. Write the Elephant Word you see.   I

Silly Rhymes Finish these silly sentences. Write a Basic Word to rhyme with the word in dark print.

8. My pet ____ ate a **fig**.   ___pig___

9. Can you **mix** ____ eggs with water?   ___six___

10. How did you ____ a safety **pin**?   ___win___

Independent Practice

Spelling Strategy The vowel sound in **pig** and **is** is called the short **i** sound. The short **i** sound may be spelled **i**.

Order of answers for questions 2–3 and 4–5 may vary.

Phonics Write Basic Words to answer the questions.

1. Which word begins like ?
2–3. Which two words begin like ?
4–5. Which two words begin like ?

Word Clues Write a Basic Word for each clue.

6. a farm animal
7. an even number between four and eight
8. what you must do to make a hole
9. what you must do to get first prize
10. what you could use if your button fell off

Elephant Words Write an Elephant Word to answer each question.

11. Which word is always spelled with a capital letter?
12. Which word has the short **i** sound spelled with two vowels?

Phonics

1. fix
2. is
3. if
4. his
5. hit

Word Clues

6. pig
7. six
8. dig
9. win
10. pin

Elephant Words

11. I
12. been

(37)

Objectives *Children will*

- practice spelling list words
- apply spelling strategies
- identify Basic Words by using meaning clues
- identify Elephant Words by using spelling clues

Daily Proofreading Practice
He wanted to **whin** the prize. (*win*)
Can you **fiks** my skate? (*fix*)

Meeting Individual Needs
auditory

Extra Support Check Independent Practice to determine who needs extra support. Help children learn to distinguish between the |ĭ| and the |ĕ| sounds. Say simple words, such as *pin, get, big, fix, hen, in, dig, ten,* and *his,* that have these vowel sounds. Tell children to shiver as if in an igloo if they hear the |ĭ| sound or to pretend to crack an egg if they hear the |ĕ| sound.

Name _____ Level 2 / Unit 3 ▲

Basic Words
1. pig
2. win
3. is
4. six
5. his
6. if
7. hit
8. fix
9. pin
10. dig

Elephant Words
been
I

PRACTICE B
Spelling the Short i Sound

Fill-In Fun Write the missing Basic or Elephant Word.

1. needle and _____
2. _____ or lose
3. _____ and seven
4. Mike and _____
5. _____ or miss
6. _____ and hers

1. pin
2. win
3. six
4. I
5. hit
6. his

Tick-Tack-Code Use the code below to write Basic or Elephant Words. Look at the letters and the shape of the lines around each letter.

	b	d	g
	f	i	e	n
	p	s	x

Example: ⌐p⌐ |i⌐ ⌐n⌐ = pin

7. fix
8. is
9. dig
10. been
11. pig
12. if

7. ⌐i⌐
8. ⌐i⌐
9. ⌐i⌐
10. ⌐i⌐
11. ⌐i⌐
12. ⌐i⌐

Applying Spelling Strategies
To Spell New Words

- Read aloud: **The gift was wrapped in beautiful paper.**
- Have children attempt to spell *gift* on their Have-a-Go charts.
- Model the following strategies as children try to spell *gift*.

> This word has the short *i* sound. The short *i* sound is probably spelled *i*.

> First, I hear the sound for *g* that I hear at the beginning of *ghost*.

gift

> I hear the sounds for *f* and *t* blended together at the end of the word.

Day 3

Objectives *Children will*
- alphabetize groups of words to the first letter
- review Basic and Review Words

Daily Proofreading Practice
Where have you **bin**? (*been*)
Papa could not find **hiz** keys. (*his*)

ABC Order

1. pig

2. I

3. fix

4. big

5. been

6. his

Letter Math

7. did

8. hit

9. if

10. his

11. been

12. pin

38

Dictionary

ABC Order Words in a dictionary are in ABC order. Look at the first letter of each of these words. The words are in ABC order.

big   **d**ig   **f**ix

Practice Look at the first letter in each word. Write the word in each group that would come first in ABC order.

1. win   pig   six
2. six   pin   I
3. pig   fix   win
4. is   six   big
5. hit   I   been
6. pin   his   win

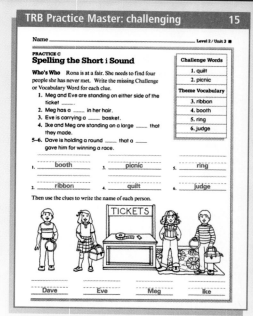

Review: Spelling Spree

Letter Math Add and take away letters to make Basic or Review Words. Write each word.

Example: w + p i n – p = **win**

7. d a d – a + i = _____
8. h + p i t – p = _____
9. i + o f – o = _____
10. h a s – a + i = _____
11. b e a n – a + e = _____
12. p a i n t – a – t = _____

> ✓ **How Are You Doing?**
> Write each spelling word as a partner reads it aloud. Did you spell any words wrong?

TEACHING OPTIONS

Cooperative Learning Activity
Vowel Swap
visual/kinesthetic

Have partners use letter cards or Scrabble® pieces to spell simple words that have the short *i* vowel sound. Ask them to see how many new words they can make by swapping the vowel. Children might build word groups such as the following:

hit: hat, hot, hut   **tin:** tan, ten, ton
pin: pan, pen   **tip:** tap, top
pit: pat, pet, pot, put

Pairs can record the words they make. Volunteers may write the word groups on a poster for the class word wall.

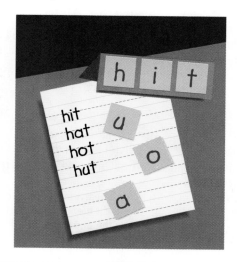

TRB Practice Master: challenging   **15**

Name _____   Level 2 / Unit 3

PRACTICE C
Spelling the Short i Sound

Who's Who Rona is at a fair. She needs to find four people she has never met. Write the missing Challenge or Vocabulary Word for each clue.

1. Meg and Eve are standing on either side of the ticket.
2. Meg has a _____ in her hair.
3. Eve is carrying a _____ basket.
4. Ike and Meg are standing on a large _____ that they made.
5–6. Dave is holding a round _____ that a _____ gave him for winning a race.

Challenge Words
1. quilt
2. picnic
Theme Vocabulary
3. ribbon
4. booth
5. ring
6. judge

1. booth   3. picnic   5. ring
2. ribbon   4. quilt   6. judge

Then use the clues to write the name of each person.

TICKETS

Dave   Eve   Meg   Ike

Proofreading and Writing

Proofread for Spelling Proofread this sign. Use proofreading marks to fix six spelling mistakes.

Example: Tony gave ~~hizz~~ his prize to Lisa.

The Ames Fair ~~iz~~ is great fun!

See the world's biggest pig!

Hit the balloons!

~~Whin bigg~~ Win big prizes!

~~Deg~~ Dig into your pockets!

Tickets are ~~siks~~ six dollars!

~~Eye~~ I know you will have a great time!

Basic

1. pig
2. win
3. is
4. six
5. his
6. if
7. hit
8. fix
9. pin
10. dig
11. been
12. I

Review
13. did
14. big

Challenge
15. quilt
16. picnic

Proofreading Marks
∧ Add
⌐ Delete
≡ Make a capital letter
/ Make a small letter

Write a Story

Rudy

Pretend you saw the world's biggest pig. Write a story telling about the pig. Try to use spelling words. You may want to make a tape recording of your story to share with a friend.

Proofreading Tip Read each word slowly to make sure there are no extra letters.

39

Objectives *Children will*
■ proofread for spelling
■ write and proofread an original composition

Daily Proofreading Practice
She **het** a home run! (*hit*)
I will **pinn** the blue ribbon on Ed. (*pin*)

Day 5 Posttest

Sentences 1–5 test the first five Basic Words. Sentences 6–10 test the next five Basic Words. Sentences 11–12 test the Elephant Words.

Basic Words
1. Sam got <u>his</u> hat.
2. Do you see that big <u>pig</u>?
3. Kit <u>is</u> here.
4. We will play <u>six</u> games.
5. Did she <u>win</u>?
6. Look in the box for a <u>pin</u>.
7. I can <u>fix</u> the kite.
8. Clap <u>if</u> you like.
9. We may get a <u>hit</u>.
10. Let me <u>dig</u> this time.
11. She and <u>I</u> may go.
12. He has <u>been</u> here.

Review Words
13. They <u>did</u> not see me.
14. That is a <u>big</u> bag.

Challenge Words
15. We had a <u>picnic</u> by the river.
16. Mom put a warm <u>quilt</u> on my bed.

TRB Unit 3 Test 16

Name _____ Level 2 / Unit 3 ●▲

Unit 3 Test: Spelling the Short i Sound

Read each sentence. Is the underlined word spelled right or wrong? Mark your answer.

	Right	Wrong
Sample: Sasha <u>did</u> her work.	●	○

Items 1–7 test Basic Words 1–5 and the Elephant Words.
Items 8–12 test Basic Words 6–10.

	Right	Wrong
1. Who will <u>win</u> the new book?	●	○
2. Jory has <u>benn</u> very busy.	○	●
3. Tony gave the book to <u>hiz</u> sister.	○	●
4. Aunt Brenda just fed the <u>pig</u>.	●	○
5. This <u>iss</u> my teacher Mr. Taylor.	○	●
6. Lou asked <u>if</u> I would go to the game.	●	○
7. There are <u>sics</u> boys on my team.	○	●
8. Will you <u>fix</u> my radio?	●	○
9. I will be happy <u>iv</u> you visit.	○	●
10. Andy can <u>deg</u> a hole in the sand.	○	●
11. That <u>pin</u> is sharp.	●	○
12. Chen was able to hit the ball.	●	○

 Meeting Individual Needs

Challenge Words Practice
Have children make crossword puzzles on graph paper, using the Challenge Words and other short *i* words. Suggest children exchange puzzles with a partner.

Another Writing Idea Ask children to draw pictures of booths or events they might see at a country fair. Below each picture, have them write a descriptive label or sentence that includes a spelling word.

Unit 3 BONUS

Day by Day Planner

These pages can be used at any time during the study of this unit.

Objectives *Children will*

- build words with short *i* phonograms
- identify rhyming words
- write an original composition

Rhyming Words

Short i Words Make rhyming words that have the short **i** vowel sound. Use the letters in the picture.
Order of answers for each phonogram may vary.

sk sp
th
f

in

fl t
z
sk

ip

1. fin	5. skip
2. thin	6. zip
3. skin	7. flip
4. spin	8. tip

Show What You Know! On another sheet of paper, write an ad for a country fair. Use words that you wrote on this page.

40

EXTENSION OPTIONS

Learning Center Activity

visual/oral/kinesthetic

Word Toss Partners can create their own booths for a country fair from empty half-gallon milk cartons by cutting a window on one side and covering the carton with colored paper. On each booth, they write a short *i* phonogram.

Children use letter cards or Spill & Spell® tiles to build rhyming words with the short *i* sound then write the words on tagboard disks. They take turns choosing a disk, reading and spelling the word, and tossing it into the correct booth.

Vocabulary Enrichment

Social Studies

A Country Fair All the words in the box have something to do with a country fair. Write those words to finish this program. Use your Spelling Dictionary.

Spelling Word Link

win

ribbon
booth
ring
judge

Horse Show

1st PLACE

12:00 **Buy your tickets at the __(1)__.**

12:30 **See the horses jump into the __(2)__.**

1:00 **The __(3)__ will choose the best horse and give the winner a blue __(4)__.**

Try This CHALLENGE

Yes or No? Write **yes** or **no** to answer each question.

5. Is a **ring** a good place to sleep?
6. Would a **judge** pick a winner?
7. Could a **ribbon** be made of cloth?
8. Would you wear a **booth** on your foot?

1. booth
2. ring
3. judge
4. ribbon

5. no
6. yes
7. yes
8. no

41

★ Fact File

Grandma Moses began painting when she was more than 70 years old. She painted more than 1,500 pictures. One of her paintings is called **Country Fair**.

Objectives *Children will*

- expand their vocabulary by using words related to a country fair
- show their understanding of the vocabulary words by completing context activities

Vocabulary Checkup

Have children use the vocabulary words in sentences or use the words to answer the questions below.

1. Where might contests or shows be held? in a *ring*
2. What could you win as a prize in a contest? a *ribbon*
3. Where do people buy tickets to see a show? at a *booth*
4. Who chooses the winner of a contest? a *judge*

Fact File

Grandma Moses

Grandma Moses was Anna Mary Robertson Moses (1860–1961). She lived and worked on farms most of her life. When arthritis made it hard for her to embroider, she began to paint scenes based on her childhood memories. She painted until her death at age 101.

Integrating Literature

Easy	Average	Challenging
Grandma's Smile *by Elaine Moore* Kim and her grandma enter pumpkins in the local fair.	**The Hog Call to End All!** *by SuAnn Kiser* Minerva and her pig win a blue ribbon in a hog calling contest.	**Country Fair** *by Gail Gibbons* The sights, sounds, and tastes of a country fair.
That Kookoory! *by Margaret Walden Froehlich* The rooster Kookoory tricks a fox on his way to a fair.	**Sam Johnson and the Blue Ribbon Quilt** *by Lisa Campbell Ernst* A farmer wins a quilting contest.	**A Week at the Fair** *by Patricia Easton* A girl describes her week at a county fair in Pennsylvania.

Spelling the Short *o* Sound

WORD LISTS

Spelling

Basic

1. job
2. pot
3. nod
4. top
5. not
6. dot
7. fox
8. mop
9. spot
10. hop
11. of

Review

12. on
13. box

Challenge

14. block
15. hospital

Vocabulary

Health: Safety at Home and at School

careful
injure
exit
alarm

Introducing the Lesson

Read Aloud

Write the Basic Words on the board.

Staying Safe at Home

Did you know that every ten seconds someone is injured at home? Staying safe in your own home is **not** an easy **job**. See if you can answer these safety questions. What can happen if you **hop** or jump from the **top** to the bottom **of** the stairs? If you **spot** something that spilled on the floor, why should you **mop** it up? Why should you never touch a hot **pot** on the stove? Why is it a good idea to **nod** your head instead of speaking when you have food in your mouth? Should you feed a wild animal like a **fox** if it comes into your back yard? Could a pin or a needle no bigger than a **dot** on the floor hurt you? Can you think **of** important safety rules for your home?

Responding Reread the questions in the selection, allowing children to respond to each one. Ask children which spelling word names what you use to clean a floor. *(mop)* Ask which two spelling words rhyme with it. *(top, hop)*

Day 1 *page 42*

Objectives *Children will*

- take the pretest
- pronounce the list words
- learn about the spelling principle
- analyze words by their short vowel pattern

Planning Checklist

☑ Pretest (TE)
☑ Spelling principle/word list
☐ Review/Challenge Words
☐ Teaching the Principle (TE)
☐ Enrichment (TE)
☐ Additional Spelling Words (TE)

Assessment

Pretest

1. Jim got a <u>job</u> in town.
2. Put water in the <u>pot</u>.
3. Did you <u>nod</u> your head?
4. That box has no <u>top</u>.
5. They did <u>not</u> go.
6. A <u>dot</u> is a round mark.
7. That <u>fox</u> runs fast.
8. I will <u>mop</u> the floor.
9. Is that a red <u>spot</u>?
10. I can <u>hop</u> on one foot.
11. Take my box <u>of</u> cups.

Day 2 *page 43*

Objectives *Children will*

- practice spelling list words
- apply spelling strategies
- classify Basic Words into groups
- identify an Elephant word by using context clues

Planning Checklist

☑ Spelling Strategy
☑ Independent Practice
☐ Daily Proofreading Practice (TE)
☐ Informal Assessment (TE)
☐ Extra Support (TE)
☐ Applying Spelling Strategies (TE)

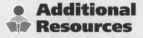

Management Tip You might suggest that children complete one or both of the Bonus pages as extra work to be done, independently or in small groups, after they take the Posttest.

Day 3 *page 44*   **Day 4** *page 45*   **Day 5** *page 45*

Objective *Children will*
• review Basic and Review Words

Planning Checklist
☐ Review: Spelling Spree
☐ How Are You Doing?
☐ Daily Proofreading Practice (TE)
☐ Ongoing Assessment (TE)

Objectives *Children will*
• proofread for spelling, capital letters, and end marks
• write and proofread an original composition

Planning Checklist
☐ Proofread: Spelling and Questions
☐ Write a Safety Quiz
☐ Daily Proofreading Practice (TE)
☐ Challenge Words Practice (TE)
☐ Another Writing Idea (TE)

Objective *Children will*
• take the posttest

Assessment
☐ **Posttest** (TE) *See Day 5*
☐ Unit 4 Test

Teacher's Resource Book
Practice Masters, pages 17–19
Unit Test, page 20
Bulletin Board, page 25

Practice Plus
Take-Home Word List 4
Games

Spelling Transparencies
Spelling Word List 4
Daily Proofreading Practice, Unit 4
Graphic Organizers

Teacher's Resource Disk
Macintosh® or Windows® software. Houghton Mifflin

Spelling CD-ROM
Macintosh® or Windows® software. Houghton Mifflin

Internet
http://www.eduplace.com

Phonics Practice
Houghton Mifflin Phonics
The Listening Corner
Phonics Home Connection

Meeting Individual Needs
Students Acquiring English

Spanish There is no |ŏ| sound in Spanish.
Activity Distribute blank cards. Children print a short o word on one side and a matching word with a different vowel sound on the other, for example: *not/net, top/tap, hot/hit, mop/map, pot/pet,* and *stop/step.* Have children practice reading the words on each card and telling which one has the |ŏ| sound.

Asian The American |ŏ| may be difficult for Asian children to pronounce.
Activity Have children repeat each spelling word after you. Then use the activity for Spanish-speaking children.

Other Activities for Any Day

• Bonus activities from pages 46–47
• Practice Masters (easy, average, challenging)
  Teacher's Resource Book, pages 17–19
• Take-Home Word List 4
  Practice Plus

Spelling the Short o Sound

Objectives *Children will*
- take the pretest
- pronounce the list words
- learn about the spelling principle
- analyze words by their short vowel pattern

Teaching the Principle

This lesson teaches the short vowel pattern for the |ŏ| sound (o followed by a consonant). Children learn the strategy of thinking of this pattern when they hear the short o sound.

To sum up the lesson, ask:

- What vowel spells the short o sound in each word? *(the vowel o)*
- What kind of letter follows the vowel o in each word? *(a consonant)*

Note: The Elephant Word *of* may be pronounced |ŭv| or |ŏv|. Call children's attention to the |v| sound for the letter *f*.

Enrichment

Vocabulary: Multiple Meanings
Have children use a dictionary to look up *top* and *spot*. Discuss the different meanings.

ŏ
top

A. jo̱b
_____

----

po̱t
_____

----

no̱d
_____

----

to̱p
_____

----

no̱t
_____

----

do̱t
_____

----

fo̱x
_____

----

mo̱p
_____

----

spo̱t
_____

----

ho̱p
_____

B. of
_____

42

Read and Say

READ the sentences. **SAY** each word in dark print.

Basic Words

1.	job	Jim got a **job** in town.
2.	pot	Put water in the **pot**.
3.	nod	Did you **nod** your head?
4.	top	That box has no **top**.
5.	not	They did **not** go.
6.	dot	A **dot** is a round mark.
7.	fox	That **fox** runs fast.
8.	mop	I will **mop** the floor.
9.	spot	Is that a red **spot**?
10.	hop	I can **hop** on one foot.
11.	of	Take my box **of** cups.

Think and Write

Most of the words have the short **o** vowel sound. It is the first sound you hear in 🐙.

the short **o** sound → j**o**b, p**o**t

How is the Elephant Word different? *The o in of is pronounced |ŭ|.*

A. Write the first **ten** Basic Words. Then draw a line under the letter that spells the short **o** sound in each word.

B. Now write the Elephant Word.

Order of answers for each category may vary.

Review		Challenge	
12. on	**13.** box	**14.** block	**15.** hospital

TEACHING OPTIONS

Meeting Individual Needs
Word Lists

You may want to assign Basic Words 1–5, the Elephant Word, and the Review Words to children who misspelled more than five words on the pretest. Assign the Challenge Words as appropriate. (You may want to have children write sentences, using the Challenge Words.)

Additional Spelling Words

Basic	Challenge	Words Often Misspelled
pop	pocket	our
doll	goggles	down
drop	copy	
trot	donkey	
rob	blond	
	follow	

Home/School Involvement
Take-Home Word List • Goal-Setting

Have children set goals for the week on Take-Home Word List 4.

TRB Practice Master: easy   17

Name _____   Level 2 / Unit 4

PRACTICE A
Spelling the Short o Sound

Basic Words
1. job
2. pot
3. nod
4. top
5. not

Summing Up
The vowel sound in job and pot is called the short o sound. The short o sound may be spelled o.

Elephant Word
of

Short o Nest Use the consonant letters on the eggs and the letter o to write four Basic Words. Draw a line under the letter that spells the short o sound in each word. Order of answers may vary.

Color the eight eggs you used. Find the answer to this riddle by writing the uncolored letters from the nest.

Riddle: What kind of bird is also a person's name?

Answer: r o b i n

Into the Woods Write the missing Basic or Elephant Words to finish the sentences in Cara's notebook.

My family went for a walk in the woods. It was my (5) to find a bird's nest. At first I could (6) see one. Then I looked up to the (7) of the oak tree. There was a nest full (8) eggs!

1. not
2. pot
3. nod
4. top
5. job
6. not
7. top
8. of

UNIT
4

Independent Practice

Spelling Strategy   The vowel sound in **job** and **pot** is called the short **o** sound. The short **o** sound may be spelled **o**.

Order of answers for question 4–5 may vary.

Phonics   Write Basic Words to answer the questions.

1. Which word rhymes with **Bob**?
2. Which word rhymes with **dot** and has almost the same meaning?
3. Which word begins like ?
4–5. Which two words begin like ?

Word Groups   Think how the words in each group are alike. Write the missing Basic Words.

6. broom, rag, _____
7. bowl, pan, _____
8. deer, rabbit, _____
9. jump, skip, _____
10. bottom, middle, _____

Elephant Word   Write the missing Elephant Word.
11. Be careful getting out _____ the bathtub.

Phonics

1. job
2. spot
3. dot
4. nod
5. not

Word Groups

6. mop
7. pot
8. fox
9. hop
10. top

Elephant Word

11. of

43

Objectives *Children will*
- practice spelling list words
- apply spelling strategies
- classify Basic Words into groups
- identify an Elephant word by using context clues

Day 2

Daily Proofreading Practice

There is soup in the **pawt**. (*pot*)
Do **nott** swim alone. (*not*)

Meeting Individual Needs
visual/oral/auditory/kinesthetic

Extra Support   Check Independent Practice to determine who needs extra support. Print Basic Words 1–10 on word cards. Distribute to children. Write rhyming words such as *rob, box, hot, rod,* and *flop* on another set of cards. Display and read these cards one at a time. Children who have a word that rhymes hold up their card, say the word, and write it on the chalkboard.

TRB Practice Master: average   18

Name _____   Level 2 / Unit 4 ▲

Basic Words
1. job
2. pot
3. nod
4. top
5. not
6. dot
7. fox
8. mop
9. spot
10. hop
Elephant Word
🐘 of

PRACTICE B
Spelling the Short o Sound

Buckle Up!   All of the seat belts need to be closed. Draw lines to match the parts of the seat belts to spell Basic or Elephant Words. Write the words.

m   d   f   j   n   o

ot   op   ob   od   f   ox

Order of answers may vary.

1. _____ mop _____   4. _____ job _____
2. _____ dot _____   5. _____ nod _____
3. _____ fox _____   6. _____ of _____

Park the Car   Draw a line to match each meaning with a Basic Word. Write the Basic Words.

7. | a deep pan | → hop
8. | a no word | → pot
9. | jump | → top
10. | a cover | → spot
11. | see | → not

7. _____ pot _____
8. _____ not _____
9. _____ hop _____
10. _____ top _____
11. _____ spot _____

Applying Spelling Strategies
To Read New Words

- Write this sentence on the chalkboard:
  I saw a robin on the first day of spring.

- Have children read the sentence silently.
- Model the following strategies as children try to decode *robin*.

> I see that the letter *o* is followed by the consonant *b*. I think this is the short *o* vowel pattern.

> I know that the letter *r* makes the sound I hear at the beginning of *rabbit*.

robin

> I recognize the word *in* at the end of this longer word.

> Rob-in. Robin. The word *robin* makes sense in the sentence.

Day 3

Objective *Children will*
■ review Basic and Review Words

Daily Proofreading Practice
We saw a **foks** in the woods. (*fox*)
I climbed to the **tup** of the hill. (*top*)

UNIT 4

Rhyming Clues

1. hop

2. job

3. nod

4. dot

5. fox

6. mop

Letter Scramble

7. pot

8. not

9. spot

Fill–In Fun

10. on

11. of

12. box

44

Review: Spelling Spree

Rhyming Clues   Write a Basic Word for each clue.

1. It rhymes with **drop**. It begins like .
2. It rhymes with **knob**. It begins like ▧.
3. It rhymes with **rod**. It begins like ▧.
4. It rhymes with **got**. It begins like ▧.
5. It rhymes with **ox**. It begins like ▧.
6. It rhymes with **pop**. It begins like ▧.

Letter Scramble   Write a Basic Word by changing
the order of letters in each word below.

7. top   8. ton   9. tops

Fill-In Fun   Write the missing Basic or Review Words.

10. off and _____
11. glass _____ milk
12. jack-in-the- _____

SAFETY FIRST!

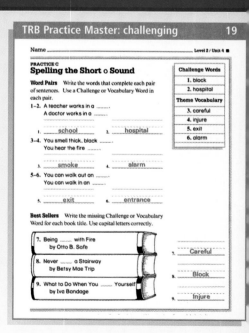

✓ How Are You Doing?
Write each spelling word in a sentence. Practice with a partner any words you spelled wrong.

TEACHING OPTIONS

Ongoing Assessment
Misspelling Short Vowel Sounds

Occasionally, children still spell a short vowel sound by selecting the letter whose name is closest in terms of sound and feel—where and how the letter name is pronounced in the mouth. For example, *pet* is spelled PAT, *wet* is WAT, *win* is WEN, and *hop* is HIP. It is rare that a child at this level will spell *all* short vowels according to this strategy; usually it is one or at most two short vowel sounds that are consistently spelled incorrectly. Review of these vowel patterns as they occur in children's sight vocabularies is the best way to "lock in" understanding of the patterns.

TRB Practice Master: challenging 19

Name _____   Level 2 / Unit 4 ■

PRACTICE C
Spelling the Short o Sound

Challenge Words
1. block
2. hospital
Theme Vocabulary
3. careful
4. injure
5. exit
6. alarm

Word Pairs   Write the words that complete each pair of sentences. Use a Challenge or Vocabulary Word in each pair.

1–2. A teacher works in a _____.
A doctor works in a _____.

1. _____school_____   2. _____hospital_____

3–4. You smell thick, black _____.
You hear the fire _____.

3. _____smoke_____   4. _____alarm_____

5–6. You can walk out an _____.
You can walk in an _____.

5. _____exit_____   6. _____entrance_____

Best Sellers   Write the missing Challenge or Vocabulary Word for each book title. Use capital letters correctly.

7. Being _____ with Fire
by Otto B. Safe   7. _____Careful_____

8. Never _____ a Stairway
by Betsy Mae Trip   8. _____Block_____

9. What to Do When You _____ Yourself
by Iva Bandage   9. _____Injure_____

Proofreading and Writing

Proofread: Spelling and Questions

A **question** begins with a capital letter and ends with a question mark.

Do you work and play safely?

Proofread this note. Use proofreading marks to fix four spelling mistakes, two missing capital letters, and two end marks.

Example: who read the list ~~ov~~ of safety rules?

Mia,

Will you help me ~~onn~~ on this job, please mop up
every ~~sopt~~ spot of water. I do ~~nawt~~ not want someone to slip.
could you wipe the table ~~tup~~ top too. Thank you.

Jenna

Basic

1. job
2. pot
3. nod
4. top
5. not
6. dot
7. fox
8. mop
9. spot
10. hop
11. of

Review

12. on
13. box

Challenge

14. block
15. hospital

Proofreading Marks

∧ Add
‿ Delete
≡ Make a capital letter
/ Make a small letter

Write a Safety Quiz

Write some questions about home safety. Try to use spelling words. Then have a friend or family member answer your questions.

Proofreading Tip

Check that you began each question with a capital letter and ended with a question mark.

45

Objectives *Children will*

■ proofread for spelling, capital letters, and end marks

■ write and proofread an original composition

Day 4

Daily Proofreading Practice

Meg has a new box **ov** paints. (*of*)
It is my **gob** to rake the leaves. (*job*)

Day 5 Posttest

Sentences 1–5 test the first five Basic Words. Sentences 6–10 test the next five Basic Words. Sentence 11 tests the Elephant Word.

Basic Words

1. That is a big <u>pot</u>.
2. This is <u>not</u> a cat.
3. I have a <u>job</u>.
4. Sam will <u>nod</u> to me.
5. Is it on <u>top</u>?
6. We must <u>mop</u> up.
7. There is a red <u>spot</u>.
8. Is it a fast <u>fox</u>?
9. The frog will not <u>hop</u>.
10. That is a green <u>dot</u>.
11. He had a day <u>of</u> fun.

Review Words

12. The cat is <u>on</u> the hat.
13. Kim gave me a <u>box</u>.

Challenge Words

14. The doctor works at the <u>hospital</u>.
15. Do not <u>block</u> the fire exit.

Meeting Individual Needs

Challenge Words Practice
Have children make safety posters using the Challenge Words and other words they've learned in this unit.

Another Writing Idea Have children write and illustrate one safety rule on large paper. Bind the pages together to make a class Big Book of home safety rules and another for school safety rules. Encourage children to use spelling words in their text.

Unit 4 BONUS

Day by Day Planner

These pages can be used at any time during the study of this unit.

Objectives *Children will*

- learn to use a thesaurus
- use context to help them choose appropriate synonyms from a thesaurus
- use words found in a thesaurus in their writing

Unit 4 BONUS

Vocabulary Enrichment

Word Builder

Spelling Word Link
job

Using a Thesaurus Look in a **thesaurus** to find just the right word to say what you mean. Read page 262 to learn how to use a thesaurus.

Write a word you could use in place of the word in dark print. Use your Thesaurus.

1. a hard **job**   **2.** **find** the trouble   **3.** a **nice** teacher

| **1.** task *or* chore | **2.** spot *or* locate | **3.** friendly *or* kind |

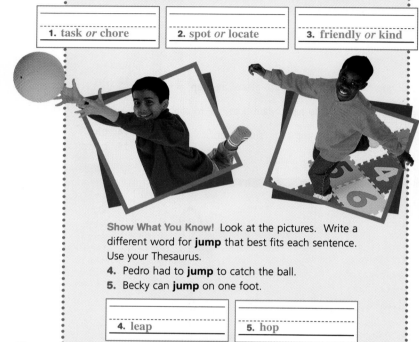

Show What You Know! Look at the pictures. Write a different word for **jump** that best fits each sentence. Use your Thesaurus.

4. Pedro had to **jump** to catch the ball.
5. Becky can **jump** on one foot.

| **4.** leap | **5.** hop |

46

EXTENSION OPTIONS

Learning Center Activity

visual/kinesthetic

Synonym Word Posters Ask children to fold a piece of large drawing paper in thirds. Have them look up the short *o* word *knock* in their Thesaurus and choose two of the synonyms listed. Ask them to write a sentence at the bottom of each section—one for *knock* (or form of) and one for each of the synonyms. Then have children illustrate each sentence.

Vocabulary Enrichment

Health

Safety at Home and at School All the words in the box have something to do with safety at home and at school. Write those words to finish this safety poster. Use your Spelling Dictionary.

Spelling Word Link

hospital

careful
injure
exit
alarm

Fire Drill Rules

→ When the fire __(1)__ rings, stop what you are doing.

→ Walk to the __(2)__ quickly.

→ Be __(3)__ going down the stairs. You do not want to __(4)__ yourself.

EXIT

1. alarm

2. exit

3. careful

4. injure

Try This CHALLENGE

Yes or No? Is the word in dark print used correctly? Write **yes** or **no**.

5. We used the window as a fire **exit**.
6. I could **injure** myself on a rusty nail.
7. The **alarm** made me sleepy.
8. If you are **careful**, you will fall.

5. yes

6. yes

7. no

8. no

Fact File

If you are ever in a room that fills up with smoke, drop to the floor and crawl out. Smoke rises, so the air near the floor will be easier to breathe.

47

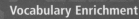

Day by Day Planner

Objectives *Children will*

■ expand their vocabulary by using words related to safety

■ show their understanding of the vocabulary words by completing context activities

Vocabulary Checkup

Have children use the vocabulary words in sentences or match the words to the definitions below.

1. a way out *exit*
2. taking steps to keep from being hurt *careful*
3. a bell that rings when there is danger *alarm*
4. to hurt *injure*

Fact File

Fire Safety

You may wish to discuss other appropriate procedures children should follow during a fire. Local fire departments often work with teachers to instruct children about fire safety techniques, such as checking doors for heat and rolling to smother flames on clothes.

Integrating Literature

Easy

Dinosaurs Beware: A Safety Guide
by Marc Brown
Dinosaurs teach children about safety.

Shy Charles
by Rosemary Wells
Shy Charles calls for help when his babysitter gets hurt.

Average

Left Behind
by Carol Carrick
Christopher gets lost during a class trip.

Officer Buckle and Gloria
by Peggy Rathmann
Officer Buckle's dog, Gloria, enlivens his boring safety lectures.

Challenging

Safety at Home
by Kyle Carter
How to avoid accidents that might happen around the house.

Safety on Bicycles
by Kyle Carter
How to signal for turning and other tips for safe cycling.

Spelling the Short *u* Sound

WORD LISTS

Spelling

Basic

1. sun
2. mud
3. bug
4. fun
5. but
6. hug
7. bun
8. nut
9. bus
10. rug
11. some
12. from

Review

13. up
14. run

Challenge

15. thunder
16. puddle

Vocabulary

Science: Seasons of the Year

summer
winter
season
weather

Introducing the Lesson

Read Aloud

Write the Basic Words on the board.

A New Season

Pretend it is early in the morning. You wake up, walk across the **rug**, and look out the window. Something is different. The **sun** is just coming up, **but** it is not in quite the same place it was a few weeks ago. You get dressed, eat your cereal, and maybe eat a **bun**. Then you **hug** your mom and run outside. You have **fun** jumping over the squishy **mud**. As you wait for the school **bus**, you see **some** geese flying overhead. They are returning **from** the South now that it is warmer. A squirrel runs across a branch with a **nut** in its mouth. The buds on the tree are beginning to open. A tiny **bug** buzzes in your ear. Can you guess what season of the year it is?

Responding Ask what season is described in the story. *(spring)* Then ask what spelling word names something that gives off light and heat. *(sun)* Have children name and spell two other Basic Words that rhyme with sun. *(fun, bun)*

Day 1 *page 48*

Objectives *Children will*

- take the pretest
- pronounce the list words
- learn about the spelling principle
- analyze words by their short vowel pattern

Planning Checklist

- ☑ Pretest (TE)
- ☑ Spelling principle/word list
- ☐ Review/Challenge Words
- ☐ Teaching the Principle (TE)
- ☐ Enrichment (TE)
- ☐ Additional Spelling Words (TE)

Assessment

Pretest

1. The <u>sun</u> is hot.
2. Buddy got <u>mud</u> on me.
3. An ant is a <u>bug</u>.
4. Was the ride <u>fun</u>?
5. I like red <u>but</u> not pink.
6. He gave me a <u>hug</u>.
7. She ate a <u>bun</u>.
8. An acorn is a <u>nut</u>.
9. I take a <u>bus</u> to school.
10. The cat is on the <u>rug</u>.
11. We saw <u>some</u> trees.
12. You ran <u>from</u> the bee.

Day 2 *page 49*

Objectives *Children will*

- practice spelling list words
- apply spelling strategies
- complete analogies with Basic Words
- identify Elephant Words by using context clues

Planning Checklist

- ☑ Spelling Strategy
- ☑ Independent Practice
- ☐ Daily Proofreading Practice (TE)
- ☐ Informal Assessment (TE)
- ☐ Extra Support (TE)
- ☐ Applying Spelling Strategies (TE)

Teacher's Resource Book
Practice Masters, pages 21–23
Unit Test, page 24
Bulletin Board, page 25

Practice Plus
Take-Home Word List 5
Games

Spelling Transparencies
Spelling Word List 5
Daily Proofreading Practice, Unit 5
Graphic Organizers

Teacher's Resource Disk
Macintosh® or Windows®
software. Houghton Mifflin

Spelling CD-ROM
Macintosh® or Windows®
software. Houghton Mifflin

Internet
http://www.eduplace.com

Phonics Practice
Houghton Mifflin Phonics
The Listening Corner
Phonics Home Connection

 Day 3 *page 50*   **Day 4** *page 51*   **Day 5** *page 51*

Objectives *Children will*
- identify words according to their position in a dictionary
- review Basic and Review Words

Planning Checklist
☐ Dictionary
☐ Review: Spelling Spree
☐ How Are You Doing?
☐ Daily Proofreading Practice (TE)
☐ Cooperative Learning Activity (TE)

Objectives *Children will*
- proofread for spelling
- write and proofread an original composition

Planning Checklist
☐ Proofread for Spelling
☐ Write a List
☐ Daily Proofreading Practice (TE)
☐ Challenge Words Practice (TE)
☐ Another Writing Idea (TE)

Objective *Children will*
- take the posttest

Assessment
☐ **Posttest** (TE) *See Day 5*
☐ Unit 5 Test

Meeting Individual Needs
Students Acquiring English

Spanish In Spanish there is no |ŭ| sound. Spanish-speaking children may spell the |ŭ| sound a or o.
Activity Write *hot, bag, cap,* and *not* on the board. Say each word. Ask children to repeat. Have volunteers change each vowel to spell the |ŭ| sound. Have children say each word.
Asian Most Asian languages have the |ŭ| sound, often represented by the letter *a.* The letter *u* is pronounced |o͞o| or |o͝o|.
Activity Model how to print the list words. Say each word as you write it, pointing to the *u.* Have children read and copy each word.

Other Activities for Any Day

- Bonus activities from pages 52–53
- Practice Masters (easy, average, challenging)
  Teacher's Resource Book, pages 21–23
- Take-Home Word List 5
  Practice Plus

Objectives *Children will*

- take the pretest
- pronounce the list words
- learn about the spelling principle
- analyze words by their short vowel pattern

Teaching the Principle

This lesson teaches the short vowel pattern for the |ŭ| sound (*u* followed by a consonant sound). Children learn the strategy of thinking of this pattern when they hear the short *u* sound.

To sum up the lesson, ask:

- What vowel spells the short u sound in each word? *(the vowel u)*
- What kind of letter follows the vowel *u* in each word? *(a consonant)*

Note: The Elephant Word *from* can be pronounced several ways: |frŭm|, |frŏm|, or unstressed |frəm|.

Enrichment

Vocabulary: Multiple Meanings
Have children use a dictionary to look up *sun, bug, but,* and *nut.* Discuss the meanings.

Read and Say

READ the sentences. **SAY** each word in dark print.

Basic Words

1.	sun	The **sun** is hot.
2.	mud	Buddy got **mud** on me.
3.	bug	An ant is a **bug**.
4.	fun	Was the ride **fun**?
5.	but	I like red **but** not pink.
6.	hug	He gave me a **hug**.
7.	bun	She ate a **bun**.
8.	nut	An acorn is a **nut**.
9.	bus	I take a **bus** to school.
10.	rug	The cat is on the **rug**.
11.	some	We saw **some** trees.
12.	from	You ran **from** the bee.

A. sun

mud

bug

fun

but

hug

bun

nut

bus

rug

B. some

from

48

Think and Write

Each word has the short **u** vowel sound. It is the first sound you hear in 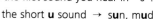.

the short **u** sound → s**u**n, m**u**d

How are the Elephant Words different? The |ŭ| sound is spelled *o* in each Elephant Word.

A. Write the first **ten** Basic Words. Then draw a line under the letter that spells the short **u** sound in each word.

B. Now write the **two** Elephant Words.
Order of answers for each category may vary.

Review	Challenge
13. up 14. run	15. thunder 16. puddle

TEACHING **OPTIONS**

Meeting Individual Needs
Word Lists

You may want to assign Basic Words 1–5, the Elephant Words, and the Review Words to children who misspelled more than five words on the pretest. Assign the Challenge Words as appropriate. (You may want to have children write sentences, using the Challenge Words.)

Additional Spelling Words

Basic	Challenge	Words Often Misspelled
plus	muffin	would
tug	shrug	could
jump	bucket	
drum	ugly	
hum	number	
	jungle	

Home/School Involvement
Take-Home Word List • Goal-Setting

Have children set goals for the week on Take-Home Word List 5.

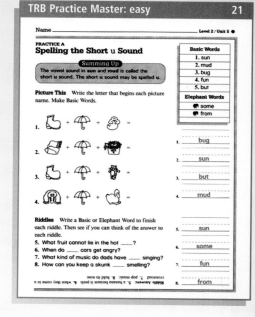

Independent Practice

 Spelling Strategy The vowel sound in **sun** and **mud** is called the short **u** sound. The short **u** sound may be spelled **u**.

Order of answers for question 4–6 may vary.

Phonics Write Basic Words to answer the questions.

1. Which word begins and ends like **bat**?
2. Which word begins and ends like **mad**?
3. Which word rhymes with **us**?
4–6. Which three words rhyme with **run**?

Word Pairs Write a Basic Word to finish the second sentence in each pair.

7. A **bed** is covered by a **blanket**.
   A **floor** is covered by a _____.
8. A **rose** is a kind of **flower**.
   A **cricket** is a kind of _____.
9. A **peel** covers an **orange**.
   A **shell** covers a _____.
10. You use your **legs** to **walk**.
    You use your **arms** to _____.

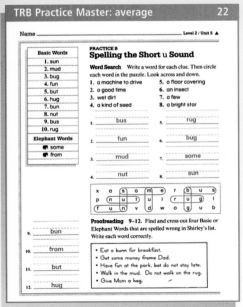

Elephant Words Write the missing Elephant Words.

11. Every fall we pick _____ apples.
12. They come _____ the old tree in our yard.

Phonics

1. but

2. mud

3. bus

4. sun

5. fun

6. bun

Word Pairs

7. rug

8. bug

9. nut

10. hug

Elephant Words

11. some

12. from

(49)

 Day 2

Objectives *Children will*

- practice spelling list words
- apply spelling strategies
- complete analogies with Basic Words
- identify Elephant Words by using context clues

Daily Proofreading Practice

We took the **buss** downtown. (*bus*)
Gus picked **som** apples. (*some*)

Meeting Individual Needs
visual/oral/auditory

Extra Support Check Independent Practice to determine who needs extra support. Write the following on the board:

t__b   r__n   c__t   h__g   s__n

Have children say each word, writing in the missing vowel *u*. Then say a sentence using each word. Children can copy from the board the short *u* word they hear in each sentence.

Name _____ Level 2 / Unit 5 ▲

Basic Words
1. sun
2. mud
3. bug
4. fun
5. but
6. hug
7. bun
8. nut
9. bus
10. rug

Elephant Words
some
from

PRACTICE B
Spelling the Short u Sound

Word Search Write a word for each clue. Then circle each word in the puzzle. Look across and down.

1. a machine to drive
2. a good time
3. wet dirt
4. a kind of seed
5. a floor covering
6. an insect
7. a few
8. a bright star

1. bus   5. rug
2. fun   6. bug
3. mud   7. some
4. nut   8. sun

x	a	s	o	m	e	r	b	u	s
p	n	u	t	u	i	r	u	g	t
f	u	n	v	d	w	o	g	u	b

Proofreading 9–12. Find and cross out four Basic or Elephant Words that are spelled wrong in Shirley's list. Write each word correctly.

- Eat a bunn for breakfast.
- Get some money frome Dad.
- Have fun at the park, bot do not stay late.
- Walk in the mud. Do not walk on the rug.
- Give Mom a heg.

9. bun
10. from
11. but
12. hug

 Applying Spelling Strategies
To Spell New Words

- Read aloud: **Jake is someone I can trust.**
- Have children attempt to spell *trust* on their Have-a-Go charts.

- Model the following strategies as children try to spell *trust*.

> This word has the short *u* sound. The short *u* sound is probably spelled *u*.

> I hear the sounds for *t* and *r* blended together at the beginning of the word.

trust

> I hear the sounds for *s* and *t* blended together at the end of the word.

Day 3

Objectives *Children will*

■ identify words according to their position in a dictionary

■ review Basic and Review Words

Daily Proofreading Practice

A **bugg** landed on Fred's nose. (*bug*)

We got a post card **frum** Nana. (*from*)

Parts of a Dictionary

1. bus
_____

2. fun
_____

3. hug
_____

4. nut
_____

5. run
_____

6. up
_____

Hink Pinks

7. bug
_____

8. nut
_____

9. hug
_____

Word Hunt

10. bun
_____

11. sun
_____

12. rug
_____

50

Dictionary

Parts of a Dictionary A dictionary lists words in ABC order. How would you find the word **run** in the dictionary? You would turn to the end and find the words that begin with **r**.

BEGINNING	MIDDLE	END
abcdefg	hijklmnopq	rstuvwxyz

Practice Write words from the box to answer the questions. Order of answers for each question may vary.

run	hug	bus	nut	up	fun

1–2. Which two words are found at the beginning of the dictionary?

3–4. Which two words are found in the middle?

5–6. Which two words are found at the end?

Review: Spelling Spree

Hink Pinks Write the Basic Word that answers the question and rhymes with the word in dark print.

7. What is a cup for an ant? a _____ **mug**

8. What is a home for a peanut? a _____ **hut**

9. What is a tight squeeze? a **snug** _____

Word Hunt Write the Basic Word you see in each longer word.

10. bunch

11. sunny

12. shrug

How Are You Doing?
Write each spelling word as a family member reads it aloud. Did you spell any words wrong?

TEACHING OPTIONS

Cooperative Learning Activity
Picture This
visual/kinesthetic

Have children choose a season, write the name of the season at the top of drawing paper, and draw a picture that depicts both the season and spelling words from this unit. Ask partners to switch drawings and see how many spelling words they can find pictured. Together, they can add spelling word labels to their drawings.

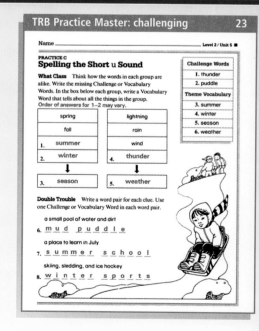

Proofreading and Writing

Proofread for Spelling Proofread this weather report. Use proofreading marks to fix five spelling mistakes.

Example: We will ~~runn~~ in the rain. *(run)*

TODAY'S WEATHER

Rain will fall ~~frum~~ *from* now until noon, ~~butt~~ *but* then the sky will clear up. The rain may be heavy, so watch out for the ~~mudd~~ *mud*! Later the sun will shine. Go outside and have ~~sun font~~ *some fun*!

Basic

1. sun
2. mud
3. bug
4. fun
5. but
6. hug
7. bun
8. nut
9. bus
10. rug
11. some
12. from

Review

13. up
14. run

Challenge

15. thunder
16. puddle

Write a List

Mr. Travis owns a store that sells only summer things. Help him make a list of some things he might sell. Then think of a good name for the store. Try to use spelling words.

Proofreading Tip
Make sure you have written your u's and w's the right way.

Proofreading Marks

∧ Add
⌐ Delete
≡ Make a capital letter
/ Make a small letter

51

Objectives *Children will*

■ proofread for spelling
■ write and proofread an original composition

Day 4

Daily Proofreading Practice

Our pig rolled in the **mod**. *(mud)*
Plants need the **son** to grow. *(sun)*

Day 5 **Posttest**

Sentences 1–5 test the first five Basic Words. Sentences 6–10 test the next five Basic Words. Sentences 11–12 test the Elephant Words.

Basic Words

1. Look at that big <u>bug</u>!
2. The frog sat in the <u>mud</u>.
3. Did they have <u>fun</u>?
4. The <u>sun</u> is in the sky.
5. Nan is little <u>but</u> fast.
6. They ran for the <u>bus</u>.
7. Step on the <u>rug</u>!
8. This is a hot <u>bun</u>.
9. I see a <u>nut</u> in the tree.
10. Dan gave me a <u>hug</u>.
11. There are <u>some</u> kites in the sky.
12. The game came <u>from</u> the box.

Review Words

13. Ted can <u>run</u> so fast!
14. Look <u>up</u> at that tree!

Challenge Words

15. The <u>thunder</u> scared our cat.
16. Kim splashed in the <u>puddle</u>.

TRB Unit 5 Test 24

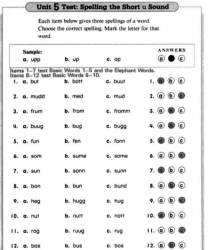

Name _____ Level 2 / Unit 5 ●▲

Unit 5 Test: Spelling the Short u Sound

Each item below gives three spellings of a word. Choose the correct spelling. Mark the letter for that word.

Sample:			ANSWERS
a. upp	b. up	c. op	ⓐ ● ⓒ

Items 1–7 test Basic Words 1–5 and the Elephant Words.
Items 8–12 test Basic Words 6–10.

1. a. but	b. bott	c. buut	1. ● ⓑ ⓒ
2. a. mudd	b. med	c. mud	2. ⓐ ⓑ ●
3. a. frum	b. from	c. fromm	3. ⓐ ● ⓒ
4. a. buug	b. bug	c. bugg	4. ⓐ ● ⓒ
5. a. fun	b. fen	c. fonn	5. ● ⓑ ⓒ
6. a. som	b. sume	c. some	6. ⓐ ⓑ ●
7. a. sun	b. sonn	c. sunn	7. ● ⓑ ⓒ
8. a. bon	b. bun	c. bund	8. ⓐ ● ⓒ
9. a. heg	b. hugg	c. hug	9. ⓐ ⓑ ●
10. a. nut	b. nutt	c. nott	10. ● ⓑ ⓒ
11. a. rog	b. ruug	c. rug	11. ⓐ ⓑ ●
12. a. bas	b. bus	c. bos	12. ⓐ ● ⓒ

Meeting Individual Needs

Challenge Words Practice
Children can make a national, regional, or local weather map, describing the weather in various locations with labels that include the Challenge Words and other weather words they know.

Another Writing Idea Ask children to write a journal entry about something fun they did on a summer day. Encourage them to use spelling words.

These pages can be used at any time during the study of this unit.

Day by Day Planner

Objectives *Children will*

■ build words with short *u* phonograms

■ identify rhyming words

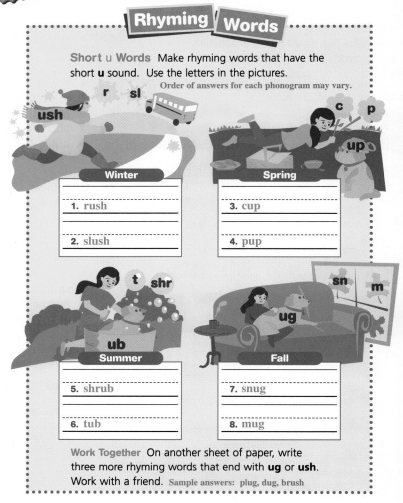

Rhyming Words

Short u Words Make rhyming words that have the short **u** sound. Use the letters in the pictures.

Order of answers for each phonogram may vary.

r   sl

ush

Winter

1. rush

2. slush

c   p

up

Spring

3. cup

4. pup

t   shr

ub

Summer

5. shrub

6. tub

sn   m

ug

Fall

7. snug

8. mug

Work Together On another sheet of paper, write three more rhyming words that end with **ug** or **ush**. Work with a friend. Sample answers: plug, dug, brush

52

EXTENSION OPTIONS

Learning Center Activity

visual/kinesthetic

Word Builder Bugs Ask children to think of a bug and draw its home in the center of a poster. On the bug home, have them write the phonogram *ug*. Around the home, children can draw or paste pictures of the bug. On each bug, have them write a word that ends with *ug*.

More -*ug* Words		
chug	lug	shrug
dug	plug	tug
jug	slug	

Vocabulary Enrichment

Science

Seasons of the Year All the words in the box have something to do with the seasons of the year. Write those words to finish this letter. Use your Spelling Dictionary.

Spelling Word Link

sun

summer
winter
season
weather

July 19, 1998

Dear Grandpa,

School is over, and I have started my _(1)_ vacation. Today's _(2)_ is too hot and sticky for me. My favorite _(3)_ of the year is _(4)_ . I can't wait to play in the snow!

Love,
Taneesha

1. summer

2. weather

3. season

4. winter

Try This CHALLENGE

Write a Letter Write a letter to a friend who is thinking of moving to your town. Tell your friend what the weather is like during the different seasons. Try to use some words from the box.

Fact File

In the fall, the days get shorter and colder. The green color on the leaves of many trees fades, leaving bright red, orange, or yellow colors.

53

Day by Day Planner

Objectives *Children will*

- expand their vocabulary by using words related to seasons of the year
- show their understanding of the vocabulary words by completing context and writing activities

Vocabulary Checkup

Have children use the vocabulary words in sentences or use the words to answer the questions below.

1. During which part of the year would you wear boots and mittens? *winter*
2. In which part of the year would you have a picnic and swim in a lake? *summer*
3. What do you call each of the four parts of the year? *season*
4. What makes a day hot or cold, sunny or cloudy, wet or dry? *weather*

Fact File

Chlorophyll

Chlorophyll, the green pigment found in most leaves, takes in sunlight that trees convert into food-producing energy. When the weather begins to turn cold, trees prepare for winter by stopping the production of chlorophyll, and the familiar yellow, orange, red, and purple colors of autumn are unmasked.

Integrating Literature

Easy	Average	Challenging
Frog and Toad All Year *by Arnold Lobel* Five seasonal stories about friends Frog and Toad.	**A Year in the City** *by Kathy Henderson* A month-by-month description of activity in a city.	**The Reasons for Seasons** *by Gail Gibbons* An explanation of the causes for seasonal changes.
Have You Seen Trees? *by Joanne Oppenheim* A poem celebrates the beauty of trees throughout the seasons.	**Pond Year** *by Kathryn Lasky* Two friends explore pond life over the course of a year.	**The Stranger** *by Chris Van Allsburg* A stranger staying with a farmer seems to have an effect on the weather.

Review: Units 1–5

WORD LISTS

Spelling

Basic Words

Unit 1	Unit 4
bag	job
am	nod
has	top
sad	dot
ran	fox
sat	hop

Unit 2	Unit 5
leg	mud
yes	fun
bed	but
went	hug
pen	bus
wet	rug

Unit 3

pig
win
his
if
hit
fix

Elephant Words

Units 1–5

was	I
said	of
been	from

The Review Unit

Word Lists

Half of the Basic Words from Units 1–5 are reviewed in this Review Unit. The remaining Basic Words from Units 1–5 are reviewed in the Extra Practice section of the Student's Handbook. Each of the Elephant Words is practiced in either the Review Unit or the Extra Practice section.

Day 1 *page 54*

Objectives *Children will*

- take the pretest
- review a spelling pattern for the |ă| sound
- review a spelling pattern for the |ĕ| sound

Planning Checklist

☐ Daily Proofreading Practice (TE)

☐ Extra Support, pages 25, 31 (TE)

☐ Extra Practice, page 241

☐ Practice Masters, pages 5, 6, 9, 10 (TRB)

Day 2 *page 55*

Objectives *Children will*

- review a spelling pattern for the |ĭ| sound
- review a spelling pattern for the |ŏ| sound

Planning Checklist

☐ Daily Proofreading Practice (TE)

☐ Extra Support, pages 37, 43 (TE)

☐ Extra Practice, page 242

☐ Practice Masters, pages 13, 14, 17, 18 (TRB)

Assessment

Pretest

1. Do not be <u>sad</u>.
2. They <u>ran</u> fast.
3. He will say <u>yes</u>.
4. It is time for <u>bed</u>.
5. That is a big <u>pig</u>.
6. You can <u>fix</u> it for me.
7. They will do my <u>job</u>.
8. That is a fast <u>fox</u>.
9. You can <u>hug</u> me.
10. The red <u>rug</u> is his.

Day 3 *page 56*

Day 4 *page 57*

Day 5 *page 57*

Objectives *Children will*
- review a spelling pattern for the |ŭ| sound
- review the Elephant Words

Planning Checklist
- ☐ Daily Proofreading Practice (TE)
- ☐ Extra Support, page 49 (TE)
- ☐ Extra Practice, page 243
- ☐ Practice Masters, pages 21, 22 (TRB)

Objective *Children will*
- analyze the spelling and meaning relationship of words in the *help* family

Planning Checklist
- ☐ Spelling-Meaning Strategy

Objective *Children will*
- take the posttest

Assessment

- ☐ **Posttest** (TE) *See Day 5*
- ☐ Unit 6 Review Tests A–B (TRB)

● Additional Resources

Teacher's Resource Book
Practice Masters, pages 5–7, 9–11, 13–15, 17–19, 21–23
Multiple-Choice Tests, pages 29–30
Bulletin Board, page 25
Spelling Newsletters: English and Spanish, pages 26–27
Spelling Game, page 28

🏠 **Practice Plus**
Take-Home Word List 6

Spelling Transparencies
Spelling Word List 6
Daily Proofreading Practice, Unit 6
Spelling-Meaning Strategy
Multiple-Choice Test

Teacher's Resource Disk
Macintosh® or Windows® software. Houghton Mifflin

Spelling CD-ROM
Macintosh® or Windows® software. Houghton Mifflin

Internet
http://www.eduplace.com

Meeting Individual Needs

You may wish to create your own pretest, using the words that children missed most often in the last five units. Children can check their own work, or a partner's, by looking up the words in the previous units' word lists or in their Spelling Dictionary.

In each Review lesson, the Basic Words are selected from both halves of the unit word list to accommodate individual needs. In Units 1–5, the top row of words is from Basic Words 1–5 and the bottom row from Basic Words 6–10.

Other Activities for Any Day

- Literature and Writing, pages 58–59
- Spelling Game
  Teacher's Resource Book, page 28
- Bulletin Board
  Teacher's Resource Book, page 25
- Take-Home Word List 6
  Practice Plus

Objectives *Children will*

- take the pretest
- review a spelling pattern for the |ă| sound
- review a spelling pattern for the |ĕ| sound

Daily Proofreading Practice

Karl **rann** to catch the bus. (*ran*)

Mom said **yez**, I may go. (*yes*)

Meeting Individual Needs

Additional Resources

Unit 1

Extra Support page 25 (TE)

Extra Practice page 241

Practice Masters pages 5–6 (TRB)

Unit 2

Extra Support page 31(TE)

Extra Practice page 241

Practice Masters pages 9–10 (TRB)

---

6 **Review:** Units 1–5

1. bag
2. ran
3. am
4. sat
5. has
6. sad
7. bed
8. pen
9. wet
10. leg
11. went
12. yes

54

Unit 1 Spelling the Short a Sound pages 24–29

ă
h a t

bag	am	has
sad	ran	sat

Spelling Strategy   The short a sound may be spelled **a**.

Write the spelling word that rhymes with each word.

1. rag   3. ham
2. man   4. fat

Write the missing spelling words.

5. Steven's bike _____ a flat tire.
6. That is why he is _____.

Unit 2 Spelling the Short e Sound pages 30–35

ĕ
p e t

leg	yes	bed
went	pen	wet

Spelling Strategy   The short e sound may be spelled **e**.

Write the spelling word that goes with each word.

7. pillow   9. rain
8. paper   10. arm

Write the missing spelling words.

   The rain clouds ___**(11)**___ away. May we go out and play? Oh ___**(12)**___, you may!

TRB Bulletin Board   25

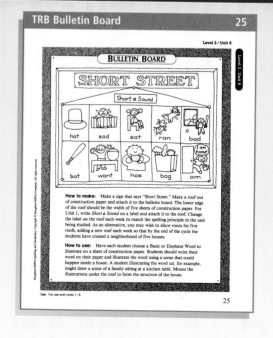

BULLETIN BOARD

SHORT STREET

Short a Sound

hat   sad   sat   ran   bad

bat   want   has   bag   am

How to make: Make a sign that says "Short Street." Make a roof out of construction paper and attach it to the bulletin board. The lower edge of the roof should be the width of five sheets of construction paper. For Unit 1, write *Short a Sound* on a label and attach it to the roof. Change the label on the roof each week to match the spelling principle in the unit being studied. As an alternative, you may wish to allow room for five roofs, adding a new roof each week so that by the end of the cycle the students have created a neighborhood of five houses.

How to use: Have each student choose a Basic or Elephant Word to illustrate on a sheet of construction paper. Students should write their word on their paper and illustrate the word using a scene that could happen inside a house. A student illustrating the word *sat*, for example, might draw a scene of a family sitting at a kitchen table. Mount the illustrations under the roof to form the structure of the house.

Use: For use with Units 1–5.

25

TRB Spelling Newsletter: English   26

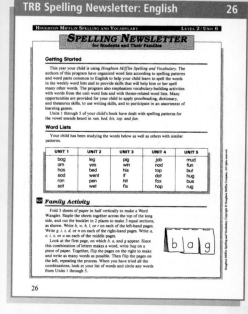

HOUGHTON MIFFLIN SPELLING AND VOCABULARY   LEVEL 2 / UNIT 6

SPELLING NEWSLETTER
for Students and Their Families

Getting Started

This year your child is using *Houghton Mifflin Spelling and Vocabulary.* The authors of this program have organized word lists according to spelling patterns and word parts common to English to help your child learn to spell the words in the weekly word lists and to provide skills that will help him or her spell many other words. The program also emphasizes vocabulary-building activities with words from the unit word lists and with theme-related word lists. Many opportunities are provided for your child to apply proofreading, dictionary, and thesaurus skills, to use writing skills, and to participate in an assortment of learning games.

Units 1 through 5 of your child's book have dealt with spelling patterns for the vowel sounds heard in *ran, bed, his, top,* and *fun.*

Word Lists

Your child has been studying the words below as well as others with similar patterns.

UNIT 1	UNIT 2	UNIT 3	UNIT 4	UNIT 5
bag	leg	pig	job	mud
am	yes	win	nod	fun
has	bed	his	top	but
sad	went	if	dot	hug
ran	pen	hit	fox	bus
sat	wet	fix	hop	rug

Family Activity

Fold 3 sheets of paper in half vertically to make a Word Wrangler. Staple the sheets together across the top of the long side, and cut the booklet in 2 places to make 3 equal sections, as shown. Write *b, w, h, l,* or *r* on each of the left-hand pages. Write *g, l, s, d,* or *n* on each of the right-hand pages. Write *a, e, i, o,* or *u* on each of the middle pages.

Look at the first page, on which *b, a,* and *g* appear. Since this combination of letters makes a word, write *bag* on a piece of paper. Together, flip the pages on the right to make and write as many words as possible. Then flip the pages on the left, repeating the process. When you have tried all the combinations, look at your list of words and circle any words from Units 1 through 5.

b | a | g

26

Unit 3 Spelling the Short i Sound pages 36–41

pig	win	his
if	hit	fix

ĭ pig

Spelling Strategy
The short **i** sound may be spelled **i**.

Write the spelling word that means the opposite.

13. lose **14.** break

Write the missing spelling words.

Jon can __(15)__ the balls hard with __(16)__ new bat. Our pet __(17)__ will chase the balls __(18)__ we don't catch them quickly!

Unit 4 Spelling the Short o Sound pages 42–47

job	nod	top
dot	fox	hop

ŏ top

Spelling Strategy
The short **o** sound may be spelled **o**.

Write the spelling word that means the same.

19. circle **20.** cover **21.** work

Write the missing spelling words.

We watched a rabbit __(22)__ into the woods. Suddenly a red __(23)__ came out of its hole. The two animals seemed to __(24)__ their heads and say hello!

13. win

14. fix

15. hit

16. his

17. pig

18. if

19. dot

20. top

21. job

22. hop

23. fox

24. nod

55

Objectives *Children will*

- review a spelling pattern for the |ĭ| sound
- review a spelling pattern for the |ŏ| sound

Daily Proofreading Practice
I will get a blue ribbon **ef** I win. (*if*)
Can you **hawp** across the room? (*hop*)

Meeting Individual Needs

Additional Resources

Unit 3
Extra Support page 37 (TE)
Extra Practice page 242
Practice Masters pages 13–14 (TRB)

Unit 4
Extra Support page 43 (TE)
Extra Practice page 242
Practice Masters pages 17–18 (TRB)

Objectives *Children will*

■ review a spelling pattern for the |ŭ| sound

■ review the Elephant Words

Daily Proofreading Practice

Grandma gave me a big **hugg**. (*hug*)

Katy **sed** she loved our play! (*said*)

Meeting Individual Needs

Additional Resources

Unit 5

Extra Support page 49 (TE)

Extra Practice page 243

Practice Masters pages 21–22 (TRB)

Reviewing Elephant Words

Extra Practice page 243

UNIT
6

_____

25. rug

_____

26. hug

_____

27. but

_____

28. fun

_____

29. bus

_____

30. mud

_____

31. I

_____

32. from

_____

33. been

_____

34. was

_____

35. of

_____

36. said

_____

56

Unit 5 Spelling the Short u Sound pages 48–53

mud	fun	but
hug	bus	rug

Spelling Strategy The short **u** sound may be spelled **u**.

Change the letter in dark print. Write a spelling word.

25. r**a**g   **27.** b**a**t

26. h**o**g   **28.** f**i**n

Write the missing spelling words.

29. A big yellow _____ just went by.

30. It splashed _____ all over my new shoes!

Elephant Words   Units 1–5   pages 24–53

was	said	been
I	of	from

Spelling Strategy Elephant Words have unusual spellings. Check them carefully when you write them.

Write the missing spelling words.

Mom and __**(31)**__ just got back __**(32)**__ the zoo. I had __**(33)**__ to the zoo once before when I __**(34)**__ small. Today we saw a lot __**(35)**__ new animals. Mom __**(36)**__ she liked the bears best.

EXTENSION OPTIONS

TRB Review Test A   29

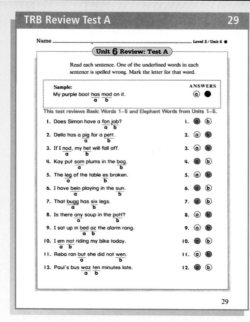

TRB Review Test B   30

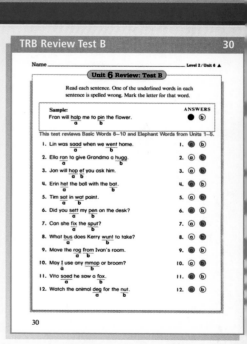

UNIT
6

Spelling-Meaning Strategy

Word Families

You know that people have families. Words have families too! Look at this word family.

| help |
| helper |
| helpful |
| helpless |

Anna will **help** you paint.

She is a good **helper**.

Anna is **helpful** in many ways.

She is not **helpless** like a baby.

Think How are the words in this family alike in meaning? How are they alike in spelling?

Apply and Extend

Write a word from the help **family in each sentence.**

1. Mark is the class _____ today.

2. Can he _____ me move the rug?

3. He is _____ when he sweeps.

4. I am not _____, so I will dust.

With a partner, think of words in these families.
Make a list for each family. See TE margin.

 sad   fish   stop

Check the Word Families list that begins on page 272. Did you miss any words? Add them to your lists.

----
1. helper
----
2. help
----
3. helpful
----
4. helpless

57

Objective *Children will*
- analyze the spelling and meaning relationship of words in the *help* family

Day **4**

Answers to *Think* Questions

- They all have some form of the meaning "to give or do what someone needs or can use."

- All of the words begin with *help*.

Day **5**   **Posttest**

The Posttest tests twenty of the Basic Words reviewed in this unit. Sentences 1–10 test words selected from Basic Words 1–5 in Units 1–5. The Elephant Words sentences test all six words reviewed in this unit.

Basic Words

1. I have a big bag.
2. Can you hop on one leg?
3. Do you like your job?
4. That is my pet pig.
5. Do they fly kites for fun?
6. The box has my name on it.
7. The cat was on the bed.
8. Nan will win the game.
9. They went up to the top.
10. Do not step in the mud.
11. Tim ran fast.
12. They went into the shop.
13. See if you can do it.
14. Look at that red fox!
15. You can step on the rug.
16. She sat on the bus.
17. Did you get wet?
18. I will hit it with a bat.
19. Can he hop up and down?
20. I will ride the bus.

Elephant Words

21. We said he could go.
22. Have you been there?
23. Ken was not here.
24. That is a big bag of cups.
25. Pam and I have fun.
26. Did I get this from you?

 Writing Model:
Class Story

Objectives *Children will*

■ read a literature passage modeling a class story

■ analyze the model to identify point of view and details

Warm-Up

Qualities of a Good Class Story

Discuss how shared experiences make the best topics for class stories, allowing everyone to participate and contribute. Then read aloud the following groups of sentences and ask children to identify the group that has the most interesting details about a class visitor. *(Group 2)*

1. Dr. Ling came to our class. She brought a tooth and a toothbrush.
2. Dr. Ling is a dentist. She came to our class with a giant pretend tooth and toothbrush.

Answers to *Think and Discuss*

1. The class told that they made money from their carnival and they told about two of the games.
2. It is interesting to know that there were one hundred dominoes in the Domino Push.
3. The word *we* is used because this is a class story and many children participated in telling it.

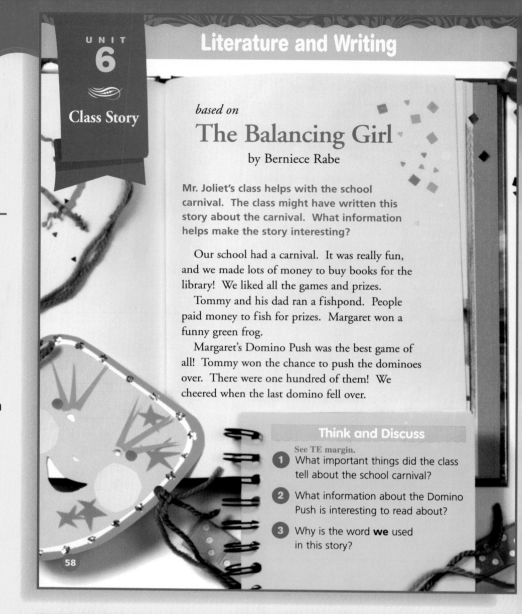

Literature and Writing

UNIT
6

Class Story

based on

The Balancing Girl

by Berniece Rabe

Mr. Joliet's class helps with the school carnival. The class might have written this story about the carnival. What information helps make the story interesting?

Our school had a carnival. It was really fun, and we made lots of money to buy books for the library! We liked all the games and prizes.

Tommy and his dad ran a fishpond. People paid money to fish for prizes. Margaret won a funny green frog.

Margaret's Domino Push was the best game of all! Tommy won the chance to push the dominoes over. There were one hundred of them! We cheered when the last domino fell over.

Think and Discuss

See TE margin.

1. What important things did the class tell about the school carnival?

2. What information about the Domino Push is interesting to read about?

3. Why is the word **we** used in this story?

58

EXTENSION **OPTIONS**

Integrating Literature *Class Story*

Easy	Average	Challenging
Arthur Writes a Story *by Marc Brown* Arthur's classmates help him write a story.	**Time Train** *by Paul Fleischman* Miss Pym's class goes back in time to the Jurassic period.	**The Magic Schoolbus®** **Inside a Bee Hive** *by Joanna Cole* Ms. Frizzle's class takes a trip through a beehive.
How the Second Grade Got $8,205.50 to Visit the Statue of Liberty *by Nathan Zimmelman* Students raise money to visit the famous statue.	**Song Lee and the Leech Man** *by Suzy Kline* Song Lee's class takes a trip to study insects.	**Pet Parade** *by Patricia Reilly Giff* Ms. Rooney's class brings their pets to school for Pet Week.

The Writing Process
Class Story

What special things have you and your class done together? Write a class story about one special thing. Follow the guidelines. Use the Writing Process below.

1 Prewriting
- Make a web. Write your story idea in the middle. Write what you want to tell about it in the other circles.

2 Draft
- Help your teacher write interesting things about your topic.

3 Revise
- Be sure the story events are in order.
- Cross out sentences that do not fit.
- Remember to use your Thesaurus to find exact words.

4 Proofread
- Is each word spelled correctly?
- Does each sentence begin and end correctly?

5 Publish
- Copy your story neatly. Draw a picture for it.
- Make a class book. Think of a title for your book.

Guidelines for Writing a Class Story

✓ Write the story events in an order that makes sense.
✓ Tell about important things that will make the story interesting for your reader.

Compostion Words

was
went
said
win
not
fun

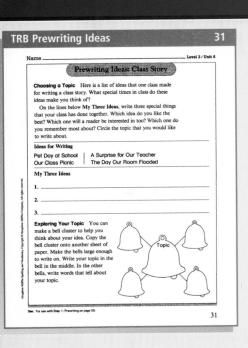

Our Puppet Show

59

Objective *Children will*
- follow the Writing Process to write a class story, using the criteria given in the guidelines

Additional Resource

To help children generate and explore topics for their class story, have them use the Prewriting Ideas in the *Teacher's Resource Book,* page 31.

Evaluating Writing

The Class Story is a collaborative effort, with each child contributing one sentence. There is no formal scoring rubric for the Class Story. After children have written their story, you may wish to review the guidelines on the student book page.

TRB Prewriting Ideas   31

Name _____   Level 2 / Unit 6

Prewriting Ideas: Class Story

Choosing a Topic Here is a list of ideas that one class made for writing a class story. What special times in class do these ideas make you think of?

On the lines below **My Three Ideas**, write three special things that your class has done together. Which idea do you like the best? Which one will a reader be interested in too? Which one do you remember most about? Circle the topic that you would like to write about.

Ideas for Writing

| Pet Day at School | A Surprise for Our Teacher |
| Our Class Picnic | The Day Our Room Flooded |

My Three Ideas

1. _____
2. _____
3. _____

Exploring Your Topic You can make a bell cluster to help you think about your idea. Copy the bell cluster onto another sheet of paper. Make the bells large enough to write on. Write your topic in the bell in the middle. In the other bells, write words that tell about your topic.

Topic

Use: For use with Step 1: Prewriting on page 59.

31

Vowel-Consonant-*e* Spellings

WORD LISTS

Spelling

Basic

1. five
2. late
3. nine
4. made
5. side
6. ate
7. fine
8. same
9. hide
10. line
11. give
12. have

Review

13. gave
14. bike

Challenge

15. mistake
16. write

Vocabulary

Social Studies: Schools

pupil

absent

locker

gym

Introducing the Lesson

Read Aloud

Write the Basic Words on the board.

Schools of Long Ago

Long ago in America, schools were not the **same** as they are today. The school-house was a one-room building **made** of wood. It was very bare, with wooden benches and desks and a single fireplace on one **side**. In winter, when there were fewer daylight hours, school lasted only four or **five** hours a day. But in **fine** summer weather, the children stayed **late**, and the school day was **nine** hours long! Usually only one man taught all the children in town. He earned very little money. Sometimes the towns-people would **give** him a piece of land on which he could grow the food that he **ate**. Of course, some things **have** not changed since long ago. Children still **line** up for recess, and they still like to play **hide**-and-seek or tag.

Responding Ask children what the school buildings of long ago were made of. *(wood)* Have them name the spelling word that tells how many hours long a school day was in summer. *(nine)*

Day 1 *page 60*

Day 2 *page 61*

Objectives *Children will*

- take the pretest
- pronounce the list words
- learn about the spelling principle
- sort words by their vowel sounds

Planning Checklist

- ☑ Pretest (TE)
- ☑ Spelling principle/word list
- ☐ Review/Challenge Words
- ☐ Teaching the Principle (TE)
- ☐ Enrichment (TE)
- ☐ Additional Spelling Words (TE)

Assessment

Pretest

1. My class has <u>five</u> frogs.
2. The bus is <u>late</u>.
3. I read <u>nine</u> books.
4. We <u>made</u> a poster.
5. Sit on this <u>side</u>.
6. Nick <u>ate</u> an apple.
7. Do you feel <u>fine</u> now?
8. We have the <u>same</u> job.
9. Did Prince <u>hide</u> his ball?
10. They got in <u>line</u>.
11. Did he <u>give</u> you a pen?
12. I <u>have</u> a pet turtle.

Objectives *Children will*

- practice spelling list words
- apply spelling strategies
- identify Basic Words by using meaning clues
- identify Elephant Words by given vowel sounds

Planning Checklist

- ☑ Spelling Strategy
- ☑ Independent Practice
- ☐ Daily Proofreading Practice (TE)
- ☐ Informal Assessment (TE)
- ☐ Extra Support (TE)
- ☐ Applying Spelling Strategies (TE)

Research Notes The selection of appropriate spelling words to study rests on a number of criteria: the words should occur frequently in printed materials; the words should be those children use frequently in their writing; the words should contain patterns children are likely to misspell. *See the Bibliography on page xv.*

 Day 3 *page 62*

 Day 4 *page 63*

 Day 5 *page 63*

Objective *Children will*
- review Basic and Review Words

Planning Checklist
- ☐ Review: Spelling Spree
- ☐ How Are You Doing?
- ☐ Daily Proofreading Practice (TE)
- ☐ Ongoing Assessment (TE)

Objectives *Children will*
- proofread for spelling and capital letters
- write and proofread an original composition

Planning Checklist
- ☐ Proofread: Spelling and Capital Letters
- ☐ Write a Daily Plan
- ☐ Daily Proofreading Practice (TE)
- ☐ Challenge Words Practice (TE)
- ☐ Another Writing Idea (TE)

Objective *Children will*
- take the posttest

Assessment
☐ **Posttest** (TE) *See Day 5*
☐ Unit 7 Test

Additional Resources

Teacher's Resource Book
Practice Masters, pages 33–35
Unit Test, page 36
Bulletin Board, page 53

Practice Plus
Take-Home Word List 7
Games

Spelling Transparencies
Spelling Word List 7
Daily Proofreading Practice, Unit 7
Graphic Organizers

Teacher's Resource Disk
Macintosh® or Windows® software. Houghton Mifflin

Spelling CD-ROM
Macintosh® or Windows® software. Houghton Mifflin

Internet
http://www.eduplace.com

Phonics Practice
Houghton Mifflin Phonics
The Listening Corner
Phonics Home Connection

Meeting Individual Needs
Students Acquiring English

Spanish In Spanish, there is nothing comparable to the final silent e.

Activity Write *mad, at,* and *cap* on the board. Say the words and have children repeat. Identify the /ă/ vowel sound. Then add an e to each word. Say the new words and have children repeat. Elicit that the final e has no sound but that it makes the vowel sound long. Repeat with *fin* and *hid.*

Asian Before introducing the vowel-consonant-e pattern, be sure children understand consonants and short vowel sounds.

Activity Use the activity for Spanish-speaking children above.

Other Activities for Any Day

- Bonus activities from pages 64–65
- Practice Masters (easy, average, challenging)
  Teacher's Resource Book, pages 33–35
- Take-Home Word List 7
  Practice Plus

Day 1

Objectives *Children will*
- take the pretest
- pronounce the list words
- learn about the spelling principle
- sort words by their vowel sounds

Teaching the Principle

This lesson teaches the vowel-consonant-e pattern for the |ā| and the |ī| sounds. Children learn the strategy of thinking of this pattern when they hear the long *a* or the long *i* sound.

To sum up the lesson, ask:

- What letter do you see at the end of each word? *(e)* Does it have any sound? *(no)*

- What letters spell the vowel-consonant-e pattern in each word? *(five, late, nine, made, side, ate, fine, same, hide, line)*

Enrichment

Vocabulary: Multiple Meanings
Have children use a dictionary to look up *late, side, fine,* and *line.* Discuss the different meanings.

ī
five

A. late
_____
made
_____
ate
_____
same
_____
B. five
_____
nine
_____
side
_____
fine
_____
hide
_____
line
_____
C. give
_____
have

60

Read and Say

READ the sentences. **SAY** each word in dark print.

Basic Words

1.	five	My class has **five** frogs.
2.	late	The bus is **late**.
3.	nine	I read **nine** books.
4.	made	We **made** a poster.
5.	side	Sit on this **side**.
6.	ate	Nick **ate** an apple.
7.	fine	Do you feel **fine** now?
8.	same	We have the **same** job.
9.	hide	Did Prince **hide** his ball?
10.	line	They got in **line**.
11.	give	Did he **give** you a pen?
12.	have	I **have** a pet turtle.

Think and Write

Most of the words have the long **a** or long **i** vowel sound spelled with the vowel-consonant-**e** pattern. These long vowel sounds begin 🏠 and 🎣.

long **a** sound → l**a**te   long **i** sound → f**i**ve

How are the Elephant Words different? In *give* and *have,* the vowel-consonant-*e* pattern spells a short rather than a long vowel sound.
A. Write **four** Basic Words with the long **a** sound.
B. Write **six** Basic Words with the long **i** sound.
C. Now write the **two** Elephant Words.
Order of answers for each category may vary.

Review		**Challenge**	
13. gave	**14.** bike	**15.** mistake	**16.** write

TEACHING OPTIONS

Meeting Individual Needs
Word Lists

You may want to assign Basic Words 1–5, the Elephant Words, and the Review Words to children who misspelled more than five words on the pretest. Assign the Challenge Words as appropriate. (You may want to have children write sentences, using the Challenge Words.)

Additional Spelling Words

Basic	**Challenge**	**Words Often Misspelled**
face	state	am
rake	stripe	and
bite	trace	
cave	maze	
mine	sunshine	
	beside	

Home/School Involvement
Take-Home Word List • Goal-Setting

Have children set goals for the week on Take-Home Word List 7.

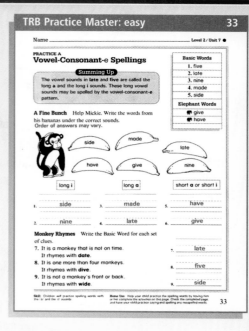

Independent Practice

Spelling Strategy The vowel sounds in **late** and **five** are called the long **a** and the long **i** sounds. These long vowel sounds may be spelled by the vowel-consonant-**e** pattern.

Order of answers for question 4–5 may vary.
Phonics Write Basic Words to answer the questions.

1. Which word begins like ?
2. Which word begins like ?
3. Which word begins like ?
4–5. Which two words begin like 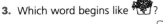?

Word Clues Write a Basic Word for each clue.
6. when you might get to school if you miss the bus
7. what you do if you do not want to be seen
8. what you might stand or write on
9. how you feel if you are not sick
10. how many fingers you have on one hand

Elephant Words
Write an Elephant Word to answer each question.
11. Which word has the short **a** sound?
12. Which word has the short **i** sound?

Phonics

1. ate
2. made
3. nine
4. side
5. same

Word Clues

6. late
7. hide
8. line
9. fine
10. five

Elephant Words

11. have
12. give

61

Day 2

Objectives *Children will*
- practice spelling list words
- apply spelling strategies
- identify Basic Words by using meaning clues
- identify Elephant Words by given vowel sounds

Daily Proofreading Practice
Pat drew a **lien** in the sand. (*line*)
Please **giv** me a push. (*give*)

Meeting Individual Needs
visual/oral/auditory/kinesthetic

Extra Support Check Independent Practice to determine who needs extra support. Write the words *late* and *five* in two columns on the board. Have children say the words and identify the vowels sounds. Say the other Basic Words in turn. Ask volunteers to write them under *late* or *five,* telling them to match the vowel sound. Have children underline the VCe pattern in each word.

Name _____   Level 2 / Unit 7 ▲

Basic Words
1. five
2. late
3. nine
4. mode
5. side
6. ate
7. fine
8. same
9. hide
10. line
Elephant Words
give
have

PRACTICE B
Vowel-Consonant-e Spellings

Crossword Clues Write a Basic or Elephant Word for each clue.

Across
2. built
5. almost ten
6. not the top or bottom
7. to own

Down
1. a long, thin mark
3. rhymes with **late**
4. less than six

In the Family Write the Basic or Elephant Word that is the opposite of the word in dark print.
8. Mr. Opposite is always **early**.
   Mrs. Opposite is always _____.
9. Mr. Opposite wears a **different** hat every day.
   Mrs. Opposite always wears the _____ one.
10. Mr. Opposite wants to **get** some new books.
    Mrs. Opposite wants to _____ away her old ones.
11. Mr. Opposite likes to **show** his paintings.
    Mrs. Opposite likes to _____ hers.
12. Mr. Opposite thinks the weather is **awful**.
    Mrs. Opposite thinks it is just _____.

8. late
9. same
10. give
11. hide
12. fine

34

Applying Spelling Strategies
To Read New Words

- Write this sentence on the chalkboard: **The baby bird was still alive after falling from its nest.**
- Have children read the sentence silently.
- Elicit the following strategies as children try to decode *alive.*

> I see the letter *a* at the beginning of the word.

> The letter *i* is followed by a consonant and e. I think this is the vowel-consonant-e pattern for the long *i* sound.

alive

> Then I see the letter *l.* I know that *l* makes the sound I hear at the beginning of *lamp.*

> A-l-ive. A-live. Alive. The word *alive* makes sense in the sentence.

UNIT 7

Objective *Children will*
■ review Basic and Review Words

Day 3

Daily Proofreading Practice

Do not be **layt** for school. (*late*)

Beth **maed** me a bookmark. (*made*)

UNIT 7

Puzzle Play

1. hide
2. have
3. same
4. bike
5. fine
6. line
7. late
8. gave

Code Breaker

9. give
10. side
11. ate
12. made

62

Review: Spelling Spree

Puzzle Play Write a Basic or Review Word for each clue. Use the letters that would be in the boxes to spell two things found in a school.

1. to cover up __ __ ☐ __
2. to own __ __ __ ☐
3. alike ☐ __ __ __
4. a bicycle __ __ ☐ __
5. good ☐ __ __ __
6. a row ☐ __ __ __
7. not on time __ ☐ __ __
8. handed ☐ __ __ __

Secret Words: d e s k   f l a g

Code Breaker Use the code to write Basic Words.

▲ = a	∩ = g	● = s
) = d	* = i	⊖ = t
☆ = e	☐ = m	◇ = v

Example:
●▲☐☆ = same

9. ∩*◇☆
10. ●*) ☆
11. ▲⊖☆
12. ☐▲) ☆

How Are You Doing?
List the spelling words that are still hard for you. Practice them with a family member.

TEACHING OPTIONS

Ongoing Assessment
Inclusion of Extra Silent Letters

Most children at the second grade level will be in the "within-word pattern" phase of spelling development. A common spelling error in this stage is the inclusion of a silent letter along with a long vowel. For example, *late* might be spelled LAIT or LAET.

By comparing and contrasting different spellings for the same long vowel sound, children will learn the various ways that long vowels are spelled in different contexts.

TRB Practice Master: challenging 35

Name _____ Level 2 / Unit 7 ■

PRACTICE C
Vowel-Consonant-e Spellings

School Books Write the missing Challenge or Vocabulary Word for each book title. Use capital letters.

1. How to Be a Smart _____ by Iva Brain
2. Games to Play in the _____ by P. E. Time
3. How to Correct a _____ by E. Raser

1. __Pupil__   3. __Mistake__

2. __Gym__

| Challenge Words |
| 1. mistake |
| 2. write |
| **Theme Vocabulary** |
| 3. pupil |
| 4. absent |
| 5. locker |
| 6. gym |

Addagrams Write a word for each clue. Then write the correct letters in the numbered boxes. The letters will spell a Challenge or Vocabulary Word.

4. a rubber wheel = t i r e (4 3 2 5)
   a thin piece of metal = w i r e (1 3 2 5) → | 1 2 3 4 5 | w r i t e |

5. something a key fits = l o c k (1 2 3 4)
   the middle of an apple = c o r e (3 2 6 5) → | 1 2 3 4 5 6 | l o c k e r |

6. an animal that flies = b a t (2 1 6)
   mailed = s e n t (3 4 5 6) → | 1 2 3 4 5 6 | a b s e n t |

35

62   Review: Spelling Spree

Proofreading and Writing

Proofread: Spelling and Capital Letters
Always begin the name of a person or pet with a capital letter.

Carlos   **N**ita   **F**luffy

Proofread this math problem. Use proofreading marks to fix four spelling mistakes and three missing capital letters.

Example: Was jason ~~lat~~ to the school fair?
      late

Ann and sarah made ~~nien~~ bookmarks.
          nine

They sold ~~fiv~~ bookmarks at the school fair.
       five

Their dog sparks ate one bookmark, and

they ~~gaev~~ one to their teacher. How many
   gave

bookmarks did Sarah and ann ~~hav~~ left?
              have

Answer: two

Write a Daily Plan

Pick a day of the week. Make a list of things you do in school on that day. Tell the time you do each thing. Try to use spelling words. Have a friend read your plan.

Monday List
8:00 _____
8:30 _____
9:00 _____

Proofreading Tip

Check that you began the name of each person and pet with a capital letter.

Basic

1. five
2. late
3. nine
4. made
5. side
6. ate
7. fine
8. same
9. hide
10. line
11. give
12. have

Review

13. gave
14. bike

Challenge

15. mistake
16. write

Proofreading Marks

∧ Add
⌐ Delete
≡ Make a capital letter
/ Make a small letter

63

TRB Unit 7 Test   **36**

Name _____ Level 2 / Unit 7 ●▲

Unit 7 Test: Vowel-Consonant-e Spellings

Read each sentence. Is the underlined word spelled right or wrong? Mark your answer.

Sample:	Right	Wrong
Freda gave me a funny hat.	●	○

Items 1–7 test Basic Words 1–5 and the Elephant Words.
Items 8–12 test Basic Words 6–10.

		Right	Wrong
1.	Wave from the <u>sied</u> of the road.	○	●
2.	The library has <u>nine</u> new books.	●	○
3.	Bruno is never <u>late</u> for school.	●	○
4.	Edith <u>moed</u> a big mistake.	○	●
5.	I will <u>have</u> another muffin.	●	○
6.	They will leave in <u>five</u> minutes.	●	○
7.	Will Gabe <u>gife</u> you his skates?	○	●
8.	Draw a red <u>line</u> across the paper.	●	○
9.	Who will <u>hied</u> the gift?	○	●
10.	Nelson <u>ate</u> all of his dinner.	●	○
11.	Stan and Nina have the <u>soem</u> shoes.	○	●
12.	You did a <u>finn</u> job on the report.	○	●

36

Meeting Individual Needs

Challenge Words Practice
Suggest children make a word search puzzle for a classmate. Have them write the Challenge Words and other spelling words on graph paper, then fill in the empty squares with random letters. Partners search for and circle the hidden words.

Another Writing Idea Have children use spelling words to write about what they think schools might be like in the future.

Objectives *Children will*

■ proofread for spelling and capital letters

■ write and proofread an original composition

Day 4

Daily Proofreading Practice
There are **fiv** clowns on the bike. (*five*)

We **hav** a pony in the barn. (*have*)

Day 5   **Posttest**

Sentences 1–5 test the first five Basic Words. Sentences 6–10 test the next five Basic Words. Sentences 11–12 test the Elephant Words.

Basic Words
1. The bus is <u>late</u>.
2. We see <u>five</u> fish.
3. She is on my <u>side</u>.
4. I had <u>nine</u> frogs.
5. We <u>made</u> a rug.
6. We like the <u>same</u> game.
7. A big hat is <u>fine</u>.
8. The pig <u>ate</u> a nut.
9. We all ride in a <u>line</u>.
10. I may <u>hide</u> my sled.
11. I <u>have</u> some cups.
12. I may <u>give</u> him one.

Review Words
13. She <u>gave</u> me a hug.
14. Is his <u>bike</u> wet?

Challenge Words
15. I made a <u>mistake</u> adding the numbers.
16. Dan likes to <u>write</u> stories.

These pages can be used at any time during the study of this unit.

Objectives *Children will*

- build words with the phonograms *-ate* and *-ape*
- identify rhyming words

Rhyming Words

Long a Words Make rhyming words that have the long **a** vowel sound. Use the letters in the picture.
Order of answers for each phonogram may vary.

ape
1. cape
2. tape
3. grape
4. scrape

ate
5. skate
6. gate
7. plate
8. crate

Work Together On another sheet of paper, write three rhyming words that end with **ine** like the word **nine**. Work with a friend. Sample answers: shine, vine, whine

64

EXTENSION OPTIONS

Learning Center Activity
visual/oral/kinesthetic

Schoolhouse Rhymes Have children draw a school with several windows. Ask them to cut along the center, top, and bottom of each window, making shutters that can be opened and closed. Children glue their drawing to another piece of paper. They write the letters *ake* on the roof of the school.

Next, children brainstorm a list of words that rhyme with *make*. Have them write one *-ake* word behind each set of window shutters. Have

them print the consonant or consonant cluster that begins the word on the shutters. Children can trade schools and see if they can guess what *-ake* word is behind the shutters.

More *-ake* Words		
bake	flake	shake
brake	lake	snake
cake	make	stake
fake	rake	take

Vocabulary Enrichment

Social Studies

Schools All the words in the box have something to do with school. Write those words to finish this note. Use your Spelling Dictionary.

Roberto,

Will you walk to school with me on Friday? I am never __(1)__ on a Friday because we get to play in the __(2)__. Before we start to play, every __(3)__ must put on sneakers. I keep mine in my __(4)__ at school.

Dillon

Spelling Word Link

write

pupil
absent
locker
gym

1. absent
2. gym
3. pupil
4. locker

Try This CHALLENGE

Yes or No? Write **yes** or **no** to answer each question.

5. Is a **pupil** a kind of teacher?
6. Would you say "here" if you were **absent**?
7. Would you keep a desk in your **locker**?
8. Could you play basketball in a **gym**?

5. no
6. no
7. no
8. yes

Fact File

Long ago in the United States, there were few books. Children studied from flat paddles called hornbooks. Most hornbooks showed the alphabet.

65

 Objectives *Children will*

■ expand their vocabulary by using words related to schools

■ show their understanding of the vocabulary words by completing context activities

Vocabulary Checkup

Have children use the vocabulary words in sentences or match the words to the definitions below.

1. a person who is being taught in school *pupil*
2. a place that can be locked for keeping clothes and valuables *locker*
3. a room for exercise and sports *gym*
4. away; not present *absent*

Fact File

Hornbooks

Tacked to one side of each hornbook was a sheet of paper with the student's lesson on it. Because the paper was so expensive, a thin, transparent sheet made from animal horns was used to protect it. Hornbooks were used until the early 1800s, when books became cheaper and easier to obtain.

Integrating Literature

Easy	Average	Challenging
Amazing Grace *by Mary Hoffman* Grace wants to be Peter Pan in the school play.	**Insects Are My Life** *by Megan McDonald* Amanda finds a class-mate as interested in reptiles as she is in insects.	**The School Mouse** *by Dick King-Smith* Flora, a mouse who lives in a school, learns to read.
Miss Nelson Is Missing *by Harry Allard* The kids in Room 207 wonder what happened to their nice teacher.	**Hog-Eye** *by Susan Meddaugh* A pig escapes from a wolf after boarding the wrong bus to school.	**Song Lee and the Leech Man** *by Suzy Kline* Song Lee's class takes a field trip to a pond.

More Vowel-Consonant-*e* Spellings

WORD LISTS

Spelling

Basic
1. bone
2. nose
3. use
4. these
5. rope
6. home
7. cute
8. close
9. hope
10. those
11. one
12. goes

Review
13. make
14. ride

Challenge
15. globe
16. mule

Vocabulary

Science: Dinosaurs
huge
sharp
reptile
fossil

Introducing the Lesson

Read Aloud

Write the Basic Words on the board.

Animals of Long Ago

At one time, Earth was **home** to the dinosaurs. Some of **these** creatures were huge. Others looked like **cute**, tiny lizards. **One** type of dinosaur had a duckbill and made honking noises through its **nose**. When the dinosaurs died, hard parts such as shell, **bone**, and teeth became fossils. Fossils are the remains of plants or animals that lived in the past. Scientists **use** fossils to find out about dinosaurs and other living things from the past. Fossils found **close** to the earth's surface are usually more recent than **those** found deep in the ground. When scientists find a fossil, they **rope** off the area to protect it. As time **goes** by, scientists **hope** to learn more about dinosaurs from fossils.

Responding Ask children what animals they learned about. *(dinosaurs)* Reread the sentence with *rope* in it. Ask children to name the spelling word they hear and another spelling word that rhymes with it. *(rope, hope)*

Day 1 *page 66*

Objectives *Children will*
- take the pretest
- pronounce the list words
- learn about the spelling principle
- sort words by their vowel sounds

Planning Checklist
- ☑ Pretest (TE)
- ☑ Spelling principle/word list
- ☐ Review/Challenge Words
- ☐ Teaching the Principle (TE)
- ☐ Enrichment (TE)
- ☐ Additional Spelling Words (TE)

Assessment

Pretest
1. I fell and broke a <u>bone</u>.
2. Star has a pink <u>nose</u>.
3. Did you <u>use</u> the brush?
4. Take <u>these</u> books.
5. Tie the <u>rope</u>.
6. A bird's <u>home</u> is a nest.
7. Leo has a <u>cute</u> puppy.
8. Stay <u>close</u> to me!
9. We <u>hope</u> to see you.
10. Look at <u>those</u> lions!
11. I have <u>one</u> hat.
12. The bus <u>goes</u> by here.

Day 2 *page 67*

Objectives *Children will*
- practice spelling list words
- apply spelling strategies
- classify Basic Words into groups
- identify Elephant Words by a given vowel sound or spelling pattern

Planning Checklist
- ☑ Spelling Strategy
- ☑ Independent Practice
- ☐ Daily Proofreading Practice (TE)
- ☐ Informal Assessment (TE)
- ☐ Extra Support (TE)
- ☐ Applying Spelling Strategies (TE)

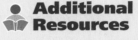

 Management Tip Encourage self-assessment. Have children check their own pretest and practice activity answers against the word list in the pupil book. This is an effective way to help children identify the words they find difficult and to help them improve their proofreading skills.

Objectives *Children will*

- alphabetize given entry words to the first letter
- review Basic and Review Words

Planning Checklist

- ☐ Dictionary
- ☐ Review: Spelling Spree
- ☐ How Are You Doing?
- ☐ Daily Proofreading Practice (TE)
- ☐ Cooperative Learning Activity (TE)

Objectives *Children will*

- proofread for spelling
- write and proofread an original composition

Planning Checklist

- ☐ Proofread for Spelling
- ☐ Write a Story
- ☐ Daily Proofreading Practice (TE)
- ☐ Challenge Words Practice (TE)
- ☐ Another Writing Idea (TE)

Objective *Children will*

- take the posttest

Assessment

- ☐ **Posttest** (TE) *See Day 5*
- ☐ Unit 8 Test

Additional Resources

Teacher's Resource Book
Practice Masters, pages 37–39
Unit Test, page 40
Bulletin Board, page 53

Practice Plus
Take-Home Word List 8
Games

Spelling Transparencies
Spelling Word List 8
Daily Proofreading Practice, Unit 8
Graphic Organizers

Teacher's Resource Disk
Macintosh® or Windows® software. Houghton Mifflin

Spelling CD-ROM
Macintosh® or Windows® software. Houghton Mifflin

Internet
http://www.eduplace.com

Phonics Practice
Houghton Mifflin Phonics
The Listening Corner
Phonics Home Connection

Meeting Individual Needs
Students Acquiring English

Spanish There is nothing in Spanish comparable to the final silent e.

Activity Write *hop* and *hope* on the board and say them. Ask children to identify the vowel sounds. Then write *bone, cute,* and *these.* Have children identify the long vowel sound and the V-C-e pattern in each word.

Asian Asian languages do not have the |*th*| sound.

Activity Demonstrate how to place the tongue to pronounce the |*th*| sound. Write these word pairs: *see/the, sees/these, sews/those.* Have children practice repeating each pair after you.

Other Activities for Any Day

- Bonus activities from pages 70–71
- Practice Masters (easy, average, challenging) Teacher's Resource Book, pages 37–39
- Take-Home Word List 8 Practice Plus

Day 1

Objectives *Children will*

- take the pretest
- pronounce the list words
- learn about the spelling principle
- sort words by their vowel sounds

Teaching the Principle

This lesson teaches the vowel-consonant-*e* pattern for the |ō|, the |yōō|, and the |ē| sounds. Children learn the strategy of thinking of this pattern when they hear the long *o*, the long *u*, or the long *e* sound.

To sum up the lesson, ask:

- What letter do you see at the end of each word? *(e)* Does it have any sound? *(no)*

- What letters spell the vowel-consonant-*e* pattern in each word? *(bone, hose, use, these, rope, home, cute, close, hope, those)*

Note: The word *use* can be pronounced |yōōz| or |yōōs| and the word *close* |klōz| or |klōs|.

Enrichment

Vocabulary: Multiple Meanings
Have children use a dictionary to look up *nose, home,* and *close.* Discuss the meanings.

ō
bone

A. bone

____ nose

____ use

____ these

____ rope

____ home

____ cute

____ close

____ hope

____ those

B. one

____ goes

66

Read and Say

READ the sentences. **SAY** each word in dark print.

Basic Words

1.	bone	I fell and broke a **bone**.
2.	nose	Star has a pink **nose**.
3.	use	Did you **use** the brush?
4.	these	Take **these** books.
5.	rope	Tie the **rope**.
6.	home	A bird's **home** is a nest.
7.	cute	Leo has a **cute** puppy.
8.	close	Stay **close** to me!
9.	hope	We **hope** to see you.
10.	those	Look at **those** lions!
11.	one	I have **one** hat.
12.	goes	The bus **goes** by here.

Think and Write

Most of the words have the long **o**, long **u**, or long **e** vowel sound spelled with the vowel-consonant-**e** pattern. These long vowel sounds begin 🐟, 🦓, and 🐍.

long **o** → b**o**ne   long **u** → **u**se   long **e** → th**e**se

How are the Elephant Words different? *One has the V-C-e pattern but no long vowel sound. Goes has a long vowel sound spelled oe.*

A. Write the first **ten** Basic Words. Then draw a line under the letters that spell the vowel-consonant-**e** pattern in each word.

B. Now write the **two** Elephant Words.
Order of answers for each category may vary.

Review		Challenge	
13. make	14. ride	15. globe	16. mule

TEACHING OPTIONS

Meeting Individual Needs
Word Lists

You may want to assign Basic Words 1–5, the Elephant Words, and the Review Words to children who misspelled more than five words on the pretest. Assign the Challenge Words as appropriate. (You may want to have children write sentences, using the Challenge Words.)

Additional Spelling Words

Basic	Challenge	Words Often Misspelled
joke	wrote	here
cube	alone	were
robe	excuse	
note	chose	
stove	refuse	
	awoke	

Home/School Involvement
Take-Home Word List • Goal-Setting

Have children set goals for the week on Take-Home Word List 8.

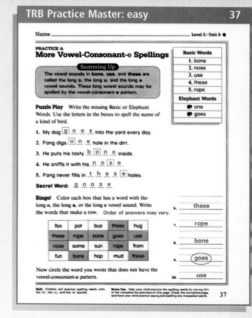

Independent Practice

Spelling Strategy The vowel sounds in **bone**, **use**, and **these** are called the long **o**, the long **u**, and the long **e** vowel sounds. These long vowel sounds may be spelled by the vowel-consonant-**e** pattern.

Order of answers for question 4–5 may vary.

Phonics Write Basic Words to answer the questions.

1. Which word begins with a vowel sound?
2. Which word rhymes with **stone**?
3. Which word begins with the same two letters as **clock**?
4–5. Which two words begin like **then**?

Word Groups Think how the words in each group are alike. Write the missing Basic Words.

6. string, ribbon, _____
7. house, apartment, _____
8. eyes, ears, _____
9. pretty, beautiful, _____
10. dream, wish, _____

Elephant Words Write an Elephant Word to answer each question.

11. Which word has the long **o** sound?
12. Which word has the vowel-consonant-**e** pattern but no long vowel sound?

Phonics

1. use
2. bone
3. close
4. these
5. those

Word Groups

6. rope
7. home
8. nose
9. cute
10. hope

Elephant Words

11. goes
12. one

(67)

Day **2**

Objectives *Children will*

- practice spelling list words
- apply spelling strategies
- classify Basic Words into groups
- identify Elephant Words by a given vowel sound or spelling pattern

Daily Proofreading Practice
I have **wun** little sister. (*one*)
My puppy chewed the **boen**. (*bone*)

Meeting Individual Needs
visual/oral/auditory

Extra Support Check Independent Practice to determine who needs extra support. Write the letters *a, e, i, o,* and *u* on the board. Remind children that the letter names and long vowel sounds are the same. Then say the following words, asking children to name the vowel sound and to write the word under the appropriate letter: *late, fine, bone, use, same, side, these, rope,* and *cute.*

Applying Spelling Strategies
To Spell New Words

- Read aloud: **We saw black smoke coming out of the oven!**
- Have children attempt to spell *smoke* on their Have-a-Go charts.

- Elicit the following strategies as children try to spell *smoke*.

I hear the sounds for *s* and *m* blended together at the beginning of the word.

The |k| sound could be spelled *c* or *k*. I think the long vowel pattern may be spelled *oke*. I'll have to check a dictionary.

smoke

This word has the long *o* sound. I hear a consonant sound after the *o*. Maybe the long *o* sound is spelled by the vowel-consonant-e pattern.

Objectives *Children will*
- alphabetize given entry words to the first letter
- review Basic and Review Words

Daily Proofreading Practice

Matt gave me **theez** paints. (*these*)

We ran **hom** before the storm. (*home*)

U N I T
8

Entry Words

1. cute

2. nose

3. ride

4. those

Fill-In Fun

5. ride

6. home

7. one

8. close

Hidden Words

9. goes

10. nose

11. those

12. cute

68

Dictionary

Entry Words The words you look up in a dictionary are called **entry words**. Entry words are in dark print. They are listed in ABC order.

entry word

nose The part of the head that a person or animal smells with.

meaning

Practice 1–4. Write these entry words in the order you would find them in the dictionary. Use ABC order.

ride	nose	those	cute

Review: Spelling Spree

Fill-In Fun Write the missing Basic or Review Words.

5. a bus _____

6. a _____ run

7. three, two, _____

8. a _____ call

Hidden Words Find the hidden Basic Word in each box. Write the word.

9. anogoeshan

10. cizsnosecz

11. epathoseds

12. khoqucutet

How Are You Doing?
Write each spelling word as a partner reads it aloud. Did you spell any words wrong?

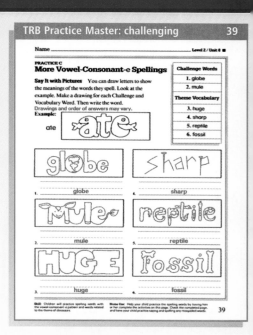

TEACHING OPTIONS

Cooperative Learning Activity

Spelling Word Crisscross
visual/oral

Have partners work together to spell pairs of words using letter cards or Scrabble® pieces. The first child choses a word and spells it on a desk or tabletop with the cards or Scrabble pieces. The second child thinks of another word that has a letter in common with the first. This child places down letters to spell this word, crossing it with the first word.

Have children read the words they have formed and make up a sentence that uses both words. Partners begin again, thinking of and spelling two more words.

TRB Practice Master: challenging   39

Name _____   Level 2 / Unit 8 ■

PRACTICE C
More Vowel-Consonant-e Spellings

Say It with Pictures You can draw letters to show the meanings of the words they spell. Look at the example. Make a drawing for each Challenge and Vocabulary Word. Then write the word. Drawings and order of answers may vary.
Example:

Challenge Words
1. globe
2. mule
Theme Vocabulary
3. huge
4. sharp
5. reptile
6. fossil

ate

globe   sharp
1. globe   4. sharp

Mule   reptile
2. mule   5. reptile

HUGE   fossil
3. huge   6. fossil

39

Proofreading and Writing

Proofread for Spelling Proofread this report. Use proofreading marks to fix six spelling mistakes.

Example: They dug ~~wone~~ ^{one} big hole.

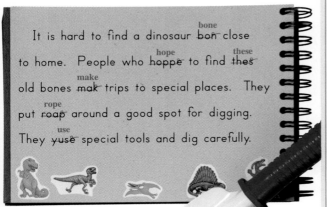

It is hard to find a dinosaur ~~bon~~ ^{bone} close to home. People who ~~hoppe~~ ^{hope} to find ~~thes~~ ^{these} old bones ~~mak~~ ^{make} trips to special places. They put ~~roap~~ ^{rope} around a good spot for digging. They ~~yuse~~ ^{use} special tools and dig carefully.

Basic

1. bone
2. nose
3. use
4. these
5. rope
6. home
7. cute
8. close
9. hope
10. those
11. one
12. goes

Review
13. make
14. ride

Challenge
15. globe
16. mule

Write a Story

Pretend you traveled back to the time when dinosaurs lived. Write a story that begins like this: **I looked around and saw dinosaurs everywhere!** Try to use spelling words. Draw pictures to go with your story.

Proofreading Tip Read each word slowly to make sure no letters have been left out.

Proofreading Marks

∧ Add
⟍ Delete
≡ Make a capital letter
/ Make a small letter

69

 Day 4

Objectives *Children will*
■ proofread for spelling
■ write and proofread an original composition

Daily Proofreading Practice
I pulled the wagon with a **roap**. *(rope)*
Which glass did you **yuze**? *(use)*

Day 5 **Posttest**

Sentences 1–5 test the first five Basic Words. Sentences 6–10 test the next five Basic Words. Sentences 11–12 test the Elephant Words.

Basic Words
1. I can <u>use</u> the cup.
2. That is a <u>bone</u>.
3. Can you see your <u>nose</u>?
4. Get us a <u>rope</u>.
5. Are <u>these</u> my pens?
6. The hat is <u>cute</u>.
7. We are <u>close</u> to it.
8. They are not at <u>home</u>.
9. Are <u>those</u> bags his?
10. I <u>hope</u> the cup is green.
11. I see just <u>one</u> kite.
12. It <u>goes</u> up so fast.

Review Words
13. Did Nan <u>ride</u> her bike?
14. Art can <u>make</u> a kite.

Challenge Words
15. The <u>mule</u> slept in the barn.
16. We found the North Pole on our <u>globe</u>.

TRB Unit 8 Test 40

Name _____ Level 2 / Unit 8 ●▲

Unit 8 Test: More Vowel-Consonant-e Spellings

Each item below gives three spellings of a word. Choose the correct spelling. Mark the letter for that word.

Sample:			ANSWERS
a. ridde	b. ride	c. ried	ⓐ ● ⓒ

Items 1–7 test Basic Words 1–5 and the Elephant Words.
Items 8–12 test Basic Words 6–10.

1. a. rope	b. rop	c. ropp	1. ● ⓑ ⓒ
2. a. oon	b. une	c. one	2. ⓐ ⓑ ●
3. a. thes	b. these	c. tese	3. ⓐ ● ⓒ
4. a. bonn	b. bone	c. bon	4. ⓐ ● ⓒ
5. a. uze	b. uss	c. use	5. ⓐ ⓑ ●
6. a. goes	b. gos	c. gose	6. ● ⓑ ⓒ
7. a. nos	b. noes	c. nose	7. ⓐ ⓑ ●
8. a. close	b. clos	c. cloes	8. ● ⓑ ⓒ
9. a. kute	b. cute	c. cutt	9. ⓐ ● ⓒ
10. a. hup	b. hoep	c. hope	10. ⓐ ⓑ ●
11. a. home	b. hom	c. homm	11. ● ⓑ ⓒ
12. a. thos	b. those	c. tose	12. ⓐ ● ⓒ

40

 Meeting Individual Needs

Challenge Words Practice
Suggest children write a silly sentence for each Challenge Word, then draw a picture or cartoon to go with each sentence.
Example: *The <u>mule</u> went to school with his dinosaur friends.*

Another Writing Idea Have children draw a picture or make a mural of the land where dinosaurs lived. Ask them to add descriptive labels that include spelling words.

These pages can be used at any time during the study of this unit.

Objectives *Children will*

- build words with the phonograms *-one, -ose,* and *-oke*
- write an original composition

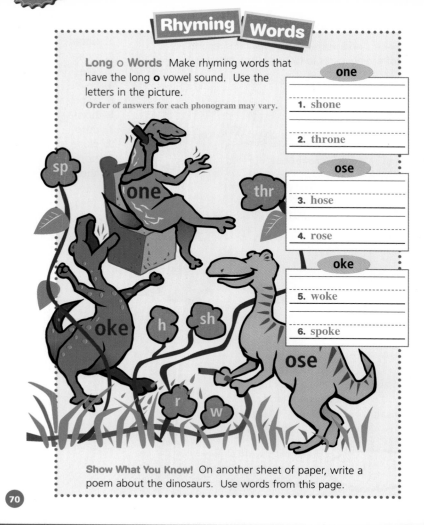

Rhyming Words

Long o Words Make rhyming words that have the long **o** vowel sound. Use the letters in the picture.
Order of answers for each phonogram may vary.

one
1. shone
2. throne

ose
3. hose
4. rose

oke
5. woke
6. spoke

Show What You Know! On another sheet of paper, write a poem about the dinosaurs. Use words from this page.

70

EXTENSION OPTIONS

Learning Center Activity
visual/kinesthetic

An *-ole* Poster Children can work alone or with a partner to brainstorm words that end with the phonogram *-ole*. Suggest they write their words in a list, then check the spellings in a dictionary.

Children can then write their *-ole* words on a poster, adding an illustration for each word to help reinforce the meaning. Some children may wish to hang their poster on the classroom word wall.

More *-ole* Words		
hole	role	stole
mole	sole	whole
pole		

Vocabulary Enrichment

Unit 8 BONUS

Science

Dinosaurs All the words in the box have something to do with dinosaurs. Write those words to finish this newspaper story. Use your Spelling Dictionary.

Spelling Word Link

bone

huge
sharp
reptile
fossil

Dinosaur Bones Found!

Mike Tang went for a walk in the woods last Sunday. He found a __(1)__ of a dinosaur's footprint! Its claws were pointed and __(2)__. Mike could tell from the footprint that the dinosaur had a __(3)__ body. The people who work at the Science Museum believe that this __(4)__ was a good hunter.

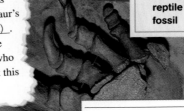

1. fossil

2. sharp

3. huge

4. reptile

Try This CHALLENGE

Write a Journal Page Pretend you found a large dinosaur fossil. What kind of dinosaur fossil is it? Where and how did you find it? Write a page for a science journal. Tell about your fossil. Try to use some words from the box.

Fact File

Not all dinosaurs were huge! The smallest known dinosaur was the compsognathus. It was about the size of a chicken.

71

Day by Day Planner

Objectives *Children will*

■ expand their vocabulary by using words related to dinosaurs

■ show their understanding of the vocabulary words by completing context and writing activities

Vocabulary Checkup

Have children use the vocabulary words in sentences or match the words to the definitions below.

1. an animal that crawls on the ground and whose body is covered with scales or a bony plate *reptile*
2. very large *huge*
3. pointed or having an edge that cuts *sharp*
4. the outline or parts left, usually in rock, of an animal that lived long ago *fossil*

Fact File

Compsognathus

The compsognathus |**kämp**´ säg nə thəs| was a theropod. Theropods were meat-eating dinosaurs. They walked on their hind legs and had small front legs that they used for eating. The tiny compsognathus was in fact related to the tyrannosaurus rex, which could grow to be as long as 40 feet.

Integrating Literature

Easy	Average	Challenging
Young Cam Jansen and the Dinosaur Game *by David A. Adler* Robert cheats to win a jar of plastic dinosaurs at a party.	**Tyrannosaurus Tex** *by Betty G. Birney* A dinosaur becomes friends with a group of cowboys.	**The Magic Schoolbus® in the Time of the Dinosaurs** *by Joanna Cole* Ms. Frizzle's class goes back to prehistoric times.
Dinosaur Questions *by Bernard Most* Questions about dinos are asked and answered.	**How I Captured a Dinosaur** *by Henry Schwartz* Liz takes an unusual pet home from vacation.	**Digging Up Dinosaurs** *by Aliki* How scientists uncover, preserve, and study dinosaur bones.

Words with Consonant Clusters

WORD LISTS

Spelling

Basic
1. trip
2. swim
3. step
4. nest
5. club
6. stone
7. next
8. brave
9. glad
10. lost

Review
11. flat
12. slip

Challenge
13. branches
14. storm

Vocabulary

Recreation: Camping and Hiking

gear
cabin
clearing
camper

Introducing the Lesson

Read Aloud

Write the Basic Words on the board.

Outdoor Fun

Why not take a camping **trip** for your **next** family vacation? You will be **glad** if you do. You do not have to be **brave** to spend time outdoors, but you should prepare well for your **trip.** Your local library or nature **club** has many good books on camping to help you. Most campsites have a place cleared for tents, and a **stone** pit or charcoal grill for cooking. A lake campsite is great for people who like to **swim** or fish. If your family is camping in the woods, carry a compass or a map in case you get **lost.** Watch your **step** and be careful not to disturb any animal or **nest** along the way.

Responding Ask children what kind of vacation is described in the selection. *(a camping trip)* Have children name activities people can do on a camping trip. Then reread the last sentence aloud. Discuss the meaning of the idiom "watch your step."

Day 1 *page 72*

Objectives *Children will*
- take the pretest
- pronounce the list words
- learn about the spelling principle
- sort words by initial or final consonant clusters

Planning Checklist
- ☑ Pretest (TE)
- ☑ Spelling principle/word list
- ☐ Review/Challenge Words
- ☐ Teaching the Principle (TE)
- ☐ Enrichment (TE)
- ☐ Additional Spelling Words (TE)

Assessment

Pretest
1. I took a <u>trip</u> to the lake.
2. She knows how to <u>swim</u>.
3. Please <u>step</u> into the bus.
4. Is the bird in its <u>nest</u>?
5. Did your <u>club</u> go hiking?
6. A <u>stone</u> is a small rock.
7. Is she <u>next</u> in line?
8. He tried to be <u>brave</u>.
9. I am <u>glad</u> you helped.
10. Pedro <u>lost</u> his cap.

Day 2 *page 73*

Objectives *Children will*
- practice spelling list words
- apply spelling strategies
- complete analogies with Basic Words
- identify antonyms

Planning Checklist
- ☑ Spelling Strategy
- ☑ Independent Practice
- ☐ Daily Proofreading Practice (TE)
- ☐ Informal Assessment (TE)
- ☐ Extra Support (TE)
- ☐ Applying Spelling Strategies (TE)

Day 3 *page 74*   **Day 4** *page 75*   **Day 5** *page 75*

Objective *Children will*

- review Basic and Review Words

Planning Checklist

☐ Review: Spelling Spree

☐ How Are You Doing?

☐ Daily Proofreading Practice (TE)

☐ Cooperative Learning Activity (TE)

Objectives *Children will*

- proofread for spelling and capital letters
- write and proofread an original composition

Planning Checklist

☐ Proofread: Spelling and Capital Letters

☐ Write an Ad

☐ Daily Proofreading Practice (TE)

☐ Challenge Words Practice (TE)

☐ Another Writing Idea (TE)

Objective *Children will*

- take the posttest

Assessment

☐ **Posttest** (TE) *See Day 5*

☐ Unit 9 Test

Additional Resources

Teacher's Resource Book

Practice Masters, pages 41–43

Unit Test, page 44

Bulletin Board, page 53

Practice Plus

Take-Home Word List 9

Games

Spelling Transparencies

Spelling Word List 9

Daily Proofreading Practice, Unit 9

Graphic Organizers

Teacher's Resource Disk

Macintosh® or Windows® software. Houghton Mifflin

Spelling CD-ROM

Macintosh® or Windows® software. Houghton Mifflin

Internet

http://www.eduplace.com

Phonics Practice

Houghton Mifflin Phonics

The Listening Corner

Phonics Home Connection

Meeting Individual Needs
Students Acquiring English

Spanish Spanish usually has no final consonant clusters. The vowel *e*, pronounced |ā|, usually precedes an *s* followed by a consonant.

Activity Write *stone, spot, step, slip, smoke,* and *snake* on the board. Point to each word and say it. Have children repeat.

Asian Clusters with *l* and *r* are difficult for East Asians who do not have |l| or |r| differentiation.

Activity Write *trip* on the board. Cover the *t*. Say *rip* slowly. Add the *t* to *rip*. Say the word slowly and have children repeat. Continue with the other list words in this way.

Other Activities for Any Day

- Bonus activities from pages 76–77
- Practice Masters (easy, average, challenging)
  Teacher's Resource Book, pages 41–43
- Take-Home Word List 9
  Practice Plus

Objectives *Children will*
- take the pretest
- pronounce the list words
- learn about the spelling principle
- sort words by initial or final consonant clusters

Teaching the Principle

This lesson teaches the concept of consonant clusters. Children learn the strategy of thinking of this consonant pattern when they hear the sounds of two consonants blended together at the beginning or the end of a word.

To sum up the lesson, ask:

- What letters spell the consonant clusters at the beginnings of words? *(tr, sw, st, cl, br, gl)*
- What consonant cluster does *next* end with? *(xt)*
- What consonant cluster does *nest* end with? *(st)*

Enrichment

Vocabulary: Multiple Meanings
Have children use a dictionary to look up *trip, club,* and *lost.* Discuss the meanings.

Words with Consonant Clusters

sw
swim

A. trip
____

swim
____

step
____

club
____

stone
____

brave
____

glad
____

B. nest
____

next
____

lost
____

72

Read and Say

READ the sentences. **SAY** each word in dark print.

Basic Words

1.	trip	I took a **trip** to the lake.
2.	swim	She knows how to **swim**.
3.	step	Please **step** into the bus.
4.	nest	Is the bird in its **nest**?
5.	club	Did your **club** go hiking?
6.	stone	A **stone** is a small rock.
7.	next	Is she **next** in line?
8.	brave	He tried to be **brave**.
9.	glad	I am **glad** you helped.
10.	lost	Pedro **lost** his cap.

Think and Write

Each word begins or ends with a **consonant cluster**. A consonant cluster is two consonant letters whose sounds are blended together.

consonant clusters → **tr**ip, **sw**im, **st**ep, **cl**ub, ne**xt**, **br**ave, **gl**ad

A. Write **seven** Basic Words that begin with a consonant cluster.
B. Write **three** Basic Words that end with a consonant cluster.

Order of answers for each category may vary.

Review	Challenge
11. flat 12. slip	13. branches 14. storm

TEACHING OPTIONS

Meeting Individual Needs
Word Lists

You may want to assign Basic Words 1–5 and the Review Words to children who misspelled more than five words on the pretest. Assign the Challenge Words as appropriate. (You may want to have children write sentences, using the Challenge Words.)

Additional Spelling Words

Basic	Challenge	Words Often Misspelled
stamp	climb	friend
swan	trumpet	from
test	swallow	
trade	breeze	
bride	toast	
	trapeze	

Home/School Involvement
Take-Home Word List • Goal-Setting

Have children set goals for the week on Take-Home Word List 9.

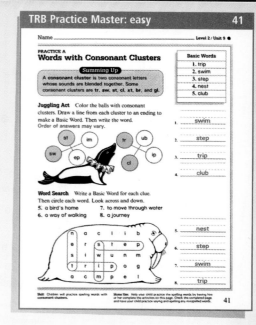

Name _____ Level 2 / Unit 9

PRACTICE A
Words with Consonant Clusters

Basic Words
1. trip
2. swim
3. step
4. nest
5. club

Summing Up
A consonant cluster is two consonant letters whose sounds are blended together. Some consonant clusters are tr, sw, st, cl, xt, br, and gl.

Juggling Act Color the balls with consonant clusters. Draw a line from each cluster to an ending to make a Basic Word. Then write the word.
Order of answers may vary.

1. swim
2. step
3. trip
4. club

Word Search Write a Basic Word for each clue. Then circle each word. Look across and down.
5. a bird's home   7. to move through water
6. a way of walking 8. a journey

5. nest
6. step
7. swim
8. trip

41

Independent Practice

Spelling Strategy A **consonant cluster** is two consonant letters whose sounds are blended together. Some consonant clusters are **tr**, **sw**, **st**, **cl**, **xt**, **br**, and **gl**. st stone

Order of answers for each question may vary.

Phonics Write Basic Words to answer the questions.

1–3. Which three words have the short **e** sound?

4–5. Which two words are spelled with the vowel-consonant-**e** pattern?

Word Pairs Write a Basic Word to finish the second sentence in each pair.

6. You bring a **picnic basket** on a **picnic**.
   You bring a **suitcase** on a _____.

7. A **player** is part of a team.
   A **member** is part of a _____.

8. You go to a **track** to run.
   You go to a **pool** to _____.

Word Meaning Write the Basic Word that means the opposite of each word in dark print.

9. We **found** our map near the tents.

10. I was **unhappy** that the trail was easy.

Phonics

1. step

2. nest

3. next

4. stone

5. brave

Word Pairs

6. trip

7. club

8. swim

Word Meaning

9. lost

10. glad

73

Day 2

Objectives *Children will*

■ practice spelling list words

■ apply spelling strategies

■ complete analogies with Basic Words

■ identify antonyms

Daily Proofreading Practice

Dad found two eggs in the **nesst**. (*nest*)

We slept in a tent on our **terip**. (*trip*)

 Meeting Individual Needs
visual/oral/auditory

Extra Support Check Independent Practice to determine who needs extra support. Write these word pairs on the board: *rip/trip, lad/glad, top/stop,* and *lake/flake*. Point to *rip*. Say it aloud and have children repeat. Do the same with *trip*. Point out and underline the consonant or consonant cluster that begins each word. Repeat this procedure with each word pair.

Name _____   Level 2 / Unit 9 ▲

Basic Words
1. trip
2. swim
3. step
4. nest
5. club
6. stone
7. next
8. brave
9. glad
10. lost

PRACTICE B

Words with Consonant Clusters

Puzzle Play Write a Basic Word for each clue. Use the letters in the boxes to spell two words that tell what the bee in the cartoon is.

1. a heavy stick of wood   c l u b
2. where birds live   n e s t
3. to float or move in water   s w i m
4. coming right after   n e x t
5. put a foot forward   s t e p
6. not afraid   b r a v e
7. happy   g l a d
8. the opposite of found   l o s t
9. a piece of rock   s t o n e
10. vacation   t r i p

Secret Words:

the b e s t   s p e l l e r

EXTRA! Draw your own cartoon. Write a word pair to tell about it. Use at least one Basic Word.

42   Skill: Children will practice spelling words with consonant clusters.   Home Use: Help your child practice the spelling words by having him or her complete the activities on this page. Check the completed page and have your child practice saying and spelling any misspelled words.

Applying Spelling Strategies
To Spell New Words

■ Read aloud: **There was a clump of daisies growing beside our tent.**

■ Have children attempt to spell *clump* on their Have-a-Go charts.

■ Elicit the following strategies as children try to spell *clump*.

I hear the sounds |k| and |l| blended together at the beginning of the word. This may be the consonant cluster *cl* that I know begins the word *club*.

I hear the sounds |m| and |p| blended together at the end of the word. I think this is the consonant cluster *mp*.

clump

This word has the short *u* sound. The short *u* sound is probably spelled *u*.

Day 3

Objective *Children will*

■ review Basic and Review Words

Daily Proofreading Practice

Would you like to join our **clob**? (*club*)
I threw a **stown** into the pond.
(*stone*)

U N I T
9

Cluster Swap

1. swim

2. flat

3. brave

4. glad

5. club

6. next

Rhyming Clues

7. nest

8. lost

9. trip

10. step

11. slip

12. stone

74

Review: Spelling Spree

Cluster Swap Make Basic or Review Words by using a consonant cluster from the box in place of each letter in dark print. Write the words.

gl	fl	cl	xt	br	sw

1. **h**im   3. **w**ave   5. **r**ub
2. **m**at   4. **p**ad   6. ne**t**

Rhyming Clues Write a Basic or Review Word for each clue.

7. It rhymes with **best**. It begins like 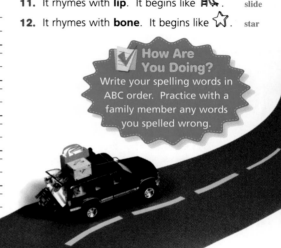.   net
8. It rhymes with **cost**. It begins like ☞.   leaf
9. It rhymes with **sip**. It begins like 🚚.   truck
10. It rhymes with **pep**. It begins like ☆.   star
11. It rhymes with **lip**. It begins like 🛝.   slide
12. It rhymes with **bone**. It begins like ☆.   star

How Are You Doing?
Write your spelling words in ABC order. Practice with a family member any words you spelled wrong.

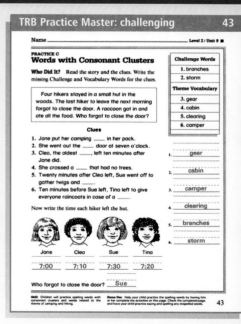

TEACHING OPTIONS

Cooperative Learning Activity
Climb the Mountain!
visual/oral/auditory

Children can play this game with a partner or small group. Have groups draw a large mountain on construction paper. Then have them add a winding trail that leads to the top of the mountain. The trail should be divided into spaces. Children write these consonant clusters on the faces of a cube: *tr, sw, st, cl, br,* and *gl.* Players take turns rolling the cube, thinking of a word that includes the cluster, and spelling the word aloud. Players who spell correctly move three spaces on the trail. The first player to reach the top wins!

TRB Practice Master: challenging   **43**

Name _____   Level 2/ Unit 9 ■

PRACTICE C
Words with Consonant Clusters

Who Did It? Read the story and the clues. Write the missing Challenge and Vocabulary Words for the clues.

Four hikers stayed in a small hut in the woods. The last hiker to leave the next morning forgot to close the door. A raccoon got in and ate all the food. Who forgot to close the door?

Clues
1. Jane put her camping _____ in her pack.
2. She went out the _____ door at seven o'clock.
3. Cleo, the oldest _____, left ten minutes after Jane did.
4. She crossed a _____ that had no trees.
5. Twenty minutes after Cleo left, Sue went off to gather twigs and _____.
6. Ten minutes before Sue left, Tina left to give everyone raincoats in case of a _____.

Now write the time each hiker left the hut.

Jane   Cleo   Sue   Tina
7:00   7:10   7:30   7:20

Who forgot to close the door? **Sue**

Challenge Words
1. branches
2. storm
Theme Vocabulary
3. gear
4. cabin
5. clearing
6. camper

1. gear
2. cabin
3. camper
4. clearing
5. branches
6. storm

43

Proofreading and Writing

Proofread: Spelling and Capital Letters

Begin the names of streets, towns, and cities with capital letters.

Stone **R**oad **W**eston **A**tlanta

Proofread these directions. Use proofreading marks to fix four spelling mistakes and three missing capital letters.

Example: We began our ~~tripe~~ in portland.
trip

Get a map at the hiking ~~clob~~ in jackson.
club

Begin your hike at webster road. Follow the

stone trail markers so you don't get lost.

Watch your ~~stap~~! The trail is not ~~flatt~~, and
step   flat

you might ~~slep~~.
slip

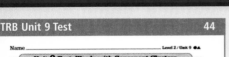

Write an Ad

Write an ad for a great summer camp. Remember to write the name of the camp and the address. Try to use spelling words. Share your ad with a friend.

Camp Green Wood

Proofreading Tip

Check that you began the names of streets, towns, and cities with capital letters.

75

Basic

1. trip
2. swim
3. step
4. nest
5. club
6. stone
7. next
8. brave
9. glad
10. lost

Review

11. flat
12. slip

Challenge

13. branches
14. storm

Proofreading Marks

∧ Add
⌐ Delete
≡ Make a capital letter
/ Make a small letter

Day 4

Objectives *Children will*

■ proofread for spelling and capital letters

■ write and proofread an original composition

Daily Proofreading Practice

Mia will have the **nekst** turn. (*next*)
I am **galad** you came to visit. (*glad*)

Day 5 Posttest

Sentences 1–5 test the first five Basic Words. Sentences 6–10 test the next five Basic Words.

Basic Words

1. Can the frog <u>swim</u>?
2. Did Meg go on a <u>trip</u>?
3. Is this the <u>nest</u>?
4. He did not <u>step</u> on the box.
5. She came to the <u>club</u>.
6. Ann is <u>brave</u>.
7. The <u>next</u> day was fun.
8. Tom is <u>glad</u> to see you.
9. We <u>lost</u> the red kite.
10. Did they see the <u>stone</u>?

Review Words

11. Did he <u>slip</u> on the step?
12. The box is <u>flat</u>.

Challenge Words

13. The <u>branches</u> were covered with snow.
14. The wind blew hard during the <u>storm</u>.

TRB Unit 9 Test 44

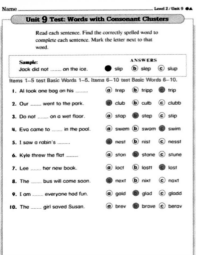

Name _____ Level 2 / Unit 9 ●A

Unit 9 Test: Words with Consonant Clusters

Read each sentence. Find the correctly spelled word to complete each sentence. Mark the letter next to that word.

Sample:	ANSWERS
Jack did not ____ on the ice.	● slip ⓑ slep ⓒ slup

Items 1–5 test Basic Words 1–5. Items 6–10 test Basic Words 6–10.

1. Al took one bag on his ____ ⓐ trep ⓑ tripp ● trip
2. Our ____ went to the park. ● club ⓑ cutb ⓒ clubb
3. Do not ____ on a wet floor. ⓐ stap ● step ⓒ stip
4. Eva came to ____ in the pool. ⓐ swem ⓑ swom ● swim
5. I saw a robin's ____ ● nest ⓑ nist ⓒ nesst
6. Kyle threw the flat ____ ⓐ ston ● stone ⓒ stune
7. Lee ____ her new book. ⓐ loct ⓑ lostt ● lost
8. The ____ bus will come soon. ● next ⓑ nixt ⓒ naxt
9. I am ____ everyone had fun. ⓐ gald ● glad ⓒ gladd
10. The ____ girl saved Susan. ⓐ brev ● brave ⓒ berav

Meeting Individual Needs

Challenge Words Practice

Ask children to draw two tents. In one have them write *branches* and other words that tell about things they might see when camping. In the second, have them write *storm* and words that tell about weather they might experience while camping.

Another Writing Idea

Suggest children use spelling words to make a picture dictionary for camping and hiking.

44

Unit 9 BONUS

These pages can be used at any time during the study of this unit.

Day by Day Planner

Objectives *Children will*

- use context to help them choose appropriate synonyms from a thesaurus

- use words found in a thesaurus in their writing

Unit 9 BONUS

Vocabulary Enrichment

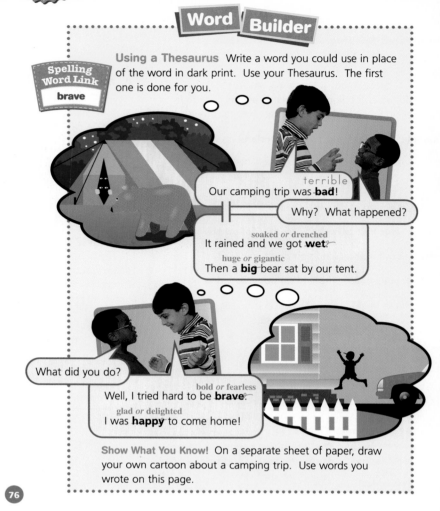

Word Builder

Using a Thesaurus Write a word you could use in place of the word in dark print. Use your Thesaurus. The first one is done for you.

Spelling Word Link
brave

terrible
Our camping trip was **bad**!

Why? What happened?

soaked *or* drenched
It rained and we got **wet**.

huge *or* gigantic
Then a **big** bear sat by our tent.

What did you do?

bold *or* fearless
Well, I tried hard to be **brave**.

glad *or* delighted
I was **happy** to come home!

Show What You Know! On a separate sheet of paper, draw your own cartoon about a camping trip. Use words you wrote on this page.

76

EXTENSION OPTIONS

Learning Center Activity

oral/auditory

Synonym Game In this game, one player tries to get a partner to say a particular word by naming synonyms or related words.

Have one child find a word in their Thesaurus that is spelled with a consonant cluster. This player names synonyms listed for the entry word. For example, the child might say "crack," "shatter," and "smash," trying to get his or her partner to say "break." If the partner guesses the correct word, he or she should then spell it aloud.

Children can play this game in teams, taking turns giving word clues and scoring one point for each word their partner guesses and spells correctly.

Vocabulary Enrichment

Recreation

Camping and Hiking All the words in the box have something to do with camping and hiking. Write those words to finish this page from a diary. Use your Spelling Dictionary.

Spelling Word Link

trip

gear
cabin
clearing
camper

June 24

Today I was the only __(1)__ walking on the trail. My __(2)__ was in a backpack. I rested at a log __(3)__. It was in a __(4)__ in the woods.

1. camper
2. gear
3. cabin
4. clearing

Try This CHALLENGE

Yes or No? Is the word in the dark print used correctly? Write **yes** or **no**.

5. There are six apartments in our **cabin**.
6. The **camper** set up her tent.
7. I hid behind some trees in the **clearing**.
8. Sid keeps a bathtub in his camping **gear**.

5. no
6. yes
7. no
8. no

Fact File

Do you want to take a long hike? Follow the Appalachian Trail. It is about 2,000 miles long and passes through 14 states from Maine to Georgia.

77

Integrating Literature

Easy	Average	Challenging
Amelia Bedelia Goes Camping *by Peggy Parish* Amelia Bedelia misinterprets camping terms like "pitching the tent."	**Ronald Morgan Goes to Camp** *by Patricia Reilly Giff* Ronald gets a camp medal for being a good friend.	**When I Go Camping with Grandma** *by Marion Dane Bauer* A girl and her grandmother go camping together.
Camp Big Paw *by Doug Cushman* Cyril runs into trouble with a bully at summer camp.	**Petey Maroni's Camp Runamok Diary** *by Pat Cummings* Raccoons outwit campers by stealing their snacks.	**Summer Camp** *by Bobbi Kalman* A description of activities enjoyed at summer camp.

Objectives *Children will*

■ expand their vocabulary by using words related to camping and hiking

■ show their understanding of the vocabulary words by completing context activities

Vocabulary Checkup

Have children use the vocabulary words in sentences or match the words to the definitions below.

1. a person who lives in a tent or a cabin for a little while *camper*
2. a small, simple house *cabin*
3. a place in the woods without trees *clearing*
4. tools, clothes, and other things used for an activity *gear*

Fact File

The Appalachian Trail

You may wish to point out the Appalachian Trail on a U.S. map. Each year about 100 people hike the full length of the trail. There are shelters built along it for hikers to camp in.

Words Spelled with *k* or *ck*

WORD LISTS

Spelling

Basic

1. lake
2. rock
3. ask
4. pick
5. truck
6. black
7. back
8. bake
9. clock
10. kick

Review

11. kite
12. take

Challenge

13. dock
14. snake

Vocabulary

Science: Rivers and Lakes

wade
shore
brook
flow

Introducing the Lesson

Read Aloud

Write the Basic Words on the board.

The Great Salt Lake

Pick a spot in the western United States and turn **back** the **clock** a few million years. Would it look the same as it does today? If you were to **ask** scientists who study the earth, they would tell you that during the time of the dinosaurs, a huge **lake** covered much of the state of Utah. All that is left of it is the Great Salt Lake. It is still big. It takes hours for a car or a **truck** to go around it. The Great Salt Lake is much saltier than the ocean. No fish— only tiny shrimp and **black** flies—can live in its waters. If you slipped on a **rock** and fell in, you would not sink. Even if you could not swim, you could lie on your **back**, **kick** your feet, and float. It is that salty! In fact, the salt you use when you **bake** may come from there!

Responding Ask children to name the lake they learned about. (*Great Salt Lake*) Then discuss the meaning of the phrase "turn **back** the **clock**." (*It means "imagine an earlier time."*)

 Day 1 *page 78*

Objectives *Children will*

- take the pretest
- pronounce the list words
- learn about the spelling principle
- sort words by their spelling patterns

Planning Checklist

- ☑ Pretest (TE)
- ☑ Spelling principle/word list
- ☐ Review/Challenge Words
- ☐ Teaching the Principle (TE)
- ☐ Enrichment (TE)
- ☐ Additional Spelling Words (TE)

Assessment

Pretest

1. They swim in the <u>lake</u>.
2. Step over that <u>rock</u>.
3. Did you <u>ask</u> him to go?
4. I will <u>pick</u> out a toy.
5. John drives a <u>truck</u>.
6. She has <u>black</u> mittens.
7. We sat in the <u>back</u> row.
8. Eva had bread to <u>bake</u>.
9. A <u>clock</u> tells the time.
10. I can <u>kick</u> the ball!

Day 2 *page 79*

Objectives *Children will*

- practice spelling list words
- apply spelling strategies
- classify Basic Words into groups
- identify synonyms

Planning Checklist

- ☑ Spelling Strategy
- ☑ Independent Practice
- ☐ Daily Proofreading Practice (TE)
- ☐ Informal Assessment (TE)
- ☐ Extra Support (TE)
- ☐ Applying Spelling Strategies (TE)

 Management Tip You may wish to write the Daily Proofreading Practice activity on the chalkboard as a warm-up for the class, to be done before children begin work on their spelling pages.

● **Additional Resources**

Teacher's Resource Book
Practice Masters, pages 45–47
Unit Test, page 48
Bulletin Board, page 53

Practice Plus
Take-Home Word List 10
Games

Spelling Transparencies
Spelling Word List 10
Daily Proofreading Practice,
   Unit 10
Graphic Organizers

Teacher's Resource Disk
Macintosh® or Windows® software.
   Houghton Mifflin

Spelling CD-ROM
Macintosh® or Windows® software.
   Houghton Mifflin

Internet
http://www.eduplace.com

Phonics Practice
Houghton Mifflin Phonics
The Listening Corner
Phonics Home Connection

 Day 3 *page 80*   **Day 4** *page 81*   **Day 5** *page 81*

Objectives *Children will*
- identify the first alphabetical word in groups of words with the same first letter
- review Basic and Review Words

Planning Checklist
☐ Dictionary
☐ Review: Spelling Spree
☐ How Are You Doing?
☐ Daily Proofreading Practice (TE)
☐ Ongoing Assessment(TE)

Objectives *Children will*
- proofread for spelling
- write and proofread an original composition

Planning Checklist
☐ Proofread for Spelling
☐ Write a Post Card
☐ Daily Proofreading Practice (TE)
☐ Challenge Words Practice (TE)
☐ Another Writing Idea (TE)

Objective *Children will*
- take the posttest

Assessment
☐ **Posttest** (TE) *See Day 5*
☐ Unit 10 Test

Meeting Individual Needs
Students Acquiring English

Spanish In Spanish the |k| sound is spelled *c* or *qu*. **Activity** Create two columns labeled *k* and *ck* on the board. Write the Basic Words in the appropriate columns. Say each word and have a volunteer underline the *k* or *ck* spelling.

Asian Children may have difficulty understanding that the |k| sound has both *k* and *ck* spellings. **Activity** Say the list words and have children repeat them. Explain that the |k| sound has two different spellings. Spell the words aloud one by one. Repeat the words. Tell children to clap once if the |k| sound is spelled *k* and twice if it is spelled *ck*.

Other Activities for Any Day

- Bonus activities from pages 82–83
- Practice Masters (easy, average, challenging)
  Teacher's Resource Book, pages 45–47
- Take-Home Word List 10
  Practice Plus

Objectives *Children will*

■ take the pretest
■ pronounce the list words
■ learn about the spelling principle
■ sort words by their spelling patterns

Teaching the Principle

This lesson teaches the *k* and *ck* spellings for the |k| sound. Children learn the strategy of thinking of the letter *k* when the |k| sound follows a long vowel or is part of a consonant cluster. They learn to think of the letters *ck* when the |k| sound follows a short vowel.

To sum up the lesson, ask:

• What one letter spells the last consonant sound in *bake*? (*k*) Is the vowel sound before *k* short or long? (*long*)

• What two letters spell the last consonant sound in *black*? (*ck*) Is the vowel sound before *ck* short or long? (*short*)

Enrichment

Vocabulary: Multiple Meanings
Have children use a dictionary to look up *rock*, *pick*, and *back*. Discuss the different meanings.

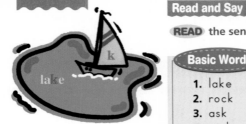

10 Words Spelled with k or ck

Read and Say

READ the sentences. **SAY** each word in dark print.

Basic Words

1.	lake	They swim in the **lake**.
2.	rock	Step over that **rock**.
3.	ask	Did you **ask** him to go?
4.	pick	I will **pick** out a toy.
5.	truck	John drives a **truck**.
6.	black	She has **black** mittens.
7.	back	We sat in the **back** row.
8.	bake	Eva had bread to **bake**.
9.	clock	A **clock** tells the time.
10.	kick	I can **kick** the ball!

A. lake

ask

bake

B. rock

pick

truck

black

back

clock

kick

Think and Write

Each word ends with the same sound. It is the first sound you hear in 🔑. This consonant sound is spelled two different ways.

k → la**k**e, as**k**   **ck** → ro**ck**, pi**ck**

Is the vowel sound before **ck** short or long? *The vowel sound before ck is short.*

A. Write **three** Basic Words that have the last consonant spelled **k**.

B. Write **seven** Basic Words that have the last consonant sound spelled **ck**.

Order of answers for each category may vary.

Review	Challenge
11. kite **12.** take	**13.** dock **14.** snake

TEACHING OPTIONS

Meeting Individual Needs
Word Lists

You may want to assign Basic Words 1–5 and the Review Words to children who misspelled more than five words on the pretest. Assign the Challenge Words as appropriate. (You may want to have children write sentences, using the Challenge Words.)

Additional Spelling Words

Basic	Challenge	Words Often Misspelled
fork	work	name
neck	squeak	time
hike	basket	
pack	knock	
cake	rocket	
	snack	

Home/School Involvement
Take-Home Word List • Goal-Setting

Have children set goals for the week on Take-Home Word List 10.

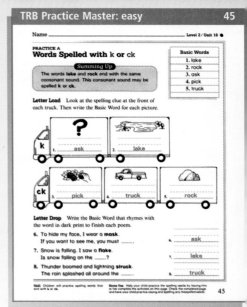

Name _____   Level 2/ Unit 10 ●

PRACTICE A
Words Spelled with k or ck

Summing Up
The words **lake** and **rock** end with the same consonant sound. This consonant sound may be spelled **k** or **ck**.

Basic Words
1. lake
2. rock
3. ask
4. pick
5. truck

Letter Load Look at the spelling clue at the front of each truck. Then write the Basic Word for each picture.

k   1. ask   2. lake

ck   3. pick   4. truck   5. rock

Letter Drop Write the Basic Word that rhymes with the word in dark print to finish each poem.

6. To hide my face, I wear a **mask**.
   If you want to see me, you must _____   6. ask

7. Snow is falling. I saw a **flake**.
   Is snow falling on the _____?   7. lake

8. Thunder boomed and lightning **struck**.
   The rain splashed all around the _____   8. truck

45

Independent Practice

Spelling Strategy The words **lake** and **rock** end with the same consonant sound. This consonant sound may be spelled **k** or **ck**.

Order of answers for each question may vary.

Phonics Write Basic Words to answer the questions.

1–2. Which two words are spelled with the vowel-consonant-**e** pattern?

3–5. Which three words begin with a consonant cluster?

Word Groups Think how the words in each group are alike. Write the missing Basic Words.

6. say, tell, _____
7. side, front, _____
8. catch, throw, _____

Word Meaning Write the Basic Word that means the same or almost the same as the word in dark print.

9. Can you skip a **stone** across the water?
10. Try to **choose** one that is smooth and flat.

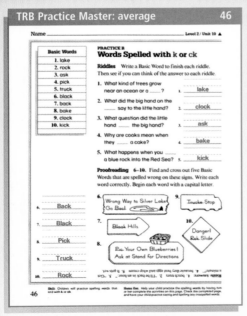

Phonics

1. lake
2. bake
3. truck
4. black
5. clock

Word Groups

6. ask
7. back
8. kick

Word Meaning

9. rock
10. pick

(79)

Objectives *Children will*
- practice spelling list words
- apply spelling strategies
- classify Basic Words into groups
- identify synonyms

Day 2

Daily Proofreading Practice
My sister drives a red **truk**. (*truck*)
We will **baek** two apple pies. (*bake*)

Meeting Individual Needs
visual/oral/auditory/kinesthetic

Extra Support Check Independent Practice to determine who needs extra support. Write each Basic Word on the board, drawing a blank for each final *k* or *ck*. (for example, ro __ __ and la __ e) Say each word one at a time. Have a volunteer repeat the word, fill in the missing letter or letters, and tell what spells the final |k| sound in that word.

Applying Spelling Strategies
To Read New Words

- Write this sentence on the chalkboard: **My friend's nickname is Wheels.**
- Have children read the sentence silently.
- Elicit the following strategies as children try to decode *nickname*.

Next, I see the letter *i* followed by *ck*. The letters *ck* make the |k| sound. I know that *ck* usually follows a short vowel sound. The letter *i* probably stands for the short *i* sound.

I know that *n* makes the sound I hear at the beginning of *nest*.

nickname

I recognize the short word *name* at the end of this longer word.

N-ick-name. Nick-name. Nickname. The word *nickname* makes sense in the sentence.

Day 3

Objectives *Children will*

- identify the first alphabetical word in groups of words with the same first letter
- review Basic and Review Words

Daily Proofreading Practice

The bedroom **klock** ticks loudly. (*clock*)

Tara dove into the cold **lacke**. (*lake*)

UNIT 10

Entry Words

1. any
   _____
2. clock
   _____
3. time
   _____
4. bake
   _____
5. take
   _____
6. key

Rhyme Time

7. clock
   _____
8. lake
   _____
9. kick
   _____
10. bake
    _____
11. kite
    _____
12. rock

80

Dictionary

Entry Words To find entry words in a dictionary, you use ABC order. When entry words begin with the same letter, you must look at the second letter. See how these entry words are put in ABC order.

l**a**ke   l**e**g   l**i**st

Practice Write the entry word in each group that would come first in the dictionary.

1. ask   apple   any
2. crown   cup   clock
3. top   time   truck
4. black   bake   bent
5. tell   told   take
6. key   know   kite

Review: Spelling Spree

Rhyme Time Finish the sentences. Write a Basic or Review Word to rhyme with the word in dark print.

7. Tick and **tock** are the sounds of a ___.
8. The wind will **shake** the homes by the ___.
9. The player is **quick**, but can he ___?
10. To cook a **cake**, you must know how to ___.
11. If the fish do not **bite**, go fly your ___.
12. The lump in my **sock** is a gray ___.

How Are You Doing?
Write each word in a sentence. Practice with a partner any words you spelled wrong.

TEACHING OPTIONS

Ongoing Assessment

The Final |k| Sound

Children will learn that the final |k| sound is spelled differently in single-syllable words, depending on whether the vowel sound is short or long. Common errors are TRUC for *truck* and BACKE for *bake* or *back*.

TRB Practice Master: challenging   **47**

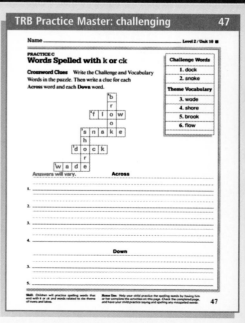

Proofreading and Writing

Proofread for Spelling Proofread this post card. Use proofreading marks to fix six spelling mistakes.

Example: Did you swim and fly your ~~kit~~? kite

May 26, 1998

Dear Rosa,

The ~~truk~~ ride around the lake was bumpy! Don't (truck)

~~aks~~ me how we ever got ~~bak~~! We are going to ~~tak~~ a (ask) (back) (take)

boat trip on Sunday. I can try to ~~pik~~ up a ~~blak~~ rock (pick) (black)

for your collection.

Your friend,

Megan

Basic

1. lake
2. rock
3. ask
4. pick
5. truck
6. black
7. back
8. bake
9. clock
10. kick

Review

11. kite
12. take

Challenge

13. dock
14. snake

Proofreading Marks

∧ Add
⌐ Delete
≡ Make a capital letter
/ Make a small letter

Write a Post Card

Pretend you are on a trip with your family. Write a post card to a friend. What exciting things do you do? Try to use spelling words. Draw a picture on your post card. Share it with a friend.

Proofreading Tip

Check each word to make sure you have not switched the order of the letters.

81

Meeting Individual Needs

Challenge Words Practice Have children draw a snake and a dock. On the snake, have them write *snake* and other *-ake* words that rhyme with it. On the dock, have them write *dock* and other *-ock* words that rhyme with it.

Another Writing Idea Ask children to pretend they are a fish that lives in a river or a lake. Have them use spelling words to write a letter to a pen pal, telling about their underwater life.

Objectives *Children will*

■ proofread for spelling
■ write and proofread an original composition

Day 4

Daily Proofreading Practice

I will **pic** out a movie to watch. (*pick*)
Please **aks** Sarah to help us. (*ask*)

Day 5 **Posttest**

Sentences 1–5 test the first five Basic Words. Sentences 6–10 test the next five Basic Words.

Basic Words

1. Tom sees a <u>rock</u> in the mud.
2. I must <u>ask</u> his name.
3. A frog is in the <u>lake</u>.
4. We must fix the <u>truck</u>.
5. Peg may <u>pick</u> a game.
6. He gave the bag <u>back</u> to him.
7. She did not <u>kick</u> the hat.
8. I will use this <u>clock</u>.
9. Let me <u>bake</u> this time.
10. The spot is <u>black</u>.

Review Words

11. We can <u>take</u> the bus.
12. I have a <u>kite</u> at home.

Challenge Words

13. I saw a green <u>snake</u> in the garden.
14. Five boats were tied at the <u>dock</u>.

These pages can be used at any time during the study of this unit.

Day by Day Planner

Objectives *Children will*

■ identify pictures to build *k* and *ck* words

■ identify rhyming words

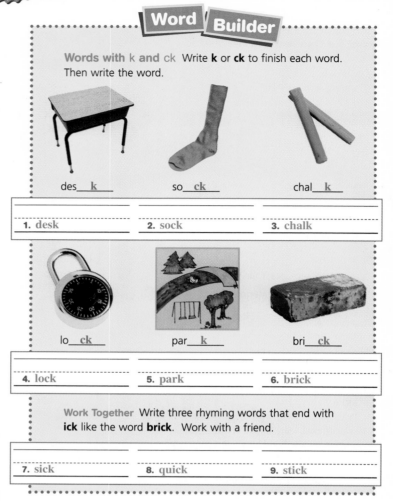

Word Builder

Words with k and ck Write **k** or **ck** to finish each word. Then write the word.

des__k__   so__ck__   chal__k__

1. desk   2. sock   3. chalk

lo__ck__   par__k__   bri__ck__

4. lock   5. park   6. brick

Work Together Write three rhyming words that end with **ick** like the word **brick**. Work with a friend.

7. sick   8. quick   9. stick

82

EXTENSION OPTIONS

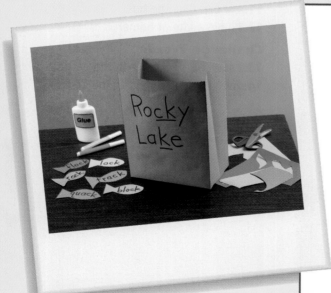

Learning Center Activity

visual/oral/auditory/kinesthetic

Rocky Lake Place in a Learning Center cutouts of fish, markers, and a paper bag that has been colored or painted blue. On the bag, print "Rocky Lake," underlining the letters *ck* and *k*.

Have children write on the fish rhyming words that end with the |k| sound. For example, they might write words that end with *-ick, -ack, -ock,* or *-ike*.

Children can then take turns pulling fish from the "lake," asking a partner to spell them or sorting them according to categories they determine.

Vocabulary Enrichment

Science

Rivers and Lakes All the words in the box have something to do with rivers and lakes. Write those words to finish this page from a report. Use your Spelling Dictionary.

Spelling Word Link

lake

wade
shore
brook
flow

This little __(1)__ has cool water.

It will __(2)__ into a big river. Birds

__(3)__ in the water. They live on

the rocky __(4)__ .

1. brook

2. flow

3. wade

4. shore

Try This CHALLENGE

Yes or No? Is the word in dark print used correctly? Write **yes** or **no**.

5. Bob is **shore** we can swim in this lake.
6. I am going to **wade** into the river.
7. The huge ship sailed up to the **brook**.
8. This water will **flow** into the ocean.

5. no

6. yes

7. no

8. yes

★ Fact File

The longest river in the world is the Nile in Africa. It is more than 4,000 miles long. A trip down the Nile would be longer than a trip across the whole United States!

83

Objectives *Children will*

- expand their vocabulary by using words related to rivers and lakes
- show their understanding of the vocabulary words by completing context activities

Vocabulary Checkup

Have children use the vocabulary words in sentences or match the words to the definitions below.

1. the land along the edge of water *shore*
2. to walk into water *wade*
3. to move freely like water in a stream *flow*
4. a small stream of fresh water *brook*

Fact File

The Nile River

Point out the Nile on a world map or a map of Africa. The Nile River flows from Lake Victoria through northeastern Africa to the Mediterranean Sea. The Nile floods yearly, depositing rich soils and creating in its valley some of the world's most fertile farmland.

Integrating Literature

Easy	Average	Challenging
Come a Tide *by George Ella Lyon* A family moves to higher ground when snow and rain cause flooding.	**Up River** *by Frank Asch* Two friends participate in a community cleanup of a river.	**Letting Swift River Go** *by Jane Yolen* The town where Sally Jane lived is flooded to create a reservoir.
All Night Near the Water *by Jim Arnosky* Ducklings spend their first night on a lake with their mother.	**All I See** *by Cynthia Rylant* A painter's picture of a lake looks different than what Charlie sees.	**Everglades** *by Jean Craighead George* The evolution of the Everglades from sea to river.

Words With Double Consonants

WORD LISTS

Spelling

Basic
1. bell
2. off
3. dress
4. add
5. hill
6. well
7. egg
8. will
9. grass
10. tell

Review
11. at
12. hot

Challenge
13. brass
14. skill

Vocabulary

Music: Songs and Instruments
tune
harp
tuba
pit

Introducing the Lesson

Read Aloud

Write the Basic Words on the board.

Folk Songs

Did you know that people have played and sung folk music for thousands of years? Many folk songs are very old and **tell** stories about things that happened long ago. A folk song passes from person to person through the years, and sometimes people **will** change or **add** to it a bit as they learn it **well**. Folk songs can be about anything. Some describe the beauty of the land, such as the green **grass** of spring or a robin's blue **egg**. Sailors who have gone **off** to sea may make up songs about the home they miss. Farmers planting crops on a **hill** may make up songs to pass the time until the dinner **bell** rings. Many folk songs are very silly and can be about anything from a favorite doll to a new **dress**.

Responding Ask children what kind of song they learned about. (*folk song*) Reread the selection slowly. Ask children to put their hands on their head whenever they hear a spelling word. Call on a volunteer to say each word.

Day 1 *page 84*

Day 2 *page 85*

Objectives *Children will*
- take the pretest
- pronounce the list words
- learn about the spelling principle
- analyze words by their final consonant spellings

Planning Checklist
- ☑ Pretest (TE)
- ☑ Spelling principle/word list
- ☐ Review/Challenge Words
- ☐ Teaching the Principle (TE)
- ☐ Enrichment (TE)
- ☐ Additional Spelling Words (TE)

Assessment

Pretest
1. Who will ring the <u>bell</u>?
2. Take that hat <u>off</u>.
3. She likes this <u>dress</u>.
4. I will <u>add</u> those numbers.
5. Jason ran up the <u>hill</u>.
6. Did you sleep <u>well</u>?
7. The <u>egg</u> was cracked.
8. Maria <u>will</u> feed Duke.
9. Please cut the <u>grass</u>.
10. I cannot <u>tell</u> you to go.

Objectives *Children will*
- practice spelling list words
- apply spelling strategies
- identify antonyms
- identify Basic Words by using meaning clues

Planning Checklist
- ☑ Spelling Strategy
- ☑ Independent Practice
- ☐ Daily Proofreading Practice (TE)
- ☐ Informal Assessment (TE)
- ☐ Extra Support (TE)
- ☐ Applying Spelling Strategies (TE)

Additional Resources

Teacher's Resource Book
Practice Masters, pages 49–51
Unit Test, page 52
Bulletin Board, page 53

Practice Plus
Take-Home Word List 11
Games

Spelling Transparencies
Spelling Word List 11
Daily Proofreading Practice,
  Unit 11
Graphic Organizers

Teacher's Resource Disk
Macintosh® or Windows® software.
  Houghton Mifflin

Spelling CD-ROM
Macintosh® or Windows® software.
  Houghton Mifflin

Internet
http://www.eduplace.com

Phonics Practice
Houghton Mifflin Phonics
The Listening Corner
Phonics Home Connection

Day 3 *page 86*

Day 4 *page 87*

Day 5 *page 87*

Objectives *Children will*
- identify entry words that would be found between given guide words
- review Basic and Review Words

Planning Checklist
☐ Dictionary
☐ Review: Spelling Spree
☐ How Are You Doing?
☐ Daily Proofreading Practice (TE)
☐ Cooperative Learning Activity (TE)

Objectives *Children will*
- proofread for spelling
- write and proofread an original composition

Planning Checklist
☐ Proofread for Spelling
☐ Write a List
☐ Daily Proofreading Practice (TE)
☐ Challenge Words Practice (TE)
☐ Another Writing Idea (TE)

Objective *Children will*
- take the posttest

Assessment
☐ **Posttest** (TE) See Day 5
☐ Unit 11 Test

Meeting Individual Needs
Students Acquiring English

Spanish Consonant sounds in Spanish are represented by a single consonant letter.
Activity Put the following on the chalkboard:

Words					
1. be △	3. dre ○	5. we △	7. te △		
2. o ▢	4. a ▽	6. gra ○	8. hi △		
Key ⚠ll	⬡ss	▽dd	▢ff		

Have children write the letters that complete the word in each shape. As each word is completed, have them say and spell it.
Asian Use the activity for Spanish-speaking children.

Other Activities for Any Day

- Bonus activities from pages 88–89
- Practice Masters (easy, average, challenging)
  Teacher's Resource Book, pages 49–51
- Take-Home Word List 11
  Practice Plus

Objectives *Children will*

- take the pretest
- pronounce the list words
- learn about the spelling principle
- analyze words by their final consonant spellings

Teaching the Principle

This lesson teaches the concept that a single consonant sound at the end of a word may be spelled with two consonant letters that are the same. Children learn the strategy of thinking of the double consonant spelling for particular sounds, such as |l|, |f|, and |s|, at the end of one-syllable words.

To sum up the lesson, ask:

- How many letters spell the final consonant sound in each word? *(two)*
- What letters spell the final consonant sound in each word? *(bell, off, dress, add, hill, well, egg, will, grass, tell)*

Enrichment

Vocabulary: Multiple Meanings
Have children use a dictionary to look up *off, dress,* and *well.* Discuss the meanings.

Words with Double Consonants

egg
gg

Read and Say

READ the sentences. **SAY** each word in dark print.

Basic Words

1.	bell	Who will ring the **bell**?
2.	off	Take that hat **off**.
3.	dress	She likes this **dress**.
4.	add	I will **add** those numbers.
5.	hill	Jason ran up the **hill**.
6.	well	Did you sleep **well**?
7.	egg	The **egg** was cracked.
8.	will	Maria **will** feed Duke.
9.	grass	Please cut the **grass**.
10.	tell	I cannot **tell** you to go.

A. be<u>ll</u>

o<u>ff</u>

dre<u>ss</u>

a<u>dd</u>

hi<u>ll</u>

we<u>ll</u>

e<u>gg</u>

wi<u>ll</u>

gra<u>ss</u>

te<u>ll</u>

84

Think and Write

Each word ends with a consonant sound. The last consonant sound is spelled with two letters that are the same.

be**ll**, o**ff**, dre**ss**, a**dd**, e**gg**

How many vowel sounds do you hear in each word? one
Do any of the words have a long vowel sound? no

A. Write the Basic Words. Then draw a line under the letters that spell the last consonant sound in each word. Order of answers may vary.

Review		Challenge	
11. at	**12.** hot	**13.** brass	**14.** skill

TEACHING OPTIONS

Meeting Individual Needs
Word Lists

You may want to assign Basic Words 1–5 and the Review Words to children who misspelled more than five words on the pretest. Assign the Challenge Words as appropriate. (You may want to have children write sentences, using the Challenge Words.)

Additional Spelling Words

Basic	Challenge	Words Often Misspelled
sell	address	little
pass	across	some
kiss	guess	
mess	cliff	
boss	pull	
	windowsill	

Home/School Involvement
Take-Home Word List • Goal-Setting

Have children set goals for the week on Take-Home Word List 11.

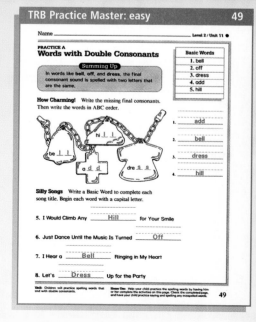

TRB Practice Master: easy   49

Name _____   Level 2 / Unit 11 ●

PRACTICE A
Words with Double Consonants

Summing Up
In words like **bell, off,** and **dress,** the final consonant sound is spelled with two letters that are the same.

Basic Words
1. bell
2. off
3. dress
4. add
5. hill

How Charming! Write the missing final consonants. Then write the words in ABC order.

1. ____ add
2. ____ bell
3. ____ dress
4. ____ hill

Silly Songs Write a Basic Word to complete each song title. Begin each word with a capital letter.

5. I Would Climb Any _____ Hill _____ for Your Smile

6. Just Dance Until the Music Is Turned _____ Off

7. I Hear a _____ Bell _____ Ringing in My Heart

8. Let's _____ Dress _____ Up for the Party

49

Independent Practice

 Spelling Strategy In words like **bell**, **off**, and **dress**, the final consonant sound is spelled with two letters that are the same.

Order of answers for question 3–4 may vary.

Phonics Write Basic Words to answer the questions.

1. Which word begins with the same consonant cluster as ? drum
2. Which word begins with the same consonant cluster as ? grapes
3–4. Which two words rhyme with **spill**?

Word Meaning Write the Basic Word that means the opposite of each word below.

5. sick   6. ask   7. on

Word Clues Write a Basic Word for each clue.

8. what you do to one and two to get three
9. what a mother or father bird keeps warm
10. what you ring at someone's door

Phonics

1. dress

2. grass

3. hill

4. will

Word Meaning

5. well

6. tell

7. off

Word Clues

8. add

9. egg

10. bell

85

Objectives *Children will*

- ■ practice spelling list words
- ■ apply spelling strategies
- ■ identify antonyms
- ■ identify Basic Words by using meaning clues

Daily Proofreading Practice
He put the **agg** in the frying pan. (*egg*)
Sam does not feel **wel** today. (*well*)

Meeting Individual Needs
visual/oral/auditory

Extra Support Check Independent Practice to determine who needs extra support. Write the Basic Words on the board. Say *feather*. Ask children to tell what letter they hear at the beginning of *feather*. (f) Have a volunteer find a word on the board that ends with the |f| sound, read the word, and underline the final double consonant. Repeat, using the key words *lamp, sock, duck,* and *ghost.*

TRB Practice Master: average   50

Name _____ Level 2 / Unit 11 ▲

Basic Words
1. bell
2. off
3. dress
4. add
5. hill
6. well
7. egg
8. will
9. grass
10. tell

PRACTICE B
Words with Double Consonants

Tick-Tack-Code Use the code below to write Basic Words. Look at the letters and the shape of the lines around each letter.

	b	d	e
	w		
	t	r	s

1. ⅃⌐⊏⊏   1. well
2. ⅂⌐⊏⊏   2. tell
3. ⊔⌐⊓⌐⌐   3. dress
4. ⅃⌐⊏⊏   4. bell

5. Off
6. Egg
7. Grass
8. Hill
9. Will
10. Add

Mother Goose Times Write the missing Basic Words in these headlines. Begin each word with a capital letter.

Humpty Dumpty Falls (5) Well

Goose Lays Gold (6) in Green (7)

Jack and Jill Climb (8) ; Jack Hurt in Fall

Tommy Tucker (9) Sing for His Supper

Snow White Can't Count!
Dwarfs Don't (10) up to Seven

50

Applying Spelling Strategies
To Spell New Words

- ■ Read aloud: **Can you stuff these socks into your backpack?**
- ■ Have children attempt to spell *stuff* on their Have-a-Go charts.

I hear the sounds for *s* and *t* blended together at the beginning of the word. I think this is the consonant cluster *st*.

- ■ Elicit the following strategies as children try to spell *stuff*.

This word has the short *u* sound. The short *u* sound is probably spelled *u*.

stuff

I hear a final |f| sound. I know this final sound is often spelled *ff* in a word with only one vowel sound.

Objectives *Children will*

■ identify entry words that would be found between given guide words

■ review Basic and Review Words

Daily Proofreading Practice

Please **tele** me what time it is. (*tell*)

The baby wore a pink **dres**. (*dress*)

UNIT
11

Guide Words

1. grass

2. hill

3. hot

4. give

Picture Clues

5. dress

6. add

7. well

8. hill

Jobs Match

9. grass

10. dress

11. egg

12. bell

86

Dictionary

Guide Words The two words at the top of a dictionary page are called **guide words**. They help you find entry words because they name the first and last entry word on the page.

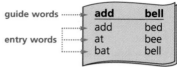

guide words →	**add**	**bell**
entry words →	add	bed
	at	bee
	bat	bell

Practice **1–4.** Write the four entry words from the box that you would find on the same page as the guide words **fun** and **ice**.

| grass | hill | egg | dress | hot | give |

Review: Spelling Spree

Picture Clues Write a Basic Word for each picture.

5.   6. $\begin{array}{r} +\,\frac{4}{5} \\ \hline 9 \end{array}$ 7.   8.

Jobs Match Look at the list of workers. Write a Basic Word that names something each person makes, uses, or works with on the job.

9. gardener
10. tailor
11. chicken farmer
12. firefighter

How Are You Doing?
List the spelling words that are hard for you. Practice them with a partner.

TEACHING OPTIONS

Cooperative Learning Activity
For the Record
visual/kinesthetic

Have children work with a partner to make records or CD's. First, have them cut out several circles from black construction paper. Next, they cut out smaller white circles to make the record labels. Have them paste a label on the center of each "record/CD." Finally, ask children to make up song or album titles using spelling words. Have them write one title on each label, underlining the spelling word or words.

TRB Practice Master: challenging   51

Name _____ Level 2 / Unit 11 ■

PRACTICE C
Words with Double Consonants

| Challenge Words |
| 1. brass |
| 2. skill |
| **Theme Vocabulary** |
| 3. tune |
| 4. harp |
| 5. tuba |
| 6. pit |

Mystery Music Find out what instrument each boy plays. Use the clues and the chart. Mark an X in the boxes under the instruments each boy does not play. Draw a star in the box that shows the instrument each boy does play.

Clues
• Each boy plays a different instrument.
• No boy's name begins with the same letter as the instrument he plays.
• Ted does not play the violin.

	harp	tuba	violin
Hal	X	X	☆
Ted	☆	X	X
Vic	X	☆	X

Write each missing Challenge Word, Vocabulary Word, or boy's name to finish the story. Use the chart to help you.

At two o'clock, the boys took their seats in the orchestra __(1)__. Soon, __(2)__ began to __(3)__ his violin. Then Ted plucked at the strings of his __(4)__. Finally, __(5)__ put the __(6)__ to his mouth and blew a few notes. He was proud of his shiny __(7)__ instrument. He hoped he had the __(8)__ to play it well.

1. pit
2. Hal
3. tune
4. harp
5. Vic
6. tuba
7. brass
8. skill

51

Proofreading and Writing

Proofread for Spelling Proofread this ad. Use proofreading marks to fix five spelling mistakes.

Example: Start singing when you hear the ~~bel~~. _bell_

Sing-Along Songs

You ~~wil~~ love these songs! They all ~~tel~~ a story. _will_ _tell_

Sing them on a hill. Hum them on the grass. Whistle them ~~att~~ home. Play them on a ~~hawt~~ day when you _at_ _hot_ go ~~of~~ to the beach. They can add to your fun! _off_

Write a List

Which instrument do you like to play or listen to? Make a list that tells why this instrument is your favorite. Give two or three reasons. Try to use spelling words. Discuss your list with a friend.

Proofreading Tip

If you use a computer when you write, use a spell checker.

Basic
1. bell
2. off
3. dress
4. add
5. hill
6. well
7. egg
8. will
9. grass
10. tell

Review
11. at
12. hot

Challenge
13. brass
14. skill

Proofreading Marks
∧ Add
⌐ Delete
≡ Make a capital letter
/ Make a small letter

87

Meeting Individual Needs

Challenge Words Practice Suggest children use the Challenge Words and other music words they know to make a music "pictionary" that tells about different instruments and how they are played.

Another Writing Idea Have children write a speech to introduce the performance of a favorite musical group. Encourage them to include spelling words.

Objectives _Children will_
- proofread for spelling
- write and proofread an original composition

Day 4

Daily Proofreading Practice
The sheep ate the soft **grazz**. (_grass_)
We all climbed up the **hil**. (_hill_)

Day 5 **Posttest**

Sentences 1–5 test the first five Basic Words. Sentences 6–10 test the next five Basic Words.

Basic Words
1. Look at my new <u>dress</u>!
2. He can <u>add</u> that for us.
3. This is a big <u>hill</u>.
4. I have a <u>bell</u> on my sled.
5. Get <u>off</u> that box.
6. Do not step on the <u>grass</u>.
7. The <u>egg</u> is for her.
8. What did she <u>tell</u> you?
9. Can you see <u>well</u>?
10. She <u>will</u> not see you.

Review Words
11. It is a <u>hot</u> day.
12. I will see you <u>at</u> nine.

Challenge Words
13. He played the tuba in a <u>brass</u> band.
14. It takes <u>skill</u> to play the violin.

These pages can be used at any time during the study of this unit.

Day by Day Planner

Objectives *Children will*

■ build words with the phonogram -*ill*

■ write original sentences

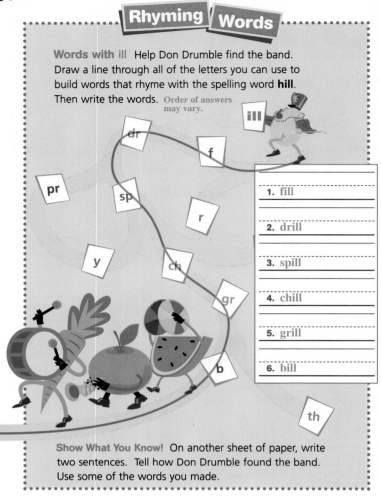

Phonics and Spelling

Rhyming Words

Words with ill Help Don Drumble find the band. Draw a line through all of the letters you can use to build words that rhyme with the spelling word **hill**. Then write the words. *Order of answers may vary.*

ill

dr

f

pr

sp

r

y

ch

gr

b

th

1. fill
2. drill
3. spill
4. chill
5. grill
6. bill

Show What You Know! On another sheet of paper, write two sentences. Tell how Don Drumble found the band. Use some of the words you made.

88

EXTENSION OPTIONS

Learning Center Activity

visual/oral/kinesthetic

My *ell* Songbook Have children take several pieces of paper, fold them in half, and staple them at the left side to make a book. On the front cover of the book, have children write "My *ell* Songbook." Children then brainstorm a list of -*ell* words. On each page of their book, they draw or paste a musical note and write an -*ell* word on it. Under each note, children write a song lyric that includes the word on the note. Some children may wish to sing their lyrics for the class.

More -*ell* Words		
bell	shell	tell
cell	smell	well
fell	spell	yell
sell	swell	

Vocabulary Enrichment

Music

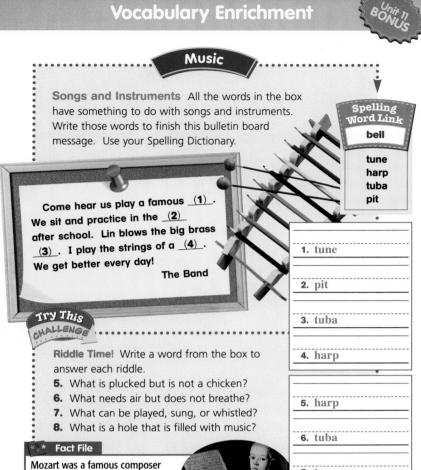

Songs and Instruments All the words in the box have something to do with songs and instruments. Write those words to finish this bulletin board message. Use your Spelling Dictionary.

Come hear us play a famous __(1)__. We sit and practice in the __(2)__ after school. Lin blows the big brass __(3)__. I play the strings of a __(4)__. We get better every day!

The Band

Spelling Word Link

bell

tune
harp
tuba
pit

1. tune

2. pit

3. tuba

4. harp

Try This CHALLENGE

Riddle Time! Write a word from the box to answer each riddle.

5. What is plucked but is not a chicken?
6. What needs air but does not breathe?
7. What can be played, sung, or whistled?
8. What is a hole that is filled with music?

5. harp

6. tuba

7. tune

8. pit

Fact File

Mozart was a famous composer who lived in Austria during the 1700s. He started playing music at the age of four. He began writing music when he was only five years old!

89

Day by Day Planner

Objectives *Children will*

- expand their vocabulary by using words related to songs and instruments
- show their understanding of the vocabulary words by completing context activities

Vocabulary Checkup

Have children use the vocabulary words in sentences or match the words to the definitions below.

1. a large brass wind instrument, low in pitch *tuba*
2. an instrument with strings stretched on a frame, which are plucked to make sounds *harp*
3. the place in front of and lower than the stage, where the musicians sit *pit*
4. a group of musical notes that make up a song; a melody *tune*

Fact File

Mozart

You may wish to play a recording of one of Mozart's more well-known pieces. At age six, Wolfgang Amadeus Mozart began giving concerts with his father and his sister. Mozart wrote more than 600 compositions in his lifetime, including symphonies, operas, and church music.

Integrating Literature

Easy

Charlie Parker Played Be Bop
by Chris Raschka
A rhythmic tribute to jazz great Charlie Parker.

What a Wonderful World
by George D. Weiss and Bob Thiele
An illustrated version of the song made famous by Louis Armstrong.

Average

Zin! Zin! Zin! A Violin
by Lloyd Moss
An introduction to the different sounds orchestral instruments make.

Tukama Tootles the Flute
by Phyllis Gershator
Tukama's flute helps him escape from a giant.

Challenging

Berlioz the Bear
by Jan Brett
Berlioz's orchestra gets into trouble on the way to a concert.

Meet the Marching Smithereens
by Ann Hayes
An introduction to a marching band.

Review: Units 7–11

WORD LISTS

Spelling
Basic Words

Unit 7	Unit 10
five	lake
made	ask
side	truck
ate	black
same	back
line	kick

Unit 8	Unit 11
bone	off
nose	add
these	hill
home	well
cute	egg
hope	grass

Unit 9

trip
swim
club
stone
next
glad

Elephant Words
Units 7–11

give	one
have	goes

The Review Unit
Word Lists

Half of the Basic Words from Units 7–11 are reviewed in this Review Unit. The remaining Basic Words from Units 7–11 are reviewed in the Extra Practice section of the Student's Handbook. All of the Elephant Words are practiced in both the Review Unit and the Extra Practice section.

Day 1 *page 90*

Day 2 *page 91*

Objectives *Children will*
- take the pretest
- review the vowel-consonant-e spelling pattern for the |ā|, |ī|, |ō|, |yo͞o|, and |ē| sounds

Planning Checklist
- ☐ Daily Proofreading Practice (TE)
- ☐ Extra Support, pages 61, 67 (TE)
- ☐ Extra Practice, page 244
- ☐ Practice Masters, pages 33, 34, 37, 38 (TRB)

Objectives *Children will*
- review words with consonant clusters
- review the spelling of words with the |k| sound

Planning Checklist
- ☐ Daily Proofreading Practice (TE)
- ☐ Extra Support, pages 73, 79 (TE)
- ☐ Extra Practice, page 245
- ☐ Practice Masters, pages 41, 42, 45, 46 (TRB)

Assessment

Pretest
1. He <u>ate</u> the fish.
2. Is she in <u>line</u>?
3. The pig is <u>cute</u>.
4. I <u>hope</u> she is fine.
5. Did he have the <u>stone</u>?
6. I am <u>glad</u>.
7. She has a blue <u>truck</u>.
8. Did he <u>kick</u> the box?
9. The frog is in the <u>well</u>.
10. The <u>grass</u> is green.

Day 3 *page 92*

 Day 4 *page 93*

 Day 5 *page 93*

Objectives *Children will*
- review the double-letter spelling of final consonant sounds
- review the Elephant Words

Planning Checklist
- ☐ Daily Proofreading Practice (TE)
- ☐ Extra Support, page 85 (TE)
- ☐ Extra Practice, page 246
- ☐ Practice Masters, pages 49, 50 (TRB)

Objective *Children will*
- analyze the spelling and meaning relationship of words in the *bake* family

Planning Checklist
- ☐ Spelling-Meaning Strategy

Objective *Children will*
- take the posttest

Assessment

- ☐ **Posttest** (TE) *See Day 5*
- ☐ Scoring Rubric
- ☐ Unit 12 Review Tests A–B (TRB)

Additional Resources

Teacher's Resource Book
Practice Masters, pages 33–35, 37–39, 41–43, 45–47, 49–51
Multiple-Choice Tests, pages 57–58
Bulletin Board, page 53
Spelling Newsletters, English and Spanish, pages 54–55
Spelling Game, page 56

Practice Plus
Take-Home Word List 12

Spelling Transparencies
Spelling Word List 12
Daily Proofreading Practice, Unit 12
Spelling-Meaning Strategy
Multiple-Choice Test

Teacher's Resource Disk
Macintosh® or Windows® software. Houghton Mifflin

Spelling CD-ROM
Macintosh® or Windows® software. Houghton Mifflin

Internet
http://www.eduplace.com

Meeting Individual Needs

You may wish to create your own pretest, using the words that children missed most often in the last five units. Children can check their own work, or a partner's, by looking up the words in the previous units' word lists or in their Spelling Dictionary.

In each Review lesson, the Basic Words are selected from both halves of the unit word list to accommodate individual needs. In Units 7–11, the top row of words is from Basic Words 1–5 and the bottom row from Basic Words 6–10.

Other Activities for Any Day

- Literature and Writing, pages 94–95
- Spelling Game
  Teacher's Resource Book, page 56
- Bulletin Board
  Teacher's Resource Book, page 53
- Take-Home Word List 12
  Practice Plus

Objectives *Children will*

■ take the pretest

■ review the vowel-consonant-*e* spelling pattern for the |ā|, |ī|, |ō|, |yōō|, and |ē| sounds

---

Daily Proofreading Practice

Al and I live on the **saem** street. (*same*)

My kitten has a pink **noze**. (*nose*)

Meeting Individual Needs

Additional Resources

Unit 7

Extra Support page 61 (TE)

Extra Practice page 244

Practice Masters pages 33–34 (TRB)

Unit 8

Extra Support page 67 (TE)

Extra Practice page 244

Practice Masters pages 37–38 (TRB)

---

12 **Review:** Units 7–11

| Unit 7 | Vowel-Consonant-*e* | pages 60-65 |

2+3=5

ī
five

| five | made | side |
| ate | same | line |

Spelling Strategy The long **a** and the long **i** vowel sounds may be spelled by the vowel-consonant-**e** pattern.

Write the spelling word that rhymes with each word.

1. mine **2.** name **3.** trade **4.** hive

Write the missing spelling words.

5. We _____ all the food Dad cooked.

6. Then we played tag by the _____ of our house.

| Unit 8 | More Vowel-Consonant-*e* | pages 66–71 |

ō
bone

| bone | nose | these |
| home | cute | hope |

Spelling Strategy The long **o**, **u**, and **e** vowel sounds may be spelled by the vowel-consonant-**e** pattern.

Change the letter in dark print. Write a spelling word.

7. **r**ope **8.** th**o**se **9.** c**u**be **10.** **r**ose

Write the missing spelling words.

11. Spot likes to eat dinner in his new _____.

12. We put his bowl and favorite _____ inside.

---

1. line

2. same

3. made

4. five

5. ate

6. side

7. hope

8. these

9. cute

10. nose

11. home

12. bone

90

EXTENSION OPTIONS

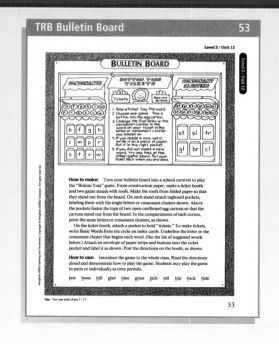

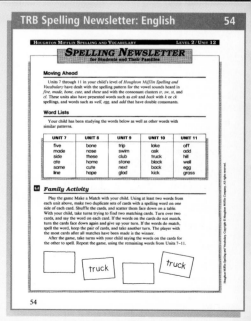

Unit 9   Consonant Clusters   pages 72–77

trip	swim	club
stone	next	glad

sw
swim

Spelling Strategy A **consonant cluster** is two consonant letters whose sounds are blended together.

Write the spelling word that means the same.

13. happy   **14.** after   **15.** rock

Write the missing spelling words.

Six people are in our sports ___(16)___. We will take a ___(17)___ to the beach and ___(18)___ all day.

Unit 10   Words Spelled with k or ck   pages 78–83

lake	ask	truck
black	back	kick

lake

Spelling Strategy The final consonant sound in **lake** and **truck** may be spelled **k** or **ck**.

Write the spelling word that means the opposite.

19. tell   **20.** front   **21.** white

Write the missing spelling words.

We went to the ___(22)___ in our new red ___(23)___. Mom showed me how to ___(24)___ my legs in the water.

13. glad

14. next

15. stone

16. club

17. trip

18. swim

19. ask

20. back

21. black

22. lake

23. truck

24. kick

91

Objectives *Children will*
- review words with consonant clusters
- review the spelling of words with the |k| sound

Day 2

Daily Proofreading Practice

I **sawim** in a pond all summer. (*swim*)
The **blak** clouds filled the sky. (*black*)

Meeting Individual Needs

Additional Resources

Unit 9

Extra Support page 73 (TE)

Extra Practice page 245

Practice Masters pages 41–42 (TRB)

Unit 10

Extra Support page 79 (TE)

Extra Practice page 245

Practice Masters pages 45–46 (TRB)

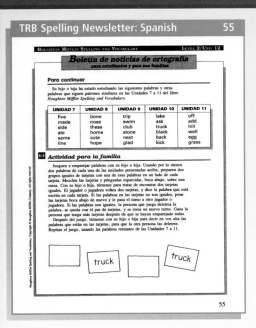

Objectives *Children will*
- review the double-letter spelling of final consonant sounds
- review the Elephant Words

Daily Proofreading Practice
Please turn the radio **auff**. (*off*)
My dog **goez** everywhere I do!
(*goes*)

Meeting Individual Needs

Additional Resources

Unit 11
Extra Support page 85 (TE)
Extra Practice page 246
Practice Masters pages 49–50 (TRB)

Reviewing Elephant Words
Extra Practice page 246

UNIT 12

25. egg

26. hill

27. grass

28. well

29. off

30. add

31. have

32. one

33. goes

34. give

35. goes

36. have

92

Unit 11   Double Consonants   pages 84-89

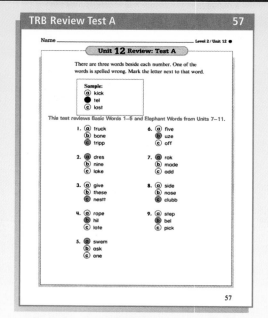

off	add	hill
well	egg	grass

Spelling Strategy   A final consonant sound may be spelled with two letters that are the same.

Write the spelling word that goes with each word.
25. hen   27. cut
26. climb   28. pail

Write the missing spelling words.
29. Take _____ your coats and sit down.
30. Today we will _____ more to our class story.

Elephant Words   Units 7–11   pages 60–89

O N E

give	have
one	goes

Spelling Strategy   Elephant Words have unusual spellings. Check them carefully when you write them.

Write the missing words. Use some words two times.
I __(31)__ six brothers. Each __(32)__ of us __(33)__ to school every day. Some days Mom will __(34)__ us a ride. When she __(35)__ to work on the train, we __(36)__ to take the bus.

EXTENSION OPTIONS

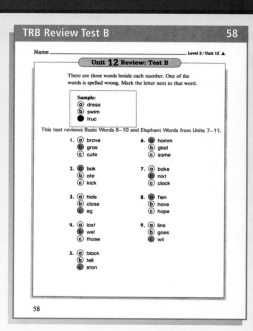

TRB Review Test A   57

Name _____   Level 2 / Unit 12 ●

Unit 12 Review: Test A

There are three words beside each number. One of the words is spelled wrong. Mark the letter next to that word.

Sample:
ⓐ kick
● tel
ⓒ lost

This test reviews Basic Words 1–5 and Elephant Words from Units 7–11.

1. ⓐ truck   6. ⓐ five
   ⓑ bone   ⓑ uze
   ⓒ tripp   ⓒ off

2. ⓐ dres   7. ⓐ rok
   ⓑ nine   ⓑ made
   ⓒ loke   ⓒ add

3. ⓐ give   8. ⓐ side
   ⓑ these   ⓑ nose
   ⓒ nestt   ⓒ clubb

4. ⓐ rope   9. ⓐ step
   ⓑ hil   ⓑ bel
   ⓒ lote   ⓒ pick

5. ⓐ swem
   ⓑ ask
   ⓒ one

57

TRB Review Test B   58

Name _____   Level 2 / Unit 12 ▲

Unit 12 Review: Test B

There are three words beside each number. One of the words is spelled wrong. Mark the letter next to that word.

Sample:
ⓐ dress
ⓑ swim
● truc

This test reviews Basic Words 6–10 and Elephant Words from Units 7–11.

1. ⓐ brave   6. ⓐ homm
   ⓑ gras   ⓑ glad
   ⓒ cute   ⓒ same

2. ⓐ bok   7. ⓐ bake
   ⓑ ate   ⓑ nixt
   ⓒ kick   ⓒ clock

3. ⓐ hide   8. ⓐ fien
   ⓑ close   ⓑ have
   ⓒ eg   ⓒ hope

4. ⓐ lost   9. ⓐ line
   ⓑ wel   ⓑ goes
   ⓒ those   ⓒ wil

5. ⓐ black
   ⓑ tell
   ⓒ ston

58

UNIT
12

Spelling-Meaning Strategy

Word Families

You know that words have families. Words in the same family are alike in spelling and meaning.

bake
baker
baked
baking

I like to **bake** cookies.
Dad says I am a good **baker**.
I **baked** a cake this morning.
Baking is fun on rainy days.

Think How are words in this family alike in meaning? How are they alike in spelling?

Apply and Extend

Write a word from the bake family in each sentence.

1. The _____ wears a white hat.
2. He _____ bread this morning.
3. We saw it _____ in the oven.
4. He can _____ good muffins too.

With a partner, think of words in these families. Make a list for each family. See TE margin.

use   dress   clear

Check the Word Families list that begins on page 272. Did you miss any words? Add them to your lists.

1. baker
2. baked
3. baking
4. bake

93

Objective *Children will*

■ analyze the spelling and meaning relationship of words in the *bake* family

Day **4**

Answers to *Think* Questions

- They all have some form of the meaning "to cook in an oven."
- They all have the *bake* spelling.

Day **5** **Posttest**

The Posttest tests twenty of the Basic Words reviewed in this unit. Sentences 1–10 test words selected from Basic Words 1–5 in Units 6–11. The Elephant Words sentences test all four words reviewed in this unit.

Basic Words
1. She <u>made</u> the kite.
2. Did Meg take a <u>trip</u>?
3. I will <u>ask</u> the man.
4. The men are in the <u>club</u>.
5. I had <u>five</u> frogs.
6. That is a big green <u>truck</u>.
7. The car is on the <u>hill</u>.
8. I will <u>add</u> the cups.
9. He had a cut on his <u>nose</u>.
10. The box had a <u>bone</u> in it.
11. I am <u>glad</u> you are at the game.
12. This is my <u>home</u>.
13. He <u>ate</u> the nut.
14. I cut the <u>egg</u>.
15. I <u>hope</u> you like this.
16. Did she see the <u>stone</u>?
17. She said to get in <u>line</u>.
18. He cut the <u>grass</u>.
19. She came <u>back</u>.
20. I will <u>kick</u> the box.

Elephant Words
21. Do you <u>have</u> a sled?
22. I will <u>give</u> him the hat.
23. The pig <u>goes</u> fast.
24. She had <u>one</u> kite.

Writing Model:
A Story About Yourself

Objectives *Children will*

- read a literature excerpt modeling a personal narrative

- analyze the model to identify a character's feelings and the main idea

Warm-Up

Qualities of a Good Story About Yourself

Discuss ideas children might include if they were writing a story about the good time they had at a picinic.

- Ask children if they would tell where the picnic was. (*Yes. The location might have contributed to making the picnic enjoyable.*)

- Ask if they would tell about a time they missed going to another picnic because they got lost. (*No. This information doesn't tell about the picnic they're writing about.*)

- Ask children if they would tell about the activities at the picnic that they enjoyed most. (*Yes. This would help readers know why they had a good time.*)

Answers to *Think and Discuss*

1. Marcia did not like school. No one noticed her new shirt, the children called her by the wrong name, she did not know where the lunchroom was, and she did not know how to do subtraction.

2. Marcia told about her first day at school.

UNIT
12

A Story
About
Yourself

Literature and Writing

from

The New Girl at School

by Judy Delton

Marcia told what happened on her first day at a new school. How does Marcia feel about her new school?

When I walked into school, everyone stared. Everyone was with a friend but me.

I had on my new shirt with the grasshopper on it. (No one even looked at the grasshopper.)

The children called me Martha. (My name is Marcia.)

Everyone knew where the lunchroom was. (I had to ask.)

Everyone could do subtraction. (I was the only one who couldn't.)

"I don't like this school," I said to my mother that night. "It will get better," she said.

Think and Discuss

See TE margin.

1. How did Marcia feel on her first day at school? What things happened to make her feel that way?

2. What **one idea** does Marcia tell about, her first day at school or her new clothes?

94

EXTENSION OPTIONS

Integrating Literature *A Story About Yourself*

Easy	Average	Challenging
I Know a Lady *by Charlotte Zolotow* A girl describes an elderly woman who befriends the neighborhood children.	**Owl Moon** *by Jane Yolen* A girl describes how she and her father go owling one wintry evening.	**Samuel Eaton's Day** *by Kate Waters* A day in the life of a Pilgrim boy.
My Hen Is Dancing *by Karen Wallace* A boy tells interesting facts about his pet hen.	**Anthony Reynoso** *by Ginger Gordon* A boy learns to rope and ride Mexican rodeo style from his father.	**My Two Worlds** *by Ginger Gordon* A girl tells why she considers New York City and the Domican Republic her home.

The Writing Process
A Story About Yourself

Write a story about something that happened to you. Follow the guidelines. Use the Writing Process.

1 Prewriting
- List special things you have done.
- Choose one idea that would make the best story.

2 Draft
- Draw the beginning of your story. Then write about it.

3 Revise
- Make sure all your sentences tell about one idea.
- Remember to use your Thesaurus to find exact words.
- Read your story to a friend. Make changes.

4 Proofread
- Did you spell each word correctly?
- Did you begin the names of people, pets, and places with capital letters?

5 Publish
- Copy your story neatly. Add a good title. Act out your story.

Guidelines for Writing a Story About Yourself

✓ The story should tell about one idea.
✓ Use enough details to make your story interesting.

Composition Words
made
home
those
glad
ask
tell

95

Objective *Children will*
- follow the Writing Process to write a personal narrative, using the criteria given in the guidelines

Additional Resource

To help children generate and explore topics for their personal narrative, have them use the Prewriting Ideas in the *Teacher's Resource Book,* page 59.

Scoring Rubric

Evaluating Writing

The scoring rubric is based on the guidelines on the student book page. Mechanics and usage errors are also considered in general. Explain to children that the guidelines will be used to evaluate their papers.

TRB Prewriting Ideas   59

Name _____ Level 2 / Unit 12

Prewriting Ideas: A Story About Yourself

Choosing a Topic Here is a list of ideas that one student thought of for writing a story. What special times of your own do these ideas make you think of?

On the lines below **My Three Ideas**, write three funny, scary, or happy things that have happened to you. Is each topic about only one idea? Which topic do you remember most about? Circle the topic that you would like to write about.

Ideas for Writing

My First Swimming Lesson	My Magic Trick That Failed
The Day I Got Lost	How I Helped a Friend

My Three Ideas

1. _____
2. _____
3. _____

Exploring Your Topic You can use a map like this one to help you plan your story. Copy the map onto another sheet of paper. Make it large enough to write on. Write your topic in the box at the top. In the circles, write **who** the story is about, **what** happens, and **where** the story takes place.

Topic

who   what   where

Use: For use with Step 1: Prewriting on page 95.

59

Scoring Rubric

Evaluating Writing

Score 4

The personal narrative meets all the evaluation criteria and reflects a meaningful experience for the child. It is also well ordered and keeps to the topic. The writer has effectively used details that make the story come alive for the reader.

Score 3

The personal narrative is coherent and keeps to a meaningful topic. Details help the reader understand the writer's experience.

Score 2

The personal narrative has an orderly progression but is still sketchy. There are not enough details to help the reader fully understand the story. Some parts do not keep to the topic.

Score 1

The work is not a personal narrative, or it meets the criteria only minimally. The telling of a personal experience is poorly developed. Few details are used. There is little order to the story, leaving the reader confused.

More Long *a* Spellings

WORD LISTS

Spelling

Basic

1. train
2. way
3. mail
4. play
5. trail
6. pay
7. sail
8. hay
9. nail
10. rain
11. they
12. great

Review

13. stay
14. day

Challenge

15. railroad
16. subway

Vocabulary

Social Studies: Trains

caboose
engine
crossing
coach

Introducing the Lesson

Read Aloud

Write the Basic Words on the board.

Freight Trains

Before railroads were built, farmers may have traveled over a rough **trail** on horses to sell their goods. Sea captains bringing **mail** had to **sail** over stormy water. Often, the crew had to **nail** crates to the deck to keep them on board. Today a freight **train** may carry everything from the food we eat to the games we **play**. There are different kinds of cars on a freight **train**. A flatcar has no top, but a boxcar is covered so **rain** along the **way** will not spoil the things inside. A stock car carries animals and the **hay** that **they** eat. A freight **train** can move a **great** amount at one time—as much as 1,800 tons! That's why people **pay** less to send things by **train**.

Responding Ask what kind of train has flatcars, boxcars, and stock cars. *(a freight train)* Have children listen for a spelling word that rhymes with *hay* in this sentence: "For this reason, people **pay** less to send things by **train**." Have a volunteer name the word, point to it on the board, and spell it.

 Day 1 *page 96*

Objectives *Children will*

- take the pretest
- pronounce the list words
- learn about the spelling principle
- sort words by their long vowel spelling patterns

Planning Checklist

- ☑ Pretest (TE)
- ☑ Spelling principle/word list
- ☐ Review/Challenge Words
- ☐ Teaching the Principle (TE)
- ☐ Enrichment (TE)
- ☐ Additional Spelling Words (TE)

Assessment

Pretest

1. He rode on the <u>train</u>.
2. We found our <u>way</u> home.
3. Can you <u>mail</u> the letter?
4. She can <u>play</u> with me.
5. They hiked the <u>trail</u>.
6. Let me <u>pay</u> for the toy.
7. I will <u>sail</u> on the lake.
8. Horses like to eat <u>hay</u>.
9. I need a longer <u>nail</u>.
10. Will it <u>rain</u> all day?
11. Did <u>they</u> buy a car?
12. The game was <u>great</u>!

Day 2 *page 97*

Objectives *Children will*

- practice spelling list words
- apply spelling strategies
- classify Basic Words into groups
- identify Elephant Words from given sounds and spelling patterns

Planning Checklist

- ☑ Spelling Strategy
- ☑ Independent Practice
- ☐ Daily Proofreading Practice (TE)
- ☐ Informal Assessment (TE)
- ☐ Extra Support (TE)
- ☐ Applying Spelling Strategies (TE)

Research Notes With very few exceptions, the words children most frequently misspell have remained constant over the years. Many of these are high-utility words and eventually need to be learned to the point where they are automatic. *See the Bibliography on page xv.*

 Day 3 *page 98* **Day 4** *page 99* **Day 5** *page 99*

Objective *Children will*

• review Basic and Review Words

Planning Checklist

☐ Review: Spelling Spree
☐ How Are You Doing?
☐ Daily Proofreading Practice (TE)
☐ Ongoing Assessment (TE)

Objectives *Children will*

• proofread for spelling and usage of *I*
• write and proofread an original composition

Planning Checklist

☐ Proofread: Spelling and Using I
☐ Write a Story
☐ Daily Proofreading Practice (TE)
☐ Challenge Words Practice (TE)
☐ Another Writing Idea (TE)

Objective *Children will*

• take the posttest

Assessment
☐ **Posttest** (TE) *See Day 5*
☐ Unit 13 Test

● Additional Resources

Teacher's Resource Book
Practice Masters, pages 61–63
Unit Test, page 64
Bulletin Board, page 81

Practice Plus
Take-Home Word List 13
Games

Spelling Transparencies
Spelling Word List 13
Daily Proofreading Practice, Unit 13
Graphic Organizers

Teacher's Resource Disk
Macintosh® or Windows® software. Houghton Mifflin

Spelling CD-ROM
Macintosh® or Windows® software. Houghton Mifflin

Internet
http://www.eduplace.com

Phonics Practice
Houghton Mifflin Phonics
The Listening Corner
Phonics Home Connection

 Meeting Individual Needs
Students Acquiring English

Spanish In Spanish, the vowel pairs ay and ai spell the |ī| sound, and the |ā| sound is spelled with the letter e.
Activity Write ay and ai on the chalkboard. Point to them and explain that these letters spell the vowel sound in way and train. Next, write Basic Words 1–10 on the chalkboard. Say each word and have children repeat it. Then erase the letters ay or ai in each word. As you say each word, have a volunteer go to the chalkboard and write the vowel pair that completes the word. You may want to practice the unit principle with chil-
Asian You may want to practice the unit principle with children by using the activity for Spanish-speaking children.

Other Activities for Any Day

• Bonus activities from pages 100–101
• Practice Masters (easy, average, challenging)
  Teacher's Resource Book, pages 61–63
• Take-Home Word List 13
  Practice Plus

Objectives *Children will*
- take the pretest
- pronounce the list words
- learn about the spelling principle
- sort words by their long vowel spelling patterns

Teaching the Principle

This lesson teaches the *ai* and *ay* spelling patterns for the |ā| sound. Children learn the strategy of thinking of the *ay* pattern when they hear the long *a* sound at the end of a word and the *ai* pattern when the long *a* sound is followed by a consonant.

To sum up the lesson, ask:

- How is the long *a* sound spelled at the end of a word? *(ay)*
- How is the long *a* sound spelled in the middle of a word? *(ai)*

Enrichment

Vocabulary: Multiple Meanings
Have children use a dictionary to look up *way*, *play*, *nail*, and *great*. Discuss the different meanings.

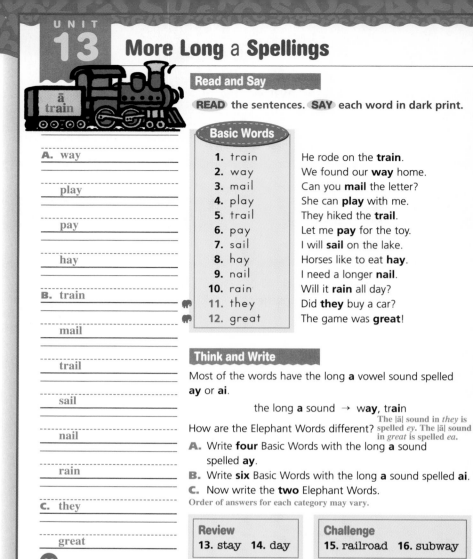

UNIT
13 More Long a Spellings

Read and Say

READ the sentences. **SAY** each word in dark print.

ā
train

Basic Words

1.	train	He rode on the **train**.
2.	way	We found our **way** home.
3.	mail	Can you **mail** the letter?
4.	play	She can **play** with me.
5.	trail	They hiked the **trail**.
6.	pay	Let me **pay** for the toy.
7.	sail	I will **sail** on the lake.
8.	hay	Horses like to eat **hay**.
9.	nail	I need a longer **nail**.
10.	rain	Will it **rain** all day?
11.	they	Did **they** buy a car?
12.	great	The game was **great**!

A. way
___ play
___ pay
___ hay
B. train
___ mail
___ trail
___ sail
___ nail
___ rain
C. they
___ great

96

Think and Write

Most of the words have the long **a** vowel sound spelled **ay** or **ai**.

the long **a** sound → **way**, tr**ai**n

The |ā| sound in *they* is spelled *ey*. The |ā| sound in *great* is spelled *ea*.

How are the Elephant Words different?

A. Write **four** Basic Words with the long **a** sound spelled **ay**.

B. Write **six** Basic Words with the long **a** sound spelled **ai**.

C. Now write the **two** Elephant Words.

Order of answers for each category may vary.

Review	Challenge
13. stay 14. day	15. railroad 16. subway

TEACHING OPTIONS

Meeting Individual Needs
Word Lists

You may want to assign Basic Words 1–5, the Elephant Words, and the Review Words to children who misspelled more than five words on the pretest. Assign the Challenge Words as appropriate. (You may want to have children write sentences, using the Challenge Words.)

Additional Spelling Words

Basic	Challenge	Words Often Misspelled
aim	playpen	right
braid	raisin	write
tray	afraid	
paid	straight	
bay	highway	
	daisy	

Home/School Involvement
Take-Home Word List • Goal-Setting

Have children set goals for the week on Take-Home Word List 13.

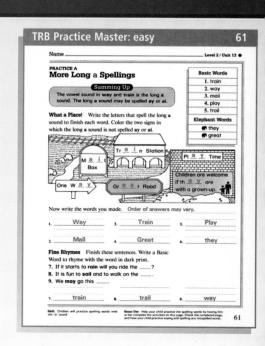

TRB Practice Master: easy   61

Name _____ Level 2 / Unit 13

PRACTICE A
More Long a Spellings

Basic Words
1. train
2. way
3. mail
4. play
5. trail

Elephant Words
- they
- great

Summing Up
The vowel sound in way and train is the long a sound. The long a sound may be spelled ay or ai.

What a Place! Write the letters that spell the long a sound to finish each word. Color the two signs in which the long a sound is not spelled ay or ai.

Tr **a i** n Station
M **a i l** Box
One W **a y**
Pl **a y** Time
Children are welcome if the **a y** sign is with a grown-up.
Gr **e a t** Road

Now write the words you made. Order of answers may vary.

1. Way   3. Train   5. Play
2. Mail   4. Great   6. they

Fine Rhymes Finish these sentences. Write a Basic Word to rhyme with the word in dark print.
7. If it starts to **rain** will you ride the _____?
8. It is fun to **sail** and to walk on the _____.
9. We **may** go this _____.

7. train   8. trail   9. way

61

Independent Practice

Spelling Strategy The vowel sound in **way** and **train** is the long **a** sound. The long **a** sound may be spelled **ay** or **ai**.

Order of answers for question 2–5 may vary.
Phonics Write Basic Words to answer the questions.
1. Which word begins and ends like **meal**?
2–5. Which four words rhyme with **stay** and end in **ay**?

Word Groups Think how the words in each group are alike. Write the missing Basic Words.
6. sidewalk, path, _____
7. hammer, saw, _____
8. drive, fly, _____
9. snow, sleet, _____
10. plane, boat, _____

Elephant Words Write an Elephant Word to answer each question.
11. Which word has the long **a** sound spelled **ey**?
12. Which word has the long **a** sound spelled **ea**?

Phonics
1. mail
2. way
3. play
4. pay
5. hay

Word Groups
6. trail
7. nail
8. sail
9. rain
10. train

Elephant Words
11. they
12. great

(97)

UNIT
13

Objectives *Children will*
- practice spelling list words
- apply spelling strategies
- classify Basic Words into groups
- identify Elephant Words from given sounds and spelling patterns

Day 2

Daily Proofreading Practice
Dan got a present in the **mayl**. (*mail*)
The farmers cut and tied the **hai**. (*hay*)

Meeting Individual Needs
visual/auditory/kinesthetic

Extra Support Check Independent Practice to determine who needs extra support. Give children two index cards. Have them write *ai* on one and *ay* on the other. Remind children that the *ay* spelling for long *a* usually comes at the end of a word and the *ai* spelling in the middle. Then say Basic Words 1–10 one at a time, asking children to hold up the card with the correct spelling of the |ā| sound.

Name _____   Level 2 / Unit 13 ▲

Basic Words
1. train
2. way
3. mail
4. play
5. trail
6. pay
7. sail
8. hay
9. nail
10. rain
Elephant Words
they
great

PRACTICE B
More Long a Spellings

Puzzle Play Write the Basic or Elephant Word for each clue. Use the letters in the boxes to spell a nice word to say.

1. give money   p a y
2. have fun   p l a y
3. very large   g r e a t
4. how to do something   w a y
5. travel across water   s a i l
6. he and she   t h e y

Secret Word: p l e a s e

Subtraction Facts Take away one word from the letters in each box. Write the Basic Word that is left.

Example: Take away **toys**. Find fun. | toplayys
7. Take away **stamp**. Find letters. | stamailmp
8. Take away **woods**. Find a path. | wotrailods
9. Take away **rose**. Find dried grass. | rohayse
10. Take away **track**. Find a railroad. | tratrainrck
11. Take away **tool**. Find sharp metal. | tonailol
12. Take away **cloud**. Find water. | clorainud

7. mail
8. trail
9. hay
10. train
11. nail
12. rain

EXTRA! Make **Subtraction Facts** of your own, and have a classmate find the Basic Words that are left.

62

Applying Spelling Strategies
To Spell New Words

- Read aloud: **Our class will paint a mural on the bank downtown.**
- Have children attempt to spell *paint* on their Have-a-Go charts.

- Elicit the following strategies as children try to spell *paint*.

First, I hear the sound for *p* that I hear at the beginning of *pig*.

paint

I hear the sounds for *n* and *t* blended together at the end of the word.

This word has the long *a* sound. The long *a* sound is probably spelled *ai* since it is in the middle of the word.

Objective *Children will*
■ review Basic and Review Words

Daily Proofreading Practice

We saw flowers along the **trale**.
(*trail*)

Alex knows a quick **wey** home! (*way*)

Review: Spelling Spree

Code Breaker

1. way

2. they

3. day

4. stay

5. great

6. pay

Word Match

7. mail

8. hay

9. nail

10. sail

11. rain

12. trail

98

Code Breaker Use the code to write Basic or Review Words.

▲ = a	∩ = g	+ = r	↑ = w
☆ = d	∞ = h	● = s	□ = y
) = e	⊥ = p	⊝ = t	

Example: ∞ ▲ □ = **hay**

1. ↑▲□   4. ● ⊝ ▲ □
2. ⊝ ∞) □   5. ∩ +) ▲ ⊝
3. ☆ ▲ □   6. ⊥ ▲ □

Word Match Write the Basic Word that goes with each place or thing.

7. post office   9. toolbox   11. cloud
8. barn   10. boat   12. mountain

How Are You Doing?
Write each word in a sentence. Practice with a partner any words you spelled wrong.

TEACHING OPTIONS

Ongoing Assessment

Misspellings for Long a

The vowel-consonant-e pattern is the basic long vowel pattern in English. The next most frequent pattern is the vowel/vowel pattern; for long a these spellings are *ai* and *ay*.

Children learn that *ai* almost always occurs in the middle of a word and *ay* at the end. Common invented spellings include RAIK and RAYK for *rake*.

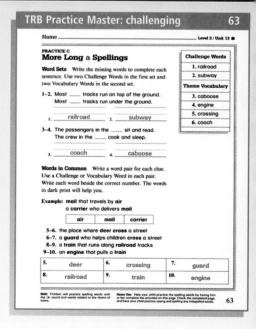

TRB Practice Master: challenging   63

Name _____ Level 2 / Unit 13 ■

PRACTICE C
More Long a Spellings

Challenge Words
1. railroad
2. subway
Theme Vocabulary
3. caboose
4. engine
5. crossing
6. coach

Word Sets Write the missing words to complete each sentence. Use two Challenge Words in the first set and two Vocabulary Words in the second set.

1–2. Most _____ tracks run on top of the ground.
Most _____ tracks run under the ground.

1. railroad   2. subway

3–4. The passengers in the _____ sit and read.
The crew in the _____ cook and sleep.

3. coach   4. caboose

Words in Common Write a word pair for each clue. Use a Challenge or Vocabulary Word in each pair. Write each word beside the correct number. The words in dark print will help you.

Example: **mail** that travels by **air**
a **carrier** who delivers **mail**

| air | mail | carrier |

5–6. the place where **deer cross** a street
6–7. a **guard** who helps children **cross** a street
8–9. a train that runs along **railroad** tracks
9–10. an **engine** that pulls a **train**

| 5. deer | 6. crossing | 7. guard |
| 8. railroad | 9. train | 10. engine |

Skill: Children will practice spelling words with the /ā/ sound and words related to the theme of trains.   Home Use: Help your child practice the spelling words by having him or her complete the activities on the page. Check the completed page, and have your child practice saying and spelling any misspelled words.   63

Proofreading and Writing

Proofread: Spelling and Using I When you talk about another person and yourself, always name yourself last.

Ben and I will buy the tickets.

Proofread these sentences from a diary. Use proofreading marks to fix four spelling mistakes and two mistakes using **I**.

Example:

I and Ana will pay for the trip.

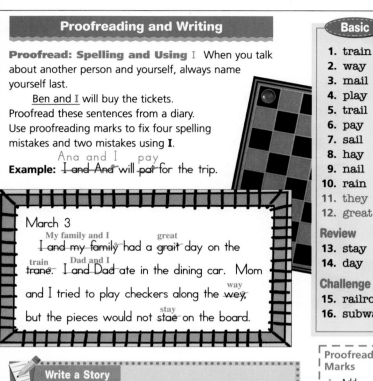

March 3

My family and I   great
I and my family had a grait day on the

train   Dad and I
trane. I and Dad ate in the dining car. Mom

and I tried to play checkers along the wey,
way

stay
but the pieces would not stae on the board.

Basic
1. train
2. way
3. mail
4. play
5. trail
6. pay
7. sail
8. hay
9. nail
10. rain
11. they
12. great

Review
13. stay
14. day

Challenge
15. railroad
16. subway

Proofreading Marks
∧ Add
⌐ Delete
≡ Make a capital letter
/ Make a small letter

Write a Story

Write a story about something special you and a friend did together. What made it fun? Try to use spelling words. Have your friend draw pictures to go with the story.

Proofreading Tip Check your writing. Make sure that you named yourself last.

99

Day 4

Objectives *Children will*
- proofread for spelling and usage of *I*
- write and proofread an original composition

Daily Proofreading Practice
Will **thay** come to the parade? (*they*)
I like to walk in the **rane**. (*rain*)

Day 5

Posttest

Sentences 1–5 test the first five Basic Words. Sentences 6–10 test the next five Basic Words. Sentences 11–12 test the Elephant Words.

Basic Words
1. The mail came late.
2. Did he ride on the train?
3. We did play with the kite.
4. Was the frog on the trail?
5. He went that way.
6. Did she pay for the cup?
7. The hay is wet.
8. When will it rain?
9. Did he fix the sail?
10. I see a big nail.
11. That is a great kite!
12. Did they go to the game?

Review Words
13. This is the best day.
14. Did she stay?

Challenge Words
15. Many people take a subway to work.
16. We always cross railroad tracks carefully.

TRB Unit 13 Test   **64**

Name _____   Level 2 / Unit 13 ●▲

Unit 13 Test: More Long a Spellings

Read each sentence. Find the correctly spelled word to complete each sentence. Mark the letter next to that word.

Sample: ANSWERS
We spent the ____ at home.   ⓐ dai ⓑ doe ● day

Items 1–7 test Basic Words 1–5 and the Elephant Words.
Items 8–12 test Basic Words 6–10.
1. We ____ on the swings.   ⓐ plae ⓑ play ⓒ plai
2. Henry song on his ____ home. ● way ⓑ wai ⓒ wey
3. My aunts said ____ like her. ⓐ thay ⓑ thaye ● they
4. Jon will follow the ____.   ⓐ tral ⓑ trail ⓒ trayl
5. Do you ride on the ____?   ⓐ tran ⓑ trayn ● train
6. Mr. Davis is a ____ teacher. ⓐ gret ⓑ great ⓒ grayt
7. I got a card in the ____.   ● mail ⓑ mal ⓒ mael
8. He ran quickly in the ____.   ⓐ raen ⓑ rone ● rain
9. Leon will ____ on the lake.   ● sail ⓑ sayl ⓒ sael
10. Do horses eat ____?   ⓐ hae ⓑ hay ⓒ hai
11. I will ____ for your ticket. ⓐ pai ⓑ paiy ● pay
12. Don't step on that ____!   ● nail ⓑ nayl ⓒ nale

64

Meeting Individual Needs

Challenge Words Practice
Suggest children make a map of a real or fictitious city, labeling locations on the map with the Challenge Words, other long *a* words, and additional words they choose.

Another Writing Idea Ask children to write rhyming couplets or a poem about a train trip or other type of journey. Encourage them to use spelling words.

These pages can be used at any time during the study of this unit.

Objectives *Children will*

- use context to help them choose appropriate synonyms from a thesaurus
- use words found in a thesaurus in their writing

Word Builder

Spelling Word Link
great

Using a Thesaurus Write a word you could use in place of the word in dark print. Use your Thesaurus.

1. The children **look** out the window.
2. The white stars are **bright**.
3. The night sky is **pretty**.
4. They are having a **great** ride!

1. stare *or* gaze	**3.** beautiful *or* lovely
2. sparkling *or* gleaming	**4.** wonderful *or* terrific

Show What You Know! On another sheet of paper, write a sentence about this picture. Use another word for **fast** found in your Thesaurus.
Sentences will vary, but should include the word swiftly or quickly.

100

EXTENSION OPTIONS

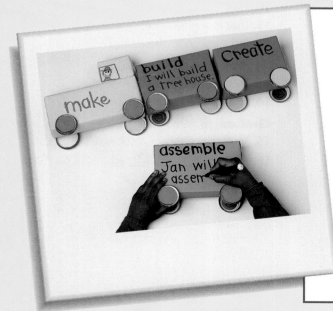

Learning Center Activity

visual/kinesthetic

Take the "A" Train Have children draw a train that has an engine and several cars, or have them construct one using materials such as empty milk cartons, small boxes, and small bottle lids.

Ask children to look up a long *a* word, such as *afraid*, *brave*, *make*, or *say*, in their Thesaurus. Have them write the entry word on the train engine. On each car, have them write one synonym and a sentence that uses the synonym.

Vocabulary Enrichment

Social Studies

Trains All of the words in the box have something to do with trains. Write those words to finish this ad. Use your Spelling Dictionary.

Spelling Word Link

train

caboose
engine
crossing
coach

Come for a Ride on Tobo Train!

A steam __(1)__ pulls Tobo Train into the station every day. Sit in the __(2)__ and read. Watch the red lights flash when the train comes to a __(3)__ . Visit the workers in the __(4)__ at the end of the train.

1. engine

2. coach

3. crossing

4. caboose

Try This CHALLENGE

Write an Ad How is a train trip better than a trip by bus, car, or plane? Write an ad for a railroad company. Tell why traveling by train is fun. Use words from the box on this page.

★ ★ Fact File

Trains have changed over the years. One of the first trains used a horse as an engine! The horse ran on a belt and that made the wheels of the train turn.

101

Day by Day Planner

Objectives *Children will*

- expand their vocabulary by using words related to trains
- show their understanding of the vocabulary words by completing context and writing activities

Vocabulary Checkup

Have children use the vocabulary words in sentences or match the words to the definitions below.

1. the railroad car that pulls the rest of the train *engine*
2. a railroad car for people *coach*
3. a place with flashing lights where people or cars can pass over railroad tracks *crossing*
4. a car at the end of a train, where the crew can cook and sleep *caboose*

Fact File

The Cyclopede

The horse-run train, or cyclopede, was used briefly in the 1820s. The vehicle ran on train rails and was powered by a circular belt. Steam-powered engines, introduced at about the same time, soon made the cyclopede obsolete.

Integrating Literature

Easy	Average	Challenging
The Train to Lulu's *by Elizabeth Fitzgerald Howard* Two sisters travel by train to visit their aunt.	**Shortcut** *by Donald Crews* A group of children take the railroad tracks as a shortcut home.	**The Polar Express** *by Chris Van Allsburg* A boy takes a magical train ride to the North Pole.
I've Been Working on the Railroad *by Nadine B. Westcott* A picture book version of the beloved folk song.	**Train** *by Charles Temple* Passengers enjoy the ride as a train chuffs and clacks down the tracks.	**Tracks** *by David Galef* Passengers on a new railroad line have a wildly exciting trip.

More Long *e* Spellings

WORD LISTS

Spelling

Basic

1. clean
2. keep
3. please
4. green
5. we
6. be
7. eat
8. tree
9. mean
10. read
11. the
12. people

Review

13. he
14. feet

Challenge

15. stream
16. street

Vocabulary

Science: Protecting Our Earth

trash
dump
collect
sewer

Introducing the Lesson

Read Aloud

Write the Basic Words on the board.

Saving Our Forests

Long ago, **green** forests covered much of North America. Gradually, **people** needed more space to build farms and cities, so they cut down trees. They used **the** wood to build houses and furniture and as fuel for heating and cooking. They also used wood to make paper for **the** books **we read**. Over **the** years, **the** forests began to diminish.

Today **we** realize that because forests **mean** so much to us, we must learn to protect them. Forests produce oxygen in **the** air that **we** breathe. They **keep** soil from washing away. Farmers need good soil to grow **the** food that **we eat**.

You can protect our forests when you go camping. **Please** be careful to **clean** up after yourself, and never build a fire next to a **tree**.

Responding Ask children what things are made from trees. *(houses, furniture, fuel, paper)* Then ask which spelling word names something that grows in a forest. *(tree)*

Day 1 *page 102* **Day 2** *page 103*

Objectives *Children will*

- take the pretest
- pronounce the list words
- learn about the spelling principle
- sort words by their long vowel spelling patterns

Planning Checklist

- ☑ Pretest (TE)
- ☑ Spelling principle/word list
- ☐ Review/Challenge Words
- ☐ Teaching the Principle (TE)
- ☐ Enrichment (TE)
- ☐ Additional Spelling Words (TE)

Assessment

Pretest

1. His shop is <u>clean</u>.
2. You can <u>keep</u> playing.
3. Will you <u>please</u> stay?
4. My truck is <u>green</u>.
5. Did <u>we</u> win?
6. Amanda will <u>be</u> late.
7. I want to <u>eat</u> now.
8. A nest is in that <u>tree</u>.
9. She did not <u>mean</u> it.
10. I love to <u>read</u>!
11. Can Emil fix <u>the</u> sail?
12. Many <u>people</u> have pets.

Objectives *Children will*

- practice spelling list words
- apply spelling strategies
- identify Basic Words by using meaning clues
- identify Elephant Words by using context clues

Planning Checklist

- ☑ Spelling Strategy
- ☑ Independent Practice
- ☐ Daily Proofreading Practice (TE)
- ☐ Informal Assessment (TE)
- ☐ Extra Support (TE)
- ☐ Applying Spelling Strategies (TE)

Day 3 *page 104*   **Day 4** *page 105*   **Day 5** *page 105*

Objectives *Children will*

- identify entry words found on the same dictionary page as given guide words
- review Basic and Review Words

Planning Checklist

- ☐ Dictionary
- ☐ Review: Spelling Spree
- ☐ How Are You Doing?
- ☐ Daily Proofreading Practice (TE)
- ☐ Cooperative Learning Activity (TE)

Objectives *Children will*

- proofread for spelling
- write and proofread an original composition

Planning Checklist

- ☐ Proofread for Spelling
- ☐ Write a Speech
- ☐ Daily Proofreading Practice (TE)
- ☐ Challenge Words Practice (TE)
- ☐ Another Writing Idea (TE)

Objective *Children will*

- take the posttest

| Assessment |

- ☐ **Posttest** (TE) *See Day 5*
- ☐ Unit 14 Test

 Additional Resources

Teacher's Resource Book
Practice Masters, pages 65–67
Unit Test, page 68
Bulletin Board, page 81

Practice Plus
Take-Home Word List 14
Games

Spelling Transparencies
Spelling Word List 14
Daily Proofreading Practice, Unit 14
Graphic Organizers

Teacher's Resource Disk
Macintosh® or Windows® software. Houghton Mifflin

Spelling CD-ROM
Macintosh® or Windows® software. Houghton Mifflin

Internet
http://www.eduplace.com

Phonics Practice
Houghton Mifflin Phonics
The Listening Corner
Phonics Home Connection

 Meeting Individual Needs
Students Acquiring English

Spanish In Spanish, the letter *i* spells the |ē| sound. Children may have difficulty with the e, ee, and ea spellings of the |ē| sound.

Activity Write e, ee, and ea as column headings on the chalkboard. Under the headings, write Basic Words 1–10. Say the words and have children repeat them. Then erase the vowel letter or letters in each word. Have volunteers write missing vowels and spell the words aloud.

Other Activities for Any Day

- Bonus activities from pages 106–107
- Practice Masters (easy, average, challenging)
  Teacher's Resource Book, pages 65–67
- Take-Home Word List 14
  Practice Plus

Objectives *Children will*

- take the pretest
- pronounce the list words
- learn about the spelling principle
- sort words by their long vowel spelling patterns

Teaching the Principle

This lesson teaches the *e, ee,* and *ea* spelling patterns for the |ē| sound. Children learn the strategy of thinking of these patterns when they hear the long *e* sound.

To sum up the lesson, have children tell how the long *e* sound is spelled in each word.

Note: The word *read* may be pronounced |rēd| or |rĕd|. The Elephant Word *the* is pronounced |thē| or |thə|.

Enrichment

Vocabulary: Multiple Meanings

Have children use a dictionary to look up *please, mean,* and *green.* Discuss the different meanings.

More Long e Spellings

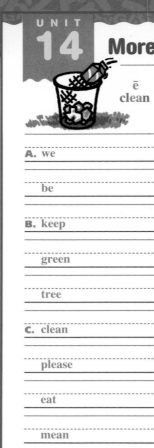

ē
clean

Read and Say

READ the sentences. **SAY** each word in dark print.

Basic Words

1.	clean	His shop is **clean**.
2.	keep	You can **keep** playing.
3.	please	Will you **please** stay?
4.	green	My truck is **green**.
5.	we	Did **we** win?
6.	be	Amanda will **be** late.
7.	eat	I want to **eat** now.
8.	tree	A nest is in that **tree**.
9.	mean	She did not **mean** it.
10.	read	I love to **read**!
11.	the	Can Emil fix **the** sail?
12.	people	Many **people** have pets.

Think and Write

Most of the words have the long **e** vowel sound spelled **e**, **ee**, or **ea**.

the long **e** sound → w**e**, k**ee**p, cl**ea**n

Which Elephant Word can you say two ways?
How is the other Elephant Word different?
The can be said two ways, |thē| or |thə|. The |ē| sound in *people* is spelled *eo*.

A. Write **two** Basic Words with the long **e** sound spelled **e**.

B. Write **three** Basic Words with the long **e** sound spelled **ee**.

C. Write **five** Basic Words with the long **e** sound spelled **ea**.

D. Now write the **two** Elephant Words. Order of answers may vary.

Review	Challenge
13. he 14. feet	15. stream 16. street

A. we

be

B. keep

green

tree

C. clean

please

eat

mean

read

D. the

people

102

Meeting Individual Needs
Word Lists

You may want to assign Basic Words 1–5, the Elephant Words, and the Review Words to children who misspelled more than five words on the pretest. Assign the Challenge Words as appropriate. (You may want to have children write sentences, using the Challenge Words.)

Additional Spelling Words

Basic	Challenge	Words Often Misspelled
three	beehive	coming
beach	beaver	getting
team	between	
need	sneeze	
feel	reason	
	least	

Home/School Involvement
Take-Home Word List • Goal-Setting

Have children set goals for the week on Take-Home Word List 14.

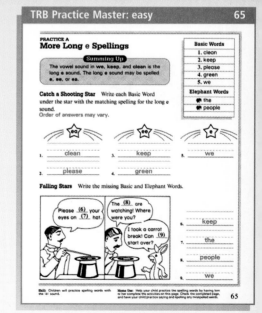

PRACTICE A
More Long e Spellings

Basic Words
1. clean
2. keep
3. please
4. green
5. we

Elephant Words
- the
- people

Summing Up
The vowel sound in we, keep, and clean is the long e sound. The long e sound may be spelled e, ee, or ea.

Catch a Shooting Star Write each Basic Word under the star with the matching spelling for the long e sound.
Order of answers may vary.

1. clean   3. keep   5. we
2. please   4. green

Falling Stars Write the missing Basic and Elephant Words.

Please (6) your eyes on (7) hat.

The (8) are watching! Where were you?

I took a carrot break! Can (9) start over?

6. keep
7. the
8. people
9. we

Skill: Children will practice spelling words with the |ē| sound.
Home Use: Help your child practice the spelling words by having him or her complete the activities on this page. Check the completed page, and have your child practice saying and spelling any misspelled words.

65

Independent Practice

Spelling Strategy The vowel sound in **we**, **keep**, and **clean** is the long **e** sound. The long **e** sound may be spelled **e**, **ee**, or **ea**.

Order of answers for question 4–6 may vary.

Phonics Write Basic Words to answer the questions.

1. Which word rhymes with **sleep**?
2. Which word begins and ends like **moon**?
3. Which word begins with the same consonant cluster as **play**?
4–6. Which three words end with the long **e** sound?

Word Clues Write a Basic Word for each clue.

7. what you do when you are hungry
8. what you might do with a good book
9. how you feel after a bath
10. how a frog or leaf looks

Elephant Words Write the missing Elephant Words.

11. Many _____ helped clean up that dirty lake.
12. Now _____ fish have a clean home!

Phonics

1. keep
2. mean
3. please
4. we
5. be
6. tree

Word Clues

7. eat
8. read
9. clean
10. green

Elephant Words

11. people
12. the

(103)

Objectives *Children will*

- ■ practice spelling list words
- ■ apply spelling strategies
- ■ identify Basic Words by using meaning clues
- ■ identify Elephant Words by using context clues

Day 2

Daily Proofreading Practice

I put a **grean** bug in the jar. (*green*)
Ben helps me **cleen** my room. (*clean*)

Meeting Individual Needs
visual/auditory/kinesthetic

Extra Support Check Independent Practice to determine who needs extra support. Give children three cards. Have them write *e* on one, *ee* on another, and *ea* on the third. Then say Basic Words 1–10 one at a time, asking children to hold up the card with the correct vowel pattern. Say the words again and have volunteers write them on the board.

Basic Words	**PRACTICE B**
1. clean	**More Long e Spellings**
2. keep	**Crossword Clues** Write a Basic or Elephant Word for
3. please	each clue.
4. green	
5. we	
6. be	
7. eat	
8. tree	
9. mean	
10. read	
Elephant Words	
● the	
● people	

Across
2. _____ and write
4. opposite of **dirty**
6. _____ and thank you

Down
1. a color
3. men and women
5. a tall plant

Letter Math Add and take away letters to make Basic or Elephant Words. Write each word.

7. win − in + e = ?
8. b + he − h = ?
9. e + bat − b = ?
10. this − is + e = ?
11. k + sheep − sh = ?
12. m + clean − cl = ?

7. we
8. be
9. eat
10. the
11. keep
12. mean

66

Applying Spelling Strategies
To Read New Words

- ■ Write this sentence on the chalkboard:
  Ana fed the elephant a peanut.
- ■ Have children read the sentence silently.

- ■ Elicit the following strategies as children try to decode *peanut*.

> I know that the letter *p* makes the |p| sound I hear at the beginning of *pig*.

> P-ea-nut. Pea-nut. Peanut. The word *peanut* makes sense in the sentence.

peanut

> The letters *ea* spell one vowel pattern for the long *e* sound.

> I see the short *u* vowel pattern and recognize the short word *nut* at the end of this longer word.

Objectives *Children will*

■ identify entry words found on the same dictionary page as given guide words

■ review Basic and Review Words

Daily Proofreading Practice

Luis planted a **tre** by the river. (*tree*)

When can **wea** visit Grandfather? (*we*)

Guide Words

1. yes

2. no

3. no

4. yes

Hidden Words

5. the

6. be

7. he

8. read

9. feet

10. mean

11. eat

12. tree

104

Dictionary

Guide Words Use guide words and ABC order to help you find words in a dictionary. If the guide words begin with the same letter as the word you are looking for, look at the second letter of each word.

guide words	**lake**	**man**	**mean**	**my**
entry words	lake	lock	mean	mud
	leaf	lunch	milk	my
	lid	man	moon	

Practice Write **yes** or **no** to tell if each entry word below would be on the same page as the guide words **feet** and **fry**.

1. flag   2. funny   3. green   4. fox

Review: Spelling Spree

Hidden Words 5–12. Find the Basic and Review Words hidden in each row. Write the words.

m t h e x b e l n h e c
r e a d o f e e t b k s
m e a n n e a t t r e e

How Are You Doing?
Write each word as a family member reads it aloud. Did you spell any words wrong?

TEACHING OPTIONS

Cooperative Learning Activity
Our Long *e* Tree
visual/kinesthetic

Ask partners or small groups to work together to make a long e tree. Have children draw or paste a tree trunk with branches on large paper. Then have them cut out yellow, orange, and red leaves.

On the yellow leaves, children print words that have the e spelling for long e. On the orange leaves, they print words with the ea spelling, and on the red leaves, words with the ee spelling. Have children paste the leaves on the branches of their tree and write "Our Long e Tree" on the trunk.

TRB Practice Master: challenging 67

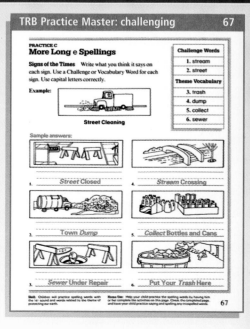

PRACTICE C
More Long e Spellings

Signs of the Times Write what you think it says on each sign. Use a Challenge or Vocabulary Word for each sign. Use capital letters correctly.

Challenge Words
1. stream
2. street

Theme Vocabulary
3. trash
4. dump
5. collect
6. sewer

Example: Street Cleaning

Sample answers:
1. Street Closed
2. Town Dump
3. Sewer Under Repair
4. Stream Crossing
5. Collect Bottles and Cans
6. Put Your Trash Here

67

Proofreading and Writing

Proofread for Spelling Proofread this sign. Use proofreading marks to fix six spelling mistakes.

tree
Example: Who put a sign on this tre?

Campers, Please Read!

green   we
This grene forest is where wea animals live.

people   please
All popul are welcome to visit, but pleaz be

keep   clean
careful! Help keap our home kleen!

Write a Speech

Write a speech. Tell why children should throw their trash away when they are on the playground. Try to use spelling words. Have some friends listen to your speech.

Proofreading Tip

Proofread your paper. Circle any words you are not sure of.

Proofreading Marks
∧ Add
⌐ Delete
≡ Make a capital letter
/ Make a small letter

105

Basic
1. clean
2. keep
3. please
4. green
5. we
6. be
7. eat
8. tree
9. mean
10. read
11. the
12. people

Review
13. he
14. feet

Challenge
15. stream
16. street

Day 4

Objectives *Children will*
■ proofread for spelling
■ write and proofread an original composition

Daily Proofreading Practice
Will you **pleeze** set the table? (*please*)
May I **keap** the mice as pets? (*keep*)

Day 5 **Posttest**

Sentences 1–5 test the first five Basic Words. Sentences 6–10 test the next five Basic Words. Sentences 11–12 test the Elephant Words.

Basic Words
1. May I <u>please</u> have a pet?
2. Did <u>we</u> win that game?
3. His grass is <u>green</u>.
4. I will <u>clean</u> a pot.
5. They will <u>keep</u> the bat.
6. The nest is in a <u>tree</u>.
7. It is time to <u>read</u>.
8. I am not <u>mean</u> to frogs.
9. She will <u>eat</u> a nut.
10. I will <u>be</u> late.
11. Some <u>people</u> use this trail.
12. I see a kite in <u>the</u> sky.

Review Words
13. A bug has six <u>feet</u>.
14. Why is <u>he</u> sad?

Challenge Words
15. There are lots of stores on our <u>street</u>.
16. We waded in the <u>stream</u>.

TRB Unit 14 Test   **68**

Unit 14 Test: More Long e Spellings

Read each sentence. Is the underlined word spelled right or wrong? Mark your answer.

Sample:	Right	Wrong
We put our <u>feet</u> in the water.	●	○

Items 1–7 test Basic Words 1–5 and the Elephant Words.
Items 8–12 test Basic Words 6–10.

		Right	Wrong
1. Tyler will try to <u>keap</u> quiet.	1.	○	●
2. Is your house white or <u>grene</u>?	2.	○	●
3. Rex asked for <u>the</u> answer.	3.	●	○
4. Will you <u>please</u> do this?	4.	●	○
5. Chris has to <u>cleen</u> his room.	5.	○	●
6. Can <u>we</u> join you on the trip?	6.	●	○
7. Some <u>peeple</u> work in the city.	7.	○	●
8. Lou has a fruit <u>trea</u> in his yard.	8.	○	●
9. What book did you <u>read</u> this week?	9.	●	○
10. Kara will <u>be</u> home soon.	10.	●	○
11. Ethan loves to <u>eet</u> corn.	11.	○	●
12. That was a <u>mean</u> thing to do.	12.	●	○

Meeting Individual Needs

Challenge Words Practice
Have children create two lists—one that includes *street* and synonyms for it (e.g., *road, lane, avenue*) and another that includes *stream* and other words for bodies of water (e.g., *ocean, lake*).

Another Writing Idea Ask children to make a poster to remind people of something they can do to help protect the earth. Encourage them to use spelling words.

These pages can be used at any time during the study of this unit.

Day by Day Planner

Objectives *Children will*

■ build words with the phonograms *-eat, -een,* and *-eam*

■ write an original composition

Rhyming Words

Long e Words Make rhyming words that have the long **e** vowel sound. Use the letters in the picture. Write each word under the correct bin.
Order of answers for each phonogram may vary.

1. neat	4. seen	7. dream
2. seat	5. teen	8. steam
3. treat	6. queen	9. scream

Show What You Know! On another sheet of paper, write a sign for the picture above. Use words that you wrote on this page.

106

EXTENSION OPTIONS

Learning Center Activity
visual/oral/auditory/kinesthetic

Folding Word Strips Have children brainstorm words that end with *-eak* and check the spellings in a dictionary. Provide children with strips of paper. On the left side of each strip, have them write the beginning consonant or consonant cluster for each word they thought of. Have them fold the right side of each strip over to make a flap. On the flap, they write *eak*. Children can exchange word strips with a partner. Partners look at each open strip and try to guess the *-eak* word. Then they fold the flap to confirm their prediction and use the word in a sentence.

More -*eak* Words		
beak	sneak	streak
leak	speak	weak
peak	squeak	

Vocabulary Enrichment

Unit 14
BONUS

Vocabulary Enrichment

Unit 14
BONUS

Science

Protecting Our Earth All the words in the box have something to do with protecting our earth. Write those words to finish this story from a town newspaper. Use your Spelling Dictionary.

Spelling Word Link

clean

trash
dump
collect
sewer

Section A

Smithtown Is in Trouble!

Where will all our __(1)__ go? Our town __(2)__ is getting full. Rain is even washing leaves and paper into the __(3)__. We need a new way to __(4)__ our papers, cans, and bottles. Let's come up with some answers!

1. trash

2. dump

3. sewer

4. collect

Try This CHALLENGE

Yes or No? Write **yes** or **no** to answer each question.

5. Would you find a **dump** on a camel?
6. Is **trash** something you throw away?
7. Would you wash a car in a **sewer**?
8. Could you **collect** litter in a bag?

5. no

6. yes

7. no

8. yes

★ Fact File

Paper is made from trees. It can also be made from many kinds of used paper. You can save a tree! Take used paper to a place that will make it into new paper.

WE RECYCLE

107

Day by Day Planner

Objectives *Children will*

- expand their vocabulary by using words related to protecting our earth
- show their understanding of the vocabulary words by completing context activities

Vocabulary Checkup

Have children use the vocabulary words in sentences or match the words to the definitions below.

1. a drain built to carry away dirty water
   sewer
2. a special place where garbage is taken
   dump
3. to gather or bring together in a group
   collect
4. things to be thrown away *trash*

Fact File

Recycling Paper

Each person in the United States uses about 700 pounds of paper every year. About forty percent of used paper products are collected for recycling. Conservation, recycling, and reforestation all help preserve endangered forests.

Integrating Literature

Easy

Where Once There Was a Wood
by Denise Fleming
Land that was once home to animals becomes a housing development.

The Earth and I
by Frank Asch
A boy respects the world around him.

Average

Someday a Tree
by Eve Bunting
A girl plants an acorn after chemicals kill her favorite oak.

Just a Dream
by Chris Van Allsburg
Because of a dream, a litterbug learns to care for his environment.

Challenging

The Big Book for Our Planet
by Ann Durell
A collection of poems and stories about the earth.

Grandfather's Dream
by Holly Keller
Restoring the wetland brings cranes back to a Vietnamese village.

The Vowel Sound in *ball*

WORD LISTS

Spelling

Basic

1. dog
2. paw
3. call
4. saw
5. ball
6. all
7. draw
8. small
9. log
10. fall

Review

11. best
12. came

Challenge

13. stall
14. claw

Vocabulary

Careers: Animal Doctor

clip
healthy
ill
cure

Introducing the Lesson

Read Aloud

Write the Basic Words on the board.

Veterinarian

Suppose that you were playing **ball** with your **dog**. You **saw** that it hurt its **paw** on a **log**. What would you do? **Call** the vet, of course. *Vet* is short for *veterinarian*, the name of an animal doctor. At the animal hospital, the vet would put your **dog** on a table in the examining room. You would hold your **dog** so it could not **fall** or jump off. The vet would first clean the **paw**. Then she would put a **small** bandage on the cut. She might say jokingly, "His **paw** will heal quickly, and he will be able to **draw** again in no time. **All** he needs is a few days of rest!"

Responding Ask children what the veterinarian in the story took care of. *(a dog's paw)* Reread the sentence with *small* in it. Ask children to name the spelling word they hear and another word that rhymes with it. *(call, ball, all, fall)*

Day 1 *page 108*

Objectives *Children will*

- take the pretest
- pronounce the list words
- learn about the spelling principle
- sort words by their spelling patterns

Planning Checklist

- ☑ Pretest (TE)
- ☑ Spelling principle/word list
- ☐ Review/Challenge Words
- ☐ Teaching the Principle (TE)
- ☐ Enrichment (TE)
- ☐ Additional Spelling Words (TE)

Assessment

Pretest

1. My dog likes bones.
2. My cat hurt its paw.
3. I will call you at home.
4. Marie saw a baby bird.
5. That is my ball.
6. We are all sleepy.
7. Can you draw a tree?
8. The kitten is small.
9. Pat cut the log.
10. Did she fall down?

Day 2 *page 109*

Objectives *Children will*

- practice spelling list words
- apply spelling strategies
- complete analogies with Basic Words
- identify Basic Words that are synonyms of given words

Planning Checklist

- ☑ Spelling Strategy
- ☑ Independent Practice
- ☐ Daily Proofreading Practice (TE)
- ☐ Informal Assessment (TE)
- ☐ Extra Support (TE)
- ☐ Applying Spelling Strategies (TE)

Management Tip The Ongoing Assessment Tips found throughout the Teacher's Edition will help you to identify common errors that children make with particular spelling patterns and to evaluate children's spelling progress in their own writing.

Additional Resources

Teacher's Resource Book
Practice Masters, pages 69–71
Unit Test, page 72
Bulletin Board, page 81

Practice Plus
Take-Home Word List 15
Games

Spelling Transparencies
Spelling Word List 15
Daily Proofreading Practice, Unit 15
Graphic Organizers

Teacher's Resource Disk
Macintosh® or Windows® software. Houghton Mifflin

Spelling CD-ROM
Macintosh® or Windows® software. Houghton Mifflin

Internet
http://www.eduplace.com

Phonics Practice
Houghton Mifflin Phonics
The Listening Corner
Phonics Home Connection

 Day 3 *page 110*   **Day 4** *page 111*   **Day 5** *page 111*

Objectives *Children will*
- look up meanings and sample sentences for given words, using their Spelling Dictionary
- review Basic and Review Words

Planning Checklist
☐ Dictionary
☐ Review: Spelling Spree
☐ How Are You Doing?
☐ Daily Proofreading Practice (TE)
☐ Cooperative Learning Activity (TE)

Objectives *Children will*
- proofread for spelling
- write and proofread an original composition

Planning Checklist
☐ Proofread for Spelling
☐ Write Instructions
☐ Daily Proofreading Practice (TE)
☐ Challenge Words Practice (TE)
☐ Another Writing Idea (TE)

Objective *Children will*
- take the posttest

Assessment
☐ **Posttest** (TE) *See Day 5*
☐ Unit 15 Test

Meeting Individual Needs
Students Acquiring English

Spanish There is no |ô| sound in Spanish. Children may find the aw spelling especially difficult because Spanish has no w.
Activity Write *paw, saw,* and *draw* on the chalkboard. Say the words, and have children repeat. Ask volunteers to trace each word as they say and spell it. Repeat with other Basic Words.
Asian Asian children may have trouble pronouncing the final *l.*
Activity Explain that to make the *l* sound the tip of the tongue touches the roof of the mouth behind the teeth. Say *la, la, la,* and have children repeat. Write *call, ball,* and *fall* on the board. Say each word slowly. Have children practice saying the words.

Other Activities for Any Day

- Bonus activities from pages 112–113
- Practice Masters (easy, average, challenging)
  Teacher's Resource Book, pages 69–71
- Take-Home Word List 15
  Practice Plus

Objectives *Children will*

- take the pretest
- pronounce the list words
- learn about the spelling principle
- sort words by their spelling patterns

Teaching the Principle

This lesson teaches three spelling patterns for the |ô| sound: *o*, *aw*, and *a* before *ll*. Children learn the strategy of thinking of these patterns when they hear the |ô| sound.

To sum up the lesson, ask:

- What letter spells the |ô| sound in *dog* and *log*? (*o*)
- What letters spell the |ô| sound in *paw* and *saw*? (*aw*)
- What letters spell the |ô| sound in *all* and *small*? (*a followed by ll*)

Enrichment

Vocabulary: Multiple Meanings

Have children use a dictionary to look up *call*, *ball*, *draw*, and *fall*. Discuss the different meanings.

UNIT 15 The Vowel Sound in ball

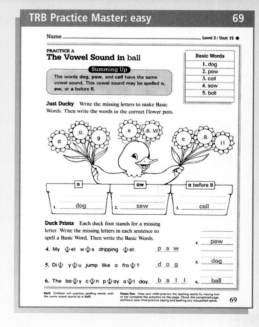

a ball

Read and Say

READ the sentences. **SAY** each word in dark print.

Basic Words

1.	dog	My **dog** likes bones.
2.	paw	My cat hurt its **paw**.
3.	call	I will **call** you at home.
4.	saw	Marie **saw** a baby bird.
5.	ball	That is my **ball**.
6.	all	We are **all** sleepy.
7.	draw	Can you **draw** a tree?
8.	small	The kitten is **small**.
9.	log	Pat cut the **log**.
10.	fall	Did she **fall** down?

A. dog

___ log

B. paw

___ saw

___ draw

C. call

___ ball

___ all

___ small

___ fall

Think and Write

Each word has the same vowel sound. It is the vowel sound you hear in 🏀 ball. This vowel sound is spelled **o**, **aw**, or **a** when **a** comes before **ll**.

the 🏀 vowel sound → d**o**g, p**aw**, c**a**ll

A. Write **two** Basic Words with the vowel sound spelled **o**.

B. Write **three** Basic Words with the vowel sound spelled **aw**.

C. Write **five** Basic Words with the vowel sound spelled **a** before **ll**.

Order of answers for each category may vary.

Review	Challenge
11. best 12. came	13. stall 14. claw

108

TEACHING OPTIONS

Meeting Individual Needs
Word Lists

You may want to assign Basic Words 1–5 and the Review Words to children who misspelled more than five words on the pretest. Assign the Challenge Words as appropriate. (You may want to have children write sentences, using the Challenge Words.)

Additional Spelling Words

Basic	Challenge	Words Often Misspelled
lawn	seesaw	want
cost	strawberry	was
tall	cloth	
hog	waterfall	
yawn	jaws	
	wallpaper	

Home/School Involvement
Take-Home Word List • Goal-Setting

Have children set goals for the week on Take-Home Word List 15.

TRB Practice Master: easy 69

Name _____ Level 2 / Unit 15

PRACTICE A
The Vowel Sound in ball

Basic Words
1. dog
2. paw
3. call
4. saw
5. ball

Summing Up
The words **dog**, **paw**, and **call** have the same vowel sound. This vowel sound may be spelled **o**, **aw**, or **a** before **ll**.

Just Ducky Write the missing letters to make Basic Words. Then write the words in the correct flower pots.

o	aw	a before ll
1. _dog_	2. _saw_	3. _call_

Duck Prints Each duck foot stands for a missing letter. Write the missing letters in each sentence to spell a Basic Word. Then write the Basic Words.

4. My 🦆et w🦆s dripping 🦆et.   p a w   4. _paw_

5. Di🦆 y🦆u jump like a fro🦆?   d o g   5. _dog_

6. The ba🦆y c🦆n p🦆ay a🦆l day.   b a l l   6. _ball_

Skill: Children will practice spelling words with the same vowel sound as in **ball**.

Home Use: Help your child practice the spelling words by having him or her complete the activities on this page. Check the completed page and have your child practice saying and spelling any misspelled words.

69

Independent Practice

 Spelling Strategy The words **dog**, **paw**, and **call** have the same vowel sound. This vowel sound may be spelled **o**, **aw**, or **a** before **ll**.

Order of answers for each question may vary.

Phonics Write Basic Words to answer the questions.

1–2. Which two words rhyme with **fog**?

3–4. Which two words begin with a consonant cluster?

Word Pairs Write a Basic Word to finish the second sentence in each pair.

5. Summer comes after **spring**.
Winter comes after _____.

6. You use a **hammer** to hit a **nail**.
You use a **bat** to hit a _____.

7. You cut **paper** with **scissors**.
You cut **wood** with a _____.

8. A **horse** has a **hoof**.
A **cat** has a _____.

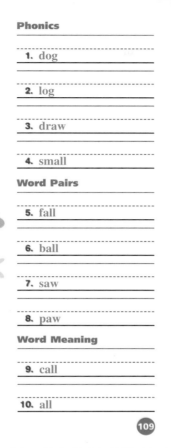

Word Meaning Write the Basic Word that means the same or almost the same as each word below.

9. shout **10.** every

Phonics

1. dog

2. log

3. draw

4. small

Word Pairs

5. fall

6. ball

7. saw

8. paw

Word Meaning

9. call

10. all

109

 Day 2

Objectives *Children will*

- practice spelling list words
- apply spelling strategies
- complete analogies with Basic Words
- identify Basic Words that are synonyms of given words

Daily Proofreading Practice

He **sau** six baby pigs. (*saw*)
Amy kicked the **bal** into the goal. (*ball*)

 Meeting Individual Needs
visual/oral/kinesthetic

Extra Support Check Independent Practice to determine who needs extra support. Write the spelling words on cards and distribute. Print the headings *o*, *aw*, and *a* on the board. Have children take turns reading their word, printing it under the correct heading, and underlining the letter(s) that spell the |ô| sound. Remind children that the words in the *a* column have the letters *ll* after the *a*.

TRB Practice Master: average 70

Name _____ Level 2 / Unit 15 ▲

Basic Words
1. dog
2. paw
3. call
4. saw
5. ball
6. all
7. draw
8. small
9. log
10. fall

PRACTICE B
The Vowel Sound in ball

Proofreading 1–4. Find and cross out four Basic Words that are spelled wrong in this ad. Write each word correctly.

DOG FOR SALE
I have one white paww.
I am small and cuddly.
You never saw a cuter dog!
Please call or come to see me at Jane's house.
(My owner did draw the frame,
but I made the picture!)

1. paw   3. saw

2. small   4. draw

Riddles Write a Basic Word to finish each riddle. Then see if you can think of the answer to each riddle.

5. What is black and white and red _____ over?

6. What do you _____ a bull when he is sleeping?

7. Why did Humpty Dumpty have a great _____?

8. How is a scrambled egg like a losing team?

9. Where does a fireplace _____ keep its money?

10. What kind of furry _____ keeps the best time?

5.	all
6.	call
7.	fall
8.	ball
9.	log
10.	dog

70

 Applying Spelling Strategies
To Spell New Words

- Read aloud: **We saw a hawk circling above us.**
- Have children attempt to spell *hawk* on their Have-a-Go charts.

- Elicit the following strategies as children try to spell *hawk*.

> This word has the |ô| sound. This sound is probably spelled *o* or *aw*. I'll have to check a dictionary.

> I hear the sound for *h* that I hear at the beginning of *hat*.

hawk

> The |k| sound could be spelled *k* or *ck*.

Objectives Children will

Day 3

- look up meanings and sample sentences for given words, using their Spelling Dictionary
- review Basic and Review Words

Daily Proofreading Practice

Don't **fawl** on the icy steps! (*fall*)

My kitten was licking her **pawe**. (*paw*)

UNIT 15

Hink Pinks

5. best _____

6. small _____

7. log _____

8. dog _____

9. saw _____

10. call _____

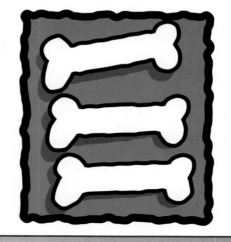

How Are You Doing?

Write your words in ABC order. Practice with a family member any words you spelled wrong.

110

Dictionary

Word Meanings A dictionary gives the **meaning** of an entry word you look up. It may also give a **sample sentence** to help make the meaning clear.

entry word   meaning

paw The foot of a four-footed animal that has claws: *My dog stuck her **paw** in the mud.*

sample sentence

Practice Follow the directions below. Use your Spelling Dictionary. Write your answers on another sheet of paper.

1. Look up **draw**. Write the meaning.
   To make a picture with lines.
2. Look up **log**. Write the sample sentence.
   We burned the log in the fire.
3. Look up **small**. Write the meaning.
   Little in size or amount.
4. Look up **best**. Write the sample sentence.
   Emily made the best picture of all.

Review: Spelling Spree

Hink Pinks Write a Basic or Review Word that answers the question and rhymes with the word in dark print.

5. What is the most wonderful nap?
   the _____ **rest**
6. What is a tiny room? a _____ **hall**
7. What is a tree trunk for a pig? a **hog** _____
8. What is a run with a puppy? a _____ **jog**
9. What is a tool for a kitten? a **paw** _____
10. What is a yell in October? a **fall** _____

Cooperative Learning Activity

Be a Word Doctor
visual/kinesthetic

Tell children that they are going to be word doctors. Give each child ten dog bones that you have cut from construction paper. Have them write one spelling word on each bone, spelling some words correctly and some incorrectly.

Children then trade bones with a partner. Partners become word doctors, crossing out any words that are spelled wrong and "fixing them up." Partners check one another's corrections, then combine all the bones and sort them into categories they determine.

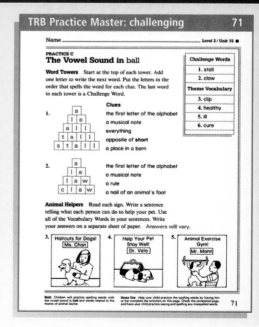

TRB Practice Master: challenging   71

Name _____   Level 2 / Unit 15

PRACTICE C
The Vowel Sound in ball

Challenge Words
1. stall
2. claw

Theme Vocabulary
3. clip
4. healthy
5. ill
6. cure

Word Towers Start at the top of each tower. Add one letter to write the next word. Put the letters in the order that spells the word for each clue. The last word in each tower is a Challenge Word.

Clues

1.
   the first letter of the alphabet
   a musical note
   everything
   opposite of **short**
   a place in a barn

2.
   the first letter of the alphabet
   a musical note
   a rule
   a nail of an animal's foot

Animal Helpers Read each sign. Write a sentence telling what each person can do to help your pet. Use all of the Vocabulary Words in your sentences. Write your answers on a separate sheet of paper. Answers will vary.

3. Haircuts for Dogs! Ms. Chan
4. Help Your Pet Stay Well! Dr. Veto
5. Animal Exercise Gym! Mr. Mann

71

Proofreading and Writing

Proofread for Spelling Proofread this letter. Use proofreading marks to fix six spelling mistakes.

Example: Rufus ~~sor~~ <u>saw</u> the doctor on Monday.

July 31, 1998

Dear Doctor Walsh,

We are ~~al~~ ^{all} glad you ~~kame~~ ^{came} to fix our dog

Pal's ~~pau~~ ^{paw} after his ~~fawl~~ ^{fall}. Today he chased a

~~boll~~ ^{ball}! I will ~~drow~~ ^{draw} a picture of him for you.

Best wishes,

Kate Rizzo

Write Instructions

Pretend you are going on vacation, and you have to leave your pet at home. Write sentences that tell a pet sitter what to do to take care of your pet. Try to use spelling words. Have a friend read your instructions. Are they clear?

Proofreading Tip

Make sure you have written your a's and o's the right way.

111

Basic

1. dog
2. paw
3. call
4. saw
5. ball
6. all
7. draw
8. small
9. log
10. fall

Review
11. best
12. came

Challenge
13. stall
14. claw

Proofreading Marks

∧ Add
ᴤ Delete
≡ Make a capital letter
/ Make a small letter

Objectives *Children will*
- proofread for spelling
- write and proofread an original composition

Daily Proofreading Practice
Nick put a **logg** on the fire. (*log*)
Gina likes to **drawe** horses. (*draw*)

Day 5 **Posttest**

Sentences 1–5 test the first five Basic Words. Sentences 6–10 test the next five Basic Words. Sentences 11–12 test the Elephant Words.

Basic Words
1. I will <u>call</u> you.
2. We <u>saw</u> a kite.
3. He can give me his <u>paw</u>.
4. She has a red <u>ball</u>.
5. That is a cute <u>dog</u>.
6. The cat is <u>small</u>.
7. Do not <u>fall</u>.
8. He will <u>draw</u> a fish.
9. I see <u>all</u> the cups.
10. The <u>log</u> is big.

Review Words
11. She <u>came</u> for my sled.
12. That is my <u>best</u> coat.

Challenge Words
13. We cleaned out the horse's <u>stall</u>.
14. The cat's <u>claw</u> is sharp.

TRB Unit 15 Test   72

Name _____   Level 2 / Unit 15 ●▲

Unit 15 Test: The Vowel Sound in ball

Each item below gives three spellings of a word. Choose the correct spelling. Mark the letter for that word.

Sample:			ANSWERS
a. wal	b. wawl	c. wall	ⓐ ⓑ ●

Items 1–6 test Basic Words 1–5. Items 6–10 test Basic Words 6–10.

1. a. paw	b. po	c. pawe	1. ⓐ ⓑ ⓒ
2. a. cawl	b. cal	c. call	2. ⓐ ⓑ ●
3. a. sawe	b. saw	c. sa	3. ⓐ ● ⓒ
4. a. dolg	b. dawg	c. dog	4. ⓐ ⓑ ●
5. a. ball	b. bal	c. bol	5. ● ⓑ ⓒ
6. a. logg	b. log	c. lawg	6. ⓐ ● ⓒ
7. a. droh	b. dro	c. draw	7. ⓐ ⓑ ●
8. a. fawl	b. fall	c. fal	8. ⓐ ● ⓒ
9. a. small	b. smal	c. smawl	9. ● ⓑ ⓒ
10. a. oll	b. al	c. all	10. ⓐ ⓑ ●

72

Meeting Individual Needs

Challenge Words Practice
Suggest children make up animal book or movie titles using the Challenge Words. (Example: Our Summer on Cat's Claw Island)

Another Writing Idea Have children draw or create from cardboard tubes, yarn, colored paper, toothpicks, etc., an imaginary animal. Then have them write about their animal, using spelling words.

These pages can be used at any time during the study of this unit.

Objectives *Children will*

- build words with the phonograms -*all* and -*aw*
- use context and picture clues to complete sentences

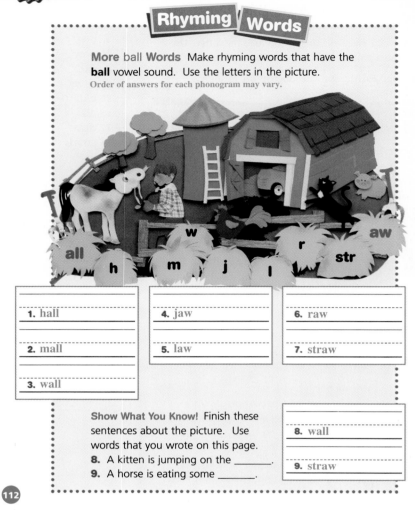

Phonics and Spelling

Rhyming Words

More ball Words Make rhyming words that have the **ball** vowel sound. Use the letters in the picture.

Order of answers for each phonogram may vary.

1. hall
2. mall
3. wall

4. jaw
5. law

6. raw
7. straw

Show What You Know! Finish these sentences about the picture. Use words that you wrote on this page.
8. A kitten is jumping on the _____.
9. A horse is eating some _____.

8. wall
9. straw

112

EXTENSION OPTIONS

Learning Center Activity

visual/kinesthetic

-og Word Wheels Cut small and large circles from tagboard. Have children write the letters *og* on a small circle and these consonants and clusters around the outer edge of a large circle: *b, cl, d, f, fr, h, j, l,* and *sm*. Then have them draw an arrow or a line from the letters *og* to the outer edge. Children attach the small circle to the center of the larger one with a paper fastener. They then spin the wheels to build rhyming words. Have children write the words they make in a list or in sentences. Some children may wish to illustrate their words or sentences.

More -og Words		
bog	fog	jog
clog	frog	log
dog	hog	smog

Vocabulary Enrichment

Careers

Animal Doctors All the words in the box have something to do with animal doctors. Write those words to finish this diary. Use your Spelling Dictionary.

Spelling Word Link

dog

clip
healthy
ill
cure

September 9

Rusty is still very __(1)__ with a cold. The doctor will __(2)__ him. She will even __(3)__ his nails. My dog will be __(4)__ again.

1. ill
2. cure
3. clip
4. healthy

Try This CHALLENGE

Yes or No? Is the word in the dark print used correctly? Write **yes** or **no**.

5. Rex is **ill** with a terrible haircut.
6. Walking a dog will keep it **healthy**.
7. I will use a hose to **clip** Koko's claws.
8. Dr. Ming has a **cure** for the leash.

5. no
6. yes
7. no
8. no

★ **Fact File**

Long ago, many towns did not have an animal doctor nearby. In those towns, the blacksmith, who made horseshoes, also worked as the horse doctor!

113

Day by Day Planner

Objectives *Children will*

■ expand their vocabulary by using words related to animal doctors

■ show their understanding of the vocabulary words by completing context activities

Vocabulary Checkup

Have children use the vocabulary words in sentences or match the words to the definitions below.

1. not sick or hurt *healthy*
2. to cut with scissors or shears *clip*
3. to bring back to good health *cure*
4. sick *ill*

Fact File

Blacksmith or Horse Doctor?

Before the automobile, forging horseshoes was often a blacksmith's most important job. Blacksmiths who tended and put shoes on horses were called farriers. Eventually, anyone who tended a sick horse was called a farrier.

Integrating Literature

Easy	Average	Challenging

Henry and Mudge Get the Cold Shivers
by Cynthia Rylant
Both Henry and his dog, Mudge, catch colds.

Island Baby
By Holly Keller
A boy helps his grandfather care for a hurt baby flamingo.

Taking My Dog to the Vet
by Susan Kuklin
A boy describes his dog's checkup at the vet's.

Taking My Cat to the Vet
by Susan Kuklin
This photo-essay records a cat's visit to a vet.

Say Woof!
by Gail Gibbons
A day in the life of a country veterinarian.

What's It Like to Be a Veterinarian
by Judith Samper
A description of the work a vet does to care for animals.

Words Spelled with *sh* or *ch*

WORD LISTS

Spelling

Basic

1. sheep
2. chase
3. wish
4. much
5. chop
6. each
7. dish
8. such
9. wash
10. ship
11. catch
12. sure

Review

13. she
14. chin

Challenge

15. shout
16. lunch

Vocabulary

Social Studies: Ranching

graze
cattle
herd
stray

Introducing the Lesson

Read Aloud

Write the Basic Words on the board.

Sheep Ranching

Have you ever had a lamb **chop** or a **dish** of lamb and potatoes? Perhaps you **wish** you had a new wool coat. Lamb and wool come from **sheep**. Wool does not spoil, so a rancher can **ship** it over long distances. Things made from wool will last a long time if you **wash** them carefully. There are many ranches in the West where **sheep** are raised today. You can be **sure** that it takes hard work to raise **such** animals. **Each** day while the animals graze, the ranch hands and their dogs keep watch for coyotes. They also **chase** and **catch** animals that may have wandered off. **Sheep** do not need **much** water, so they can be raised on dry plains.

Responding Ask children what kind of ranch they learned about. *(sheep ranch)* Then ask children to name some things made from wool. *(clothing, blankets, rugs)*

 Day 1 *page 114*

Objectives *Children will*

- take the pretest
- pronounce the list words
- learn about the spelling principle
- sort words by their spelling patterns

Planning Checklist

- ☑ Pretest (TE)
- ☑ Spelling principle/word list
- ☐ Review/Challenge Words
- ☐ Teaching the Principle (TE)
- ☐ Enrichment (TE)
- ☐ Additional Spelling Words (TE)

Assessment

Pretest

1. The farmer has <u>sheep</u>.
2. Did he <u>chase</u> the cat?
3. Make a <u>wish</u>.
4. We stayed <u>much</u> longer.
5. Anna will <u>chop</u> the log.
6. They like <u>each</u> puppy.
7. Marco broke a <u>dish</u>.
8. I am <u>such</u> a good cook.
9. Will you <u>wash</u> the cup?
10. We saw the <u>ship</u> sail.
11. Did Sing <u>catch</u> a fish?
12. Are you <u>sure</u> you saw her?

Day 2 *page 115*

Objectives *Children will*

- practice spelling list words
- apply spelling strategies
- identify Basic Words that are synonyms of given words
- identify Elephant Words by using context clues

Planning Checklist

- ☑ Spelling Strategy
- ☑ Independent Practice
- ☐ Daily Proofreading Practice (TE)
- ☐ Informal Assessment (TE)
- ☐ Extra Support (TE)
- ☐ Applying Spelling Strategies (TE)

Day 3 *page 116*

 Day 4 *page 117*

 Day 5 *page 117*

Additional Resources

Teacher's Resource Book
Practice Masters, pages 73–75
Unit Test, page 76
Bulletin Board, page 81

Practice Plus
Take-Home Word List 16
Games

Spelling Transparencies
Spelling Word List 16
Daily Proofreading Practice,
 Unit 16
Graphic Organizers

Teacher's Resource Disk
Macintosh® or Windows® software.
 Houghton Mifflin

Spelling CD-ROM
Macintosh® or Windows® software.
 Houghton Mifflin

Internet
http://www.eduplace.com

Phonics Practice
Houghton Mifflin Phonics
The Listening Corner
Phonics Home Connection

Day 3

Objective *Children will*
• review Basic and Review
 Words

Planning Checklist
☐ Review: Spelling Spree
☐ How Are You Doing?
☐ Daily Proofreading Practice
 (TE)
☐ Cooperative Learning
 Activity (TE)

Day 4

Objectives *Children will*
• proofread for spelling and
 usage of *er* and *est*
• write and proofread an original composition

Planning Checklist
☐ Proofread: Spelling and
 Using *er* and *est*
☐ Write a Description
☐ Daily Proofreading Practice
 (TE)
☐ Challenge Words Practice
 (TE)
☐ Another Writing Idea (TE)

Day 5

Objective *Children will*
• take the posttest

Assessment
☐ **Posttest** (TE) *See Day 5*
☐ Unit 16 Test

 Meeting Individual Needs
Students Acquiring English

Spanish There is no |sh| sound in Spanish.
Activity Say *chop/shop, sheep/cheap, chip/ship*. Have children raise their hands when they hear the |sh| sound. Write Basic Words with *sh* on the board. Point to a word, say it, and have children repeat it. Have a volunteer circle the *sh*'s.

Asian Asians may pronounce the |ĭ| sound as the |ē| sound.
Activity Write *hit/heat* and *ship/sheep* on the board. Say each word and have children repeat it. Ask children what vowel sound they hear in each word. Underline the vowels. Then ask volunteers to name the word with the |ĭ| sound in each pair.

**Other Activities
for Any Day**

• Bonus activities from pages 118–119

• Practice Masters (easy, average,
 challenging)
 Teacher's Resource Book,
 pages 73–75

• Take-Home Word List 16
 Practice Plus

Objectives *Children will*

■ take the pretest

■ pronounce the list words

■ learn about the spelling principle

■ sort words by their spelling patterns

Teaching the Principle

This lesson teaches the *sh* and the *ch* spelling patterns for the |sh| and |ch| sounds. Children learn the strategy of thinking of *sh* when they hear the |sh| sound and *ch* when they hear the |ch| sound.

To sum up the lesson, ask:

• What is the sound of *sh*? |sh|

• What is the sound of *ch*? |ch|

Enrichment

Vocabulary: Multiple Meanings

Have children use a dictionary to look up *chase, chop, dish,* and *ship*. Discuss the different meanings.

16 Words Spelled with sh or ch

sh sheep

Read and Say

READ the sentences. **SAY** each word in dark print.

Basic Words

1.	sheep	The farmer has **sheep**.
2.	chase	Did he **chase** the cat?
3.	wish	Make a **wish**.
4.	much	We stayed **much** longer.
5.	chop	Anna will **chop** the log.
6.	each	They like **each** puppy.
7.	dish	Marco broke a **dish**.
8.	such	I am **such** a good cook.
9.	wash	Will you **wash** the cup?
10.	ship	We saw the **ship** sail.
11.	catch	Did Sing **catch** a fish?
12.	sure	Are you **sure** you saw her?

A. sheep

_____ wish

_____ dish

_____ wash

_____ ship

B. chase

_____ much

_____ chop

_____ each

_____ such

C. catch

_____ sure

114

Think and Write

Each word begins or ends with the first sound you hear in 👞 *shoe* or 🪑 *chair*.

the **sh** sound → **sh**eep, wi**sh**

the **ch** sound → **ch**ase, mu**ch**

How are the Elephant Words different?

In *catch*, the letters *tch* spell the |ch| sound. In *sure*, the letter *s* spells the |sh| sound.

A. Write **five** Basic Words spelled with **sh**.

B. Write **five** Basic Words spelled with **ch**.

C. Now write the **two** Elephant Words.

Order of answers for each category may vary.

Review		**Challenge**	
13. she	14. chin	15. shout	16. lunch

TEACHING OPTIONS

Meeting Individual Needs
Word Lists

You may want to assign Basic Words 1–5, the Elephant Words, and the Review Words to children who misspelled more than five words on the pretest. Assign the Challenge Words as appropriate. (You may want to have children write sentences, using the Challenge Words.)

Additional Spelling Words

Basic	**Challenge**	**Words Often Misspelled**
sheet	goldfish	
chest	spinach	went
teach	shiver	cannot
leash	checkers	
chain	chew	
	shower	

Home/School Involvement
Take-Home Word List • Goal-Setting

Have children set goals for the week on Take-Home Word List 16.

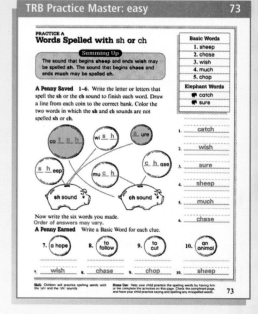

TRB Practice Master: easy   73

PRACTICE A
Words Spelled with sh **or** ch

Basic Words
1. sheep
2. chase
3. wish
4. much
5. chop

Elephant Words
🐘 catch
🐘 sure

Summing Up
The sound that begins sheep and ends wish may be spelled sh. The sound that begins chase and ends much may be spelled ch.

A Penny Saved 1–6. Write the letter or letters that spell the sh or the ch sound to finish each word. Draw a line from each coin to the correct bank. Color the two words in which the sh and ch sounds are not spelled sh or ch.

co t c h   wi s h   s ure

s h eep   mu c h   c h ase

sh sound   ch sound

1. catch
2. wish
3. sure
4. sheep
5. much
6. chase

Now write the six words you made. Order of answers may vary.

A Penny Earned Write a Basic Word for each clue.

7. a hope   8. to follow   9. to cut   10. an animal

7. wish   8. chase   9. chop   10. sheep

73

Independent Practice

Spelling Strategy The sound that begins **sheep** and ends **wish** may be spelled **sh**. The sound that begins **chase** and ends **much** may be spelled **ch**.

Order of answers for each question may vary.

Phonics Write Basic Words to answer the questions.

1–2. Which two words have the short **u** sound?

3–4. Which two words have the long **e** sound?

Word Meaning Write the Basic Word that means the same or almost the same as each word below.

5. plate
6. boat
7. hope
8. follow
9. cut
10. clean

Elephant Words Write the missing Elephant Words.

11. Watch Tex _____ the bundles of hay.

12. I am _____ he works very hard.

Phonics

1. much

2. such

3. sheep

4. each

Word Meaning

5. dish

6. ship

7. wish

8. chase

9. chop

10. wash

Elephant Words

11. catch

12. sure

(115)

Day 2

Objectives *Children will*
- practice spelling list words
- apply spelling strategies
- identify Basic Words that are synonyms of given words
- identify Elephant Words by using context clues

Daily Proofreading Practice

I ate too **mutch** ice cream! (*much*)
We **eech** had a pony ride. (*each*)

Meeting Individual Needs
visual/auditory/oral/kinesthetic

Extra Support Check Independent Practice to determine who needs extra support. Write *sh* and *ch* as headings on the board. Say *sheep, chase, wish, much,* and *chop*. Ask children to identify whether a word has the |sh| or the |ch| sound. Then write the word in the appropriate column. Have volunteers trace with a finger the *sh* or the *ch* as they say the word.

Basic Words
1. sheep
2. chase
3. wish
4. much
5. chop
6. each
7. dish
8. such
9. wash
10. ship
Elephant Words
🐘 catch
🐘 sure

PRACTICE B
Words Spelled with sh or ch

Dot-to-Dot 1–4. Find what race cars do. Connect the dots to spell Basic Words. Then write the words.

m u a s s u h e
c h w h h c s e p

1. _much_   3. _such_
2. _wash_   4. _sheep_

Word Search Write a Basic or Elephant Word for each clue. Then circle each word in the puzzle.

5. cut up   8. want   11. run after
6. a boat   9. every   12. get hold of
7. a plate   10. certain

5. _chop_   7. _dish_   9. _each_   11. _chase_
6. _ship_   8. _wish_   10. _sure_   12. _catch_

s	u	r	e	m	b	w	s	y	i
e	t	d	a	s	v	i	l	m	z
v	g	i	c	h	a	s	e	s	h
e	e	s	h	i	o	h	b	w	j
h	c	h	o	p	c	a	t	c	h

Skill: Children will practice spelling words with the |sh| and the |ch| sounds.
Home Use: Help your child practice the spelling words by having him or her complete the activities on this page. Check the completed page, and have your child practice saying and spelling any misspelled words.

74

Applying Spelling Strategies
To Read New Words

- Write this sentence on the chalkboard: **I am going skating after I finish my homework.**

- Have children read the sentence silently.
- Elicit the following strategies as children try to decode *finish*.

> I know that the letter *f* makes the sound I hear at the beginning of *feather*.

fini**sh**

> F-in-ish. Fin-ish. Finish. The word *finish* makes sense in the sentence.

> I see that the letter *i* is followed by the consonant *n*. I think this is the short *i* vowel pattern. The letters *i* and *n* spell the word *in*.

> I see that the next *i* is followed by two consonants. I think this is another short *i* vowel pattern. I know that the letters *sh* make the |sh| sound.

Objective *Children will*

■ review Basic and Review Words

Daily Proofreading Practice

It is my turn to **wach** the dishes. (*wash*)

Be **shure** you close the windows. (*sure*)

Review: Spelling Spree

Letter Swap

1. much

2. chase

3. dish

4. chin

5. each

6. such

7. ship

Puzzle Play

8. catch

9. sure

10. wash

11. chop

12. wish

Letter Swap Make Basic or Review Words by using **sh** or **ch** in place of each letter in dark print. Write the words.

1. mu**g**
2. **c**ase
3. di**g**
4. **w**in
5. eat
6. sun
7. **l**ip

Puzzle Play Write the missing Basic Words. Use the letters that would be in the boxes to spell what someone does in a classroom.

8. I __ __ ☐ __ __ the rope Mom throws to me.
9. I am not __ __ __ ☐ when the rodeo is coming.
10. We __ ☐ __ __ the sheep's dirty wool.
11. Can you ☐ __ __ __ down this tree?
12. I __ __ __ ☐ I could ride the new pony!

Secret Word: t e a c h

How Are You Doing?

List the spelling words that are hard for you. Practice them with a partner.

TEACHING OPTIONS

Cooperative Learning Activity

Beat the Clock

visual/auditory/kinesthetic

Provide pairs of children with Scrabble® pieces or letter cards and a one or two minute timer. One child thinks of a spelling word, gives a clue for the word, and starts the timer. For example, the clue might be "this is something you can do with an ax." (*chop*) The partner guesses the word and tries to spell it with the Scrabble pieces or cards before time runs out. Children score one point for each word they spell correctly within the time limit.

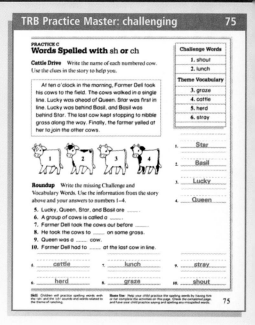

TRB Practice Master: challenging   75

PRACTICE C
Words Spelled with sh or ch

Challenge Words
1. shout
2. lunch
Theme Vocabulary
3. graze
4. cattle
5. herd
6. stray

Cattle Drive Write the name of each numbered cow. Use the clues in the story to help you.

At ten o'clock in the morning, Farmer Dell took his cows to the field. The cows walked in a single line. Lucky was ahead of Queen. Star was first in line. Lucky was behind Basil, and Basil was behind Star. The last cow kept stopping to nibble grass along the way. Finally, the farmer yelled at her to join the other cows.

1. Star
2. Basil
3. Lucky
4. Queen

Roundup Write the missing Challenge and Vocabulary Words. Use the information from the story above and your answers to numbers 1–4.

5. Lucky, Queen, Star, and Basil are ____.
6. A group of cows is called a ____.
7. Farmer Dell took the cows out before ____.
8. He took the cows to ____ on some grass.
9. Queen was a ____ cow.
10. Farmer Dell had to ____ at the last cow in line.

5. cattle
6. herd
7. lunch
8. graze
9. stray
10. shout

75

Proofreading and Writing

Proofread: Spelling and Using *er* **and** *est*
Add **er** to adjectives to compare two people or things.
Add **est** to compare more than two.
    The small**est** pony chased the other four.
Proofread this tall tale. Use proofreading marks to fix four spelling mistakes and two mistakes using **er** or **est**.

Example: Shirley is ~~mush quickest~~ than Roy is.
much quicker

L̲ong ago, Roy Ram raced with a ~~sheap~~ *sheep*
named Shirley. He was ~~shure~~ *sure* he could
~~cach~~ *catch* up to her, but Shirley was ~~fastest~~ *faster*. She
ran with such speed that ~~shee~~ *she* blew down
each tree along her path. That is why
their ranch has the ~~fewer~~ *fewest* trees of all!

Write a Description

Draw some pictures of ranch animals. Then write about them. Tell how they are alike and different. Try to use spelling words.
Example: The sheep is shorter than the horse.

Proofreading Tip

Check that you added er **or** est **to adjectives when comparing two or more people or things.**

117

| **Basic** |
| 1. sheep |
| 2. chase |
| 3. wish |
| 4. much |
| 5. chop |
| 6. each |
| 7. dish |
| 8. such |
| 9. wash |
| 10. ship |
| 11. catch |
| 12. sure |

Review
13. she
14. chin

Challenge
15. shout
16. lunch

Proofreading Marks
∧ Add
⤲ Delete
≡ Make a capital letter
╱ Make a small letter

Objectives *Children will*
◾ proofread for spelling and usage of *er* and *est*
◾ write and proofread an original composition

Day 4

Daily Proofreading Practice
The **shippe** sailed across the sea. (*ship*)
Jim is **soch** a good storyteller! (*such*)

Day 5   **Posttest**

Sentences 1–5 test the first five Basic Words. Sentences 6–10 test the next five Basic Words. Sentences 11–12 test the Elephant Words.

Basic Words
1. Dot will <u>chop</u> the log.
2. Did he have <u>much</u> help?
3. Did Sam <u>chase</u> the kite?
4. Look at the <u>sheep</u>.
5. I had a <u>wish</u>.
6. Did you <u>wash</u> the pot?
7. They gave one to <u>each</u> man.
8. This is <u>such</u> a great day!
9. Did she see the <u>ship</u>?
10. The white <u>dish</u> is big.
11. Did you <u>catch</u> it?
12. She is <u>sure</u> that she can do it.

Review Words
13. I hit my <u>chin</u>.
14. Did <u>she</u> make a dress?

Challenge Words
15. I had some soup for <u>lunch</u>.
16. We heard them <u>shout</u> our names.

TRB Unit 16 Test   76

Name _____ Level 2 / Unit 16 ●▲

Unit 16 Test: Words Spelled with *sh* **or** *ch*

Read each sentence. Find the correctly spelled word to complete each sentence. Mark the letter next to that word.

| Sample: | ANSWERS |
| Patti said _____ would be here. | ⓐ shee ⓑ che ● she |

Items 1–7 test Basic Words 1–5 and the Elephant Words.
Items 8–12 test Basic Words 6–10.
1. I will count the _____.   ⓐ chepe ⓑ sheep ⓒ shep
2. Dina will _____ the wood.   ⓐ chop ⓑ chope ⓒ chob
3. How _____ did it cost?   ⓐ mushe ⓑ moch ⓒ much
4. Scruffy likes to _____ cars.   ⓐ chas ⓑ chaze ⓒ chase
5. Are you _____ of that?   ⓐ sure ⓑ shor ⓒ chure
6. Joy made a _____.   ⓐ wich ⓑ wish ⓒ wesh
7. Doug tried to _____ the ball.   ⓐ cech ⓑ catsh ⓒ catch
8. That is _____ a great book!   ⓐ such ⓑ sush ⓒ soch
9. Give a horn to _____ child.   ⓐ ech ⓑ each ⓒ eech
10. Terry gave me a pretty _____.   ⓐ dish ⓑ dich ⓒ desh
11. A _____ took them home again.   ⓐ shup ⓑ ship ⓒ shipp
12. Carl had to _____ his hands.   ⓐ wach ⓑ wosh ⓒ wash

Meeting Individual Needs

Challenge Words Practice
Ask children to make two concept webs, writing *meals* in the center of one and *talk* in the center of the other. In the outer circles, have them add the Challenge Words and other words they choose to name different meals and ways of speaking.

Another Writing Idea Have children use the spelling words in silly tongue twisters about ranching. (Example: Shawn is sure his sheep are shy.)

These pages can be used at any time during the study of this unit.

Day by Day Planner

Objectives *Children will*

- build words with the consonant digraph *ch*
- sort *ch* words into categories

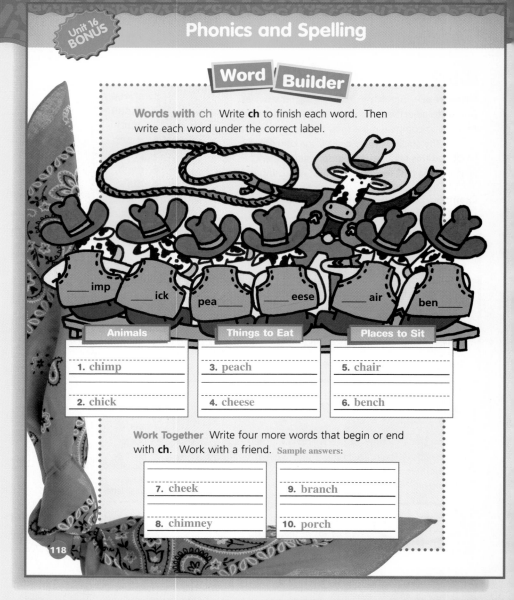

Word Builder

Words with ch Write **ch** to finish each word. Then write each word under the correct label.

____imp   ____ick   pea____   ____eese   ____air   ben____

Animals	Things to Eat	Places to Sit
1. chimp	3. peach	5. chair
2. chick	4. cheese	6. bench

Work Together Write four more words that begin or end with **ch**. Work with a friend. Sample answers:

7. cheek	9. branch
8. chimney	10. porch

118

EXTENSION OPTIONS

Cowhands brush their horses.

A flash of lightning may scare the cattle.

Learning Center Activity

visual/kinesthetic

sh Puzzle Strips Ask children to brainstorm a list of *sh* words. They might use a dictionary to find words that begin with *sh* and think of rhyming words to identify those that end with *sh*. Provide strips of drawing paper. On one end of each strip, chil-dren use an *sh* word in a sentence about ranches or ranching. On the other end, they draw a picture to go with their sentence. Children then cut each strip into two puzzle pieces and have a friend match the sentences and pictures.

More Words That End with *-sh*			
crash	smash	finish	brush
dash	splash	bush	crush
flash	fresh	push	rush
trash	squash	leash	slush

Vocabulary Enrichment

Unit 16 BONUS

Social Studies

Ranching All the words in the box have something to do with ranching. Write those words to finish the beginning of this story. Use your Spelling Dictionary.

Spelling Word Link

sheep

graze
cattle
herd
stray

Life on a Ranch

A rancher leads a __(1)__ of cows.
Her dog runs after a __(2)__ calf.
The __(3)__ are going to a field. They
will __(4)__ there all day.

1. herd
2. stray
3. cattle
4. graze

Try This CHALLENGE

Yes or No? Write **yes** or **no** to answer each question.
5. Would sheep **graze** in a barn?
6. Does a **stray** stay close to a group?
7. Is there more than one cow in a **herd**?
8. Would you call a group of pigs **cattle**?

5. no
6. no
7. yes
8. no

Fact File

Many songs and stories are about ranching. Agnes De Mille, a famous dancer, even made a dance about a cowgirl on a ranch. The dance is called **Rodeo**.

119

Objectives *Children will*

- expand their vocabulary by using words related to ranching
- show their understanding of the vocabulary words by completing context activities

Day by Day Planner

Vocabulary Checkup

Have children use the vocabulary words in sentences or match the words to the definitions below.

1. a group of animals of one kind, such as cows, that are kept together *herd*
2. to eat growing grass *graze*
3. having gone away from a group or place *stray*
4. large animals, such as cows, that have hoofs and grow horns *cattle*

Fact File

Rodeo

Agnes De Mille here dances the role of Cowgirl in the ballet *Rodeo*. Cowgirl is a lively young girl who prefers riding a horse to wearing a dress. The action takes place at the Burnt Ranch during a rodeo and square dance.

Integrating Literature

Easy	Average	Challenging
Just Like My Dad *by Tricia Gardella* A boy recounts his daily routine on his family's ranch.	**Cowboy Country** *by Ann Herbert Scott* An old buckaroo tells how he became a cowboy.	**On the Pampas** *by Maria Cristina Brusca* A girl spends time at her grandparents' ranch in Argentina.
On the Trail with Miss Pace *by Sharon Denslow* Surprising things happen when a teacher vacations at a dude ranch.	**Meanwhile Back at the Ranch** *by Trinka Hakes Noble* A bored rancher misses some wacky goings-on at his ranch.	**Cowboys** *by Joan Anderson* Two boys help out with a roundup on a New Mexican ranch.

Words Spelled with *th* or *wh*

WORD LISTS

Spelling

Basic
1. teeth
2. when
3. then
4. wheel
5. with
6. what
7. than
8. while
9. them
10. which

Review
11. white
12. bath

Challenge
13. mouth
14. whistle

Vocabulary

Careers: Dentist
toothbrush
rinse
roots
braces

Introducing the Lesson

Read Aloud

Write the Basic Words on the board.

A Visit to the Dentist

When was the last time you had your **teeth** cleaned? Do you remember **what** the dentist did? **While** you sat in the chair, the dentist first looked at your **teeth** **with** a mirror and a dental explorer, **which** is a tool **with** a hook at the end. The dentist **then** checked for cavities. He may have used a scaler to scrape away the tartar. Finally, the dentist used an electric tool **with** a round brush and a buffer, **which** looks like a tiny rubber **wheel**, to polish your **teeth**. Did you look at **them** in the mirror? Your **teeth** should have been shinier **than** pearls! Sometimes the dentist will give you a new toothbrush to help you keep your **teeth** shiny.

Responding Ask children what a dentist takes care of. *(teeth)* Then ask children why it is important to brush their teeth.

Day 1 *page 120*

Objectives *Children will*
- take the pretest
- pronounce the list words
- learn about the spelling principle
- sort words by their spelling patterns

Planning Checklist
☑ Pretest (TE)
☑ Spelling principle/word list
☐ Review/Challenge Words
☐ Teaching the Principle (TE)
☐ Enrichment (TE)
☐ Additional Spelling Words (TE)

Assessment

Pretest
1. I must brush my <u>teeth</u>.
2. You know <u>when</u> to clap.
3. Jess will leave by <u>then</u>.
4. Turn the <u>wheel</u> fast!
5. Can you play <u>with</u> me?
6. I will get <u>what</u> I want.
7. He is older <u>than</u> I am.
8. Can I read for a <u>while</u>?
9. Hit the ball to <u>them</u>.
10. Pick <u>which</u> toy you want.

Day 2 *page 121*

Objectives *Children will*
- practice spelling list words
- apply spelling strategies
- complete analogies with Basic Words
- identify Basic Words by using clues

Planning Checklist
☑ Spelling Strategy
☑ Independent Practice
☐ Daily Proofreading Practice (TE)
☐ Informal Assessment (TE)
☐ Extra Support (TE)
☐ Applying Spelling Strategies (TE)

Management Tip Encourage children to share what they are learning with their parents by having them take home the spelling list to practice with family members. You may want to share with parents any spelling games or activities that you find particularly fun and effective.

 Day 3 page 122 **Day 4** page 123 **Day 5** page 123

Objectives *Children will*

- alphabetize given words to the third letter to identify which word comes first in the dictionary
- review Basic and Review Words

Planning Checklist

- ☐ Dictionary
- ☐ Review: Spelling Spree
- ☐ How Are You Doing?
- ☐ Daily Proofreading Practice (TE)
- ☐ Ongoing Assessment

Objectives *Children will*

- proofread for spelling
- write and proofread an original composition

Planning Checklist

- ☐ Proofread for Spelling
- ☐ Write a Label
- ☐ Daily Proofreading Practice (TE)
- ☐ Challenge Words Practice (TE)
- ☐ Another Writing Idea (TE)

Objective *Children will*

- take the posttest

Assessment

- ☐ **Posttest** (TE) *See Day 5*
- ☐ Unit 17 Test

Additional Resources

Teacher's Resource Book
Practice Masters, pages 77–79
Unit Test, page 80
Bulletin Board, page 81

Practice Plus
Take-Home Word List 17
Games

Spelling Transparencies
Spelling Word List 17
Daily Proofreading Practice, Unit 17
Graphic Organizers

Teacher's Resource Disk
Macintosh® or Windows® software. Houghton Mifflin

Spelling CD-ROM
Macintosh® or Windows® software. Houghton Mifflin

Internet
http://www.eduplace.com

Phonics Practice
Houghton Mifflin Phonics
The Listening Corner
Phonics Home Connection

 Meeting Individual Needs
Students Acquiring English

Spanish The Spanish alphabet has no *w*.
Activity Write Basic Words with *wh* on the board. Underline *wh* as you say each word. Have children repeat them. Then erase the *wh* in each word. As you point to and say each word, have a volunteer fill in the blanks, say the word, and spell it.

Asian Asian children may mispronounce the voiced |th| and the unvoiced |th| sounds as |d| or |s|.
Activity Say *then* and *thin* slowly, having children repeat the words. Point out that for the |th| sound you hear in *thin*, air is pushed out forcefully.

 ## Other Activities for Any Day

- Bonus activities from pages 124–125
- Practice Masters (easy, average, challenging)
  Teacher's Resource Book, pages 77–79
- Take-Home Word List 17
  Practice Plus

Objectives *Children will*

■ take the pretest

■ pronounce the list words

■ learn about the spelling principle

■ sort words by their spelling patterns

Teaching the Principle

This lesson teaches the *th* spelling pattern for the |th| and the |th| sounds and the *wh* spelling pattern for the |hw| sound. Children learn the strategy of thinking of *th* when they hear the |th| or the |th| sound and *wh* when they hear the |hw| sound.

To sum up the lesson, ask:

● What is the sound of *th* in *then*? |th|

● What is the sound of *th* in *teeth*? |th|

● What is the sound of *wh*? |hw|

Enrichment

Vocabulary: Multiple Meanings

Have children use a dictionary to look up *then*, *what*, and *while*. Discuss the different meanings.

Words Spelled with th or wh

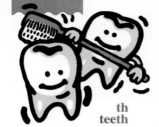

th
teeth

A. teeth

then

with

than

them

B. when

wheel

what

while

which

120

Read and Say

READ the sentences. **SAY** each word in dark print.

Basic Words

1.	teeth	I must brush my **teeth**.
2.	when	You know **when** to clap.
3.	then	Jess will leave by **then**.
4.	wheel	Turn the **wheel** fast!
5.	with	Can you play **with** me?
6.	what	I will get **what** I want.
7.	than	He is older **than** I am.
8.	while	Can I read for a **while**?
9.	them	Hit the ball to **them**.
10.	which	Pick **which** toy you want.

Think and Write

Each word is spelled with **th** or **wh**. The letters **th** spell two different sounds in these words. The letters **wh** spell one sound.

the **th** sounds → **th**en
→ tee**th**

the **wh** sound → **wh**en

A. Write **five** Basic Words spelled with **th**.

B. Write **five** Basic Words spelled with **wh**.

Order of answers for each category may vary.

Review	Challenge
11. white **12.** bath	**13.** mouth **14.** whistle

TEACHING OPTIONS

Meeting Individual Needs
Word Lists

You may want to assign Basic Words 1–5 and the Review Words to children who mis-spelled more than five words on the pretest. Assign the Challenge Words as appropri-ate. (You may want to have children write sentences, using the Challenge Words.)

Additional Spelling Words

Basic	Challenge	Words Often Misspelled
whine	thumb	pretty
both	whimper	very
math	smooth	
thaw	Thursday	
whip	thought	
	wheelbarrow	

Home/School Involvement
Take-Home Word List • Goal-Setting

Have children set goals for the week on Take-Home Word List 17.

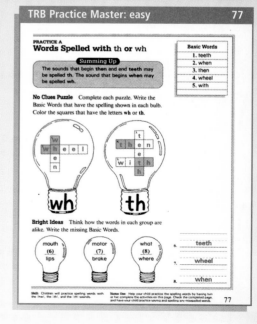

Independent Practice

 Spelling Strategy The sounds that begin **then** and end **teeth** may be spelled **th.** The sound that begins **when** may be spelled **wh.**

Order of answers for questions 3–4 and 5–6 may vary.

Phonics Write Basic Words to answer the questions.

1. Which word has the short **a** sound?
2. Which word rhymes with **smile**?
3–4. Which two words have the short **i** sound?
5–6. Which two **th** words have the short **e** sound?

Word Clues Write a Basic Word for each clue.

7. This question word has a **hat** in it.
8. This question word has a **hen** in it.

Word Pairs Write a Basic Word to finish the second sentence in each pair.

9. Some things are **square** like a **box.**
   Some things are **round** like a _____.
10. More than one **foot** is **feet.**
    More than one **tooth** is _____.

Phonics

1. than
2. while
3. with
4. which
5. then
6. them

Word Clues

7. what
8. when

Word Pairs

9. wheel
10. teeth

(121)

Objectives *Children will*

- practice spelling list words
- apply spelling strategies
- complete analogies with Basic Words
- identify Basic Words by using clues

 Day **2**

Daily Proofreading Practice

I turned the steering **wheil**. (*wheel*)
Julio is older **then** my brother. (*than*)

 Meeting Individual Needs
visual/oral/auditory

Extra Support Check Independent Practice to determine who needs extra support. Write the column headings *sh, ch, th,* and *wh* on the board. Say these words in random order: *sheep, chase, chop, ship, when, then, wheel, what, than,* and *while.* Ask children to listen carefully to each word. Have a volunteer repeat each word and tell you under which heading to write it.

 Applying Spelling Strategies
To Read New Words

- Read aloud: **The cake had a thick layer of chocolate.**
- Have children attempt to spell *thick* on their Have-a-Go charts.
- Elicit the following strategies as children try to spell *thick.*

I hear the |th| sound at the beginning of the word. I know that this sound is spelled *th.*

thick

I hear the |k| sound at the end of the word. This sound is probably spelled *ck* because it follows a short vowel sound.

This word has the short *i* sound. The short *i* sound is probably spelled *i.*

Objectives *Children will*

- alphabetize given words to the third letter to identify which word comes first in the dictionary
- review Basic and Review Words

Daily Proofreading Practice

The dentist will check my **teath**. (*teeth*)

Ali knows **wich** game to buy. (*which*)

Entry Words

1. white
_____

2. than
_____

3. play
_____

4. wheel
_____

5. baby
_____

6. side
_____

Rhyme Time

7. bath
_____

8. them
_____

9. wheel
_____

10. white
_____

11. while
_____

12. then
_____

(122)

Dictionary

Entry Words You know you use ABC order to find words in a dictionary. When entry words begin with the same two letters, you must look at the third letter of each word. See how these words are put in ABC order.

te**a**m   te**e**th   te**n**t

Practice Write the word in each group that would come first in the dictionary. Use ABC order.

1. why   white   whose
2. them   thin   than
3. play   plug   plow
4. wheel   who   while
5. bath   baby   ball
6. sink   silly   side

Review: Spelling Spree

Rhyme Time Finish the sentences. Write a Basic or Review Word to rhyme with the word in dark print.

7. I left a muddy **path** all the way to the _____.
8. I see bugs on a **stem**, and I don't like _____.
9. How would it **feel** to be round like a _____?
10. The tail of my **kite** is red, green, and _____.
11. This is the last **mile** I will run for a _____!
12. Now and _____ I count to **ten**.

How Are You Doing?

Write each spelling word in a sentence. Practice with a family member any words you spelled wrong.

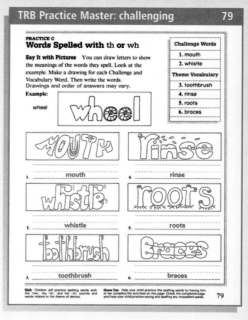

hen
when

TEACHING OPTIONS

Ongoing Assessment

The Consonant Digraph *wh*

Children often spell the *wh* digraph with a *w*. For example, *when* may spelled WEN and *which*, WICH. It's important to realize that in casual speech, most speakers—both children and adults—don't really pronounce the sound for *wh* any differently than they do the sound for *w*.

TRB Practice Master: challenging 79

PRACTICE C
Words Spelled with th or wh

Say It with Pictures You can draw letters to show the meanings of the words they spell. Look at the example. Make a drawing for each Challenge and Vocabulary Word. Then write the words. Drawings and order of answers may vary.

Example:

wheel

Challenge Words
1. mouth
2. whistle

Theme Vocabulary
3. toothbrush
4. rinse
5. roots
6. braces

1. mouth
2. whistle
3. toothbrush
4. rinse
5. roots
6. braces

79

Proofreading and Writing

Proofread for Spelling Proofread these jokes. Use proofreading marks to fix six spelling mistakes.

Example: Tell me a joke ~~wile~~ while we eat.

Marta: Do you know ~~wich~~ which teeth cry more ~~thann~~ than the others?

Nick: I know! Baby teeth do!

Carrie: Do you know ~~wat~~ what to do ~~wen~~ when your ~~teth~~ teeth fall out?

Jon: Of course! Stick them back in ~~whith~~ with white toothpaste!

Write a Label

Pretend you invented a new toothpaste. Draw a picture of your toothpaste tube and write a label for it. Tell how to use your toothpaste and why it is special. Try to use spelling words.

Proofreading Tip | **Read your paper aloud to a friend.**

(123)

Basic
1. teeth
2. when
3. then
4. wheel
5. with
6. what
7. than
8. while
9. them
10. which

Review
11. white
12. bath

Challenge
13. mouth
14. whistle

Proofreading Marks
∧ Add
⌐ Delete
≡ Make a capital letter
/ Make a small letter

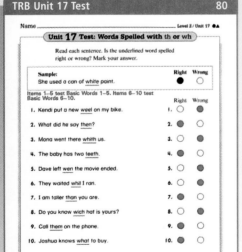

Meeting Individual Needs

Challenge Words Practice Ask children to write the Challenge Words and other *th* and *wh* words on graph paper in a crossword puzzle format. Have them write one letter in each square, "crossing" words where they have common letters.

Another Writing Idea Have children write a story about the Big Bad Wolf's, or another animal's, trip to the dentist. Suggest they use spelling words.

Objectives *Children will*
- proofread for spelling
- write and proofread an original composition

Daily Proofreading Practice
Do you know **wat** time it is? (*what*)
We played baseball **whith** Matt. (*with*)

Day 5 **Posttest**

Sentences 1–5 test the first five Basic Words. Sentences 6–10 test the next five Basic Words.

Basic Words
1. That is a small <u>wheel</u>.
2. We use our <u>teeth</u> to eat.
3. Can you go <u>with</u> me?
4. He will be home <u>when</u> I call.
5. I will play and <u>then</u> go to bed.
6. Tell <u>them</u> to pay.
7. She will draw <u>while</u> I look.
8. Can you see <u>which</u> way to go?
9. I do <u>what</u> I want.
10. I have no other game <u>than</u> that one.

Review Words
11. I will take a <u>bath</u>.
12. The ship has a <u>white</u> sail.

Challenge Words
13. My dog comes when I <u>whistle</u>.
14. I popped a grape into my <u>mouth</u>.

These pages can be used at any time during the study of this unit.

Objective *Children will*

■ build words with the consonant digraphs *th* and *wh*

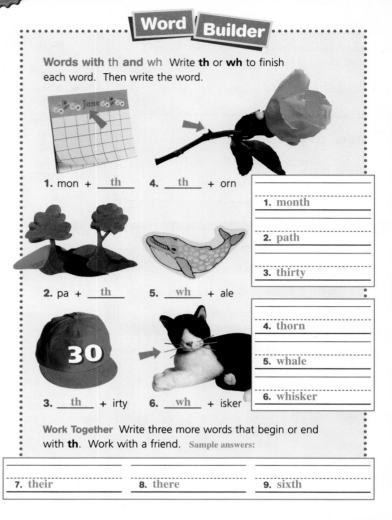

Phonics and Spelling

Word Builder

Words with th and wh Write **th** or **wh** to finish each word. Then write the word.

1. mon + ___th___

4. ___th___ + orn

2. pa + ___th___

5. ___wh___ + ale

30

3. ___th___ + irty

6. ___wh___ + isker

1. month
2. path
3. thirty

4. thorn
5. whale
6. whisker

Work Together Write three more words that begin or end with **th**. Work with a friend. **Sample answers:**

7. their   8. there   9. sixth

124

EXTENSION OPTIONS

Learning Center Activity

visual/kinesthetic

Big Mouth Poster On large paper, have children draw a big open mouth with teeth. In the center of the mouth, have them write "th and wh." Then ask them to print a *th* or a *wh* word on each tooth. To help children think of words, suggest they use a dictionary or think of rhyming words.

Big Mouth Poster

thin white
th   wh
bath thick both

More Words That End with -th

bath	health	cloth	both	tooth
path	wealth	moth		truth
			mouth	youth
birth	length	fourth	south	
earth	strength	north		

Vocabulary Enrichment

Careers

Dentist All the words in the box have something to do with dentists. Write those words to finish this list. Use your Spelling Dictionary.

Dr. Dan's Checklist

✔ Have Cara __(1)__ her mouth with water.

✔ Look at the __(2)__ of her teeth on an x-ray.

✔ Put __(3)__ on her teeth.

✔ Give her a __(4)__ when I am done.

Try This CHALLENGE

Riddle Time! Write a word from the box to answer each riddle.

5. What makes crooked things straight?
6. What do both trees and teeth have?
7. What kind of brush is not used for hair?
8. How do you get rid of soap or toothpaste?

Fact File

Did you know that President George Washington had to wear false teeth? In fact, he had four pairs! They were made of many things, such as gold and ivory.

Spelling Word Link

teeth

toothbrush
rinse
roots
braces

1. rinse

2. roots

3. braces

4. toothbrush

5. braces

6. roots

7. toothbrush

8. rinse

Day by Day Planner

Objectives *Children will*

- ◼ expand their vocabulary by using words related to dentists
- ◼ show their understanding of the vocabulary words by completing context activities

Vocabulary Checkup

Have children use the vocabulary words in sentences or match the words to the definitions below.

1. wires and bands used to straighten crooked teeth *braces*
2. to clear out or off with water *rinse*
3. a small brush used to clean the teeth *toothbrush*
4. parts of the teeth that are in the gums *roots*

Fact File

George Washington's Teeth

Popular belief has it that Washington's dentures were wooden. In fact, they were made with hippopotamus, walrus and cow teeth; elephant tusks, metals, and springs. The false teeth fit poorly, which may be one reason you never see Washington smile in portraits.

Integrating Literature

Easy	Average	Challenging

Arthur's Tooth
by Marc Brown
His first loose tooth causes Arthur the aardvark some worry.

Cousin Ruth's Tooth
by Amy McDonald
The entire Fister family helps Cousin Ruth look for her missing tooth.

Milo's Toothache
by Ida Luttrell
Milo the pig's toothache makes his friends panic.

What's It Like to Be a Dentist
by Judith Stamper
A dentist tells a patient about what she does and the equipment she uses.

Dr. DeSoto
by William Steig
A mouse dentist and his wife outwit a fox who plans to eat them.

When I See My Dentist
by Susan Kuklin
This photo essay describes a girl's trip to the dentist.

Review: Units 13–17

WORD LISTS

Spelling
Basic Words

Unit 13	Unit 16
train	sheep
mail	chase
play	chop
pay	each
hay	dish
rain	ship

Unit 14	Unit 17
clean	teeth
please	then
green	wheel
be	than
tree	while
read	them

Unit 15

dog
call
saw
all
draw
log

Elephant Words
Units 13–17

they	people
great	catch
the	sure

The Review Unit

Word Lists

Half of the Basic Words from Units 13–17 are reviewed in this Review Unit. The remaining Basic Words from Units 13–17 are reviewed in the Extra Practice section of the Student's Handbook.

All of the Elephant Words are practiced in both the Review Unit and the Extra Practice section.

Day 1 *page 126*

Objectives *Children will*
- take the pretest
- review spelling patterns for the |ā| sound
- review spelling patterns for the |ē| sound

Planning Checklist
- ☐ Daily Proofreading Practice (TE)
- ☐ Extra Support, pages 97, 103 (TE)
- ☐ Extra Practice, page 247
- ☐ Practice Masters, pages 61, 62, 65, 66 (TRB)

Day 2 *page 127*

Objectives *Children will*
- review spelling patterns for the |ô| sound
- review the spelling of words with the |sh| or |ch| sound

Planning Checklist
- ☐ Daily Proofreading Practice (TE)
- ☐ Extra Support, pages 109, 115 (TE)
- ☐ Extra Practice, page 248
- ☐ Practice Masters, pages 69, 70, 73, 74 (TRB)

Assessment

Pretest
1. It is fun to get <u>mail</u>.
2. I will help <u>pay</u>.
3. Fix my clock, <u>please</u>.
4. A train will <u>be</u> late.
5. Did you <u>call</u> me?
6. I cut a big <u>log</u>.
7. I must <u>chop</u> it up.
8. A sail is on his <u>ship</u>.
9. I will wave <u>while</u> you go.
10. Please read to <u>them</u>.

Day 3 *page 128* **Day 4** *page 129* **Day 5** *page 129*

Objectives *Children will*
- review the spelling of words with the |*th*|, the |th|, or the |hw| sound
- review the Elephant Words

Planning Checklist
- ☐ Daily Proofreading Practice (TE)
- ☐ Extra Support, page 121 (TE)
- ☐ Extra Practice, page 249
- ☐ Practice Masters, pages 77, 78 (TRB)

Objective *Children will*
- analyze the spelling and meaning relationship of words in the *play* family

Planning Checklist
- ☐ Spelling-Meaning Strategy

Objective *Children will*
- take the posttest

Assessment
- ☐ **Posttest** (TE) *See Day 5*
- ☐ Scoring Rubric
- ☐ Unit 18 Review Tests A–B (TRB)

Additional Resources

Teacher's Resource Book
Practice Masters, pages 61–63, 65–67, 69–71, 73–75, 77–79
Multiple-Choice Tests, pages 86–87
Bulletin Board, page 81
Spelling Newsletters: English and Spanish, pages 82–83
Spelling Game, pages 84–85
Midyear Test, pages 89–90

Practice Plus
Take-Home Word List 18

Spelling Transparencies
Spelling Word List 18
Daily Proofreading Practice, Unit 18
Spelling-Meaning Strategy
Multiple-Choice Test

Teacher's Resource Disk
Macintosh® or Windows® software. Houghton Mifflin

Spelling CD-ROM
Macintosh® or Windows® software. Houghton Mifflin

Internet
http://www.eduplace.com

Meeting Individual Needs

You may wish to create your own pretest, using the words that children missed most often in the last five units. Children can check their own work, or a partner's, by looking up the words in the previous units' word lists or in their Spelling Dictionary.

In each Review lesson, the Basic Words are selected from both halves of the unit word list to accommodate individual needs. In Units 13–17, the top row of words is from Basic Words 1–5 and the bottom row from Basic Words 6–10.

Other Activities for Any Day

- Literature and Writing, pages 130–131
- Spelling Game
  Teacher's Resource Book, pages 84–85
- Bulletin Board
  Teacher's Resource Book, page 81
- Take-Home Word List 18
  Practice Plus

Objectives *Children will*

■ take the pretest

■ review spelling patterns for the |ā| sound

■ review spelling patterns for the |ē| sound

Daily Proofreading Practice

That **trane** has fifty cars! (*train*)

I **rede** books with my brother. (*read*)

Meeting Individual Needs

Additional Resources

Unit 13

Extra Support page 97 (TE)

Extra Practice page 247

Practice Masters pages 61–62 (TRB)

Unit 14

Extra Support page 103 (TE)

Extra Practice page 247

Practice Masters pages 65–66 (TRB)

---

18 Review: Units 13–17

Unit 13   More Long a Spellings   pages 96–101

ā
train

train	mail	play
pay	hay	rain

1. train

2. mail

3. play

4. rain

5. hay

6. pay

7. green

8. clean

9. tree

10. read

11. please

12. be

Spelling Strategy   The long **a** sound may be spelled **ay** or **ai**.

Change the letters in dark print. Write spelling words.

1. trai**l**   **2.** mai**d**   **3.** **gr**ay   **4.** rai**l**

Write the missing spelling words.

5. The _____ in our field is high.

6. We will _____ someone to cut it.

Unit 14   More Long e Spellings   pages 102–107

ē
clean

clean	please	green
be	tree	read

Spelling Strategy   The long **e** sound may be spelled **e, ee,** or **ea**.

Write the spelling word that goes with each word.

7. color   **8.** wash   **9.** branch   **10.** story

Write the missing spelling words.

11. Will you _____ help me wash the dishes?

12. Then we will _____ done with our work.

126

EXTENSION OPTIONS

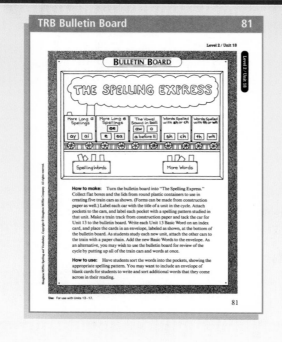

TRB Bulletin Board   81

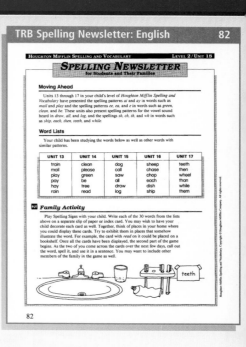

TRB Spelling Newsletter: English   82

Unit 15 The Vowel Sound in ball pages 108–113

dog	call	saw
all	draw	log

a ball

Spelling Strategy The vowel sound in **dog** may be spelled **o**, **aw**, or **a** before **ll**.

Write the missing spelling words.

Gram and Papa ___(13)___ us in for lunch. We ___(14)___ wash quickly. I bring in a ___(15)___ for the fire.

Write the spelling word that goes with each place.

16. tool shed   **17.** art class   **18.** pet shop

Unit 16 Words with sh or ch pages 114–119

sheep	chase	chop
each	dish	ship

sh
sheep

Spelling Strategy
the **sh** sound → **sheep**, **dish**
the **ch** sound → **chop**, **each**

Write the spelling word that rhymes with each word.

19. peach   **21.** trip
20. stop   **22.** deep

Write the missing spelling words.

23. One day the cat ate from the dog's _____.
24. Then the dog began to _____ the cat!

---

13. call

14. all

15. log

16. saw

17. draw

18. dog

19. each

20. chop

21. ship

22. sheep

23. dish

24. chase

127

Objectives *Children will*
- review spelling patterns for the |ô| sound
- review the spelling of words with the |sh| or |ch| sound

Daily Proofreading Practice
My rabbit comes when I **cawl**. (*call*)
The **sheap** rested on the hill. (*sheep*)

Meeting Individual Needs

Additional Resources

Unit 15
Extra Support page 109 (TE)
Extra Practice page 248
Practice Masters pages 69–70 (TRB)
Unit 16
Extra Support page 115 (TE)
Extra Practice page 248
Practice Masters pages 73–74 (TRB)

TRB Spelling Newsletter: Spanish 83

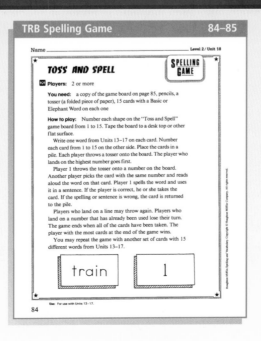

HOUGHTON MIFFLIN SPELLING AND VOCABULARY   LEVEL 2/UNIT 18

Boletín de noticias de ortografía
para estudiantes y para sus familias

Para continuar

Su hijo o hija ha estado estudiando las siguientes palabras y otras palabras que siguen patrones similares en las Unidades 13 a 17 del libro *Houghton Mifflin Spelling and Vocabulary*.

UNIDAD 13	UNIDAD 14	UNIDAD 15	UNIDAD 16	UNIDAD 17
train	clean	dog	sheep	teeth
mail	please	call	chase	then
play	green	saw	chop	wheel
pay	be	all	each	than
hay	tree	draw	dish	while
rain	read	log	ship	them

Actividad para la familia

Jueguen con anuncios para deletrear con su hijo o hija. Escriban cada una de las 30 palabras de las listas de arriba en un pedazo de papel o en una tarjeta aparte. Si lo desean, hagan que su hijo o hija decore las tarjetas. Piensen juntos en lugares de su casa donde puedan poner las tarjetas a la vista. Traten de ponerlas en lugares que de alguna forma ilustren la palabra. Por ejemplo, la tarjeta que tiene la palabra *read* puede colocarse en un estante de libros. Una vez que se hayan colocado a la vista todas las tarjetas, comienza la segunda parte del juego. Cuando ustedes encuentren las palabras durante los días siguientes, digan la palabra en voz alta, deletréenla y úsenla en una oración. Si lo desean, incluyan a otros miembros de la familia en el juego.

83

TRB Spelling Game 84–85

Name _____   Level 2/Unit 18

TOSS AND SPELL   SPELLING GAME

Players: 2 or more

You need: a copy of the game board on page 85, pencils, a tosser (a folded piece of paper), 15 cards with a Basic or Elephant Word on each one

How to play: Number each shape on the "Toss and Spell" game board from 1 to 15. Tape the board to a desk top or other flat surface.

Write one word from Units 13–17 on each card. Number each card from 1 to 15 on the other side. Place the cards in a pile. Each player throws a tosser onto the board. The player who lands on the highest number goes first.

Player 1 throws the tosser onto a number on the board. Another player picks the card with the same number and reads aloud the word on that card. Player 1 spells the word and uses it in a sentence. If the player is correct, he or she takes the card. If the spelling or sentence is wrong, the card is returned to the pile.

Players who land on a line may throw again. Players who land on a number that has already been used lose their turn. The game ends when all of the cards have been taken. The player with the most cards at the end of the game wins.

You may repeat the game with another set of cards with 15 different words from Units 13–17.

train   1

84   **Use:** For use with Units 13–17.

Objectives *Children will*

- review the spelling of words with the |*th*|, the |th|, or the |hw| sound
- review the Elephant Words

Daily Proofreading Practice

Mom read **wile** Greg painted. (*while*)

Lin and I play **kach** in the yard. (*catch*)

Meeting Individual Needs

Additional Resources

Unit 17

Extra Support page 121 (TE)

Extra Practice page 249

Practice Masters pages 77–78 (TRB)

Reviewing Elephant Words

Extra Practice page 249

UNIT
18

_____
25. than

_____
26. them

_____
27. teeth

_____
28. then

_____
29. wheel

_____
30. while

_____
31. great

_____
32. the

_____
33. people

_____
34. catch

_____
35. they

_____
36. sure

128

Unit 17   Words with th or wh   pages 120–125

| teeth | then | wheel |
| than | while | them |

th
teeth

Spelling Strategy   the **th** sounds → **t**ee**th**, **th**en
the **wh** sound → **wh**eel

Change the letters in dark print. Write spelling words.

25. **pl**an   26. **st**em

Write the missing spelling words.

27. brush your _____   29. steering _____

28. now and _____   30. once in a _____

Elephant Words   Units 13–17   pages 96–125

S U R E

| they | great | the |
| people | catch | sure |

Spelling Strategy   Elephant Words have unusual spellings. Check them carefully when you write them.

Write the missing spelling words.

We had a __(31)__ time at __(32)__ ball game.
Many __(33)__ came to see Mike Magoo __(34)__ balls.
One player hit the balls so hard, __(35)__ almost knocked
Mike down! I am __(36)__ Mike is the best player.

EXTENSION **OPTIONS**

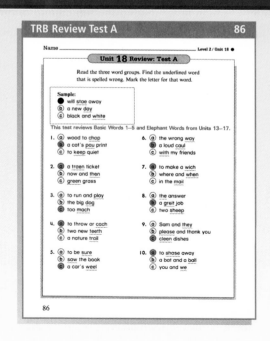

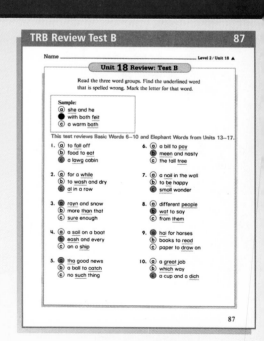

UNIT
18

Spelling-Meaning Strategy

Word Families

Look at this word family. Remember that words in the same family are alike in spelling and meaning.

play
player
played
playful

Kim loves to **play** tennis.

She is a good **player**.

She **played** a game on Monday.

Her **playful** dog chased the balls.

Think How are the words in this family alike in meaning? How are they alike in spelling?

Apply and Extend

Write a word from the play family in each sentence.
1. We watched the seals _____.
2. One _____ seal had a ball.
3. He _____ with it in the water.
4. He looked like a soccer _____!

With a partner, think of words in these families. Make a list for each family. See TE margin.

 clean   sail   rain

Check the Word Families list that begins on page 272. Did you miss any words? Add them to your lists.

1. play

2. playful

3. played

4. player

129

Day 4

Objective *Children will*
- analyze the spelling and meaning relationship of words in the *play* family

Answers to *Think* Questions
- They all share the meaning of "to have fun or to take part in a game of."
- They all contain the word *play*.

Day 5   **Posttest**

The Posttest tests twenty of the Basic Words reviewed in this unit. Sentences 1–10 test words selected from Basic Words 1–5 in Units 13–17. The Elephant Words sentences test all six words reviewed in this unit.

Basic Words
1. Pick a pot, <u>please</u>.
2. My dress is <u>green</u>.
3. I want to <u>play</u>.
4. Will a frog <u>chase</u> a bug?
5. A bus lost a <u>wheel</u>.
6. I like to ride on a <u>train</u>.
7. I will <u>call</u> my pet.
8. Does a fish have <u>teeth</u>?
9. I have a brave <u>dog</u>.
10. Do <u>sheep</u> like grass?
11. I will use his <u>dish</u>.
12. A nest is in a <u>tree</u>.
13. I can <u>draw</u> a bus.
14. We got wet in the <u>rain</u>.
15. Help <u>them</u> fix my bed.
16. Sit on a <u>log</u>.
17. My trip will <u>be</u> fun.
18. I cut some <u>hay</u>.
19. He will play <u>while</u> I swim.
20. Do you see a <u>ship</u>?

Elephant Words
21. Did <u>they</u> see a man?
22. I like <u>the</u> clock.
23. It is a <u>great</u> game.
24. Some <u>people</u> like frogs.
25. I am <u>sure</u> I will win.
26. We will <u>catch</u> fish.

Writing Model:
Story

Day by Day Planner

Objectives *Children will*

■ read a literature excerpt modeling a story

■ analyze the model to identify story elements and to predict an outcome

Warm-Up

Qualities of a Good Story

Ask children to think of favorite stories they have read or heard. Use the following prompts to discuss features of these stories and to review important story elements:

• What is the title of a favorite story? How does the title make you want to find out more?

• How does the story begin? How did the author make you want to keep reading or listening?

• What happens in the beginning, the middle, and the end of the story?

• What problem do the characters have? How do they solve the problem?

Answers to *Think and Discuss*

1. The story is about Yukio, who finds a whale stuck between some rocks.

2. Yukio must find a way to get the whale back into the sea.

3. This is the beginning of the story because it introduces the main character and explains the problem he must solve.

4. Answers will vary.

UNIT 18

Story

Literature and Writing

from

A Thousand Pails of Water

by Ronald Roy

The story is about a little boy who lived in Japan. Who is the boy in this story, and what is the story about?

Yukio lived in a village where people fished to make their living.

One day Yukio walked down to the sea. As he walked by the edge of the water, he saw a whale. The whale was stuck between some rocks.

Yukio knew that the whale would not live long out of the sea.

"I will help you," he said to the whale. But how? The whale was huge.

Think and Discuss

See TE margin.

1 Who is this story about? What does he find by the water?

2 What problem must Yukio solve?

3 Do you think this is the **beginning**, the **middle**, or the **end** of the story? Why?

4 What do you think will happen in the rest of this story?

130

EXTENSION OPTIONS

Integrating Literature *Story*

Easy	Average	Challenging
The Golden Goose *by Uri Shulevitz* A simpleton's kindness wins him a princess bride.	**Strega Nona: Her Story** *by Tomie dePaola* Strega Nona relates how she learned to cast spells and cure maladies.	**The Bunyans** *by Audrey Wood* The gigantic Bunyan family creates some of America's natural wonders.
Young Mouse and Elephant *by Pamela J. Farris* A mouse sets off to prove he is the strongest animal on the plain.	**Tops and Bottoms** *by Janet Stevens* Hare reverses his bad luck by striking a clever bargain with Bear.	**Kongi and Potgi** *by Oki S. Han* A Korean retelling of the Cinderella story.

The Writing Process
Story

What kinds of stories do you like? Write a story you would like to read. Follow the guidelines. Use the Writing Process.

1 Prewriting
- Make a story map. Draw or write about what happens in the beginning, the middle, and the end of your story.

2 Draft
- Write two beginnings. Which one do you like better?

3 Revise
- Add details that tell what your characters say and do.
- Remember to use your Thesaurus to find exact words.
- Read your story to a friend. Make changes.

4 Proofread
- Did you spell each word correctly?
- Did you use words that compare correctly?

5 Publish
- Copy your story neatly.
- Add a title.
- Read your story aloud to classmates.

Guidelines for Writing a Story

✓ Use details that will make your characters interesting.
✓ The story should have a beginning, a middle, and an end.
✓ Write a title that will make the reader want to find out more.

Composition Words
they
people
saw
wish
when
which

131

Objective *Children will*
- follow the Writing Process to write a story, using the criteria given in the guidelines

Additional Resource

To help children generate and explore topics for their story, have them use the Prewriting Ideas in the *Teacher's Resource Book*, page 88.

Scoring Rubric

Evaluating Writing

The scoring rubric is based on the guidelines on the student book page. Mechanics and usage errors are also considered in general. Explain to children that the guidelines will be used to evaluate their papers.

TRB Prewriting Ideas   88

Name _____ Level 2 / Unit 18

Prewriting Ideas: Story

Choosing A Topic Here is a list of ideas that one student made for writing a story. What story ideas of your own do these make you think of?

On the lines below **My Three Ideas**, write three ideas that you think would make a good make-believe story. Which idea do you like the best? Which one can you tell enough about? Which one will other people enjoy? Circle the topic that you would like to write about.

Ideas for Writing

The Dinosaur That Needed Help | The Magic Whistle
The Runaway Bicycle | The Secret Subway

My Three Ideas

1. _____

2. _____

3. _____

Exploring Your Topic You can use a puzzle map to help you plan your story. Copy the map onto another sheet of paper. Make it large enough to write on. In each piece, write what will happen in the **beginning**, the **middle**, and the **end** of your story.

| Beginning | Middle | End |

Use: For use with Step 1: Prewriting on page 131.

88

Scoring Rubric

Story

Score 4

While meeting the criteria for a story, the work also shows an imaginative approach. There is a creative plot, an interesting main character, and a strong beginning, middle, and end.

Score 2

The work is in the form of a story, but it may need more details. The story follows a sequence, but it may need a stronger beginning or end.

Score 3

The story follows a sequence. The writer has provided sufficient detail to develop the character and the plot.

Score 1

The work is not in the form of a story, or it meets the story criteria minimally. Events have no clear sequence and are confusing. The writer used little or no detail.

Words That End with *nd, ng,* or *nk*

WORD LISTS

Spelling

Basic

1. king
2. thank
3. hand
4. sing
5. and
6. think
7. bring
8. long
9. end
10. thing

Review

11. an
12. men

Challenge

13. grand
14. young

Vocabulary

Social Studies: Castles and Kings

throne
castle
page
feast

Introducing the Lesson

Read Aloud

Write the Basic Words on the board.

May I Bring a Friend?

Did you ever **think** about what it would be like to have lunch with a **king**? *May I Bring a Friend?* is a story about a boy who visits a **king and** queen every day for a week. He chooses a different friend to **bring** with him each day. The **king and** queen love to **sing and** play with their guests, but there is one unusual **thing** about each of the boy's friends. One friend has an extremely **long** neck, **and** another likes to hang by one **hand** from the chandelier. One friend is almost too large to fit in the palace! At the **end** of the story, the friends **thank** the **king and** queen and invite them to visit their homes.

Responding Ask children what two special people the boy visited. *(a king and a queen)* Ask children which spelling word means "a man who rules a country." *(king)* Have them name three other spelling words that rhyme with it. *(sing, bring, thing)*

Day 1 *page 132*

Objectives *Children will*

- take the pretest
- pronounce the list words
- learn about the spelling principle
- sort words by their final consonant sounds

Planning Checklist

☑ Pretest (TE)

☑ Spelling principle/word list

☐ Review/Challenge Words

☐ Teaching the Principle (TE)

☐ Enrichment (TE)

☐ Additional Spelling Words (TE)

Assessment

Pretest

1. A king rules a country.
2. Will you thank her today?
3. Hold my hand.
4. I like to hear you sing.
5. He has a dog and a cat.
6. I think you are nice.
7. Did you bring the ball?
8. Swans have long necks.
9. It is the end of the day.
10. What is that thing?

Day 2 *page 133*

Objectives *Children will*

- practice spelling list words
- apply spelling strategies
- classify Basic Words into groups
- identify antonyms

Planning Checklist

☑ Spelling Strategy

☑ Independent Practice

☐ Daily Proofreading Practice (TE)

☐ Informal Assessment (TE)

☐ Extra Support (TE)

☐ Applying Spelling Strategies (TE)

Research Notes The errors young children make in their invented spellings reflect how they are categorizing sounds— these errors usually are not auditory discrimination problems. *See the Bibliography on page xv.*

 Day 3 *page 134*   **Day 4** *page 135*   **Day 5** *page 135*

Objective *Children will*

- review Basic and Review Words

Planning Checklist

- ☐ Review: Spelling Spree
- ☐ How Are You Doing?
- ☐ Daily Proofreading Practice (TE)
- ☐ Ongoing Assessment (TE)

Objectives *Children will*

- proofread for spelling and capital letters
- write and proofread an original composition

Planning Checklist

- ☐ Proofread: Spelling and Capital Letters
- ☐ Write a Weekly Plan
- ☐ Daily Proofreading Practice (TE)
- ☐ Challenge Words Practice (TE)
- ☐ Another Writing Idea (TE)

Objective *Children will*

- take the posttest

Assessment

- ☐ **Posttest** (TE) *See Day 5*
- ☐ Unit 19 Test

 Additional Resources

Teacher's Resource Book
Practice Masters, pages 91–93
Unit Test, page 94
Bulletin Board, page 111

Practice Plus
Take-Home Word List 19
Games

Spelling Transparencies
Spelling Word List 19
Daily Proofreading Practice, Unit 19
Graphic Organizers

Teacher's Resource Disk
Macintosh® or Windows® software. Houghton Mifflin

Spelling CD-ROM
Macintosh® or Windows® software. Houghton Mifflin

Internet
http://www.eduplace.com

Phonics Practice
Houghton Mifflin Phonics
The Listening Corner
Phonics Home Connection

Meeting Individual Needs
Students Acquiring English

Spanish The *ng* sounds may be difficult for children to hear. **Activity** Write *wing, king, sing,* and *long* on the board. Say each word and have children repeat it. Ask children which letters spell the |ng| sounds. Then erase the *ng* endings and have volunteers go to the board, complete the words, and say them.

Asian Asians may have trouble pronouncing the final *nd* or *ng*. **Activity** Write the Basic Words on the board. Say each word, emphasizing the final sounds. Have children repeat. Say *fin, leg,* and *king.* Ask which ends with the same sounds as *wing.* Repeat with *log, lone, long* and *brain, bring, brag.*

Other Activities for Any Day

- Bonus activities from pages 136–137
- Practice Masters (easy, average, challenging)
  Teacher's Resource Book, pages 91–93
- Take-Home Word List 19
  Practice Plus

Day 1

Objectives *Children will*
- take the pretest
- pronounce the list words
- learn about the spelling principle
- sort words by their final consonant sounds

Teaching the Principle

This lesson teaches the spellings of the final consonant pairs *nd, ng,* and *nk.* Children learn the strategy of thinking of these spelling patterns when they hear the |nd|, the |ng|, and the |nk| sounds.

To sum up the lesson, ask:

- Which words are spelled with *-and* or *-end*? *(hand, and, end)*

- Which words are spelled with *-ing* or *-ong*? *(king, sing, bring, thing, long)*

- Which words are spelled with *-ank* or *-ink*? *(thank, think)*

Enrichment

Vocabulary: Multiple Meanings
Have children use a dictionary to look up *hand, long,* and *end.* Discuss the different meanings.

ng
king

A. hand

_____

and

_____

end

B. king

_____

sing

_____

bring

_____

long

_____

thing

C. thank

_____

think

132

Read and Say

READ the sentences. **SAY** each word in dark print.

Basic Words

1.	king	*king*	A **king** rules a country.
2.	thank	*thank*	Will you **thank** her today?
3.	hand	*hand*	Hold my **hand**.
4.	sing	*sing*	I like to hear you **sing**.
5.	and	*and*	He has a dog **and** a cat.
6.	think	*think*	I **think** you are nice.
7.	bring	*bring*	Did you **bring** the ball?
8.	long	*long*	Swans have **long** necks.
9.	end	*end*	It is the **end** of the day.
10.	thing	*thing*	What is that **thing**?

Think and Write

Each word ends with the consonants **nd**, **ng**, or **nk**. In words that end with the consonant cluster **nd**, you hear the sounds of **n** and **d**. In words that end with **ng** or **nk**, you may not hear the **n** sound.

nd → ha**nd**
ng → ki**ng**
nk → tha**nk**

A. Write **three** Basic Words that end with **nd**.
B. Write **five** Basic Words that end with **ng**.
C. Write **two** Basic Words that end with **nk**.

Order of answers for each category may vary.

Review		**Challenge**	
11. an	12. men	13. grand	14. young

TEACHING OPTIONS

Meeting Individual Needs
Word Lists

You may want to assign Basic Words 1–5 and the Review Words to children who misspelled more than five words on the pretest. Assign the Challenge Words as appropriate. (You may want to have children write sentences, using the Challenge Words.)

Additional Spelling Words

Basic	**Challenge**	**Words Often Misspelled**
wink	skunk	for
bang	wrong	on
song	friend	
send	sandwich	
bend	belong	
	second	

Home/School Involvement
Take-Home Word List • Goal-Setting

Have children set goals for the week on Take-Home Word List 19.

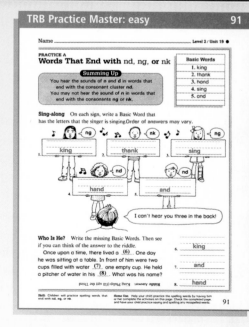

Name _____ Level 2 / Unit 19

PRACTICE A
Words That End with nd, ng, **or** nk

Basic Words
1. king
2. thank
3. hand
4. sing
5. and

Summing Up
You hear the sounds of n and d in words that end with the consonant cluster nd. You may not hear the sound of n in words that end with the consonants ng or nk.

Sing-along On each sign, write a Basic Word that has the letters that the singer is singing. Order of answers may vary.

1. king
2. thank
3. sing
4. hand
5. and

I can't hear you three in the back!

Who Is He? Write the missing Basic Words. Then see if you can think of the answer to the riddle.

Once upon a time, there lived a (6) ___. One day he was sitting at a table. In front of him were two cups filled with water (7) ___ one empty cup. He held a pitcher of water in his (8) ___. What was his name?

6. king
7. and
8. hand

Skill: Children will practice spelling words that end with nd, ng, or nk.

Home Use: Help your child practice the spelling words by having him or her complete the activities on this page. Check the completed page and have your child practice saying and spelling any misspelled words.

Riddle Answer: King Philip (fill up) the Third

91

Independent Practice

 Spelling Strategy You hear the sounds of **n** and **d** in words that end with the consonant cluster **nd**. You may not hear the sounds of **n** in words that end with the consonants **ng** or **nk**.

Order of answers for question 2–4 may vary.

Phonics Write Basic Words to answer the questions.

1. Which word begins with a vowel sound and rhymes with **stand**?

2–4. Which three words begin with the same sound?

Word Groups Think how the words in each group are alike. Write the missing Basic Words.

5. shoulder, arm, _____
6. take, carry, _____
7. prince, queen, _____
8. hum, whistle, _____

Word Meaning Write the Basic Word that means the opposite of each word in dark print.

9. We want to hear the **beginning** of the story.
10. It is a **short** fairy tale about a wise princess.

Phonics

1. and

2. thank

3. think

4. thing

Word Groups

5. hand

6. bring

7. king

8. sing

Word Meaning

9. end

10. long

(133)

Day 2 **Objectives** *Children will*

- practice spelling list words
- apply spelling strategies
- classify Basic Words into groups
- identify antonyms

Daily Proofreading Practice
I **thik** it will snow today. (*think*)
The **ind** of the story was funny. (*end*)

Meeting Individual Needs
visual/oral/auditory

Extra Support Check Independent Practice to determine who needs extra support. Write *hand, sing,* and *thank* on the board. Underline the letters *nd, ng,* and *nk*. Point to and say each word. Say *king*. Ask if *king* ends with the same ending sounds as *hand, sing,* or *thank*. Write *king* under *sing* and underline *ng*. Repeat with *think, bring, and, long, end,* and *thing*.

Applying Spelling Strategies
To Spell New Words

- Read aloud: **A chipmunk scurried across the trail.**
- Have children attempt to spell *chipmunk* on their Have-a-Go charts.

- Elicit the following strategies as children try to spell *chipmunk*.

> I hear the word *chip* at the beginning of this longer word. I know that the |ch| sound is spelled *ch*. *Chip* has the short *i* vowel sound followed by *p*.

> Next, I hear the sound for *m* that I hear at the beginning of *monster*.

chipmunk

> This part of the word has the short *u* sound. The short *u* sound is probably spelled *u*.

> I hear the same |nk| sound that I hear at the end of *thank*. I know that the |nk| sound is spelled *nk*.

Day 3

Objective *Children will*
■ review Basic and Review Words

Daily Proofreading Practice

What is that **thang** on your hat?
(*thing*)
We **sig** songs while we work. (*sing*)

UNIT
19

Fill–In Fun

1. men

2. long

3. king

4. end

5. hand

6. sing

Word Search

7. bring

8. think

9. an

10. thank

11. and

12. thing

(134)

Review: Spelling Spree

Fill-In Fun Write the missing Basic or Review Words.
1. _____ and women
2. short and _____
3. _____ and queen
4. beginning and _____
5. _____ and foot
6. _____ and dance

Word Search Write the Basic or Review Word that is hidden in each sentence. Each hidden word is made with letters from the end of one word and the beginning of the next.

Example: You must co**me n**ow! **men**

7. We ru**b r**ings to make them shine.
8. Where are the three **thin k**nights?
9. They built **a n**ew stone tower.
10. Do the queen's birds fly higher **than k**ites?
11. The dragon be**ga n** dreaming of caves.
12. Prince Hal has **thin g**reen gloves.

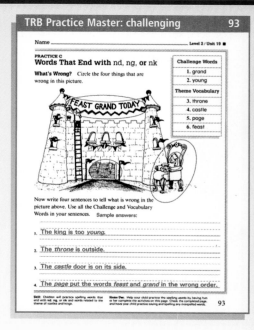

✓ How Are You Doing?
Write your spelling words in ABC order. Practice with a partner any words you spelled wrong.

TEACHING OPTIONS

Ongoing Assessment

The Letter *n* in Consonant Pairs

At this point in the year, some second grade children will still omit *n* before other consonants. For example, they may write HAD for *hand*, THAK for *thank*, and THIG for *thing*.

This does not mean that they cannot hear the |n| sound; rather, they categorize it as part of the vowel sound. With continued exposure, they will begin to include *n* in this context.

TRB Practice Master: challenging 93

Name _____ Level 2 / Unit 19 ■

PRACTICE C
Words That End with nd, ng, or nk

What's Wrong? Circle the four things that are wrong in this picture.

Challenge Words
1. grand
2. young
Theme Vocabulary
3. throne
4. castle
5. page
6. feast

FEAST GRAND TODAY

Now write four sentences to tell what is wrong in the picture above. Use all the Challenge and Vocabulary Words in your sentences. Sample answers:

1. The king is too *young*.
2. The *throne* is outside.
3. The *castle* door is on its side.
4. The *page* put the words *feast* and *grand* in the wrong order.

Skill: Children will practice spelling words that end with nd, ng, or nk and words related to the theme of castles and kings.

Home Use: Help your child practice the spelling words by having him or her complete the activities on this page. Check the completed page, and have your child practice saying and spelling any misspelled words.

93

Proofreading and Writing

Proofread: Spelling and Capital Letters
Always begin the names of the days of the week with capital letters.

Monday   Wednesday   Sunday

Proofread this sign. Use proofreading marks to fix four spelling mistakes and two missing capital letters.

Example: On friday the queen will ~~thenk~~ us.

thank

The king returns on wednesday night.

men   and
All ~~min an~~ women will meet him on

end
thursday morning. Come to the ~~ind~~ of

the great hall to sing a song for him. If

bring
you play an instrument, ~~birng~~ it with you.

Basic

1. king
2. thank
3. hand
4. sing
5. and
6. think
7. bring
8. long
9. end
10. thing

Review

11. an
12. men

Challenge

13. grand
14. young

Proofreading Marks

∧ Add
⌐ Delete
≡ Make a capital letter
/ Make a small letter

Write a Weekly Plan

Pretend you are a king or a queen. Make a plan for the week. Tell one or two things you would do on each day. Try to use spelling words.

Queen's Plan

Proofreading Tip
Check that you began the names of the days of the week with capital letters.

(135)

Day 4

Objectives *Children will*
- proofread for spelling and capital letters
- write and proofread an original composition

Daily Proofreading Practice

He wears a ring on one **hend**. (*hand*)
Please **thanc** Yoko for her help. (*thank*)

Day 5 **Posttest**

Sentences 1–5 test the first five Basic Words. Sentences 6–10 test the next five Basic Words.

Basic Words
1. Take my <u>hand</u> as we go.
2. I like to <u>sing</u>.
3. I will <u>thank</u> her.
4. You <u>and</u> I can play ball.
5. The man is a <u>king</u>.
6. Do not let go of the <u>end</u>.
7. Give me that <u>thing</u>.
8. You can <u>bring</u> a top.
9. It is a <u>long</u> ride.
10. Do you <u>think</u> you can go?

Review Words
11. The <u>men</u> play ball.
12. She had <u>an</u> egg.

Challenge Words
13. The queen lives in a <u>grand</u> palace.
14. The boy is too <u>young</u> to be king.

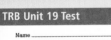

TRB Unit 19 Test   94

Name _____   Level 2 / Unit 19 ●▲

Unit 19 Test: Words That End with nd, ng, or nk

Each item below gives three spellings of a word. Choose the correct spelling. Mark the letter for that word.

Sample:			ANSWERS
a. send	b. sen	c. seng	● ⓑ ⓒ

Items 1–5 test Basic Words 1–5. Items 6–10 test Basic Words 6–10.

1. a. onk	b. and	c. ong	1. ⓐ ● ⓒ
2. a. thangk	b. thang	c. thank	2. ⓐ ⓑ ●
3. a. king	b. kig	c. kingg	3. ● ⓑ ⓒ
4. a. sig	b. sing	c. sind	4. ⓐ ● ⓒ
5. a. hend	b. hant	c. hand	5. ⓐ ⓑ ●
6. a. think	b. thind	c. thinc	6. ● ⓑ ⓒ
7. a. lonk	b. logn	c. long	7. ⓐ ⓑ ●
8. a. enk	b. end	c. eng	8. ⓐ ● ⓒ
9. a. birng	b. brind	c. bring	9. ⓐ ⓑ ●
10. a. thing	b. thind	c. thign	10. ● ⓑ ⓒ

94

Meeting Individual Needs

Challenge Words Practice
Ask children to use letter cards to build the Challenge Words on a tabletop. Have them add other *nd, ng,* or *nk* words in a crossword puzzle format, joining words where they have common letters.

Another Writing Idea Have children write a fairy tale about a king or queen who rules over a very unusual kingdom. Encourage them to use spelling words.

These pages can be used at any time during the study of this unit.

Objectives *Children will*

▨ build words with the phonograms *-and* and *-ing*

▨ write rhyming words to complete a poem

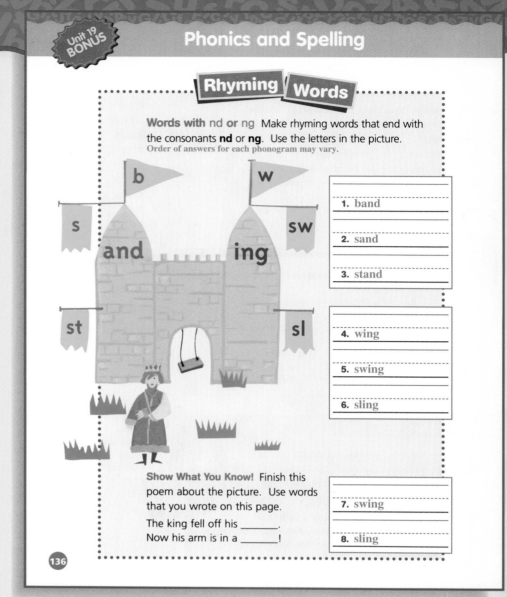

Rhyming Words

Words with nd or ng Make rhyming words that end with the consonants **nd** or **ng**. Use the letters in the picture.
Order of answers for each phonogram may vary.

b

w

s

sw

and   **ing**

st

sl

1. band
2. sand
3. stand

4. wing
5. swing
6. sling

Show What You Know! Finish this poem about the picture. Use words that you wrote on this page.

The king fell off his _____.
Now his arm is in a _____!

7. swing
8. sling

136

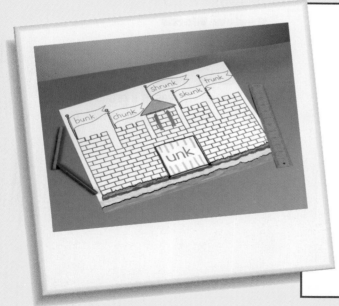

Learning Center Activity

visual/auditory/kinesthetic

An -*unk* Castle Have children draw their own castle with towers, a drawbridge, and a moat. On the drawbridge, have them write the letters *unk*. Then ask them to brainstorm a list of words that end in *-unk* and write them on flags and banners flying from the castle towers. Children might enjoy writing *-unk* words that tell about something related to the moat in that part of their drawing.

More Words That End with *-unk*		
bunk	plunk	stunk
chunk	shrunk	sunk
dunk	skunk	trunk
junk		

Vocabulary Enrichment

Social Studies

Castles and Kings All the words in the box have something to do with castles and kings. Write the words to finish this invitation. Use your Spelling Dictionary.

Spelling Word Link

king

throne
castle
page
feast

July 2, 1998

Dear People of the Kingdom,

Please come to the King's birthday party on Sunday, July 11. The doors to the __(1)__ will open at one o'clock. The King will sit on his __(2)__ and greet everyone. The cooks are making a big __(3)__! When lunch is ready, a young __(4)__ will tell you where to sit.

Your friend,
The Queen

1. castle
2. throne
3. feast
4. page

Try This CHALLENGE

Clue Match Write a word from the box for each clue.

5. This can be made of sand or stone.
6. This can be found in a book or in a castle.
7. This is a chair for a very special person.
8. Many people can enjoy this together.

5. castle
6. page
7. throne
8. feast

Fact File

Castles were damp and chilly! To help keep the cold out, heavy pieces of cloth were hung on the walls. Colorful pictures or designs were woven into them.

137

Integrating Literature

Easy	Average	Challenging
Rollo & Tweedy & the Ghost at Dougal Castle *by Laura J. Allen* Two mice investigate a mystery at a castle.	**King Bidgood's in the Bathtub** *by Audrey Wood* A king refuses to leave the bathtub to rule.	**Castles** *by Jason Cooper* An investigation of how different castles were built.
Bub, or the Very Best Thing *by Natalie Babbitt* A king and queen disagree over what's best for the baby prince.	**The Castle Builder** *by Dennis Nolan* A boy builds a sand-castle and imagines being a knight.	**The King and the Tortoise** *by Tololwa Mollel* A tortoise fulfills a king's request for a robe of smoke.

Objectives *Children will*

■ expand their vocabulary by using words related to castles and kings

■ show their understanding of the vocabulary words by completing context activities

Vocabulary Checkup

Have children use the vocabulary words in sentences or match the words to the definitions below.

1. a special chair that a king or a queen sits on *throne*
2. a big, fancy meal *feast*
3. a child who delivers messages and runs errands in a castle *page*
4. a large stone building or fort with high, thick walls and towers *castle*

Fact File

Tapestries

The photograph shows a section of a late fifteenth-century tapestry from a series called "The Lady and the Unicorn." Most tapestries from the Middle Ages were made of wool and depicted scenes from the Bible, mythology, or everyday life.

Words That End with *s* or *es*

WORD LISTS

Spelling

Basic
1. dishes
2. dresses
3. bells
4. boxes
5. beaches
6. days
7. bikes
8. wishes
9. things
10. names
11. children

Review
12. cups
13. frogs

Challenge
14. coins
15. classes

Vocabulary

Math: Earning Money

earn
sale
change
chores

Introducing the Lesson

Read Aloud

Write the Basic Words on the board.

A Yard Sale

Instead of playing at the **beaches** or parks every day this summer, why not have a yard sale? You can give the money you make to a charity or a special fund for **children**. Ask your friends and neighbors for **bells, bikes,** shirts, **dresses, dishes,** and anything else they no longer need. It may take many **days** to collect everything. Store all the **things** in **boxes**. Make signs to post in your neighborhood. Put price tags on everything. Then have your yard sale. Although you may never know the **names** of the people you have helped through your donation, you will help make their **wishes** come true.

Responding Ask children what special project they learned about. *(a yard sale)* Ask them what things they might sell at a yard sale. Ask which spelling word means more than one dress *(dresses)*, more than one thing *(things)*, and more than one box *(boxes)*. Ask volunteers to point to each spelling word on the board as it is named.

 Day 1 *page 138*

Objectives *Children will*
- take the pretest
- pronounce the list words
- learn about the spelling principle
- sort words by their spelling patterns

Planning Checklist
☑ Pretest (TE)
☑ Spelling principle/word list
☐ Review/Challenge Words
☐ Teaching the Principle (TE)
☐ Enrichment (TE)
☐ Additional Spelling Words (TE)

Assessment

Pretest
1. I will wash the <u>dishes</u>.
2. Try on these <u>dresses</u>.
3. Did you ring the <u>bells</u>?
4. Jacob packed the <u>boxes</u>.
5. The <u>beaches</u> are sandy.
6. I was away for two <u>days</u>.
7. Ride your <u>bikes</u> home.
8. Liza made six <u>wishes</u>.
9. He has ten <u>things</u> to do.
10. They told us their <u>names</u>.
11. Are the <u>children</u> home?

Day 2 *page 139*

Objectives *Children will*
- practice spelling list words
- apply spelling strategies
- identify Basic Words by using meaning clues
- identify an Elephant Word by adding missing letters

Planning Checklist
☑ Spelling Strategy
☑ Independent Practice
☐ Daily Proofreading Practice (TE)
☐ Informal Assessment (TE)
☐ Extra Support (TE)
☐ Applying Spelling Strategies (TE)

Additional Resources

Teacher's Resource Book
Practice Masters, pages 95–97
Unit Test, page 98
Bulletin Board, page 111

Practice Plus
Take-Home Word List 20
Games

Spelling Transparencies
Spelling Word List 20
Daily Proofreading Practice,
  Unit 20
Graphic Organizers

Teacher's Resource Disk
Macintosh® or Windows®
  software. Houghton Mifflin

Spelling CD-ROM
Macintosh® or Windows®
  software. Houghton Mifflin

Internet
http://www.eduplace.com

Phonics Practice

Houghton Mifflin Phonics
The Listening Corner
Phonics Home Connection

 Day 3 *page 140*

 Day 4 *page 141*

 Day 5 *page 141*

Objective *Children will*
- review Basic and Review Words

Planning Checklist
- ☐ Review: Spelling Spree
- ☐ How Are You Doing?
- ☐ Daily Proofreading Practice (TE)
- ☐ Cooperative Learning Activity (TE)

Objectives *Children will*
- proofread for spelling and capital letters
- write and proofread an original composition

Planning Checklist
- ☐ Proofread: Spelling and Capital Letters
- ☐ Write an Ad
- ☐ Daily Proofreading Practice (TE)
- ☐ Challenge Words Practice (TE)
- ☐ Another Writing Idea (TE)

Objective *Children will*
- take the posttest

Assessment

- ☐ **Posttest** (TE) *See Day 5*
- ☐ Unit 20 Test

Other Activities for Any Day

- Bonus activities from pages 142–143
- Practice Masters (easy, average, challenging)
  Teacher's Resource Book, pages 95–97
- Take-Home Word List 20
  Practice Plus

Meeting Individual Needs
Students Acquiring English

Spanish There is no |sh| sound in Spanish.
Activity Say *wish/which, ditch/dish*, and *bush/beach*, asking children to show one finger if the |sh| sound is in the first word and two if it is in the second. Write *wish* and *dish* on the board. Say the words and have a volunteer circle the letters *sh*.

Asian In most Asian languages, nouns have only one form.
Activity On cards, write the singular form of Basic Words 1–10 with the plural form below it. Make the *s* and *es* endings a different color. Show the cards, pronouncing each word and having the children repeat it. Use both forms in sentences.

UNIT 20

Objectives *Children will*

- take the pretest
- pronounce the list words
- learn about the spelling principle
- sort words by their spelling patterns

Teaching the Principle

This lesson teaches the formation of regular plural nouns by adding -s or -es. Children learn the strategy of spelling plurals by adding -s to most singular nouns and adding -es to singular nouns that end with *s, x, sh,* or *ch*.

To sum up the lesson, ask:

- When do you add -s to name more than one? *(You add -s to most words.)*
- When do you add -es to name more than one? *(You add -es to words that end with s, x, sh, or ch.)*

Enrichment

Vocabulary: Multiple Meanings
Have children use a dictionary to look up *dresses, names,* and *things*. Discuss the meanings.

UNIT 20 — Words That End with s or es

es
bikes

A. bells

_____ days

_____ bikes

_____ things

_____ names

B. dishes

_____ dresses

_____ boxes

_____ beaches

_____ wishes

C. children

138

Read and Say

READ the sentences. **SAY** each word in dark print.

Basic Words

1. dishes	*dishes*	I will wash the **dishes**.
2. dresses	*dresses*	Try on these **dresses**.
3. bells	*bells*	Did you ring the **bells**?
4. boxes	*boxes*	Jacob packed the **boxes**.
5. beaches	*beaches*	The **beaches** are sandy.
6. days	*days*	I was away for two **days**.
7. bikes	*bikes*	Ride your **bikes** home.
8. wishes	*wishes*	Liza made six **wishes**.
9. things	*things*	He has ten **things** to do.
10. names	*names*	They told us their **names**.
11. children	*children*	Are the **children** home?

Think and Write

Each word names more than one of something. The **s** and **es** endings make these words mean more than one.

    s → bell**s**, bike**s**

    es → dress**es**, box**es**, di**sh**es, beach**es**

How is the Elephant Word different? *It is plural but does not end with s or es.*

A. Write **five** Basic Words that have the **s** ending.
B. Write **five** Basic Words that have the **es** ending.
C. Now write the Elephant Word.

Order of answers for each category may vary.

Review	Challenge
12. cups 13. frogs	14. coins 15. classes

TEACHING OPTIONS

Meeting Individual Needs
Word Lists

You may want to assign Basic Words 1–5, the Elephant Word, and the Review Words to children who misspelled more than five words on the pretest. Assign the Challenge Words as appropriate. (You may want to have children write sentences, using the Challenge Words.)

Additional Spelling Words

Basic	Challenge	Words Often Misspelled
stamps	giraffes	started
bushes	robots	where
grapes	circuses	
kisses	watches	
foxes	paintbrushes	
	helmets	

Home/School Involvement
Take-Home Word List • Goal-Setting

Have children set goals for the week on Take-Home Word List 20.

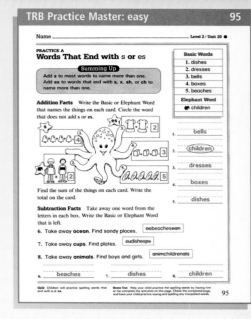

TRB Practice Master: easy   95

Name _____   Level 2 / Unit 20 ●

PRACTICE A
Words That End with s or es

Summing Up
Add **s** to most words to name more than one.
Add **es** to words that end with **s, x, sh,** or **ch** to name more than one.

Addition Facts Write the Basic or Elephant Word that names the things on each card. Circle the word that does not add s or es.

Find the sum of the things on each card. Write the total on the card.

Subtraction Facts Take away one word from the letters in each box. Write the Basic or Elephant Word that is left.

6. Take away **ocean**. Find sandy places. oebeachesean

7. Take away **cups**. Find plates. oudishesps

8. Take away **animals**. Find boys and girls. animchildrenals

6. _beaches_   7. _dishes_   8. _children_

Basic Words
1. dishes
2. dresses
3. bells
4. boxes
5. beaches
Elephant Word
🐘 children

1. bells
2. (children)
3. dresses
4. boxes
5. dishes

95

Independent Practice

Spelling Strategy

Add **s** to most words to name more than one. Add **es** to words that end with **s**, **x**, **sh**, or **ch** to name more than one.

Phonics Write Basic Words to answer the questions.

1. Which word begins like  ? *thirty*
2. Which word begins with the same consonant cluster as ? *drum*
3. Which word has the long **i** sound?
4. Which word rhymes with **tells**?

Word Clues Write a Basic Word for each clue.

5. People make them at birthday parties.
6. Sand castles may be found there.
7. People are known by them.
8. Gifts may come in them.
9. Nights come after them.
10. Food is put on them.

Elephant Word Think of the missing letters in the Elephant Word. Write the word.

11. The **child** __ __ __ sold juice to earn money.

Phonics

1. things
2. dresses
3. bikes
4. bells

Word Clues

5. wishes
6. beaches
7. names
8. boxes
9. days
10. dishes

Elephant Word

11. children

139

Objectives *Children will*

■ practice spelling list words
■ apply spelling strategies
■ identify Basic Words by using meaning clues
■ identify an Elephant Word by adding missing letters

Day 2

Daily Proofreading Practice

I put the cake on new **dishez**. (*dishes*)
It rained hard for two **daze**. (*days*)

Meeting Individual Needs
visual/kinesthetic

Extra Support Check Independent Practice to determine who needs extra support. Hold up a pen. Write *pen*. Repeat, showing several pens and writing *pens*. Elicit how the spelling changes. Then write *dish/dishes, box/boxes, dress/dresses, bell/bells,* and *beach/beaches.* Have volunteers circle the *-s* and *-es* endings. Review how *-es* is added to form the plural of words.

Applying Spelling Strategies
To Read New Words

■ Write this sentence on the chalkboard:
I grew two inches this year!
■ Have children read the sentence silently.

■ Elicit the following strategies as children try to decode *inches*.

inches

I know that the letters *ch* make the |ch| sound.

The letters *es* after *ch* probably make this word plural. I think these letters are pronounced |ez|.

I see that the letter *i* is followed by the consonant *n*. I think this is the short *i* vowel pattern. I know that *n* makes the sound I hear at the beginning of *nest*.

I-n-ch-es. In-ches. Inches. The word *inches* makes sense in the sentence.

Objective *Children will*
- review Basic and Review Words

Daily Proofreading Practice
He made two birthday **wishis**.
(*wishes*)
We heard all the **belles** ringing. (*bells*)

Code Breaker

1. dishes

2. bells

3. things

4. wishes

Letter Math

5. dresses

6. children

7. frogs

Letter Swap

8. cups

9. beaches

10. days

11. bikes

12. names

140

Review: Spelling Spree

Code Breaker Use the code to write Basic Words.

⊖ = w	⊥ = d	☆ = s	☽ = g
∗ = n	● = i	◇ = h	□ = t
∩ = e	↑ = b	▲ = l	

Example: ☆ ∩ □ ☆ = **sets**

1. ⊥ ● ☆ ◇ ∩ ☆   3. □ ◇ ● ∗ ☽ ☆
2. ↑ ∩ ▲ ▲ ☆   4. ⊖ ● ☆ ◇ ∩ ☆

Letter Math Add and take away letters to make Basic or Review Words. Write the words.

5. d r + l e s s − l + e s = _____
6. c h + w i l d − w + r e n = _____
7. f r + l o g − l + s = _____

Letter Swap Change the first letter in each word to make a Basic or Review Word. Write the words.

8. **p**ups   10. **r**ays   12. **g**ames
9. **p**eaches   11. **h**ikes

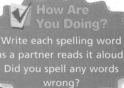
How Are You Doing?
Write each spelling word as a partner reads it aloud. Did you spell any words wrong?

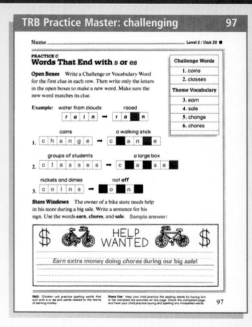

TEACHING OPTIONS

Cooperative Learning Activity
Learn and Earn
visual/oral/kinesthetic

Provide pairs of children with blank cards. Children write the singular form of a spelling word on each card. They color the back of each card green and print "$1" on it. Partners place the cards in a pile, face-down. They take turns pulling a card, reading the word, then saying and spelling the plural form. A player who spells the plural correctly keeps the card; otherwise, it goes back in the pile. The player who "earns" the most $1 bills wins.

TRB Practice Master: challenging 97

Name _____ Level 2 / Unit 20 ▪

PRACTICE C
Words That End with s or es

Challenge Words
1. coins
2. classes
Theme Vocabulary
3. earn
4. sale
5. change
6. chores

Open Boxes Write a Challenge or Vocabulary Word for the first clue in each row. Then write only the letters in the open boxes to make a new word. Make sure the new word matches its clue.

Example: water from clouds   raced
r a i n → r a ▪ n

1. coins   a walking stick
c h a n g e → c ▪ a n ▪ e

2. groups of students   a large box
c l a s s e s → c ▪ ▪ s e

3. nickels and dimes   not off
c o i n s → ▪ o ▪ n

Store Windows The owner of a bike store needs help in his store during a big sale. Write a sentence for his sign. Use the words **earn**, **chores**, and **sale**. Sample answer:

Earn extra money doing chores during our big sale!

97

Proofreading and Writing

Proofread: Spelling and Capital Letters

Always begin the names of holidays with capital letters.

Columbus **D**ay   Thanksgiving **D**ay

Proofread this list of club plans. Use proofreading marks to fix four spelling mistakes and four missing capital letters.

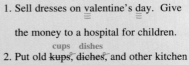

Example: We raked the ~~beeches~~ on labor day.

1. Sell dresses on valentine's day. Give

   the money to a hospital for children.

2. Put old ~~kups~~, ~~diches~~, and other kitchen
   cups   dishes

   things   boxes
   ~~tings~~ in ~~boxs~~. Sell them at the fair

   on flag day.

Write an Ad

Write an ad for a holiday fair. What kinds of things will be for sale? Include the name of the holiday in your ad. Try to use spelling words. Draw pictures to go with your ad.

FAIR!

Proofreading Tip Check that you began the name of each holiday with a capital letter.

Basic
1. dishes
2. dresses
3. bells
4. boxes
5. beaches
6. days
7. bikes
8. wishes
9. things
10. names
11. children

Review
12. cups
13. frogs

Challenge
14. coins
15. classes

Proofreading Marks
∧ Add
⌐ Delete
≡ Make a capital letter
/ Make a small letter

141

Meeting Individual Needs

Challenge Words Practice
Ask children to use the Challenge Words to make acrostic puzzles. Have them write the words down the left side of their paper, then use each letter as the first letter in a phrase that tells something people might sell to earn money.

Another Writing Idea Have children use spelling words to make a mail-order catalog that includes prices, pictures, and descriptions of the items being sold.

Day 4

■ proofread for spelling and capital letters

■ write and proofread an original composition

Daily Proofreading Practice
Do your goats have **namz**? (*names*)
The swings are for **childrun**.
(*children*)

Day 5 **Posttest**

Sentences 1–5 test the first five Basic Words. Sentences 6–10 test the next five Basic Words. Sentence 11 tests the Elephant Word.

Basic Words
1. I made two new <u>dresses</u>.
2. I see the <u>boxes</u>.
3. She has nine <u>bells.</u>
4. I like the <u>beaches</u>.
5. Did he wash the <u>dishes</u>?
6. The <u>days</u> are fun.
7. Do the cats have <u>names</u>?
8. We like the <u>bikes</u>.
9. He made five <u>wishes</u>.
10. I have to get ten <u>things</u>.
11. The <u>children</u> went to the game.

Review Words
12. Did the <u>frogs</u> chase the bug?
13. I will wash the <u>cups</u>.

Challenge Words
14. Both <u>classes</u> are studying math.
15. I put the <u>coins</u> in my pocket.

Unit 20
BONUS

These pages can be used at any time during the study of this unit.

Day by Day Planner

Objectives *Children will*

■ build words with the suffix *-less*

■ replace phrases with suffixes

Unit 20
BONUS

Vocabulary Enrichment

Word Builder

Spelling Word Link
names

Building Words with less When you add **less** to a word, it changes the meaning of the word.

name + less = name**less**

The word **nameless** means "without a name."

Finish the chart below.

1. use + less = useless
2. end + less = endless
3. job + less = jobless
4. home + less = homeless

Work Together Write a word that means the same as each group of words in dark print. Use the words you made in the chart. Work with a friend.

5. The stray cat is **without a home**.
6. Jake has been **without a job** since April.
7. The car ride seemed to be **without an end**.
8. My broken bike is **without use**.

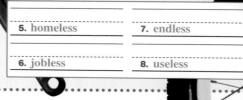

5. homeless	7. endless
6. jobless	8. useless

142

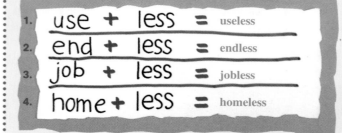

EXTENSION OPTIONS

Learning Center Activity
visual/oral/auditory/kinesthetic/

A *-less* Word Bank Use a covered box to make a Word Bank for your Learning Center. Make a slit in the top. Cut "coins" from construction paper. Children can make deposits to the Word Bank by thinking of *-less* words, writing them on the coins, and placing them in the bank. They can then work independently or with a partner to read the words on the coins and use them in oral or written sentences.

Vocabulary Enrichment

Math

Earning Money All the words in the box have something to do with earning money. Write those words to finish this story from a school newspaper. Use your Spelling Dictionary.

Spelling Word Link

coins

earn
sale
change
chores

Second-Grade Class Saves the Day!

Mrs. Garrett's class did all of the __(1)__ for the school bake __(2)__ . The children set up the tables and put prices on the food. They even made cookies to __(3)__ some money. Thanks to Mrs. Garrett's class, there is lots of __(4)__ to count!

1. chores

2. sale

3. earn

4. change

Try This CHALLENGE

Yes or No? Is the word in dark print used correctly? Write **yes** or **no**.

5. We bought a **sale** at the new store.
6. We saved **chores** for extra money.
7. Pam has **change** in her piggy bank.
8. I started working to **earn** money.

5. no

6. no

7. yes

8. yes

★ Fact File

Coins used on the Yap Islands are too big to carry in your pocket! The smallest coin is one foot wide, and the largest is twelve feet!

coin

143

Day by Day Planner

Objectives *Children will*

- expand their vocabulary by using words related to earning money
- show their understanding of the vocabulary words by completing context activities

Vocabulary Checkup

Have children use the vocabulary words in sentences or match the words to the definitions below.

1. coins *change*
2. the act of selling *sale*
3. small jobs *chores*
4. to get by working *earn*

Fact File

The Yap Islands

Yap is 514 miles southwest of Guam, in the Pacific Ocean. The stone used for making the coins was quarried in Palau and carried by canoe across about 275 miles of open ocean to Yap. Each stone has its own legend, and its value is based on the difficulty of the trip.

Integrating Literature

Easy	Average	Challenging
Jelly Beans for Sale *by Bruce McMillan* Children buy and sell jelly beans using combinations of coins.	**Pigs Will Be Pigs** *by Amy Axelrod* The Pigs search their house for money to eat out.	**Alexander, Who Used to Be Rich Last Sunday** *by Judith Viorst* Alexander has only bus tokens by Sunday's end.
Arthur's Funny Money *by Lillian Hoban* Arthur the chimp tries to earn money to buy a T-shirt.	**Music, Music for Everyone** *by Vera Williams* Rosa organizes her friends into the Oak Street Band to earn money.	**Max Malone Makes a Million** *by Charlotte Herman* Max and a friend make cookies and sell lemonade to earn money.

More Long *o* Spellings

WORD LISTS

Spelling

Basic

1. boat
2. cold
3. go
4. slow
5. no
6. old
7. coat
8. grow
9. told
10. show
11. toe
12. do

Review

13. so
14. say

Challenge

15. coast
16. rainbow

Vocabulary

Science: The Seashore

ocean
jellyfish
shrimp
crab

Introducing the Lesson

Read Aloud

Write the Basic Words on the board.

One Morning in Maine

Has anyone ever **told** you that you can make a wish on a baby tooth after it falls out? The book *One Morning in Maine* by Robert McCloskey is about a girl named Sal who lives on an island and has her first loose tooth. She worries that **no** new teeth will **grow** when the baby teeth fall out. Sal runs to **show** her father her loose tooth. Then Sal's tooth falls out while she is wading in **cold** water to dig for clams. She comes out covered in a **coat** of mud from head to **toe**. Sal wishes on her baby tooth. Then she gets ready to **go** on a **boat** trip into town with her dad, but the **old** motor won't start. It is a **slow** trip, but they **do** get to town and Sal gets her wish. What was the wish? Read the book and find out!

Responding Ask how Sal gets into town from the island. *(by boat)* Ask children to describe losing their own baby teeth. Read aloud the sentence with the word **cold** in it. Ask children what **cold** means in the sentence. *(the opposite of hot)* Have a volunteer go to the chalkboard and circle the two spelling words that rhyme with *cold*. *(told, old)*

Day 1 *page 144*

Objectives *Children will*

- take the pretest
- pronounce the list words
- learn about the spelling principle
- sort words by their spelling patterns

Planning Checklist

- ☑ Pretest (TE)
- ☑ Spelling principle/word list
- ☐ Review/Challenge Words
- ☐ Teaching the Principle (TE)
- ☐ Enrichment (TE)
- ☐ Additional Spelling Words (TE)

Assessment

Pretest

1. I want to sail the <u>boat</u>.
2. The lake is <u>cold</u>.
3. We will <u>go</u> home.
4. Snails are very <u>slow</u>.
5. A fish has <u>no</u> feet.
6. I like to fix <u>old</u> bikes.
7. Eva put on her <u>coat</u>.
8. The plant will <u>grow</u>.
9. Dan <u>told</u> me a joke.
10. I will <u>show</u> you my toy.
11. She bumped her <u>toe</u>!
12. He must <u>do</u> the dishes.

Day 2 *page 145*

Objectives *Children will*

- practice spelling list words
- apply spelling strategies
- identify antonyms
- identify Elephant Words according to spelling patterns and vowel sounds

Planning Checklist

- ☑ Spelling Strategy
- ☑ Independent Practice
- ☐ Daily Proofreading Practice (TE)
- ☐ Informal Assessment (TE)
- ☐ Extra Support (TE)
- ☐ Applying Spelling Strategies (TE)

UNIT 21

FYI As children practice the spelling words, you might have them work with spelling partners to check each other's work.

 page 146

Objectives *Children will*
- use context clues and a dictionary entry to determine the meaning of a given word
- review Basic and Review Words

Planning Checklist
☐ Dictionary
☐ Review: Spelling Spree
☐ How Are You Doing?
☐ Daily Proofreading Practice (TE)
☐ Cooperative Learning Activity (TE)

 page 147

Objectives *Children will*
- proofread for spelling
- write and proofread an original composition

Planning Checklist
☐ Proofread for Spelling
☐ Write a Program
☐ Daily Proofreading Practice (TE)
☐ Challenge Words Practice (TE)
☐ Another Writing Idea (TE)

 page 147

Objective *Children will*
- take the posttest

Assessment
☐ Posttest (TE) *See Day 5*
☐ Unit 21 Test

Additional Resources

Teacher's Resource Book
Practice Masters, pages 99–101
Unit Test, page 102
Bulletin Board, page 111

Practice Plus
Take-Home Word List 21
Games

Spelling Transparencies
Spelling Word List 21
Daily Proofreading Practice, Unit 21
Graphic Organizers

Teacher's Resource Disk
Macintosh® or Windows® software. Houghton Mifflin

Spelling CD-ROM
Macintosh® or Windows® software. Houghton Mifflin

Internet
http://www.eduplace.com

Phonics Practice
Houghton Mifflin Phonics
The Listening Corner
Phonics Home Connection

Other Activities for Any Day

- Bonus activities from pages 148–149
- Practice Masters (easy, average, challenging) Teacher's Resource Book, pages 99–101
- Take-Home Word List 21 Practice Plus

Meeting Individual Needs
Students Acquiring English

Spanish The *ld* ending is rare in Spanish. **Activity** Write *cool/cold, old/pole, tool/told* on the board. Say the words and have children raise one or two fingers to show whether the first or second word ends with *ld*. Then write *cold, old,* and *told* on the board, omitting the letters *ld*. Say each word and have children repeat it. Ask a volunteer to write in the missing letters.

Asian Some children may have difficulty with the *ld* ending. They may omit the |l| or add an extra vowel at the end. **Activity** Use the activity for Spanish-speaking children.

Objectives *Children will*

■ take the pretest

■ pronounce the list words

■ learn about the spelling principle

■ sort words by their spelling patterns

Teaching the Principle

This lesson teaches the *o*, *oa*, and *ow* spelling patterns for the |ō| sound. Children learn the strategy of thinking of these patterns when they hear the long *o* sound.

To sum up the lesson, ask:

• How is the long *o* sound spelled in *go* and *cold*? (*o*)

• How is the long *o* sound spelled in *boat* and *coat*? (*oa*)

• How is the long *o* sound spelled in *slow* and *grow*? (*ow*)

Note: The Elephant Word *do* is pronounced |dōō| when it is used as a verb and |dō| when it names a musical tone.

Enrichment

Vocabulary: Multiple Meanings

Have children use a dictionary to look up *cold*, *coat*, and *show*. Discuss the meanings.

UNIT 21 More Long o Spellings

ō
boat

Read and Say

READ the sentences. **SAY** each word in dark print.

Basic Words

1.	boat	*boat*	I want to sail the **boat**.
2.	cold	*cold*	The lake is **cold**.
3.	go	*go*	We will **go** home.
4.	slow	*slow*	Snails are very **slow**.
5.	no	*no*	A fish has **no** feet.
6.	old	*old*	I like to fix **old** bikes.
7.	coat	*coat*	Eva put on her **coat**.
8.	grow	*grow*	The plant will **grow**.
9.	told	*told*	Dan **told** me a joke.
10.	show	*show*	I will **show** you my toy.
11.	toe	*toe*	She bumped her **toe**!
12.	do	*do*	He must **do** the dishes.

A. cold

go

no

old

told

B. boat

coat

C. slow

grow

show

D. toe

do

144

Think and Write

Most of the words have the long **o** vowel sound spelled **o**, **oa**, or **ow**.

the long **o** sound → g**o**, b**oa**t, sl**ow**

How are the Elephant Words different?
In *toe*, the |ō| sound is spelled *oe*. In *do*, the *o* spells the |ōō| sound.

A. Write **five** Basic Words with the long **o** sound spelled **o**.

B. Write **two** Basic Words with the long **o** sound spelled **oa**.

C. Write **three** Basic Words with the long **o** sound spelled **ow**.

D. Now write the **two** Elephant Words.

Order of answers for each category may vary.

Review	Challenge
13. so 14. say	15. coast 16. rainbow

TEACHING OPTIONS

Meeting Individual Needs
Word Lists

You may want to assign Basic Words 1–5, the Elephant Words, and the Review Words to children who misspelled more than five words on the pretest. Assign the Challenge Words as appropriate. (You may want to have children write sentences, using the Challenge Words.)

Additional Spelling Words

Basic	Challenge	Words Often Misspelled
soap	yellow	have
most	poster	said
low	pillow	
hold	pony	
toad	rowboat	
	oatmeal	

Home/School Involvement
Take-Home Word List • Goal-Setting

Have children set goals for the week on Take-Home Word List 21.

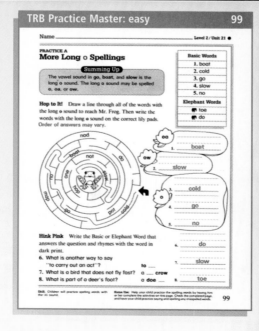

UNIT 21

Independent Practice

Spelling Strategy The vowel sound in **go**, **boat**, and **slow** is the long **o** sound. The long **o** sound may be spelled **o**, **oa**, or **ow**.

Order of answers for questions 3–4 and 5–6 may vary.

Phonics Write Basic Words to answer the questions.

1. Which word begins with a vowel sound?
2. Which word begins with the first sound you hear in ? *shoe*
3–4. Which two words rhyme with **float**?
5–6. Which two words begin with the same consonant clusters as **slide** and **green**?

Word Meaning Write the Basic Word that means the opposite of each word below.

7. come   8. asked   9. yes   10. hot

Elephant Words Write an Elephant Word to answer each question.

11. Which word ends with the letter **o** but does not have the long **o** sound?
12. Which word has the long **o** sound spelled **oe**?

Phonics

1. old
2. show
3. boat
4. coat
5. slow
6. grow

Word Meaning

7. go
8. told
9. no
10. cold

Elephant Words

11. do
12. toe

(145)

Day 2

Objectives *Children will*

■ practice spelling list words
■ apply spelling strategies
■ identify antonyms
■ identify Elephant Words according to spelling patterns and vowel sounds

Daily Proofreading Practice

I love my **oald** teddy bear. (*old*)
These beans need sun to **groe**. (*grow*)

Meeting Individual Needs
visual/auditory/kinesthetic

Extra Support Check Independent Practice to determine who needs extra support. Give children three cards. Have them write *o* on one, *oa* on another, and *ow* on the third. As you say each Basic Word, have children hold up the card with the corresponding spelling of the long *o* sound. Ask a volunteer to write the word on the board, underlining the letter/letters that spell the vowel sound.

Applying Spelling Strategies
To Spell New Words

■ Read aloud: **Eva pulled the loaf of warm bread from the oven.**
■ Have children attempt to spell *loaf* on their Have-a-Go charts.

■ Elicit the following strategies as children try to spell *loaf*.

> I hear the sound for *l* that I hear at the beginning of *lamp*.

> The |f| sound is the sound I hear at the beginning of *feather*. It is probably spelled *f*.

loaf

> This word has the long *o* sound. The long *o* sound is probably spelled *oa* or *ow*. I'll have to check a dictionary.

Objectives *Children will*

■ use context clues and a dictionary entry to determine the meaning of a given word

■ review Basic and Review Words

Daily Proofreading Practice

I rowed the **bote** across the lake. (*boat*)

Karla likes to **goe** to the zoo. (*go*)

Dictionary

1. 1

2. 2

3. 2

4. 1

Word Hunt

5. say

6. boat

7. no

8. go

9. old

10. toe

11. do

12. so

146

Dictionary

Finding the Right Meaning Some words have more than one meaning. A dictionary lists all the meanings of a word. Each meaning is numbered.

> **coat** **1.** A type of outer clothing with sleeves: *I wore a warm **coat**.* **2.** An outer covering of fur or hair on an animal: *I brushed the horse's **coat**.*

Practice Write **1** or **2** to tell which meaning of **coat** is used in each sentence.
1. The fisherman wore a wool **coat**.
2. Rags licked his sandy **coat** clean.
3. A seal's thick **coat** helps keep it warm.
4. I bought a heavy **coat** to wear sailing.

Review: Spelling Spree

Word Hunt Write the Basic or Review Word you see in each longer word.
5. sayings
6. tugboat
7. nosy
8. goat
9. folder
10. tiptoe
11. hairdo
12. also

How Are You Doing?
Write each word in a sentence. Practice with a family member any words you spelled wrong.

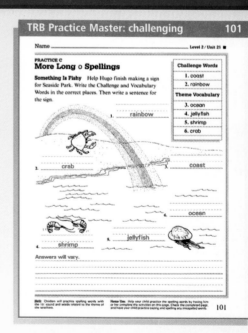

TEACHING OPTIONS

Cooperative Learning Activity

Spelling Stars
visual/auditory/kinesthetic

Ask partners or small groups to draw starfish on construction paper. In the center of each star, have them write one spelling for the long o sound (*o, oa,* or *ow*). On each star point, have them write a word that has the same long o spelling.

Suggest children brainstorm words for each long o spelling by thinking of rhyming words and checking them in a dictionary.

Proofreading and Writing

Proofread for Spelling Proofread these tips for whale watching. Use proofreading marks to fix six spelling mistakes.

do
Example: How long doe whales live?

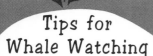

Tips for Whale Watching

coat
• Take a warm ~~koat~~. The boat

slow   cold
is ~~sloe~~. You will be out in the ~~coald~~

wind for a long time.

told
• Listen to the captain. You will be ~~toweld~~ how

grow
the whales live and how they ~~gro~~ to be so big.

show
• Don't forget to ~~sho~~ me your pictures!

Write a Program

The animals in the ocean are having a talent show! Write a program for the show. List all the animals and tell what they might do. Try to use spelling words.

TALENT SHOW

Proofreading Tip Proofread for one kind of error at a time.

147

Basic

1. boat
2. cold
3. go
4. slow
5. no
6. old
7. coat
8. grow
9. told
10. show
11. toe
12. do

Review

13. so
14. say

Challenge

15. coast
16. rainbow

Proofreading Marks

∧ Add
⌒ Delete
≡ Make a capital letter
/ Make a small letter

Day 4

Objectives *Children will*

■ proofread for spelling

■ write and proofread an original composition

Daily Proofreading Practice

Ron will **sho** me the seashells. (*show*)

I have a warm wool **cowt**. (*coat*)

Day 5   **Posttest**

Sentences 1–5 test the first five Basic Words. Sentences 6–10 test the next five Basic Words. Sentences 11–12 test the Elephant Words.

Basic Words

1. My clock is <u>slow</u>.
2. I must <u>go</u> home.
3. The <u>boat</u> is long.
4. We had <u>no</u> rope.
5. It is <u>cold</u> here.
6. She <u>told</u> me five things.
7. Wash the <u>old</u> pot.
8. Please <u>show</u> me the flag.
9. I see a spot on the <u>coat</u>.
10. The grass will <u>grow</u>.
11. I have a job I must <u>do</u>.
12. I kick with my big <u>toe</u>.

Review Words

13. What did the man <u>say</u>?
14. The bus is <u>so</u> late.

Challenge Words

15. We saw a <u>rainbow</u> after the storm.
16. She walked along the rocky <u>coast</u>.

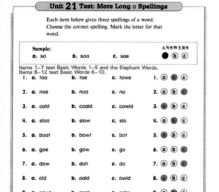

TRB Unit 21 Test   102

Name _____   Level 2 / Unit 21 ●▲

Unit 21 Test: More Long o Spellings

Each item below gives three spellings of a word. Choose the correct spelling. Mark the letter for that word.

Sample:
a. so   b. soa   c. soe   ANSWERS ● ⓑ ⓒ

Items 1–7 test Basic Words 1–5 and the Elephant Words.
Items 8–12 test Basic Words 6–10.

1. a. toa   b. toe   c. towe   1. ⓐ ● ⓒ
2. a. noe   b. noa   c. no   2. ⓐ ⓑ ●
3. a. cold   b. coald c. cowld   3. ● ⓑ ⓒ
4. a. sloa   b. slow   c. slo   4. ⓐ ● ⓒ
5. a. boat   b. bowt   c. bot   5. ● ⓑ ⓒ
6. a. goe   b. gow   c. go   6. ⓐ ⓑ ●
7. a. dow   b. doh   c. do   7. ⓐ ⓑ ●
8. a. old   b. oald   c. owld   8. ● ⓑ ⓒ
9. a. cowt   b. coat   c. cofe   9. ⓐ ● ⓒ
10. a. sho   b. showe c. show   10. ⓐ ⓑ ●
11. a. gro   b. grow   c. groe   11. ⓐ ● ⓒ
12. a. told b. towld c. toald   12. ● ⓑ ⓒ

102

Meeting Individual Needs

Challenge Words Practice
Have children write tongue twisters, using the Challenge Words and other words that begin with the same consonant sounds. (Example: Ken calmly caught a crab and a clam near his cottage by the coast.)

Another Writing Idea
Suggest children write a poem about the ocean. Encourage them to use spelling words.

These pages can be used at any time during the study of this unit.

Day by Day Planner

Objectives *Children will*

- use context to help them choose appropriate synonyms from a thesaurus

- use words found in a thesaurus in their writing

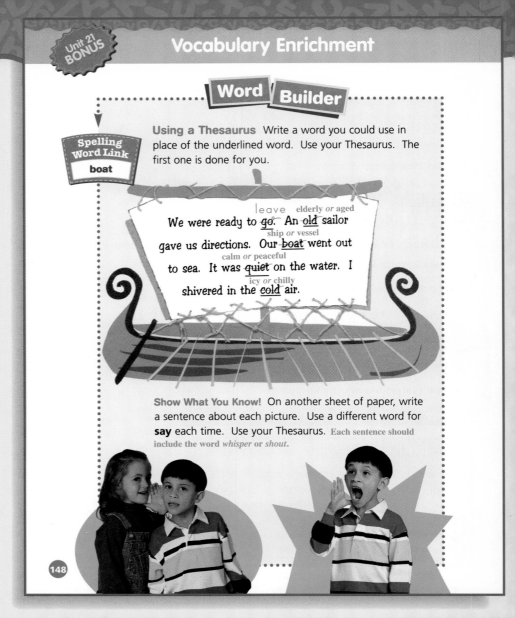

Unit 21 BONUS

Vocabulary Enrichment

Word Builder

Using a Thesaurus Write a word you could use in place of the underlined word. Use your Thesaurus. The first one is done for you.

Spelling Word Link

boat

leave

We were ready to go. An old sailor
elderly *or* aged

gave us directions. Our boat went out
ship *or* vessel

to sea. It was quiet on the water. I
calm *or* peaceful

shivered in the cold air.
icy *or* chilly

Show What You Know! On another sheet of paper, write a sentence about each picture. Use a different word for **say** each time. Use your Thesaurus. Each sentence should include the word *whisper* or *shout*.

148

EXTENSION OPTIONS

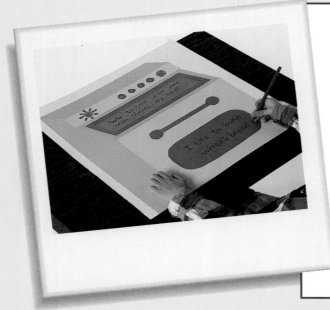

Learning Center Activity

visual/kinesthetic

Cooking Up Exact Words Have children look up *cook* in their Thesaurus and find two long *o* words (*toast, roast*) as well as other exact words for *cook*. Ask them to choose one word and look it up in a dictionary. Have children draw a cooking implement to represent their word, then write the word on their drawing along with the dictionary definition and a sentence. Children may want to cut out their pictures and post them on a bulletin board or on the class word wall.

Vocabulary Enrichment

Science

The Seashore All the words in the box have something to do with the seashore. Write those words to finish this poster. Use your Spelling Dictionary.

SEA ANIMALS

Many animals live in the __(1)__. A __(2)__ has a fan-shaped tail. A __(3)__ is hard and has claws. A __(4)__ has a very soft body.

Spelling Word Link

boat

ocean
jellyfish
shrimp
crab

1. ocean

2. shrimp

3. crab

4. jellyfish

Try This CHALLENGE

Riddle Time! Write a word from the box to answer each riddle.

5. I am not angry, but I might pinch you.
6. My waves do not mean "good-bye."
7. You might make fun of me for being small.
8. Part of my name tastes good with peanut butter.

5. crab

6. ocean

7. shrimp

8. jellyfish

★ Fact File

There are many different kinds of whales. The blue whale is the largest animal in the world. It can weigh more than 200,000 pounds.

149

Day by Day Planner

Objectives *Children will*

■ expand their vocabulary by using words related to the seashore

■ show their understanding of the vocabulary words by completing context activities

Vocabulary Checkup

Have children use the vocabulary words in sentences or match the words to the definitions below.

1. an animal with a flat body, five pairs of legs, claws on the front pair of legs, and often a hard shell *crab*
2. a sea animal with a soft body and long arms that can sting *jellyfish*
3. the great body of salt water that covers most of the earth *ocean*
4. a small animal with a shell and a tail shaped like a fan *shrimp*

Fact File

Blue Whales

Blue whales live in all of the oceans, but they are extremely rare. At birth, blue whales average about two tons in weight and twenty-three feet in length. They may grow to be one hundred feet long and live for eighty years.

Integrating Literature

Easy	Average	Challenging
Sail Away *by Donald Crews* A family spending the day sailing weathers a storm.	**What's It Like to Be a Fish?** *by Wendy Pfeffer* An explanation of why fish are perfectly suited to live in the water.	**Night of the Pufflings** *by Bruce McMillan* Icelandic children help young pufflings get safely to the ocean.
Beach Feet *by Lynn Reiser* Rhyming text reveals the many kinds of feet found at the beach.	**Into the Sea** *by Brenda K. Guiberson* A description of the life cycle of the turtle.	**The Magic School Bus® on the Ocean Floor** *by Joanna Cole* Ms. Frizzle's class goes on an undersea adventure.

The Vowel Sounds in *moon* and *book*

WORD LISTS

Spelling

Basic

1. zoo
2. food
3. look
4. moon
5. book
6. soon
7. took
8. good
9. room
10. foot
11. you
12. who

Review

13. clap
14. like

Challenge

15. hoof
16. moose

Vocabulary

Science: Zoos

tame
diet
groom
perch

Introducing the Lesson

Read Aloud

Write the Basic Words on the board.

Feed the Animals!

Have **you** ever known anyone **who took** a hippopotamus to lunch? **You** may say that your mother would let **you** take a trip to the **moon** before letting this animal set **foot** in your dining **room**. Although zoos will not let **you** take a hippo home, **you** could help buy **food** for one. The Detroit Zoo and the St. Louis Zoo will let **you** help feed an animal for a year. Your local **zoo** may too. Just call them. **Look** in the telephone **book** for the number. The **zoo** will send **you** information about the animals **you** can help take care of. **Good** luck! **Soon you** may be the proud parent of a hippopotamus!

Responding Ask children where they can go to see many different types of animals. *(the zoo)* Ask children to name the two words that rhyme in this sentence: "**Look** in the telephone **book** for the number." *(look, book)* Then have a volunteer go to the chalkboard and point to the spelling word that rhymes with *moon*. *(soon)*

Day 1 *page 150*

Objectives *Children will*

- take the pretest
- pronounce the list words
- learn about the spelling principle
- sort words by their vowel sounds

Planning Checklist

- ☑ Pretest (TE)
- ☑ Spelling principle/word list
- ☐ Review/Challenge Words
- ☐ Teaching the Principle (TE)
- ☐ Enrichment (TE)
- ☐ Additional Spelling Words (TE)

Assessment

Pretest

1. We saw bears at the <u>zoo</u>.
2. He will eat his <u>food</u>.
3. I like to <u>look</u> at the fish.
4. The <u>moon</u> is in the sky.
5. Read this <u>book</u>.
6. They will come <u>soon</u>.
7. Rafi <u>took</u> my hat.
8. She had a <u>good</u> time.
9. Kim has a big <u>room</u>.
10. I have a cut on my <u>foot</u>.
11. Did <u>you</u> feed the goats?
12. Seth knows <u>who</u> called.

Day 2 *page 151*

Objectives *Children will*

- practice spelling list words
- apply spelling strategies
- complete analogies with Basic Words
- identify Elephant Words by given vowel sounds and spellings

Planning Checklist

- ☑ Spelling Strategy
- ☑ Independent Practice
- ☐ Daily Proofreading Practice (TE)
- ☐ Informal Assessment (TE)
- ☐ Extra Support (TE)
- ☐ Applying Spelling Strategies (TE)

Additional Resources

Teacher's Resource Book
Practice Masters, pages 103–105
Unit Test, page 106
Bulletin Board, page 111

 Practice Plus
Take-Home Word List 22
Games

Spelling Transparencies
Spelling Word List 22
Daily Proofreading Practice, Unit 22
Graphic Organizers

Teacher's Resource Disk
Macintosh® or Windows® software. Houghton Mifflin

Spelling CD-ROM
Macintosh® or Windows® software. Houghton Mifflin

Internet
http://www.eduplace.com

Phonics Practice
Houghton Mifflin Phonics
The Listening Corner
Phonics Home Connection

 Day 3 *page 152*

Objective *Children will*
• review Basic and Review Words

Planning Checklist
☐ Review: Spelling Spree
☐ How Are You Doing?
☐ Daily Proofreading Practice (TE)
☐ Cooperative Learning Activity (TE)

 Day 4 *page 153*

Objectives *Children will*
• proofread for spelling and capital letters
• write and proofread an original composition

Planning Checklist
☐ Proofread: Spelling and Capital Letters
☐ Write Some Riddles
☐ Daily Proofreading Practice (TE)
☐ Challenge Words Practice (TE)
☐ Another Writing Idea (TE)

 Day 5 *page 153*

Objective *Children will*
• take the posttest

Assessment
☐ **Posttest** (TE) *See Day 5*
☐ Unit 22 Test

Meeting Individual Needs
Students Acquiring English

Spanish Spanish has a sound similar to the |o͞o| sound, but it is spelled *u*. Spanish has no |o͝o|.
Activity Say Basic Words 1–10, exaggerating the vowel sounds, and have children repeat them. Write the words on the board. Then make columns labeled *moon* and *book*. Ask children to tell you whether the vowel sound in each word matches that of *moon* or *book*, and write the word in the correct column.
Asian Some children may have difficulty hearing the difference between the |o͞o| and the |o͝o| sounds.
Activity Use the activity for Spanish-speaking students.

Other Activities for Any Day

• Bonus activities from pages 154–155
• Practice Masters (easy, average, challenging)
  Teacher's Resource Book, pages 103–105
• Take-Home Word List 22
  Practice Plus

Day 1

Objectives *Children will*

- take the pretest
- pronounce the list words
- learn about the spelling principle
- sort words by their vowel sounds

Teaching the Principle

This lesson teaches the *oo* spelling pattern for the |o͞o| and the |o͝o| sounds. Children learn the strategy of thinking of this *oo* spelling pattern when they hear these vowel sounds.

To sum up the lesson, ask:

- What vowel sounds do the letters *oo* make in *moon* and *zoo*? |o͞o|

- What vowel sounds do the letters *oo* make in *book* and *foot*? |o͝o|

Note: The word *room* may be pronounced |r¢m| in some regions.

Enrichment

Vocabulary: Multiple Meanings

Have children use a dictionary to look up *look, good,* and *foot.* Discuss the different meanings.

The Vowel Sounds in moon and book

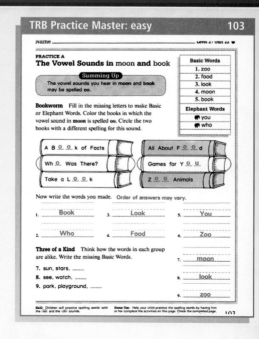

o͞o book   o͞o moon

A. zoo

____ food ____

____ moon ____

____ soon ____

____ room ____

____ you ____

____ who ____

B. look

____ book ____

____ took ____

____ good ____

____ foot ____

150

Read and Say

READ the sentences. **SAY** each word in dark print.

Basic Words

1. zoo	*zoo*	We saw bears at the **zoo**.
2. food	*food*	He will eat his **food**.
3. look	*look*	I like to **look** at the fish.
4. moon	*moon*	The **moon** is in the sky.
5. book	*book*	Read this **book**.
6. soon	*soon*	They will come **soon**.
7. took	*took*	Rafi **took** my hat.
8. good	*good*	She had a **good** time.
9. room	*room*	Kim has a big **room**.
10. foot	*foot*	I have a cut on my **foot**.
11. you	*you*	Did **you** feed the goats?
12. who	*who*	Seth knows **who** called.

Think and Write

Most of the words are spelled with the letters **oo**. These letters make two different vowel sounds.

the (moon) ☾ vowel sound → z**oo**, f**oo**d
the (book) 📖 vowel sound → l**oo**k, t**oo**k

How are the Elephant Words different? The |o͞o| sound is spelled *ou* in *you* and *o* in *who*.

A. Write **seven** Basic Words with the ☾ vowel sound. Remember the Elephant Words.

B. Write **five** Basic Words with the 📖 vowel sound.

Order of answers for each category may vary.

Review	Challenge
13. clap 14. like	15. hoof 16. moose

TEACHING OPTIONS

Meeting Individual Needs
Word Lists

You may want to assign Basic Words 1–5, the Elephant Words, and the Review Words to children who misspelled more than five words on the pretest. Assign the Challenge Words as appropriate. (You may want to have children write sentences, using the Challenge Words.)

Additional Spelling Words

Basic	Challenge	Words Often Misspelled
spoon	cartoon	goes
boot	balloon	going
noon	cookbook	
cook	choose	
cool	rooster	
	crook	

Home/School Involvement
Take-Home Word List • Goal-Setting

Have children set goals for the week on Take-Home Word List 22.

Independent Practice

 Spelling Strategy The vowel sounds in **moon** and **book** may be spelled **oo**.

moon book

Order of answers for questions 2–3 and 4–6 may vary.

Phonics Write Basic Words to answer the questions.

1. Which word rhymes with **wood**?
2–3. Which two words rhyme with **noon**?
4–6. Which three words rhyme with **cook**?

Word Pairs Write the missing Basic Words.

7. You see **paintings** at a **museum**.
You see **animals** at a _____.
8. A **jet** is one kind of **plane**.
A **kitchen** is one kind of _____.
9. You **drink** your **milk**.
You **eat** your _____.
10. You **catch** with your **hand**.
You **kick** with your _____.

Elephant Words Write an Elephant Word to answer each question.

11. Which word has the ☾ sound spelled **o**?
12. Which word has the ☾ sound spelled **ou**?

Phonics
_____
1. good
_____
2. moon
_____
3. soon
_____
4. look
_____
5. book
_____
6. took

Word Pairs
_____
7. zoo
_____
8. room
_____
9. food
_____
10. foot

Elephant Words
_____
11. who
_____
12. you

(151)

 Day 2

Objectives *Children will*

- practice spelling list words
- apply spelling strategies
- complete analogies with Basic Words
- identify Elephant Words by given vowel sounds and spellings

Daily Proofreading Practice
Men have walked on the **mune**. (*moon*)
Do **yoo** like to dance? (*you*)

Meeting Individual Needs
visual/oral/auditory

Extra Support Check Independent Practice to determine who needs extra support. Draw a moon and a book on the board. Say *moon* and *book* as you label the drawings. Elicit from children that the vowel sounds in the words are different. Write Basic Words 1–10 on the board. Have volunteers read each word and draw a moon or a book beside each word to identify its vowel sound.

TRB Practice Master: average   104

Basic Words	PRACTICE B
1. zoo	**The Vowel Sounds in moon and book**
2. food	**Hidden Words** Find and circle the hidden Basic Word
3. look	in each box. Then write the word.
4. moon	
5. book	1. omibooketou 4. roopufoody
6. soon	2. bougoodoolu 5. stookowoon
7. took	3. tulookenyoo 6. zoufootsoo
8. good	
9. room	1. book 4. food
10. foot	2. good 5. took
Elephant Words	3. look 6. foot
you	
who	

Word Search Write the missing Basic or Elephant Words. Then circle each word in the puzzle. Look across and down.

7. _____ moon
8. _____ you
9. _____ soon
10. _____ zoo
11. _____ room
12. _____ who

7. sun and _____   10. _____ keeper
8. _____ and I   11. lots of _____ to move
9. coming _____   12. _____ or what

104

Applying Spelling Strategies
To Read New Words

- Write this sentence on the chalkboard:
The new shampoo came in a dinosaur bottle.

- Have children read the sentence silently.
- Elicit the following strategies as children try to decode *shampoo*.

 shampoo

The letter *p* makes the sound I hear at the beginning of *pig*. And I know that *oo* can make the |o͞o| or the |o͝o| sound. I'll try both to see which makes sense.

I know that the letters *sh* make the |sh| sound.

I see that *a* is followed by a consonant. I think this is the short *a* vowel pattern. I know that the consonant *m* makes the sound I hear at the beginning of *monster*.

Sh-am-po͞o. Sh-am-po͞o. Sham-po͞o. Shampoo. The word *shampoo* makes sense in the sentence.

Day 3

Objective *Children will*
- review Basic and Review Words

Daily Proofreading Practice

She wore a red sock on one **fut**.
(foot)
I know **hoo** hit the home run. *(who)*

Puzzle Play

1. roo(m)
2. g(o)od
3. soo(n)
4. loo(k)
5. lik(e)
6. (y)ou

Hidden Words

7. who
8. took
9. clap

Jobs Match

10. moon
11. zoo
12. book

(152)

Review: Spelling Spree

Puzzle Play Write a Basic or Review Word for each clue. Use the letters that would be in the boxes to spell an animal in the zoo.

1. a place with four walls __ __ __ ☐
2. the opposite of **bad** __ ☐ __ __
3. a short time from now __ __ __ ☐
4. to see with your eyes __ __ __ ☐
5. to think someone or something is nice __ __ __ ☐
6. a person who is not me, him, or her ☐ __ __

Secret Word: m o n k e y

Hidden Words Find the hidden Basic or Review Word in each box. Write the word.

7. wethwholle   8. stuttookom   9. kasclappat

Jobs Match Write the Basic Word that tells where the person works or what the person makes or works with on the job.

10. astronaut
11. animal trainer
12. author

How Are You Doing?
List the spelling words that are hard for you. Practice them with a family member.

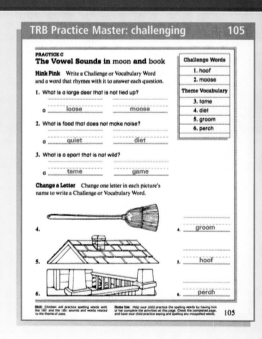

TEACHING OPTIONS

Cooperative Learning Activity
Crazy Crosswords
visual/kinesthetic

Have partners or small groups build two-dimensional crossword puzzles, using UpWords® tiles or letter cards. Children take turns using the letters to spell a word with the *oo* pattern. Players add to what previous players have spelled, either by building *out* in a regular crossword formation, or by building *up,* covering letters that have already been placed down. For example, if one player spells *book,* the next player might cover the *b* with a *t* to spell *took.*

PRACTICE C
The Vowel Sounds in moon and book

Challenge Words
1. hoof
2. moose

Theme Vocabulary
3. tame
4. diet
5. groom
6. perch

Hink Pink Write a Challenge or Vocabulary Word and a word that rhymes with it to answer each question.

1. What is a large deer that is not tied up?
   a _loose_ _moose_

2. What is food that does not make noise?
   a _quiet_ _diet_

3. What is a sport that is not wild?
   a _tame_ _game_

Change a Letter Change one letter in each picture's name to write a Challenge or Vocabulary Word.

4. _groom_
5. _hoof_
6. _perch_

105

Proofreading and Writing

Proofread: Spelling and Capital Letters

Always begin the names of the months of the year with capital letters.

January   April   November

Proofread this page from a travel book. Use proofreading marks to fix four spelling mistakes and two missing capital letters.

Example: Is december a ~~goud~~ good time to go?

You will ~~lik~~ *like* Betty's Wild Animal Park in june or july.

There is ~~rume~~ *room* for animals to run there and plenty of ~~fode~~ *food*

for them to eat. The best way to explore the zoo is on ~~fot~~ *foot*.

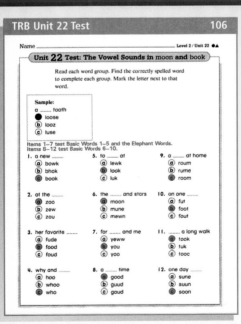

Write Some Riddles

I am orange. You can pick me in October. What am I? Write riddles. Try to use spelling words and months of the year in your clues. Have a friend guess the answers.

Proofreading Tip

Check that you began the name of each month with a capital letter.

Basic

1. zoo
2. food
3. look
4. moon
5. book
6. soon
7. took
8. good
9. room
10. foot
11. you
12. who

Review

13. clap
14. like

Challenge

15. hoof
16. moose

Proofreading Marks

∧ Add
⌐ Delete
≡ Make a capital letter
/ Make a small letter

153

Objectives *Children will*

■ proofread for spelling and capital letters

■ write and proofread an original composition

Day 4

Daily Proofreading Practice

Mario **tok** his mitt to school. *(took)*
We fed monkeys at the **zew**. *(zoo)*

Day 5 **Posttest**

Sentences 1–5 test the first five Basic Words. Sentences 6–10 test the next five Basic Words. Sentences 11–12 test the Elephant Words.

Basic Words

1. Will you <u>look</u> for the pen?
2. I see a big <u>moon</u>.
3. We will go to the <u>zoo</u>.
4. The <u>book</u> is about a cat.
5. I ate the hot <u>food</u>.
6. I will go to my <u>room</u>.
7. We will bake it <u>soon</u>.
8. She put her <u>foot</u> on the box.
9. He <u>took</u> the box.
10. That is a <u>good</u> kite.
11. I saw <u>who</u> did it.
12. Can <u>you</u> clean it?

Review Words

13. We <u>like</u> to play.
14. He can <u>clap</u> for me.

Challenge Words

15. The <u>moose</u> ate twigs and bark.
16. She took a stone from the horse's <u>hoof</u>.

TRB Unit 22 Test   106

Name _____   Level 2 / Unit 22 ●▲

Unit 22 Test: The Vowel Sounds in moon and book

Read each word group. Find the correctly spelled word to complete each group. Mark the letter next to that word.

Sample:
a _____ tooth
ⓐ loose
ⓑ looz
ⓒ luse

Items 1–7 test Basic Words 1–5 and the Elephant Words.
Items 8–12 test Basic Words 6–10.

1. a new _____
ⓐ bowk
ⓑ bhok
ⓒ book

5. to _____ at
ⓐ lewk
ⓑ look
ⓒ luk

9. a _____ at home
ⓐ roum
ⓑ rume
ⓒ room

2. at the _____
ⓐ zoo
ⓑ zew
ⓒ zou

6. the _____ and stars
ⓐ moon
ⓑ mune
ⓒ mewn

10. on one _____
ⓐ fut
ⓑ foot
ⓒ fout

3. her favorite _____
ⓐ fude
ⓑ food
ⓒ foud

7. for _____ and me
ⓐ yeww
ⓑ you
ⓒ yoo

11. a long walk
ⓐ took
ⓑ tuk
ⓒ tooc

4. why and _____
ⓐ hoo
ⓑ whoo
ⓒ who

8. a _____ time
ⓐ good
ⓑ guud
ⓒ goud

12. one day _____
ⓐ sune
ⓑ suun
ⓒ soon

Meeting Individual Needs

Challenge Words Practice

Ask children to write a description of a make-believe zoo animal, using the Challenge Words. Have them draw a picture of the animal to accompany their description.

Another Writing Idea

Suggest children write a guidebook or a brochure for a zoo. Encourage them to include spelling words.

Unit 22 BONUS

These pages can be used at any time during the study of this unit.

Objectives *Children will*

- build words with the phonograms -*oom*, -*ook*, and -*ool*
- write original sentences

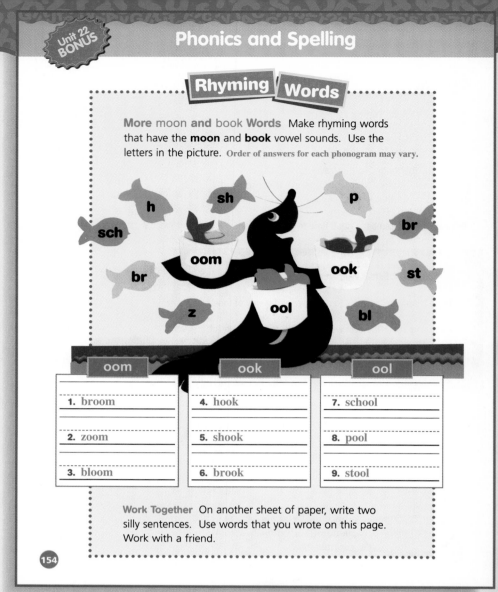

Phonics and Spelling

Rhyming Words

More moon and book Words Make rhyming words that have the **moon** and **book** vowel sounds. Use the letters in the picture. Order of answers for each phonogram may vary.

oom	ook	ool
1. broom	4. hook	7. school
2. zoom	5. shook	8. pool
3. bloom	6. brook	9. stool

Work Together On another sheet of paper, write two silly sentences. Use words that you wrote on this page. Work with a friend.

154

EXTENSION OPTIONS

Learning Center Activity

visual/auditory/kinesthetic

Oops . . . Two Word Webs Have children make a word web of *oop* words. Ask them to write *oop* in the center circle, then think of and write rhyming *oop* words in the outer circles. You may also wish to have children make a "human word web" like the one pictured.

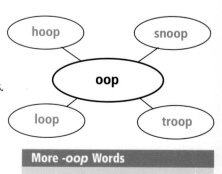

More -oop Words		
droop	scoop	stoop
hoop	sloop	swoop
loop	snoop	troop

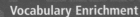 

Vocabulary Enrichment

Unit 22 BONUS

Science

Zoos All the words in the box have something to do with zoos. Write those words to finish this sign. Use your Spelling Dictionary.

Spelling Word Link

zoo

tame
diet
groom
perch

Parrots like to __(1)__ on branches. They __(2)__ their own feathers. Fruit is part of their __(3)__ . A __(4)__ parrot makes a good pet.

1. perch
2. groom
3. diet
4. tame

Try This CHALLENGE

Yes or No? Write **yes** or **no** to answer each question.

5. Would a **tame** monkey live in a jungle?
6. Do some animals **groom** themselves?
7. Could an elephant **perch** on a branch?
8. Could a bear live on a **diet** of rocks?

5. no
6. yes
7. no
8. no

★ Fact File

The biggest parrots are called **macaws**. They can be as big as three feet long from head to tail! Macaws live in Mexico and in Central and South America.

155

Day by Day Planner

Objectives *Children will*

■ expand their vocabulary by using words related to zoos

■ show their understanding of the vocabulary words by completing context activities

Vocabulary Checkup

Have children use the vocabulary words in sentences or match the words to the definitions below.

1. to make neat in appearance *groom*
2. the usual food and drink taken in by a person or an animal every day *diet*
3. to rest or sit on a branch or a rod *perch*
4. trained to live with people *tame*

Fact File

Macaws

Macaws are quite intelligent and are sometimes able to get out of locked cages. You might hear a squawk, a screech, or even a "hello" from a macaw, as they can be very vocal. As a result of deforestation, macaws that live in the wild are endangered.

Integrating Literature

Easy	Average	Challenging
Going to the Zoo by Tom Paxton Three siblings go to the zoo in this song.	**Baby Zoo** by Bruce McMillan An introduction to young members of the animal kingdom.	**A Lion Named Shirley Williamson** by Bernard Waber The lions at the Brooklyn Zoo resent the attention the new lioness receives.
What Do You Do at a Petting Zoo? by Hana Machotka Readers guess the identity of seven zoo animals.	**Zoo** by Gail Gibbons An inside look at the workings of a zoo, from morning to night.	**Zoo Dooings** by Jack Prelutsky A collection of funny animal poems.

Homophones

WORD LISTS

Spelling

Basic
1. plane
2. plain
3. tail
4. tale
5. rode
6. road
7. hole
8. whole
9. to
10. too
11. two

Review
12. see
13. by

Challenge
14. threw
15. through

Vocabulary

Social Studies: Things That Fly
pilot
glide
land
crew

Introducing the Lesson

Read Aloud

Write the Basic Words on the board.

Up, Up, and Away

Many of you have probably been in a **plane,** but have you ever been in a hot-air balloon? The first balloon was made in 1783 by **two** brothers, Joseph and Jacques Montgolfier. They made a large, **plain** cloth bag and lined the **whole** thing with paper. They floated the bag over a fire. As hot air entered the **hole** in the bottom, the bag rose up, with a **tail** of smoke trailing behind. Later they tied a cage **to** the balloon. Inside the cage **rode** a sheep, a duck, and a rooster. The brothers thought that flying was **too** dangerous for people! Today ballooning is safe and enjoyable. In a hot-air balloon you could go for a fun ride in the countryside without having **to** follow a **road.** Then you would have a **tale to** tell your friends!

Responding Ask children to name something that flies when filled with hot air. *(a hot-air balloon)* Say the word *plain* as you point to it on the board. Ask children to say and spell another spelling word that sounds like this word but means something you fly in. *(plane)*

Day 1 *page 156*

Objectives *Children will*
- take the pretest
- pronounce the list words
- learn about the spelling principle
- identify homophones

Planning Checklist
- ☑ Pretest (TE)
- ☑ Spelling principle/word list
- ☐ Review/Challenge Words
- ☐ Teaching the Principle (TE)
- ☐ Enrichment (TE)
- ☐ Additional Spelling Words (TE)

Assessment

Pretest
1. Zack can fly a <u>plane</u>.
2. She likes <u>plain</u> food.
3. My dog Pal wags his <u>tail</u>.
4. Mom told us a <u>tale</u>.
5. Mia <u>rode</u> on the bus.
6. Stay on this <u>road</u>.
7. How deep is that <u>hole</u>?
8. I ate the <u>whole</u> cake!
9. We will go <u>to</u> the club.
10. Can they play <u>too</u>?
11. Eric has <u>two</u> bikes.

Day 2 *page 157*

Objectives *Children will*
- practice spelling list words
- apply spelling strategies
- complete analogies with Basic Words
- identify Elephant Words by using context clues

Planning Checklist
- ☑ Spelling Strategy
- ☑ Independent Practice
- ☐ Daily Proofreading Practice (TE)
- ☐ Informal Assessment (TE)
- ☐ Extra Support (TE)
- ☐ Applying Spelling Strategies (TE)

 FYI You may want to set up a Spelling Corner in a learning center, stocked with different kinds of manipulatives, such as magnetic letters, letter tiles, punchouts, alphabet posters, and word walls.

 Day 3 *page 158*

Objectives *Children will*
- identify homophones that complete sentences by using the Spelling Dictionary
- review Basic and Review Words

Planning Checklist
- ☐ Dictionary
- ☐ Review: Spelling Spree
- ☐ How Are You Doing?
- ☐ Daily Proofreading Practice (TE)
- ☐ Ongoing Assessment

 Day 4 *page 159*

Objectives *Children will*
- proofread for spelling
- write and proofread an original composition

Planning Checklist
- ☐ Proofread for Spelling
- ☐ Write a Description
- ☐ Daily Proofreading Practice (TE)
- ☐ Challenge Words Practice (TE)
- ☐ Another Writing Idea (TE)

Day 5 *page 159*

Objective *Children will*
- take the posttest

Assessment
☐ **Posttest** (TE) *See Day 5*
☐ Unit 23 Test

● 📖 Additional Resources

Teacher's Resource Book
Practice Masters, pages 107–109
Unit Test, page 110
Bulletin Board, page 111

🏠 **Practice Plus**
🔲 Take-Home Word List 23
Games

Spelling Transparencies
Spelling Word List 23
Daily Proofreading Practice, Unit 23
Graphic Organizers

Teacher's Resource Disk
Macintosh® or Windows® software. Houghton Mifflin

Spelling CD-ROM
Macintosh® or Windows® software. Houghton Mifflin

Internet
http://www.eduplace.com

Phonics Practice
Houghton Mifflin Phonics
The Listening Corner
Phonics Home Connection

👤📖 Meeting Individual Needs
Students Acquiring English

Spanish In Spanish, a final *e* spells a sound. **Activity** Write *plane, tale, rode,* and *whole* on the board. Say each word and have children repeat it. Tell them the final *e* has no sound, but helps the long vowel sound. Have volunteers circle the final *e* in each word, say the word, and spell it.

Asian Using flash cards can clarify confusing word pairs. **Activity** Draw and label a plane, a tail, and a road on flash cards. Write Basic Words 1–10 in pairs on the board and say them. Show each card and have children say the word it represents, spell the word, and then spell its homophone.

Other Activities for Any Day

- Bonus activities from pages 160–161
- Practice Masters (easy, average, challenging)
  Teacher's Resource Book, pages 107–109
- Take-Home Word List 23
  Practice Plus

Day 1

Objectives *Children will*
- take the pretest
- pronounce the list words
- learn about the spelling principle
- identify homophones

Teaching the Principle

This lesson teaches the concept that homophones are words that sound alike but have different spellings and meanings. Children learn the strategy of using word meaning as a clue in determining spelling.

To sum up the lesson, have children read and spell aloud each homophone, then use it correctly in an oral sentence.

Enrichment

Vocabulary: Multiple Meanings
Have children use a dictionary to look up *plain* and *tail.* Discuss the different meanings.

plain

plane

A. plane

plain

tail

tale

rode

road

hole

whole

B. to

too

two

156

Read and Say

READ the sentences. **SAY** each word in dark print.

Basic Words

1.	plane	*plane*	Zack can fly a **plane**.
2.	plain	*plain*	She likes **plain** food.
3.	tail	*tail*	My dog Pal wags his **tail**.
4.	tale	*tale*	Mom told us a **tale**.
5.	rode	*rode*	Mia **rode** on the bus.
6.	road	*road*	Stay on this **road**.
7.	hole	*hole*	How deep is that **hole**?
8.	whole	*whole*	I ate the **whole** cake!
9.	to	*to*	We will go **to** the club.
10.	too	*too*	Can they play **too**?
11.	two	*two*	Eric has **two** bikes.

Think and Write

Each word is a homophone. **Homophones** are words that sound alike but do not have the same spelling or the same meaning.

HOMOPHONE	MEANING
pl**ane**	an airplane
pl**ain**	not fancy

How are the Elephant Words different? The first eight words are pairs of homophones. The Elephant Words are a set of three homophones.

A. Write the first **eight** Basic Words in order. Then draw a circle around each pair of homophones.

B. Now write the **three** Elephant Words.

Order of answers for each category may vary.

Review	Challenge
12. see 13. by	14. threw 15. through

TEACHING OPTIONS

Meeting Individual Needs
Word Lists

You may want to assign Basic Words 1–4, the Elephant Words, and the Review Words to children who misspelled more than five words on the pretest. Assign the Challenge Words as appropriate. (You may want to have children write sentences, using the Challenge Words.)

Additional Spelling Words

Basic	Challenge	Words Often Misspelled
hour	blue	other
our	blew	letter
week	deer	
weak	dear	
pail	sent	
pale	cent	

Home/School Involvement
Take-Home Word List • Goal-Setting

Have children set goals for the week on Take-Home Word List 23.

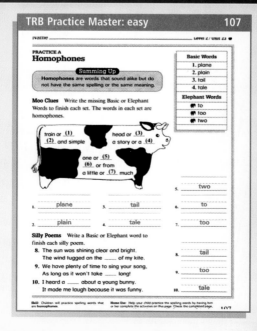

TRB Practice Master: easy   107

Independent Practice

Spelling Strategy **Homophones** are words that sound alike but do not have the same spelling or the same meaning.

Order of answers may vary.

Phonics Write Basic Words to answer the question.

1–3. Which three words have the long **o** sound spelled with the **o-consonant-e** pattern?

Word Meaning Write the Basic Word that means the same or almost the same as each word below.

4. street **5.** simple **6.** story

Word Pairs Write a Basic Word to finish the second sentence in each pair.

7. A bird **flaps** its **wings**.
A dog **wags** its _____.

8. You **drive** a car.
You **fly** a _____.

Elephant Words Write the missing Elephant Words.

9. Sam and I have _____ kites.
10. Do you have a kite _____?
11. We can all go _____ the park and fly them!

Phonics

1. rode

2. hole

3. whole

Word Meaning

4. road

5. plain

6. tale

Word Pairs

7. tail

8. plane

Elephant Words

9. two

10. too

11. to

(157)

Day 2

Objectives *Children will*

- practice spelling list words
- apply spelling strategies
- complete analogies with Basic Words
- identify Elephant Words by using context clues

Daily Proofreading Practice
The **plain** flew over the clouds. (*plane*)
I gave a bird feeder **too** Aunt Polly. (*to*)

Meeting Individual Needs
visual/oral/auditory

Extra Support Check Independent Practice to determine who needs extra support. Write *plane, tail, rode, hole,* and *to* in one column on the board. Write *plain, tale, road, whole,* and *too* in a second column. Ask children to draw lines between the homophones. Use each word in a sentence. Have volunteers identify the word on the board that matches the word in your sentence.

TRB Practice Master: average 108

Basic Words	
1. plane	
2. plain	
3. tail	
4. tale	
5. rode	
6. road	
7. hole	
8. whole	

Elephant Words
to
too
two

PRACTICE B
Homophones

Crossword Clues Write a Basic or Elephant Word for each clue.

Across
2. a place for cars
3. the opposite of *from*
4. a story

Down
1. something that flies
2. drove in a car

Proofreading 5–10. Find and cross out six Basic or Elephant Words that are spelled wrong on this menu. Write each word correctly.

5. two
6. whole
7. tail
8. hole
9. plain
10. too

Dom's Diner

Scrambled eggs with to muffins $2.50
A hole pizza $1.95
Lobster tale soup $3.25
Doughnut with or without a whole 45¢
Pudding
  plane 75¢
  with topping 90¢
Turkey (and the stuffing to) $3.75

108

Skill: Children will practice spelling words that are homophones. **Home Use:** Help your child practice the spelling words by having him or her complete the activities on this page. Check the completed page.

Applying Spelling Strategies
To Spell New Words

- Read aloud: **Jeff said he'd meet me at Foxwood Park after school.**
- Have children attempt to spell *meet* on their Have-a-Go charts.
- Elicit the following strategies as children try to spell *meet*.

meet

I hear the sound for *m* that I hear at the beginning of *monster*.

The final |t| sound is the sound I hear at the beginning of *tiger*. This sound is spelled *t*.

This word has the long *e* sound, which is probably spelled *ea* or *ee*.

This word could be spelled *m-e-a-t* or *m-e-e-t*. When I look in a dictionary, I see that *meet* is spelled *ee* when it means "to come face to face."

UNIT 23

Day 3

Objectives *Children will*

■ identify homophones that complete sentences by using the Spelling Dictionary

■ review Basic and Review Words

Daily Proofreading Practice

Tad **road** his bike by the river. *(rode)*

I painted the **hole** fence green. *(whole)*

UNIT 23

Using Homophones

1. by
2. tale
3. two

Hink Pinks

4. plain
5. plane
6. whole
7. hole

Letter Swap

8. rode
9. tale
10. tail
11. road

158

Dictionary

Using Homophones When you do not know which homophone to write, look up the words in a dictionary. The meanings will help you decide.

hole An opening into or through something: *I found a **hole** in my shoe.*
♦ *These sound alike* **hole**, **whole**.

Practice Write the correct word in dark print to finish each sentence. Use your Spelling Dictionary.

1. Grandma lives _____ the airport. **(buy, by)**
2. Dad read me a _____ about jets. **(tale, tail)**
3. Do all jets have only _____ wings? **(two, to)**

Review: Spelling Spree

Hink Pinks Write two Basic Words to answer each question. The two words must rhyme.

4–5. What is a jet that is not fancy? a ____ ____
6–7. What is all of something you dig? a ____ ____

Letter Swap Make Basic Words by changing the letters in dark print. Write the words.

8. **r**ide
9. **s**ale
10. **p**ail
11. **l**oad

How Are You Doing?
Write your words in ABC order. Practice with a family member any words you spelled wrong.

TEACHING OPTIONS

Ongoing Assessment

Homophones and Meaning

Children often confuse homophones, writing RODE for *road* and HOLE for *whole,* for example. The best way to help children remember which spelling to use is to point out that these homophones are spelled differently because they mean different things. Also, whenever possible, homophones should be presented and discussed in meaningful contexts.

TRB Practice Master: challenging 109

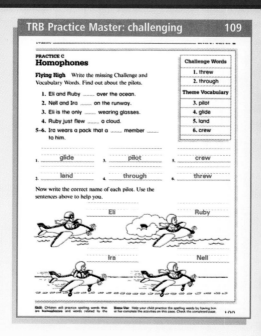

Proofreading and Writing

Proofread for Spelling Proofread this ad. Use proofreading marks to fix five spelling mistakes.

Example: We ~~road~~ rode high in the sky.

BALLOON RIDES
by
Float ~~biy~~ by a cloud! Fly as high as a plane! The whole world looks different when you ~~sea~~ see it from a balloon. It is not ~~two~~ too late ~~too~~ to sign up! Bring ~~to~~ two friends for free.

Write a Description

Pretend you invented a new flying machine. Tell about the machine and how it works. Try to use spelling words. Read your description to a friend. Have your friend draw a picture of the machine from your description.

Proofreading Tip
A computer spell checker cannot tell you if you have used the correct homophone.

(159)

Basic
1. plane
2. plain
3. tail
4. tale
5. rode
6. road
7. hole
8. whole
9. to
10. too
11. two

Review
12. see
13. by

Challenge
14. threw
15. through

Proofreading Marks
∧ Add
⌐ Delete
≡ Make a capital letter
/ Make a small letter

Objectives *Children will*
- proofread for spelling
- write and proofread an original composition

Daily Proofreading Practice
He told us a **tail** about a lost cat. *(tale)*
Sara has **to** frogs and a fish. *(two)*

Posttest

Sentences 1–4 test the first four Basic Words. Sentences 5–8 test the next four Basic Words. Sentences 9–11 test the Elephant Words.

Basic Words
1. She told us a <u>tale</u>.
2. Did he ride on the <u>plane</u>?
3. The kite had a <u>tail</u>.
4. I like the <u>plain</u> cup best.
5. That is a big <u>hole</u>.
6. We can see the <u>road</u>.
7. I <u>rode</u> my bike home.
8. Is that the <u>whole</u> play?
9. It is <u>too</u> hot.
10. I will go <u>to</u> the game.
11. She had <u>two</u> frogs.

Review Words
12. The bus is <u>by</u> the truck.
13. Did he <u>see</u> the kite?

Challenge Words
14. The catcher <u>threw</u> the ball to me.
15. We drove <u>through</u> the tunnel.

TRB Unit 23 Test 110

Unit 23 Test: Homophones

Read each sentence. Is the underlined word spelled right or wrong? Mark your answer.

Sample:	Right	Wrong
I can <u>sea</u> a bird in the sky.	○	●

Items 1–7 test Basic Words 1–4 and the Elephant Words.
Items 8–11 test Basic Words 5–8.

	Right	Wrong
1. Angelo can sing well <u>two</u>.	○	●
2. We made a very <u>plane</u> dinner.	○	●
3. Rosie told us a funny <u>tale</u>.	●	○
4. Are you going <u>to</u> Sandra's party?	●	○
5. Fred watched the <u>plain</u> fly by.	○	●
6. My dog chases his own <u>tail</u>.	●	○
7. Would Irene like <u>too</u> go with us?	○	●
8. Carl <u>road</u> the horse to work.	○	●
9. The mask covered her <u>whole</u> face.	●	○
10. Vera and I live on the same <u>rode</u>.	○	●
11. There is a big <u>hole</u> in my shoe.	●	○

110

Meeting Individual Needs

Challenge Words Practice Ask children to draw a picture for each Challenge Word and other homophone pairs. Have them write the homophones on word cards and see if a friend can match the words and pictures.

Another Writing Idea Ask children to pretend they are sky-writers. Have them write messages they might write in the sky with their planes. Encourage them to include spelling words.

Day
by
Day
Planner

*These pages can be used at any
time during the study of this unit.*

Objectives *Children will*

■ build word families for the homophones *see* and *sea*

■ show their understanding of vocabulary by completing context activities

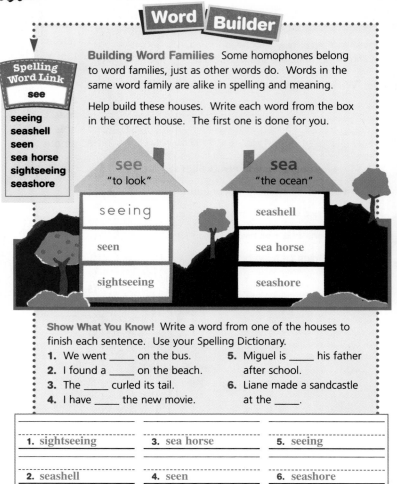

Vocabulary Enrichment

Word Builder

Spelling Word Link

see

seeing
seashell
seen
sea horse
sightseeing
seashore

Building Word Families Some homophones belong to word families, just as other words do. Words in the same word family are alike in spelling and meaning.

Help build these houses. Write each word from the box in the correct house. The first one is done for you.

see "to look"

seeing

seen

sightseeing

sea "the ocean"

seashell

sea horse

seashore

Show What You Know! Write a word from one of the houses to finish each sentence. Use your Spelling Dictionary.

1. We went _____ on the bus.
2. I found a _____ on the beach.
3. The _____ curled its tail.
4. I have _____ the new movie.
5. Miguel is _____ his father after school.
6. Liane made a sandcastle at the _____.

1. sightseeing	3. sea horse	5. seeing
2. seashell	4. seen	6. seashore

160

EXTENSION OPTIONS

Learning Center Activity

visual/kinesthetic

Homophone Word Families Have children build their own word families. Suggest they "build" a house for each of the homophones *sail* and *sale,* using a dictionary to find related words.

Vocabulary Enrichment

Social Studies

Things That Fly All the words in the box have something to do with things that fly. Use those words to finish this timetable. Use your Spelling Dictionary.

Spelling Word Link

plane

pilot
glide
land
crew

12:30	The __(1)__ turns on the engines and flies the plane.
1:00	Some __(2)__ members serve you lunch.
2:00	The plane will __(3)__ over Swan Lake.
2:30	You should __(4)__ in Swanville.

1. pilot
2. crew
3. glide
4. land

Try This CHALLENGE

Write a Message Pretend you are a skywriter. Write one or two messages. Try to use some words from the box on this page.

★ Fact File

In 1903, Orville Wright made the first flight in an airplane. His famous ride lasted only 12 seconds. He flew just 120 feet, which is about as long as three school buses!

161

Integrating Literature

Easy	Average	Challenging
Feathers for Lunch *by Lois Ehlert* A cat tries to catch a backyard bird for his lunch.	**Crosby** *by Dennis Haseley* A boy named Crosby discovers and fixes up an old kite.	**First Flight** *by George Shea* A boy named Tom Tate sees the Wright Brothers build the first plane.
Curious George Flies a Kite *by H. A. Rey* The mischievous monkey George has a funny adventure with a kite.	**Isla** *by Arthur Dorros* Rosa and her grandmother fly to the Caribbean in their imaginations.	**Nobody Owns the Sky** *by Reeve Lindbergh* A picture book biography of African American aviatrix Bessie Coleman.

Day by Day Planner

Objectives *Children will*

- expand their vocabulary by using words related to things that fly
- show their understanding of the vocabulary words by completing context activities

Vocabulary Checkup

Have children use the vocabulary words in sentences or match the words to the definitions below.

1. the people who work together to fly an airplane or sail a ship *crew*
2. to move smoothly and quietly *glide*
3. a person who flies an airplane *pilot*
4. to come down or bring to rest on the ground *land*

Fact File

The Wright Brothers

Pictured is the Wright brothers' first flight at Kitty Hawk, North Carolina, on December 17, 1903. Orville is at the controls of the plane. Wilbur is standing at the right of the picture. Later that day, Wilbur flew the biplane for fifty-nine seconds and covered 852 feet.

Review: Units 19–23

WORD LISTS

Spelling
Basic Words

Unit 19	Unit 22
thank	food
sing	look
and	moon
think	took
bring	good
end	room

Unit 20	Unit 23
dresses	tail
boxes	tale
beaches	rode
days	road
bikes	hole
wishes	whole

Unit 21
boat
go
slow
old
coat
told

Elephant Words
Units 19–23

children	to
do	too
who	two

The Review Unit
Word Lists

Half of the Basic Words from Units 19–23 are reviewed in this Review Unit. The remaining Basic Words from Units 19–23 are reviewed in the Extra Practice section of the Student's Handbook. Each of the Elephant Words is practiced in either the Review Unit or the Extra Practice section.

Day 1 *page 162*

Objectives *Children will*
- take the pretest
- review words that end with the consonant pairs *nd*, *ng*, and *nk*
- review plural words ending in *s* or *es*

Planning Checklist
- ☐ Daily Proofreading Practice (TE)
- ☐ Extra Support, pages 133, 139 (TE)
- ☐ Extra Practice, page 250
- ☐ Practice Masters, pages 91, 92, 95, 96 (TRB)

Assessment

Pretest
1. I can <u>sing</u> for them.
2. This is the <u>end</u> of the ride.
3. I have some white <u>dresses</u>.
4. The <u>days</u> are hot.
5. He can <u>go</u> with her.
6. My <u>coat</u> is big.
7. The <u>moon</u> is white.
8. This is a <u>good</u> game.
9. He <u>told</u> me a <u>tale</u>.
10. She will take the <u>whole</u> thing.

Day 2 *page 163*

Objectives *Children will*
- review spelling patterns for the |ō| sound
- review a spelling pattern for the |ōō| and the |o͞o| sounds

Planning Checklist
- ☐ Daily Proofreading Practice (TE)
- ☐ Extra Support, pages 145, 151(TE)
- ☐ Extra Practice, page 251
- ☐ Practice Masters, pages 99, 100, 103, 104 (TRB)

Day 3 *page 164*   **Day 4** *page 165*   **Day 5** *page 165*

Objectives *Children will*

- review homophones
- review the Elephant Words

Planning Checklist

☐ Daily Proofreading Practice (TE)

☐ Extra Support, page 157 (TE)

☐ Extra Practice, page 252

☐ Practice Masters, pages 107, 108 (TRB)

Objective *Children will*

- analyze the spelling and meaning relationship of words in the *thank* word family

Planning Checklist

☐ Spelling-Meaning Strategy

Objective *Children will*

- take the posttest

Assessment

☐ **Posttest** (TE) *See Day 5*

☐ Scoring Rubric

☐ Unit 24 Review Tests A–B (TRB)

 Additional Resources

Teacher's Resource Book
Practice Masters, pages 91–93, 95–97, 99–101, 103–105, 107–109
Multiple-Choice Tests, pages 116–117
Bulletin Board, page 111
Spelling Newsletters, English and Spanish, pages 112–113
Spelling Game, pages 114–115

Practice Plus
Take-Home Word List 24

Spelling Transparencies
Spelling Word List 24
Daily Proofreading Practice, Unit 24
Spelling-Meaning Strategy
Multiple-Choice Test

Teacher's Resource Disk
Macintosh® or Windows® software. Houghton Mifflin

Spelling CD-ROM
Macintosh® or Windows® software. Houghton Mifflin

Internet
http://www.eduplace.com

Other Activities for Any Day

- Literature and Writing, pages 166–167
- Spelling Game
  Teacher's Resource Book, pages 114–115
- Bulletin Board
  Teacher's Resource Book, page 111
- Take-Home Word List 24
  Practice Plus

Meeting Individual Needs

You may wish to create your own pretest, using the words that children missed most often in the last five units. Children can check their own work, or a partner's, by looking up the words in the previous units' word lists or in their Spelling Dictionary.

In each Review lesson, the Basic Words are selected from both halves of the unit word list to accommodate individual needs. In Units 19–22, the top row of words is from Basic Words 1–5 and the bottom row from Basic Words 6–10. In Unit 23, the first two words in the top row are from Basic Words 1–4 and the remaining words are from Basic Words 5–8.

Day 1

Objectives *Children will*

- take the pretest
- review words that end with the consonant pairs *nd*, *ng*, and *nk*
- review plural words ending in *-s* or *-es*

Daily Proofreading Practice

Did you **brang** a lunch box? (*bring*)

We filled the **boxez** with toys. (*boxes*)

Meeting Individual Needs

Additional Resources

Unit 19

Extra Support page 133 (TE)

Extra Practice page 250

Practice Masters pages 91–92 (TRB)

Unit 20

Extra Support page 139 (TE)

Extra Practice page 250

Practice Masters pages 95–96 (TRB)

---

24 Review: Units 19–23

Unit 19   Words with nd, ng, or nk   pages 132–137

king ng

thank	sing	and
think	bring	end

Spelling Strategy   Some words end with the consonants **nd**, **ng**, or **nk**.

Write the spelling word that rhymes with each word.

1. send   2. bank   3. pink   4. land

Write the missing spelling words.

5. We will _____ songs at home tonight.
6. Grandpa will _____ his banjo and play for us.

Unit 20   Words with s or es   pages 138–143

bikes es

dresses	boxes	beaches
days	bikes	wishes

Spelling Strategy

s → days, bikes

es → dresses, boxes, wishes, beaches

Write the spelling word that goes with each word.

7. skirts   8. cardboard   9. sand   10. tires

Write the missing words.

11. How many _____ are there until my birthday?
12. I will make _____ as I blow out the candles.

1. end
2. thank
3. think
4. and
5. sing
6. bring
7. dresses
8. boxes
9. beaches
10. bikes
11. days
12. wishes

162

EXTENSION OPTIONS

TRB Bulletin Board   111

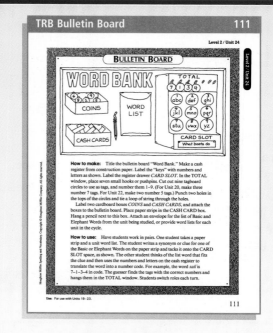

TRB Spelling Newsletter: English   112

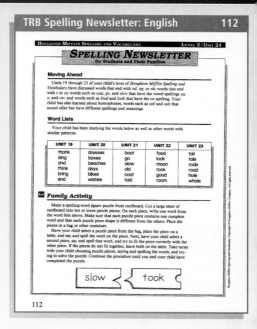

Unit 21   More Long o Spellings   pages 144–149

boat	go	slow
old	coat	told

ō
boat

Spelling Strategy   The long **o** sound may be spelled **o**, **oa**, or **ow**.

Write the spelling word that means the opposite.
13. fast   14. new   15. stop

Write the missing spelling words.
Dad __(16)__ me I could go for a ride in the __(17)__ . I put on my __(18)__ and ran to the dock.

Unit 22   Sounds in moon and book   pages 150–155

food	look	moon
took	good	room

ōō
book

ōō
moon

Spelling Strategy   The vowel sounds in **moon** and **look** may be spelled **oo**.

Write the spelling word that is hidden in each box.
19. uslookim   20. pagoodye   21. otookacg

Write the missing spelling words.
We had a snack in our __(22)__ late last night. We ate our __(23)__ by the light of the __(24)__ .

13. slow _____

14. old _____

15. go _____

16. told _____

17. boat _____

18. coat _____

19. look _____

20. good _____

21. took _____

22. room _____

23. food _____

24. moon _____

(163)

Day 2

Objectives *Children will*
■ review spelling patterns for the |ō| sound
■ review a spelling pattern for the |ōō| and the |ōō| sounds

Daily Proofreading Practice
Grandma **towld** me an old story. (*told*)
The **rume** was full of people. (*room*)

Meeting Individual Needs

Additional Resources
Unit 21
Extra Support page 145 (TE)
Extra Practice page 251
Practice Masters pages 99–100 (TRB)
Unit 22
Extra Support page 151 (TE)
Extra Practice page 251
Practice Masters pages 103–104 (TRB)

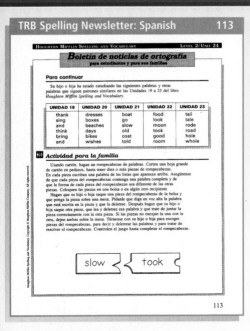

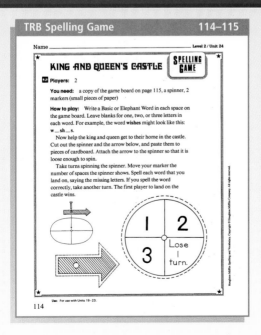

Objectives *Children will*

■ review homophones

■ review the Elephant Words

Daily Proofreading Practice

She has a **whole** in her sock. (*hole*)

May Elsa play this game **to**? (*too*)

Meeting Individual Needs

Additional Resources

Unit 23

Extra Support page 157 (TE)

Extra Practice page 252

Practice Masters pages 107–108 (TRB)

Reviewing Elephant Words

Extra Practice page 252

UNIT 24

Unit 23   Homophones   pages 156–161

plain

plane

tail	tale	rode
road	hole	whole

Spelling Strategy   **Homophones** sound alike but do not have the same spelling or the same meaning.

Change the letter in dark print. Write a spelling word.

25. r**o**le   26. ho**m**e   27. **t**oad

Write the missing spelling words.

I read a ___**(28)**___ about how the squirrel got a bushy ___**(29)**___ . I read the ___**(30)**___ story in one night!

25. rode

26. hole

27. road

28. tale

29. tail

30. whole

31. children

32. who

33. to

34. two

35. too

36. do

Elephant Words   Units 19–23   pages 132–161

 who

children	do	who
to	too	two

Spelling Strategy   Elephant Words have unusual spellings. Check them carefully when you write them.

Write the missing spelling words.

There are six ___**(31)**___ from school ___**(32)**___ are coming ___**(33)**___ my house today. We will play in my tree house. We will ride on my swing. Can you bring ___**(34)**___ friends and come ___**(35)**___ ? Please ___**(36)**___ !

164

EXTENSION OPTIONS

TRB Review Test A   116

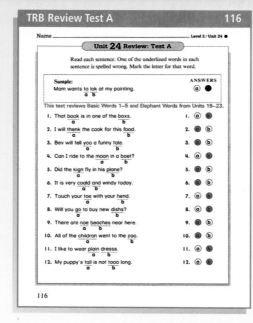

TRB Review Test B   117

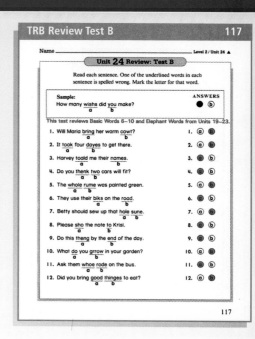

UNIT 24

Spelling-Meaning Strategy

Word Families

Look at this word family. Remember that words in the same family are alike in spelling and meaning.

thank	It is important to **thank** people.
thankful	I am **thankful** for many things.
thanks	I give **thanks** for a good home.
thanked	I **thanked** my Mom for helping me.

Think How are the words in this family alike in meaning? How are they alike in spelling?

Apply and Extend

Write a word from the thank **family in each sentence.**

1. The Pilgrims were very _____.
2. How could they _____ the Indians?
3. They _____ them by making a meal.
4. Everyone gave _____ for their food.

With a partner, think of words in these families. Make a list for each family. See TE margin.

 wish   hand   slow

Check the Word Families list that begins on page 272. Did you miss any words? Add them to your lists.

1. thankful

2. thank

3. thanked

4. thanks

(165)

Day 4

Objective *Children will*

■ analyze the spelling and meaning relationship of words in the *thank* word family

Answers to *Think* Questions

- They all have some form of the meaning "to say that you are grateful."

- They all have the *thank* spelling.

Day 5 **Posttest**

The Posttest tests twenty of the Basic Words reviewed in this unit. Sentences 1–10 test words selected from Basic Words 1–5 in Units 19–23. The Elephant Words sentences test all six words reviewed in this unit.

Basic Words

1. May I <u>sing</u>?
2. The <u>dresses</u> are red.
3. He <u>and</u> I can go.
4. The <u>boat</u> is fast.
5. Her dog has a white <u>tail</u>.
6. We ate all the <u>food</u>.
7. Nine <u>boxes</u> are in my room.
8. She can <u>go</u> with me.
9. Will you <u>look</u> at that?
10. I <u>rode</u> in the car.
11. I <u>think</u> I will play a game.
12. Some <u>days</u> we play.
13. I see a <u>good</u> hat.
14. The <u>bikes</u> are big.
15. Can we take this <u>road</u>?
16. You have an <u>old</u> book.
17. He will <u>bring</u> it with him.
18. My <u>coat</u> is black.
19. We <u>took</u> a game with us.
20. The box has a <u>hole</u> in it.

Elephant Words

21. The <u>children</u> will play.
22. She can <u>do</u> it for me.
23. Did he see <u>who</u> it was?
24. We have <u>to</u> get the cups.
25. He has <u>two</u> cats.
26. She has a white flag <u>too</u>.

Writing Model:
Instructions

Objectives *Children will*

- read a passage modeling instructions

- analyze the model to identify the order of steps, order words, and the topic sentence

Warm-Up

Qualities of Good Instructions

Read aloud the following groups of sentences that give instructions. Have children tell which group is easiest to follow and why. (*Group 2*)

1. Then you dry the dishes. You put soap in the water. Put the dishes away. Next, wash the dishes.

2. First, put dishwashing liquid in some water in the sink. Next, wash the dishes in the soapy water. Then rinse the dishes with clear, hot water. Finally, dry the dishes.

Answers to *Think and Discuss*

1. The steps are: 1) Take a piece of white paper. 2) Get a paintbrush and a bowl of milk. 3) Write your message with the brush and milk. 4) Let the message dry.

2. The steps are written in the order someone should do them.

3. The order words used are *first, next, then,* and *finally.*

4. The first sentence tells the main idea.

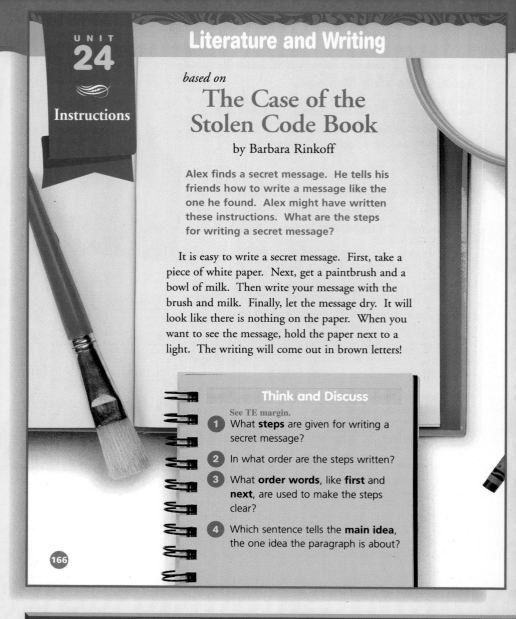

UNIT 24

Instructions

Literature and Writing

based on

The Case of the Stolen Code Book

by Barbara Rinkoff

Alex finds a secret message. He tells his friends how to write a message like the one he found. Alex might have written these instructions. What are the steps for writing a secret message?

It is easy to write a secret message. First, take a piece of white paper. Next, get a paintbrush and a bowl of milk. Then write your message with the brush and milk. Finally, let the message dry. It will look like there is nothing on the paper. When you want to see the message, hold the paper next to a light. The writing will come out in brown letters!

Think and Discuss

See TE margin.

1. What **steps** are given for writing a secret message?

2. In what order are the steps written?

3. What **order words**, like **first** and **next**, are used to make the steps clear?

4. Which sentence tells the **main idea**, the one idea the paragraph is about?

166

EXTENSION OPTIONS

Integrating Literature *Instructions*

Easy	Average	Challenging
My Drum *by Kay Davies* Easy instructions for making and playing a drum.	**Loo-Loo, Boo, and Art You Can Do** *by Denis Roche* A girl and a dog lead children through easy art projects.	**Hopscotch Around the World** *by Mary D. Lankford* Rules for playing hopscotch games from around the world.
Pin the Tail on the Donkey *by Joanna Cole* Directions for children's favorite party games.	**Peas and Honey** *by Kimberly Colen* Simple recipes for kids include a pinch of poetry.	**Jacks Around the World** *by Mary D. Lankford* Rules for playing variations of the game jacks.

The Writing Process
Instructions

Think of some things you know how to do well. Write instructions for one of your ideas. Follow the guidelines. Use the Writing Process.

1 Prewriting
- Write a few words about each step on a sheet of paper.
- Draw a picture to go with each step.

2 Draft
- Write the steps in an order that makes sense.

3 Revise
- Cross out steps that do not belong.
- Remember to use your Thesaurus to find exact words.
- Read your instructions to a friend. Make changes.

4 Proofread
- Did you spell each word correctly?
- Did you begin the names of holidays and months with capital letters?

5 Publish
- Copy your instructions neatly. Then tape-record your instructions. Have a friend follow your instructions.

•• Guidelines for Writing Instructions

✓ Begin with a sentence that tells the main idea.
✓ List the steps in order.
✓ Use order words to make the steps clear.

Composition Words

bring
things
show
soon
you
whole

167

Objective *Children will*
- follow the Writing Process to write instructions, using the criteria given in the guidelines

Additional Resource

To help children generate and explore topics for their personal narrative, have them use the Prewriting Ideas in the *Teacher's Resource Book,* page 118.

Scoring Rubric

Evaluating Writing

The scoring rubric is based on the guidelines on the student book page. Mechanics and usage errors are also considered in general. Explain to children that the guidelines will be used to evaluate their papers.

TRB facsimile: TRB Prewriting Ideas   118

Name _____   Level 2 / Unit 24

Prewriting Ideas: Instructions

Choosing a Topic   Here is a list of ideas that one student made for writing instructions. What things that you can do well do these ideas make you think of?
On the lines below **My Three Ideas**, write three things that you know how to do or make. Which idea do you know all the steps for? For which idea can you explain each step clearly? Circle the topic that you would like to write about.

Ideas for Writing

| How to Make a Code | How to Eat Corn on the Cob |
| How to Whistle | How to Make a Mud Pie |

My Three Ideas

1. _____
2. _____
3. _____

Exploring Your Topic   You can use a picture like this one to help you plan your instructions. Copy the picture onto another sheet of paper. Make it large enough to write on. Write your topic on the big stone. Then write a few words about each step on the small stepping stones. Write the steps in order.

Topic → step 1 → step 2 → step 3 → step 4

Use: For use with Step 1: Prewriting on page 167.

118

Scoring Rubric

Instructions

Score 4

The instructions are easy to follow and interesting to read. The steps are in the proper sequence, and the writer has used time-order words. The object of the instructions is creative or unusual.

Score 2

The work is in the form of instructions. There is a sequence of steps, but it is not very logical. Time-order words are used minimally or inappropriately.

Score 3

The instructions follow a logical sequence of steps. Time-order words are used correctly to advance the understanding of the reader. There is a goal that can be achieved.

Score 1

The work does not relate to instructions. There are no steps to follow. There is no goal to be achieved. The writing is confused and without focus.

More Long *i* Spellings

WORD LISTS

Spelling

Basic

1. sky
2. find
3. night
4. high
5. fly
6. try
7. light
8. dry
9. right
10. kind
11. eye
12. buy

Review

13. why
14. cry

Challenge

15. flight
16. behind

Vocabulary

Science: Stars and Planets

Mars
space
planet
Pluto

Introducing the Lesson

Read Aloud

Write the Basic Words on the board.

Star Light, Star Bright

On a clear, **dry night**, look **high** above your head at the **sky**. Look to the left and to the **right**. You will **find** that the **sky** is filled with stars. Did you ever **try** to count them? With the human **eye**, you cannot see all the stars in the universe. Even if you **buy** a telescope, you will not see them all. Many stars are the same size as the Sun, but because they are so far away they look like tiny points of **light**. It would take a rocket thousands of years to **fly** to the stars. The closest star to Earth is the Sun. It is an ordinary **kind** of star, neither the biggest nor the brightest. Without the Sun, however, there would be no life on Earth!

Responding Ask children what star is closest to Earth. *(the Sun)* Ask them to name the spelling word that tells the time when it is easiest to see the stars. *(night)* Ask which spelling words rhyme with *night*. *(light, right)*

Day 1 page 168   **Day 2** page 169

Objectives *Children will*

- take the pretest
- pronounce the list words
- learn about the spelling principle
- sort words by their spelling patterns

Planning Checklist

- ☑ Pretest (TE)
- ☑ Spelling principle/word list
- ☐ Review/Challenge Words
- ☐ Teaching the Principle (TE)
- ☐ Enrichment (TE)
- ☐ Additional Spelling Words (TE)

Objectives *Children will*

- practice spelling list words
- apply spelling strategies
- identify antonyms
- identify Elephant Words as homophones

Planning Checklist

- ☑ Spelling Strategy
- ☑ Independent Practice
- ☐ Daily Proofreading Practice (TE)
- ☐ Informal Assessment (TE)
- ☐ Extra Support (TE)
- ☐ Applying Spelling Strategies (TE)

Assessment

Pretest

1. I see a star in the sky.
2. Help me find my book.
3. Mom works at night.
4. How high can you jump?
5. Can you fly a plane?
6. I will try to draw a pig.
7. It is light outside.
8. The brown grass is dry.
9. Show me the right way.
10. Jon is kind to animals.
11. He can close one eye.
12. They will buy a car.

Research Notes Analogy is a powerful learning strategy. It can be used to show children how words are related in groups or "families." Uncertain about the spelling of *found*, for example, children can be shown the words *ground* and *pound*.

 Day 3 *page 170*

 Day 4 *page 171*

Day 5 *page 171*

Objectives *Children will*
- use a dictionary entry and context clues to identify the multiple meanings of a given word
- review Basic and Review Words

Planning Checklist
- ☐ Dictionary
- ☐ Review: Spelling Spree
- ☐ How Are You Doing?
- ☐ Daily Proofreading Practice (TE)
- ☐ Ongoing Assessment

Objectives *Children will*
- proofread for spelling
- write and proofread an original composition

Planning Checklist
- ☐ Proofread for Spelling
- ☐ Write Some Captions
- ☐ Daily Proofreading Practice (TE)
- ☐ Challenge Words Practice (TE)
- ☐ Another Writing Idea (TE)

Objective *Children will*
- take the posttest

Assessment
☐ **Posttest** (TE) *See Day 5*
☐ Unit 25 Test

Additional Resources

Teacher's Resource Book
Practice Masters, pages 119–121
Unit Test, page 122
Bulletin Board, page 139

Practice Plus
Take-Home Word List 25
Games

Spelling Transparencies
Spelling Word List 25
Daily Proofreading Practice, Unit 25
Graphic Organizers

Teacher's Resource Disk
Macintosh® or Windows® software. Houghton Mifflin

Spelling CD-ROM
Macintosh® or Windows® software. Houghton Mifflin

Internet
http://www.eduplace.com

Phonics Practice
Houghton Mifflin Phonics
The Listening Corner
Phonics Home Connection

 Meeting Individual Needs
Students Acquiring English

Spanish In Spanish, the |ī| sound is spelled *ai* or *ay*. The letter *i* spells the |ē| sound. Some children may also have difficulty with words that end with *t*.

Activity Write *sky, fly, try,* and *dry* on the board. Say each word and have children repeat it. Then erase the *y* endings and have volunteers go to the board and complete the words. Repeat the activity with the letter *i* in *find* and *kind*. Say *nice/night, lie/light,* and *rice/right*. Ask children which word in each pair ends with the |t| sound. Say the words with the final |t| sound, emphasizing the ending. Have children repeat after you.

Other Activities for Any Day

- Bonus activities from pages 172–173
- Practice Masters (easy, average, challenging)
  Teacher's Resource Book, pages 119–121
- Take-Home Word List 25
  Practice Plus

Objectives *Children will*
- take the pretest
- pronounce the list words
- learn about the spelling principle
- sort words by their spelling patterns

Teaching the Principle

This lesson teaches the *y, i,* and *igh* spelling patterns for the |ī| sound. Children learn the strategy of thinking of these patterns when they hear the long *i* sound.

To sum up the lesson, ask:

- What are three ways the long *i* vowel sound is spelled in these words? (*y, i, igh*)

- What long *i* spelling has two silent letters? What are the letters? (*igh; g* and *h*)

Enrichment

Vocabulary: Multiple Meanings
Have children use a dictionary to look up *light* and *right.* Discuss the different meanings.

ī
f ly

Read and Say

READ the sentences. **SAY** each word in dark print.

Basic Words

1.	sky	*sky*	I see a star in the **sky**.
2.	find	*find*	Help me **find** my book.
3.	night	*night*	Mom works at **night**.
4.	high	*high*	How **high** can you jump?
5.	fly	*fly*	Can you **fly** a plane?
6.	try	*try*	I will **try** to draw a pig.
7.	light	*light*	It is **light** outside.
8.	dry	*dry*	The brown grass is **dry**.
9.	right	*right*	Show me the **right** way.
10.	kind	*kind*	Jon is **kind** to animals.
11.	eye	*eye*	He can close one **eye**.
12.	buy	*buy*	They will **buy** a car.

A. sky
___ fly
___ try
___ dry

B. find
___ kind

C. night
___ high
___ light
___ right

D. eye
___ buy

(168)

Think and Write

Most of the words have the long **i** vowel sound spelled **y, i,** or **igh**.

the long **i** sound → sk**y**, f**i**nd, n**igh**t

How are the Elephant Words different? The |ī| sound is spelled *eye* and *uy*.

A. Write **four** Basic Words with the long **i** sound spelled **y**.
B. Write **two** Basic Words with the long **i** sound spelled **i**.
C. Write **four** Basic Words with the long **i** sound spelled **igh**.
D. Now write the **two** Elephant Words.

Order of answers for each category may vary.

Review	Challenge
13. why 14. cry	15. flight 16. behind

TEACHING OPTIONS

Meeting Individual Needs
Word Lists

You may want to assign Basic Words 1–5, the Elephant Words, and the Review Words to children who misspelled more than five words on the pretest. Assign the Challenge Words as appropriate. (You may want to have children write sentences, using the Challenge Words.)

Additional Spelling Words

Basic	Challenge	Words Often Misspelled
July	tiny	family
wild	tiger	really
fight	nightmare	
spy	siren	
mind	tightrope	
	firefly	

Home/School Involvement
Take-Home Word List • Goal-Setting

Have children set goals for the week on Take-Home Word List 25.

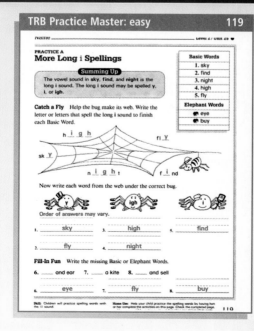

TRB Practice Master: easy 119

Name ___ Level 2 / Unit 25

PRACTICE A
More Long i Spellings

Summing Up
The vowel sound in sky, find, and night is the long i sound. The long i sound may be spelled y, i, or igh.

Basic Words
1. sky
2. find
3. night
4. high
5. fly

Elephant Words
eye
buy

Catch a Fly Help the bug make its web. Write the letter or letters that spell the long i sound to finish each Basic Word.

h i g h   fl Y
sk Y
n i g h t   f i nd

Now write each word from the web under the correct bug.

Order of answers may vary.

1. sky   3. high   5. find
2. fly   4. night

Fill-In Fun Write the missing Basic or Elephant Words.

6. ___ and ear   7. ___ a kite   8. ___ and sell
9. eye   ___. fly   ___. buy

Independent Practice

 Spelling Strategy The vowel sound in **sky**, **find**, and **night** is the long **i** sound. The long **i** sound may be spelled **y**, **i**, or **igh**.

Order of answers for question 4–5 may vary.

Phonics Write Basic Words to answer the questions.

1. Which word begins with the same consonant cluster as ? flag
2. Which word begins with the same consonant cluster as ? skate
3. Which word begins with the same consonant cluster as ? truck
4–5. Which two words rhyme with **mind**?

Word Meaning Write the Basic Word that means the opposite of each word below.

6. wet　　8. dark　　10. day
7. low　　9. wrong

Elephant Words Write an Elephant Word to answer each riddle.

11. I sound like **I**, but I am what you use to look at the stars.
12. I sound like **by**, but I am something you do with money.

Phonics

1. fly
2. sky
3. try
4. find
5. kind

Word Meaning

6. dry
7. high
8. light
9. right
10. night

Elephant Words

11. eye
12. buy

(169)

Objectives Children will
- practice spelling list words
- apply spelling strategies
- identify antonyms
- identify Elephant Words as homophones

Daily Proofreading Practice
Those birds **fli** south each winter. *(fly)*
Turn **rite** at the stop sign. *(right)*

Meeting Individual Needs
visual/oral/auditory

Extra Support Check Independent Practice to determine who needs extra support. Draw three large stars on the board. Write *y*, *i*, or *igh* on each one. Draw small stars around the large ones. Write a Basic Word on each. Point to and say one word at a time. Have volunteers repeat, underline the letter(s) that spell the |ī| sound and draw a line connecting the smaller star with the matching large one.

TRB Practice Master: average　　120

Applying Spelling Strategies
To Spell New Words

- Read aloud: **We have pizza for lunch every Friday.**
- Have children attempt to spell *Friday* on their Have-a-Go charts.
- Elicit the following strategies as children try to spell *Friday*.

> I hear the sounds for *f* and *r* blended together at the beginning of the word.

> I recognize the word *day* at the end of this longer word. I know that *day* is spelled *d-a-y*.

Friday

> Next, I hear the long *i* sound. The long *i* sound could be spelled *y*, *i*, or *igh*. I'll have to check a dictionary.

UNIT 25

Day 3

Objectives *Children will*

- use a dictionary entry and context clues to identify the multiple meanings of a given word
- review Basic and Review Words

Daily Proofreading Practice

I cannot **fiend** my new boots. *(find)*
The stars shine in the dark **skigh**. *(sky)*

UNIT 25

Dictionary

1. 1
2. 3
3. 2
4. 1

ABC Words

5. buy
6. fly
7. cry
8. why
9. eye

Word Hunt

10. light
11. right
12. kind

(170)

Dictionary

Finding the Right Meaning Some entry words may have three different meanings. Each meaning is numbered.

fly **1.** To move through the air using wings: *The birds* **fly** *to their nests.* **2.** To operate a plane or a spacecraft: *Captain Roy will* **fly** *the plane.* **3.** To move quickly: *I have to* **fly***, or I will be late for school.*

Practice Write **1**, **2**, or **3** to tell which meaning of **fly** is used in each sentence below.
1. Did you see that robin **fly** by?
2. I had to **fly** to catch the school bus.
3. My uncle knows how to **fly** jets.
4. Bees **fly** from flower to flower.

Review: Spelling Spree

ABC Words Use ABC order to write the missing letter in each group. Make Basic or Review Words.
Example: r <u>s</u> t j<u>k</u>l x <u>y</u>z = **sky**
5. a__c t__v x__z
6. e__g k__m x__z
7. b__d q__s x__z
8. v__x g__i x__z
9. d__f x__z d__f

Word Hunt Write the Basic Word you see in each longer word.
10. slightly
11. brightest
12. kindness

How Are You Doing? Write each word in a sentence. Practice with a partner any words you spelled wrong.

TEACHING OPTIONS

Ongoing Assessment

Long Vowel Patterns

As children explore different spelling patterns for the same long vowel sounds, they often use an inappropriate pattern. In the case of long *i*, for example, the following are common errors: FIEND or FINDE for *find* and NITE for *night*.

For the same reason, when children reach Unit 26, they may misspell *many* as MANE and *lady* as LADEE until they learn the principle that the final long e sound in two-syllable words is usually spelled *y*.

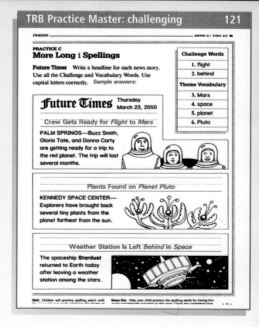

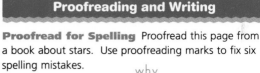

Proofreading and Writing

Proofread for Spelling Proofread this page from a book about stars. Use proofreading marks to fix six spelling mistakes.

Example: Do you know ~~wiy~~ why stars shine?

The best time to look at

stars is a ~~dri nite~~ dry night when the

~~ski~~ sky is clear. You should ~~tri~~ try

to ~~fin~~ find a ~~hi~~ high, open place. One

bright light you will see is

the North Star.

SUN

Write Some Captions

Pretend you were the first child to go to the moon. Draw some pictures that show what you did on your trip. Then write a caption for each picture. Try to use spelling words.

Proofreading Tip

Check to make sure that your n's don't look like your r's.

171

Basic
1. sky
2. find
3. night
4. high
5. fly
6. try
7. light
8. dry
9. right
10. kind
11. eye
12. buy

Review
13. why
14. cry

Challenge
15. flight
16. behind

Proofreading Marks
- ∧ Add
- ℘ Delete
- ≡ Make a capital letter
- / Make a small letter

Day 4

Objectives *Children will*
- proofread for spelling
- write and proofread an original composition

Daily Proofreading Practice
Dad tucks me in bed at **nyte**. *(night)*
I would like to **bi** some candy. *(buy)*

Day 5

Posttest

Sentences 1–5 test the first five Basic Words. Sentences 6–10 test the next five Basic Words. Sentences 11–12 test the Elephant Words.

Basic Words
1. The dog will <u>find</u> a bone.
2. We do not ride bikes at <u>night</u>.
3. Look at the <u>sky</u>.
4. I will <u>fly</u> the plane.
5. The nest is <u>high</u> in the tree.
6. Be <u>kind</u> to the dog.
7. Please fix the <u>light</u>.
8. I can hop on my <u>right</u> foot.
9. Please <u>dry</u> the dishes.
10. We will <u>try</u> to win the game.
11. Please <u>buy</u> a good book.
12. I did not hit my <u>eye</u>.

Review Words
13. Please do not <u>cry</u>.
14. Tell me <u>why</u> it is so hot.

Challenge Words
15. The sun went <u>behind</u> a cloud.
16. It was a long <u>flight</u> over the ocean.

TRB Unit 25 Test   122

Unit 25 Test: More Long i Spellings

Each item below gives three spellings of a word. Choose the correct spelling. Mark the letter for that word.

Sample:			ANSWERS
a. cri	b. cry	c. crigh	Ⓐ ● Ⓒ

Items 1–7 test Basic Words 1–5 and the Elephant Words.
Items 8–12 test Basic Words 6–10.

1. a. fly	b. fli	c. fligh	1. Ⓐ Ⓑ Ⓒ
2. a. nyt	b. night	c. nite	2. Ⓐ Ⓑ Ⓒ
3. a. bigh	b. bi	c. buy	3. Ⓐ Ⓑ ●
4. a. hy	b. hye	c. high	4. Ⓐ Ⓑ ●
5. a. skie	b. sky	c. skigh	5. Ⓐ ● Ⓒ
6. a. eigh	b. eie	c. eye	6. Ⓐ Ⓑ ●
7. a. find	b. fynd	c. fighnd	7. ● Ⓑ Ⓒ
8. a. ryt	b. right	c. rit	8. Ⓐ ● Ⓒ
9. a. try	b. tri	c. trigh	9. ● Ⓑ Ⓒ
10. a. drigh	b. dry	c. dri	10. Ⓐ ● Ⓒ
11. a. lyt	b. liht	c. light	11. Ⓐ Ⓑ ●
12. a. kind	b. kynd	c. kighnd	12. ● Ⓑ Ⓒ

Meeting Individual Needs

Challenge Words Practice
Have children make a word collage for each Challenge Word by cutting letters and pictures from magazines and assembling them to show each word visually. For example, they might show the word *flight* on a bird.

Another Writing Idea
Suggest children write a science fiction story or play about a trip to another planet. Encourage them to include spelling words.

Unit 25 BONUS

Day by Day Planner

These pages can be used at any time during the study of this unit.

Objectives *Children will*

- use context to choose appropriate synonyms from a thesaurus
- use words found in a thesaurus in their writing

Unit 25 BONUS

Vocabulary Enrichment

Word Builder

Using a Thesaurus Write a word you could use in place of the word in dark print. Use your Thesaurus. The first one is done for you.

Spelling Word Link
kind

type
Our sun is a **kind** of star. It is
sizzling *or* blazing
made of **hot** gases. Some stars
small *or* tiny   twinkle *or* glow
look so **little**. Others **shine** so
choose *or* select
brightly. I **pick** one star to watch.

Show What You Know! Write a sentence about this picture, using a different word for **cry**. Use your Thesaurus.

Sentences will vary but should include the word *weep* or *sob*.

172

EXTENSION OPTIONS

Learning Center Activity

visual/kinesthetic

Synonym Stars Have children look up long *i* words such as *bright*, *find*, *shine*, and *nice* in their Thesaurus. Ask them to draw a night sky filled with stars. Have them write the entry words and their synonyms on the stars. Children then trade papers with a partner and see if their partner can draw lines connecting each entry word and its synonyms. Partners then choose a group of three synonyms and write sentences for the words on sentence strips. Have them cut the strips apart into word cards and reassemble them, interchanging synonyms when possible.

Vocabulary Enrichment

Unit 25 BONUS

Science

Stars and Planets All the words in the box have something to do with the stars and the planets. Write those words to finish this speech. Use your Spelling Dictionary.

Spelling Word Link

sky

Mars
space
planet
Pluto

We live on the __(1)__ Earth. One day we will be able to fly through __(2)__ and land on __(3)__, which is next to Earth. Who knows, we may even travel all the way to tiny, cold __(4)__ !

1. planet
2. space
3. Mars
4. Pluto

Try This CHALLENGE

Yes or No? Write **yes** or **no** to answer each question.
5. Is **Mars** a star?
6. Do you water a **planet** to make it grow?
7. Could you take a train ride to **Pluto**?
8. Is **space** bigger than an ocean?

5. no
6. no
7. no
8. yes

Fact File

Have you ever looked up in the sky and seen the Big Dipper? It is a group of seven stars in the shape of a cup with a long handle. Two of the stars point to the North Star.

173

Objectives *Children will*
- expand their vocabulary by using words related to stars and planets
- show their understanding of the vocabulary words by completing context activities

Vocabulary Checkup

Have children use the vocabulary words in sentences or match the words to the definitions below.
1. the huge place around Earth where the stars and planets are *space*
2. the planet that is farthest from the Sun *Pluto*
3. the red planet that is fourth in distance from the Sun *Mars*
4. a body that moves around a star, such as the Sun *planet*

Fact File

The Big Dipper

The Big Dipper is part of a larger constellation called Ursa Major, or the Great Bear. The cup's handle forms the bear's tail. The stars in the Big Dipper are probably seventy to eighty light-years from Earth.

Explain to children that in the photograph the white lines connecting the stars were drawn to make it easier to see the shape of the Big Dipper.

Integrating Literature

Easy	Average	Challenging
Shooting Stars *by Holly Keller* A simple explanation of shooting stars.	**How Many Stars in the Sky?** *by Lenny Hort* A sleepless father and son count stars.	**You're Aboard Spaceship Earth** *by Patricia Lauber* An explanation of how the earth sustains life.
The Sun's Family of Planets *by Allan Fowler* This photo essay provides facts about the solar system.	**The Magic School Bus® Lost in the Solar System** *by Joanna Cole* Ms. Frizzle's class takes a trip through the solar system.	**How the Stars Fell into the Sky** *by Jerrie Oughton* This Navajo legend tells why the stars are in the sky.

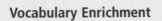

The Final Sound in *puppy*

WORD LISTS

Spelling

Basic

1. puppy
2. baby
3. lucky
4. happy
5. very
6. lady
7. funny
8. silly
9. many
10. only
11. cookie

Review

12. me
13. bee

Challenge

14. furry
15. noisy

Vocabulary

Science: Baby Animals

piglet
kid
tadpole
hatch

Introducing the Lesson

Read Aloud

Write the Basic Words on the board.

Animal Farm

Do you know the names of different farm animals? A female horse is called a mare. Usually, she has **only** one **baby** at a time. The young horse is called a foal. A female pig is a sow. She is **very lucky** because she has **many** piglets. Pigs often eat cooked garbage that may include anything from a piece of meat to an oatmeal **cookie**. A mother goose is certainly **funny** to watch! Like a busy **lady**, she hurries along with her **silly** goslings waddling behind her. Sometimes the farmer's **puppy** tags along. The animals on the farm seem **happy**. Would you like to live on a farm?

Responding Ask children to name some of the animals mentioned in the selection. Ask children what spelling word names a baby dog. *(puppy)* Reread the sentence with *baby* in it. Ask children what word in the sentence names something very young. *(baby)* Have a volunteer come to the chalkboard and point to *baby*.

Day 1 page 174

Objectives *Children will*

- take the pretest
- pronounce the list words
- learn about the spelling principle

Planning Checklist

- ☑ Pretest (TE)
- ☑ Spelling principle/word list
- ☐ Review/Challenge Words
- ☐ Teaching the Principle (TE)
- ☐ Enrichment (TE)
- ☐ Additional Spelling Words (TE)

Assessment

Pretest

1. My <u>puppy</u> has big feet.
2. A kitten is a <u>baby</u> cat.
3. I have a <u>lucky</u> penny.
4. The <u>happy</u> boy sang.
5. That nest is <u>very</u> big.
6. The <u>lady</u> made us lunch.
7. Your joke was <u>funny</u>.
8. They are acting <u>silly</u>.
9. He has <u>many</u> games.
10. I have <u>only</u> one dress.
11. Suki ate a big <u>cookie</u>.

Day 2 page 175

Objectives *Children will*

- practice spelling list words
- apply spelling strategies
- identify Basic Words by using meaning clues
- identify Elephant Words by supplying missing letters

Planning Checklist

- ☑ Spelling Strategy
- ☑ Independent Practice
- ☐ Daily Proofreading Practice (TE)
- ☐ Informal Assessment (TE)
- ☐ Extra Support (TE)
- ☐ Applying Spelling Strategies (TE)

 Management Tip Some children find certain words especially troublesome to spell. You may want to let children include those words for study in a given spelling unit, even if the new words don't follow the spelling pattern focused on in the lesson.

Day 3 *page 176*

Objective *Children will*
• review Basic and Review Words

Planning Checklist
☐ Review: Spelling Spree
☐ How Are You Doing?
☐ Daily Proofreading Practice (TE)
☐ Cooperative Learning Activity (TE)

Day 4 *page 177*

Objectives *Children will*
• proofread for spelling and titles
• write and proofread an original composition

Planning Checklist
☐ Proofread for Spelling and Titles for People
☐ Write a Letter
☐ Daily Proofreading Practice (TE)
☐ Challenge Words Practice (TE)
☐ Another Writing Idea (TE)

Day 5 *page 177*

Objective *Children will*
• take the posttest

Assessment
☐ **Posttest** (TE) *See Day 5*
☐ Unit 26 Test

● **Additional Resources**

Teacher's Resource Book
Practice Masters, pages 123–125
Unit Test, page 126
Bulletin Board, page 139

🏠 **Practice Plus**
Take-Home Word List 26
Games

Spelling Transparencies
Spelling Word List 26
Daily Proofreading Practice, Unit 26
Graphic Organizers

Teacher's Resource Disk
Macintosh® or Windows® software. Houghton Mifflin

Spelling CD-ROM
Macintosh® or Windows® software. Houghton Mifflin

Internet
http://www.eduplace.com

Phonics Practice
Houghton Mifflin Phonics
The Listening Corner
Phonics Home Connection

Meeting Individual Needs
Students Acquiring English

Spanish In Spanish, the |ē| sound is sometimes spelled *y*, but it is more often spelled *i*.

Activity Write the letters *i* and *y* on the chalkboard. Circle the *y*. Then write Basic Words 1–10 on the board. Say each word as you write it and have children repeat after you. Then erase the *y* at the end of each word. Have volunteers go to the chalkboard and add the missing final letter.

Other Activities for Any Day

• Bonus activities from pages 178–179
• Practice Masters (easy, average, challenging)
  Teacher's Resource Book, pages 123–125
• Take-Home Word List 26
  Practice Plus

Objectives *Children will*

■ take the pretest

■ pronounce the list words

■ learn about the spelling principle

Teaching the Principle

This lesson teaches the *y* spelling for the |ē| sound. Children learn the strategy of thinking of this spelling pattern when they hear the long *e* sound at the end of a two-syllable word.

To sum up the lesson, ask:

- How many syllables does each word have? *(two)*

- How is the long *e* sound spelled at the end of Basic Words 1–10? *(y)*

Note: The Elephant Word *cookie* may also be spelled *cooky*. This is an acceptable but less common spelling.

Enrichment

Vocabulary: Multiple Meanings

Have children use a dictionary to look up *very, funny, silly,* and *only.* Discuss the different meanings.

Read and Say

ē

puppy

READ the sentences. **SAY** each word in dark print.

Basic Words

1. puppy	*puppy*	My **puppy** has big feet.
2. baby	*baby*	A kitten is a **baby** cat.
3. lucky	*lucky*	I have a **lucky** penny.
4. happy	*happy*	The **happy** boy sang.
5. very	*very*	That nest is **very** big.
6. lady	*lady*	The **lady** made us lunch.
7. funny	*funny*	Your joke was **funny**.
8. silly	*silly*	They are acting **silly**.
9. many	*many*	He has **many** games.
10. only	*only*	I have **only** one dress.
11. cookie	*cookie*	Suki ate a big **cookie**.

A. puppy

baby

lucky

happy

very

lady

funny

silly

many

only

B. cookie

174

Think and Write

Each word has two parts called **syllables**. Each syllable has one vowel sound. You hear the long **e** vowel sound in the second syllable of each word. In most of the words, the long **e** sound is spelled **y**.

puppy → pup p**y**   baby → ba b**y**

How is the Elephant Word different? The |ē| sound is spelled *ie*.

A. Write the first **ten** Basic Words. Then draw a line under the letter that spells the final long **e** sound in each word.

B. Now write the Elephant Word.

Order of answers may vary.

Review	
12. me	13. bee

Challenge	
14. furry	15. noisy

TEACHING OPTIONS

Meeting Individual Needs
Word Lists

You may want to assign Basic Words 1–5, the Elephant Word, and the Review Words to children who misspelled more than five words on the pretest. Assign the Challenge Words as appropriate. (You may want to have children write sentences, using the Challenge Words.)

Additional Spelling Words

Basic	Challenge	Words Often Misspelled
muddy	city	tried
sticky	heavy	know
hobby	dirty	
daddy	carry	
study	angry	
	sorry	

Home/School Involvement
Take-Home Word List • Goal-Setting

Have children set goals for the week on Take-Home Word List 26.

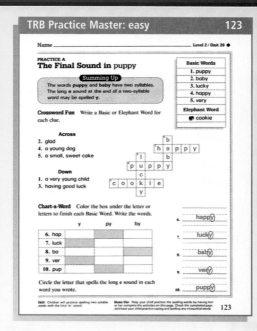

Independent Practice

Spelling Strategy The words **puppy** and **baby** have two syllables. The long **e** sound at the end of a two-syllable word may be spelled **y**.

Order of answers for question 3–4 may vary.

Phonics Write Basic Words to answer the questions.

1. Which word has the short **e** sound spelled **e**?
2. Which word has the long **o** sound in the first syllable?
3–4. Which two words have the long **a** sound in the first syllable?

Word Meaning Write a Basic Word for each meaning. Use your Spelling Dictionary.

5. feeling joy
6. having good luck
7. a young dog
8. not showing good sense
9. the opposite of **few**
10. causing laughter

Elephant Word Think of the missing letters in the Elephant Word. Write the word.

11. I baked a **cook**__ __ shaped like a little lamb.

Phonics

1. very
2. only
3. baby
4. lady

Word Meaning

5. happy
6. lucky
7. puppy
8. silly
9. many
10. funny

Elephant Word

11. cookie

Objectives *Children will*
- practice spelling list words
- apply spelling strategies
- identify Basic Words by using meaning clues
- identify an Elephant Word by supplying missing letters

Day 2

Daily Proofreading Practice
We picked **meny** oranges. (*many*)
A duckling is a **babee** duck. (*baby*)

Meeting Individual Needs
visual/oral/auditory

Extra Support Check Independent Practice to determine who needs extra support. Emphasize the two syllables in each spelling word by having children repeat them after you, clapping for each syllable. Explain that each clap represents a syllable. To reinforce the *y* spelling in the final syllable, write several of the words on the board. Ask volunteers to read each one and to underline the *y*.

Applying Spelling Strategies
To Spell New Words

- Read aloud: **The howling wind and creaking doors made the house seem spooky.**

- Have children attempt to spell *spooky* on their Have-a-Go charts.
- Elicit the following strategies as children try to spell *spooky*.

I hear the sounds for *s* and *p* blended together at the beginning of the word.

This word has two syllables, so I think the final long *e* sound is spelled *y*.

spook**y**

The |o͞o| sound is probably spelled *oo*, and the |k| sound is probably spelled *k* because it doesn't follow a short vowel.

Objective *Children will*
■ review Basic and Review Words

Daily Proofreading Practice

She wore a **funne** mask. (*funny*)
The **ladie** gave me a balloon. (*lady*)

Letter Math

1. many

2. me

3. very

4. bee

5. only

Puzzle Play

6. happy

7. silly

8. lady

9. baby

Short Cuts

10. cookie

11. puppy

12. lucky

176

Review: Spelling Spree

Letter Math Add and take away letters to make Basic or Review Words. Write each word.

1. m a n e − e + y = _____
2. m + s e e − s − e = _____
3. v e r b − b + y = _____
4. b + t r e e − t r = _____
5. o n e − e + l y = _____

Puzzle Play Write a Basic Word for each clue. Use the letters that would be in the boxes to spell what baby animals like to do.

6. glad __ __ ▢ __ __
7. foolish __ __ __ ▢ __
8. a woman __ ▢ __ __
9. a very young child __ __ __ ▢

Secret Word: p l a y

Short Cuts Write the Basic Words that have these shorter words in them.

10. cook   11. pup   12. luck

How Are You Doing?
Write each spelling word as a family member reads it aloud. Did you spell any words wrong?

TEACHING **OPTIONS**

Cooperative Learning Activity
Hidden Vowels
visual/oral

Have children work with partners. One child thinks of a spelling word. As the partner turns away, this child spells the word with letter tiles or Scrabble® pieces, turning over the vowels so they are hidden from view. The partner looks at the word with the missing vowels and predicts what the word is. This child then spells the word aloud, turning over the hidden vowels to check the spelling. After children review their spelling words in this fashion, suggest they continue with other words that have the *y* spelling for |ē|.

TRB Practice Master: challenging   125

Name _____   Level 2 / Unit 26

PRACTICE C
The Final Sound in puppy

Take a Close Look Look at Pictures 1 and 2. Circle five things in Picture 2 that are different from Picture 1.

Challenge Words
1. furry
2. noisy
Theme Vocabulary
3. piglet
4. kid
5. tadpole
6. hatch

Now write five sentences to tell how Picture 2 is different from Picture 1. Use all the Challenge and Vocabulary Words.
Sample answers:

1. There is only one *piglet*.
2. The *kid* does not have horns.
3. A *furry* dog is barking.
4. A *tadpole* swims in the pond.
5. Two *noisy* chicks *hatch* from the eggs.

125

UNIT 26

Proofreading and Writing

Proofread: Spelling and Titles for People
Always begin a person's title with a capital letter. Put a period after **Mrs.**, **Mr.**, **Dr.**, and **Ms.**, but not after **Miss**.

Mrs. Kitt   Dr. Doe   Miss Bryd

Proofread Josh's letter. Use proofreading marks to fix four spelling mistakes and three titles that are wrong.

Example: How ~~maney~~ many cats does ms. Woo have?

February 14, 1998

Dear Miss, Smith,

   I got Puff from mrs. Barnes! I am very ~~luky~~ lucky. I asked dr. Vetto why Puff acts so ~~funnie~~ funny. He told ~~mee~~ me that being ~~sily~~ silly is how kittens have fun!

     Your friend,

     Josh

Write a Letter

Pretend you have a new pet. Write a letter to a vet, asking for information on how to take care of your pet. Try to use spelling words.

Proofreading Tip **Check that you began and ended each person's title correctly.**

Basic

1. puppy
2. baby
3. lucky
4. happy
5. very
6. lady
7. funny
8. silly
9. many
10. only
11. cookie

Review
12. me
13. bee

Challenge
14. furry
15. noisy

Proofreading Marks
∧ Add
⌿ Delete
≡ Make a capital letter
/ Make a small letter

(177)

Objectives *Children will*
- proofread for spelling and titles
- write and proofread an original composition

Day 4

Daily Proofreading Practice
Her **pupy** has black spots. (*puppy*)
The clowns made **silli** faces. (*silly*)

Day 5 **Posttest**

Sentences 1–5 test the first five Basic Words. Sentences 6–10 test the next five Basic Words. Sentence 11 tests the Elephant Word.

Basic Words
1. Is she <u>happy</u>?
2. I saw a cute <u>baby</u>.
3. The fish is <u>very</u> big.
4. We are <u>lucky</u>.
5. I have a black <u>puppy</u>.
6. Is this the <u>only</u> cup?
7. We saw one <u>lady</u>.
8. My pet is <u>funny</u>.
9. I have <u>many</u> hats.
10. You are so <u>silly</u>.
11. I will make a <u>cookie</u> for you.

Review Words
12. Did you see the <u>bee</u>?
13. Give <u>me</u> the ball.

Challenge Words
14. The kitten is soft and <u>furry</u>.
15. Our roosters are <u>very</u> <u>noisy</u>.

TRB Unit 26 Test   **126**

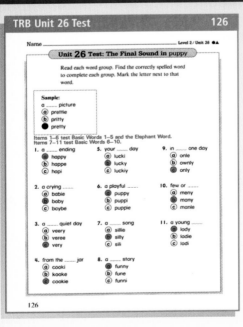

Meeting Individual Needs

Challenge Words Practice
Have children make up newspaper headlines, using each of the Challenge Words.

Another Writing Idea Ask children to imagine they own a pet that just had babies. Have them make a poster to help find good homes for the babies. The poster should include a picture of the animals and sentences that tell about them. Encourage children to use spelling words.

These pages can be used at any time during the study of this unit.

Objectives *Children will*

■ identify rhyming words

■ generate words with the |ē| sound spelled *y*

Phonics and Spelling

Rhyming Words

Words That End Like puppy Which picture names rhyme with the words below? Write each picture name next to the word it rhymes with.

Example: guppy **puppy**

Zoe's room

20

1. berry | **1. cherry**

2. belly | **2. jelly**

3. funny | **3. bunny**

4. Tony | **4. pony**

5. plenty | **5. twenty**

Work Together On another sheet of paper, write three more words that have the long **e** sound spelled **y** like **baby**. Work with a friend. Sample answers: easy, sorry, penny

178

EXTENSION OPTIONS

hilly
silly

hobby
lobby

fluffy
puffy

milky
silky

Learning Center Activity

visual/auditory/kinesthetic

A Word Ladder Provide children with cards cut from colored paper or tagboard. Have children brainstorm more rhyming pairs of two-syllable words that have the final long e sound spelled *y*. Ask children to write each rhyming pair on a card. Attach the cards with yarn to form a word ladder that you can hang on your word wall or on a bulletin board.

More Rhyming Words

candy	bumpy	baggy	creepy	leaky	foggy
handy	lumpy	shaggy	sleepy	sneaky	soggy
sandy	mummy	crabby	nearly	sticky	copy
flaky	tummy	shabby	yearly	tricky	floppy
shaky	yummy	ready	greedy	hilly	gloomy
lady	muddy	steady	speedy	silly	roomy
shady	study				

Vocabulary Enrichment

Science

Baby Animals All the words in the box have something to do with baby animals. Write those words to finish this page from a diary. Use your Spelling Dictionary.

Spelling Word Link

puppy

piglet
kid
tadpole
hatch

October 9

Dad and I went to a farm today. We saw a goat and her __(1)__ . A pink __(2)__ played in a nearby pen. A tiny __(3)__ swam in the pond. We even saw some chicks __(4)__ !

1. kid
2. piglet
3. tadpole
4. hatch

Try This CHALLENGE

Questions and Answers Write a word from the box to answer each question.

5. Which animal lives in water?
6. Which animal may have little horns?
7. What do baby birds do?
8. Which animal may have a curly tail?

5. tadpole
6. kid
7. hatch
8. piglet

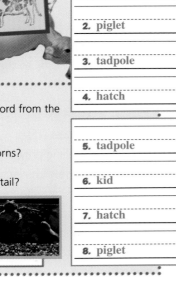

Fact File

At first a tadpole looks like a little fish. Slowly it grows legs. Then it loses its tail and becomes a frog!

179

Objectives *Children will*

- expand their vocabulary by using words related to baby animals
- show their understanding of the vocabulary words by completing context activities

Vocabulary Checkup

Have children use the vocabulary words in sentences or match the words to the definitions below.

1. to come out of an egg *hatch*
2. a young frog that has a tail and lives in water *tadpole*
3. a young goat *kid*
4. a young pig *piglet*

Fact File

Tadpoles

Tadpoles, or polliwogs, hatch from a jelly-like mass of thousands of frog eggs. Most species change into frogs within a few months, although some remain tadpoles for two years. Most tadpoles are two to six inches long.

Integrating Literature

Easy	Average	Challenging
Goose *by Molly Bang* A gosling raised by woodchucks discovers that she can fly.	**Kangaroos Have Joeys** *by Philippa-Alys Browne* Rhyming verse introduces the names of various baby animals.	**Nights of the Pufflings** *by Bruce McMillan* Icelandic children help young pufflings get safely to the ocean.
Foal *by Mary Ling* A foal narrates his growth over a period of days, weeks, and months.	**Booby Hatch** *by Betsy Lewin* Pépe, a blue-footed booby, grows up in the Galápagos Islands.	**Arctic Babies** *by Kathy Darling* A description of young animals that live in the arctic region.

The Vowel Sound in *cow*

WORD LISTS

Spelling

Basic

1. town
2. house
3. out
4. down
5. cow
6. now
7. found
8. how
9. mouse
10. brown
11. could
12. should

Review

13. name
14. cat

Challenge

15. couch
16. crowded

Vocabulary

Social Studies: Places to Live

cottage
igloo
trailer
palace

Introducing the Lesson

Read Aloud

Write the Basic Words on the board.

Home Sweet Home

How many different kinds of homes can you name? Cottages, cabins, mansions, and castles are homes. Where do you live **now**? In a **house** or an apartment? In a city or a **town**? Animals have homes too. A **mouse** lives in a hole, and a **cow** lives in a barn. A **brown** bear lives in a den in the winter. And have you ever **found** a flea on a dog? That's where fleas like to live! A whale lives **out** in the ocean and a fish lives deep **down** in the sea. **Could** you think of a place where a king and queen might live? And you **should** certainly know the name of the place where the president of the United States lives!

Responding Ask children where a mouse lives. *(in a hole)* Ask them to say the spelling word that names a place that is bigger than a village but smaller than a city. *(town)* Have volunteers go to the chalkboard and underline the spelling words that rhyme with *town*. *(down, brown)*

Day 1 *page 180*

Day 2 *page 181*

Objectives *Children will*

- take the pretest
- pronounce the list words
- learn about the spelling principle
- sort words by their spelling patterns

Planning Checklist

☑ Pretest (TE)
☑ Spelling principle/word list
☐ Review/Challenge Words
☐ Teaching the Principle (TE)
☐ Enrichment (TE)
☐ Additional Spelling Words (TE)

Assessment

Pretest

1. I live in a small <u>town</u>.
2. My <u>house</u> is by the pond.
3. Mom went <u>out</u> for a walk.
4. He ran <u>down</u> the hill.
5. Our <u>cow</u> gives us milk.
6. Will we eat <u>now</u>?
7. You <u>found</u> my kite!
8. Teach me <u>how</u> to cook.
9. Boots chased the <u>mouse</u>.
10. Can I have a <u>brown</u> bag?
11. We <u>could</u> go with you.
12. I ate more than I <u>should</u>.

Objectives *Children will*

- practice spelling list words
- apply spelling strategies
- complete analogies with Basic Words
- identify Elephant Words by supplying missing letters

Planning Checklist

☑ Spelling Strategy
☑ Independent Practice
☐ Daily Proofreading Practice (TE)
☐ Informal Assessment (TE)
☐ Extra Support (TE)
☐ Applying Spelling Strategies (TE)

Day 3 *page 182*

Day 4 *page 183*

Day 5 *page 183*

Objectives *Children will*

- use a dictionary entry and context clues to identify different meanings of a given word
- review Basic and Review Words

Planning Checklist

- ☐ Dictionary
- ☐ Review: Spelling Spree
- ☐ How Are You Doing?
- ☐ Daily Proofreading Practice (TE)
- ☐ Ongoing Assessment (TE)

Objectives *Children will*

- proofread for spelling
- write and proofread an original composition

Planning Checklist

- ☐ Proofread for Spelling
- ☐ Write a Story
- ☐ Daily Proofreading Practice (TE)
- ☐ Challenge Words Practice (TE)
- ☐ Another Writing Idea (TE)

Objective *Children will*

- take the posttest

Assessment

- ☐ **Posttest** (TE) *See Day 5*
- ☐ Unit 27 Test

● Additional Resources

Teacher's Resource Book
Practice Masters, pages 127–129
Unit Test, page 130
Bulletin Board, page 139

Practice Plus
Take-Home Word List 27
Games

Spelling Transparencies
Spelling Word List 27
Daily Proofreading Practice, Unit 27
Graphic Organizers

Teacher's Resource Disk
Macintosh® or Windows® software. Houghton Mifflin

Spelling CD-ROM
Macintosh® or Windows® software. Houghton Mifflin

Internet
http://www.eduplace.com

Phonics Practice
Houghton Mifflin Phonics
The Listening Corner
Phonics Home Connection

Meeting Individual Needs
Students Acquiring English

Spanish The sound in Spanish that is similar to the |ou| sound is spelled *au*. There is no *w* in Spanish.

Activity Be sure that children know the letter *w* and can write it. Then write these two silly sentences on the chalkboard: *I found the mouse out behind the house. Now how will the brown cow get down to town?* Have a volunteer circle all the words with the *ou* spelling. Have another volunteer circle all the words with the *ow* spelling. Then have children copy the sentences on paper and underline the *ou* or *ow* in each spelling word. Children may wish to draw pictures for the sentences.

Other Activities for Any Day

- Bonus activities from pages 184–185
- Practice Masters (easy, average, challenging)
  Teacher's Resource Book, pages 127–129
- Take-Home Word List 27
  Practice Plus

Objectives *Children will*

- take the pretest
- pronounce the list words
- learn about the spelling principle
- sort words by their spelling patterns

Teaching the Principle

This lesson teaches the *ow* and the *ou* spelling patterns for the |ou| sound. Children learn the strategy of thinking of these patterns when they hear the |ou| sound. They learn that the |ou| sound is usually spelled *ow* at the end of a word.

To sum up the lesson, ask:

- How is the vowel sound spelled in *town* and *cow*? *(ow)*

- How is the vowel sound spelled in *house* and *out*? *(ou)*

- How is the vowel sound spelled when it comes at the end of a word? *(ow)*

Enrichment

Vocabulary: Multiple Meanings
Have children use a dictionary to look up *down*, *out*, and *house*. Discuss the meanings.

The Vowel Sound in COW

ow
COW

A. town
_____
_____
down
_____
_____
cow
_____
_____
now
_____
_____
how
_____
_____
brown
_____

B. house
_____
_____
out
_____
_____
found
_____
_____
mouse
_____

C. could
_____
_____
should

(180)

Read and Say

READ the sentences. **SAY** each word in dark print.

Basic Words

1. town	*town*	I live in a small **town**.
2. house	*house*	My **house** is by the pond.
3. out	*out*	Mom went **out** for a walk.
4. down	*down*	He ran **down** the hill.
5. cow	*cow*	Our **cow** gives us milk.
6. now	*now*	Will we eat **now**?
7. found	*found*	You **found** my kite!
8. how	*how*	Teach me **how** to cook.
9. mouse	*mouse*	Boots chased the **mouse**.
10. brown	*brown*	Can I have a **brown** bag?
11. could	*could*	We **could** go with you.
12. should	*should*	I ate more than I **should**.

Think and Write

Most of the words have the same vowel sound. It is the vowel sound you hear in .

the 🐄 vowel sound → t**ow**n, h**ou**se

How are the Elephant Words different? *Ou* spells the |ōō| sound.

A. Write **six** Basic Words with the 🐄 vowel sound spelled **ow**.

B. Write **four** Basic Words with the 🐄 vowel sound spelled **ou**.

C. Now write the **two** Elephant Words.
Order of answers for each category may vary.

Review	Challenge
13. name 14. cat	15. couch 16. crowded

TEACHING OPTIONS

Meeting Individual Needs
Word Lists

You may want to assign Basic Words 1–5, the Elephant Words, and the Review Words to children who misspelled more than five words on the pretest. Assign the Challenge Words as appropriate. (You may want to have children write sentences, using the Challenge Words.)

Additional Spelling Words

Basic	Challenge	Words Often Misspelled
cloud	tower	knew
growl	meow	new
blouse	towel	
clown	around	
sour	outside	
	snowplow	

Home/School Involvement
Take-Home Word List • Goal-Setting

Have children set goals for the week on Take-Home Word List 27.

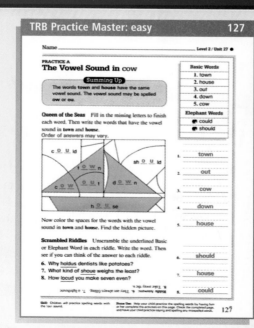

Name _____ Level 2 / Unit 27 ●

PRACTICE A
The Vowel Sound in COW

Summing Up
The words **town** and **house** have the same vowel sound. The vowel sound may be spelled **ow** or **ou**.

Basic Words
1. town
2. house
3. out
4. down
5. cow
Elephant Words
● could
● should

Queen of the Seas Fill in the missing letters to finish each word. Then write the words that have the vowel sound in **town** and **house**.
Order of answers may vary.

c_O_U_d   sh_O_U_ld
t_OW_n
c_OW_   _OU_t   d_OW_n
h_OU_se

Now color the spaces for the words with the vowel sound in **town** and **house**. Find the hidden picture.

Scrambled Riddles Unscramble the underlined Basic or Elephant Word in each riddle. Write the word. Then see if you can think of the answer to each riddle.

6. Why holdus dentists like potatoes?
7. What kind of shoue weighs the least?
8. How locud you make seven even?

1. _____ town
2. _____ out
3. _____ cow
4. _____ down
5. _____ house
6. _____ should
7. _____ house
8. _____ could

127

Independent Practice

Spelling Strategy The words **town** and **house** have the same vowel sound. This vowel sound may be spelled **ow** or **ou**.

Order of answers for question 4–6 may vary.
Phonics Write Basic Words to answer the questions.

1. Which word begins with a consonant cluster?
2. Which word begins and ends like **den**?
3. Which word begins and ends like **tin**?
4–6. Which three words rhyme with **plow**?

Word Pairs Write a Basic Word to finish the second sentence in each pair.

7. **People** means more than one **person**.
   Mice means more than one _____.
8. If you **lose** something, it is **lost**.
   If you **find** something, it is _____.
9. The opposite of **left** is **right**.
   The opposite of **in** is _____.
10. A **bear** lives in a **cave**.
    A **person** lives in a _____.

Elephant Words Think of the missing letters in each Elephant Word. Write each word.

11. sh __ __ ld
12. c __ __ ld

Phonics

1. brown

2. down

3. town

4. cow

5. now

6. how

Word Pairs

7. mouse

8. found

9. out

10. house

Elephant Words

11. should

12. could

(181)

Objectives *Children will*

■ practice spelling list words
■ apply spelling strategies
■ complete analogies with Basic Words
■ identify Elephant Words by supplying missing letters

Daily Proofreading Practice

They built a log **howse**. (*house*)
I slid **douwn** the hill on a sled.
(*down*)

Meeting Individual Needs
visual/oral/auditory

Extra Support Check Independent Practice to determine who needs extra support. Give children two index cards. Have them write *ow* on one and *ou* on the other. Say a Basic Word and have children repeat it. Have them tell if the |ou| sound is in the beginning, middle, or end of the word. Then ask them to hold up the card that shows the spelling of the vowel sound in that word.

Applying Spelling Strategies
To Read New Words

■ Write this sentence on the chalkboard:
Mom raises one eyebrow when she is upset.

■ Have children read the sentence silently.
■ Elicit the following strategies as children try to decode *eyebrow*.

I recognize the word *eye* at the beginning of this longer word.

This looks like a consonant cluster. I'll blend the sounds for *b* and *r* together.

eyebrow

Eye-br-ow. Eye-brow. Eyebrow. The word *eyebrow* makes sense in the sentence.

I see the letters *ow*. I know that these letters make the |ou| sound at the end of a word.

Objectives *Children will*

■ use a dictionary entry and context clues to identify different meanings of a given word

■ review Basic and Review Words

Daily Proofreading Practice

You **shood** read every day. (*should*)

Do you know **hauw** to skip? (*how*)

Dictionary

1. 3
_____
2. 4
_____
3. 1
_____
4. 2
_____

Hidden Words

5. how
_____
6. town
_____
7. now
_____

Letter Swap

8. cat
_____
9. name
_____
10. found
_____
11. out
_____
12. brown
_____

182

Dictionary

Finding the Right Meaning You know that words may have more than one meaning. Use a dictionary to find all the different meanings of a word.

> **brown** **1.** The color of chocolate: *Zia has long **brown** hair.* **2.** To cook until brown on the outside: *I can **brown** the rolls in the oven.*

Practice Look up the word **out** in your Spelling Dictionary. Write **1**, **2**, **3**, or **4** to tell which meaning of the word is used in each sentence.

1. The lights were **out** in my house all day.
2. The stars come **out** at night.
3. We went **out** to see the play.
4. My teacher was **out** this morning.

Review: Spelling Spree

Hidden Words Find the hidden Basic Word in each box. Write the word.

5. cithowwer   **6.** fostownick   **7.** maunnowus

Letter Swap Change each letter in dark print. Write a Basic or Review Word.

8. **c**ap
9. **s**ame
10. **r**ound
11. **o**ur
12. **f**rown

How Are You Doing?
Write your words in ABC order. Practice with a family member any words you spelled wrong.

TEACHING **OPTIONS**

Ongoing Assessment
Diphthongs and Contractions

Spellings of diphthongs, where one vowel sound blends into another, will vary as children "lock in" the appropriate pattern. Common errors for the |ou| sound, for example, are FAUND, FAUWND, FOUWND (*found*) and DOUWN (*down*).

When children study the contractions in Unit 29, misspellings may involve misplacement or omission of the apostrophe: DONT, WEVE, DID'NT, HAS'NT, DIDINT. The contraction *you're* is also commonly misspelled as its homophone, *your*.

TRB Practice Master: challenging   129

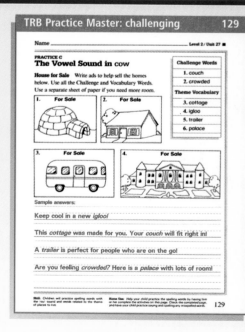

Name _____   Level 2 / Unit 27 ■

PRACTICE C
The Vowel Sound in cow

Challenge Words
1. couch
2. crowded
Theme Vocabulary
3. cottage
4. igloo
5. trailer
6. palace

House for Sale Write ads to help sell the homes below. Use all the Challenge and Vocabulary Words. Use a separate sheet of paper if you need more room.

1. For Sale   2. For Sale
3. For Sale   4. For Sale

Sample answers:

Keep cool in a new *igloo!*

This *cottage* was made for you. Your *couch* will fit right in!

A *trailer* is perfect for people who are on the go!

Are you feeling *crowded?* Here is a *palace* with lots of room!

129

Proofreading and Writing

Proofread for Spelling Proofread these directions.
Use proofreading marks to fix six spelling mistakes.

Example: I painted the walls broun. *brown*

Do you know how to plan a hous for a pet? *house*

First, decide how big it shoud be. A kow needs more *should* *cow*
room than a mous! Next, find out what else your *mouse*
pet needs. Most pets cood use a bed to lie doun on, *could* *down*
food, and water. Last, draw your plan on paper.

Basic
1. town
2. house
3. out
4. down
5. cow
6. now
7. found
8. how
9. mouse
10. brown
11. could
12. should

Review
13. name
14. cat

Challenge
15. couch
16. crowded

Write a Story

Think of friends you visited in their
house or apartment. Write a story
about your visit. Tell why it was fun
or exciting. Try to use spelling words.
Then share your story with a friend.

Proofreading Tip Read your paper again slowly
to see if any words have been
left out.

Proofreading Marks
∧ Add
⌿ Delete
≡ Make a capital letter
╱ Make a small letter

(183)

Meeting Individual Needs

Challenge Words Practice
Ask children to make a word
search puzzle for a classmate. Have
them write the Challenge Words
and other words with the |ou|
sound on graph paper, then fill in
the empty squares with random
letters. Partners search for and circle the hidden words.

Another Writing Idea
Suggest children draw their dream
home then write sentences about
it using spelling words.

Objectives *Children will*
■ proofread for spelling
■ write and proofread an original
composition

Daily Proofreading Practice
Liz **faund** a pretty blue stone. (*found*)
Our **towen** has two new parks.
(*town*)

Day 5 **Posttest**

Sentences 1–5 test the first five Basic Words.
Sentences 6–10 test the next five Basic
Words. Sentences 11–12 test the Elephant
Words.

Basic Words
1. We came by that <u>house</u>.
2. I like this <u>town</u>.
3. The <u>cow</u> ate the grass.
4. Look <u>down</u> the road.
5. Is it hot <u>out</u>?
6. We see <u>how</u> big you are.
7. I can go <u>now</u>.
8. Tom likes the <u>brown</u> coat.
9. The cat will chase the <u>mouse</u>.
10. She <u>found</u> that stone.
11. He took more than he <u>should</u>.
12. I <u>could</u> get my bike.

Review Words
13. What is her <u>name</u>?
14. He has a <u>cat</u>.

Challenge Words
15. The morning train was <u>crowded</u>.
16. Mom got a new <u>couch</u> for the living
room.

Unit 27 BONUS

These pages can be used at any time during the study of this unit.

Objectives *Children will*

- build words with the phonograms -*own* and -*ound*
- generate rhyming words

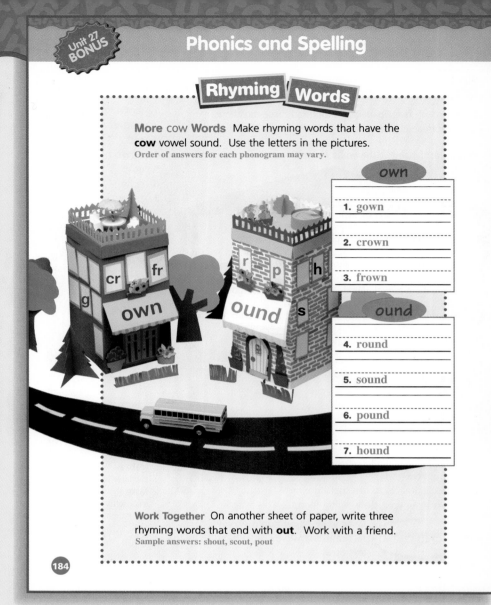

Unit 27 BONUS

Phonics and Spelling

Rhyming Words

More cow Words Make rhyming words that have the **cow** vowel sound. Use the letters in the pictures.
Order of answers for each phonogram may vary.

own

cr fr
g **own**

r p h
ound s

1. gown
2. crown
3. frown

ound

4. round
5. sound
6. pound
7. hound

Work Together On another sheet of paper, write three rhyming words that end with **out**. Work with a friend.
Sample answers: shout, scout, pout

184

EXTENSION OPTIONS

Learning Center Activity

visual/auditory/kinesthetic

Make an |ou| Town On large drawing paper, have children draw a town with two main streets, Ou Street and Ow Street. Along each street, have them draw homes. On each home, children write a pair of rhyming words with the |ou| sound spelling that matches the street name. Children can begin thinking of rhyming pairs by looking at their spelling words. Encourage them to use a dictionary to check the spellings of additional words.

More Rhyming *ou* Words

cloud	count	couch	ground	growl
loud	mount	grouch	mound	howl
proud	mouth	ouch	clown	owl
	south	pouch	drown	prowl

Vocabulary Enrichment

Social Studies

Places to Live All the words in the box have something to do with places to live. Use those words to write labels for these pictures. Use your Spelling Dictionary.

Spelling Word Link

house

cottage
igloo
trailer
palace

1. palace

2. trailer

3 igloo

4. cottage

Try This CHALLENGE

Riddle Time! Write a word from the box to answer each riddle.

5. What home might have huge, fancy rooms?
6. What has wheels but often does not move?
7. What can be a home or a kind of cheese?
8. What is frozen but can keep people warm?

5. palace

6. trailer

7. cottage

8. igloo

Fact File

People have lived in apartment houses for hundreds of years! Long ago, American Indians built homes in the sides of cliffs. Some were four stories high!

185

Day by Day Planner

Objectives *Children will*

- expand their vocabulary by using words related to places to live
- show their understanding of the vocabulary words by completing context activities

Vocabulary Checkup

Have children use the vocabulary words in sentences or match the words to the definitions below.

1. a house with wheels that can be pulled by a truck *trailer*
2. a small house in the country *cottage*
3. a house made from blocks of ice or snow *igloo*
4. a fancy house where a king or queen lives *palace*

Fact File

Cliff Dwellings

Some of the oldest and largest cliff dwellings can still be seen at Mesa Verde National Park in southwestern Colorado. These homes were built around A.D. 1200 by the Anasazi, who were ancestors of the Pueblo Indians.

Integrating Literature

Easy	Average	Challenging

Old Henry
by Joan W. Blos
Henry's run-down house causes problems for his neighbors.

It Could Always Be Worse
by Margot Zemach
A rabbi gives a man advice about his small house.

This Is My House
by Arthur Dorros
A tour of houses around the world.

Home Place
by Crescent Dragonwagon
A family out hiking imagines who lived in the remains of an old house they find.

My House Has Stars
by Megan McDonald
Children around the world describe where they live.

Homeplace
by Ann Shelby
A woman tells her granddaughter how her house has changed over time.

Compound Words

WORD LISTS

Spelling

Basic
1. bathtub
2. bedtime
3. myself
4. someone
5. maybe
6. into
7. upon
8. anyone
9. without
10. cannot

Review
11. stop
12. flag

Challenge
13. playground
14. nobody

Vocabulary

Health: Taking Care of Yourself

jog
fit
muscles
shape

Introducing the Lesson

Read Aloud

Write the Basic Words on the board.

The Wet Visitor

What would you do if you moved **into** a new house and heard strange splashing noises coming from the bathroom? **Maybe** you would be brave and go inside **without** fear, but I **myself** would run out the door! In the story *The House on East 88th Street* by Bernard Waber, Mrs. Primm finds a crocodile in the **bathtub.** Before **anyone** can panic, Lyle the crocodile begins performing tricks, such as balancing a ball **upon** the tip of his long nose. Lyle is so lovable that soon the Primms **cannot** imagine life without him. Each night at **bedtime,** they tuck him into his bed of bath water. But **someone** comes to take Lyle away. What happens next? Read the book!

Responding Ask children what was in the Primm's bathtub. *(a crocodile)* Ask which spelling word names the place where Lyle the crocodile sleeps. *(bathtub)* Ask children to name the spelling word in this sentence: "But **someone** comes to take Lyle away." *(someone)*

Day 1 page 186

Day 2 page 187

Objectives *Children will*
- take the pretest
- pronounce the list words
- learn about the spelling principle
- divide compound words

Planning Checklist

☑ Pretest (TE)
☑ Spelling principle/word list
☐ Review/Challenge Words
☐ Teaching the Principle (TE)
☐ Enrichment (TE)
☐ Additional Spelling Words (TE)

Objectives *Children will*
- practice spelling list words
- apply spelling strategies
- identify synonyms
- identify Basic Words by using meaning clues

Planning Checklist

☑ Spelling Strategy
☑ Independent Practice
☐ Daily Proofreading Practice (TE)
☐ Informal Assessment (TE)
☐ Extra Support (TE)
☐ Applying Spelling Strategies (TE)

Assessment

Pretest
1. I wash in the <u>bathtub</u>.
2. When is your <u>bedtime</u>?
3. I played by <u>myself</u>.
4. Did <u>someone</u> call me?
5. I think <u>maybe</u> I can do it.
6. We walked <u>into</u> the store.
7. The frog sat <u>upon</u> a rock.
8. Pia did not see <u>anyone</u>.
9. He cooks <u>without</u> help.
10. They <u>cannot</u> stay.

Management Tip Encourage children to add new words to their spelling lists. You may want to keep a Word Bank in the classroom. Invite children to write down words from their reading and deposit them in the Word Bank. Children can take turns drawing words from the Word Bank and adding them to their spelling lists.

 Day 3 *page 188*

Objective *Children will*
- review Basic and Review Words

Planning Checklist
- ☐ Review: Spelling Spree
- ☐ How Are You Doing?
- ☐ Daily Proofreading Practice (TE)
- ☐ Cooperative Learning Activity (TE)

 Day 4 *page 189*

Objectives *Children will*
- proofread for spelling and book title mechanics
- write and proofread an original composition

Planning Checklist
- ☐ Proofread: Spelling and Book Titles
- ☐ Write Book Titles
- ☐ Daily Proofreading Practice (TE)
- ☐ Challenge Words Practice (TE)
- ☐ Another Writing Idea (TE)

Day 5 *page 189*

Objective *Children will*
- take the posttest

Assessment

- ☐ **Posttest** (TE) *See Day 5*
- ☐ Unit 28 Test

 **Additional Resources**

Teacher's Resource Book
Practice Masters, pages 131–133
Unit Test, page 134
Bulletin Board, page 139

Practice Plus
Take-Home Word List 28
Games

Spelling Transparencies
Spelling Word List 28
Daily Proofreading Practice, Unit 28
Graphic Organizers

Teacher's Resource Disk
Macintosh® or Windows® software. Houghton Mifflin

Spelling CD-ROM
Macintosh® or Windows® software. Houghton Mifflin

Internet
http://www.eduplace.com

Phonics Practice
Houghton Mifflin Phonics
The Listening Corner
Phonics Home Connection

Meeting Individual Needs
Students Acquiring English

Spanish Spanish has very few compound words.
Activity Say each Basic Word, clearly dividing the two parts, and have children repeat it. Write the shorter words on the board and have volunteers draw a line between the words that make up each compound.

Asian Seeing or hearing two familiar words combined to form a compound word may be difficult for some Asian children.
Activity Use the activity for Spanish-speaking children.

Other Activities for Any Day

- Bonus activities from pages 190–191
- Practice Masters (easy, average, challenging)
  Teacher's Resource Book, pages 131–133
- Take-Home Word List 28
  Practice Plus

Objectives *Children will*

■ take the pretest

■ pronounce the list words

■ learn about the spelling principle

■ divide compound words

Teaching the Principle

This lesson teaches the concept of compound words, demonstrating how some words can be made up of two shorter words. Children learn the strategy of analyzing words for this spelling pattern.

To sum up the lesson, have children tell what two words they see in each compound list word.

Enrichment

Vocabulary: Multiple Meanings

Have children use a dictionary to look up *into* and *without*. Discuss the different meanings.

bathtub

Read and Say

READ the sentences. **SAY** each word in dark print.

Basic Words

1. bathtub	*bathtub*	I wash in the **bathtub**.
2. bedtime	*bedtime*	When is your **bedtime**?
3. myself	*myself*	I played by **myself**.
4. someone	*someone*	Did **someone** call me?
5. maybe	*maybe*	I think **maybe** I can do it.
6. into	*into*	We walked **into** the store.
7. upon	*upon*	The frog sat **upon** a rock.
8. anyone	*anyone*	Pia did not see **anyone**.
9. without	*without*	He cooks **without** help.
10. cannot	*cannot*	They **cannot** stay.

A. bath | tub

bed | time

my | self

some | one

may | be

in | to

up | on

any | one

with | out

can | not

Think and Write

Each word is a **compound word**. A compound word is made up of two shorter words.

$$bath + tub \rightarrow bathtub$$
$$bed + time \rightarrow bedtime$$
$$my + self \rightarrow myself$$

A. Write the **ten** Basic Words. Then draw a line between the two words that make up each compound word.

Order of answers may vary.

Review	**Challenge**
11. stop 12. flag	13. playground 14. nobody

186

Meeting Individual Needs
Word Lists

You may want to assign Basic Words 1–5 and the Review Words to children who mis-spelled more than five words on the pretest. Assign the Challenge Words as appropri-ate. (You may want to have children write sentences, using the Challenge Words.)

Additional Spelling Words

Basic	**Challenge**	**Words Often Misspelled**
pancake	sweatshirt	there
classroom	doorbell	their
handstand	shoelace	
airplane	downstairs	
ladybug	homework	
	grasshopper	

Home/School Involvement
Take-Home Word List • Goal-Setting

Have children set goals for the week on Take-Home Word List 28.

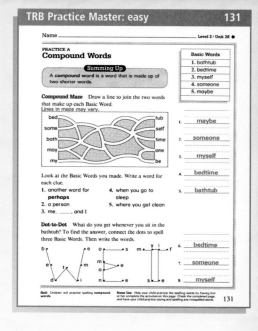

PRACTICE A
Compound Words

Summing Up
A compound word is a word that is made up of two shorter words.

Basic Words
1. bathtub
2. bedtime
3. myself
4. someone
5. maybe

Compound Maze Draw a line to join the two words that make up each Basic Word. *Lines in maze may vary.*

1. maybe
2. someone
3. myself
4. bedtime
5. bathtub

Look at the Basic Words you made. Write a word for each clue.

1. another word for **perhaps**
2. a person
3. me, _____, and I
4. when you go to sleep
5. where you get clean

Dot-to-Dot What do you get whenever you sit in the bathtub? To find the answer, connect the dots to spell three Basic Words. Then write the words.

6. bedtime
7. someone
8. myself

131

Independent Practice

 Spelling Strategy A **compound word** is a word that is made up of two shorter words.

Order of answers for questions 3–4 and 5–6 may vary.

Phonics Write Basic Words to answer the questions.

1. Which word has three syllables?
2. Which word has the long **i** sound spelled **y**?
3–4. Which two words have the short **i** sound in the first syllable?
5–6. Which two words have the short **o** sound in the second syllable?

Word Meaning Write the Basic Word that means the same or almost the same as each word below.

7. somebody   8. perhaps

Word Clues Write the Basic Word for each clue.

9. This is sometimes filled with bubbles.
10. This is when you go to sleep.

Phonics

1. anyone
2. myself
3. into
4. without
5. upon
6. cannot

Word Meaning

7. someone
8. maybe

Word Clues

9. bathtub
10. bedtime

(187)

 Day 2

Objectives *Children will*
- practice spelling list words
- apply spelling strategies
- identify synonyms
- identify Basic Words by using meaning clues

Daily Proofreading Practice

Will **sumone** win the prize? (*someone*)

I **can not** visit today. (*cannot*)

 Meeting Individual Needs
visual/oral/auditory/kinesthetic

Extra Support Check Independent Practice to determine who needs extra support. Write each Basic Word on the board, putting a plus sign between the words in each compound. Say the words and have children repeat. Then write an equal sign after each pair of words. Have volunteers go to the board and write the compound word that each pair makes. Then have them say the word.

Name _____   Level 2 / Unit 28 ▲

Basic Words
1. bathtub
2. bedtime
3. myself
4. someone
5. maybe
6. into
7. upon
8. anyone
9. without
10. cannot

PRACTICE B
Compound Words

Rhyme Time Each word in dark print rhymes with the second part of a Basic Word. Write the Basic Word.

1. Can you get a bear **cub** to sit in the _____?
2. Give them a **dime** if they know when it's _____.
3. The books on the **shelf** are only for _____.
4. Tom _____ eat the food while it is **hot**.
5. Will Mom **shout** if I leave _____ my lunch?

1. bathtub   4. cannot
2. bedtime   5. without
3. myself

Words in a Haystack Circle five Basic Words hidden in the hay. Look across and down. Then write the words. *Order of answers may vary.*

6. someone
7. into
8. upon
9. maybe
10. anyone

132

Applying Spelling Strategies
To Spell New Words

- Read aloud: **We like to build castles in the sandbox.**
- Have children attempt to spell *sandbox* on their Have-a-Go charts.
- Elicit the following strategies as children try to spell *sandbox*.

I hear the word *sand* at the beginning of this longer word. I know that *sand* is spelled s-a-n-d.

sandbox

I hear the word *box* at the end of this longer word. I know that *box* is spelled b-o-x.

Day 3

Objective *Children will*
■ review Basic and Review Words

Daily Proofreading Practice

I brush my teeth at **bedtim**. (*bedtime*)
Clara sat **apon** a tall stool. (*upon*)

Word Puzzles

1. cannot

2. someone

3. myself

4. without

Hidden Compounds

5. bedtime

6. maybe

7. bathtub

8. anyone

Fill-In Fun

9. flag

10. upon

11. stop

12. into

188

Review: Spelling Spree

Word Puzzles Make Basic Words by matching the puzzle pieces. Write the words.

1. can | self
2. some | out
3. my | not
4. with | one

any | one

Hidden Compounds Put together two words in each sentence to make a Basic Word. Write the word.
5. Do you go to bed at the same time each night?
6. You may slip, so please be careful.
7. Did you take a bath in that old tub?
8. He said any child could be the one who wins.

Fill-In Fun Write the missing Basic or Review Words.
9. raise the _____   11. _____ and go
10. once _____ a time   12. get _____ shape

How Are You Doing?
List the spelling words that are hard for you. Practice them with a family member.

TEACHING OPTIONS

Cooperative Learning Activity
Mystery Words
visual/oral

Have children play a version of Hangman using letter cards or Scrabble® pieces. One child thinks of a compound word and spells it with letter cards, turning the cards facedown while other players cover their eyes. Players take turns guessing letters that might be in the word. If the letter *is* in the word, the first child turns that card(s) over. Players score one point for each letter that is turned over and five points for guessing the word correctly. Children take turns guessing letters and selecting words. The player with the most points wins.

TRB Practice Master: challenging   133

Name _____   Level 2 / Unit 28

PRACTICE C
Compound Words

Staying in Shape Draw a picture to finish this story. Then write sentences to tell what happens in each picture. Use all the Challenge and Vocabulary Words.

Challenge Words
1. playground
2. nobody

Theme Vocabulary
3. jog
4. fit
5. muscles
6. shape

1.

2.

3.

Answers will vary.

1. _____
2. _____
3. _____

133

Proofreading and Writing

Proofread: Spelling and Book Titles Begin the first, the last, and each important word in a book title with a capital letter. Draw a line under the title.

<u>H</u>erman the <u>L</u>oser   <u>A</u>mos and <u>B</u>oris

Proofread Ariana's book report. Use proofreading marks to fix four spelling mistakes and two mistakes in book titles.

Example: Can you read swimmy ~~wifout~~ ^{without} help?

The book <u>Gregory the Terrible eater</u>
is about a goat who ~~canot stap~~ ^{cannot stop} eating
healthy food. I think ~~enyone~~ ^{anyone} would like
this funny book! It is funnier than <u>Clyde</u>
<u>Monster</u>, a book about a monster who
is afraid at bedtime. Maybe you know
~~somone~~ ^{someone} like that too!

Write Book Titles

Write three titles for some books about exercising. Try to use spelling words. Share your titles with a friend.
Example: <u>Anyone Can Exercise</u>

Proofreading Tip

Check that you wrote each book title correctly.

Basic
1. bathtub
2. bedtime
3. myself
4. someone
5. maybe
6. into
7. upon
8. anyone
9. without
10. cannot

Review
11. stop
12. flag

Challenge
13. playground
14. nobody

Proofreading Marks
∧ Add
⌐ Delete
≡ Make a capital letter
／ Make a small letter

189

Objectives *Children will*
- proofread for spelling and book title mechanics
- write and proofread an original composition

Day 4

Daily Proofreading Practice
Was **anywon** at the store? (*anyone*)
I made the cookies by **miself**.
(*myself*)

Day 5   **Posttest**

Sentences 1–5 test the first five Basic Words. Sentences 6–10 test the next five Basic Words.

Basic Words
1. Should I thank <u>someone</u>?
2. I did it <u>myself</u>.
3. I clean the <u>bathtub</u>.
4. I hope that <u>maybe</u> we can play.
5. We have the same <u>bedtime</u>.
6. I feel cold <u>without</u> a hat.
7. Did you give my bike to <u>anyone</u>?
8. We <u>cannot</u> sail in the rain.
9. He sat down <u>upon</u> the box.
10. Did she go <u>into</u> the shop?

Review Words
11. Please look at the <u>flag</u>.
12. We must <u>stop</u> the game.

Challenge Words
13. Be sure <u>nobody</u> wakes up the baby.
14. There is a slide at the <u>playground</u>.

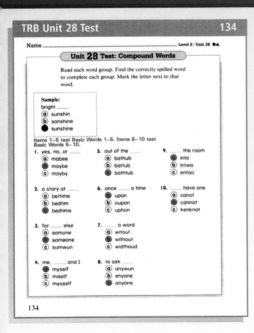

TRB Unit 28 Test   134

Name _____ Level 2 / Unit 28 ●▲

Unit 28 Test: Compound Words

Read each word group. Find the correctly spelled word to complete each group. Mark the letter next to that word.

Sample:
bright
(a) sunshin
(b) sonshine
● sunshine

Items 1–5 test Basic Words 1–5. Items 6–10 test Basic Words 6–10.

1. yes, no, or ___
   (a) mabee
   ● maybe
   (c) mayby

2. a story at ___
   (a) beltime
   (b) bedtim
   ● bedtime

3. for ___ else
   (a) somone
   ● someone
   (c) sumwun

4. me, ___, and I
   ● myself
   (b) miself
   (c) myssef

5. out of the ___
   (a) bathub
   (b) battub
   ● bathtub

6. once ___ a time
   ● upon
   (b) oupon
   (c) uphon

7. ___ a word
   (a) witout
   ● without
   (c) widthoud

8. to ask ___
   (a) anywun
   (b) enyone
   ● anyone

9. ___ the room
   ● into
   (b) intwo
   (c) entoo

10. ___ have one
    (a) canot
    ● cannot
    (c) kenknot

134

Meeting Individual Needs

Challenge Words Practice
Ask children to write some safety rules for the playground, using the two Challenge Words and other compound words they choose.

Another Writing Idea Have children write instructions for a game or an exercise that will help people stay in shape. Encourage them to use spelling words.

Unit 28 BONUS

These pages can be used at any time during the study of this unit.

Day by Day Planner

Objectives *Children will*

- build compound words
- write word clues

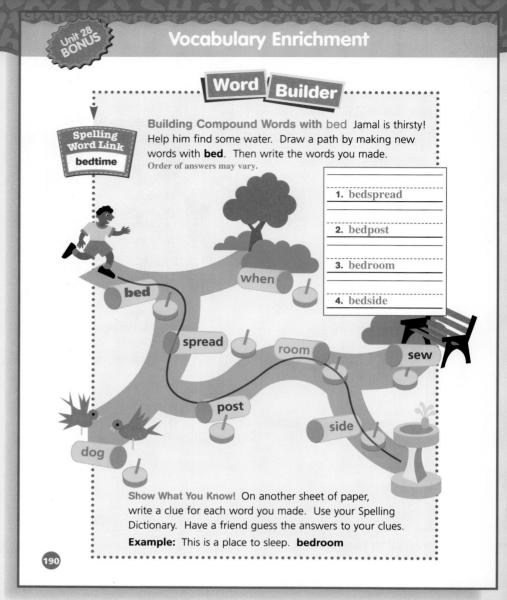

Unit 28 BONUS

Vocabulary Enrichment

Word Builder

Spelling Word Link

bedtime

Building Compound Words with bed Jamal is thirsty! Help him find some water. Draw a path by making new words with **bed**. Then write the words you made. Order of answers may vary.

1. bedspread
2. bedpost
3. bedroom
4. bedside

(path words shown: bed, when, spread, room, sew, post, side, dog)

Show What You Know! On another sheet of paper, write a clue for each word you made. Use your Spelling Dictionary. Have a friend guess the answers to your clues.

Example: This is a place to sleep. **bedroom**

190

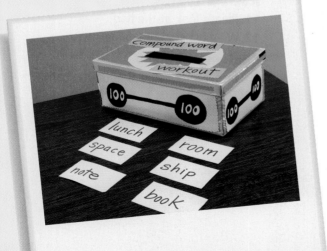

Learning Center Activity

visual/kinesthetic

Compound Word Workout In your Learning Center, place blank cards cut from tagboard or colored paper and a box labeled "Compound Word Workout." Explain that children are going to exercise their minds. Have them brainstorm compound words, write one part of each compound on a card, and put the pairs of cards in the box. Children remove cards from the box and see how many compound words they can make. Partners can time their "workouts" by seeing how many words they can form in a given time period.

Vocabulary Enrichment

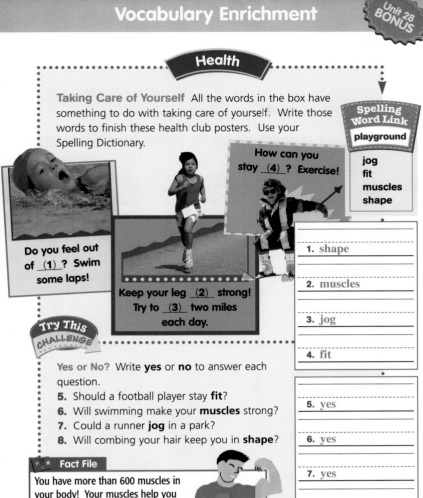

Health

Taking Care of Yourself All the words in the box have something to do with taking care of yourself. Write those words to finish these health club posters. Use your Spelling Dictionary.

Spelling Word Link

playground

jog
fit
muscles
shape

Do you feel out of **(1)**? Swim some laps!

How can you stay **(4)**? Exercise!

Keep your leg **(2)** strong! Try to **(3)** two miles each day.

1. shape

2. muscles

3. jog

4. fit

Try This CHALLENGE

Yes or No? Write **yes** or **no** to answer each question.

5. Should a football player stay **fit**?
6. Will swimming make your **muscles** strong?
7. Could a runner **jog** in a park?
8. Will combing your hair keep you in **shape**?

5. yes

6. yes

7. yes

8. no

★ Fact File

You have more than 600 muscles in your body! Your muscles help you move. You can take care of them by exercising and eating healthy foods.

191

Objectives *Children will*

- expand their vocabulary by using words related to taking care of yourself
- show their understanding of the vocabulary words by completing context activities

Vocabulary Checkup

Have children use the vocabulary words in sentences or match the words to the definitions below.

1. to run slowly *jog*
2. parts of the body under the skin that help a person move *muscles*
3. strong and healthy *fit*
4. good working order; good health *in shape*

Fact File

Exercising

One of the most important muscles, the heart, can benefit from regular exercise. Activities such as swimming, brisk walking, and dancing improve heart action and help blood circulation. Those who exercise regularly are able to maintain activities longer and tend to get tired less easily than those who do not.

Integrating Literature

Easy	Average	Challenging
Dinosaurs Alive and Well *by Laurie K. Brown and Marc Brown* Dinosaurs teach children about ways to stay healthy.	**Albert the Running Bear Gets the Jittters** *by Barbara Isenberg* Albert, a champion runner, is challenged to a race.	**Germs Make Me Sick!** *by Melvin Berger* An introduction to germs and how they make us sick.
The Vegetable Show *by Laurie Krasny Brown* Vegetable performers remind children that vegetables are part of a healthy diet.	**Yummers!** *by James Marshall* Eugene Turtle and Emily Pig try walking to lose weight.	**The Edible Pyramid** *by Loreen Leedy* Children learn good nutrition at a restaurant called The Edible Pyramid.

Contractions

WORD LISTS

Spelling

Basic
1. I'll
2. we've
3. don't
4. you're
5. isn't
6. didn't
7. you'll
8. I've
9. hasn't
10. we'll
11. can't

Review
12. it
13. us

Challenge
14. they're
15. wouldn't

Vocabulary

Science: Insects

flea
moth
beetle
crawl

Introducing the Lesson

Read Aloud

Write the Basic Words on the board.

Many Small Creatures

Isn't it amazing how many kinds of insects there are in the world? **We've** already found 800,000 types of insects, and scientists say **we'll** discover as many as 10,000 more each year. Life **hasn't** been easy for these insects, but they stay alive because of their small size and their ability to live anywhere. **You're** probably bothered by insects like bees and termites, but **I'll** bet you **didn't** know that insects help us in many ways. They help plants to grow and provide food for many animals. Although I **can't** say **I've** tried them, many people enjoy eating insects. **Don't** look so surprised! Maybe someday **you'll** find roasted ants for sale in your grocery store!

Responding Ask children what two ways insects help us. *(They help plants grow and provide food for animals.)* **Read** these words: "Life **has not** been easy for all these insects." Ask a volunteer to repeat the sentence, using the contraction for *has not*. *(hasn't)* **Repeat** this activity with some of the other contractions in the selection.

Day 1 *page 192*

Objectives *Children will*
- take the pretest
- pronounce the list words
- learn about the spelling principle
- identify the missing letters in contractions

Planning Checklist
- ☑ Pretest (TE)
- ☑ Spelling principle/word list
- ☐ Review/Challenge Words
- ☐ Teaching the Principle (TE)
- ☐ Additional Spelling Words (TE)

Day 2 *page 193*

Objectives *Children will*
- practice spelling list words
- apply spelling strategies
- identify Basic Words and an Elephant Word that mean the same as given words in sentences

Planning Checklist
- ☑ Spelling Strategy
- ☑ Independent Practice
- ☐ Daily Proofreading Practice (TE)
- ☐ Informal Assessment (TE)
- ☐ Extra Support (TE)
- ☐ Applying Spelling Strategies (TE)

Assessment

Pretest
1. I said that I'll be there.
2. I know we've had fun!
3. Why don't you rest?
4. We think you're great!
5. It isn't time to play.
6. Mom didn't eat dinner.
7. I hope you'll stay.
8. I think I've lost my pen.
9. She hasn't called yet.
10. Next time we'll sing.
11. I can't go to the park.

page 194

 page 195

 page 195

• Additional Resources

Teacher's Resource Book
Practice Masters, pages 135–137
Unit Test, page 138
Bulletin Board, page 139

Practice Plus
Take-Home Word List 29
Games

Spelling Transparencies
Spelling Word List 29
Daily Proofreading Practice,
    Unit 29
Graphic Organizers

Teacher's Resource Disk
Macintosh® or Windows®
    software. Houghton Mifflin

Spelling CD-ROM
Macintosh® or Windows®
    software. Houghton Mifflin

Internet
http://www.eduplace.com

Phonics Practice
Houghton Mifflin Phonics
The Listening Corner
Phonics Home Connection

Objective *Children will*

• review Basic and Review
  Words

Planning Checklist

☐ Review: Spelling Spree
☐ How Are You Doing?
☐ Daily Proofreading Practice
   (TE)
☐ Cooperative Learning
   Activity (TE)

Objectives *Children will*

• proofread for spelling and
  commas
• write and proofread an
  original composition

Planning Checklist

☐ Proofread: Spelling and
   Commas
☐ Write Some Diary Entries
☐ Daily Proofreading Practice
   (TE)
☐ Challenge Words Practice
   (TE)
☐ Another Writing Idea (TE)

Objective *Children will*

• take the posttest

Assessment

☐ **Posttest** (TE) *See Day 5*
☐ Unit 29 Test

Meeting Individual Needs
Students Acquiring English

Spanish Contractions do not occur in formal written Spanish. **Activity** Write *I will* and *I'll* on the board. Say them and explain that they mean the same thing. Explain that the apostrophe in *I'll* takes the place of the letters *wi* in *will*. Write the Basic Words on the board. Beside them write the words they are made from. Read the pairs and have children repeat them. Have volunteers circle the letters that were dropped to form the contractions. Then have volunteers trace the contractions—including the apostrophes—at the board.

Other Activities for Any Day

• Bonus activities from pages 196–197
• Practice Masters (easy, average, challenging)
  Teacher's Resource Book,
  pages 135–137
• Take-Home Word List 29
  Practice Plus

Objectives *Children will*

■ take the pretest

■ pronounce the list words

■ learn about the spelling principle

■ identify the missing letters in contractions

Teaching the Principle

This lesson teaches the meanings and formation of a variety of contractions. Children learn the strategy of writing contractions in place of certain words, using an apostrophe to replace the omitted letter or letters.

To sum up the lesson, have children name the word or words used to make each contraction. Have them tell what missing letter or letters each apostrophe stands for.

Answers to *Think* Questions

• The two words used to make each contraction are *I will, we have, do not, you are, is not, did not, you will, I have, has not,* and *we will.*

• The Elephant Word was formed from the compound word *cannot.*

Read and Say

READ the sentences. **SAY** each word in dark print.

Basic Words

1.	I'll	*I'll*	I said that **I'll** be there.
2.	we've	*we've*	I know **we've** had fun!
3.	don't	*don't*	Why **don't** you rest?
4.	you're	*you're*	We think **you're** great!
5.	isn't	*isn't*	It **isn't** time to play.
6.	didn't	*didn't*	Mom **didn't** eat dinner.
7.	you'll	*you'll*	I hope **you'll** stay.
8.	I've	*I've*	I think **I've** lost my pen.
9.	hasn't	*hasn't*	She **hasn't** called yet.
10.	we'll	*we'll*	Next time **we'll** sing.
11.	can't	*can't*	I **can't** go to the park.

A. I'll, wi

we've, ha

don't, o

you're, a

isn't, o

didn't, o

you'll, wi

I've, ha

hasn't, o

we'll, wi

can't, no

192

Think and Write

Each word is a **contraction.** A contraction is a short way of writing two words. One or more letters are left out, and a mark called an **apostrophe** is put in their place.

I + <u>will</u> → **I'll**   we + <u>have</u> → **we've**

What two words were used to make each contraction? Were two words used to make the Elephant Word? See TE margin.

A. Write the **eleven** Basic Words. Beside each word, write the letter or letters that the apostrophe takes the place of. Remember the Elephant Word. *Order of answers may vary.*

Review	Challenge
12. it 13. us	14. they're 15. wouldn't

TEACHING OPTIONS

Meeting Individual Needs
Word Lists

You may want to assign Basic Words 1–5, the Elephant Word, and the Review Words to children who misspelled more than five words on the pretest. Assign the Challenge Words as appropriate. (You may want to have children write sentences, using the Challenge Words.)

Additional Spelling Words

Basic	Challenge	Words Often Misspelled
she'll	won't	through
that's	weren't	school
wasn't	doesn't	
it's	aren't	
I'm	there's	
	he'd	

Home/School Involvement
Take-Home Word List • Goal-Setting

Have children set goals for the week on Take-Home Word List 29.

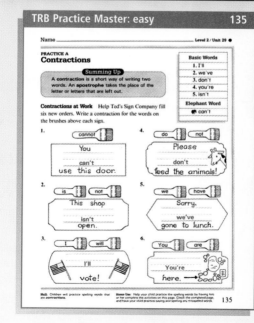

Independent Practice

 Spelling Strategy A **contraction** is a short way of writing two words. An **apostrophe** takes the place of the letter or letters that are left out.

Order of answers for question 3–4 may vary.

Phonics Write Basic Words to answer the questions.

1. Which word has the long **o** sound?
2. Which word begins like **happy**?

3–4. Which two words have the long **e** sound?

Word Meaning Write the Basic Word that means the same as the pair of words in dark print.

5. I think **I will** get an ant farm.
6. An ant farm **is not** hard to care for.
7. Perhaps **you will** be surprised to learn that ants work together in groups.
8. **I have** heard that each ant has its own job.
9. Maybe you **did not** know that a queen ant's only job is to lay eggs.
10. If **you are** interested in ants, you can buy an ant farm to set up at home.

Elephant Word Write the Elephant Word that means the same as the word in dark print.
11. An ant **cannot** tap-dance.

Phonics

1. don't
2. hasn't
3. we've
4. we'll

Word Meaning

5. I'll
6. isn't
7. you'll
8. I've
9. didn't
10. you're

Elephant Word

11. can't

(193)

 Day 2

Objectives *Children will*
- practice spelling list words
- apply spelling strategies
- identify Basic Words and an Elephant Word that mean the same as given words in sentences

Daily Proofreading Practice

I **dont** know her name. (*don't*)
Next year **we'ill** study bees. (*we'll*)

Meeting Individual Needs
visual/oral/auditory

Extra Support Check Independent Practice to determine who needs extra support. Write these sentences: *We will go to the circus. We'll go to the circus.* Read them aloud and have children repeat. Explain that *we'll* is a contraction for *we will*. Discuss the meaning and formation of the contraction. Repeat, changing the first words of the sentences to *You will* and *You'll, I will* and *I'll*, and *Do not* and *Don't*.

 Applying Spelling Strategies
To Read New Words

- Write this sentence on the chalkboard:
My sisters haven't seen my tree house yet.

- Have children read the sentence silently.
- Elicit the following strategies as children try to decode *haven't*.

> The apostrophe lets me know that this word is probably a contraction. I think that the apostrophe takes the place of *o* in the word *not*.

> I recognize the word *have* at the beginning of this longer word.

have**n't**

> Have-n't. Haven't. *Haven't* means "have not." The words *have not* make sense in the sentence.

Objective *Children will*
■ review Basic and Review Words

Daily Proofreading Practice
He **didint** finish his lunch. (*didn't*)
I think **yoo'ull** enjoy the rides.
(*you'll*)

Letter Math

1. us
2. can't
3. you're
4. it
5. we've

Word Wheels

6. don't
7. isn't
8. didn't
9. hasn't
10. you'll
11. we'll
12. I'll

194

Review: Spelling Spree

Letter Math Add and take away to make Basic or Review Words. Write the words.

1. bugs − b − g = _____
2. cannot − no + ' = _____
3. you are − a + ' = _____
4. knits − kn − s = _____
5. we have − ha + ' = _____

Word Wheels 6–12. Make contractions that are Basic Words. Join the word in the center of each wheel with another word on the same wheel. Write the contractions. *Order of answers may vary.*

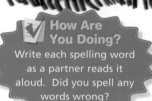

How Are You Doing?
Write each spelling word as a partner reads it aloud. Did you spell any words wrong?

TEACHING OPTIONS

Cooperative Learning Activity
Contraction Bugs
visual/kinesthetic

Suggest partners make contraction bugs. For each bug, children should cut the following from colored paper: three circles for the body, six legs, and one head.

Children glue the pieces together to make a bug, attaching two legs to each circle in the body. They write a contraction on each body segment and the two words that make up the contraction on the attached legs. Children may wish to paint a mural of a garden or a forest and paste their bugs on the mural.

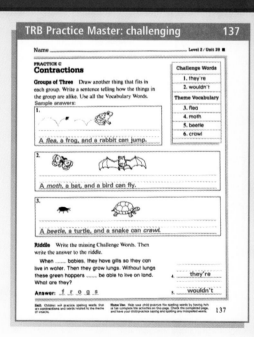

TRB Practice Master: challenging 137

Name _____ Level 2 / Unit 29 ■

PRACTICE C
Contractions

Groups of Three Draw another thing that fits in each group. Write a sentence telling how the things in the group are alike. Use all the Vocabulary Words.
Sample answers:

Challenge Words
1. they're
2. wouldn't
Theme Vocabulary
3. flea
4. moth
5. beetle
6. crawl

1. A *flea*, a frog, and a rabbit can *jump*.

2. A *moth*, a bat, and a bird can *fly*.

3. A *beetle*, a turtle, and a snake can *crawl*.

Riddle Write the missing Challenge Words. Then write the answer to the riddle.

When _____ babies, they have gills so they can live in water. Then they grow lungs. Without lungs these green hoppers _____ be able to live on land. What are they?

Answer: f r o g s

4. they're

5. wouldn't

137

Proofreading and Writing

Proofread: Spelling and Commas Always put a **comma** between the day and the year in a **date**.

Will the picnic be on June 22, 1998?

Proofread the ant's message. Use proofreading marks to fix four spelling mistakes and two missing commas.

Example: Be sure ~~youre~~ there on May 20, 1998!

> I've
> ~~Ive~~ set a date for our picnic. We ~~cant~~ have ~~et~~
> can't   it
> on July 4, 1998. People don't want ants at
> picnics, and there isn't ever enough food for all of
> you'll
> us. Instead, ~~you'ill~~ be coming on January 1, 1999.
> In winter, people will not bug us!

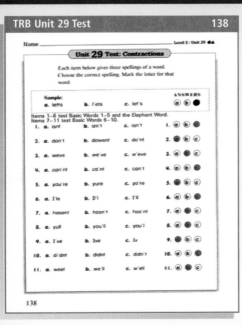

Write Some Diary Entries

Pretend you are a bee. Pick three days of the week and write a diary entry for each day. Include the date and two or three sentences about what you saw and did. Try to use spelling words.

Proofreading Tip

Check that you wrote each date correctly.

Basic
1. I'll
2. we've
3. don't
4. you're
5. isn't
6. didn't
7. you'll
8. I've
9. hasn't
10. we'll
11. can't

Review
12. it
13. us

Challenge
14. they're
15. wouldn't

Proofreading Marks
∧ Add
⌿ Delete
≡ Make a capital letter
/ Make a small letter

195

TRB Unit 29 Test   138

Unit 29 Test: Contractions

Each item below gives three spellings of a word. Choose the correct spelling. Mark the letter for that word.

Sample:
a. letts   b. l'ets   c. let's   ⓐ ⓑ ●

Items 1–6 test Basic Words 1–5 and the Elephant Word.
Items 7–11 test Basic Words 6–10.

1. a. isnt   b. izn't   c. isn't   1. ⓐ ⓑ ●
2. a. don't   b. dowen't   c. do'nt   2. ● ⓑ ⓒ
3. a. weve   b. we've   c. w'eve   3. ⓐ ● ⓒ
4. a. can'nt   b. cd'nt   c. can't   4. ⓐ ⓑ ●
5. a. you're   b. yure   c. yo're   5. ● ⓑ ⓒ
6. a. I'le   b. I'l'l   c. I'll   6. ⓐ ⓑ ●
7. a. hasent   b. hasn't   c. has'nt   7. ⓐ ● ⓒ
8. a. yull   b. you'll   c. you'l   8. ⓐ ● ⓒ
9. a. I've   b. Ive   c. Iv   9. ● ⓑ ⓒ
10. a. di'dnt   b. didnt   c. didn't   10. ⓐ ⓑ ●
11. a. weel   b. we'll   c. w'ell   11. ⓐ ● ⓒ

138

Meeting Individual Needs

Challenge Words Practice
Ask children to draw four pictures of insects then write a sentence or a caption for each picture, using a Challenge Word.

Another Writing Idea Have children pretend that a scientist has just discovered a strange bug. Ask children to write questions they would ask the scientist as well as the answers the scientist would give. Encourage them to use spelling words.

Objectives *Children will*
■ proofread for spelling and commas
■ write and proofread an original composition

Day 4

Daily Proofreading Practice
The book **is'nt** in my desk. (*isn't*)
I think **your** taller than I. (*you're*)

Day 5   Posttest

Sentences 1–5 test the first five Basic Words. Sentences 6–10 test the next five Basic Words. Sentence 11 tests the Elephant Word.

Basic Words
1. I can see <u>you're</u> hot.
2. It <u>isn't</u> the one I want.
3. That is the one <u>I'll</u> use.
4. We <u>don't</u> think it is right.
5. I think <u>we've</u> cut too much.
6. These are the best toys <u>I've</u> seen.
7. He <u>hasn't</u> come to play.
8. He will go if <u>you'll</u> go.
9. We did say <u>we'll</u> do it.
10. She <u>didn't</u> tell me.
11. I <u>can't</u> play that game.

Review Words
12. The kite is for <u>us</u>.
13. Take <u>it</u> for me.

Challenge Words
14. They can take the test when <u>they're</u> ready.
15. The cat <u>wouldn't</u> go out in the rain.

These pages can be used at any time during the study of this unit.

Objectives *Children will*

- write homophones to match illustrations
- illustrate and label homophones

Vocabulary Enrichment

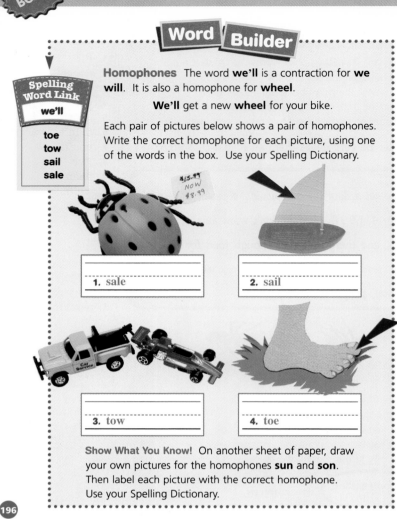

Word Builder

Homophones The word **we'll** is a contraction for **we will**. It is also a homophone for **wheel**.

We'll get a new **wheel** for your bike.

Each pair of pictures below shows a pair of homophones. Write the correct homophone for each picture, using one of the words in the box. Use your Spelling Dictionary.

Spelling Word Link

we'll

toe
tow
sail
sale

1. sale
2. sail
3. tow
4. toe

Show What You Know! On another sheet of paper, draw your own pictures for the homophones **sun** and **son**. Then label each picture with the correct homophone. Use your Spelling Dictionary.

196

EXTENSION OPTIONS

Learning Center Activity
visual/kinesthetic

My Homophone Dictionary Ask children to brainstorm and list more homophones. Then suggest they make their own homophone dictionary. Have children write each pair of homophones on facing pages, drawing a picture for each word.

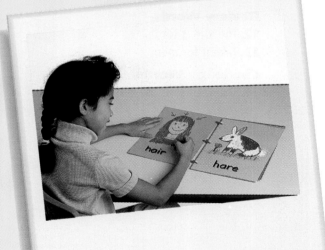

More Homophones		
ate/eight	doe/dough	in/inn
blew/blue	fir/fur	knight/night
cent/sent	flour/flower	meat/meet
close/clothes	hair/hare	rose/rows

Vocabulary Enrichment

Science

Insects All the words in the box have something to do with insects. Write those words to finish this science log. Use your Spelling Dictionary.

Spelling Word Link

they're

flea
moth
beetle
crawl

July 15

Today I saw a bug __(1)__ up a tree. Was it a tiny jumping __(2)__? Was it a __(3)__ with soft wings? No, it was a big black __(4)__. I love looking for insects, but sometimes they're hard to find!

Try This CHALLENGE

1. crawl

2. flea

3. moth

4. beetle

Write Some Riddles What insect can jump, but cannot fly? A flea! Write more insect riddles. Try to use some words from the box on this page. Have a friend guess the answers to your riddles.

★ Fact File

Did you know that there are more than 1,000,000 different kinds of insects? Insects live almost everywhere. They even live near the North Pole!

197

Objectives *Children will*

- expand their vocabulary by using words related to insects
- show their understanding of the vocabulary words by completing context and writing activities

Vocabulary Checkup

Have children use the vocabulary words in sentences or match the words to the definitions below.

1. a flying insect with soft wings and a body fatter than a butterfly's *moth*
2. an insect with hard front wings that cover the back wings when it is resting *beetle*
3. a small, jumping insect with no wings *flea*
4. to move slowly on or as if on the hands and knees *crawl*

Fact File

Insects

An insect is a six-legged animal with a segmented body that has three major divisions. Many insects have two pairs of wings. Scientists believe there may be up to ten million kinds of insects yet to be discovered.

Integrating Literature

Easy	Average	Challenging
Fireflies, Fireflies, Light My Way *by Jonathan London* Fireflies lead children through a nighttime world of nature.	**Insects Are My Life** *by Megan McDonald* Amanda's classmates can't understand her love for bugs.	**Why Mosquitoes Buzz in People's Ears** *by Verna Aardema* This African legend explains why mosquitoes buzz.
Flit, Flutter, Fly! *by Lee Bennett Hopkins* Poems about bugs and other crawly creatures.	**Buz** *by Richard Egielski* A boy takes a pill to get rid of the bug he swallowed with his cornflakes.	**The Big Bug Book** *by Margery Facklam* An introduction to thirteen of the world's largest bugs.

Review: Units 25–29

WORD LISTS

Spelling
Basic Words

Unit 25	Unit 28
find	bathtub
high	myself
fly	someone
light	into
dry	upon
kind	cannot

Unit 26	Unit 29
puppy	we've
baby	don't
very	you're
lady	didn't
silly	you'll
only	hasn't

Unit 27

house
out
down
now
found
brown

Elephant Words
Units 25–29

eye	could
buy	should
cookie	can't

The Review Unit

Word Lists

Half of the Basic Words from Units 25–29 are reviewed in this Review Unit. The remaining Basic Words from Units 25–29 are reviewed in the Extra Practice section of the Student's Handbook. All of the Elephant Words are practiced in both the Review Unit and the Extra Practice section.

Day 1 page 198

Objectives *Children will*
- take the pretest
- review spelling patterns for the |ī| sound
- review a spelling pattern for the |ē| sound at the end of a two-syllable word

Planning Checklist
- ☐ Daily Proofreading Practice (TE)
- ☐ Extra Support, pages 169, 175 (TE)
- ☐ Extra Practice, page 253
- ☐ Practice Masters, pages 119, 120, 123, 124 (TRB)

Assessment

Pretest
1. I see a green <u>light</u>.
2. The hat is <u>dry</u>.
3. I like him <u>very</u> much.
4. The dog is <u>silly</u>.
5. We have a white <u>house</u>.
6. May they clap <u>now</u>?
7. I came by <u>myself</u>.
8. I want to help <u>someone</u>.
9. I think <u>you're</u> good.
10. He <u>hasn't</u> been to that lake.

Day 2 page 199

Objectives *Children will*
- review spelling patterns for the |ou| sound
- review compound words

Planning Checklist
- ☐ Daily Proofreading Practice (TE)
- ☐ Extra Support, pages 181, 187 (TE)
- ☐ Extra Practice, page 254
- ☐ Practice Masters, pages 127, 128, 131, 132 (TRB)

Day 3 *page 200*   **Day 4** *page 201*   **Day 5** *page 201*

Objectives *Children will*
- review contractions
- review the Elephant Words

Planning Checklist
☐ Daily Proofreading Practice (TE)
☐ Extra Support, page 193 (TE)
☐ Extra Practice, page 255
☐ Practice Masters, pages 135, 136 (TRB)

Objective *Children will*
- analyze the spelling and meaning relationship of words in the *light* word family

Planning Checklist
☐ Spelling-Meaning Strategy

Objective *Children will*
- take the posttest

Assessment
☐ **Posttest** (TE) *See Day 5*
☐ Scoring Rubric
☐ Unit 30 Review Tests A–B (TRB)

Teacher's Resource Book
Practice Masters, pages 119–121, 123–125, 127–129, 131–133, 135–137
Multiple-Choice Tests, pages 144–145
Bulletin Board, page 139
Spelling Newsletters, English and Spanish, pages 140–141
Spelling Game, pages 142–143

Practice Plus
Take-Home Word List 30

Spelling Transparencies
Spelling Word List 30
Daily Proofreading Practice, Unit 30
Spelling-Meaning Strategy
Multiple-Choice Test

Teacher's Resource Disk
Macintosh® or Windows® software. Houghton Mifflin

Spelling CD-ROM
Macintosh® or Windows® software. Houghton Mifflin

Internet
http://www.eduplace.com

Meeting Individual Needs

You may wish to create your own pretest, using the words that children missed most often in the last five units. Children can check their own work, or a partner's, by looking up the words in the previous units' word lists or in their Spelling Dictionary.

In each Review lesson, the Basic Words are selected from both halves of the unit word list to accommodate individual needs. In Units 25–29, the top row of words is from Basic Words 1–5 and the bottom row from Basic Words 6–10.

Other Activities for Any Day

- Literature and Writing, pages 202–203
- Spelling Game
  Teacher's Resource Book, pages 142–143
- Bulletin Board
  Teacher's Resource Book, page 139
- Take-Home Word List 30
  Practice Plus

UNIT 30 Review

Day 1

Objectives *Children will*

- take the pretest
- review spelling patterns for the |ī| sound
- review a spelling pattern for the |ē| sound at the end of a two-syllable word

---

Daily Proofreading Practice

The plane flew **hie** above us. (*high*)

The rabbit's fur is **veree** soft. (*very*)

Meeting Individual Needs

Additional Resources

Unit 25

Extra Support page 169 (TE)

Extra Practice page 253

Practice Masters pages 119–120 (TRB)

Unit 26

Extra Support page 175 (TE)

Extra Practice page 253

Practice Masters pages 123–124 (TRB)

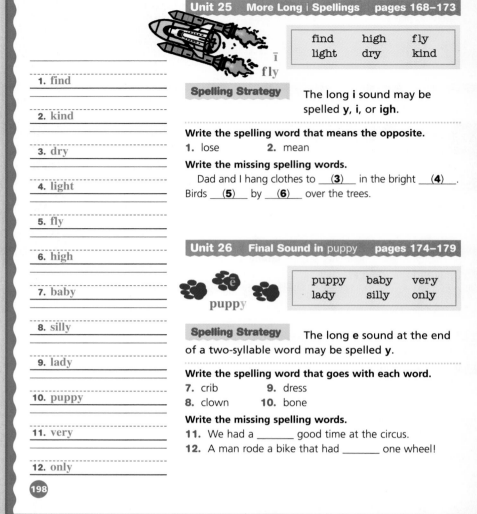

30 Review: Units 25–29

1. find
2. kind
3. dry
4. light
5. fly
6. high
7. baby
8. silly
9. lady
10. puppy
11. very
12. only

198

Unit 25 More Long i Spellings pages 168–173

find	high	fly
light	dry	kind

ī fly

Spelling Strategy The long **i** sound may be spelled **y**, **i**, or **igh**.

Write the spelling word that means the opposite.

1. lose   2. mean

Write the missing spelling words.

Dad and I hang clothes to __(3)__ in the bright __(4)__.
Birds __(5)__ by __(6)__ over the trees.

Unit 26 Final Sound in puppy pages 174–179

puppy	baby	very
lady	silly	only

ē puppy

Spelling Strategy The long **e** sound at the end of a two-syllable word may be spelled **y**.

Write the spelling word that goes with each word.

7. crib   9. dress
8. clown   10. bone

Write the missing spelling words.

11. We had a _____ good time at the circus.
12. A man rode a bike that had _____ one wheel!

EXTENSION OPTIONS

TRB Bulletin Board 139

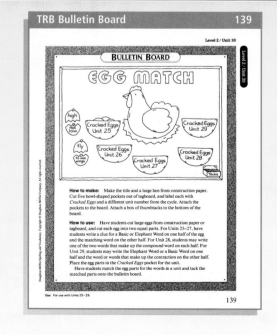

Level 2 / Unit 30

BULLETIN BOARD

EGG MATCH

How to make: Make the title and a large hen from construction paper. Cut five bowl-shaped pockets out of tagboard, and label each with *Cracked Eggs* and a different unit number from the cycle. Attach the pockets to the board. Attach a box of thumbtacks to the bottom of the board.

How to use: Have students cut large eggs from construction paper or tagboard, and cut each egg into two equal parts. For Units 25–27, have students write a clue for a Basic or Elephant Word on one half of the egg and the matching word on the other half. For Unit 28, students may write one of the two words that make up the compound word on each half. For Unit 29, students may write the Elephant Word or a Basic Word on one half and the word or words that make up the contraction on the other half. Place the egg parts in the *Cracked Eggs* pocket for the unit.

Have students match the egg parts for the words in a unit and tack the matched parts onto the bulletin board.

Use: For use with Units 25–29.

139

TRB Spelling Newsletter: English 140

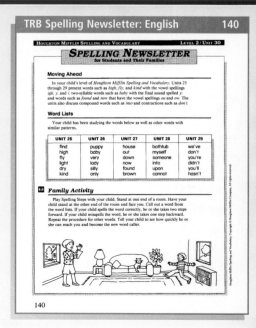

HOUGHTON MIFFLIN SPELLING AND VOCABULARY   LEVEL 2 / UNIT 30

SPELLING NEWSLETTER
for Students and Their Families

Moving Ahead

In your child's level of *Houghton Mifflin Spelling and Vocabulary*, Units 25 through 29 present words such as *high, fly,* and *kind* with the vowel spellings *igh, y,* and *i*; two-syllable words such as *baby* with the final sound spelled *y*; and words such as *found* and *now* that have the vowel spellings *ou* and *ow*. The units also discuss compound words such as *into* and contractions such as *don't*.

Word Lists

Your child has been studying the words below as well as other words with similar patterns.

UNIT 25	UNIT 26	UNIT 27	UNIT 28	UNIT 29
find	puppy	house	bathtub	we've
high	baby	out	myself	don't
fly	very	down	someone	you're
light	lady	now	into	didn't
dry	silly	found	upon	you'll
kind	only	brown	cannot	hasn't

Family Activity

Play Spelling Steps with your child. Stand at one end of a room. Have your child stand at the other end of the room and face you. Call out a word from the word lists. If your child spells the word correctly, he or she takes two steps forward. If your child misspells the word, he or she takes one step backward. Repeat the procedure for other words. Tell your child to see how quickly he or she can reach you and become the new word caller.

140

---

198 **Review**

Unit 27   The Vowel Sound in COW   pages 180–185

house	out	down
now	found	brown

ow
cow

Spelling Strategy   The vowel sound in **down** and **house** may be spelled **ow** or **ou**.

Write the spelling word that rhymes with each word.

13. round   **14.** shout   **15.** cow

Write the missing spelling words.

Joy is painting our __(16)__ white and __(17)__. She moves her brush up and __(18)__ on the door.

Unit 28   Compound Words   pages 186–191

bathtub	myself	someone
into	upon	cannot

bathtub

Spelling Strategy   A **compound word** is a word that is made up of two shorter words.

Change the word in dark print. Write a spelling word.

19. some**time**   **21.** up**set**
20. in**side**   **22.** him**self**

Write the missing spelling words.

23. Mom is filling the _____ with warm water.
24. I _____ wait to play with my toy boat!

13. found
14. out
15. now
16. house
17. brown
18. down
19. someone
20. into
21. upon
22. myself
23. bathtub
24. cannot

199

Objectives *Children will*
- review spelling patterns for the |ou| sound
- review compound words

Daily Proofreading Practice

A clown popped **owt** of the box. (*out*)
Bubbles filled the **baftub**. (*bathtub*)

Meeting Individual Needs

Additional Resources

Unit 27
Extra Support page 181 (TE)
Extra Practice page 254
Practice Masters pages 127–128 (TRB)

Unit 28
Extra Support page 187 (TE)
Extra Practice page 254
Practice Masters pages 131–132 (TRB)

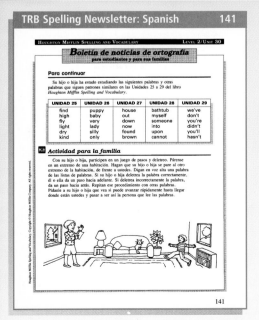

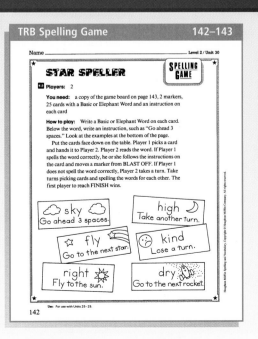

Objectives *Children will*

Day 3

■ review contractions

■ review the Elephant Words

Daily Proofreading Practice

Mary **haz'nt** read that book. (*hasn't*)

He **cood** help us find the trail. (*could*)

Meeting Individual Needs

Additional Resources

Unit 29

Extra Support page 193 (TE)

Extra Practice page 255

Practice Masters pages 135–136 (TRB)

Reviewing Elephant Words

Extra Practice page 255

UNIT
30

25. hasn't

26. don't

27. didn't

28. you're

29. you'll

30. we've

31. eye

32. could

33. should

34. can't

35. buy

36. cookie

200

Unit 29   Contractions   pages 192–197

we've	don't	you're
didn't	you'll	hasn't

Spelling Strategy   we + <u>h</u>ave → **we've**
do + n<u>ot</u> → **don't**

Write the spelling word that means the opposite.

25. has   **26.** do   **27.** did

Write the missing spelling words.

I know __(28)__ a good camper. If __(29)__ help, we can camp here. It feels as if __(30)__ been hiking all day long!

Elephant Words   Units 25–29   pages 168–197

eye	buy	cookie
could	should	can't

Spelling Strategy   Elephant words have unusual spellings. Check them carefully when you write them.

Write the missing spelling words.

Mom and I went to the __(31)__ doctor together. I tried, but I __(32)__ not read the chart. The doctor said I __(33)__ get glasses. Then if I __(34)__ see well, I can put them on. Mom let me __(35)__ a __(36)__ on the way home.

EXTENSION OPTIONS

TRB Review Test A 144

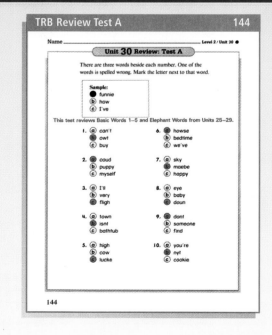

TRB Review Test B 145

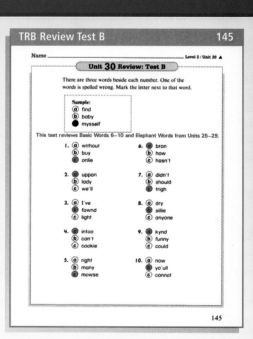

UNIT
30

Spelling-Meaning Strategy

Word Families

Look at this word family. Remember that words in the same family are alike in spelling and meaning.

light	The **light** of the moon was bright.
lights	The stars were twinkling **lights**.
lighted	Fireworks **lighted** the sky.
lighthouse	I watched from the **lighthouse**.

Think How are the words in this family alike in meaning? How are they alike in spelling?

Apply and Extend

Write a word from the light family in each sentence.
1. What is one of the brightest _____?
2. This _____ helps sailors at sea.
3. It has _____ the way for lost ships.
4. It is found on top of a tall _____.

With a partner, think of words in these families. Make a list for each family. See TE margin.

 kind high bright

Check the Word Families list that begins on page 272. Did you miss any words? Add them to your lists.

1. lights

2. light

3. lighted

4. lighthouse

201

Day **4**

Objective *Children will*
■ analyze the spelling and meaning relationship of words in the *light* word family

Answers to *Think* Questions

• They all have some form of the meaning "a form of energy that enables one to see."

• They all have the *light* spelling.

Day **5**   **Posttest**

The Posttest tests twenty of the Basic Words reviewed in this unit. Sentences 1–10 test words selected from Basic Words 1–5 in Units 25–29. The Elephant Words sentences test all six words reviewed in this unit.

Basic Words
1. I will do it <u>myself</u>.
2. He will step <u>out</u> of the train.
3. I will <u>find</u> the bikes.
4. She has a <u>puppy</u>.
5. The sheep <u>don't</u> chase the truck.
6. I saw a cute <u>baby</u>.
7. I will wash the <u>bathtub</u>.
8. I live in that <u>house</u>.
9. I think <u>we've</u> seen this show.
10. This is a <u>high</u> hill.
11. The old boat <u>cannot</u> go fast.
12. I gave one to the <u>lady</u>.
13. The sheep <u>found</u> some green grass.
14. It went <u>into</u> the nest.
15. This is the <u>only</u> one.
16. I have a <u>brown</u> book.
17. Can you fix the <u>light</u>?
18. My feet will be <u>dry</u>.
19. Look and <u>you'll</u> see the flag.
20. The ship <u>hasn't</u> sailed.

Elephant Words
21. You can stay, but I <u>should</u> go home.
22. Did you <u>buy</u> that truck?
23. Will you take this <u>cookie</u>?
24. She <u>can't</u> ride a bike.
25. He has a cut on his <u>eye</u>.
26. I ran as fast as I <u>could</u>.

Writing Model:
Description

Objectives *Children will*

■ read a literature excerpt modeling a description

■ analyze the model to identify
exact words and details

Warm-Up

Qualities of a Good Description

Use these discussion prompts to help children
think about how to write a good description:

• Imagine that you went swimming. How
could you describe how the water
looked? felt? smelled?

• Think about your favorite place. What
words could you use to paint a clear picture for the reader?

Read aloud the following groups of sentences. Have children tell which group gives
the clearest description and why. *(Group 1)*

1. The Bakerman Farm has cows, horses,
pigs, chickens, and goats. We got to
watch Mavis milk the goats. When I fed
the pigs, they grunted happily.

2. The Bakerman Farm has some animals.
There are buildings. We got to do things
there. The farm is not too far away.

Answers to *Think and Discuss*

1. The exact words *stamping* and *stormed*
tell how the giant walked.

2. The exact words *yelled* and *roared* tell
how the giant sounded.

3. He hit his head against a tree until the
leaves shook off like snowflakes; he
pulled up a tree and whirled it around
his head and knocked down twenty-one
other trees.

4. The little boy must have felt surprised
and frightened by the angry giant.

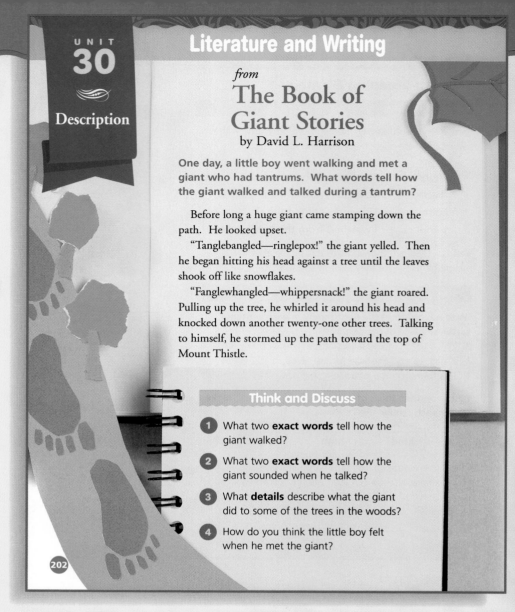

U N I T
30
~
Description

Literature and Writing

from

The Book of Giant Stories
by David L. Harrison

One day, a little boy went walking and met a
giant who had tantrums. What words tell how
the giant walked and talked during a tantrum?

Before long a huge giant came stamping down the
path. He looked upset.

"Tanglebangled—ringlepox!" the giant yelled. Then
he began hitting his head against a tree until the leaves
shook off like snowflakes.

"Fanglewhangled—whippersnack!" the giant roared.
Pulling up the tree, he whirled it around his head and
knocked down another twenty-one other trees. Talking
to himself, he stormed up the path toward the top of
Mount Thistle.

Think and Discuss

1 What two **exact words** tell how the
giant walked?

2 What two **exact words** tell how the
giant sounded when he talked?

3 What **details** describe what the giant
did to some of the trees in the woods?

4 How do you think the little boy felt
when he met the giant?

202

EXTENSION OPTIONS

Integrating Literature *Description*

Easy	Average	Challenging

**Journey of the
Nightly Jaguar**
by Burton Albert
This Mayan legend
reveals how the sun
becomes a jaguar at
night.

Animals in Winter
by Henrietta Bancroft
A description of how
animals cope with harsh
weather.

Secret Place
by Eve Bunting
A boy describes the
patch of wilderness he
finds in his city.

Home Lovely
by Lynn Rae Perkins
A girl makes her trailer
home beautiful by plant-
ing flowers.

Market Day
by Eve Bunting
A girl describes the
sights and sounds of
market day in her Irish
village.

Desert Trip
by Barbara A. Steiner
A girl tells about her trip
backpacking in the
desert with her mother.

The Writing Process

Description

Think of your favorite people, things, or places. Write a description of one of them. Follow the guidelines. Use the Writing Process.

1 Prewriting
• Draw a picture of what you are going to describe. Show it to a friend. Add more details if you need to.

2 Draft
• Write sentences that describe your topic. Put them in an order that makes sense.

3 Revise
• Add exact words and details.
• Remember to use your Thesaurus to find exact words.
• Read your description to a friend.
• Make changes.

4 Proofread
• Did you spell each word correctly?
• Did you begin the titles of people with capital letters?

5 Publish
• Copy your description neatly. Read it to a friend.

Guidelines for Writing a Description

✓ Use exact words and details to tell how things look, sound, smell, taste, and feel.
✓ Put the details in an order that is clear.

Composition Words
kind
happy
very
funny
brown
without

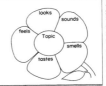

My Grandfather

(203)

Objective *Children will*
■ follow the Writing Process to write a description, using the criteria given in the guidelines

Additional Resource

To help children generate and explore topics for their description, have them use the Prewriting Ideas in the *Teacher's Resource Book*, page 146.

Scoring Rubric

Evaluating Writing

The scoring rubric is based on the guidelines on the student book page. Mechanics and usage errors are also considered in general. Explain to children that the guidelines will be used to evaluate their papers.

Scoring Rubric

Description

Score 4

The description is engaging and creative. The writer uses sensory language to create a vivid picture. Details are relevant and help paint a clear image of what is being described. The description is unusual and imaginative.

Score 3

The work identifies and describes a topic. Several details contribute to a complete and clear picture of what is being described. The writer has included sensory language. The topic can be identified by the description.

Score 2

The work is in the form of a description. The writer has identified the topic being described but uses few details or little sensory language in the writing. A clear picture has not been drawn.

Score 1

The work is not a description, or it meets the criteria minimally. There is no identifiable topic being described. The writing is confused and without focus.

The Vowel + *r* Sound in *car*

WORD LISTS

Spelling

Basic

1. car
2. start
3. arm
4. far
5. yard
6. part
7. barn
8. hard
9. party
10. farm
11. are
12. warm

Review

13. cut
14. fast

Challenge

15. large
16. carpet

Vocabulary

Social Studies:
Automobiles

hood
motor
trunk
traffic

Introducing the Lesson

Read Aloud

Write the Basic Words on the board.

Cars of Yesterday

What was it like to ride in one of the first automobiles? Going to a picnic or a **party** was a real adventure! First of all, the **car** was **hard** to **start**. The driver leaned against the front **part** of the **car** and turned a crank. He had to have strong muscles in his **arm** to turn it! The car itself had no top, no windows, and no heater. In snowy weather, the **car** was often stored in the **barn** or **yard**. Roads were not covered with a smooth surface as they **are** today. Riders wore long coats and goggles to protect themselves from the dust and to keep **warm**. No one traveled very **far**. If the **car** broke down, the driver walked to the nearest **farm** to ask for help.

Responding Ask children what the crank on an old car was used for. *(to start the car)* Reread aloud the sentence with the word *yard* in it. Ask children what *yard* means in the sentence. *(ground near a building; lawn)* Ask children which spelling word rhymes with *yard*. *(hard)*

Day 1 *page 204*

Objectives *Children will*

- take the pretest
- pronounce the list words
- learn about the spelling principle
- analyze words according to their |är| sound

Planning Checklist

- ☑ Pretest (TE)
- ☑ Spelling principle/word list
- ☐ Review/Challenge Words
- ☐ Teaching the Principle (TE)
- ☐ Enrichment (TE)
- ☐ Additional Spelling Words (TE)

Assessment

Pretest

1. Our car had a flat tire.
2. Dad will start the truck.
3. I broke my arm.
4. My home is not far.
5. Trees grow in my yard.
6. A leaf is part of a tree.
7. The cow is in the barn.
8. That old bun is hard.
9. Taj came to my party.
10. Sheep live on a farm.
11. They are sleeping.
12. The sun is warm.

Day 2 *page 205*

Objectives *Children will*

- practice spelling list words
- apply spelling strategies
- classify Basic Words into groups
- identify Elephant Words by their sounds and spelling patterns

Planning Checklist

- ☑ Spelling Strategy
- ☑ Independent Practice
- ☐ Daily Proofreading Practice (TE)
- ☐ Informal Assessment (TE)
- ☐ Extra Support (TE)
- ☐ Applying Spelling Strategies (TE)

FYI **Research Notes** When children consistently spell the past tense *-ed* ending correctly, regardless of how it sounds, it is a sign that they are learning how pattern can override sound in spelling—a critical understanding in English spelling. *See Bibliography on page xv.*

 Day 3 *page 206* **Day 4** *page 207* **Day 5** *page 207*

Objectives *Children will*
- use a dictionary entry and context clues to identify the right meaning of a given word
- review Basic and Review Words

Planning Checklist
- ☐ Dictionary
- ☐ Review: Spelling Spree
- ☐ How Are You Doing?
- ☐ Daily Proofreading Practice (TE)
- ☐ Cooperative Learning Activity (TE)

Objectives *Children will*
- proofread for spelling
- write and proofread an original composition

Planning Checklist
- ☐ Proofread for Spelling
- ☐ Write Some Bumper Stickers
- ☐ Daily Proofreading Practice (TE)
- ☐ Challenge Words Practice (TE)
- ☐ Another Writing Idea (TE)

Objective *Children will*
- take the posttest

Assessment
☐ **Posttest** (TE) *See Day 5*
☐ Unit 31 Test

 Additional Resources

Teacher's Resource Book
Practice Masters, pages 147–149
Unit Test, page 150
Bulletin Board, page 167

Practice Plus
Take-Home Word List 31
Games

Spelling Transparencies
Spelling Word List 31
Daily Proofreading Practice, Unit 31
Graphic Organizers

Teacher's Resource Disk
Macintosh® or Windows® software. Houghton Mifflin

Spelling CD-ROM
Macintosh® or Windows® software. Houghton Mifflin

Internet
http://www.eduplace.com

Phonics Practice
Houghton Mifflin Phonics
The Listening Corner
Phonics Home Connection

 Meeting Individual Needs
Students Acquiring English

Spanish No Spanish words end with the |t| or the |d| sound. **Activity** Write *boat* on the board and say it, emphasizing the final |t|. Say *coat, coal, part, start, stick, cart,* having children raise their hands when they hear a word that ends like *boat.* Call on volunteers to say the words. Repeat the activity for the final |d|, using *yard* with *barn, said, man, mud, ham,* and *hard.*

Asian Asian children may have difficulty with the |r| sound. **Activity** Say |ar| before saying each of the Basic Words, and have children repeat after you. Show children how the jaw drops for the |a| sound and rises for the |r| sound.

Other Activities for Any Day

- Bonus activities from pages 208–209
- Practice Masters (easy, average, challenging)
  Teacher's Resource Book, pages 147–149
- Take-Home Word List 31
  Practice Plus

Day 1

Objectives *Children will*
- take the pretest
- pronounce the list words
- learn about the spelling principle
- analyze words according to their |är| sound

Teaching the Principle

This lesson teaches the *ar* spelling pattern for the |är| sound. Children learn the strategy of thinking of this pattern when they hear the vowel + r sound in *car*.

To sum up the lesson, ask:

- What letters spell the vowel + r sound in *start* and *arm*? (ar)

- Is this vowel sound the same as the short *a* sound in *at*? (no) Is it the same as the long *a* sound in *ate*? (no)

Enrichment

Vocabulary: Multiple Meanings
Have children use a dictionary to look up *start*, *yard,* and *part.* Discuss the different meanings.

ar
car

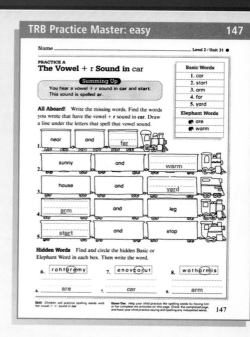

Read and Say

READ the sentences. **SAY** each word in dark print.

A. car

start

arm

far

yard

part

barn

hard

party

farm

B. are

warm

Basic Words

1. car	*car*	Our **car** had a flat tire.
2. start	*start*	Dad will **start** the truck.
3. arm	*arm*	I broke my **arm**.
4. far	*far*	My home is not **far**.
5. yard	*yard*	Trees grow in my **yard**.
6. part	*part*	A leaf is **part** of a tree.
7. barn	*barn*	The cow is in the **barn**.
8. hard	*hard*	That old bun is **hard**.
9. party	*party*	Taj came to my **party**.
10. farm	*farm*	Sheep live on a **farm**.
11. are	*are*	They **are** sleeping.
12. warm	*warm*	The sun is **warm**.

Think and Write

Each word has a vowel sound that is not short or long. The vowel sound is different because the vowel is followed by **r**.

the vowel + **r** sound → **car**, st**ar**t

How are the Elephant Words different? *Are* has the |är| sound but the *a-consonant-e* pattern. *Warm* is spelled *ar* but has the |ôr| sound.

A. Write the first **ten** Basic Words. Then draw a line under the letters that spell the vowel + r sound in each word.

B. Now write the **two** Elephant Words.
Order of answers for each category may vary.

Review		Challenge	
13. cut	14. fast	15. large	16. carpet

204

TEACHING OPTIONS

Meeting Individual Needs
Word Lists

You may want to assign Basic Words 1–5, the Elephant Words, and the Review Words to children who misspelled more than five words on the pretest. Assign the Challenge Words as appropriate. (You may want to have children write sentences, using the Challenge Words.)

Additional Spelling Words

Basic	Challenge	Words Often Misspelled
dark	target	something
park	garden	outside
art	market	
march	apartment	
smart	charcoal	
	cartwheel	

Home/School Involvement
Take-Home Word List • Goal-Setting

Have children set goals for the week on Take-Home Word List 31.

TRB Practice Master: easy 147

Name _____ Level 2 / Unit 31

PRACTICE A
The Vowel + r Sound in car

Summing Up
You hear a vowel + r sound in car and start. This sound is spelled ar.

Basic Words
1. car
2. start
3. arm
4. far
5. yard

Elephant Words
are
warm

All Aboard! Write the missing words. Find the words you wrote that have the vowel + r sound in car. Draw a line under the letters that spell that vowel sound.

1. near and far
2. sunny and warm
3. house and yard
4. arm and leg
5. start and stop

Hidden Words Find and circle the hidden Basic or Elephant Word in each box. Then write the word.

6. raht**are**my → are
7. enov**car**ut → car
8. woth**arm**is → arm

Skill: Children will practice spelling words with the vowel + r sound in car.
Home Tip: Help your child practice the spelling words by having him or her complete the activities on this page. Check the completed page, and have your child practice saying and spelling any misspelled words.

147

UNIT 31

Independent Practice

 Spelling Strategy You hear the vowel + **r** sound in **car** and **start**. This sound is spelled **ar**.

Phonics Write Basic Words to answer the questions.
1. Which word ends with the long **e** sound?
2. Which word begins and ends like **head**?
3. Which word begins and ends like **form**?
4. Which word rhymes with **yarn**?

Word Groups Think how the words in each group are alike. Write the missing Basic Words.
5. finger, hand, _____   7. bus, truck, _____
6. inch, foot, _____   8. close, nearby, _____

Word Meaning Write the Basic Word that means the same or almost the same as each word below.
9. piece   10. begin

Elephant Words Write an Elephant Word to answer each question.
11. Which word has the vowel + **r** spelling but not the vowel + **r** sound?
12. Which word has the vowel + **r** sound but is spelled **a**-consonant-**e**?

Phonics

1. party
2. hard
3. farm
4. barn

Word Groups

5. arm
6. yard
7. car
8. far

Word Meaning

9. part
10. start

Elephant Words

11. warm
12. are

(205)

Day 2

Objectives *Children will*
- practice spelling list words
- apply spelling strategies
- classify Basic Words into groups
- identify Elephant Words by their sounds and spelling patterns

Daily Proofreading Practice
The horses sleep in the **barne**. (*barn*)
We planned a **partey** for Ray. (*party*)

 Meeting Individual Needs
visual/auditory/oral

Extra Support Check Independent Practice to determine who needs extra support. Write *am/arm* and *had/hard* on the board. Say the words and have children repeat. Underline the *ar* in *arm* and *hard*. Explain that the *r* adds the |r| sound and also changes the vowel sound. Ask children to repeat the word pairs several times, listening for the difference between the |ă| and the |är| sounds.

Name _____   Level 2 / Unit 31 ▲

PRACTICE B
The Vowel + r Sound in car

Basic Words
1. car
2. start
3. arm
4. far
5. yard
6. part
7. barn
8. hard
9. party
10. farm

Elephant Words
🐘 are
🐘 warm

Picture Math Write the word for each clue.

1. _____ – n + d = yard
2. _____ n + r + t = part
3. f + _____ = farm
4. _____ – c + e = are
5. _____ – o + a = warm
6. _____ – d = car

Word Pairs Write a Basic Word to finish the second sentence in each pair.
7. Your **foot** is part of your **leg**.
Your **hand** is part of your _____   arm
8. People sleep in a **house**.
Animals sleep in a _____   barn
9. A pillow is **soft**.
A rock is _____   hard
10. At the **end**, you **stop**.
At the beginning, you _____   start
11. The opposite of **low** is **high**.
The opposite of **near** is _____   far
12. On the **Fourth of July**, you have a **parade**.
On your **birthday**, you have a _____   party

148

 Applying Spelling Strategies
To Spell New Words

- Read aloud: **She wrapped a long, wool scarf around her neck.**

  I hear the |s| and the |k| sounds blended together. I think these sounds could be spelled by the consonant cluster sc or sk. I'll have to check a dictionary.

- Have children attempt to spell *scarf* on their Have-a-Go charts.
- Elicit the following strategies as children try to spell *scarf*.

  The |f| sound is the sound I hear at the beginning of feather. I know this sound is usually spelled f.

sc**rf**

This word has the same vowel + r sound I hear in car. I know this sound is spelled ar.

Independent Practice   205

Objectives *Children will*

■ use a dictionary entry and con-text clues to identify the right meaning of a given word

■ review Basic and Review Words

Daily Proofreading Practice

Alma fed the pigs at the **farem**. (*farm*)

Where **ar** you going? (*are*)

Dictionary

----
1. 3

----
2. 2

----
3. 1

Hink Pinks

----
4. barn

----
5. start

----
6. part

----
7. farm

----
8. fast

Word Match

----
9. warm

----
10. arm

----
11. party

206

Dictionary

Finding the Right Meaning Use a dictionary to find all the different meanings of a word.

> **hard** **1.** The opposite of **soft**: *The glass broke when it hit the **hard** floor.* **2.** The opposite of **easy**; difficult: *That problem is too **hard** for first graders.*

Practice Write **1**, **2**, or **3** to tell which meaning of **part** or **start** is used in each sentence. Use your Spelling Dictionary.

1. Did you get a **part** in the play?
2. The engine needs a new **part**.
3. We want to **start** a softball club.

Review: Spelling Spree

Hink Pinks Write the Basic or Review Word that answers the question and rhymes with the word in dark print.

4. Where do animals like to knit? a **yarn** _____
5. What is a clever beginning? a **smart** _____
6. What is a wagon piece? a **cart** _____
7. What is a warning on a ranch? a _____ **alarm**
8. What is a quick takeoff? a _____ **blast**

Word Match Write the Basic Word that goes with each word.

9. heat
10. sleeve
11. birthday

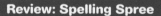

How Are You Doing?

List the spelling words that are hard for you. Practice them with a partner.

TEACHING OPTIONS

Cooperative Learning Activity

Automobile Pull-Throughs
visual/oral/auditory/kinesthetic

Have children make automobile pull-throughs like the one shown. Provide them with a tag board stencil of a car, scissors, and paper strips. Help children write their spelling words on a paper strip and cut two slits in the car window.

Partners use the pull-throughs to play vari-ous games. For example, one child might pull the strip through, reading one word at a time for a partner to spell. Or a child might give a clue for a spelling word. The partner pulls the strip until the word that matches the clue appears in the car window.

barn

car

farm

TRB Practice Master: challenging 149

Name _____ Level 2 / Unit 31

PRACTICE C
The Vowel + r Sound in *car*

Crossword Clues Write the Challenge and Vocabulary Words in the puzzle. Then write a clue for each **Across** word and each **Down** word.

| Challenge Words |
| 1. large |
| 2. carpet |
| Theme Vocabulary |
| 3. hood |
| 4. motor |
| 5. trunk |
| 6. traffic |

Answers will vary.   **Across**

1. _____
3. _____
5. _____

Down

1. _____
2. _____
3. _____

149

Proofreading and Writing

Proofread for Spelling Proofread these directions. Use proofreading marks to fix six spelling mistakes.

Example: How ~~fas~~ ^fast^ can you go?

Start the toy ~~kar~~ ^car^ in a part
of the ~~yord~~ ^yard^ where the grass is ~~kut~~ ^cut^
short. Stay ~~farr~~ ^far^ away from trees.
Have a friend give you a ~~hrad~~ ^hard^
push. When you ~~ar~~ ^are^ ready to stop,
pull the red bar.

Finish

Write Some Bumper Stickers

I ♥ my car!

A bumper sticker can tell people what you think of something. Write messages for bumper stickers on colored paper. Try to use spelling words. Add some pictures.

Proofreading Tip
Check that you used correct end marks.

207

Basic
1. car
2. start
3. arm
4. far
5. yard
6. part
7. barn
8. hard
9. party
10. farm
11. are
12. warm
Review
13. cut
14. fast
Challenge
15. large
16. carpet

Proofreading Marks
∧ Add
↗ Delete
≡ Make a capital letter
/ Make a small letter

Day 4

Objectives *Children will*
■ proofread for spelling
■ write and proofread an original composition

Daily Proofreading Practice
Mimi planted peas in our **yerd**. (*yard*)
We will **starte** dance class today. (*start*)

Day 5

Posttest

Sentences 1–5 test the first five Basic Words. Sentences 6–10 test the next five Basic Words. Sentences 11–12 test the Elephant Words.

Basic Words
1. The truck will not <u>start</u> in the cold.
2. He has a green <u>car</u>.
3. The club is not <u>far</u> from my home.
4. She is in the <u>yard</u>.
5. The ball hit his <u>arm</u>.
6. The sheep are in the <u>barn</u>.
7. I live on a <u>farm</u>.
8. This book is <u>hard</u>.
9. We will go to the <u>party</u>.
10. I will take <u>part</u> of it.
11. The food is <u>warm</u>.
12. See how clean we <u>are</u>?

Review Words
13. She ran <u>fast</u>.
14. The tree was <u>cut</u> down.

Challenge Words
15. The van has <u>large</u> doors.
16. The floor is covered with a <u>carpet</u>.

TRB Unit 31 Test 150

Name _____ Level 2 / Unit 31 ●▲

Unit 31 Test: The Vowel + r Sound in car

Read each sentence. Find the correctly spelled word to complete each sentence. Mark the letter next to that word.

Sample:		ANSWERS	
Fill the glass ___	ⓐ jur	● jar	ⓒ jer

Items 1–7 test Basic Words 1–5 and the Elephant Words.
Items 8–12 test Basic Words 6–10.
1. May we ___ to play? ⓐ stirt ⓑ stert ● start
2. Bert travels near and ___ ● far ⓑ fer ⓒ furr
3. We ___ the winners! ⓐ ar ⓑ arr ● are
4. I like my old ___ ⓐ kar ● car ⓒ cor
5. Marty works in the ___ ● yard ⓑ yarde ⓒ yerd
6. Dora has a ___ blanket. ⓐ warme ● warm ⓒ wurm
7. Move your left ___ ⓐ arme ⓑ arn ● arm
8. Is that ___ or soft? ⓐ haad ● hard ⓒ hird
9. Come to my birthday ___ ● party ⓑ parti ⓒ pardy
10. The cow is in the red ___ ⓐ bern ⓑ barrn ● barn
11. Paul has a ___ in the play. ⓐ pard ● part ⓒ parte
12. My class will visit a ___ ● farm ⓑ farn ⓒ ferm

150

Meeting Individual Needs

Challenge Words Practice
Ask children to draw a car of their own design. Have them add labels or write an ad for their car using the Challenge Words.

Another Writing Idea
Suggest children write about a real or an imaginary car trip or auto race. Encourage them to use spelling words.

These pages can be used at any time during the study of this unit.

Objectives *Children will*

- build words with the |är| vowel sound
- write word clues

Word Builder

Words with Vowel + r Make words that have the same vowel sound you hear in **car**. Write an **ar** word for each clue. The letters on the tires will help you.

Beginning Letters

Ending Letters

1. the sound a dog makes
2. what jam comes in
3. a birthday _____
4. sun, moon, and _____
5. a kind of string
6. On your _____, get set, go!

1. bark	4. star
2. jar	5. yarn
3. card	6. mark

Show What You Know! On another sheet of paper, write your own clue for an **ar** word. Have a friend try and guess the answer to your clue.

208

EXTENSION OPTIONS

Learning Center Activity
visual/kinesthetic

An *ar* "Wordmobile" Suggest children make *ar* "wordmobiles." They can draw a car on a paper plate or on tag board and attach it to a hanger. Have them write *ar* words on tires and hang them from the car. Children may find it helpful to think of rhyming words to identify new *ar* words.

More -*ar* Words

dark	art	bar
lark	cart	tar
park	chart	
spark	smart	
shark		

Vocabulary Enrichment

Unit 31 BONUS

Social Studies

Automobiles All the words in the box have something to do with automobiles. Write those words from the box to finish this diagram. Use your Spelling Dictionary.

Spelling Word Link

car

hood
motor
trunk
traffic

What a __4__ jam!

1. hood

2. motor

3. trunk

4. traffic

Try This CHALLENGE

Riddle Time! Write a word from the box to answer each riddle.

5. What kind of jam does not go on toast?
6. What do both a car and an elephant have?
7. What might be part of a car and a coat?
8. What runs but has no legs?

5. traffic

6. trunk

7. hood

8. motor

★ Fact File

Do all cars need gas? Long ago, the motors in some cars ran on steam from boiling water. Today, some special cars run on power from the sun!

209

Day by Day Planner

Objectives *Children will*

- expand their vocabulary by using words related to automobiles
- show their understanding of the vocabulary words by completing a diagram

Vocabulary Checkup

Have children use the vocabulary words in sentences or match the words to the definitions below.

1. a machine that gives the power to make something move or run; an engine *motor*
2. the covered storage area of a car *trunk*
3. cars, buses, and trucks moving along roads and streets *traffic*
4. the metal cover over the motor of a car, bus, or truck *hood*

Fact File

Solar Cars

Gasoline-powered automobiles are a major cause of air pollution, but alternatives are being developed. General Motors' "Impact" is an electricity-powered car that can go about 125 miles before its batteries need recharging, and can travel at speeds above 65 miles per hour. You may wish to point out that the word *gas* is short for *gasoline*.

Integrating Literature

Easy	Average	Challenging
Taxi! Taxi! *by Cari Best* Tina's favorite Sunday activity is going out with her papi, a taxi driver.	**Good Driving, Amelia Bedelia** *by Herman Parish* The daffy housekeeper goes for a birthday ride in the country.	**The Rattlebang Picnic** *by Margaret Mahy* The McTavish family uses a pizza as a wheel when their car breaks down.
The Car Washing Street *by Denise L. Patrick* On Saturdays, all the people in a city neighborhood wash their car.	**Night Driving** *by John Coy* A father and son take a nighttime road trip through the desert to the mountains.	**Cars and How They Go** *by Joanna Cole* An explanation of how the various parts of a car work.

The Vowel + *r* Sound in *store*

WORD LISTS

Spelling

Basic

1. store
2. corn
3. for
4. more
5. or
6. morning
7. short
8. born
9. story
10. horn
11. four
12. your

Review

13. fish
14. game

Challenge

15. afford
16. before

Vocabulary

Social Studies:

Supermarkets

dairy
counter
price
cart

Introducing the Lesson

Read Aloud

Write the Basic Words on the board.

To Market, To Market

Did you know that before **your** grandparents were **born**, there were no supermarkets? People had to go to **four or more** shops to buy all of their groceries. Most were a **short** distance away, and people would do their food shopping each **morning**. Each **store** sold different things. Shoppers would go to one shop to buy dairy products such as milk, to another shop to buy meat, and to still another shop **for corn** and other produce. Today, supermarkets sell everything from a frozen dinner to a party **horn**. Maybe older members of your family could tell you a **story** about the way they did their shopping. What things have changed? What things are still the same?

Responding   Ask children where people bought their groceries before there were supermarkets. *(in small stores or shops)* Reread these words from the selection: "Most were a **short** distance away." Ask what *short* means here. *(a small distance)* Ask children if they can think of another meaning for *short*.

Day 1 *page 210*

Objectives *Children will*

- take the pretest
- pronounce the list words
- learn about the spelling principle
- analyze words according to their |ôr| sound

Planning Checklist

☑ Pretest (TE)

☑ Spelling principle/word list

☐ Review/Challenge Words

☐ Teaching the Principle (TE)

☐ Enrichment (TE)

☐ Additional Spelling Words (TE)

Assessment

Pretest

1. I got eggs at the <u>store</u>.
2. The pig ate the <u>corn</u>.
3. I looked <u>for</u> my book.
4. Nate wants <u>more</u> food.
5. I will go by car <u>or</u> bus.
6. I jog every <u>morning</u>.
7. We took <u>short</u> trip.
8. When were you <u>born</u>?
9. Will you tell me a <u>story</u>?
10. The car <u>horn</u> beeped.
11. Anna has <u>four</u> boxes.
12. Is that <u>your</u> house?

Day 2 *page 211*

Objectives *Children will*

- practice spelling list words
- apply spelling strategies
- identify Basic Words that match given meanings
- identify Elephant Words that are homophones of given words

Planning Checklist

☑ Spelling Strategy

☑ Independent Practice

☐ Daily Proofreading Practice (TE)

☐ Informal Assessment (TE)

☐ Extra Support (TE)

☐ Applying Spelling Strategies (TE)

Objective *Children will*
• review Basic and Review Words

Planning Checklist
☐ Review: Spelling Spree
☐ How Are You Doing?
☐ Daily Proofreading Practice (TE)
☐ Ongoing Assessment (TE)

Objectives *Children will*
• proofread for spelling and commas
• write and proofread an original composition

Planning Checklist
☐ Proofread for Spelling and Commas
☐ Write a List
☐ Daily Proofreading Practice (TE)
☐ Challenge Words Practice (TE)
☐ Another Writing Idea (TE)

Objective *Children will*
• take the posttest

Assessment

☐ **Posttest** (TE) *See Day 5*
☐ Unit 32 Test

 Additional Resources

Teacher's Resource Book
Practice Masters, pages 151–153
Unit Test, page 154
Bulletin Board, page 167

Practice Plus
Take-Home Word List 32
Games

Spelling Transparencies
Spelling Word List 32
Daily Proofreading Practice, Unit 32
Graphic Organizers

Teacher's Resource Disk
Macintosh® or Windows® software.
Houghton Mifflin

Spelling CD-ROM
Macintosh® or Windows® software.
Houghton Mifflin

Internet
http://www.eduplace.com

Phonics Practice
Houghton Mifflin Phonics
The Listening Corner
Phonics Home Connection

 Meeting Individual Needs
Students Acquiring English

Spanish Although Spanish has a sound similar to the |ôr| sound in English, it is spelled or, never ore.
Activity Write *store, corn, for, more,* and *morning* on the board. Say each word and have children repeat it. Underline the or and ore pattern in each word and explain that there are two ways to spell the |ôr| sound. Then erase the or and ore patterns. Make two large cards, one with or and one with ore. Point to and say a word on the board. Have a volunteer hold the correct card up near the blanks, say the word, and spell it. Repeat with other words.

Other Activities for Any Day

• Bonus activities from pages 214–215
• Practice Masters (easy, average, challenging)
  Teacher's Resource Book, pages 151–153
• Take-Home Word List 32
  Practice Plus

Objectives *Children will*

■ take the pretest

■ pronounce the list words

■ learn about the spelling principle

■ analyze words according to their |ôr| sound

Teaching the Principle

This lesson teaches the *or* and the *ore* spelling patterns for the |ôr| sound. Children learn the strategy of thinking of these patterns when they hear the vowel + *r* sound in *store*.

To sum up the lesson, ask:

• What letters spell the vowel + *r* sound in *for* and *corn*? *(or)*

• What letters spell the vowel + *r* sound in *store* and *more*? *(ore)*

Enrichment

Vocabulary: Multiple Meanings

Have children use a dictionary to look up *store, short,* and *story.* Discuss the different meanings.

UNIT

32 The Vowel + r Sound in *store*

A. store

_____ corn

_____ for

_____ more

_____ or

_____ morning

_____ short

_____ born

_____ story

_____ horn

B. four

_____ your

210

Read and Say

READ the sentences. **SAY** each word in dark print.

Basic Words

1. store	*store*	I got eggs at the **store**.
2. corn	*corn*	The pig ate the **corn**.
3. for	*for*	I looked **for** my book.
4. more	*more*	Nate wants **more** food.
5. or	*or*	I will go by car **or** bus.
6. morning	*morning*	I jog every **morning**.
7. short	*short*	We took a **short** trip.
8. born	*born*	When were you **born**?
9. story	*story*	Will you tell me a **story**?
10. horn	*horn*	The car **horn** beeped.
11. four	*four*	Anna has **four** boxes.
12. your	*your*	Is that **your** house?

Think and Write

Each word has the vowel + **r** sound.

the vowel + **r** sound → c**or**n, st**ore**

How are the Elephant Words different?
In the Elephant Words, the |ôr| sound is spelled *our.*

A. Write the first **ten** Basic Words. Then draw a line under the letters that spell the vowel + **r** sound in each word.

B. Now write the **two** Elephant Words.

Order of answers for each category may vary.

Review	Challenge
13. fish **14.** game	**15.** afford **16.** before

TEACHING OPTIONS

Meeting Individual Needs
Word Lists

You may want to assign Basic Words 1–5, the Elephant Words, and the Review Words to children who misspelled more than five words on the pretest. Assign the Challenge Words as appropriate. (You may want to have children write sentences, using the Challenge Words.)

Additional Spelling Words

Basic	Challenge	Words Often Misspelled
sport	report	I'm
fork	anymore	that's
snore	corner	
north	forty	
fort	horse	
	order	

Home/School Involvement
Take-Home Word List • Goal-Setting

Have children set goals for the week on Take-Home Word List 32.

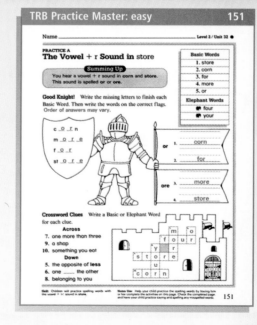

Independent Practice

Spelling Strategy You hear a vowel + **r** sound in **corn** and **store**. This sound is spelled **or** or **ore**.

Order of answers for question 3–5 may vary.
Phonics Write Basic Words to answer the questions.

1. Which word begins like and sounds like **four**?
2. Which word begins with a vowel?
3–5. Which three words rhyme with **torn**?

Word Meaning Write a Basic Word for each meaning. Use your Spelling Dictionary.

6. a place where things are sold
7. the early part of the day
8. greater in number
9. the opposite of **tall**
10. a tale you may read or hear

Elephant Words Write an Elephant Word to answer each question.

11. Which word is a homophone for **for**?
12. Which word is a homophone for **you're**?

Phonics

1. for

2. or

3. corn

4. born

5. horn

Word Meaning

6. store

7. morning

8. more

9. short

10. story

Elephant Words

11. four

12. your

211

Day 2

Objectives *Children will*

- practice spelling list words
- apply spelling strategies
- identify Basic Words that match given meanings
- identify Elephant Words that are homophones of given words

Daily Proofreading Practice
I made lunch **fore** Grandpa. *(for)*
Should we buy **mor** cheese? *(more)*

Meeting Individual Needs
visual/oral/auditory/kinesthetic

Extra Support Check Independent Practice to determine who needs extra support. Write *shot/short, stop/store,* and *mop/more* on the board. Say the words and have children repeat. Explain that the *r* adds the |r| sound and changes the sound of the letter *o*. Have volunteers say the words and underline the letters that spell the vowel + *r* sound in the second word of each pair.

TRB Practice Master: average   **152**

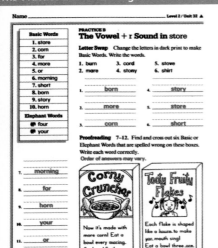

Applying Spelling Strategies
To Read New Words

- Write this sentence on the chalkboard:
We dug for clams at the seashore.
- Have children read the sentence silently.

- Elicit the following strategies as children try to decode *seashore.*

Sea-sh-ore. Sea-shore. Seashore. The word *seashore* makes sense in the sentence.

I recognize the word *sea* at the beginning of this longer word.

seashore

I know that the letters *sh* make the |sh| sound.

I remember that the letters *ore* make the vowel + *r* sound that I hear in *store.*

Objective *Children will*
- review Basic and Review Words

Daily Proofreading Practice

I eat toast in the **morening**.
(morning)
Carlos told me a funny **storey**. *(story)*

UNIT
32

Word Tricks

1. corn

2. morning

3. horn

4. store

5. game

6. story

Fill-In Fun

7. or

8. born

9. for

10. your

11. more

12. short

212

Review: Spelling Spree

Word Tricks Take away one word from the letters in each box. Write the Basic or Review Word that is left.

1. Take away **apple**. Find a vegetable. coapplern
2. Take away **night**. Find early day. mornnighting
3. Take away **song**. Find an instrument. hosongrn
4. Take away **farm**. Find a shop. stofarmre
5. Take away **work**. Find what you play. gaworkme
6. Take away **poem**. Find a tale. stopoemry

Fill-In Fun Write the missing Basic Words.

7. laugh _____ cry
8. a newly _____ baby
9. house _____ sale
10. on _____ mark
11. _____ or less
12. tall or _____

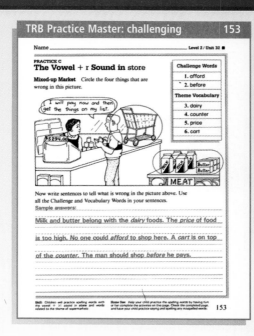

How Are You Doing?
Write each word in a sentence. Practice with a partner any words you spelled wrong.

TEACHING OPTIONS

Ongoing Assessment

r-Influenced Vowels

As children learn the spellings of "*r*-influenced" vowel sounds, you will often see them experiment with and overgeneralize other vowel patterns, for example: FORE *(for)*, MORENING *(morning)*, and STOREY *(story)*.

When children begin studying the words in Unit 33, they may spell the final |ər| sound *ir* or *or:* SISTIR *(sister),* FLOWOR *(flower),* and WATIR *(water).* As they examine words that share the same spelling for |ər|, children learn to apply the same spelling pattern across a number of words rather than "reinventing" the spelling each time this sound is encountered.

TRB Practice Master: challenging 153

Name _____ Level 2 / Unit 32

PRACTICE C
The Vowel + r Sound in store

Mixed-up Market Circle the four things that are wrong in this picture.

Challenge Words
1. afford
2. before

Theme Vocabulary
3. dairy
4. counter
5. price
6. cart

Now write sentences to tell what is wrong in the picture above. Use all the Challenge and Vocabulary Words in your sentences.
Sample answers:

Milk and butter belong with the *dairy* foods. The *price* of food

is too high. No one could *afford* to shop here. A *cart* is on top

of the *counter*. The man should shop *before* he pays.

153

Proofreading and Writing

Proofread: Spelling and Commas Use a comma between the name of a city and the name of a state.

The supermarket is in Atlanta, Georgia.

Proofread this sign. Use proofreading marks to fix four spelling mistakes and two missing commas.

Example: We buy ~~carn~~ corn at a farm in Ames, Iowa.

> <u>more</u>   <u>your</u>
> Get ~~Mor~~ for ~~Yer~~ Money!
>
> Come to Mick's Market in Portland, Oregon.
> Taste our fresh ~~fich~~ fish and vegetables.
> We open every morning at eight and close at ~~for~~ four.
> Our new store will open soon in Salem, Oregon!

Write a List

Pretend you have won the Super Shopper contest at your supermarket. The prize is a trip to any three cities you choose! List the cities you would like to visit. Tell why you would like to go there. Try to use spelling words.

Proofreading Tip Make sure you put a comma between the name of a city and the name of a state.

Basic
1. store
2. corn
3. for
4. more
5. or
6. morning
7. short
8. born
9. story
10. horn
11. four
12. your

Review
13. fish
14. game

Challenge
15. afford
16. before

Proofreading Marks
∧ Add
⌐ Delete
≡ Make a capital letter
/ Make a small letter

213

Objectives *Children will*

Day 4
■ proofread for spelling and commas
■ write and proofread an original composition

Daily Proofreading Practice
I picked fresh **coren** for dinner. *(corn)*
Mike put **for** apples in the cart. *(four)*

Day 5 ### Posttest

Sentences 1–5 test the first five Basic Words. Sentences 6–10 test the next five Basic Words. Sentences 11–12 test the Elephant Words.

Basic Words
1. Is he happy <u>or</u> sad?
2. She and I will go to the <u>store</u>.
3. Jim likes to eat <u>corn</u>.
4. The kite is <u>for</u> us.
5. I wish I had <u>more</u> dishes.
6. The baby was <u>born</u> at night.
7. It is fun to play a <u>horn</u>.
8. The book is <u>short</u>.
9. Please tell me a <u>story</u>.
10. He eats an egg in the <u>morning</u>.
11. May I pet <u>your</u> dog?
12. We found <u>four</u> frogs.

Review Words
13. Can you swim like a <u>fish</u>?
14. We will start the <u>game</u>.

Challenge Words
15. Have you been here <u>before</u>?
16. We cannot <u>afford</u> a new car.

TRB Unit 32 Test   154

Name _____   Level 2 / Unit 32 ●▲

Unit 32 Test: The Vowel + r Sound in store

Each item below gives three spellings of a word. Choose the correct spelling. Mark the letter for that word.

				ANSWERS
Sample:				
a. befor	b. before	c. befour		ⓐ ● ⓒ

Items 1–7 test Basic Words 1–5 and the Elephant Words.
Items 8–12 test Basic Words 6–10.

1. a. or	b. orr	c. oure	1. ⓐ ⓑ ⓒ
2. a. mor	b. mour	c. more	2. ⓐ ⓑ ⓒ
3. a. corne	b. corn	c. korn	3. ⓐ ⓑ ⓒ
4. a. fer	b. for	c. forr	4. ⓐ ⓑ ⓒ
5. a. yor	b. youre	c. your	5. ⓐ ⓑ ⓒ
6. a. store	b. stour	c. stor	6. ⓐ ⓑ ⓒ
7. a. forr	b. foure	c. four	7. ⓐ ⓑ ⓒ
8. a. horne	b. horn	c. honn	8. ⓐ ⓑ ⓒ
9. a. morning	b. moring	c. morening	9. ⓐ ⓑ ⓒ
10. a. short	b. shorte	c. chort	10. ⓐ ⓑ ⓒ
11. a. stori	b. story	c. story	11. ⓐ ⓑ ⓒ
12. a. bron	b. born	c. boren	12. ⓐ ⓑ ⓒ

154

Meeting Individual Needs

Challenge Words Practice
Have children make crossword puzzles on graph paper, using the Challenge Words and other |ôr| words. Suggest children exchange puzzles with a partner.

Another Writing Idea Ask children to write a radio jingle or television commercial for a local supermarket. Encourage them to include spelling words.

These pages can be used at any time during the study of this unit.

Objectives *Children will*

■ build words with the *ore* spelling of the |ôr| sound

■ write an original composition

Phonics and Spelling

Rhyming Words

Words with Vowel + r Use the letter or letters that make the beginning sound of each picture name to make words that rhyme with **store.** Order of answers may vary.

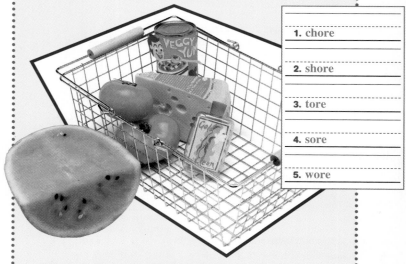

1. chore
2. shore
3. tore
4. sore
5. wore

Show What You Know! Pork chops are on sale at Wilson's Store. Write an ad for the sale. Use **or** and **ore** words.

214

EXTENSION OPTIONS

Learning Center Activity

visual/kinesthetic

Stock the Shelves Provide children with small empty boxes, plain brown bags, cardboard tubes, colored paper, markers, and other art supplies. Explain that children are going to create products for a grocery store. Have them make the package for each product, using words that have the |ôr| sound. Ask children to underline the *or* and *ore* words on their products.

Vocabulary Enrichment

Social Studies

Supermarkets All the words in the box have something to do with supermarkets. Write those words to finish these sentences. Use your Spelling Dictionary.

Spelling Word Link

store

dairy
counter
price
cart

The milk just arrived from the __(1)__.
The __(2)__ of a carton is $1.89. Evan put two cartons in his __(3)__. He paid for them at the __(4)__.

1. dairy

2. price

3. cart

4. counter

Try This CHALLENGE

Yes or No? Is the word in dark print used correctly? Write **yes** or **no**.

5. Kristen writes in her **dairy** every day.
6. Manuel placed the cans on the **counter**.
7. The winner's **price** was a new bike.
8. Put the food in the shopping **cart**.

5. no

6. yes

7. no

8. yes

Fact File

If a dozen is twelve, what is a "baker's dozen"? Bakers sometimes add one extra for every twelve things they sell. That is why a baker's dozen is thirteen, not twelve!

215

Objectives *Children will*

■ expand their vocabulary by using words related to supermarkets

■ show their understanding of the vocabulary words by completing context activities

Vocabulary Checkup

Have children use the vocabulary words in sentences or match the words to the definitions below.

1. a container or basket with wheels that is moved by hand *cart*
2. a place in a store where things are paid for *counter*
3. a farm that produces milk *dairy*
4. the amount of money asked or paid for something *price*

Fact File

A Baker's Dozen

"Baker's dozen" goes back to an act of the English Parliament in 1266. The act set weight standards for bread. To be sure they were meeting the standard, bakers began giving an extra loaf for each dozen sold to customers.

Integrating Literature

Easy	Average	Challenging
Big Squeak, Little Squeak *by Robert Kraus* Two mice run into trouble when they they buy cheese at Mr. Kit Kat's shop.	**Tom** *by Tomie dePaola* Tom spends time with his grandfather, who runs a grocery store.	**At the Supermarket** *by David Hautzig* A photo-essay shows how workers keep a grocery store running.
We Keep a Store *by Anne Shelby* A young girl enjoys helping out at her parents' country store.	**Down the Road** *by Alice Schertle* For the first time, Hetty's parents send her to the store alone to buy eggs.	**Onion Sundaes** *by David Adler* Two cousins help nab a crook at a supermarket.

Words That End with *er*

WORD LISTS

Spelling

Basic
1. flower
2. water
3. under
4. over
5. better
6. sister
7. brother
8. mother
9. father
10. after

Review
11. that
12. shop

Challenge
13. gather
14. center

Vocabulary

Science: Gardening

soil
petals
shoot
hoe

Introducing the Lesson

Read Aloud

Write the Basic Words on the board.

Growing Plants

Would you like to grow a **flower** or a vegetable garden? You don't need a lot of land. You can grow plants in a pot even if you live in a small apartment. First, open the top of an empty milk carton. Put some small stones at the bottom. Fill two-thirds of the carton with soil. The darker the soil, the **better** it is! Press the seeds into the soil, put more soil **over** them, and add some **water**. Place a sheet of plastic wrap **over** the carton. Roots will grow **under** the soil, and soon you will see plants. **After** a couple of weeks, remove some plants so that others will have room to grow. Later, you and your **mother**, **father**, **sister**, or **brother** will enjoy fresh flowers or vegetables!

Responding Ask what two kinds of plants you learned about that can grow in small indoor pots. *(flowers and vegetables)* Ask children to name the pair of spelling words that mean the same as *mom* and *dad*. *(mother* and *father)* Then have children name the other pair of family words from the list on the chalkboard. *(sister, brother)*

Day 1 page 216

Objectives *Children will*
- take the pretest
- pronounce the list words
- learn about the spelling principle
- analyze words that end with the |ər| sound

Planning Checklist
- ☑ Pretest (TE)
- ☑ Spelling principle/word list
- ☐ Review/Challenge Words
- ☐ Teaching the Principle (TE)
- ☐ Enrichment (TE)
- ☐ Additional Spelling Words (TE)

Assessment

Pretest
1. Can I smell the <u>flower</u>?
2. The plants need <u>water</u>.
3. My doll is <u>under</u> the bed.
4. Our car went <u>over</u> a bump.
5. I can swim <u>better</u> than you.
6. My baby <u>sister</u> is crying.
7. Is that your <u>brother</u>?
8. I will call my <u>mother</u>.
9. My <u>father</u> is at home.
10. Champ ran <u>after</u> me.

Day 2 page 217

Objectives *Children will*
- practice spelling list words
- apply spelling strategies
- complete analogies with Basic Words
- identify antonyms

Planning Checklist
- ☑ Spelling Strategy
- ☑ Independent Practice
- ☐ Daily Proofreading Practice (TE)
- ☐ Informal Assessment (TE)
- ☐ Extra Support (TE)
- ☐ Applying Spelling Strategies (TE)

Management Tips You may want to have children select samples of their best spelling tests to include in their cumulative folders.

Teacher's Resource Book
Practice Masters, pages 155–157
Unit Test, page 158
Bulletin Board, page 167

🏠 **Practice Plus**
Take-Home Word List 33
Games

Spelling Transparencies
Spelling Word List 33
Daily Proofreading Practice,
Unit 33
Graphic Organizers

Teacher's Resource Disk
Macintosh® or Windows®
software. Houghton Mifflin

Spelling CD-ROM
Macintosh® or Windows®
software. Houghton Mifflin

Internet
http://www.eduplace.com

Phonics Practice
Houghton Mifflin Phonics
The Listening Corner
Phonics Home Connection

 page 218

 page 219

Day 5 . *page 219*

Objective *Children will*
• review Basic and Review Words

Planning Checklist
☐ Review: Spelling Spree
☐ How Are You Doing?
☐ Daily Proofreading Practice (TE)
☐ Cooperative Learning Activity (TE)

Objectives *Children will*
• proofread for spelling and commas
• write and proofread an original composition

Planning Checklist
☐ Proofread: Spelling and Commas
☐ Write a Letter
☐ Daily Proofreading Practice (TE)
☐ Challenge Words Practice (TE)
☐ Another Writing Idea (TE)

Objective *Children will*
• take the posttest

Assessment
☐ **Posttest** (TE) *See Day 5*
☐ Unit 33 Test

 Meeting Individual Needs
Students Acquiring English

Spanish In Spanish there is no |ər| sound. **Activity** Write the Basic Words on the chalkboard, using different-colored chalk for the er endings. Say the words, have children repeat them, and ask volunteers to underline the spelling pattern for the vowel + r sound. Then erase the endings and say each word again. Have volunteers complete the words at the board.

Other Activities for Any Day

• Bonus activities from pages 220–221
• Practice Masters (easy, average, challenging)
  Teacher's Resource Book, pages 155–157
• Take-Home Word List 33
  Practice Plus

Objectives *Children will*

■ take the pretest

■ pronounce the list words

■ learn about the spelling principle

■ analyze words that end with the |ər| sound

Teaching the Principle

This lesson teaches the *er* spelling pattern for the |ər| sound at the end of two-syllable words. Children learn the strategy of thinking of this pattern when they hear the vowel + *r* sound at the end of *flower*.

To sum up the lesson, ask:

• How many syllables are there in each word? *(two)*

• In which syllable do you hear the vowel + *r* sound? *(second)*

• What letters spell the vowel + *r* sound at the end of each word? *(er)*

Enrichment

Vocabulary: Multiple Meanings
Have children use a dictionary to look up *under, over,* and *after.* Discuss the different meanings.

UNIT 33 Words That End with er

er water

er flower

A. flower
_____
water
_____
under
_____
over
_____
better
_____
sister
_____
brother
_____
mother
_____
father
_____
after

Read and Say

READ the sentences. **SAY** each word in dark print.

Basic Words

1. flower	*flower*	Can I smell the **flower**?
2. water	*water*	The plants need **water**.
3. under	*under*	My doll is **under** the bed.
4. over	*over*	Our car went **over** a bump.
5. better	*better*	I can swim **better** than you.
6. sister	*sister*	My baby **sister** is crying.
7. brother	*brother*	Is that your **brother**?
8. mother	*mother*	I will call my **mother**.
9. father	*father*	My **father** is at home.
10. after	*after*	Champ ran **after** me.

Think and Write

Each word ends with the vowel + **r** sound you hear at the end of flower.

the vowel + **r** sound → flow**er**, wat**er**

Does each word on the list have more than one syllable? yes

How many syllables are there in each word? two

In which syllable do you hear the vowel + **r** sound? second

A. Write the **ten** Basic Words. Then draw a line under the letters that spell the vowel + **r** sound in each word.

Review	Challenge
11. that 12. shop	13. gather 14. center

TEACHING OPTIONS

Meeting Individual Needs
Word Lists

You may want to assign Basic Words 1–5 and the Review Words to children who misspelled more than five words on the pretest. Assign the Challenge Words as appropriate. (You may want to have children write sentences, using the Challenge Words.)

Additional Spelling Words

Basic	Challenge	Words Often Misspelled
ever	feather	
zipper	wonder	it
antler	danger	it's
later	finger	
power	fever	
	chapter	

Home/School Involvement
Take-Home Word List • Goal-Setting

Have children set goals for the week on Take-Home Word List 33.

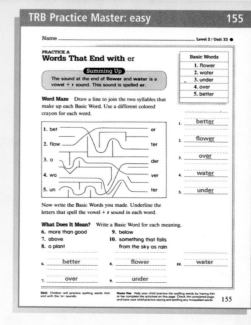

Independent Practice

 Spelling Strategy The sound at the end of **flower** and **water** is a vowel + r sound. This sound is spelled **er**.

Order of answers for question 3–4 may vary.

Phonics Write Basic Words to answer the questions.

1. Which word has the short **i** sound in the first syllable?
2. Which word has the short **e** sound in the first syllable?
3–4. Which two words have **other** in them?

Word Pairs Write a Basic Word to finish the second sentence in each pair.

5. A **plane** travels in the **air**.
   A **boat** travels in the _____.
6. A **woman** may be a **mother**.
   A **man** may be a _____.
7. You go **down** to go **under**.
   You go **up** to go _____.
8. A **trunk** is part of a **tree**.
   A **stem** is part of a _____.

Word Meaning Write the Basic Word that means the opposite of each word below.

9. before
10. above

Phonics

1. sister
2. better
3. brother
4. mother

Word Pairs

5. water
6. father
7. over
8. flower

Word Meaning

9. after
10. under

(217)

 Day 2

Objectives *Children will*

- practice spelling list words
- apply spelling strategies
- complete analogies with Basic Words
- identify antonyms

Daily Proofreading Practice
My **fathir** drives a truck. (*father*)
There is a **flowor** on her hat. (*flower*)

 Meeting Individual Needs
visual/oral/auditory/kinesthetic

Extra Support Check Independent Practice to determine who needs extra support. Write the Basic Words on the board. Say each word, exaggerating the two syllables. Underline the *er* ending in *flower*. Explain that these letters spell the |ər| sound. Have volunteers repeat each remaining word after you, tell where they hear the |ər| sound, and trace the final *er* with colored chalk.

Name _____ Level 2 / Unit 33 ▲

Basic Words
1. flower
2. water
3. under
4. over
5. better
6. sister
7. brother
8. mother
9. father
10. after

PRACTICE B
Words That End with er

Billy Goat Books Write the missing Basic Word for each book title. Begin each word with a capital letter.

My Home in the Water (1) a Bridge by J. Troll
Greener Grass Tastes (2) by the Gruff Brothers
My Life (3) I Met the Troll by Little Willie Gruff
New Ways to Cross (4) a Stream by Big Bill Gruff

1. _____ Under
2. _____ Better
3. _____ After
4. _____ Over

Family Picture Write the Basic Words that name the people and things in this picture.

father
mother
sister
brother
water
flower

 Applying Spelling Strategies
To Read New Words

- Write this sentence on the chalkboard:
  Gino spread peanut butter on the cracker.
- Have children read the sentence silently.
- Elicit the following strategies as children try to decode *cracker*.

cracker

This looks like a consonant cluster. I'll blend the sounds for *c* and *r* together.

I see that the letter *a* is followed by the consonants *ck*. I think this is the short *a* vowel pattern. I know that the letters *ck* make the |k| sound.

I've learned that the letters *er* at the end of a two-syllable word make the vowel + *r* sound that I hear at the end of *flower*.

Cr-ack-er. Crack-er. Cracker. The word *cracker* makes sense in the sentence.

Objective *Children will*

■ review Basic and Review Words

Daily Proofreading Practice

His **muther** plays the flute. (*mother*)
The tooth is **undur** my pillow. (*under*)

Puzzle Play

1. f a ther
2. m o ther
3. o ver
4. w ater
5. sist e r
6. aft e r

Rhyme Time

7. better
8. shop
9. brother
10. under
11. flower
12. that

(218)

Review: Spelling Spree

Puzzle Play Write a Basic Word for each clue. Use the letters that would be in the boxes to spell something you use to cut grass.

1. a man in a family __ ☐ __ __ __ __
2. a woman in a family ☐ __ __ __ __ __
3. on top of ☐ __ __ __
4. melted ice ☐ __ __ __ __
5. a girl in a family __ __ __ __ ☐ __
6. behind __ __ __ __ ☐

Secret Words: a   m o w e r

Rhyme Time Finish the sentences. Write a Basic or Review Word to rhyme with the word in dark print.

7. Your **letter** is so much _____ than mine.
8. Did you buy your **mop** at that little _____ ?
9. My **other** _____ loves to work in his garden.
10. When I hear **thunder**, I hide _____ my quilt!
11. A rain **shower** may help your _____ grow.
12. The **hat** _____ you sat on is mine!

How Are You Doing?
Write your words in ABC order. Practice with a family member any words you spelled wrong.

TEACHING OPTIONS

Cooperative Learning Activity

Shake and Spell
visual/oral

Have partners choose a spelling word, read it, and spell it using letter dice or Boggle® cubes. One partner then places the dice in a cup, spills out the letters, and tries to spell as much of the word as possible with the letters that face up. The player puts the unusable letters back in the cup, then shakes and spills the dice again. Play continues until the word is completed. The second partner repeats the activity, trying to spell the word using fewer rolls of the dice. Partners continue with different spelling words.

TRB Practice Master: challenging   157

Name _____   Level 2 / Unit 33 ■

PRACTICE C
Words That End with er

Word Change Write the Challenge or Vocabulary Word for each clue. Then follow the directions to change that word to another word.

1. Write a Vocabulary Word that means **a plant that has just begun to grow**.
2. Change the second vowel to a consonant to write a word that means **the opposite of tall**.

1. ___shoot___   2. ___short___

3. Write a Challenge Word that means **to bring together**.
4. Change one consonant to write a word that means **a male parent**.

3. ___gather___   4. ___father___

		Challenge Words
		1. gather
		2. center
		Theme Vocabulary
		3. soil
		4. petals
		5. shoot
		6. hoe

What Class Think how the words in each group are alike. Write the missing Challenge or Vocabulary Word. In the box next to each group, write a word or words that tell about all the things in the group.

Sample answers:

5.	rake	shovel	hoe	→ tools
6.	side	top	center	→ positions
7.	earth	dirt	soil	→ ground
8.	stem	leaf	petals	→ flower parts

Skill: Children will practice spelling words that end with the /ər/ sound and words related to the theme of gardening.

Home Tip: Help your child practice the spelling words by having him or her complete the activities on this page. Check the completed page and have your child practice saying and spelling any misspelled words.

157

Proofreading and Writing

Proofread: Spelling and Commas Use a comma after the **greeting** and after the **closing** in a letter.

Dear Tashia,   Your friend,

Proofread this letter. Use proofreading marks to fix five spelling mistakes and two missing commas.

Example: Dear ~~Muther~~, Mother

May 24, 1998

Dear Terrance,
   My ~~fathar~~ father has a new garden ~~thet~~ that is better than the old one. My ~~sistur~~ sister and I put in the plants. My ~~bruther~~ brother tried to help, but he sprayed ~~watter~~ water all over us!

Your cousin,
Nicole

Basic

1. flower
2. water
3. under
4. over
5. better
6. sister
7. brother
8. mother
9. father
10. after

Review

11. that
12. shop

Challenge

13. gather
14. center

Proofreading Marks

∧ Add
~~ Delete
≡ Make a capital letter
/ Make a small letter

Write a Letter

Pretend you are a rabbit and have just found a great vegetable garden. Write a letter to your family. Tell them about your adventure. Try to use spelling words.

Proofreading Tip

Check your letter to make sure that you put a comma after the greeting and closing.

219

TRB Unit 33 Test   158

Name _____ Level 2 / Unit 33 ⬤▲

Unit 33 Test: Words That End with er

Read each word group. Find the correctly spelled word to complete each group. Mark the letter next to that word.

Sample:
a very hot _____
ⓐ sommer
ⓑ sumer
● summer

Items 1–5 test Basic Words 1–5. Items 6–10 test Basic Words 6–10.

1. up and _____
ⓐ ower
● over
ⓒ ovver

2. cool, fresh _____
● water
ⓑ watter
ⓒ warter

3. for _____ or worse
ⓐ beter
● better
ⓒ battur

4. a pretty red _____
ⓐ floer
ⓑ flowr
● flower

5. down and _____
● under
ⓑ ander
ⓒ undr

6. father and _____
ⓐ mothr
ⓑ muther
● mother

7. sister or _____
ⓐ bruther
● brother
ⓒ brouther

8. before and _____
ⓐ afer
ⓑ aftor
● aftr

9. my little _____
ⓐ sistr
ⓑ sester
● sister

10. son and _____
ⓐ fowther
ⓑ father
ⓒ fathar

158

Meeting Individual Needs

Challenge Words Practice
Ask children to make *er* flowers. Have them write *er* in the center of the flower, then write the Challenge Words and other *er* words on the petals. Children can draw their flowers or make them from cut paper.

Another Writing Idea
Suggest children write a tall tale about a plant that grows to a gigantic size. Encourage them to use spelling words.

Day 4

Objectives *Children will*

▪ proofread for spelling and commas

▪ write and proofread an original composition

Daily Proofreading Practice
Are you feeling **bettor** today? (*better*)
The horse jumped **ovir** the fence. (*over*)

Day 5

Posttest

Sentences 1–5 test the first five Basic Words. Sentences 6–10 test the next five Basic Words.

Basic Words
1. The car ran <u>over</u> the ball.
2. The cat hid <u>under</u> the bed.
3. We want to have some <u>water</u>.
4. She can play the game <u>better</u> than I can.
5. Do you have a red <u>flower</u>?
6. You can ask your <u>brother</u> to go.
7. Give the cup to my <u>father</u>.
8. Pat sat next to her <u>mother</u>.
9. I see my <u>sister</u>.
10. The bee came <u>after</u> me.

Review Words
11. We will go to the <u>shop</u>.
12. I saw <u>that</u> frog.

Challenge Words
13. Put the plate in the <u>center</u> of the table.
14. We will <u>gather</u> flowers in the field.

Day by Day Planner

These pages can be used at any time during the study of this unit.

Objectives *Children will*

■ identify and write antonyms

■ draw and label antonyms

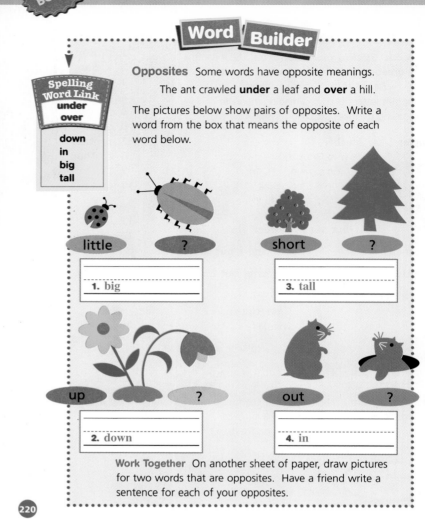

Vocabulary Enrichment

Word Builder

Opposites Some words have opposite meanings.
The ant crawled **under** a leaf and **over** a hill.

The pictures below show pairs of opposites. Write a word from the box that means the opposite of each word below.

Spelling Word Link

under
over

down
in
big
tall

little   ?   short   ?

_____
1. big

_____
3. tall

up   ?   out   ?

_____
2. down

_____
4. in

Work Together On another sheet of paper, draw pictures for two words that are opposites. Have a friend write a sentence for each of your opposites.

220

EXTENSION OPTIONS

Learning Center Activity
visual/oral/auditory/kinesthetic

Growing Opposites Invite children to draw a picture of a vegetable garden and label it with words that are opposites. Discuss the different things children might include in their pictures, such as specific vegetables, gardening tools, baskets for the vegetables, and the gardeners themselves. To help children complete this activity, you might first brainstorm a list of opposites as a group, then post the list on your classroom word wall for reference.

Opposites

above/below	front/back
dark/light	hard/soft
different/same	huge/tiny
dirty/clean	left/right
dry/wet	smooth/rough
empty/full	thick/thin
top/bottom	young/old

Vocabulary Enrichment

Science

Gardening All the words in the box have something to do with gardening. Write those words to finish these directions. Use your Spelling Dictionary.

Spelling Word Link

flower

soil
petals
shoot
hoe

How to Grow a Flower Garden
First, get a __(1)__ from the tool shed. Next, dig into the __(2)__ with it. Then plant the seeds and water them. In a few days, you will see the first long green __(3)__. Before you know it, your flowers will have pretty __(4)__!

1. hoe

2. soil

3. shoot

4. petals

Try This CHALLENGE

Clue Match Write a word from the box for each clue.
5. A rose might have red ones.
6. Digging in it can make you dirty.
7. You hold it by a handle.
8. It is a plant that has just begun to grow.

5. petals

6. soil

7. hoe

8. shoot

Fact File

Some people think that plants grow only on land. Actually, most of the world's plants live in ocean water or grow on the ocean floor!

221

Day by Day Planner

Objectives *Children will*
- expand their vocabulary by using words related to gardening
- show their understanding of the vocabulary words by completing context activities

Vocabulary Checkup

Have children use the vocabulary words in sentences or match the words to the definitions below.

1. a tool with a flat blade on a long handle *hoe*
2. the loose top layer of dirt in which plant life can grow *soil*
3. a plant that has just begun to grow *shoot*
4. the brightly colored parts of a flower *petals*

Fact File

Ocean Plant Life

Plants can only live where there is sunlight. In oceans, light can penetrate the first 300 to 600 feet of water. Even microscopic plants must live near the surface, on the ocean floor in shallow water, or along the shoreline.

Integrating Literature

Easy	Average	Challenging
How a Seed Grows *by Helene J. Jordan* Two children watch as the seeds they plant grow into bean plants.	**Watermelon Day** *by Kathi Appelt* Jesse can't wait until the watermelon in her garden is ready to eat.	**The Garden of Happiness** *by Erika Tamar* Marisol and her neighbors turn a vacant lot into a community garden.
Oliver's Vegetables *by Vivian French* Oliver discovers he likes vegetables after exploring his grandfather's garden.	**The Empty Pot** *by Demi* A boy named Ping cannot get a seed the emperor has given him to sprout.	**Jack's Garden** *by Henry Cole* Jack plants seeds that turn into a beautiful flower garden.

Words That End with *ed* or *ing*

WORD LISTS

Spelling

Basic

1. batted
2. running
3. clapped
4. stopped
5. getting
6. shopping
7. stepped
8. hugging
9. pinned
10. sitting
11. missed
12. telling

Review

13. this
14. must

Challenge

15. jogging
16. flipped

Vocabulary

**Physical Education:
Sports**

score
tie
goal
match

Introducing the Lesson

Read Aloud

**Write the Basic Words
on the board.**

Baseball

Baseball players have been **getting** hits, **running** the bases, and **hugging** each other after games for over a hundred years. Fans have always **clapped** when their team won, but other things have changed. At first, players did not have the equipment they use today. **Sitting** on the bench was safe, but there was no **telling** what might happen when a player **batted**. A catcher once **stopped** playing because he nearly got hit on the nose when the batter **missed** the ball. In the next game, the catcher wore a wire mask. Another time, a player **stepped** onto the field wearing a glove and the fans laughed. But soon players were wearing gloves with pads **pinned** inside. Today, **shopping** for a baseball team's equipment can take as long as playing a game!

Responding Ask children which sport they learned about. *(baseball)* Read aloud these words from the selection: "**Sitting** on the bench was safe . . . ." Ask children to name other Basic words with the same ending as *sitting*. *(running, getting, shopping, hugging, telling)*

Day 1 page 222

Objectives *Children will*

- take the pretest
- pronounce the list words
- learn about the spelling principle
- sort words by their endings

Planning Checklist

☑ Pretest (TE)
☑ Spelling principle/word list
☐ Review/Challenge Words
☐ Teaching the Principle (TE)
☐ Enrichment (TE)
☐ Additional Spelling Words (TE)

Assessment

Pretest

1. The girl <u>batted</u> the ball.
2. He is <u>running</u> in a race.
3. I <u>clapped</u> my hands.
4. She <u>stopped</u> the car.
5. My dog is <u>getting</u> big.
6. Will you go <u>shopping</u>?
7. You <u>stepped</u> on a bee!
8. He is <u>hugging</u> my cat.
9. Mom <u>pinned</u> my dress.
10. I am <u>sitting</u> next to you.
11. They <u>missed</u> the train.
12. Matt is <u>telling</u> a story.

Day 2 page 223

Objectives *Children will*

- practice spelling list words
- apply spelling strategies
- identify Basic Words by using meaning clues
- identify Elephant Words by using context clues

Planning Checklist

☑ Spelling Strategy
☑ Independent Practice
☐ Daily Proofreading Practice (TE)
☐ Informal Assessment (TE)
☐ Extra Support (TE)
☐ Applying Spelling Strategies (TE)

Management Tips You may want to have children select samples of their best spelling tests to include in their cumulative folders.

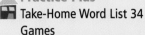 **Additional Resources**

Teacher's Resource Book
Practice Masters, pages 159–161
Unit Test, page 162
Bulletin Board, page 167

Practice Plus
Take-Home Word List 34
Games

Spelling Transparencies
Spelling Word List 34
Daily Proofreading Practice, Unit 34
Graphic Organizers

Teacher's Resource Disk
Macintosh® or Windows® software. Houghton Mifflin

Spelling CD-ROM
Macintosh® or Windows® software. Houghton Mifflin

Internet
http://www.eduplace.com

Phonics Practice
Houghton Mifflin Phonics
The Listening Corner
Phonics Home Connection

 Day 3 *page 224* **Day 4** *page 225* **Day 5** *page 225*

Objectives *Children will*
• identify the dictionary entry that would list a given verb form
• review Basic and Review Words

Planning Checklist
☐ Dictionary
☐ Review: Spelling Spree
☐ How Are You Doing?
☐ Daily Proofreading Practice (TE)
☐ Ongoing Assessment

Objectives *Children will*
• proofread for spelling
• write and proofread an original composition

Planning Checklist
☐ Proofread for Spelling
☐ Write a Speech
☐ Daily Proofreading Practice (TE)
☐ Challenge Words Practice (TE)
☐ Another Writing Idea (TE)

Objective *Children will*
• take the posttest

Assessment
☐ **Posttest** (TE) *See Day 5*
☐ Unit 34 Test

Meeting Individual Needs
Students Acquiring English

Spanish In Spanish there are no |ing| sounds. **Activity** Say batted/batting, clapping/clapped, stopped/stopping. Ask children to name the words ending with |ing|. Then write the Basic Words ending in -ing on the board. As you say each word, have volunteers circle the ing.

Asian Children may need help pronouncing the -ed ending. **Activity** Write the Basic Words ending in -ed on the board. Say each word, emphasizing the |t| sound in clapped, stopped, and stepped, the |ĭd| sound in batted, and the |d| sound in pinned. Call on children to pronounce the words.

Other Activities for Any Day
• Bonus activities from pages 226–227
• Practice Masters (easy, average, challenging) Teacher's Resource Book, pages 159–161
• Take-Home Word List 34 Practice Plus

Day 1

Objectives *Children will*

- take the pretest
- pronounce the list words
- learn about the spelling principle
- sort words by their endings

Teaching the Principle

This lesson teaches the spellings of words that are formed by joining a base word and the ending *-ed* or *-ing*. Children learn the strategy of doubling the final consonant before adding *-ed* or *-ing* when a word ends with a short vowel and a single consonant.

Answers to *Think* Questions

- The last letter is doubled.
- In the Elephant Words, the last letter is not doubled before the ending is added.

Enrichment

Vocabulary: Multiple Meanings
Have children use a dictionary to look up *stopped, getting, pinned,* and *sitting.* Discuss the different meanings.

UNIT 34 Words That End with *ed* or *ing*

A. batted

___ clapped

___ stopped

___ stepped

___ pinned

___ missed

B. running

___ getting

___ shopping

___ hugging

___ sitting

___ telling

222

Read and Say

READ the sentences. **SAY** each word in dark print.

Basic Words

1.	batted	*batted*	The girl **batted** the ball.
2.	running	*running*	He is **running** in a race.
3.	clapped	*clapped*	I **clapped** my hands.
4.	stopped	*stopped*	She **stopped** the car.
5.	getting	*getting*	My dog is **getting** big.
6.	shopping	*shopping*	Will you go **shopping**?
7.	stepped	*stepped*	You **stepped** on a bee!
8.	hugging	*hugging*	He is **hugging** my cat.
9.	pinned	*pinned*	Mom **pinned** my dress.
10.	sitting	*sitting*	I am **sitting** next to you.
11.	missed	*missed*	They **missed** the train.
12.	telling	*telling*	Matt is **telling** a story.

Think and Write

Each word is made up of a base word and the ending **ed** or **ing**. The base word has a short vowel sound followed by a consonant.

bat + t + ed → bat**ted**
run + n + ing → run**ning**

What happens to the last letter in each base word before the ending **ed** or **ing** is added? See TE margin.
How are the Elephant Words different?

A. Write **six** Basic Words with the **ed** ending.
B. Write **six** Basic Words with the **ing** ending.

Order of answers for each category may vary.

Review	**Challenge**
13. this 14. must	15. jogging 16. flipped

TEACHING OPTIONS

Meeting Individual Needs
Word Lists

You may want to assign Basic Words 1–5, the Elephant Words, and the Review Words to children who misspelled more than five words on the pretest. Assign the Challenge Words as appropriate. (You may want to have children write sentences, using the Challenge Words.)

Additional Spelling Words

Basic	**Challenge**	**Words Often Misspelled**
napping	wrapping	because
popped	strapped	before
rubbed	hummed	
cutting	snapped	
dipped	chopping	
	skipping	

Home/School Involvement
Take-Home Word List • Goal-Setting

Have children set goals for the week on Take-Home Word List 34.

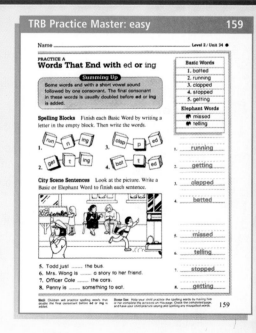

Name ___   Level 2 / Unit 34

PRACTICE A
Words That End with ed or ing

Summing Up
Some words end with a short vowel sound followed by one consonant. The final consonant in these words is usually doubled before **ed** or **ing** is added.

Spelling Blocks Finish each Basic Word by writing a letter in the empty block. Then write the words.

Basic Words
1. batted
2. running
3. clapped
4. stopped
5. getting

Elephant Words
6. missed
7. telling

1. running
2. getting
3. clapped
4. batted
5. missed
6. telling
7. stopped
8. getting

City Scene Sentences Look at the picture. Write a Basic or Elephant Word to finish each sentence.

5. Todd just ___ the bus.
6. Mrs. Wong is ___ a story to her friend.
7. Officer Cole ___ the cars.
8. Penny is ___ something to eat.

159

Independent Practice

Spelling Strategy Some words end with a short vowel sound followed by one consonant. The final consonant in these words is usually doubled before **ed** or **ing** is added.

Order of answers for question 3–4 may vary.

Phonics Write Basic Words to answer the questions.

1. Which word rhymes with **grinned**?
2. Which word rhymes with **tugging**?
3–4. Which two words have the short **e** sound in the base word and begin like **go** or **stay**?

Word Clues Write a Basic Word for each clue.

5. what the car did at the red light
6. what the children did at the end of the show
7. what you feel like doing when you are tired
8. what you would be doing at a store
9. what the baseball player did to hit the ball
10. what the racer was doing around the track

Elephant Words Write the missing Elephant Words.

11. Roberto _____ the first part of practice.
12. The coach was _____ the team what to do.

Phonics

1. pinned

2. hugging

3. getting

4. stepped

Word Clues

5. stopped

6. clapped

7. sitting

8. shopping

9. batted

10. running

Elephant Words

11. missed

12. telling

223

Objectives *Children will*

- practice spelling list words
- apply spelling strategies
- identify Basic Words by using meaning clues
- identify Elephant Words by using context clues

Daily Proofreading Practice

We **clapt** for the singers. (*clapped*)
I went **shoping** at the mall. (*shopping*)

Meeting Individual Needs
visual/oral/auditory

Extra Support Check Independent Practice to determine who needs extra support. Write *bat* + __ + *ed* = *batted* on the board. Ask children what letter to add in the blank to make *batted*. (*t*) Write the missing *t* and read the equation. Write similar equations for the remaining words, asking volunteers to supply the missing letters and to spell the completed words.

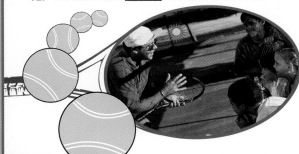

Applying Spelling Strategies
To Spell New Words

- Read aloud: **I knew my brother had fooled me when I saw him grinning.**
- Have children attempt to spell *grinning* on their Have-a-Go charts.

- Elicit the following strategies as children try to spell *grinning*.

> I know that the word *grin* is spelled with the consonant cluster *gr* and the short vowel pattern *i-n*.

grinning

> Because the base word *grin* has a short *i* sound followed by the single consonant *n*, I know I have to add another *n* before I write the *-ing* ending.

Objectives *Children will*

■ identify the dictionary entry that would list a given verb form

■ review Basic and Review Words

Daily Proofreading Practice

He was **sittin** on the swings. (*sitting*)
Lee **stepded** over the big hole. (*stepped*)

U N I T
34

Dictionary

1. tell

2. shop

3. pin

4. miss

Picture Clues

5. running

6. sitting

7. hugging

Letter Swap

8. clapped

9. stopped

10. telling

11. shopping

12. batted

224

Dictionary

Finding Words with Endings Words with endings like **ed** and **ing** are usually listed in the dictionary with their base word. To find **clapped**, you would look up the entry word **clap**.

entry word

clap To slap hands together: *Do not clap until the end of the song.* **clapped, clapping**

words with endings

Practice Write the entry word you would look up to find each of these words in the dictionary.

1. telling   2. shopping   3. pinned   4. missed

Review: Spelling Spree

Picture Clues Write a Basic Word for each picture.

5.   6.   7.

Letter Swap Change the letters in dark print to make Basic Words. Write the words.

8. **sn**apped
9. **dr**opped
10. **s**elling
11. **dr**opping
12. **p**atted

☑ **How Are You Doing?**
Write each word as a partner reads it aloud. Did you spell any words wrong?

TEACHING OPTIONS

Ongoing Assessment

Inflectional Endings

The consistent spelling of inflectional endings takes time to develop. Common misspellings are as follows: CLAPT, CLAPDED, CLAPED (*clapped*); GETING (*getting*); and HIDDING, HIDEING (*hiding*). Particularly in the case of *-ed*, most children require time and appropriate exposure to sort out the common *-ed* spelling for the three sounds this ending can represent: |t|, |d|, and |əd|.

TRB Practice Master: challenging 161

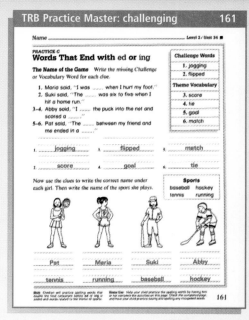

Proofreading and Writing

Proofread for Spelling Proofread this newspaper story. Use proofreading marks to fix six spelling mistakes.

running
Example: The girls are ~~runing~~ fast!

- City News Today -

A Great Race

stepped
The crowd stopped talking as Lisa ~~steped~~
getting
ahead of Amy on the track. Was Amy ~~gettin~~
must   this
tired? Amy knew she ~~mast~~ win ~~thes~~ race.

Could she do it? Later, people clapped as the
pinned
judge ~~penned~~ a ribbon on Amy's shirt. If
missed
you weren't there, you ~~missd~~ a great race!

Write a Speech

Pretend you are a famous sports star. Write a thank-you speech for a prize you have won. Tell about yourself and your sport. Try to use spelling words. Give your speech in front of a small group.

My Speech

Proofreading Tip

Use your mouse to highlight each line so that you can proofread one line at a time.

225

Basic

1. batted
2. running
3. clapped
4. stopped
5. getting
6. shopping
7. stepped
8. hugging
9. pinned
10. sitting
11. missed
12. telling

Review

13. this
14. must

Challenge

15. jogging
16. flipped

Proofreading Marks

∧ Add
⤵ Delete
≡ Make a capital letter
/ Make a small letter

Meeting Individual Needs

Challenge Words Practice

Ask children to build the Challenge Words with letter tiles or cards, crossing them at their common letter *i*. Have them add other *-ed* and *-ing* words that double the final consonant, using a crossword puzzle format.

Another Writing Idea

Suggest children use spelling words to write a journal entry about a sports event that they watched or participated in.

Objectives *Children will*
- proofread for spelling
- write and proofread an original composition

Daily Proofreading Practice

Papa likes **teling** jokes. (*telling*)
I **pind** the tail on the donkey. (*pinned*)

Posttest

Sentences 1–5 test the first five Basic Words. Sentences 6–10 test the next five Basic Words. Sentences 11–12 test the Elephant Words.

Basic Words
1. The grass is <u>getting</u> greener.
2. She <u>batted</u> the ball.
3. At the top of the hill, we <u>stopped</u> for a look.
4. The dog is <u>running</u> after the cat.
5. When she found the lost dog, we all <u>clapped</u>.
6. Tim is <u>hugging</u> the cat.
7. A big man <u>stepped</u> out of the car.
8. They went <u>shopping</u> at the store.
9. I <u>pinned</u> a flower on the hat.
10. All the boys are <u>sitting</u> on the steps.
11. The king is <u>telling</u> a tale.
12. I was late and <u>missed</u> the play.

Review Words
13. The cat hid in <u>this</u> box.
14. The bus <u>must</u> stop here.

Challenge Words
15. We go <u>jogging</u> around the track.
16. The diver <u>flipped</u> in the air.

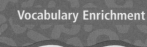

Day by Day Planner

These pages can be used at any time during the study of this unit.

Objectives *Children will*

- identify the correct definitions of homographs
- identify and write sentences for homographs

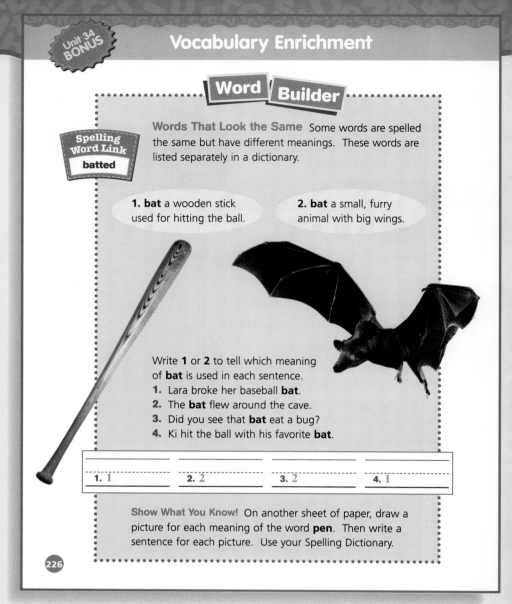

Unit 34
BONUS

Vocabulary Enrichment

Word Builder

Spelling Word Link
batted

Words That Look the Same Some words are spelled the same but have different meanings. These words are listed separately in a dictionary.

1. bat a wooden stick used for hitting the ball.

2. bat a small, furry animal with big wings.

Write **1** or **2** to tell which meaning of **bat** is used in each sentence.
1. Lara broke her baseball **bat**.
2. The **bat** flew around the cave.
3. Did you see that **bat** eat a bug?
4. Ki hit the ball with his favorite **bat**.

| 1. 1 | 2. 2 | 3. 2 | 4. 1 |

Show What You Know! On another sheet of paper, draw a picture for each meaning of the word **pen**. Then write a sentence for each picture. Use your Spelling Dictionary.

226

EXTENSION OPTIONS

Learning Center Activity
visual/kinesthetic

A Sports Dictionary Remind children that some words have two separate entries in the dictionary. Provide children with large paper. Have them each make a page for a sports dictionary of homographs. On the top half of the page, have children list the word, write a sentence using the sports-related meaning of the word, and draw a picture. On the bottom, have them do the same for another meaning of the word. Children can bind their pages together to make a class Big Book.

Sports Homographs

ball	count	fast	pick
bat	cricket	fit	pitcher
batter	duck	jam	racket
box	fan	match	row

Vocabulary Enrichment

Physical Education

Sports All the words in the box have something to do with sports. Write those words to finish this sports report. Use your Spelling Dictionary.

Spelling Word Link

running

score
tie
goal
match

The Tigers and the Bears see the __(1)__ on the board. Will it be a __(2)__ game? The __(3)__ is almost over. Which team will make the next __(4)__?

2	2
Tigers	Bears

1. score

2. tie

3. match

4. goal

Try This CHALLENGE

Yes or No? Write **yes** or **no** to answer each question.

5. Does a **tie** game mean one team wins?
6. Does making a **goal** help you win a game?
7. Can a **match** be played with only one team?
8. Do you use numbers when you keep **score**?

5. no

6. yes

7. no

8. yes

★ Fact File

Every four years, people from more than 170 countries play in the Olympic Games. The first games were held in Greece about 2,500 years ago!

227

Objectives *Children will*
- expand their vocabulary by using words related to sports
- show their understanding of the vocabulary words by completing context activities

Vocabulary Checkup

Have children use the vocabulary words in sentences or match the words to the definitions below.

1. a score given for driving a ball or puck into a special part of the playing area *goal*
2. a game or contest that ends with the same score for both sides *tie*
3. a sports contest *match*
4. a record of points made by each person or team in a game or contest *score*

Fact File

The Olympics

Modern Olympics were organized to promote world peace and amateur athletics. The five rings in the Olympic symbol stand for the continents of Africa, Asia, Australia, Europe, and North and South America. You may wish to show children these areas and Greece on a world map.

Integrating Literature

Easy	Average	Challenging
Willy the Wimp *by Anthony Browne* Willy the chimp thinks his skill at soccer comes from magic cleats.	**Riding Silver Star** *by Joanna Cole* A girl prepares her horse Star for an upcoming competition.	**Wilma Unlimited** *by Kathleen Krull* The story of African American runner Wilma Rudolph, an Olympic gold medalist.
Play Ball, Amelia Bedelia *by Peggy Parish* Taking instructions literally, Amelia Bedelia wreaks havoc on a ballgame.	**JoJo's Flying Side Kick** *by Brian Pinkney* To earn her yellow belt in tae kwon do class, JoJo must break a board with a flying side kick.	**Zero's Slider** *by Matt Christopher* Zero suddenly develops the ability to pitch perfect sliders.

More Words with *ed* or *ing*

WORD LISTS

Spelling

Basic

1. liked
2. hoping
3. baked
4. using
5. chased
6. making
7. closed
8. hiding
9. named
10. riding

Review

11. time
12. sleep

Challenge

13. teasing
14. decided

Vocabulary

Social Studies: Friendship

neighbor
share
welcome
invite

Introducing the Lesson

Read Aloud

Write the Basic Words on the board.

Friendship

A best friend is wonderful to have. In a book by James Marshall, two hippos **named** George and Martha are best friends. Martha **baked** and cooked for George, and she **liked making** him pea soup. George hated pea soup! One day, **hoping** Martha wouldn't notice, George poured the soup into his shoes. What a mess! Another time, George scared Martha by **hiding** behind her. Later, **riding** in the Tunnel of Love, Martha got George back by scaring *him*. Then, **using** a tree branch to spy from, George tried to read Martha's diary one day. She **closed** the book and **chased** him away. What other kinds of silly adventures do these two friends have? Read *George and Martha* and find out!

Responding Ask children to name the two best friends in the selection. *(George and Martha)* Then ask them to name spelling words that tell some of the things that George and Martha did. *(You may want to reread the selection.)* Write the words that children name on the chalkboard under the headings *ed* and *ing*.

Day 1 *page 228*

Objectives *Children will*

- take the pretest
- pronounce the list words
- learn about the spelling principle
- sort words by their endings

Planning Checklist

- ☑ Pretest (TE)
- ☑ Spelling principle/word list
- ☐ Review/Challenge Words
- ☐ Teaching the Principle (TE)
- ☐ Enrichment (TE)
- ☐ Additional Spelling Words (TE)

Assessment

Pretest

1. I <u>liked</u> the show.
2. We are <u>hoping</u> for rain.
3. Rose <u>baked</u> a cake.
4. Are you <u>using</u> the mop?
5. The fox <u>chased</u> the sheep.
6. They are <u>making</u> a kite.
7. The store is <u>closed</u>.
8. The dog is <u>hiding</u> a bone.
9. Have you <u>named</u> the cat?
10. Dad is <u>riding</u> his bike.

Day 2 *page 229*

Objectives *Children will*

- practice spelling list words
- apply spelling strategies
- identify synonyms
- classify Basic Words into groups

Planning Checklist

- ☑ Spelling Strategy
- ☑ Independent Practice
- ☐ Daily Proofreading Practice (TE)
- ☐ Informal Assessment (TE)
- ☐ Extra Support (TE)
- ☐ Applying Spelling Strategies (TE)

FYI **Management Tip** Children can evaluate their own spelling progress by comparing papers they wrote at the beginning of the school year with papers they have written recently. Encourage children to think about how they feel their spelling and proofreading skills have changed over the year.

Day 3 *page 230*

Day 4 *page 231*

Day 5 *page 231*

Objectives *Children will*
- identify the dictionary entry that would list a given verb form
- review Basic and Review Words

Planning Checklist
- ☐ Dictionary
- ☐ Review: Spelling Spree
- ☐ How Are You Doing?
- ☐ Daily Proofreading Practice (TE)
- ☐ Cooperative Learning Activity (TE)

Objectives *Children will*
- proofread for spelling
- write and proofread an original composition

Planning Checklist
- ☐ Proofread for Spelling
- ☐ Write a Story
- ☐ Daily Proofreading Practice (TE)
- ☐ Challenge Words Practice (TE)
- ☐ Another Writing Idea (TE)

Objective *Children will*
- take the posttest

Assessment
☐ **Posttest** (TE) *See Day 5*
☐ Unit 35 Test

Additional Resources

Teacher's Resource Book
Practice Masters, pages 163–165
Unit Test, page 166
Bulletin Board, page 167

Practice Plus
Take-Home Word List 35
Games

Spelling Transparencies
Spelling Word List 35
Daily Proofreading Practice, Unit 35
Graphic Organizers

Teacher's Resource Disk
Macintosh® or Windows® software. Houghton Mifflin

Spelling CD-ROM
Macintosh® or Windows® software. Houghton Mifflin

Internet
http://www.eduplace.com

Phonics Practice
Houghton Mifflin Phonics
The Listening Corner
Phonics Home Connection

Meeting Individual Needs
Students Acquiring English

Spanish Children may not recognize the *ed* and *ing* endings.
Activity On the board write *like, liked,* and *liking*. Say the words. Have children repeat. Ask them to name the word with the *-ed* or *-ing* ending. Repeat with other Basic Words.

Asian Children may not recognize that a word ending with *ed* or *ing* may come from a base word ending with *e.*
Activity Write the Basic Words on the board in columns, following this example: *like, liked, liking*. Explain that the *e* was dropped in each word before an ending was added. Say some Basic Words. Have volunteers write the base word on the board.

Other Activities for Any Day

- Bonus activities from pages 232–233
- Practice Masters (easy, average, challenging)
  Teacher's Resource Book, pages 163–165
- Take-Home Word List 35
  Practice Plus

Objectives *Children will*

- take the pretest
- pronounce the list words
- learn about the spelling principle
- sort words by their endings

Teaching the Principle

This lesson teaches the spellings of words that are formed by joining a base word and the ending *-ed* or *-ing*. Children learn the strategy of dropping the final *e* in a base word that has the vowel-consonant-e pattern before they add *-ed* or *-ing*.

Answers to *Think* Questions

- The base words are *like, hope, bake, use, chase, make, close, hide, name,* and *ride.*
- The final *e* is dropped before the ending is added.

Enrichment

Vocabulary: Multiple Meanings
Have children use a dictionary to look up *using* and *making*. Discuss the different meanings.

More Words with ed or ing

Read and Say

READ the sentences. **SAY** each word in dark print.

Basic Words

1. liked	*liked*	I **liked** the show.
2. hoping	*hoping*	We are **hoping** for rain.
3. baked	*baked*	Rose **baked** a cake.
4. using	*using*	Are you **using** the mop?
5. chased	*chased*	The fox **chased** the sheep.
6. making	*making*	They are **making** a kite.
7. closed	*closed*	The store is **closed**.
8. hiding	*hiding*	The dog is **hiding** a bone.
9. named	*named*	Have you **named** the cat?
10. riding	*riding*	Dad is **riding** his bike.

A. liked

___
baked

___
chased

___
closed

___
named

B. hoping

___
using

___
making

___
hiding

___
riding

228

Think and Write

Each word is made up of a base word and the ending **ed** or **ing**. The base word has the vowel-consonant-**e** pattern.

$$\text{like} - e + ed \rightarrow \text{lik}\textbf{ed}$$
$$\text{hope} - e + ing \rightarrow \text{hop}\textbf{ing}$$

What is the base word for each word? *See TE margin.*
What happens to the last letter in each base word before the ending **ed** or **ing** is added?

A. Write **five** Basic Words that have the **ed** ending.
B. Write **five** Basic Words that have the **ing** ending.
Order of answers for each category may vary.

Review	Challenge
11. time 12. sleep	13. teasing 14. decided

Meeting Individual Needs
Word Lists

You may want to assign Basic Words 1–5 and the Review Words to children who misspelled more than five words on the pretest. Assign the Challenge Words as appropriate. (You may want to have children write sentences, using the Challenge Words.)

Additional Spelling Words

Basic	Challenge	Words Often Misspelled
joked	raising	again
waving	surprised	always
taped	erasing	
saved	pasted	
driving	pleased	
	voted	

Home/School Involvement
Take-Home Word List • Goal-Setting

Have children set goals for the week on Take-Home Word List 35.

TRB Practice Master: easy   163

Name _____ Level 2 / Unit 35 ●

PRACTICE A
More Words with ed or ing

Basic Words
1. liked
2. hoping
3. baked
4. using
5. chased

Summing Up
Some words end with the vowel-consonant-e pattern. The final e in these words is dropped before ed or ing is added.

Odd One Out Cross out the shape that is different from the others in the row. Write a Basic Word with the letters that are left.

1. baked
2. liked
3. using
4. hoping

A Better Letter Write the missing Basic Words to finish this letter.

January 16, 1991

Dear Mitch,
I went to the circus last night! It was funny when the clowns ran out __(5)__ each other. An elephant picked one clown up by __(6)__ its trunk! I __(7)__ it so much that I want to go again. I was __(8)__ you could come with me next time.
Your friend,
Liz

5. chased
6. using
7. liked
8. hoping

163

Independent Practice

Spelling Strategy Some words end with the vowel-consonant-**e** pattern. The final **e** in these words is dropped before **ed** or **ing** is added.

ed ing

Order of answers for question 3–4 may vary.
Phonics Write Basic Words to answer the questions.

1. Which word has two syllables and has the long **a** sound?
2. Which word begins with a vowel?
3–4. Which two words have two syllables and have the long **i** sound?

Word Meaning Write the Basic Word that means the same or almost the same as each word below.

5. followed   6. enjoyed
7. shut   8. called

Word Groups Think how the words in each group are alike. Write the missing Basic Words.

9. wanting, wishing, _____
10. fried, boiled, _____

Phonics

1. making
2. using
3. hiding
4. riding

Word Meaning

5. chased
6. liked
7. closed
8. named

Word Groups

9. hoping
10. baked

(229)

UNIT
35

Objectives *Children will*
- practice spelling list words
- apply spelling strategies
- identify synonyms
- classify Basic Words into groups

Day 2

Daily Proofreading Practice
Zak is **yuzing** finger paints. (*using*)
Our cat is **nammed** Snowball. (*named*)

Meeting Individual Needs
visual/auditory

Extra Support Check Independent Practice to determine who needs extra support. Write the following word "equation" on the board:

like + ed =

Read the equation. Cross out the final e in *like*, then write *liked* to complete the equation. Write equations for the remaining words, asking volunteers to follow your example in completing them.

Name _____   Level 2 / Unit 35 ▲

Basic Words	PRACTICE B
1. liked	**More Words with ed or ing**
2. hoping	**Proofreading** 1–4. Find and cross out four Basic
3. baked	Words that are spelled wrong in this news story. Write
4. using	each word correctly.
5. chased	
6. making	Chip Baker was namd Cook of the Year.
7. closed	He baked 1000 cookies in two hours.
8. hiding	Everyone liked the cookies. Next year
9. named	he will be making a new kind of
10. riding	cookie, useing nuts. He is hopeing
	the new cookies will be even better.

1. named   2. using
3. making   4. hoping

Word Search Write a Basic Word for each clue. Then find the word in the puzzle and circle it.

5. cooked   8. shut
6. covering up   9. moving on a bike
7. enjoyed   10. followed

5. baked
6. hiding
7. liked
8. closed
9. riding
10. chased

k e l c l o s e d y
v p u r i d i n g q
l e b a k e d r n c
c h a s e d t w i e
o b h i d i n g f s

164

Applying Spelling Strategies
To Spell New Words

- Read aloud: **I almost choked from eating too fast.**
- Have children attempt to spell *choked* on their Have-a-Go charts.

I know that the |ch| sound is spelled *ch*.

choked

I hear the long *o* sound followed by the |k| sound. I think this is probably spelled with the vowel-consonant-*e* pattern *o-k-e*.

- Elicit the following strategies as children try to spell *choked*.

Because the base word *choke* is spelled with the vowel-consonant-*e* pattern, I know I have to drop the final e before I write the ending *-ed*.

Day 3

Objectives *Children will*

■ identify the dictionary entry that would list a given verb form

■ review Basic and Review Words

Daily Proofreading Practice

Anita **likt** to jump rope. (*liked*)

We are **makeing** a snowman. (*making*)

Dictionary

Dictionary
1. make
2. name
3. chase
4. ride
5. use
6. close

ABC Words
7. using
8. sleep
9. liked
10. hoping
11. closed
12. hiding

230

Dictionary

Finding Words with Endings Remember that words with endings like **ed** and **ing** are usually listed in the dictionary with their base word. To find **hoping**, you would look up the entry word **hope**.

entry word

hope To wish for something: *I hope that I will win this race.* **hoped, hoping**

words with endings

Practice Write the entry word you would look up to find each of these words in the dictionary.

1. making   3. chased   5. using
2. named   4. riding   6. closed

Review: Spelling Spree

ABC Words Use ABC order to write the missing letter in each group. Make Basic or Review Words.

7. t _ v   r _ t   h _ j   m _ o   f _ h
8. r _ t   k _ m   d _ f   d _ f   o _ q
9. k _ m   h _ j   j _ l   d _ f   c _ e
10. g _ i   n _ p   o _ q   h _ j   m _ o   f _ h
11. b _ d   k _ m   n _ p   r _ t   d _ f   c _ e
12. g _ i   h _ j   c _ e   h _ j   m _ o   f _ h

How Are You Doing?

Write each spelling word in a sentence. Practice with a family member any words you spelled wrong.

TEACHING OPTIONS

Cooperative Learning Activity

Friendly Pairs

visual/kinesthetic

Invite children to work together to make paper people. Have them fold a piece of colored paper in half and draw a person on one half. Explain that one arm of the person must touch the fold. With the paper still folded, children cut out the figure, being sure not to cut through the fold where the arm touches.

Children then unfold their paper figures. They write a spelling word on one and its base word on the other. Small groups might enjoy making a friendship chain by taping all their paper people together.

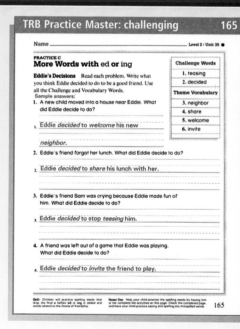

TRB Practice Master: challenging   165

Proofreading and Writing

Proofread for Spelling Proofread this page from a television guide. Use proofreading marks to fix six spelling mistakes.

Example: Wag loves to ~~slep~~ sleep on Pete's bed.

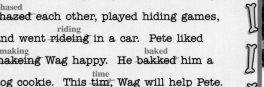

For Pete's Sake is about a boy ~~naemd~~ named Pete and his dog, Wag. Last week, they ~~chazed~~ chased each other, played hiding games, and went ~~rideing~~ riding in a car. Pete liked ~~makeing~~ making Wag happy. He ~~bakked~~ baked him a dog cookie. This ~~tim~~ time, Wag will help Pete.

Watch and find out how!

Write a Story

Write a story about a time when you had a problem and a friend helped you. Try to use spelling words. Draw pictures to go with your story. Share your story with a friend.

Proofreading Tip Read your paper again. Put a check mark on each word to show that you have looked at it.

231

Basic

1. liked
2. hoping
3. baked
4. using
5. chased
6. making
7. closed
8. hiding
9. named
10. riding

Review

11. time
12. sleep

Challenge

13. teasing
14. decided

Proofreading Marks

∧ Add
⌐ Delete
≡ Make a capital letter
/ Make a small letter

Objectives *Children will*

- proofread for spelling
- write and proofread an original composition

Day 4

Daily Proofreading Practice

Is he **hidding** behind the tree? (*hiding*)
She **clozd** the big red doors. (*closed*)

Day 5 **Posttest**

Sentences 1–5 test the first five Basic Words. Sentences 6–10 test the next five Basic Words.

Basic Words

1. Can you fix the saw I am <u>using</u>?
2. This food was <u>baked</u>.
3. The children are <u>hoping</u> for a puppy.
4. A cat <u>chased</u> a mouse.
5. My mother <u>liked</u> the play.
6. The baby was <u>named</u> after his father.
7. This book is <u>making</u> me think.
8. A mouse is <u>hiding</u> in a hole.
9. The box is now <u>closed</u>.
10. My father is <u>riding</u> in a train.

Review Words

11. The puppy will go to <u>sleep</u>.
12. We had a good <u>time</u>.

Challenge Words

13. I <u>decided</u> to write a story.
14. My sister is always <u>teasing</u> me.

TRB Unit 35 Test   166

Name _____ Level 2 / Unit 35 ●▲

Unit 35 Test: More Words with ed or ing

Read each word group. Find the correctly spelled word to complete each group. Mark the letter next to that word.

Sample:
a trip
ⓐ facing
● taking
ⓒ takeng

Items 1–5 test Basic Words 1–5. Items 6–10 test Basic Words 6–10.

1. boiled or ____
ⓐ bakked
ⓑ backeg
● baked

2. ____ your head
● using
ⓑ ussig
ⓒ uzing

3. ____ that book
ⓐ likked
ⓑ liked
ⓒ liket

4. wishing and ____
ⓐ hoping
ⓑ hopeink
ⓒ hopeng

5. ____ up a tree
ⓐ chasd
ⓑ chasaed
ⓒ chased

6. ____ and seeking
ⓐ hideing
ⓑ hiding
ⓒ hidding

7. a dog ____ Frank
ⓐ namd
ⓑ nammed
ⓒ named

8. ____ a mud pie
ⓐ making
ⓑ mackcing
ⓒ makeind

9. ____ the door
ⓐ closd
ⓑ clozed
ⓒ closed

10. ____ a horse
ⓐ riddign
ⓑ riding
ⓒ rideig

166

Meeting Individual Needs

Challenge Words Practice Ask children to make acrostic puzzles. Have them write each Challenge Word vertically, then use each letter to begin a phrase that tells something friends do.

Another Writing Idea Have children use spelling words to write questions they could use to interview a friend. (Examples: Do you like <u>riding</u> bikes? Have you ever <u>baked</u> a cake?) Suggest children conduct their interviews.

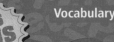

These pages can be used at any time during the study of this unit.

Day by Day Planner

Objectives *Children will*

■ build words with the suffix *-ful*

■ write words with the suffix *-ful* to replace phrases

Unit 35 BONUS

Vocabulary Enrichment

Word Builder

Building Words with *ful* When you add **ful** to a word, it changes the meaning of the word.

hope + ful = hope**ful**

The word **hopeful** means "full of hope."

Spelling Word Link
hoping

Finish the chart below.

1. help + ful =   helpful

2. thank + ful =   thankful

3. play + ful =   playful

4. pain + ful =   painful

Work Together Make these sentences easier to read. Write a word that means the same as each group of words in dark print. Use the words you made in the chart. Work with a friend.

5. Rina's new kitten is **full of play**.

6. David is **full of help** around the house.

7. Dad was **full of thanks** when the car started.

8. My broken foot is **full of pain** when I stand on it.

5. playful	7. thankful
6. helpful	8. painful

232

EXTENSION OPTIONS

Learning Center Activity
visual/kinesthetic

A Friendship Quilt Cut out large squares of colored paper. Have each child select one to make a quilt square. The square should include a word that ends with the suffix *-ful* and a sentence or sentences that use the word. The sentence should tell about friend-ship in general or about a specific person or pet who is a friend. Children might decorate their word or cut the letters from magazines. They might also add illustrations to their square. Post the squares on a bulletin board to form a friendship quilt.

More *-ful* Words			
bashful	forgetful	mouthful	spoonful
careful	graceful	peaceful	useful
cheerful	handful	powerful	watchful
fearful	joyful	skillful	wonderful

Vocabulary Enrichment

Unit 35 BONUS

Social Studies

Friendship All the words in the box have something to do with friendship. Write those words to finish this note. Use your Spelling Dictionary.

Spelling Word Link

liked

neighbor
share
welcome
invite

Dear Ariana,
    Can you come to my house on Sunday? My new __(1)__ moved in next door. I will __(2)__ her to play with us. We can make her feel __(3)__ . We can __(4)__ our toys with her.
                        Sarah

1. neighbor

2. invite

3. welcome

4. share

Try This CHALLENGE

Write a Play Write a short play about two people who are best friends. Tell about some of the things that they do together. Try to use words from the box on this page.

★ Fact File

Eleanor Roosevelt was a special friend to people who needed help. The wife of a president, she worked to make life better for people all over the world.

233

Objectives *Children will*

- expand their vocabulary by using words related to friendship
- show their understanding of the vocabulary words by completing context and writing activities

Vocabulary Checkup

Have children use the vocabulary words in sentences or match the words to the definitions below.

1. to ask someone to come somewhere or do something *invite*
2. a person who lives next door to or near another *neighbor*
3. to have, use, or do with another or others *share*
4. greeted or accepted warmly *welcome*

Fact File

Eleanor Roosevelt and Marian Anderson

In 1939, Marian Anderson, a famous singer, was not allowed to perform in Washington's Constitution Hall because she was black. Eleanor Roosevelt helped arrange for Anderson to sing from the steps of the Lincoln Memorial instead, where a huge crowd gathered to hear her. Later that year, Anderson was awarded the Spingarn Medal for her achievements.

Integrating Literature

Easy	Average	Challenging
Yo! Yes? *by Chris Raschka* Two boys meet on the street and decide to become friends.	**Gina** *by Bernard Waber* A new girl in the neighborhood makes friends with the boys.	**Metropolitan Cow** *by Tim Egan* Bennet the cow makes friends with his new neighbor, Webster the pig.
Jamaica and Brianna *by Juanita Havill* Jamaica is jealous of her friend Brianna's new boots.	**The Iguana Brothers** *by Tony Johnston* Two iguana brothers discover that they can be best friends.	**Gooseberry Park** *by Cynthia Rylant* An unusual trio of animal friends work to reunite a squirrel and her babies.

Review: Units 31–35

WORD LISTS

Spelling

Basic Words

Unit 31	Unit 34
start	running
arm	clapped
far	getting
barn	shopping
hard	stepped
party	pinned

Unit 32	Unit 35
store	liked
corn	hoping
or	chased
morning	making
short	named
story	riding

Unit 33

flower
water
better
sister
father
after

Elephant Words

Units 31–35

are	your
warm	missed
four	telling

The Review Unit

Word Lists

Half of the Basic Words from Units 31–35 are reviewed in this Review Unit. The remaining Basic Words from Units 31–35 are reviewed in the Extra Practice section of the Student's Handbook. All of the Elephant Words are practiced in both the Review Unit and the Extra Practice section.

 Day 1 *page 234*

Objectives *Children will*
- take the pretest
- review a spelling pattern for the |är| sound
- review spelling patterns for the |ôr| sound

Planning Checklist
- ☐ Daily Proofreading Practice (TE)
- ☐ Extra Support, pages 205, 211 (TE)
- ☐ Extra Practice, page 256
- ☐ Practice Masters, pages 147, 148, 151, 152 (TRB)

Day 2 *page 235*

Objectives *Children will*
- review the *er* spelling for the |ər| sound in two-syllable words
- review adding *ed* and *ing*

Planning Checklist
- ☐ Daily Proofreading Practice (TE)
- ☐ Extra Support, pages 217, 223 (TE)
- ☐ Extra Practice, page 257
- ☐ Practice Masters, pages 155, 156, 159, 160 (TRB)

Assessment

Pretest
1. The car did not <u>start</u>.
2. I had fun at the <u>party</u>.
3. Please go to the <u>store</u>.
4. I see the sun in the <u>morning</u>.
5. Kim likes cold <u>water</u>.
6. I will go with my <u>sister</u>.
7. The cat is <u>running</u> fast.
8. He <u>stepped</u> on a bug.
9. I am <u>hoping</u> it will rain.
10. The puppy <u>chased</u> the frog.

Teacher's Resource Book
Practice Masters, pages 147–149, 151–153, 155–157, 159–161, 163–165
Multiple-Choice Tests, pages 172–173
Bulletin Board, page 167
Spelling Newsletters, English and Spanish, pages 168–169
Spelling Game, pages 170–171
End-of-Year Test, pages 175–176

Practice Plus
 Take-Home Word List 36
Spelling Transparencies
Spelling Word List 36
Daily Proofreading Practice, Unit 36
Spelling-Meaning Strategy
Multiple-Choice Test

Teacher's Resource Disk
Macintosh® or Windows® software. Houghton Mifflin

Spelling CD-ROM
Macintosh® or Windows® software. Houghton Mifflin

Internet
http://www.eduplace.com

Day 3 *page 236*

Objectives *Children will*
• review adding *ed* and *ing*
• review the Elephant Words

Planning Checklist

☐ Daily Proofreading Practice (TE)

☐ Extra Support, page 229 (TE)

☐ Extra Practice, page 258

☐ Practice Masters, pages 163, 164 (TRB)

Day 4 *page 237*

Objective *Children will*
• analyze the spelling and meaning relationship of words in the *farm* word family

Planning Checklist

☐ Spelling-Meaning Strategy

Day 5 *page 237*

Objective *Children will*
• take the posttest

Assessment

☐ **Posttest** (TE) *See Day 5*

☐ Scoring Rubric

☐ Unit 36 Review Tests A–B (TRB)

Meeting Individual Needs

You may wish to create your own pretest, using the words that children missed most often in the last five units. Children can check their own work, or a partner's, by looking up the words in the previous units' word lists or in their Spelling Dictionary. In each Review lesson, the Basic Words are selected from both halves of the unit word list to accommodate individual needs. In Units 31–35, the top row of words is from Basic Words 1–5 and the bottom row from Basic Words 6–10.

Other Activities for Any Day

• Literature and Writing, pages 238–239

• Spelling Game
Teacher's Resource Book, pages 170–171

• Bulletin Board
Teacher's Resource Book, page 167

• Take-Home Word List 36
Practice Plus

Objectives *Children will*

- take the pretest
- review a spelling pattern for the |är| sound
- review spelling patterns for the |ôr| sound

Daily Proofreading Practice

The lid was **harde** to twist off. (*hard*)

A toy **stor** is beside the school. (*store*)

Meeting Individual Needs

Additional Resources

Unit 31

Extra Support page 205 (TE)

Extra Practice page 256

Practice Masters pages 147–148 (TRB)

Unit 32

Extra Support page 211 (TE)

Extra Practice page 256

Practice Masters pages 151–152 (TRB)

---

36 Review: Units 31–35

Unit 31   Vowel + r Sound in car   pages 204–209

start	arm	far
barn	hard	party

1. hard

2. far

3. start

4. arm

5. party

6. barn

Spelling Strategy The vowel + **r** sound in **far** is spelled **ar**.

Write the spelling word that means the opposite.

1. easy   **2.** near   **3.** stop

Write the missing spelling words.

The doctor took the cast off Maya's **(4)** today. Tomorrow we will have a big **(5)** for her in our **(6)**.

Unit 32   Vowel + r Sound in store   pages 210–215

store	corn	or
morning	short	story

7. store

8. short

9. morning

10. story

11. or

12. corn

Spelling Strategy The vowel + **r** sound in **corn** and **store** is spelled **or** or **ore**.

Write the spelling word that means the same.

7. shop   **8.** small

Write the missing spelling words.

Every **(9)** I read a **(10)** as I eat breakfast. I like to eat toast **(11)** a big **(12)** muffin.

234

EXTENSION OPTIONS

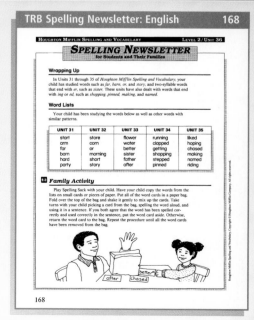

Unit 33   Words Ending with er   pages 216–221

flower	water	better
sister	father	after

er water

er flower

Spelling Strategy

The vowel + **r** sound at the end of **flower** is spelled **er**.

Write the spelling word that goes with each word.

13. man   15. girl
14. garden   16. river

Write the missing spelling words.

17. We went to the park _____ school.
18. Jill can climb the bars _____ than anyone.

Unit 34   Words with ed or ing   pages 222–227

running	clapped	getting
shopping	stepped	pinned

Spelling Strategy

run + ing → ru**nn**ing
clap + ed → cla**pp**ed

Change the letters in dark print. Write spelling words.

19. **st**opping   21. **tr**apped
20. **p**etting   22. ru**bb**ing

Write the missing spelling words.

23. I stood on a chair as Gram _____ my skirt.
24. Then I _____ down and changed my clothes.

---

13. father
_____

14. flower
_____

15. sister
_____

16. water
_____

17. after
_____

18. better
_____

19. shopping
_____

20. getting
_____

21. clapped
_____

22. running
_____

23. pinned
_____

24. stepped
_____

235

Day 2

Objectives *Children will*

- review the *er* spelling for the |ər| sound in two-syllable words
- review adding *-ed* and *-ing*

Daily Proofreading Practice

My **sistir** made me a mask. (*sister*)
I like **runing** on the beach. (*running*)

Meeting Individual Needs

Additional Resources

Unit 33

Extra Support page 217 (TE)

Extra Practice page 257

Practice Masters pages 155–156 (TRB)

Unit 34

Extra Support page 223 (TE)

Extra Practice page 257

Practice Masters pages 159–160 (TRB)

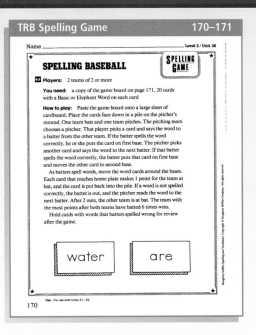

UNIT **36** Review

Day 3

Objectives *Children will*

- review adding *-ed* and *-ing*
- review the Elephant Words

Daily Proofreading Practice

Julia is **rideing** the pony. (*riding*)
I was late and **misst** the bus.
(*missed*)

Meeting Individual Needs

Additional Resources

Unit 35

Extra Support page 229 (TE)

Extra Practice page 258

Practice Masters pages 163–164 (TRB)

Reviewing Elephant Words

Extra Practice page 258

UNIT
36

25. making

26. hoping

27. liked

28. named

29. chased

30. riding

31. four

32. are

33. warm

34. missed

35. your

36. telling

236

Unit 35   More Words with ed **or** ing   **pages 228–233**

bak **ed**
e

liked	hoping	chased
making	named	riding

Spelling Strategy

like + ed → liked
name + ed → named
hope + ing → hoping
ride + ing → riding

Write the spelling word that rhymes with each word.
25. taking   26. roping   27. hiked

Write the missing spelling words.
Grandpa's dog was ___(28)___ Frisky. He always ___(29)___
us when we were ___(30)___ our bikes.

Elephant Words   Units 31–35   pages 204–233

are

are	warm	four
your	missed	telling

Spelling Strategy   Elephant Words have unusual
spellings. Check them carefully when you write them.

Write the missing spelling words.
The ___(31)___ of us ___(32)___ playing tag to keep
___(33)___. I just ___(34)___ tagging ___(35)___ coat with
my hand. You keep ___(36)___ me that you can run faster
than I can, but we will see!

EXTENSION **OPTIONS**

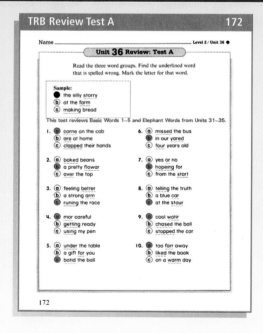
TRB Review Test A   172

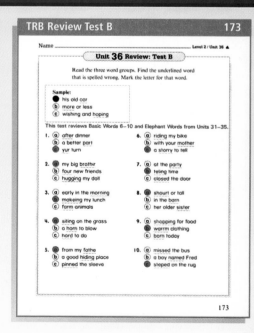
TRB Review Test B   173

UNIT
36

Spelling-Meaning Strategy

Word Families

You know that words in the same family are alike in spelling and meaning. Look at this word family.

farm	Miss Green lives on a **farm**.
farmer	She is a cattle **farmer**.
farmland	She owns a lot of **farmland**.
farming	**Farming** is hard work.

Think How are the words in this family alike in meaning? How are they alike in spelling?

Apply and Extend

Write a word from the farm **family in each sentence.**
1. We visited a big _____ today.
2. There were many miles of _____.
3. The _____ showed us the fields.
4. We learned what hard work _____ is!

With a partner, think of words in these families. Make a list for each family. See TE margin.

 warm   **shop**   **hope**

Check the Word Families list that begins on page 272. Did you miss any words? Add them to your lists.

1. farm

2. farmland

3. farmer

4. farming

(237)

Day 4

Objective *Children will*
■ analyze the spelling and meaning relationship of words in the *farm* word family

Answers to *Think* Questions

- They all have some form of the meaning "a piece of land or a ranch on which crops and animals are raised."

- They all have a form of the word *farm*.

Day 5   **Posttest**

The Posttest tests twenty of the Basic Words reviewed in this unit. Sentences 1–10 test words selected from Basic Words 1–5 in Units 31–35. The Elephant Words sentences test all six words reviewed in this unit.

Basic Words
1. A bug was on my <u>arm</u>.
2. We went to the <u>store</u>.
3. Nan is <u>better</u> now.
4. The dog sat when I <u>clapped</u>.
5. I was <u>hoping</u> to see you there.
6. When will the game <u>start</u>?
7. My pet is <u>getting</u> old.
8. He <u>liked</u> the bike.
9. I see a red <u>flower</u>.
10. Ted ate some <u>corn</u>.
11. I washed the car this <u>morning</u>.
12. A mouse is in the <u>barn</u>.
13. The bed is too <u>short</u>.
14. Bring me to my <u>father</u>.
15. The children will go <u>shopping</u>.
16. The cat <u>stepped</u> on the box.
17. Can you see my <u>sister</u>?
18. The club had a <u>party</u>.
19. Have they <u>named</u> the baby?
20. They are <u>riding</u> bikes.

Elephant Words
21. The children <u>are</u> wet.
22. I have <u>four</u> names.
23. The bed is <u>warm</u>.
24. We <u>missed</u> the bus.
25. Dot is <u>telling</u> us about her cat.
26. I found <u>your</u> coat.

Day by Day Planner

Writing Model:
Letters

Objectives *Children will*

■ read a model of a friendly letter

■ analyze the model to evaluate the content of a friendly letter and to identify its parts

Warm-Up

Qualities of a Good Friendly Letter

Have children turn to the **Letter Model** on page 261. Together, review the five parts of a friendly letter. Then use these discussion prompts to help children think about letters that appeal to readers:

• What kinds of things might a reader enjoy learning about in a letter? Is it important to say something special to the reader? Why or why not?

• Name some different reasons you might write a letter. *(to say thank you; to say get well; to invite someone to a party)*

Answers to *Think and Discuss*

1. It is about what he and Wendell did together.
2. The five parts of a letter are the date, the greeting, the body, the closing, and the name.
3. The date tells when the letter was written.
4. The name tells who wrote the letter.

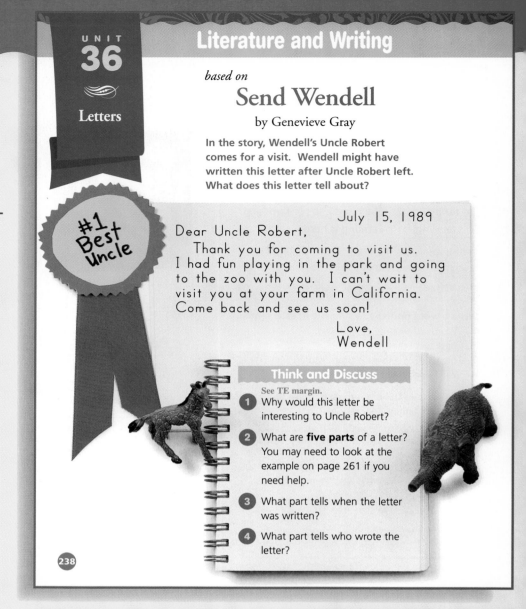

UNIT
36
Letters

Literature and Writing

based on

Send Wendell

by Genevieve Gray

In the story, Wendell's Uncle Robert comes for a visit. Wendell might have written this letter after Uncle Robert left. What does this letter tell about?

#1 Best Uncle

July 15, 1989

Dear Uncle Robert,
   Thank you for coming to visit us. I had fun playing in the park and going to the zoo with you. I can't wait to visit you at your farm in California. Come back and see us soon!

Love,
Wendell

Think and Discuss

See TE margin.

1 Why would this letter be interesting to Uncle Robert?

2 What are **five parts** of a letter? You may need to look at the example on page 261 if you need help.

3 What part tells when the letter was written?

4 What part tells who wrote the letter?

238

EXTENSION OPTIONS

Integrating Literature *Letters*

Easy	Average	Challenging
A Letter to Amy *by Ezra Jack Keats* Peter's letter to Amy causes a run-in with a pleasant ending.	**Dear Peter Rabbit** *by Alma Flor Ada* Storybook characters send letters back and forth to each other.	**Stringbean's Trip to the Shining Sea** *by Vera Williams* A boy sends post cards home during a trip to the West Coast.
Arthur's Pen Pal *by Lillian Hoban* Arthur the chimp is surprised to discover his pen pal is a girl.	**Good-bye, Curtis** *by Kevin Henkes* The family and friends of a letter carrier surprise him with a retirement party.	**Here Comes the Mail** *by Gloria Skurzynski* The story of how mail gets from one place to another.

The Writing Process
Letters

Who do you think would like to get a letter from you? Write a letter to that person. Follow the guidelines. Use the Writing Process.

1 Prewriting
• Make a list of questions to answer in your letter.

2 Draft
• Pretend that the person you are writing to is sitting next to you. Write your letter as if you were talking to that person.

3 Revise
• Add words or sentences that will make your letter more interesting.
• Remember to use your Thesaurus to find exact words.
• Read your letter to a friend. Make changes.

4 Proofread
• Did you spell each word correctly?
• Did you use commas correctly?

5 Publish
• Copy your letter, and address an envelope. Mail your letter.

Guidelines for Writing a Letter

✓ Be sure to include all five parts of the letter.
✓ Use details that help your reader picture what you are writing about.

Composition Words

are
more
your
mother
missed
liked

Maria Cassa
12 Hill Road
Boston, MA
02138

239

Objective *Children will*

☐ follow the Writing Process to write a letter, using the criteria given in the guidelines

Additional Resource

To help children generate and explore topics for their letter, have them use the Prewriting Ideas in the *Teacher's Resource Book,* page 174.

Scoring Rubric

Evaluating Writing

The scoring rubric is based on the guidelines on the student book page. Mechanics and usage errors are also considered in general. Explain to children that the guidelines will be used to evaluate their papers.

TRB Prewriting Ideas 174

Name _____ Level 2 / Unit 36

Prewriting Ideas: Letters

Choosing a Topic Here is a list of ideas that one student made for writing a letter. What ideas of your own do they give you?
On the lines below **My Three Ideas**, write three ideas that you would like to tell someone about in a letter. Which idea do you like the best? Will it interest the person that you are writing to? Circle the idea that you would like to write about.

Ideas for Writing

| My Trip to the Zoo | Why I Like Camp |
| My New Baby Brother | My Long Plane Ride |

My Three Ideas

1. _____
2. _____
3. _____

Exploring Your Topic You can use a stamp cluster to help you plan whom you will write to and what you want to say. Copy the cluster onto another sheet of paper. Make it large enough to write on. Write your topic in the big stamp. Use the smaller stamps to write some details about your idea and to tell who will get your letter.

person I will write to — Topic — detail — detail — detail

Use: For use with Step 1: Prewriting on page 239.

174

Scoring Rubric

Letters

Score 4

All five parts of the friendly letter are in place and are used correctly. The writer conveys information creatively and includes details that add interest and charm to the letter. The letter expresses the personality of the writer.

Score 3

All five parts of the friendly letter are used correctly. The letter conveys information to the reader, and some details are used.

Score 2

The work is in the form of a letter, but the writer may not have used all five parts of the letter form. The writer has not used details to make the events clear for the reader.

Score 1

The work is not a friendly letter. It does not follow the friendly-letter form. The writing does not focus on any particular topic, and it is hard to understand.

Student's Handbook

Extra Practice and Review   Cycle 1

Unit 1   Spelling the Short a Sound   pages 24–29

hat	bag	as
bat	sat	bad

ă
hat

Spelling Strategy   The short a sound may be spelled **a**.

Write the spelling word that goes with each word.

1. chair   **2.** ball   **3.** head

Write the missing spelling words.

Tilly left the store with a big ___(4)___ of food.
Just ___(5)___ she stepped outside, she tripped.
That was a ___(6)___ way to start the day!

Unit 2   Spelling the Short e Sound   pages 30–35

pet	ten	bed
help	set	went

ĕ
pet

Spelling Strategy   The short e sound may be spelled **e**.

Change the letter in dark print. Write a spelling word.

7. **d**en   **9.** **b**ad
8. **s**at   **10.** **s**ent

Write the missing spelling words.

Ben and I are going to a special zoo. We can ___(11)___ the animals' soft fur. We can even ___(12)___ feed the baby sheep and goats!

1. sat

2. bat

3. hat

4. bag

5. as

6. bad

7. ten

8. set

9. bed

10. went

11. pet

12. help

241

Extra Practice and Review

Cycle 1

13. hit

14. six

15. dig

16. win

17. is

18. pin

19. mop

20. pot

21. fox

22. nod

23. spot

24. not

Unit 3   Spelling the Short i Sound   pages 36–41

ǐ
pig

win	is	six
hit	pin	dig

Spelling Strategy

The short **i** sound may be spelled **i**.

Write the spelling word that rhymes with each word.

13. sit   **14.** mix   **15.** big

Write the missing spelling words.

16. Will Joe _____ a prize for his pumpkin?

17. The prize _____ a big blue ribbon.

18. Joe can _____ the ribbon to his shirt.

Unit 4   Spelling the Short o Sound   pages 42–47

ǒ
top

pot	nod	not
fox	mop	spot

Spelling Strategy

The short **o** sound may be spelled **o**.

Write a spelling word for each clue.

19. You use it to clean.   **21.** It has a bushy tail.

20. You use it to cook.   **22.** Your head does this.

Write the missing spelling words.

23. My broken pen left a _____ on my shirt.

24. I could _____ clean the ink off.

242

Cycle 1

Unit 5   Spelling the Short u Sound   pages 48–53

sun	mud	bug
bun	nut	bus

ŭ
sun

Spelling Strategy   The short **u** sound may be spelled **u**.

Write the spelling word for each clue.

25. ant   **26.** dirt   **27.** acorn

Write the missing spelling words.

28. Dad and I ride on the _____ to the beach.

29. The _____ is beginning to shine.

30. I eat a soft _____ from our basket.

Elephant Words   Units 1–5   pages 24–53

want	any	said
I	some	from

any

Spelling Strategy   Elephant Words have unusual spellings. Check them carefully when you write them.

Write the missing spelling words.

Mom and __(31)__ saw __(32)__ people making juice. They made it __(33)__ oranges. Mom __(34)__ that a machine took out all the seeds. I didn't find __(35)__ seeds at all. I __(36)__ a machine like that!

25. bug

26. mud

27. nut

28. bus

29. sun

30. bun

31. I

32. some

33. from

34. said

35. any

36. want

243

Extra Practice and Review

Cycle 2

Unit 7   **Vowel-Consonant-e**   **pages 60–65**

ī
five

late	nine	made
fine	same	hide

Spelling Strategy   The long **a** and the long **i** vowel sounds may be spelled by the vowel-consonant-**e** pattern.

Write a spelling word that means the opposite.
1. different   **3.** early
2. find   **4.** sick

Write the missing spelling words.
5. We _____ a list of birds that we saw today.
6. I counted _____ different kinds of birds!

Unit 8   **More Vowel-Consonant-e**   **pages 66–71**

ō
bone

use	these	rope
home	close	those

Spelling Strategy   The long **o**, **u**, and **e** vowel sounds may be spelled by the vowel-consonant-**e** pattern.

Change the letter in dark print. Write a spelling word.
7. **c**hose   **8.** ro**l**e   **9.** ho**s**e

Write the missing spelling words.
    Do you want to __(10)__ any of __(11)__ balloons right here? I think __(12)__ over there are prettier.

_____

1. same

2. hide

3. late

4. fine

5. made

6. nine

7. close

8. rope

9. home

10. use

11. these

12. those

244

Cycle 2

Unit 9   **Consonant Clusters**   pages 72–77

swim	step	nest
brave	glad	lost

sw
swim

Spelling Strategy   A **consonant cluster** is two consonant letters whose sounds are blended together.

Write the spelling word that goes with each word.

13. bird   **15.** foot

14. smile   **16.** pool

Write the missing spelling words.

17. One day I got _____ in the park.

18. I was _____ and did not get scared.

Unit 10 **Words Spelled with** k **or** ck **pages 78–83**

rock	pick	truck
bake	clock	kick

k
lake

Spelling Strategy   The final consonant sound in **bake** and **rock** may be spelled **k** or **ck**.

Write the spelling word you see in each longer word.

19. bakery   **20.** kickstand   **21.** pickle

Write the missing spelling words.

We used a __(22)__ to move broken things. A wheel hit a __(23)__, and an old __(24)__ began to tick!

13. nest

14. glad

15. step

16. swim

17. lost

18. brave

19. bake

20. kick

21. pick

22. truck

23. rock

24. clock

(245)

Extra Practice and Review   Cycle 2

Unit 11   Double Consonants   pages 84–89

gg
egg

bell	off	dress
will	grass	tell

Spelling Strategy   A final consonant sound may be spelled with two letters that are the same.

Write the spelling word that rhymes with each word.

25. pass   **26.** mess   **27.** fill

Write the missing spelling words.

We heard the ___(28)___ ring. Then Ms. Day came to ___(29)___ us it was time to get ___(30)___ the swings.

Elephant Words   Units 7–11   pages 60–89

O N E

give	have
one	goes

Spelling Strategy   Elephant Words have unusual spellings. Check them carefully when you write them.

Write the missing words. Use some words two times.

I ___(31)___ my library card to the man. He ___(32)___ to check my name. I already ___(33)___ two books, but I can take ___(34)___ more. I ___(35)___ to decide between two books. Which ___(36)___ should I take?

25. grass

26. dress

27. will

28. bell

29. tell

30. off

31. give

32 goes

33. have

34. one

35. have

36. one

Cycle 3

Unit 13   More Long a Spellings   page 96–101

way	play	trail
sail	hay	nail

ā
train

Spelling Strategy   The long a sound may be spelled **ay** or **ai**.

Write the spelling word that is hidden in each box.

1. tshaymle   **2.** adlplaymi   **3.** osptrailyk

Write the missing spelling words.

The ___(4)___ on our boat is torn. It ripped on a sharp ___(5)___ on the ___(6)___ to our picnic.

Unit 14   More Long e Spellings   pages 102–107

keep	please	we
eat	tree	mean

ē
clean

Spelling Strategy   The long e sound may be spelled **e**, **ee**, or **ea**.

Write the spelling words that go with the words.

7. food   **9.** thank-you
8. save   **10.** leaf

Write the missing spelling words.

11. At school _____ are learning about words.
12. The word **bat** can _____ different things.

1. hay

2. play

3. trail

4. sail

5. nail

6. way

7. eat

8. keep

9. please

10. tree

11. we

12. mean

247

Extra Practice and Review   Cycle 3

Unit 15   The Vowel Sound in ball   pages 108–113

a
ball

| paw | call | ball |
| small | log | fall |

Spelling Strategy

The vowel sound in **ball** may be spelled **o**, **aw**, or **a** before **ll**.

Write the spelling word for each clue.

13. tiny   **14.** foot   **15.** wood   **16.** shout

Write the missing spelling words.

17. Jeff hit the _____ high into the air.

18. We watched it _____ into the bushes.

13. small

14. paw

15. log

16. call

17. ball

18. fall

Unit 16   Words with sh or ch   pages 114–119

sh
sheep

| chase | wish | much |
| such | wash | ship |

Spelling Strategy

the **sh** sound → **sh**ip, wi**sh**

the **ch** sound → **ch**ase, mu**ch**

Write the spelling word that rhymes with each word.

19. clip   **20.** fish   **21.** case

Write the missing spelling words.

Fido splashes too __(22)__ soap and water on us.

It is __(23)__ hard work to __(24)__ him!

19. ship

20. wish

21. chase

22. much

23. such

24. wash

248

Cycle 3

Unit 17 **Words with** th **or** wh **pages 120–125**

when	then	with
what	while	which

th
teeth

Spelling Strategy the **th** sounds → wi**th**, **th**en
the **wh** sound → **wh**en

Change the letters in dark print. Write spelling words.

25. wi**ll**   **26.** **th**an   **27.** **sm**ile

Write the missing spelling words.

Now __(28)__ will I do? I can't tell __(29)__ fish is mine __(30)__ they all swim together!

Elephant Words **Units 13–17** **pages 96–125**

they	great	the
people	catch	sure

S U R E

Spelling Strategy Elephant Words have unusual spellings. Check them carefully when you write them.

Write the missing spelling words.

Many __(31)__ came to __(32)__ fishing contest. Everyone was __(33)__ that Jill would __(34)__ the most fish. Later, we had a cookout. We cooked every fish, and __(35)__ all tasted __(36)__!

25. with

26. then

27. while

28. what

29. which

30. when

31. people

32. the

33. sure

34. catch

35. they

36. great

249

Extra Practice and Review

Cycle 4

Unit 19 Words with nd, ng, or nk pages 132–137

ng
king

king	thank	hand
think	long	thing

Spelling Strategy

Some words end with the consonants **nd**, **ng**, or **nk**.

Write the spelling word that goes with each word.

1. finger **2.** idea **3.** crown

Write the missing spelling words.

I wrote a ___(4)___ letter to ___(5)___ Papa. I wish I knew the name of the ___(6)___ he sent me!

Unit 20 Words with s or es pages 138–143

bikes
es

dishes	bells	boxes
wishes	things	names

Spelling Strategy

s → bell**s**, name**s**

es → di**sh**es, bo**x**es

Write the spelling word that rhymes with each word.

7. smells **8.** wings **9.** flames

Write the missing spelling words.

Kate took the tops off the ___(10)___. Inside were toy cups and ___(11)___! Her ___(12)___ had come true!

1. hand
2. think
3. king
4. long
5. thank
6. thing
7. bells
8. things
9. names
10. boxes
11. dishes
12. wishes

250

Cycle 4

Unit 21   More Long o Spellings   pages 144–149

boat	cold	no
coat	grow	show

ō
boat

Spelling Strategy   The long **o** sound may be spelled **o**, **oa**, or **ow**.

Write the spelling word for each meaning.

13. to get big   **14.** a ship   **15.** to point out

Write the missing spelling words.

Len buttoned his __(16)__. The __(17)__ air made his ears sting. He had __(18)__ hat for his head!

Unit 22   Sounds in moon and book   pages 150–155

zoo	food	book
soon	good	foot

oo
book

ōō
moon

Spelling Strategy   The vowel sounds in **food** and **book** may be spelled **oo**.

Write the spelling word you see in each longer word.

19. cookbook   **20.** football   **21.** goodness

Write the missing spelling words.

We visited the seals at the __(22)__. We gave them some __(23)__. I hope we can go back __(24)__!

13. grow

14. boat

15. show

16. coat

17. cold

18. no

19. book

20. foot

21. good

22. zoo

23. food

24. soon

251

Extra Practice and Review

Cycle 4

25. plain

26. hole

27. plane

28. whole

29. rode

30. road

31. who

32. to

33. toe

34. two

35. you

36. too

Unit 23	Homophones	pages 156–161

plain   plane

plane	plain	rode
road	hole	whole

Spelling Strategy   **Homophones** sound alike but do not have the same spelling or the same meaning.

Change the letters in dark print. Write spelling words.

25. **tr**ain   26. hol**d**   27. plate   28. **st**ole

Write the missing spelling words.

29. We _____ in a special parade car.

30. People by the side of the _____ waved.

Elephant Words	Units 19–23	pages 132–161

who

toe	you	who
to	too	two

Spelling Strategy   Elephant Words have unusual spellings. Check them carefully when you write them.

I am looking for someone __(31)__ can teach me how __(32)__ dance. Each time I try, I step on my own __(33)__. I cannot make my __(34)__ feet work together! Maybe __(35)__ have this problem __(36)__!

Cycle 5

Unit 25　More Long i Spellings　pages 168–173

sky	find	night
try	right	kind

ī
fly

Spelling Strategy　The long **i** sound may be spelled **y**, **i**, or **igh**.

Write the spelling word that means the same.

1. evening　　**2.** correct　　**3.** friendly

Write the missing spelling words.

Tonight the ___(**4**)___ is full of stars. Tina and I will ___(**5**)___ to ___(**6**)___ the Dog Star.

Unit 26　Final Sound in puppy　pages 174–179

puppy	lucky	happy
funny	many	only

ē
puppy

Spelling Strategy　The long **e** sound at the end of a two-syllable word may be spelled **y**.

Change the letters in the dark print. Write spelling words.

7. **b**unny　　**8.** ha**nd**y　　**9.** lu**mp**y

Write the missing spelling words.

The tiny ___(**10**)___ was sleepy. It was ___(**11**)___ one week old. It had ___(**12**)___ things to learn!

___

1. night

2. right

3. kind

4. sky

5. try

6. find

7. funny

8. happy

9. lucky

10. puppy

11. only

12. many

(253)

Extra Practice and Review

Cycle 5

Unit 27   The Vowel Sound in cow   pages 180–185

ow
cow

| town | house | cow |
| how | mouse | brown |

Spelling Strategy   The vowel sound in **brown** and **mouse** may be spelled **ow** or **ou**.

Write the spelling word that goes with each word.
13. calf   **14.** color   **15.** home   **16.** city

Write the missing spelling words.
17. I saw a _____ run across the floor.
18. I wonder _____ it got in here!

Unit 28   Compound Words   pages 186–191

bathtub

| bedtime | myself | maybe |
| upon | anyone | without |

Spelling Strategy   A **compound word** is a word that is made up of two shorter words.

Change the word in dark print. Write a spelling word.
19. any**thing**   **20.** bed**room**   **21.** **your**self

Write the missing spelling words.
Look at the bird sitting ___**(22)**___ that branch.
Oh, ___**(23)**___ you can't see it ___**(24)**___ these glasses.

13. cow

14. brown

15. house

16. town

17. mouse

18. how

19. anyone

20. bedtime

21. myself

22. upon

23. maybe

24. without

254

Cycle 5

Unit 29   Contractions   pages 192–197

I'll	you're	isn't
didn't	I've	we'll

Spelling Strategy   I + <u>will</u> → **I'll**

is + n<u>ot</u> → **isn't**

Write the contraction for each pair of words.

25. did not   **26.** we will   **27.** you are

Write the missing spelling words.

I think ___**(28)**___ need a new coat soon. The one that ___**(29)**___ been wearing ___**(30)**___ big enough.

Elephant Words   Units 25–29   pages 168–197

eye	buy	cookie
could	should	can't

Spelling Strategy   Elephant Words have unusual spellings. Check them carefully when you write them.

Write the missing spelling words.

Mom lets me ___**(31)**___ a ___**(32)**___ at the bakery. I ___**(33)**___ decide which one I want. I wish I ___**(34)**___ take them all. Maybe I ___**(35)**___ just close one ___**(36)**___ and choose without looking!

25. didn't

26. we'll

27. you're

28. I'll

29. I've

30. isn't

31. buy

32. cookie

33. can't

34. could

35. should

36. eye

255

Extra Practice and Review

Cycle 6

1. part
2. car
3. barn
4. farm
5. yard
6. start
7. more
8. short
9. store
10. horn
11. for
12. born

Unit 31   Vowel + r Sound in car   pages 204–209

car	start	yard
part	barn	farm

Spelling Strategy   The vowel + **r** sound in **car** is spelled **ar**.

Change the letter in dark print. Write a spelling word.
1. par**k**   2. **j**ar   3. **y**arn   4. **h**arm

Write the missing spelling words.
5. I have a small garden in my back _____.
6. I will _____ planting seeds there soon.

Unit 32   Vowel + r Sound in store   pages 210–215

store	for	more
short	born	horn

Spelling Strategy   The vowel + **r** sound in **for** and **store** is spelled **or** or **ore**.

Write the spelling word that means the opposite.
7. less   8. long

Write the missing spelling words.
    Jed went to the __(**9**)__ and bought a bike __(**10**)__.
He also got a toy __(**11**)__ his newly __(**12**)__ son.

Cycle 6

Unit 33   Words Ending with er   pages 216–221

under	over	better
brother	mother	after

er water

er flower

Spelling Strategy   The vowel + **r** sound at the end of **under** is spelled **er**.

Write the spelling word that means the same.

13. above   **14.** below   **15.** mom

Write the missing spelling words.

My little ___(16)___ Zane plays the drums each night ___(17)___ supper. I hope he plays ___(18)___ soon!

Unit 34   Words with ed or ing   pages 222–227

batted	getting	stopped
hugging	pinned	sitting

Spelling Strategy

stop + ed → stop**p**ed

hug + ing → hug**g**ing

Write the spelling word that rhymes.

19. popped   **20.** hitting   **21.** letting   **22.** patted

Write the missing spelling words.

23. The judge _____ a ribbon on Sarah's picture.

24. Then everyone began _____ Sarah.

---

13. over

14. under

15. mother

16. brother

17. after

18. better

19. stopped

20. sitting

21. getting

22. batted

23. pinned

24. hugging

257

Extra Practice and Review

Cycle 6

25. baked

26. riding

27. closed

28. using

29. hoping

30. hiding

31. telling

32. missed

33. four

34. your

35. are

36. warm

Unit 35 More Words with ed or ing pages 228–233

bak → ed
e

| hoping | baked | using |
| closed | hiding | riding |

Spelling Strategy

bake + ed → baked
close + ed → closed
hope + ing → hoping
hide + ing → hiding

Write the spelling word that goes with each word.

25. cake   **26.** horse   **27.** door

Write the missing spelling words.

Dad was __(28)__ his special glasses. He was __(29)__ to see Mars, but it was __(30)__ behind a cloud.

Elephant Words   Units 31–35   pages 204–233

are

| are | warm | four |
| your | missed | telling |

Spelling Strategy   Elephant Words have unusual spellings. Check them carefully when you write them.

Write the missing spelling words.

The baker was __(31)__ us a very long story. Now we have __(32)__ the bus. The bakery is __(33)__ blocks from __(34)__ house. We do not even have coats! How __(35)__ we going to stay __(36)__ ?

Writer's Resources

Capitalization and Punctuation Guide

Rules for Capitalization

Sentences	**Begin every sentence with a capital letter.** **T**he girl looked at the picture. **W**hat did the picture show?
People, Places, Pets	**Begin the names of people, places, and pets with capital letters.** My friend **D**ean lives on **E**lm **S**treet in **L**akewood. He has a dog named **W**ags.
I	**Always write the pronoun I as a capital letter.** Stan and **I** rode our bikes.
Days	**Begin the names of the days of the week with capital letters.** Is the picnic on **S**aturday?
Holidays	**Begin the names of holidays with capital letters.** There are parades on **C**olumbus **D**ay.
Months	**Begin the names of months with capital letters.** Were you born in **J**anuary?
Titles for People	**Begin titles for people with capital letters. Put a period after most titles.** **M**rs. Mann **M**r. Chan **D**r. Rogers **M**s. Willis **M**iss Gomez **The title** Miss **does not end with a period.**

259

Writer's Resources

Capitalization and Punctuation Guide

Book Titles

> **Begin the first word, the last word, and each important word in a book title with a capital letter. Draw a line under the title.**
>
> The book **T**he **C**at in the **H**at is funny.
>
> I read **T**he **S**nowy **D**ay yesterday.

Rules for Punctuation

End Marks

> **End a telling sentence with a period.**
> The squirrel is brown**.**

> **End a question with a question mark.**
> Does the squirrel see the nut**?**

Apostrophes

> **Use an apostrophe in a contraction to show where letters are left out.**
>
> do not → don't   I have → I've
> you are → you're   we will → we'll

Commas

> **Use a comma between the day and the year in a date.**
> Penny was born on June 21, 1982.
> She started school on August 31, 1988.

> **Use a comma between the name of a city or a town and the name of a state.**
> We watched fireworks in Tampa, Florida.
> We went to a fair in Carmel, California.

> **Use a comma after the greeting and after the closing in a letter.**
> Dear Daniel,   Yours truly,

Writer's Resources

Letter Model

Friendly Letter

Remember that a letter has **five** parts.

1 The **date** tells when the letter was written.

2 The **greeting** means "hello."

3 The **body** is the main part of the letter.

4 The **closing** means "good-by."

5 The **name** tells who wrote the letter.

Use all five parts when you write a letter. Put capital letters and commas where they belong.

Study this letter model.

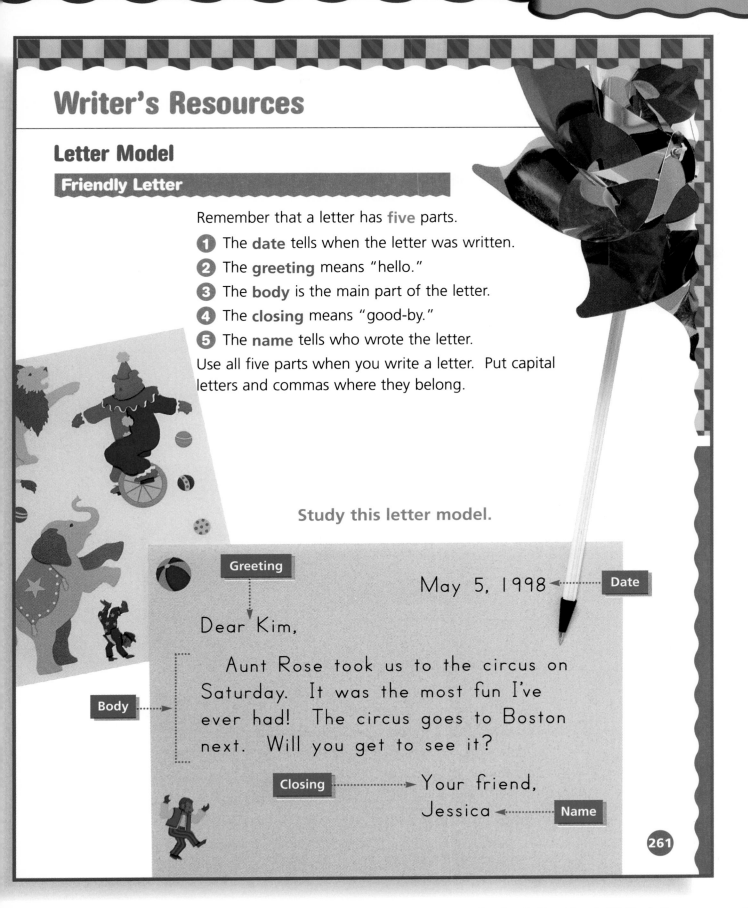

Greeting

May 5, 1998 ← Date

Dear Kim,

Body → Aunt Rose took us to the circus on Saturday. It was the most fun I've ever had! The circus goes to Boston next. Will you get to see it?

Closing → Your friend,

Jessica ← Name

261

My First Thesaurus

How to Use This Thesaurus

A thesaurus can help you find just the right words to use when you write. Imagine you wrote this sentence:

My birthday gift came in a big box.

You decide that **big** doesn't tell how big the box really was. You need a more exact word.

You can find other words for **big** in this thesaurus. The entry words in a thesaurus are in ABC order, so you turn to the **B** section and find **big**.

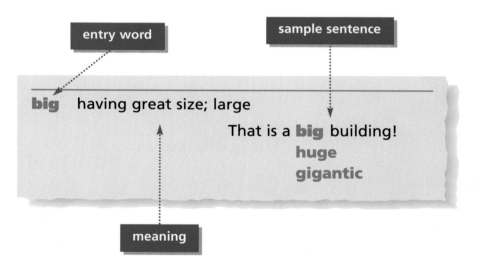

entry word

sample sentence

big   having great size; large

That is a **big** building!
huge
gigantic

meaning

You read the meaning of the word **big**. Then you read the sample sentence. You see that **huge** and **gigantic** are words you could use in place of **big**.

You decide that **huge** is the word that tells how big the box really was. You write your sentence again, using the word **huge** in place of **big**.

My birthday gift came in a huge box.

My First Thesaurus

afraid   filled with fear

My dog is **afraid** of water.
   scared
   frightened

argue   to fight using words

We **argue** about what to play.
   quarrel
   disagree

bad   not pleasant

The **bad** weather made us sad.
   terrible
   awful

big   having great size; large

That is a **big** building!
   huge
   gigantic

boat   a small craft that floats and moves on water

We like to ride on a **boat**.
   ship
   vessel

(continued)

My First Thesaurus

brave   able to face danger or pain without fear

Officer Day is a **brave** woman.
>>> **bold**
>>> **fearless**

break   to cause to come apart

Word Bank	
burst	shatter
destroy	tear
split	crush
crack	smash

bright   giving off light

Look at Sarah's **bright** new bike!
>>> **sparkling**
>>> **gleaming**

close   to move something so that it is not open

Mike will **close** the car door.
>>> **slam**
>>> **shut**

cold   having no warmth

The air here is very **cold**.
>>> **icy**
>>> **chilly**

264

My First Thesaurus

cook   to use heat to prepare food

Word Bank

bake	grill
fry	warm
toast	broil
boil	roast

cry   to have tears fall from your eyes

The sad movie made me **cry**.

weep
sob

F

fast   with great speed

Can you run as **fast** as Tia?

quickly
swiftly

find   to look for and discover

We hope to **find** Pablo's keys.

spot
locate

fix   to make something work right

Fran will **fix** the zipper.

repair
mend

265

My First Thesaurus

 go   to move from one place to another

Is it time to **go** yet?
>   leave
>   depart

great   very good

You did a **great** job!
>   wonderful
>   terrific

 happy   showing or feeling joy

We were **happy** to see Grandpa.
>   glad
>   delighted

help   to do what is needed or useful

Will you **help** me?
>   assist
>   aid

hot   giving off much heat

Dad built a **hot** fire.
>   sizzling
>   blazing

My First Thesaurus

job   work that needs to be done

Doing the dishes is my **job**!
>> task
>> chore

jump   to spring into the air

Jon will **jump** over the puddle.
>> hop
>> leap

junk   things that are of no use

I threw out all the **junk**!
>> trash
>> rubbish

kind   a group of things that are alike

This **kind** of fruit is best.
>> type
>> variety

knock   to hit

Word Bank	
bang	strike
rap	whack
thump	pound
beat	tap

267

My First Thesaurus

L

little   not big

Gus waved to the **little** girl.
> small
> tiny

---

look   to watch or see

Dan likes to **look** at flowers.
> stare
> gaze

M

make   to put together

Word Bank	
build	produce
mold	shape
create	construct
form	assemble

N

nice   pleasant; not mean

My friends are very **nice**.
> friendly
> kind

O

old   having lived a long time

The **old** man was very helpful.
> elderly
> aged

268

My First Thesaurus

part   a bit; not the whole thing

What do you call that **part**?
> piece
> section

pick   to decide on one of a group of things

Which one would you **pick**?
> choose
> select

pile   many objects bunched one on top of another

Look at this **pile** of clothes!
> stack
> mound

pretty   pleasing to look at

The butterfly is **pretty**.
> beautiful
> lovely

quiet   having little or no noise

My favorite place is **quiet**.
> calm
> peaceful

My First Thesaurus

R **run** to move quickly on foot

bolt	gallop
jog	trot
sprint	dash
dart	race

S **say** to speak aloud

What did the coach **say**?

whisper

shout

shine to give off light

Clara's eyes seemed to **shine**.

twinkle

glow

smart able to learn quickly

Chet is very **smart** in school.

clever

intelligent

strange not usual

Beth's lamp is very **strange**.

odd

unusual

My First Thesaurus

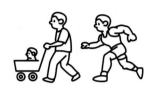 **walk** to move on foot at a steady pace

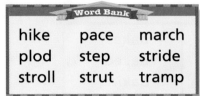

Word Bank

hike	pace	march
plod	step	stride
stroll	strut	tramp

wet not dry

Is your coat still **wet**?
         soaked
         drenched

work to stay in motion; go

Does the tractor **work** at all?
         run
         operate

271

Spelling and Meaning   Word Families

B bake
bakes
baked
baking
baker
bakery

B bright
brighter
brightest
brightly
brighten
brightness

C care
cares
cared
caring
careful
carefully
careless

C clean
cleans
cleaned
cleaning
cleaner
cleanest

C clear
clears
cleared
clearing
clearer
clearest
clearly

D dress
dresses
dressed
dressing
dresser

F farm
farms
farmed
farming
farmer
farmhouse
farmland

F fish
fishes
fished
fishing
fishy
fisherman

H hand
hands
handed
handing
handful
handle
handmade

Word Families (continued)

H **happy**
- **happ**ier
- **happ**iest
- **happ**ily
- **happ**iness

H **help**
- **help**s
- **help**ed
- **help**ing
- **help**er
- **help**ful
- **help**less

H **high**
- **high**er
- **high**est
- **high**ly
- **high**way

H **hope**
- **hope**s
- **hop**ed
- **hop**ing
- **hope**ful
- **hope**less

K **kind**
- **kind**er
- **kind**est
- **kind**ly
- **kind**ness

L **land**
- **land**s
- **land**ed
- **land**ing
- **land**lord
- **land**mark
- **land**scape

L **light**
- **light**s
- **light**ed
- **light**ing
- **light**ning
- **light**er
- **light**house

O **out**
- **out**door
- **out**er
- **out**ing
- **out**line
- **out**side

P **paint**
- **paint**s
- **paint**ed
- **paint**ing
- **paint**er
- **paint**brush

273

Word Families (continued)

P play

plays
played
playing
player
playful
playground

P please

pleases
pleased
pleasing
pleasant
pleasure

R race

races
raced
racing
racer
racetrack

R rain

rains
rained
raining
rainy
rainbow
raincoat

S sad

sadder
saddest
sadly
sadness

S sail

sails
sailed
sailing
sailboat
sailor

S ship

ships
shipped
shipping
shipment
shipwreck

S shop

shops
shopped
shopping
shopper
shopkeeper

S slow

slows
slowed
slowing
slower
slowest
slowly

Word Families (continued)

S spot

spots
spotted
spotter
spotless
spotlight

S stop

stops
stopped
stopping
stopper
stoplight

S sun

sunflower
sunglasses
sunny
sunrise
sunset
sunshine

T thank

thanks
thanked
thanking
thankful
thankless

T time

times
timed
timing
timer
timekeeper

U use

uses
used
using
user
useful
useless

W warm

warmed
warming
warmer
warmest
warmly
warmth

W water

waters
watered
watering
waterfall
waterproof
watery

W wish

wishes
wished
wishing
wishbone

Spelling Dictionary

How to Use a Dictionary

Finding an Entry Word

Entry Words

A word you look up in a dictionary is called an entry word. Entry words are listed in ABC order.

To find a word that has an ending, like **ed** or **ing**, you usually look up the base word. For example, to find **sailed**, you would look up the entry word **sail**.

Guide Words

At the top of each page in a dictionary, you will see two guide words. The guide words name the first and last entry on the page. Use the guide words and ABC order to find an entry word.

Reading an Entry

Look carefully at the dictionary entry below.

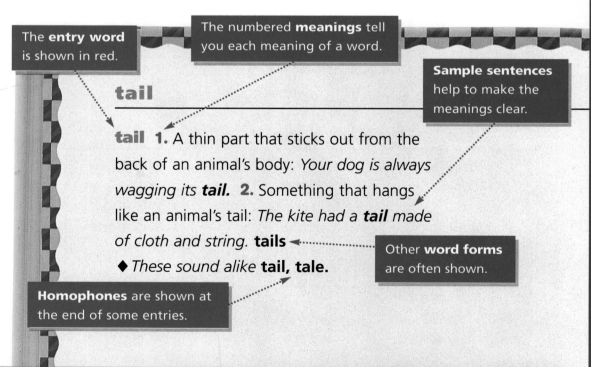

The **entry word** is shown in red.

The numbered **meanings** tell you each meaning of a word.

Sample sentences help to make the meanings clear.

tail

tail 1. A thin part that sticks out from the back of an animal's body: *Your dog is always wagging its **tail**.* **2.** Something that hangs like an animal's tail: *The kite had a **tail** made of cloth and string.* **tails**
◆ *These sound alike **tail, tale**.*

Other **word forms** are often shown.

Homophones are shown at the end of some entries.

Spelling Dictionary

a 1. One: *I didn't hear **a** word you said.* **2.** Any; each: ***A** circus has clowns and elephants.*

absent Not present in a place or with someone: *Two children are **absent** from school today.*

add 1. To find the sum of two or more numbers: *If you **add** 6 to 8, you get 14.* **2.** To put on as a new part: *We want to **add** a new deck to the house.* **3.** To put in something more: *I **add** carrots to the soup.* **added, adding**

afford To be able to pay for or spend: *We can **afford** the small car but not the large one.* **afforded, affording**

after 1. The opposite of **before:** *The children will nap **after** lunch.* **2.** Behind: *The clowns came **after** the elephants in the parade.* **3.** At a time later than: ***After** a few hours, we went home.*

alarm A bell that rings when there is danger: *When we hear the **alarm** for a fire drill, we leave the school.* **alarms**

all 1. The total number of; every: ***All** five children are good friends.* **2.** Completely: *I was sick, but I'm **all** better now.* **3.** Each and every one: ***All** of us like Marcie.*

am A form of **be:** *I **am** happy.*

an The form of **a** that is used before words beginning with a vowel or with a silent **h:** *I saw **an** elephant and a tiger. Sarah rode a horse for **an** hour.*

and Together with or along with; as well as: *My sister **and** I went to the store and to the park.*

any One or some in a group of three or more: *Take **any** book or books you want.*

anyone Any person; anybody: ***Anyone** in the class may play this game.*

are A form of **be:** *You **are** at home. We **are** coming to your party.*

arm The part of the body that connects the hand and wrist to the shoulder: *Your elbow is part of your **arm**.* **arms**

as 1. In just the same way: *You'll never meet anyone **as** nice.* **2.** For example: *At the zoo we saw large animals, such **as** tigers and lions.* **3.** At the same time that: *I sang a song **as** I worked.*

ask The opposite of **tell;** to question. *Did you **ask** me what time it is?* **asked, asking**

at Used to show where: *Will you be **at** school?*

ate The past form of **eat:** *We **ate** sandwiches and fruit for lunch.*

baby A very young child or animal: *A duck's **baby** is a duckling.* **babies**

baby ducklings

(277)

Spelling Dictionary

back **1.** The part of the body on the other side from the chest: *I could not scratch my* **back** *between my shoulders.* **2.** The opposite of **front:** *The teacher asked the children in the* **back** *of the room to stand up.* **backs**

bad Not good; awful: *The apple tasted* **bad,** *so Jon did not eat it.* **worse, worst**

bag A sack made of paper or cloth: *Mom put a sandwich and an orange in a* **bag** *for Li's lunch.* **bags**

bake To cook in an oven: *We will bake bread today.* **baked, baking**

baked The past form of **bake:** *We* **baked** *cookies yesterday.*

baker A person who bakes: *The* **baker** *made bread and cakes to sell.* **bakers**

baking A form of **bake:** *We like* **baking** *cakes.*

ball A round object used in a game or sport: *Molly throws the* **ball,** *and Polly catches it.* **balls**

barn A large building where farm animals live and where grain and hay are kept: *There are cows and horses in the* **barn. barns**

barn

bat **1.** A strong wooden stick or club used for hitting a ball, as in baseball: *Ben got a new baseball* **bat** *for his birthday.* **bats** **2.** To hit a ball with or as if with a strong wooden stick: *Rosa* **batted** *the ball across the field.* **batted, batting**

bat A small, furry animal that looks like a mouse with big wings: *A* **bat** *sleeps during the day and hunts at night.* **bats**

bath The act of washing in water: *Bill gave his muddy dog a* **bath. baths**

bathtub A large tub that you sit in to wash yourself: *Nick washed himself in the* **bathtub. bathtubs**

be **1.** To live: *There once* **was** *a beautiful princess.* **2.** To have a certain place: *Please* **be** *home in five minutes.* **3.** To have a certain feeling: *We* **are** *glad to see them.* **was, being**
♦ *These sound alike* **be, bee.**

beach The sandy shore of the sea or a lake: *Children built castles of sand on the* **beaches. beaches**

bear To give birth to: *Dogs* **bear** *several puppies at one time.* **bore, born, bearing**

bed A piece of furniture or a place for sleeping: *I put clean sheets on my* **bed. beds**

bedpost A post at the corner of a bed: *Each* **bedpost** *on my brother's bed has one of his hats on it.* **bedposts**

bedroom A room for sleeping: *My dog likes to sleep in my* **bedroom. bedrooms**

bedside The space beside a bed: *I have a table with a lamp at my* **bedside.**

bedspread   **born**

bedspread A top cover for a bed: *My aunt bought me a new **bedspread** for my birthday.* **bedspreads**

bedtime The time when a person goes to bed: *Dad reads us a story at **bedtime**.* **bedtimes**

bee An insect that has four wings and a hairy body. Most bees have a stinger. *A **bee** may make honey in its hive.* **bees**
◆ *These sound alike **bee, be**.*

been A past form of **be**: *Ollie has **been** to the circus.*

beetle An insect with hard front wings that cover the back wings when the beetle is resting. Some beetles are black: *This kind of **beetle** eats the farmer's crops.* **beetles**

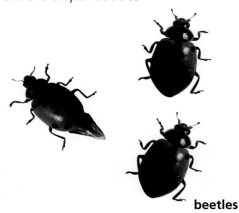

beetles

before 1. Ahead of; earlier than: *My sister got home **before** me.* 2. In the past: *I've heard that **before**.*

behind At the back of or in the rear of: *He looked quickly **behind** him.*

bell A piece of metal that makes a sound when it is struck: *After I ring the **bell**, Suki will come to the door.* **bells**

best A form of **good** that compares more than two people or things: *Emily made the **best** picture of all.*

better 1. A form of **good** that compares two people or things: *Caleb is a **better** swimmer than Peter is.* 2. More excellent or higher in quality: *I know that my work will be **better** next year.*

big 1. Large: *Elephants are **big** animals.* 2. Important: *She is a **big** star on TV.* **bigger, biggest**

bike A machine with two wheels, a seat for the rider, and pedals; a bicycle: *Clara and Patrick ride their **bikes** to school.* **bikes**

black The opposite of **white**: *Black is the color of the sky at night.* **blacker, blackest**

block 1. A piece of wood, plastic, or stone that is usually shaped like a square or a rectangle: *The baby is playing with a toy **block**.* 2. An area of a city or town that has streets on four sides: *I took a walk around the **block**.* **blocks**

boat A small ship that travels on water: *We rowed a **boat** across the lake.* **boats**

bone One of the many hard pieces inside the body: *Can you feel a **bone** in your elbow?* **bones**

book A set of pages put together and placed between covers: *Allison read a **book** to me.* **books**

booth A small stand or place where things such as tickets are sold: *The woman in the **booth** sold us tickets for the show.* **booths**

born A past form of **bear**: *A new baby was **born**.*

279

Spelling Dictionary

box **1.** A container with four sides, a bottom, and a top: *We put the presents in the cardboard **boxes** and tied them with ribbons.* **2.** The amount that this kind of container holds: *We sold a **box** of old books.* **boxes**

braces Wires and bands used for making crooked teeth straight: *Mike will need to wear **braces** on his teeth for two years.*

branch One of the parts that grow out from the trunk of a tree or shrub: *A leaf fell from the **branch** of the tree.* **branches**

brass A kind of metal. Some musical instruments are made out of brass: *Chris plays a trumpet made of **brass**.* **brasses**

brave Not afraid: *I tried to be **brave** when I bumped my toe.* **braver, bravest**

bright Giving off or filled with a lot of light: *The **bright** sun lit up the forest.* **brighter, brightest**

bring To take with or to: *I **bring** a peach to school every day.* **brought, bringing**

brook A small stream: *Children can walk in the **brook** because the water is not deep.* **brooks**

brother A boy or man who has the same mother and father as another person: *My **brother** is two years older than I am.* **brothers**

brown **1.** The color of chocolate: *Zia has long **brown** hair.* **2.** To cook until brown on the outside: *I can **brown** the rolls in the oven.*

bug An insect, such as a cricket or an ant: *A bee is a **bug** that buzzes and has wings.* **bugs**

bun A roll made of bread: *Beth ate a **bun** for breakfast.* **buns**

bus A large machine with a motor, wheels, and many seats used for carrying people from place to place: *Some children ride the **bus** to school.* **buses**

but Even so; just the same; anyhow: *Andrew wore his jacket, **but** he was still cold.*

buy To get by paying money for: *I want to **buy** a new kite, so I am saving my money.* **bought, buying**
♦ *These sound alike* **buy, by.**

by Past, beyond, or near: *The school bus goes **by** my house.*
♦ *These sound alike* **by, buy.**

C

cabin A small, simple house: *The **cabin** in the forest was made of logs.* **cabins**

cabin

caboose A car at the end of a train, where the crew can cook and sleep: *The first car of the train is the engine, and the last car is the **caboose**.* **cabooses**

280

call   **children**

call **1.** To shout: *When I call my dog's name, he comes.* **2.** To send for: *When our parents call us, we come in.* **3.** To speak with on the phone: *I call Mom at work when I get home from school.* **called, calling**

came The past form of **come:** *Grandma came to our house today.*

camper A person who lives outside in a tent or a cabin for a little while: *The camper slept in a tent in the woods.* **campers**

can To be able to: *Elmer can run faster than his brother.* **could**

can A metal or plastic container: *Paul bought a can of tomato soup* at the store. **cans**

cannot Not able to: *The baby cannot walk yet.*

can't A short way to write **cannot:** *I can't find my lunch!*

cape A warm coat that is worn over the shoulders: *The princess wore a long gold cape over her dress.* **capes**

car A machine with a motor and wheels, used for carrying people and things: *The family packed the car and went on a trip.* **cars**

careful Taking steps to keep from being hurt: *Be careful to look both ways before you cross the street.*

carpet A thick covering for a floor; rug: *The dog loves to lie on the new carpet.* **carpets**

cart A container or basket with wheels that is moved by hand: *He pushed the cart full of toys to the front of the store.* **carts**

castle A large stone building or fort with high, thick walls and towers: *The king and queen lived in a castle with all their servants and friends.* **castles**

cat A soft, furry animal with sharp claws, whiskers, and a long tail: *Our cat played with a ball of yarn.* **cats**

catch To get hold of something that is moving: *I'll throw the ball and you catch it.* **caught, catching**

cattle Large animals, such as cows, that have hoofs and grow horns: *The rancher gives the cattle hay to eat in winter.*

cattle

center **1.** the middle: *They put the flowers in the center of the table.* **2.** A place where many activities take place: *The town built a new center.* **centers**

change Coins: *Do you need change for the bus?*

chase **1.** To run after in order to catch; to follow: *We chase our dog every time it runs away.* **2.** To drive away: *A cat chased the bird from the tree.* **chased, chasing**

child A young boy or girl: *That game would be a good gift for a child.* **children**

children More than one child: *There are twenty children in the class.*

281

Spelling Dictionary

chin The part of the face below the mouth: *Dad has whiskers on his **chin.*** **chins**

chop To cut by hitting with a sharp tool, such as an ax: *I **chop** each piece of wood in two.* **chopped, chopping**

chore A small job: *My weekly **chores** are to empty the trash and sweep the stairs.* **chores**

clap To slap hands together: *Do not **clap** until the end of the song.* **clapped, clapping**

class A group of students who learn together: *There are two new children in **class** starting today.* **classes**

claw A sharp, curved nail on the toe of an animal or bird: *The rooster has sharp **claws.*** **claws**

claw

clean 1. Not dirty: *Please put the dirty clothes in the washer, then fold the **clean** clothes.* **cleaner, cleanest** 2. To get rid of dirt; to wash: *We **clean** the house every Saturday.* **cleaned, cleaning**

clear Free from clouds, mist, or dust: *Today the sky was **clear.*** **clearer, clearest**

clearing An open place without trees in a forest: *We saw deer in a **clearing** in the woods.* **clearings**

clip To cut: *I **clip** my nails once a week.* **clipped, clipping**

clock A machine that shows time: *Please look at the **clock** and tell me what time it is.* **clocks**

close 1. Near: *The market is **close** to our house.* **closer, closest** 2. To shut: *Have you **closed** the door?* **closed, closing**

club A group with members who join together to do special things, such as hiking: *Our **club** went swimming today.* **clubs**

coach A railroad car for people: *We rode in the **coach.*** **coaches**

coast The land touching the sea: *Clams and shrimp are found along the **coast.*** **coasts**

coat 1. A type of outer clothing with sleeves: *I wore a warm **coat.*** 2. An outer layer of fur or hair on an animal: *I brushed the horse's **coat.*** **coats**

coin A kind of money: *I found an old **coin** on the sidewalk.* **coins**

cold The opposite of **hot:** *The lake was too **cold** for swimming.* **colder, coldest**

collect To gather or bring together in a group: *Who will **collect** the trash and bring it to the dump?* **collected, collecting**

come To move toward the person who is speaking or toward a certain place: *The children **come** quickly when the teacher calls them.* **came, come, coming**

cookie A small, sweet cake: *You may have a **cookie** after dinner.* **cookies**

282

corn   **cute**

corn A tall vegetable grown for its large yellow ears. Corn is used as food or ground up for use in baking: *We ate corn and hamburgers for lunch.* **corn**

cottage A small house in the country: *The cottage had only three rooms and a garden in the back.* **cottages**

cottage cheese A soft white cheese made from skim milk: *Jane really enjoys cottage cheese with fruit.*

couch A sofa: *The cat ran under the couch.* **couches**

could The past form of **can**: *We were happy that Uncle Bob could come for dinner.*

counter A place in a store where things are paid for: *When you finish shopping, please pay at the counter.* **counters**

cow A large animal with horns and hoofs. Cows are raised for milk: *A young cow is called a calf.* **cows**

crab An animal from the same group as lobsters and shrimp. Crabs have flat bodies and five pairs of legs. The front pair of legs are large and have claws. Crabs often have hard shells: *We saw a crab on the beach.* **crabs**

crab

crawl To move slowly on or as if on the hands and knees: *Ants crawl across the picnic table.* **crawled, crawling**

crew The people who work together to sail a ship or fly an airplane: *I asked someone in the crew to show me around the ship.* **crews**

crossing A place with flashing lights where railroad tracks may be crossed: *Cars stopped at the crossing as the train went by.* **crossings**

crowd To fill with people or things: *We like to crowd around the fireplace on cold winter nights.* **crowded, crowding**

crowded The past form of **crowd**: *The children crowded into the gym.*

crown A head covering made of gold with jewels. A crown is worn by a king or queen: *The queen wore a crown made of gold and bright rubies.* **crowns**

cry To weep: *Babies cry when they are hungry.* **cried, crying**

cup A small, open container with a handle. Cups are used for drinking: *Roberto set the table with plates and cups.* **cups**

cure 1. Something that makes a sick person get better: *Rest and good food may be a cure for your cold.* **cures** 2. To bring back to good health: *Doctors and nurses try to cure sick people.* **cured, curing**

cut To shorten or trim: *I cut the grass every week.* **cut, cutting**

cute Very pretty: *Kate is wearing a cute dress with flowers and bows on it.* **cuter, cutest**

283

Spelling Dictionary

dairy A farm that produces milk: *The store gets milk and cheese from a* **dairy.** **dairies**

day The time between when the sun rises and when it sets: *She begins the* **day** *with a good breakfast.* **days**

decide To make up one's mind: *She can't* **decide** *about joining the club.* **decided, deciding**

decided The past form of **decide:** *She* **decided** *to join the chorus.*

did The past form of **do:** *John* **did** *his job well.*

didn't The opposite of **did:** a short way to write **did not:** *I* **didn't** *forget my books.*

diet The usual food and drink taken in by a person or animal every day: *A healthy* **diet** *has lots of fruits and vegetables in it.* **diets**

dig **1.** To move dirt out of the ground: *Dogs* **dig** *holes to bury bones.* **2.** To find by looking hard for: *If you* **dig** *into your desk, you will find crayons.* **dug, digging**

dish **1.** A plate for holding food: *Adam put* **dishes** *and cups on the table.* **2.** Something held or served in a dish: *I ate two* **dishes** *of fruit salad.* **dishes**

dish

do **1.** To carry out an act: *I* **do** *all of my homework.* **2.** Used to make a strong statement: *I* **do** *want to go.* **did, done, doing, does**

dock A place to tie up a boat: *Lisa ties a rope to her boat when it is at the* **dock. docks**

dog An animal with four legs that barks and eats meat. A dog is part of the same group as wolves and foxes; a pet: *Irma teaches her* **dog** *to sit up and do other tricks.* **dogs**

don't The opposite of **do;** a short way to write **do not:** *I* **don't** *need help with my homework.*

dot A small round mark, circle, or point: *Do not forget to put a* **dot** *over the letter* **i. dots**

down **1.** From a higher to a lower place: *The cat climbed* **down** *from the roof.* **2.** In or to a lower point or place: *The teacher told the children to sit* **down** *in their chairs.*

draw To make pictures with lines: *You may get out your crayons and* **draw. drew, drawn, drawing**

dress A piece of clothing with a top and skirt that is worn by women and girls: *Martha, Rosa, and Kim wore pretty* **dresses** *to my birthday party.* **dresses**

dry **1.** The opposite of **wet:** *Our sneakers were wet, so we put on* **dry** *ones.* **2.** Having little or no rain: *It was a* **dry** *summer.* **drier, driest** **3.** To make or become dry: *First we will wash the dishes, then we will* **dry** *them.* **dried, drying**

dump A special place where trash is taken: *A truck took our old stove to the* **dump. dumps**

each Every: *Speak to **each** child.*

earn To get by working: *Jason and Rigo **earn** money by taking care of little children.* **earned, earning**

eat 1. To take food into the body through the mouth: *The children **eat** apples when they are hungry for a snack.* **2.** To have a meal: *We **eat** dinner at six o'clock.* **ate, eaten, eating**

egg The round or oval object laid by a mother bird or fish. A young animal grows inside the shell and later hatches: *We watched a baby chicken hatch from an **egg.*** **eggs**

elk A large deer with very big antlers: *We saw an **elk** while hiking in the woods.* **elk** or **elks**

elk

end 1. The opposite of **beginning:** *We didn't know what would happen until the **end** of the story.* **2.** The first or last part of something that is long: *Sam sat at one **end** of the table.* **ends**

engine The railroad car that pulls the rest of the train: *The driver of the train always sits in the **engine.*** **engines**

exit A way out: *That door is an **exit** from the room.* **exits**

eye What people and animals see with: *Our puppy closed both **eyes** and went to sleep.* **eyes**
♦ *These sound alike* **eye, I.**

fabric Cloth, such as cotton or wool: *The costume is made of a light, red **fabric.*** **fabrics**

fall 1. To drop or come down quickly: *The books **fall** off the table.* **fell, fallen, falling 2.** The act of dropping down quickly, as after tripping or slipping: *Rick hurt his arm in a **fall** on the steps.* **falls 3.** The season that follows summer: *September, October, and November are months in the **fall.***

far The opposite of **near;** to or at a great distance: *I walked **far** into the woods.* **farther** or **further, farthest** or **furthest**

farm 1. A piece of land or a ranch on which crops or animals are raised: *We saw sheep and pigs at the **farm.*** **farms 2.** To raise crops or animals: *Those families **farm** in the valley.* **farmed, farming**

farmer A person who owns a farm: *The **farmer** raises pigs and sheep.* **farmers**

285

Spelling Dictionary

farming The job of growing crops and raising animals: *Farming is difficult in places where the soil is rocky.*

farmland Land used for planting and growing vegetables: *Next year my dad plans to buy more farmland.*

fast Moving, acting, or done quickly: *We need fast runners for the race.* **faster, fastest**

father A man who has children: *My friend's father is a carpenter.* **fathers**

feast A big fancy meal: *We made a feast and invited our friends to eat with us.* **feasts**

feet More than one **foot**: *After the long hike, we soaked our feet in the cool water.*

find The opposite of **lose**; to look for and discover: *Could Kip and Alex help me find my lost pen?* **found, finding**

fine **1.** Good: *Thank you for the fine job you did.* **2.** The opposite of **sick**; in good health: *I was sick yesterday, but I feel fine today.* **finer, finest**

fish Any of a large group of water animals that have a backbone, fins, and gills for breathing: *We had tuna, a kind of fish, for dinner.* **fish** or **fishes**

fit Strong and healthy: *Irene stays fit by swimming and eating well.* **fitter, fittest**

five Being one more than four: *I counted five dogs in the park.*

fix The opposite of **break**; to make work again; to mend: *They fix flat tires at the gas station.* **fixed, fixing**

flag A piece of cloth with pictures or stripes that is used to stand for a country or a club: *My dad and I raise the flag to the top of the flagpole every morning.* **flags**

flat Not bumpy; smooth: *We could see for miles across the flat land.* **flatter, flattest**

flea A small, jumping insect with no wings: *A flea jumped off my dog's back.* **fleas**

flight A trip in an airplane or space ship: *Many people would like to be on the first flight to Mars.* **flights**

flip To turn over in the air: *I like to flip the pancakes for breakfast.* **flipped, flipping**

flow To move freely like water in a stream: *The water will flow into the pipe.* **flowed, flowing**

flower A plant that makes seeds and usually has colorful petals: *A rose is a flower.* **flowers**

fly **1.** To move through the air using wings: *The birds fly to their nests.* **2.** To operate a plane or spacecraft: *Captain Roy will fly the plane.* **3.** To move quickly: *I have to fly, or I will be late for school.* **flew, flown, flying**

food Anything that an animal or person can eat: *We gave our dog his food for dinner.* **foods**

fish

foot 1. The part of the leg of a person or animal that it stands or walks on: *Julio can hop on one foot.* 2. A length equal to 12 inches: *My new ruler is one foot long.* **feet**

for In order to find, get, have, keep, or save: *I was looking for my cat.*
♦ These sound alike **for, four.**

fossil The outline or parts left of a plant or animal that lived long ago. Fossils are found in rocks: *A fossil of a dinosaur may show how big the dinosaur was.* **fossils**

fossil

found The past form of **find**: *My lost pen was found at last!*

four 1. A number written 4 that is equal to the sum of 3 + 1: *We four are best friends.* 2. Being one more than three: *There are four people in my family.*
♦ These sound alike **four, for.**

fox An animal that has a pointed nose, a long, bushy tail, and thick fur. Some foxes are red and live in holes in the ground: *We saw a deer, a rabbit, and a fox in the woods.* **foxes**

frog A small animal with smooth skin, webbed feet, and long back legs. Frogs live in or near water. They swim well and can make long jumps: *We saw two big green frogs on a rock in the pond.* **frogs**

from 1. Starting at: *We will play from now until two o'clock.* 2. Beginning in or on: *Those flowers are from our garden.* 3. Out of: *I took a book from the box.*

fun A good time: *Children have fun at the circus.*

funny Causing laughter: *My friend told me a funny joke.* **funnier, funniest**

furry Covered with fur: *We saw the new, furry puppy.*

G

game Something done for fun: *Grandma taught us a new game to play.* **games**

gather To come together or put together: *I'll gather the papers together.* **gathered, gathering**

gave The past form of **give**: *I gave my dad the tools he needed.*

gear Things, such as tools or clothes, used for a special job, game, or activity: *Ci put his sneakers, shorts, and other gear for running in his bag.*

get 1. To become: *Our new puppies get stronger every day.* 2. To earn: *He's getting a reward for finding the lost bike.* **got, got** or **gotten, getting**

287

Spelling Dictionary

give **1.** To make a gift of: *My sisters **give** me presents.* **2.** To hand over; pass: *Please **give** me the paper.* **3.** To provide; supply: *My friend will **give** us some help.* **gave, given, giving**

glad The opposite of **unhappy;** pleased; happy: *We were really **glad** to be back home again.* **gladder, gladdest**

glide To move smoothly and quietly: *The kites **glide** high in the air.* **glided, gliding**

globe **1.** A map of the world that is shaped like a ball: *We have a **globe** with a light inside it.* **2.** The earth: *Astronauts travel all around the **globe**.* **globes**

go **1.** The opposite of **come;** to leave: *I will **go** now.* **2.** To move from one place to another: *We **go** to the store every day.* **3.** The opposite of **stop;** to begin or continue to move: *The car wouldn't **go**.* **went, gone, going, goes**

goal A score given for driving a ball or puck into a special part of the playing area: *You make a **goal** in soccer by kicking the ball into the net.* **goals**

goes A form of **go:** *This bus **goes** into town.*

good The opposite of **bad:** *Every child wants to read that **good** book.* **better, best**

gown A women's long, fancy dress: *The princess wore a **gown** of silver cloth to the ball.* **gowns**

grand Very large: *The queen lives in a **grand** castle.* **grander, grandest**

grass Ground covered with green plants that have tall, thin leaves: *Dad sits on the **grass** in the yard.*

graze To eat growing grass: *Sheep **graze** in the fields all summer.* **grazed, grazing**

great **1.** Very large in size or number: *A **great** many people watched the game.* **2.** Wonderful: *We all had a **great** time at the zoo.* **greater, greatest**

green The color of most plant leaves and grass: *Peas are **green,** and carrots are orange.* **greener, greenest**

groom To make neat: *Monkeys in the jungle **groom** themselves.* **groomed, grooming**

grow To become bigger in size: *Baby lambs **grow** into big sheep.* **grew, grown, growing**

gym A large room for playing sports: *Jillian, Trisha, and Emily jog around the **gym**.* **gyms**

goal

hamster A small, furry animal with large cheeks and a short tail: *Tom's pet is a soft, furry **hamster**.* **hamsters**

hand   hide

hand The part of the arm that is below the wrist. The hand includes the fingers and thumb: *Dad held Jacob's* **hand** *when they crossed the street.* **hands**

happy Feeling joy; glad: *I'm* **happy** *that my birthday is almost here.* **happier, happiest**

hard **1.** The opposite of **soft:** *The glass broke when it hit the* **hard** *floor.* **2.** The opposite of **easy;** difficult: *That problem is too* **hard** *for first graders.* **harder, hardest**

harp A musical instrument with strings that are stretched on a frame. A player plucks the strings to make sounds: *Carlos played a beautiful song on the* **harp. harps**

harp

has A form of **have;** owns: *Jenny* **has** *a toy tiger.*

hasn't The opposite of **has;** a short way to write **has not:** *He* **hasn't** *ever been late for school.*

hat Something worn on the head: *Louis wore a* **hat** *to keep his ears warm.* **hats**

hatch To come out of an egg: *A hen sits on her eggs until her chicks* **hatch. hatched, hatching**

have **1.** To own: *I* **have** *a bicycle.* **2.** To be in a certain relationship to: *You* **have** *three sisters and two brothers.* **3.** Used to show that something has already been done: *We* **have** *eaten all the oranges.* **4.** To be forced; must: *I* **have** *to go home now.* **had, having, has**

hay Grass and other plants that are cut and dried and used as food for farm animals: *The* **hay** *is stored in the barn.*

he The man or boy talked about before: *I wrote a letter to my friend, then* **he** *wrote to me.*

healthy Not sick or hurt: *Good food and lots of sleep help keep us* **healthy. healthier, healthiest**

help To give or do what someone needs or can use: *I* **help** *my little sister pick up her toys.* **helped, helping**

helper Someone who gives help: *The teacher's* **helper** *will pick up the papers.* **helpers**

helpful Giving help; useful: *Jeb was* **helpful** *when he showed me how to fix my bike.*

herd A group of animals of one kind, such as cows, that are kept together: *Dogs help the rancher move a* **herd** *of cows to my barn.* **herds**

hide **1.** The opposite of **find;** to keep or put out of sight: *We* **hide** *the ball behind a tree.* **2.** To cover up: *Clouds can sometimes* **hide** *the sun in the sky.* **hid, hidden** or **hid, hiding**

289

Spelling Dictionary

high **1.** The opposite of **low:** *Mountains are* **high,** *and valleys are low.* **2.** At a great distance above the ground: *The balloon was* **high** *in the sky.* **higher, highest**

hill A tall, rounded part of the earth. A hill is not as high as a mountain: *Let's fly our kites from the top of the* **hill.** **hills**

his Belonging to him: *Where did he put* **his** *glasses?*

hit **1.** To strike: *The stone* **hit** *the water with a splash.* **2.** To move by striking with a bat: *I* **hit** *the ball over the fence and into the seats.* **hit, hitting**

hoe A tool with a flat blade on a long handle. A hoe is used for breaking up soil and for weeding: *Martha will use a* **hoe** *to dig weeds out of the garden.* **hoes**

hole An opening into or through something: *I found a* **hole** *in my shoe.* **holes**
♦ *These sound alike* **hole, whole.**

home **1.** The place where you live: *A* **home** *may be a house, an apartment, or a room.* **2.** A place outdoors where plants or animals may live: *The forest is the* **home** *of trees, foxes, and rabbits.* **homes**

home run A hit in baseball that allows the batter to touch all the bases and score a run: *Roberto hit a* **home run** *in the baseball game yesterday.* **home runs**

hood **1.** A covering for the head and neck, usually on a coat: *The* **hood** *on my jacket will keep my head warm.* **2.** The metal cover over the motor of a car, bus, or truck: *He lifted the* **hood** *of the car to look at the motor.* **hoods**

hoof The tough covering on the foot of some animals. Horses, cattle, deer, and pigs have hoofs: *The horse tripped over a rock and hurt his* **hoof.** **hoofs** or **hooves.**

hoof

hop **1.** To move with light, quick leaps: *The children* **hop,** *skip, and jump on the playground during recess.* **2.** To jump over: *Kimberly* **hopped** *the fence and ran to the barn.* **hopped, hopping**

hope To wish for something: *I* **hope** *that I will win this race.* **hoped, hoping**

horn **1.** A musical instrument, such as a trumpet: *Every child got a paper hat and a toy* **horn** *at the party.* **2.** A signal that makes a loud sound: *The* **horn** *in Jill's car makes a funny sound.* **horns**

hospital A building where doctors and nurses take care of people who are sick or hurt: *Did you have to stay in the* **hospital** *when you broke your leg?* **hospitals**

hot Having or giving off great heat: *The sun is* **hot.** **hotter, hottest**

house A building to live in: *My family moved into a new* **house** *last week.* **houses**

how 1. In what way; by what means: *I would like to know* ***how*** *you did that trick.* **2.** To what extent or amount: ***How*** *do you like your new bike?*

hug To put your arms around and squeeze: *I was* ***hugging*** *the stuffed dog that I love most.* **hugged, hugging**

huge Very big: *Elephants and whales are* ***huge*** *animals.* **huger, hugest**

I The person who is the speaker or writer: ***I*** *am a good friend.*
◆ *These sound alike* **I, eye.**

if 1. On the condition that: *I will go only* ***if*** *you go.* **2.** Whether: *I wonder* ***if*** *it is time for lunch.*

igloo A house made from blocks of frozen ice or hard snow: *An* ***igloo*** *is often shaped like a dome, or half of a circle.* **igloos**

ill Sick: *Fran's cats were* ***ill***, *and they kept sneezing.*

I'll A short way to write **I will** or **I shall:** ***I'll*** *color the sky blue.*

injure To hurt: *If I fall off my bike, I could* ***injure*** *my knees.* **injured, injuring**

into 1. To the inside of: *I went* ***into*** *the house.* **2.** To that state or form of: *We got* ***into*** *a real mess when we gave the dog a bath.*

invite To ask to come somewhere or do something: *How many people did you* ***invite*** *to the party?* **invited, inviting**

is A form of **be:** *Molly* ***is*** *my sister.*

isn't A short way to write **is not:** *It* ***isn't*** *raining out.*

it 1. The thing or matter talked about before: *I saw a house I liked and bought* ***it***. **2.** Used with verbs: ***It*** *has been snowing since yesterday.*

I've A short way to write **I have:** ***I've*** *been to the zoo three times.*

J

jellyfish A sea animal with a soft body. Many jellyfish have long arms that can sting: *We saw a* ***jellyfish*** *floating in the sea.* **jellyfish** or **jellyfishes**

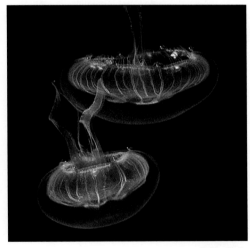

jellyfish

job Work; a task or chore: *Who gets the* ***job*** *of sweeping the floor?* **jobs**

jog To run slowly: *I* ***jog*** *around the block every morning.* **jogged, jogging**

jogging A form of **jog:** *We went* ***jogging*** *this morning.*

Spelling Dictionary

judge A person who chooses the winner of a contest or race: *The **judge** gave our cat first prize.* **judges**

keep **1.** To continue in a certain way or place: *Good foods **keep** us healthy.* **2.** To stop: *The fences **keep** the cows from getting on the road.* **kept, keeping**

kick **1.** To hit with the foot: *Ellie can **kick** the ball across the field.* **2.** To move the feet or legs, as in swimming: *The faster you **kick,** the faster you can swim.* **kicked, kicking**

kid A young goat: *The mother goat and her **kid** rubbed their horns on the fence.* **kids**

kind The opposite of **mean;** helpful and friendly: *We are always **kind** to our neighbors.* **kinder, kindest**

kind A sort or type: *I like this **kind** of sandwich.* **kinds**

king A man who rules a country: *When the **king** makes a rule, every person in the land follows it.* **kings**

kite A light frame made of wood and covered with paper. A kite flies in the wind at the end of a long string: *Fly your **kite** high in the sky on a windy day.* **kites**

lady A woman: *A **lady** on the bus gave us directions.* **ladies**

lake A body of water with land all around it: *In the summer, we go sailing on the **lake.*** **lakes**

lake

land To come down or bring to rest on the ground: *Planes **land** at the airport.* **landed, landing**

large Big; not small: *The chair came in a **large** box.* **larger, largest**

late **1.** The opposite of **early;** not on time: *Please don't be **late** for dinner.* **2.** After the right time: *The train arrived **late.*** **later, latest**

leg The part of the body between the hip and the foot: *Timmy can hop on one **leg.*** **legs**

light **1.** Something bright that you can see: *Those points of **light** in the sky are the stars.* **2.** The light of day: *We got up before **light.*** **lights 3.** The opposite of **dark:** *Sunshine coming in the windows made the room **light.*** **lighter, lightest 4.** To make or become bright with light: *We **light** the room with candles.* **5.** To guide or show with a light: *The lamps along the path will **light** our way.* **lighted** or **lit, lighting**

lighted A past form of **light:** *Lamps **lighted** the room.*

lighthouse   **Mars**

lighthouse A tower with a powerful light at the top that is used to guide ships away from dangerous shores: *The ship saw the **lighthouse** and sailed away from the rocky shore.* **lighthouses**

lights A form of **light**: *We saw the **lights** of the city.*

like To enjoy; to think someone or something is nice: *I **like** playing the drums.* **liked, liking**

line 1. A long, thin mark, such as those on a piece of writing paper: *Please write your name on the top **line** of your paper.* **2.** A row of people or things: *The children stood in a **line**.* **lines 3.** To form a row: *People **lined** up to get tickets.* **lined, lining**

lizard An animal from the same group as turtles and snakes. Lizards have scales, four legs, and a long tail: *A **lizard** eats lots of bugs.* **lizards**

lizard

locker A small closet for locking up clothes and other things: *I keep my sneakers, my jacket, and my books in my **locker** at school.* **lockers**

log A cut piece of tree trunk, used for building or for burning: *We burned the **log** in the fire.* **logs**

long The opposite of **short**: *An elephant has a **long** trunk and a short tail.* **longer, longest**

look To see with your eyes: *I **look** at the pictures in my book.* **looked, looking**

lost 1. The opposite of **found**: *I looked everywhere for my **lost** sock, but I did not find it.* **2.** Not able to find your way: *We took a wrong turn and got **lost**.*

lucky Having good luck: *A **lucky** person won the contest.* **luckier, luckiest**

lunch A meal eaten in the middle of the day: *We have **lunch** every day at noon.* **lunches**

made The past form of **make**: *The children **made** little animals out of clay.*

mail Letters and packages sent through the post office: *I got a card from Gil in the **mail**.*

make 1. To form, shape, or put together: *They **make** masks out of paper bags and colored paper.* **2.** To cause to be or become: *Those songs **make** me happy.* **3.** To carry out or do: *We **make** a trip to visit our uncle every summer.* **made, making**

man A fully grown male human being: *A boy will grow up to be a **man**.* **men**

many The opposite of **few**; adding up to a large number: *There are **many** stars in the sky.* **more, most**

Mars The red planet that is fourth in distance from the sun: ***Mars** is next to the planet Earth.*

293

Spelling Dictionary

mask Something that covers and hides the face: *The clown had a funny* **mask** *on her face.* **masks**

masks

match A sports contest: *The whole family saw the famous tennis player win the* **match.** **matches**

maybe Perhaps: **Maybe** *we can go shopping tomorrow.*

me A form of **I**: *They sent* **me** *a book for my birthday.*

mean **1.** To have as its meaning: *What does this word* **mean? 2.** To be important: *His friends* **mean** *a great deal to Robby.* **meant, meaning**

mean Not kind or good: *Hurting someone's feelings is* **mean. meaner, meanest**

men More than one **man:** *Three* **men** *were fixing the street.*

miss **1.** To fail to hit, reach, catch, meet, or get: *Harry* **missed** *the train.* **2.** To fail to be present for: *I* **missed** *one day of school.* **missed, missing**

mistake Something that was not done the right way: *Some of the children made a* **mistake** *on the last spelling test.* **mistakes**

moon The body in the sky that goes around the earth: *When the* **moon** *is full, it looks like a flat white disk in the sky.* **moons**

moose A large animal that is part of the same group as a deer: *A* **moose** *came out of the woods.* **moose**

mop **1.** A cleaning tool with a long handle, used for washing or dusting floors: *Sweep the floor with a broom and wash it with a* **mop. mops 2.** To clean or wipe with a mop: *Peter will* **mop** *the floor because he spilled glue on it.* **mopped, mopping**

more The opposite of **less;** greater in number: *There are* **more** *children in that class than in our class.*

morning The early part of the day: *We woke up in the* **morning.** **mornings**

moth A flying insect that looks like a butterfly. A moth has soft wings and a body that is fatter than a butterfly's body: *A* **moth** *ate a hole in my wool shirt.* **moths**

mother A woman who has children: *He lives with his* **mother** *and his brothers.* **mothers**

motor A machine that gives the power to make something move or run; an engine: *Pam fixed the* **motor** *in my truck and it runs better.* **motors**

mouse A small, furry animal with a thin tail. Some mice live in holes in or near houses: *Does a* **mouse** *like to eat cheese?* **mice**

mouth   no

mouth The part of the body through which an animal takes in food: *How many teeth do you have in your* **mouth? mouths**

much 1. Greatly; a lot: *This test was* **much** *harder than the last one.* **more, most** 2. A great amount: **Much** *of my work is done.*

mud Wet, sticky, soft dirt: *The soil in the garden turned to* **mud** *after the rain.*

mule An animal that looks like a horse but has longer ears and a tail like a donkey's: *The* **mule** *carried all of the packs along the hiking trail.* **mules**

muscle A part of your body that is under the skin. You use more than one muscle when you move: *Did you know that you use almost every* **muscle** *in your body when you swim?* **muscles**

must Used to show that something is necessary: *If you want good marks, you* **must** *work hard.*

myself My own self: *I can clean my room all by* **myself.**

N

nail 1. A thin, sharp piece of metal. People hammer nails into pieces of wood to hold them together: *He pounded the* **nail** *with the hammer from the toolbox.* **nails** 2. To put together with nails: *We* **nail** *the boards together to make a bed.* **nailed, nailing**

name 1. A word or words by which a person, animal, thing, or place is known: *Their* **names** *are Seth and Carrie.* **names** 2. To give a name to; to call: *We* **named** *our cat Cleo.* **named, naming**

neighbor A person who lives next door to or near another: *Our* **neighbor** *lets us play in her yard.* **neighbors**

nest A home shaped like a bowl that is made by birds. Birds lay eggs and take care of their young in the nest: *The robin made a* **nest** *of twigs.* **nests**

nest

next Coming right after: *Monday was rainy, but the* **next** *day was sunny.*

night The opposite of **day;** evening; the time between when the sun sets and when it rises: *The sky is dark at* **night. nights**

nine Being one more than eight: *The dog had* **nine** *puppies.*

no 1. The opposite of **yes: No,** *I'm not going.* 2. Not any: *There are* **no** *apples left.*

295

Spelling Dictionary

nobody No person: ***Nobody*** *was looking.*

nod To move the head down and up quickly to say yes or greet someone: *The teacher asks if the children want to draw, and they* ***nod.*** **nodded, nodding**

noisy Making a lot of noise: *The school yard is* ***noisy*** *during the day.* **noisier, noisiest**

nose The part of the head that a person or an animal smells with: *The puppy sniffs my shoes with its* ***nose.*** **noses**

not Used to make a word or words mean **no:** *I will* ***not*** *go.*

now At this time: *He's eating and can't answer the phone* ***now.***

nut A fruit or seed with a hard shell, such as a peanut or acorn: *The squirrel carried a* ***nut*** *to its nest in the oak tree.* **nuts**

nuts

ocean The great body of salt water that covers most of the earth and moves in waves: *Whales and fish live in the* ***ocean.*** **oceans**

of 1. Belonging to: *The walls* ***of*** *the room are white.* **2.** From the group making up: *Most* ***of*** *the children are here.* **3.** Holding; containing: *We carried the bag* ***of*** *food home.* **4.** From: *We hopped out* ***of*** *the car quickly.*

off 1. Away from a place: *The car drove* ***off.*** **2.** The opposite of **on:** *Turn the radio* ***off.*** **3.** So as to be no longer on: *Take your coat* ***off.***

old 1. Having lived for a long time: ***Old*** *people know a lot about life.* **2.** The opposite of **new;** showing signs of age or use: *We bought a new rug because our* ***old*** *one had holes in it.* **older, oldest**

on The opposite of **off;** in or into action: *Turn the television* ***on.***

one 1. A single person or thing: ***One*** *of us is taller than Jamie.* **ones** **2.** Being a single person or thing: *You may have just* ***one*** *apple, not two.* **3.** Some: ***One*** *day I would like to travel.*

only Just; and nothing more: *She's* ***only*** *three years old.*

or Used between words to show a choice: *I don't know whether to laugh* ***or*** *cry.*

out 1. Not in; outside: *Dad is* ***out*** *in the garden.* **2.** Not here; away: *The doctor is* ***out*** *right now.* **3.** No longer working: *Our power was* ***out*** *during the storm.* **4.** Into view: *The moon came* ***out*** *from behind a cloud.*

over 1. Higher than; above: *A sign hung* ***over*** *the door.* **2.** Upon: *Put paint* ***over*** *those walls.*

page
petal

page One side of a printed sheet of paper, as in a book: *Please turn to the next* **page. pages**

page A child who delivers messages and runs errands in a castle: *A* **page** *brought news that the queen was sick.* **pages**

palace A king's or queen's big, fancy house: *The* **palace** *had more than one hundred rooms.* **palaces**

parrot A bird with brightly colored feathers: *A* **parrot** *can learn to say funny things.* **parrots**

part **1.** A piece of a whole: *John gave me* **part** *of his apple.* **2.** A piece in a machine: *I need a new* **part** *for my radio.* **3.** A role played by an actor: *Mike has a small* **part** *in the school play.* **parts**

party A gathering of people for fun: *I had a big* **party. parties**

paw The foot of a four-footed animal that has claws: *My dog stuck her* **paw** *in the mud.* **paws**

pay To give money for things or for work done: *I* **pay** *for my lunch at school.* **paid, paying**

pen Something used for writing: *Grandpa signed his name with a* **pen. pens**

pen A small place with a fence around it where animals are kept: *The cows are in the barn, and the pigs are in the* **pen. pens**

penguin A bird that lives by the ocean. Penguins have white feathers in front and black feathers on the back. Penguins cannot fly, but they can use their wings to swim: *The* **penguin** *ate a large fish.* **penguins**

penguin

people Human beings: *The* **people** *on the bus sang songs and played games.* **people**

perch To rest or sit on a branch or rod: *Birds* **perch** *on the branches of the tree.* **perched, perching**

pet **1.** A tame animal that lives with people: *A dog, cat, or fish can be a* **pet. pets 2.** To stroke or pat in a gentle manner: *We like to* **pet** *the baby animals at the farm.* **petted, petting**

petal One of the brightly colored parts of a flower: *A daisy might have white, yellow, or pink* **petals. petals**

(297)

Spelling Dictionary

pick To choose: *I **pick** this book to read.* **picked, picking**

picnic A meal that people eat outdoors: *On Monday my class had a **picnic** in the park.* **picnics**

pig A farm animal that has short legs, a fat body, and a flat nose: *In the barn, a **pig** and her baby piglets say, "Oink, oink."* **pigs**

piglet

piglet A young pig: *The pink **piglet** that we saw at the farm had a little, curly tail.* **piglets**

pilot A person who runs the plane while it is flying: *The **pilot** was not on the plane, so we could not take off.* **pilots**

pin **1.** A short, stiff piece of wire used to hold things together: *Mom used a **pin** to put a flower on Jenny's shirt.* **pins** **2.** To put together or attach with a pin: *Eric **pinned** these pieces of cloth together.* **pinned, pinning**

pit The place in front of a stage where people playing musical instruments sit. The pit is lower than the stage: *We carried our instruments into the **pit** and began to play our music.* **pits**

plain **1.** Simple; not fancy: *He wore his **plain** white shirt instead of the one with stripes.* **plainer, plainest** **2.** A large, flat piece of land without any trees: *We could see for miles across the grassy **plain.*** **plains**
♦ *These sound alike **plain, plane.***

plane A machine with wings that can fly through the air; an airplane: *On Monday, we will fly across the country in a **plane.*** **planes**
♦ *These sound alike **plane, plain.***

planet A body that moves around a star, such as the sun: *Earth is a **planet.*** **planets**

play **1.** To have fun: *The children went out to **play.*** **2.** To take part in a game of: *Let's **play** tag after school.* **played, playing** **3.** A story acted out on stage: *Every child has a part in our **play.*** **plays**

played The past form of **play**: *We **played** a game.*

player A person who plays a game or sport: *She is a great hockey **player.*** **players**

playful Lively; liking to play: *The **playful** kitten rolled and tumbled on the rug.*

playground An outdoor area for play, sports, and games: *The class met in the **playground** after school.* **playgrounds**

please To be willing to: ***Please** tell us a story.* **pleased, pleasing**

Pluto The planet that is farthest from the sun: ***Pluto** is a cold, tiny planet.*

pot A deep, round container that is used for cooking: *After dinner we washed three dishes, a **pot,** a pan, and a bowl.* **pots**

price   **reptile**

price The amount of money asked or paid for something: *The **price** of the tent was $79.00.* **prices**

puddle A small amount of water that is collected in one place: *We splashed through the mud **puddle**.* **puddles**

pupil A young person who goes to school: *Our teacher has twenty **pupils** in his class.* **pupils**

puppy A young dog: *Our **puppy** likes to sleep on an old blanket.* **puppies**

queen **1.** A woman who is the ruler of a country: *The **queen** hoped that all people in her land would be happy.* **2.** The wife of a king: *The king and **queen** planned a huge feast for all of their friends.* **queens**

quiet The opposite of **noisy;** silent; having little or no noise: *The children in the library were very **quiet** today.* **quieter, quietest**

quilt A covering for a bed: *The **quilt** my grandmother made me keeps me warm at night.* **quilts**

railroad The metal track that trains ride on: *The **railroad** goes through our town.* **railroads**

rain **1.** Water that falls from clouds to the earth in drops: *The **rain**, sleet, and snow made our bus late for school.* **2.** A fall of rain: *The streets flood during a heavy **rain**.* **rains**

rainbow Colored light across the sky: *When the rain stopped, we saw a **rainbow**.* **rainbows**

ran The past form of **run;** raced; jogged: *The children **ran** around the park.*

read To understand the meaning of printed words: *In our class, we **read** many good stories.* **read, reading**

red The color of most apples and fire trucks: *We mixed **red** paint and blue paint to make purple paint.* **redder, reddest.**

reptile Any one of a group of animals that creep or crawl on the ground. Reptiles have backbones and are usually covered with scales. The body of a reptile gets as warm or cold as the air around it. Snakes, turtles, and lizards are reptiles: *A **reptile** does not have fur on its body.* **reptiles**

reptile

(299)

Spelling Dictionary

ribbon A strip of cloth given as a prize in a contest: *The judge gave our dog Buddy first prize, a blue* **ribbon.** **ribbons**

ride **1.** To sit on and make an object move: *I* **ride** *my bicycle to school.* **2.** To be carried in a car, bus, or plane: *I'll drive the car, and you can* **ride** *with me.* **rode, ridden, riding** **3.** A trip in a car, bus, or plane: *Dad and I went on a bus* **ride. rides**

right **1.** The side or direction opposite of **left:** *The number 3 is on the* **right** *side of a clock face.* **2.** The opposite of **wrong;** correct: *I tried to think of the* **right** *answer.*

ring A place where shows or contests take place: *The dogs in the show walk around the* **ring. rings**

rinse To clear out or off with water: **Rinse** *your mouth after you brush your teeth.* **rinsed, rinsing**

road A street: *The car drove along the* **road** *near the beach.* **roads**
◆ *These sound alike* **road, rode.**

rock A stone: *He tripped on a* **rock** *and fell down.* **rocks**

rode The past form of **ride:** *She* **rode** *her bike to the park.*
◆ *These sound alike* **rode, road.**

room **1.** Space that is or may be used: *There's* **room** *in our car for five people.* **2.** A part of a building that has four walls: *The* **room** *where we cook is the kitchen.* **rooms**

root **1.** The part of a tooth that is in the gums: *Brushing your teeth helps keep the* **roots** *healthy.* **2.** The part of a plant that grows down into the soil: *A tree's* **roots** *grow deep into the earth.* **roots**

rope **1.** A strong, thick cord: *Dad made a swing for my baby brother, using* **rope** *and a piece of wood.* **ropes** **2.** To set off with ropes: *The coaches* **rope** *off the playing field.* **roped, roping**

rope

rug A piece of thick, heavy cloth used to cover a floor: *We sat on the* **rug** *and played a game.* **rugs**

run **1.** To move quickly on foot: *My mother asked me not to* **run** *down the stairs.* **2.** To flow: *If the paints spill, they will* **run** *all over the floor.* **ran, run, running**

sad Unhappy: *Keesha was* **sad** *when Grandma went home.* **sadder, saddest**

said The past form of **say:** *Mom* **said** *we could go out and play.*

sail   **set**

sail 1. A piece of strong cloth that is stretched out to catch the wind and move a ship or boat through the water: *The **sail** on Rico's boat is red and green.* **sails 2.** To travel on a ship or boat that moves by catching the wind with large pieces of strong cloth: *They **sail** down the river on a raft made of logs.* **sailed, sailing**
♦ *These sound alike* **sail, sale.**

sale 1. The act of selling: *We hope to earn lots of money at our clothing **sale**.* **2.** A selling of goods at reduced prices: *Goodman's Store is having a shirt **sale**.* **sales**
♦ *These sound alike* **sale, sail.**

same The opposite of **different**; alike: *These two books are the **same** size and shape.*

sat The past form of **sit**: *Everyone **sat** quietly and listened to me.*

saw A tool that has a thin metal blade with sharp teeth for cutting hard things: *We used a **saw** to cut the wood.* **saws**

saw The past form of **see**: *I **saw** many stars in the sky last night.*

say To speak; talk: *"What did you **say**?" Joseph asked.* **said, saying**

score A record of points made by each person or team in a game or contest: *You may keep the **score** this time.* **scores**

sea The body of salt water that covers most of the earth; ocean: *I sit by the **sea** and watch the boats.* **seas**
♦ *These sound alike* **sea, see.**

sea horse A small ocean fish with a head that looks like the head of a horse: *The **sea horse** was hiding behind some plants.* **sea horses**

seashell The hard shell of a snail, clam, oyster, or other sea animal: *I found a yellow **seashell** in the sand.* **seashells**

seashells

seashore The land at the edge of or near the ocean: *We always rent a house by the **seashore** during the summer.* **seashores**

season One of the four parts of the year. The seasons are spring, summer, autumn, and winter: *The **season** of autumn is also called fall.* **seasons**

see To look at and take in with the eyes: *Can you **see** the writing on the board?* **saw, seen, seeing**
♦ *These sound alike* **see, sea.**

seeing A form of **see**: *I'll be **seeing** you soon.*

seen A past form of **see**: *Have you **seen** my mittens?*

set 1. To put; place: *I **set** the package on the table.* **2.** To place in order for proper use; arrange: *Please help me **set** the table for dinner.* **set, setting**

301

Spelling Dictionary

sewer A drain built to carry away dirty water: *When a pipe in the **sewer** breaks, workers must dig up the street to fix it.* **sewers**

shall 1. Used to show something will take place in the future: *We **shall** eat dinner at six.* **2.** Used to show something that must be done: *You **shall** clean your room today.* **should**

shape Good working order; good health: *Runners must stay in **shape.***

share To have, use, or do with another or others: *Would you like to **share** this last orange?* **shared, sharing**

sharp Pointed or having an edge that cuts: *A bear's claws and teeth are quite large and very **sharp.*** **sharper, sharpest**

she The woman or girl talked about before: *My mother told me that **she** would return soon.*

sheep An animal with hoofs and a thick coat of wool. Sheep are raised for their wool, skin, or meat: *A baby **sheep** is a lamb.* **sheep**

sheep

ship A boat that can travel in deep water. A ship has a motor or sails: *People can go across the ocean on a **ship.*** **ships**

shoot A plant that has just begun to grow: *The first tulip **shoot** has come up in the garden.* **shoots**

shop 1. A place where things are sold; a store: *We buy our shoes at that **shop.*** **shops 2.** To visit stores to look or buy: *They are **shopping** for new clothes.* **shopped, shopping**

shore The land along the edge of a body of water: *Children play near the rocks along the **shore** of the lake.* **shores**

short 1. The opposite of **tall;** small: *Beth is tall, but her brother is **short.*** **2.** The opposite of **long;** covering a small distance: *We took a **short** walk.* **shorter, shortest**

should The past form of **shall:** *You **should** send them a note. We **should** arrive at noon.*

shout To say something in a loud voice; yell: *I had to **shout** to get my dog to come away from the street.* **shouted, shouting**

show 1. To cause or allow to be seen: *I **show** Mom my school papers.* **2.** To point out; to explain: ***Show** me how to do that dance, please.* **showed, shown** or **showed, showing**

shrimp A small animal with a shell and a tail shaped like a fan. Shrimp live in the ocean. They are part of the same group as lobsters and crabs: *Some people earn money by fishing for **shrimp.*** **shrimp** or **shrimps**

side   **some**

side **1.** A line that forms an edge: *We will plant tulips along this* **side** *of the garden.* **2.** The space next to someone or something: *Horses stood by the side of the barn.* **sides**

sightseeing The act of visiting and touring interesting places: *We went* **sightseeing** *during our vacation in Maine.*

silly **1.** Not showing good sense; foolish: *Forgetting my socks was a* **silly** *mistake.* **2.** Not serious: *We watched the clowns acting* **silly.** **sillier, silliest**

sing To perform a song: *Our teacher plays music, and we* **sing** *songs.* **sang, sung, singing**

sister A girl or woman who has the same mother and father as another person. *My friend has a* **sister** *and a brother.* **sisters**

sit To rest on the lower part of the body where the hips and legs join: *Tyrone and Kevin* **sit** *on the bench at the game.* **sat, sitting**

six Being one more than five: *I picked* **six** *apples.*

skill Ability to do something well: *That model car has been made with great* **skill.** **skills**

sky The part of the air that seems to be over the earth: *There is an airplane up in the* **sky!** **skies**

sleep To be not awake: *I* **sleep** *during long rides in the car.* **slept, sleeping**

slip To lose your balance and fall or start to fall: *It is easy to* **slip** *on ice.* **slipped, slipping**

slow The opposite of **fast;** moving or going at a low speed: *The bus was so* **slow** *that we were late for school.* **slower, slowest**

small Little in size or amount: *An elephant is big, but a mouse is* **small.** **smaller, smallest**

snail A land or water animal with a soft body and a hard shell: *The* **snail** *moves very slowly across the rocks in the fish tank.* **snails**

snail

snake A reptile that has a long, narrow body and no legs. *We saw a* **snake** *in the field.* **snakes**

so Very; a lot: *You are always* **so** *friendly to everyone.*

soil The loose top layer of dirt in which plant life can grow: *We dug holes in the* **soil** *and planted tomato seeds.* **soils**

some A few or a little: *Dad gave us* **some** *oranges.* **Some** *snow fell, but mostly it rained.*

303

Spelling Dictionary

someone Somebody; some person: *Someone called, but I don't know who it was.*

son A male child: *Ray's parents have one* **son. sons**
◆ These sound alike **son, sun.**

soon In a short time from now: *Dinner is almost ready, so we'll eat* **soon. sooner, soonest**

space The huge place around the earth where the stars, sun, and planets are: *We use rockets to send people into* **space.**

spot **1.** A small mark: *Amy got a* **spot** *of red paint on her shirt.* **spots** **2.** To find or locate: *It was hard to* **spot** *you in the crowd.* **spotted, spotting**

dog with spots

stall A space that is closed in on all sides. Many barns and stables have stalls: *The horse tried to get out of its* **stall. stalls**

start **1.** To set up: *Ellen and Kate want to* **start** *a soccer club.* **2.** To get a machine going: *Mom could not* **start** *her truck today.* **3.** To begin to do; the opposite of stop: *Dad will* **start** *cooking dinner now.* **started, starting**

stay To remain in one place: *Let's* **stay** *here and play another game.* **stayed, staying**

step **1.** A movement made by lifting one foot and putting it down in another spot: *The baby took one* **step** *this morning.* **2.** A way of walking: *Please watch your* **step** *going across these rocks.* **steps** **3.** To move by taking steps; to walk: *She* **stepped** *up to the teacher's desk.* **stepped, stepping**

stone A rock: *Kara stopped walking because she had a* **stone** *in her shoe.* **stones**

stop To end or cause to end the moving or acting of something: *The cars* **stop** *to let the children cross the street.* **stopped, stopping**

store A place where things are sold; shop: *We can buy clothes at the* **store. stores**

storm A strong wind with rain, sleet, hail, or snow: *The campers hurried back to camp when they felt a* **storm** *coming.* **storms**

story A tale you may read or hear: *I just read a great* **story. stories**

stray **1.** An animal that has gone away from a group or the place it is supposed to stay: *The rancher looked all day for the* **stray. strays** **2.** Having gone away from a group or from a place: *The* **stray** *cat was cold and hungry.*

stream A narrow path of water that moves in one direction: *That **stream** runs into the river.* **streams**

stream

street A road in a city or town: *Our **street** is the longest one in the town.* **streets**

subway A train that travels through tunnels underground: *Taking the **subway** is a good way to travel in the city.* **subways**

such So much or so great: *You read with **such** speed!*

summer The hottest season of the year, between spring and fall: *We can swim and play outdoors in the **summer.*** **summers**

sun The star around which the earth moves: *The **sun** shines and gives light and heat to the earth.* **suns**
◆ *These sound alike* **sun, son.**

sure Certain: *I checked the spelling in the dictionary, so I'm **sure** it's right.* **surer, surest**

swim To move through the water by moving the arms, legs, or fins: *Fish **swim** in the tank of water.* **swam, swum, swimming**

T

tadpole A young frog that lives in water and has a tail: *A **tadpole** will lose its tail when it grows into a frog.* **tadpoles**

tail **1.** A thin part that sticks out from the back of an animal's body: *Your dog is always wagging its **tail.*** **2.** Something that hangs like an animal's tail: *The kite had a **tail** made of cloth and string.* **tails**
◆ *These sound alike* **tail, tale.**

take **1.** To hold: *We **take** the brushes and start to paint.* **2.** To do: *I will **take** a bath after dinner.* **3.** To carry or cause to go along with one: *Franz and Mark **take** their little brother to school.* **took, taken, taking**

tale A story: *Luis told us a funny **tale** about going to camp.* **tales**
◆ *These sound alike* **tale, tail.**

tame Used to living with people: *We had a **tame** deer in our yard.* **tamer, tamest**

tease To annoy or bother by making fun of: *I don't like my brother to **tease** me.* **teased, teasing**

teasing A form of **tease**: *The children shouldn't be **teasing** the dog.*

teeth More than one **tooth**: *When your baby **teeth** fall out, new ones grow in.*

tell **1.** The opposite of **ask**: *If you ask a question, I'll **tell** you the answer.* **2.** To say in words: *I'm going to **tell** you a story.* **told, telling**

305

Spelling Dictionary

ten Being one more than nine: *Little Paul counted his **ten** toes.*

than Compared to: *Mountains are bigger **than** hills.*

thank To say that you are grateful that you were given something: *I **thank** my friends for the new books.* **thanked, thanking**

thanked The past form of **thank:** *We **thanked** Aunt Millie for the gift.*

thankful Grateful; full of thanks: *They were **thankful** when Tim found their lost cat.*

thanks A showing or saying that you are grateful or thankful: *She gave **thanks** for her good health.*

that **1.** The one farther away or at a distance: *This is a robin, and **that** is a sparrow.* **2.** The one just talked about: ***That** animal we saw in the forest was a fox.* **those**

the Used to show that a word stands for certain persons or things: ***The** dogs have black tails.*

them A form of **they:** *Did you see **them**? The letter was from **them**.*

then **1.** At the time: *We lived in the city **then**.* **2.** After that; next: *One more game, and **then** we should go home.*

these A form of **this:** *This is my hat. Are **these** your gloves?*

they The people, animals, or things last talked about; those ones: *Elephants are large, but **they** move quickly.*

they're A short way to write **they are:** ***They're** coming to visit next week.*

thing An object or animal that is not named: *What are those **things** on the table?* **things**

think **1.** To use your mind to form ideas: *Can you **think** of a gift to make for Miss Marble?* **2.** To believe: *I **think** the storm is over.* **thought, thinking**

this **1.** The one that is present, nearby, or that was just talked about: ***This** house is mine.* **2.** The one nearer than another: ***This** is an oak tree, and that is a pine tree.* **these**

those A form of **that:** *That sock is mine. **Those** are your socks.*

threw The past form of **throw:** *She **threw** the ball well.*
◆ *These sound alike* **threw, through.**

throne The special chair that a king or queen sits on: *The king sat on a **throne** made of gold.* **thrones**

throne

through **1.** In one side and out the other: *We walked **through** the parking lot.* **2.** Among or between: *She walked **through** the flowers.*
◆ *These sound alike* **through, threw.**

throw To send through the air with a quick motion of the arm: *Most dogs like people to **throw** a ball for them to chase.* **threw, thrown, throwing**

thunder   **trailer**

thunder The rumbling or crashing noise that comes after a flash of lightning: *The **thunder** was so loud that everyone jumped.*

tie A game or contest that ends with the same score for both sides: *Both teams scored six points, so the game was a **tie.*** **ties**

time A certain point in the past, present, or future, as shown on a clock: *The **time** right now is 3:30 in the afternoon.* **times**

to **1.** Toward: *I sang a song as I walked **to** school.* **2.** So as to reach: *They came **to** my house.* **3.** On or in contact with: *Tie a bow **to** the package.* **4.** Used with action words: *I would like **to** play with that game.*
◆ *These sound alike* **to, too, two.**

toe One of the parts that stick out from the foot. *There was a hole in Ann's sock, and her big **toe** was cold!* **toes**
◆ *These sound alike* **toe, tow.**

told The past form of **tell**: *Grandpa **told** us how to make a kite.*

too **1.** Also: *I want to go **too.*** **2.** More than enough: *Don't hold your pen **too** tightly.*
◆ *These sound alike* **too, to, two.**

took The past form of **take**: *Sam took his jacket from the closet.*

tooth One of the set of hard parts in the mouth used for chewing and biting: *His front **tooth** is loose.* **teeth**

toothbrush A small brush that is used to clean the teeth: *Beth picked up her new, orange **toothbrush** and brushed her teeth.* **toothbrushes**

top **1.** The opposite of **bottom;** the highest part: *I stood on the **top** of the hill.* **2.** A lid; a cover: *Please put the **top** on the box.* **tops**

tow To pull along behind with a chain, rope, or cable: *They had to **tow** our car to the garage.* **towed, towing**
◆ *These sound alike* **tow, toe.**

town A place where people live that is larger than a village but smaller than a city: *The family lived in a **town** just a few miles from the city.* **towns**

traffic The number of cars, buses, and trucks moving along roads and streets: *I see lots of **traffic** in the morning when people are driving to work.*

trail An outdoor path or track: *I hiked along the **trail** through the woods.* **trails**

trail

trailer A house with wheels that can be pulled by a car or truck. A trailer can be used as a home when it is parked or put up on cement blocks: *Our **trailer** has a kitchen, a bathroom, and three beds.* **trailers**

Spelling Dictionary

train A string of railroad cars used to move people or things. The cars are connected together and pulled by an engine: *The **train** stopped at our station and we began our trip.* **trains**

train

trash Things to be thrown away: *We put all the **trash** in a large bag and took it to the dump.*

tree A tall plant with branches and one main stem of wood: *The **tree** has many branches and leaves.* **trees**

trip A passing from one place to another; a journey: *We rode in a bus on our **trip** across the country.* **trips**

truck A large machine with wheels and a motor that is used to carry big or heavy loads: *The movers put the tables and chairs in a **truck** and took them to our new house.* **trucks**

trunk **1.** The covered, back part of a car, used for storage: *We put all of our camping gear in the **trunk**.* **2.** The long nose of an elephant, used for holding and feeding: *The elephant used its **trunk** to pick up the log.* **trunks**

try To make an effort: *The children **try** to stay quiet during the story.* **tried, trying**

tuba A large brass wind instrument with a full, rich sound: *You need a lot of air in your lungs to play the **tuba!*** **tubas**

tune A group of musical notes that make up a simple song: *David whistled a **tune** as he worked on his model airplane.* **tunes**

two Being one more than one: *She has **two** sisters.*
◆ *These sound alike* **two, to, too.**

under The opposite of **above;** below: *A boat was passing **under** the bridge.*

up From a lower to a higher place: *I threw the ball **up.***

upon On: *We stopped and sat down **upon** a flat rock.*

us A form of **we:** *They told **us** the latest news.*

use To do something with an object: *Did you **use** soap to wash your hands?* **used, using**

very A lot; really: *I am **very** happy that Liz is my friend.*

vest A jacket without sleeves that is worn over a shirt: *Dad wears a warm **vest** under his coat in the winter.* **vests**

wade To walk into or through something, such as water or mud, that keeps the feet from moving quickly: *On our hike we had to* **wade** *across a stream.* **waded, wading**

want To wish: *We* **want** *to play outdoors.* **wanted, wanting**

warm Somewhat hot: *I took a bath in* **warm** *water.* **warmer, warmest**

was A past form of **be**: *Bobby* **was** *the winner of that race.*

wash To clean using water and soap: *Whose turn is it to* **wash** *the dishes?* **washed, washing**

water That which falls from the sky as rain and forms rivers, oceans, and lakes: *I hope it rains soon because the trees need* **water**.

way 1. How you do something: *I like the* **way** *you kick a ball.* **2.** Travel along a road or path: *Lead the* **way** *home.* **ways**

we The people who are speaking or writing: **We** *went to the circus.*

weather The way it is outdoors. The weather may be hot or cold, sunny or cloudy, or wet or dry: *The* **weather** *is warm and cloudy.*

welcome 1. To greet warmly: *We will* **welcome** *our friend by giving him a hug.* **welcomed, welcoming 2.** Greeted or accepted warmly: *You are always a* **welcome** *visitor.*

well A deep hole that is dug into the ground to get water: *We pump water from the* **well** *into a pail.* **wells**

well 1. In a way that is good: *My dog behaves* **well. 2.** The opposite of sick; in good health: *I had a cold last week, but now I'm* **well** *again.*

we'll A short way to write **we will** or **we shall**: **We'll** *help you fix lunch tomorrow.*

went The past form of **go**: *We* **went** *to the store before we came home.*

wet Being soaked with water: *Brad went out in the rain and got* **wet**. **wetter, wettest**

we've A short way to write **we have**: **We've** *had fun at the park.*

what That which; the thing that: *I saw* **what** *you did.*

wheel 1. A round thing that can turn. Cars, trucks, and buses move on wheels: *The front* **wheel** *of my bicycle is bent, so I can't ride it.* **2.** Something that is shaped like a wheel: *The driver uses a steering* **wheel** *to turn the car.* **wheels**

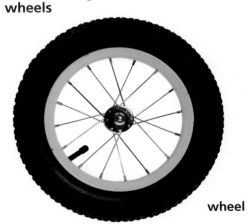

wheel

when 1. At what time: **When** *did you leave?* **2.** At or during the time that: *Jason will get off the school bus* **when** *it stops.*

309

Spelling Dictionary

which **1.** The one or ones talked about: *They bought the car, which was blue.* **2.** Being what one or ones: *Which coat is yours?*

while **1.** Some amount of time: *Please stay for a while.* **2.** During the time that: *Our vacation was great while it lasted.*

whistle To make a clear, high sound by forcing air through the teeth or lips: *Can you whistle a song?* **whistled, whistling**

white The opposite of **black**; the color of snow: *The moon looks white in the dark sky.* **whiter, whitest**

who The person or group that: *The friend who was here has left.*

whole Complete: *The whole class laughed at the joke.*
♦ *These sound alike* **whole, hole.**

why For what reason: *Why did you say that?*

will Used to show something that is going to take place in the future: *Mom will drive tomorrow.* **would**

win **1.** The opposite of **lose**; to be first in a game or contest: *Maria and Sara want to win the race.* **2.** To receive as a prize: *We may win a trip to New York.* **won, winning**

winter The coldest season of the year, between fall and spring: *This winter was very snowy.* **winters**

wish **1.** A strong hope for something: *I hope I get one of my three wishes.* **wishes** **2.** To hope for; want: *I wish to be a teacher when I grow up.* **wished, wishing**

with **1.** In the company of: *Come with me.* **2.** By means of; using: *We washed the clothes with soap.*

without Not having: *I painted that picture without help.*

would The past form of **will**: *You said that you would help me dry the dishes.*

wouldn't A short way to write **would not**: *He wouldn't play with us.*

write **1.** To form letters or words on a piece of paper with a pen or pencil: *Write your name on the top of your paper.* **2.** To make up a story, a poem, or a play for someone to read: *I like to write stories for my family and friends.* **wrote, written, writing**

yard A length equal to 3 feet or 36 inches: *A yard is less than a meter.* **yards**

yard A piece of ground near a building: *I raked the grass in the yard.* **yards**

yard

310

yes   zoo

yes **1.** It is true: *Yes, Sue is home from work.* **2.** An answer that shows something is all right or okay: *Our teacher said* **yes** *when we asked if we could stay inside.*

you The one or ones spoken or written to: *This package is addressed to* **you.**

you'll A short way to write **you will** or **you shall:** *I hope* **you'll** *come to my party next week.*

young Not old or fully grown: *The* **young** *prince hoped to become a knight.* **younger, youngest**

your Belonging to you: *Where did you put* **your** *books?*
◆ *These sound alike* **your, you're.**

you're A short way to write **you are:** **You're** *my best friend.*
◆ *These sound alike* **you're, your.**

Z

zoo A large place where living animals are kept. People can go to a zoo and see the animals: *I saw tigers at the* **zoo. zoos**

ZOO

Content Index

Numbers in **boldface** indicate pages on which a skill is introduced as well as references to the Capitalization and Punctuation Guide.

Content Index

alphabetical order, 26, 74, 110, 134, 158, 182, 218

self-assessment, 26, 32, 38, 44, 50, 62, 68, 74, 80, 86, 98, 104, 110, 116, 122, 134, 140, 146, 152, 158, 170, 176, 182, 188, 194, 206, 212, 218, 224, 230

spelling strategies, 24–25, 30–31, 36–37, 42–43, 48–49, 54–57, 60–61, 66–67, 72–73, 78–79, 84–85, 90–93, 96–97, 102–103, 108–109, 114–115, 120–121, 126–129, 132–133, 138–139, 144–145, 150–151, 156–157, 162–165, 168–169, 174–175, 180–181, 186–187, 192–193, 198–201, 204–205, 210–211, 216–217, 222–223, 228–229, 234–237
See also Vocabulary.

Spelling Across the Curriculum

art, 29
careers, 113, 125
health, 47, 191
math, 143
music, 89
physical education, 227
recreation, 77
science, 35, 53, 71, 83, 107, 149, 155, 173, 179, 197, 221

social studies, 41, 65, 101, 119, 137, 161, 185, 209, 215, 233

Spelling and Meaning

word forms, 57, 93, 129, 160, 165, 201, 237, 272–275

Thinking Skills

analogies, 31, 49, 73, 109, 121, 151, 157, 181, 217

analyzing. *See* A, B pages in each Basic Unit. *See also* 57, 93, 129, 165, 201, 237

classifying, 43, 67, 79, 97, 133, 205, 217, 229

creative thinking, 33, 39, 69, 70, 88, 101, 123, 135, 141, 147, 153, 154, 159, 161, 171, 195, 219, 225, 233

critical thinking, 29, 35, 41, 47, 65, 77, 83, 89, 107, 113, 125, 137, 143, 149, 155, 173, 179, 185, 191, 209, 215, 221, 226

drawing logical conclusions, 130, 202, 238

identifying main idea, 166
making generalizations. *See* A pages in each Basic Unit.

making inferences, 37, 50, 54, 57, 61, 85, 86, 92, 98, 103, 126, 139, 152, 162, 164, 187, 198, 223, 235, 241, 242, 243, 245, 247, 250, 254, 258

persuasion, 75, 101, 105, 141, 214

predicting outcomes, 130

sequencing, 26, 38, 50, 68, 74, 110, 122, 130–131, 134, 135, 147, 158, 166–167, 170, 182, 218, 230

using graphic organizers, 142, 232

Vocabulary

See also Spelling and Meaning.

antonyms, 55, 73, 85, 91, 133, 145, 163, 169, 198, 200, 217, 220, 234, 244, 256

base words, 57, 93, 129, 165, 201, 237, 272–275

cloze activities, 29, 31, 32, 35, 41, 43, 44, 47, 49, 50, 53–57, 65, 68, 71, 73, 80, 83, 89, 90–93, 101, 103, 107, 109–110, 112, 115, 119, 121–122, 125–129, 134, 136–137, 143, 149, 151, 155, 157–158, 160–165, 173, 181, 188, 191, 197–201, 206, 208, 212, 215, 217–218, 221, 223, 227, 233–237, 241–258

compound words, **186–190**, 199, 254

content area vocabulary, 29, 35, 41, 47, 53, 65, 71, 77, 83, 89, 101, 107, 113, 119, 125, 137, 143, 149, 155, 161, 173, 179, 185, 191, 197, 209, 215, 221, 227, 233

context clues, 54, 55, 56, 57, 71, 86, 90, 91, 92, 93, 119, 126, 127, 128, 129, 134, 158, 162, 163, 164, 165, 182, 188, 198, 199, 200, 201, 212, 234, 235, 236, 241, 242, 243, 244, 245, 246, 247, 248, 249, 250, 251, 252, 253, 254, 255, 256, 257, 258

313

Content Index

Credits

Illustrations **100** Annie Gusman **101** Lehner & Whyte **107** Lehner & Whyte **118** Jennifer Harris **134** Annie Gusman **153** Lehner & Whyte **172** Linda Davick **177** Lehner & Whyte **178** Mary Lynn Carson **190** Lehner & Whyte **209** Fred Schrier **215** Marina Thompson **220** Lehner & Whyte

Assignment Photography **22** Allan Landau, **61** (b), **82** (tl), **85** (b), **97** (m), **98** (b),**133, 139, 140** (bl) (br), **148** (b), **152** (b), **172** (b), **181** Allan Landau **167** (br), **206** (mr), **217** Parker/Boone Productions **57** (tr), **64** (t), **76** (tr) (tl), **113** (t), **115** (b), **166–167, 187** (b), **202, 238–239** Tony Scarpetta **25** (b), **31** (b), **37** (b), **43, 93** (tr) Tracey Wheeler

Photography **3** Rich Iwasaki/Allstock/PNI **8, 16** (dog) Images Copyright © 1997 PhotoDisc, Inc. **16** (web) © Archive Photos/PNI **29, 35** Images Copyright © 1997 PhotoDisc, Inc. **38** Larry Lefever/Grant Heilman Photography **41** Grandma Moses: <u>Country Fair</u> Copyright ©1996, Grandma Moses Properties Co., New York. **49** Rich Iwasaki/Allstock/PNI **53** T. Nakajima/Photonica **65** Free Library of Philadelphia **71** (t) David J. Sams/Tony Stone Images **71** (br) Image Copyright © 1997 PhotoDisc, Inc. **71** (bl) Chris Butler/Science Photo Library/Photo Researchers **77** Andre Jebby/Stock South/PNI **82** (bl) Image Copyright © 1997 PhotoDisc, Inc. **83** NASA/Mark Marten/Science Source/Photo Researchers **89** The Granger Collection **95** Lawrence Migdale/Tony Stone Images **100** David Epperson/Allstock/PNI **101** Corbis-Bettmann **103** Joe McDonald/Bruce Coleman/PNI **109** Image Copyright © 1997 PhotoDisc, Inc. **113** AKG Photo London **116** Image Copyright © 1997 PhotoDisc, Inc. **119, 125** (b) Corbis-Bettmann **129** Strauss & Curtis/The Stock Market **137** AKG Photo London **143** Jack Fields/Corbis **149** (t) Peter Scoones/Masterfile **149** (b), **151** (r) Images Copyright © 1997 PhotoDisc, Inc. **155** Jerald P. Fish/Tony Stone Images **161** The Granger Collection **165** Robert Daemmrich/Tony Stone Images **169** H. Heyn/Milon/Photo Researchers, Inc. **171** NASA **173** Frank Zullo/Science Source/Photo Researchers, Inc.

175 Kathi Lamm/Allstock/PNI **177, 178** (tl) (br) Images Copyright © 1997 PhotoDisc, Inc. **178** John Scheiber/The Stock Market **179** Patrice Ceisel/Stock, Boston/PNI **185** (tl) Dave Bartruff/Corbis **185** (tr) Martin Jones/Corbis **185** (ml) Dave Rosenberg/Tony Stone Images **185** (mr) © Cs. Rafael, 1994/Sovfoto/Eastfoto/PNI **185** (b) Michael Fogden/ Oxford Scientific Films/Earth Scenes **191** (r) David Madison/Tony Stone Images **191** (m) Robert E. Daemmrich/Tony Stone Images **191** (r) Jess Stock/Tony Stone Images **197** (tr) (b) Images Copyright © 1997 PhotoDisc, Inc. **203** (t) Peter Cade/Tony Stone Images **203** (m) Lawrence Migdale/Tony Stone Images **203** (b) Peter Beck/The Stock Market **209** (b) Joe Sohm/Chromosohm/ Stock Connection **215** Don Smetzer/Tony Stone Images **221** (b) Darryl Torckler/Tony Stone Images **223** Zigy Kaluzny/Tony Stone Images **225** Image Copyright © 1997 PhotoDisc, Inc. **226** Merlin D. Tuttle/Bat Conservation International **227** (m) Image Copyright © 1997 PhotoDisc, Inc. **227** (b) Karl Weatherly/Corbis **229** DeWitt Jones/ Corbis **232** Images Copyright © 1997 PhotoDisc, Inc. **233** Schomburg Center, NYPL **237** Roseanne Olson/Allstock/ PNI **239** Richard Hutchings/Photo Researchers, Inc. **277** Image Copyright © 1997 PhotoDisc, Inc. **278** Thomas Braise/The Stock Market **279** Image Copyright © 1997 PhotoDisc, Inc. **280** Tony Stone Images **281** Ted Mahieu/ The Stock Market **282, 283** Images Copyright © 1997 PhotoDisc, Inc. **285** Tom Brakefield/The Stock Market **286** Steve Grubman **287** James Amos/Corbis **288** Michael Hart/FPG International **289** Frank Fournier/Contact Press Images/PNI **290** Image Copyright © 1997 PhotoDisc, Inc. **291** Robert Brons/BPS/Tony Stone Images **292** Alese & Mort Pechter/The Stock Market **293, 295** Images Copyright © 1997 PhotoDisc, Inc. **297** Art Wolfe/Tony Stone Images **298** Renne Lynn/Tony Stone Images **299, 300, 301, 302, 303, 304** Images Copyright © 1997 PhotoDisc, Inc. **305** James Randkley/Tony Stone Images **306** © Christie's Images, 1995/PNI **307** David Ulmer/Stock, Boston/PNI **308** John Elk/Tony Stone Images **310** H.L. Miller/Stock South/PNI **311** Tom & Michelle Grimm/Tony Stone Images

Handwriting Models

a b c d e f g h i
j k l m n o p q r
s t u v w x y z

A B C D E F G H I
J K L M N O P Q R
S T U V W X Y Z

a b c d e f g h i
j k l m n o p q r
s t u v w x y z

A B C D E F G H I
J K L M N O P Q R
S T U V W X Y Z

Words Often Misspelled

You use many of the words on this page in your writing. Check this list if you cannot think of the spelling for a word you need. The words are in ABC order.

A
again
always
am
and
are

B
because
before

C
cannot
coming
could

D
down

F
family
for
friend
from

G
getting
girl
goes
going

H
have
here
how

I
I'm
it
it's

K
knew
know

L
letter
little

N
name
new
now

O
on
other
our
outside

P
pretty

R
really
right

S
said
school
some
something
started

T
that's
their
there
through
time
tried

V
very

W
want
was
went
were
where
would
write

Y
you
your

The effectiveness of a spelling and vocabulary program begins with its word list. The word lists in *Houghton Mifflin Spelling and Vocabulary* are based on the results of extensive research in the following areas:

1. frequency of use in student compositions,
2. frequency of appearance in reading materials,
3. reading familiarity, and
4. spelling difficulty.

RESEARCH

Among the materials used in the development of the word lists were the following studies and word sources:

- **Dolch Basic Sight Vocabulary**—Edward Dolch's list of 220 high-frequency words
- **800 Base Words**—a list of the 800 base words of highest frequency of occurrence in the American Heritage computerized study of the vocabulary of published materials used in American public schools in grades 3 and 4
- **Starter Words**—Robert L. Hillerich's list of the 190 most frequently used words in children's writing, adult print materials, and school materials for grades 3–9
- *The American Heritage Word Frequency Book*—a study by John B. Carroll, et al., of word frequency in print materials used in grades 3–9
- **Jacobson**—a study of word frequency in more than 20,000 student compositions, conducted by Milton D. Jacobson for Houghton Mifflin Company (unpublished)
- *The New Iowa Spelling Scale*—Harry A. Greene's study of spelling difficulty
- *Basic Skills Word List*—a study of reading familiarity of words by grade level
- *The Living Word Vocabulary*—a study by Edgar Dale and Joseph O'Rourke of students' familiarity with words and word meanings by grade level

The data from the existing research was compiled and stored in an electronic data base. Every word considered for inclusion in *Houghton Mifflin Spelling and Vocabulary* was then evaluated by entering it into the data base and analyzing all of the data available on that word. This use of technology ensured that the process of word selection was as thorough and meticulous as possible. The resulting word lists present the words that students need to know at the most appropriate grade level.

PLACEMENT

Careful attention was given to placing the words not only in the appropriate grade levels, but also in the appropriate type of word list. Each unit of *Houghton Mifflin Spelling and Vocabulary* contains five distinct word lists: Basic Words, Challenge Words, Review Words, Content Area Vocabulary, and Words Often Misspelled. Each word list has its own purpose, characteristics, and level of difficulty.

- The **Basic Words** exemplify the spelling principle that is the focus of the unit. Among the words that could be used to illustrate the principle, those with the highest frequency ranks were selected to be Basic Words. In terms of reading familiarity, the Basic Words are usually at or below the grade level at which they are presented. These words, however, represent a level of spelling difficulty that most students at the grade level have not yet mastered.

  As part of the Basic Words, some units also contain Elephant Words. These words represent the unit principle in spelling but are exceptions to the principle in pronunciation, or vice versa. For example, *from* is an Elephant Word in a Level 2 unit in which the principle is spelling the |ŭ| sound with *u*.

- Each of the **Challenge Words** illustrates the unit spelling principle. These words are above grade level in both reading and spelling difficulty.

- All **Review Words** in this grade level are introduced as Basic Words in previous levels. Whenever possible, the Review Words illustrate the spelling principle.

- The **Content Area Vocabulary** are words commonly used in curriculum materials and print materials found outside the classroom. Students' vocabularies are enhanced as they learn specific meanings related to a particular topic, whether or not the words are familiar to them in other contexts.

- The **Words Often Misspelled** are high-frequency words for writing that students tend to misspell in this grade level.

- **The Spelling Strategy Words** are included in the "Applying Spelling Strategies" feature in the Teacher's Edition. Students use strategies they have learned to spell or read these new words.

- **Special Words for Writing** (level 1 only) are high-frequency words taken from Hillerich's Starter Words. These words do not follow the principles taught in Level 1 but are necessary for students to learn in order to be able to write.

Examples of words used in various word lists in Level 5, Unit 4, are shown below.

Word	Type	Dolch	800 Base Words	Starter Words	American Heritage	Jacobson	Iowa	Basic Skills	Living Word
choose	Basic	—	Y	N	722	1795	5–6	3	4
group	Review	—	Y	N	319	597	4–5	3	4
pursuit	Challenge	—	Y	N	6977	5397	8–9	7	6
view	Basic	—	Y	N	1566	1339	5–6	4	4
warrant	Content Area	—	N	N	13755	—	8–9	7	6

According to the research, the word *choose* does not appear on the Dolch or Starter Word lists (since these lists apply more to the primary levels), although it does appear on the list of 800 Base Words. In the American Heritage study of word frequency, *choose* has a rank of 722 (i.e., there are 721 more frequently used words); in the Jacobson study, its rank is 1795. According to the Iowa Scale, 50% of students between grades 5 and 6 spell *choose* correctly. The grade level at which students are familiar with *choose* when they read the word is grade 3, according to the Basic Skills Word List, and grade 4, according to the *Living Word Vocabulary*. Based on this data, the word *choose* was placed as a Basic Word in Unit 4 of Level 5, a unit that teaches the |o͞o| sound.

The examples below are from Level 2, Unit 14, which teaches spellings for the |ē| sound.

Word	Type	Dolch	800 Base Words	Starter Words	American Heritage	Jacobson	Iowa	Basic Skills	Living Word
keep	Basic	2.1	Y	Y	207	204	3–4	2	—
he	Review	P	Y	Y	11	5	1–2	1	—

The word *keep* appears on the Dolch list for the first half of second grade (*he* appears on the primer level) and also appears on the list of 800 Base Words and the Starter Word list. *Keep* has a frequency rank of 207 on the American Heritage study and 204 in the Jacobson study. According to the Iowa Scale, 50% of students between grades 3 and 4 spell *keep* correctly. According to the Basic Skills Word List, *keep* is a familiar reading word to students in grade 2. (*Living Word Vocabulary* does not analyze reading familiarity below grade 4.)

Bibliography

Bear, Donald R.; Invernizzi, Marcia; Johnston, Francine; Templeton, Shane. *Words Their Way: Word Study for Phonics, Vocabulary, and Spelling Instruction.* Englewood Cliffs, New Jersey, Prentice-Hall Inc., 1996.

Carroll, John B.; Davies, Peter; and Richman, Barry. *The American Heritage Word Frequency Book*. Boston, Houghton Mifflin Company, 1971.

Dale, Edgar, and O'Rourke, Joseph. *The Living Word Vocabulary*. Field Enterprises Educational Corporation, 1976.

Dolch, Edward W. *Better Spelling*. Champaign, IL, Garrard Press, 1942.

Greene, Harry A. *The New Iowa Spelling Scale*. Iowa City, State University of Iowa, 1954.

Hillerich, Robert L. "'A Little Dab'l Do Ya'?" *Teaching K-8*, (January 1988) 23–27.

IOX, *Basic Skills Word List*, IOX, Los Angeles, 1980.

The following list contains every Basic, Review, Challenge, Content Area Vocabulary Word, Word Often Misspelled, Spelling Strategy Word, and Special Word for Writing (Level 1 only) presented in *Houghton Mifflin Spelling and Vocabulary,* Levels 1-6.

- The **numbers** following each word indicate the level(s) and unit(s) in which the word appears.

- Many numbers are followed by a **letter** indicating the type of list on which the word appears. If no letter follows the unit number, the word is presented as a Basic Word. The Word List Key shows the letters used to indicate the types of word lists.

- Words marked with an **asterisk** are included in the Additional Words Lists in each Basic Unit in the Teacher's Edition.

- Words in blue are taught in this level.

Word List Key

*	Additional Words List	**CA**	Content Area Word
C	Challenge Word	**SW**	Special Word for Writing
R	Review Word	**WOM**	Word Often Misspelled
		SS	Spelling Strategy Word

A sample entry is shown below:

around 2-27C*, 3-16WOM*, 3-34, 4-9R*, 4-17WOM*

This entry indicates that **around** appears in Level 2, Unit 27, as an Additional Challenge Word; in Level 3, Unit 16, as a Word Often Misspelled and in Unit 34 as a Basic Word; and in Level 4, Units 9 and 17 respectively, as an Additional Review Word and as a Word Often Misspelled.

A

a 1–1SW, 2–1R
a lot 3–19WOM*, 4–25WOM*, 5–20WOM*, 6–14WOM*
abandon 6–10C*
abbreviation 6–25C*
abilities 5–28, 6–26R
ablaze 4–29*
able 3–33, 4–15R
abolish 6–10CA
about 1–14SW, 3–34, 4–31R*
above 3–34*
abrupt 4–29C
absence 6–28
absent 2–7CA, 5–33, 6–17R
absorb 5–7C*
abstain 5–16C
absurd 6–5C
abundant 6–23C*
abuses 6–33CA
academy 4–31CA
Acadia 5–34CA
accelerate 6–2C*
accent 6–32C*
accept 6–17
accepted 5–20C*
accident 4–35CA, 5–33, 6–32R
accidentally 6–35
accommodate 6–32C*
accompany 6–32*
accomplish 4–4C, 6–32
accomplishment 5–22C*
according 6–32
account 6–32
accountant 6–32CA
accumulate 6–32C

accurate 6–32
accuse 5–4C, 6–32
ache 4–19
achieve 4–29, 5–26R*, 6–31R*
achievement 6–14*
acknowledged 6–33CA
acquaint 6–2SS
acquaintance 6–35C*
acquire 6–32
acre 6–9
acrobat 3–9CA
across 2–11C*, 4–32*
act 3–35CA, 5–29
action 5–29, 6–25R
active 6–22*
actively 5–22
activity 4–1C
actor 5–11, 6–11R
actual 5–17*
adapt 5–26C, 6–32*
add 1–1C*, 2–11
addition 6–32
address 2–11C*, 5–16, 6–32R
adhesive 6–22C*
adjoin 6–4C
adjourn 5–16CA, 6–32C*
adjust 6–32
admirable 6–23*
admiral 6–17
admiration 6–19
admire 6–19
admit 6–11
admitted 6–13*
admonish 6–32C*
adopt 5–29C*, 6–16
adoption 5–29C*
adorable 6–14

adore 5–19, 6–32R
adorn 6–32*
advanced 6–14
advancement 6–35
advantage 6–22
advent 6–32C*
adventure 5–23, 6–32R
advertise 6–22
advice 4–3C, 6–32
advise 6–32
advocate 6–15CA
affair 6–32
affect 6–20
affection 6–20
affiliated 6–32C
affirmative 6–32SS
afflict 6–32*
afford 2–32C, 3–28*
afraid 2–13C*, 4–29
after 2–33, 3–27R
afternoon 4–13, 5–9R
again 2–35WOM*, 3–19WOM*, 3–34, 4–17WOM*, 4–32R, 5–7WOM*, 6–15WOM*
against 4–35
age 3–16, 4–20R*
agency 6–27CA
agenda 6–15CA
agent 6–23
aggressive 6–22C
ago 1–8C*, 3–34, 4–31R*
agree 3–34C*, 4–29
agreeable 5–33*
agricultural 6–10C
ahead 3–34, 4–31R*
aid 4–1

ailment 4–28C
aim 2–13*
air 3–19, 4–10R
airplane 1–10C*, 2–28*, 3–21, 4–13R*
airport 4–13, 5–13R
aisle 5–10C*
alarm 2–4CA, 3–13C*, 4–10
alert 4–31C, 6–16
alive 2–7SS, 3–34, 4–31R
all 1–7SW, 2–15
all right 3–10C*, 4–13, 5–9R, 5–20WOM*, 6–14WOM*
allegiance 5–28CA
alley 4–17
allow 3–9C*, 4–22, 5–26R
allowance 6–28
almost 3–10, 4–32R*
alone 2–8C*, 3–34*, 4–32
along 3–34SS
aloud 4–9, 5–19R*
alphabet 4–33, 5–34R*
already 4–13
also 1–8C*, 3–10, 4–25WOM*, 4–32R*, 5–7WOM*
alter 6–19*
alteration 5–33CA, 6–19*
altered 5–21C*
alternate 5–5C*
alternative 6–22C
although 5–16
altitude 6–13CA
altos 6–26
aluminum 4–5CA
always 2–35WOM*, 3–19WOM*, 4–9, 4–25WOM*, 5–5R*,

5–20WOM*, 6–14WOM*
am 2–1, 2–7WOM*, 3–1WOM*
amateur 5–35C
amaze 4–32, 5–19R
amazing 5–20*
ambassador 6–9C
ambitious 6–25C*
ambulance 3–29C*, 6–17
amendment 5–32CA
among 3–34C, 5–26*
amount 3–9C*, 5–5*
amplifiers 5–16SS
amusement 4–28C*, 6–14
amusing 5–20
an 1–1, 2–19R
anarchy 6–9CA
ancestor 6–9SS
anchor 4–14C, 5–16*
ancient 6–25
and 1–1SW, 2–7WOM*, 2–19, 3–1WOM*
angel 5–14
angelic 4–19SS
anger 5–11
angle 5–14
angriest 4–25, 5–28R
angry 2–26C*, 3–25CA
angular 6–9C*
animal 4–33, 5–34R*
animals 3–3CA
animate 5–29C
animation 5–29C
ankle 5–14
announce 5–5C*
annoy 6–4
annual 5–17*
another 3–34WOM*,

bleachers 3–7CA
bleed 3–4*
blew 2–23C*, 3–31*, 4–7, 5–4R
blind 3–8*, 4–3
blink 3–1*
blizzard 4–25CA
block 2–4C, 4–4, 5–1R*
blockade 6–10CA
blond 2–4C*
blood 3–11CA, 4–35
bloom 6–4
blossom 5–26
blouse 2–27*
blow 3–5
blue 2–23C*, 3–31, 4–7R
bluffing 4–16C*
blur 5–8
board 3–20C*, 4–11, 5–7R
boards 3–22CA
boast 3–5SS, 5–3, 6–2R
boat 2–21, 3–5R*
body 1–4C*, 4–17
boil 3–15
bold 4–4*
bomb 4–34C*, 6–1
bone 2–8
bonus 4–4C*
book 2–22
bookkeeper 6–7C*
bookshelf 3–21C*
boost 5–4*
booster 4–29CA
boot 2–22*, 3–31, 4–8R*
booth 2–3CA, 4–8*
borders 4–31CA
bore 5–7, 6–5R*
bored 3–20C*
born 2–32
borough 6–8C
borrow 4–23
borrowed 5–20
boss 2–11*
both 2–17*, 3–5, 4–4R*
bother 4–29
bothered 6–13
bottle 4–15, 5–14R*
bottom 4–23, 5–15R
bought 3–32
boulder 4–14C*
bounce 3–9C, 4–9, 5–5R*
bountiful 5–5SS, 6–4C
bouquet 5–19C*
boutique 5–33CA
bow 3–9
bowl 3–5*, 4–4
box 1–4, 2–4R

boxes 2–20
boy 3–15
boycott 5–28CA
brace 4–20*
braces 2–17CA
bracket 4–29*
brag 3–28CA
bragging 5–21, 6–13R*
braid 2–13*
brain 5–2, 6–2R
brake 3–20C*, 6–2
branches 2–9C, 3–22CA
brand 6–22CA
brass 2–11C, 6–1
brave 1–10C*, 2–9
bread 3–1CA, 4–35*
break 3–20C*, 4–1
breakfast 4–13, 5–9R
breath 5–1, 6–3R
breathe 3–11CA, 5–2*
breathing 4–16C
breathless 5–22, 6–14R
breeze 2–9C*
breezier 4–25C
brick 4–3
bride 2–9*
bridge 4–20, 5–23R
bridle 4–11CA
brief 6–31
bright 3–8, 4–3R*
brilliant 6–23
bring 2–19
broadcast 5–29CA
broadcaster 6–11CA
broccoli 4–32SS
broil 3–15*
broke 4–4, 5–3R
bronze 4–5CA
brook 2–10CA, 4–8
brother 2–33, 3–16R, 4–29R*
brother–in–law 5–9
brought 3–22WOM*, 3–32, 4–33WOM*, 5–15WOM*, 6–10WOM*
brown 2–27, 3–9R*
bruise 5–4
brush 3–19CA, 4–7
bubble 3–33*
bucket 2–5C*, 4–29
buckle 4–19*
budget 6–21CA
buffalo 4–32CA
bug 1–7*, 2–5
build 3–22CA, 4–3
built 4–3
bulge 4–20C*
bulldozer 6–19CA
bullet 6–11

bulletin 4–8C
bulletin board 5–9C*, 6–20CA
bumblebee 3–17CA
bumpy 3–20CA
bun 2–5
bunch 5–1, 6–1R
bundle 6–10
bunk 5–1
bunnies 3–23SS
burden 6–11
burglar 5–11
burn 4–11
burnt 3–20CA, 5–8
burro 6–8C
burrow 6–8C
burst 4–11*
bury 4–5C*, 5–10, 6–8R
bus 1–7*, 2–5
bush 4–8
bushel 5–14
bushes 2–20*
busier 5–28
businesswoman 5–13C*
busy 4–27
but 1–7, 2–5
butter 3–28
butterflies 4–25*
butterfly 1–23C*
button 3–28, 4–32R*
buy 2–25, 3–19R, 4–8WOM*, 5–21WOM*
buzz 3–17CA
by 1–23, 2–23R

C

cab 2–1*
cabbage 4–20, 5–25R*
cabin 2–9CA, 4–27
cabinet 6–9CA
caboose 2–13CA, 4–31*
cactus 3–17C*, 4–32CA
cadet 4–31C
cage 3–16*, 4–20
cake 2–10*
calcium 4–5CA
calculator 5–11C*
calendar 4–14C*, 6–9
calf 3–23CA, 4–34
call 2–15, 3–10R*
caller 3–26*
calm 4–34
calmly 3–26C, 5–22*
calves 6–26
came 1–10, 2–15R
camel 5–19
camera 4–33, 5–29R
camp 1–1C*
campaign 5–2C, 6–22CA

camper 2–9CA
campfire 5–1CA
campsite 4–8CA
campus 6–11
can 1–1, 2–1R
can't 2–29, 3–10WOM*, 3–35R, 4–3WOM*, 5–19WOM*, 6–5WOM*
canal 4–31*
canaries 3–23C
canary 5–34, 6–17R*
cancel 4–15C, 6–10
canceled 5–21C*
candid 4–22C, 6–11*
candidate 5–2C
candies 3–23*
candle 4–15
cannot 2–16WOM*, 2–28, 3–10WOM*, 3–21R, 4–3WOM*, 5–19WOM*, 6–5WOM*
canoe 5–1CA
canteen 4–8CA
canvas 5–10C
canvass 5–10C
canyon 4–23, 5–26R*
capable 6–23
cape 2–1CA
Capitol 5–16CA
capsule 4–29CA
captain 4–14CA, 5–23, 6–11R*, 6–15WOM*
caption 4–33CA
captive 5–25, 6–22R*
capture 4–32, 5–23R
car 2–31
cardinal 5–5CA
care 3–19
cared 3–22, 4–16R
career 5–8C
carefree 6–7
careful 2–4CA, 3–26, 4–28R
careless 4–28, 5–22R
cargo 6–1CA
carnival 5–35*
carpenter 4–33, 5–35R*
carpentry 6–19CA
carpet 2–31C, 3–27*, 4–23
carriage 4–20, 5–25R*
carried 3–23, 4–25R
carrot 5–26
carry 2–26C*
cart 2–32CA
carton 3–13C*, 6–10*
cartoon 2–22C*, 4–33CA
cartwheel 2–31C*
carve 5–7
carving 4–16C*
cashew 4–7SS

cashier 6–5C*
casserole 5–21CA
cast 3–35CA
castle 2–19CA, 3–33C*, 4–34
casual 5–17*
cat 1–1, 2–27R
catalog 6–22CA
catch 1–1C*, 2–16, 3–11R
categories 4–25C
catering 5–21C
caterpillar 4–27CA
cattle 2–16CA, 4–15
caught 3–22WOM*, 3–32, 4–33WOM*, 5–15WOM*, 6–10WOM*
cauliflower 6–4CA
cause 4–9, 5–5R
caused 3–22C*
caution 5–15CA, 6–25
cavalry 6–10CA
cave 2–7*
cavern 4–4CA
caves 1–20*
cavity 3–31CA
cease 5–2C
cedar 6–8CA
ceiling 6–31
celebrate 6–28
celebration 6–19SS
celery 4–17C*, 5–34*
cell 5–8CA
cellar 4–14
cellos 6–26
cent 2–23C*, 3–29*, 4–15CA
center 2–33C, 3–29, 4–14R
central 5–14*
cereal 4–7CA
certain 3–29, 4–23R*, 5–23R*
chain 2–16*
chair 1–19C*, 3–19, 4–10R
chairperson 6–7*
chalk 3–10*
chalkboard 3–21C*, 5–13
challenge 4–23C
chamber 5–11C
champion 4–1C, 5–35
chance 3–29*, 4–20
chancellor 6–9C
change 2–20CA, 3–16*, 4–20
changeable 6–14
channel 5–29CA, 6–10
chapter 2–33C*, 4–14, 5–11R*
character 5–11C, 6–9*
charcoal 2–31C*, 3–10CA
charge 3–16*, 4–10, 5–7R*
charm 4–10
chart 5–7*, 6–5
charter 5–26C

chase 2–16
chased 2–35
cheap 4–2
cheat 5–2*
check 3–34CA
checkbook 6–16CA
checkers 2–16C*
checking 4–16, 5–20R
cheek 3–17*
cheer 4–10, 5–8R*
cheerful 5–22
cheerleader 5–9
cheery 4–17*
cheese 1–14C*
chef 4–2C
chemicals 5–31CA
cherries 3–23*
chest 1–16C*, 2–16*
chew 2–16C*, 3–31, 4–7R
chick 3–23*
chicken 4–29
chief 4–2
chiefs 6–26
chieftain 5–23*
child 3–8
children 2–20, 5–16R*
chime 4–3*
chimney 4–17SS
chimp 1–19C*
chin 1–19, 2–16R
chip 1–19*
chipmunk 2–19SS, 4–27CA
choice 3–15C*, 5–5*
choked 2–35SS
choose 2–22C*, 5–4
chop 1–19, 2–16, 3–2R*
chopped 3–22
chopping 2–34C*
chore 4–11
chores 2–20CA
chorus 6–16C*
chose 2–8C*, 4–4, 5–3R*
chosen 4–26
Christopher Columbus
  5–23CA
chronic 6–33C
chunk 4–19*
church 3–14*
chute 3–3C*, 5–4*
cider 3–29C*
cinema 5–20CA
cinnamon 5–21CA
circle 3–29, 4–15R
circuit 5–19CA, 6–5C*
circumstances 6–5C
circus 3–29, 4–32R*
circuses 2–20C*
cirque 6–25CA

cities 4–25, 5–28R
citizen 5–34*
citizens 6–9CA
city 2–26C*, 3–29, 4–17R,
  4–27R*
civilize 6–22
claim 5–2
clam 1–13*, 4–19CA
clamor 5–11C
clamp 4–3CA
clap 1–13, 2–22R
clapped 2–34, 3–22R*
clarify 6–15CA
clarinet 6–26CA
class 1–13C*, 3–1, 4–1R*
classes 2–20C
classified 5–28C*
classmate 5–13, 6–7R*
classroom 2–28*
clause 6–4
claw 2–15C, 5–5
clay 1–17SS, 3–4, 4–1R
clean 2–14, 3–4R*
cleanliness 4–28C
cleanse 6–3
clear 3–13, 4–10R*
clearing 2–9CA
clefs 6–26C*
clever 4–31
click 3–17*
client 6–23
cliff 2–11C*, 6–1
cliffs 6–26*
climate 6–28*
climb 2–9C*, 4–34, 5–23R
clinic 4–28CA
clip 2–15CA
clock 2–10, 3–17R*
close 2–8, 3–17R*
closed 2–35, 3–22R*
closeness 5–22
closet 4–31C*, 5–19
cloth 2–15C*, 3–10
clothes 3–5C*, 5–32WOM*,
  6–33WOM*
cloud 1–13C*, 2–27*, 3–9
cloudier 4–25
clover 5–11
clown 2–27*, 3–9, 4–9R
club 1–13, 2–9, 3–2R*
clue 4–7*, 5–4
clump 2–9SS
clumsy 4–23C*
clutter 4–14*
coach 2–13CA, 3–5
coal 4–4
coarse 5–10*
coast 2–21C, 4–4
coat 2–21, 3–17R

coat of arms 4–34CA
coax 6–2C
cobblestones 4–20CA
cocoa 4–4C*
cocoon 4–8C
code 5–3, 6–2R
coil 3–15*
coin 3–15
coins 2–20C
cold 2–21, 3–5R
coldly 3–26*
collage 4–21CA
collapsed 5–20, 6–14R
collar 3–32CA, 4–14, 5–11R
collect 2–14CA, 5–15
college 6–22
collide 5–15C
collie 4–9CA
colonel 6–10C
colonies 5–28C
color 3–33, 4–14R*, 4–27R*
colorful 3–26C*, 4–28, 5–22R*
colt 4–11CA
Columbia 4–13CA
column 6–16C*
comb 3–5C*, 4–7CA, 4–34*,
  5–3*
combination 6–19
combine 6–19
come 3–3
comedy 6–17SS, 6–28CA
comfortable 5–33, 6–35R
coming 2–14WOM*, 3–22*,
  3–28WOM*, 4–4WOM*,
  5–3WOM*, 6–4WOM*
command 5–19CA
commencement 6–14C*
comment 6–21
commerce 6–31CA
commercial 5–29CA
commission 6–21C
committee 5–16CA
commodity 6–31CA
common 4–22, 5–32R
commotion 6–21
communities 5–28C*
community 6–21
commute 4–7C
compact 6–21*
compact disk 5–9C*
companies 4–25C*
companion 5–35, 6–21R*
company 6–17
compare 3–19C, 5–32, 6–21R
compass 4–4CA, 6–21*
compassion 6–21*
compensate 6–21C
compete 6–21

complain 5–16, 6–21R*
complaint 6–21CA
complete 3–34CA, 5–32*
complex 5–16, 6–21R
compliance 6–21C
complicate 5–2C*, 6–21
compliment 6–21C*
compose 3–27C*, 4–23, 5–32R
composition 5–32C*, 6–21
compositor 6–35CA
compound 5–32
comprehensive 6–21C
compromise 5–16CA
computer 4–7C*, 5–19CA,
  6–21
con 6–34CA
conceal 6–2C*
conceit 6–31
concentration 6–21SS, 6–35
concern 5–32, 6–21R
concert 3–29C, 6–21
conch 6–7CA
concise 5–32C, 6–21*
conclude 6–20
conclusion 6–20
concrete 5–16C*, 6–19CA
condition 5–34, 6–25R
condor 5–5CA
conduct 5–32, 6–21R*
cone 3–3SS
Confederacy 6–10CA
conference 6–21
confess 5–31, 6–21R*
confession 5–31, 6–25R,
  6–35R*
confidence 6–28C*
confident 6–21C*
confirm 6–21
conflict 5–16C*, 6–21
conform 5–32*
confront 6–21
confuse 5–31C*, 6–20
confusion 5–31C*, 6–20
Congress 5–16C, 6–11*
connect 6–19
connection 6–19
conquer 6–21
conscience 5–16C
consecutively 6–14C
consent 5–32
consequence 6–21C
conservation 6–21C*
consider 5–35, 6–9R
considerable 6–23
considerate 6–28
consist 5–32
consolidate 6–21C*
constant 5–16, 6–23R
constellation 6–21C*

constitution 5–16CA, 6–21
construct 6–19
construction 6–19
consumer 6–21
contact 6–21
contagious 5–32C*, 6–27CA
contain 5–32, 6–21R
contaminate 5–31C
contamination 5–31C, 6–35*
content 6–21
contentment 5–22C
contest 3–16CA, 6–21
continent 4–4C, 6–23*
continental 6–25CA
continually 6–35C*
continue 4–7C*, 5–35, 6–21R*
contradict 6–15CA
contribute 5–31C*, 6–19
contribution 5–31C*, 6–19
control 5–16C*, 6–21
control tower 4–26CA
convene 5–32C, 6–21*
convention 5–2CA
conversation 5–32C*, 6–21
convict 5–29
conviction 5–29, 6–35R
convince 4–22C*, 5–32, 6–21R
cook 2–22*, 3–31, 4–8R
cookbook 2–22C*
cookie 2–26
cool 2–22*, 3–13CA
cooperate 6–19
cooperating 5–20SS
cooperation 6–19
cooperative 5–25C, 6–22*
coordinated 6–14C
coordinator 6–9C*
copied 4–25, 5–28R*
copper 4–5CA
copy 2–4C*, 3–34CA, 4–27*
copyright 6–35CA
coral 4–19CA
cork 5–7
corn 2–32
corner 2–32C*, 4–32, 5–15R
corporal 6–10C
corporation 6–17CA
corral 4–32C
correct 3–17C*, 5–29, 6–20R
correction 5–29, 6–20R
correspondent 6–35C*
corridor 6–9C
cost 2–15*, 3–10
costume 3–35CA
cottage 2–27CA, 4–20, 5–25R
cotton 3–28*
couch 2–27C, 4–9
cough 3–32, 4–35R*

could 1–17SW, 2–5WOM*,
  2–27, 3–19R, 3–31WOM*,
  4–11WOM*
couldn't 3–35
could've 3–35C*
councilor 6–9C
counselor 5–1CA
count 3–9, 4–9R*
counter 2–32CA
countless 5–22, 6–14R*
countries 3–23C*, 4–25*,
  5–28, 6–26R
country 4–20CA
county 5–5*
couple 4–9
coupon 6–21CA
courage 3–16C, 6–22
courier 6–9C
course 4–11, 5–10*
court 5–9CA, 6–5
courteous 6–17C*
courtesy 5–34C*
cousin 4–27, 5–33WOM*,
  6–26WOM*
cover 4–27
covered 5–21, 6–13R*
cow 2–27
coward 5–5
cowardice 5–25*
cozy 4–26C*
crab 2–21CA
crack 3–17, 4–19R*
cracker 2–33SS
craft 4–1SS, 6–1
crafts 5–1CA
crash 3–1*
crater 5–19*
crawl 2–29CA, 3–10*
crayon 3–4C
crazier 4–25
creak 4–5
cream 4–2
crease 6–2*
create 5–17, 6–19R*
creation 6–19R*
creative 5–25, 6–22R
creature 4–2C*, 5–23
credit 5–19, 6–16R
creditor 6–32CA
creek 4–5
creep 1–14C*
crescent 6–11C*
crestfallen 6–7C
crevasse 6–25CA
crevice 6–16C
crew 2–23CA, 3–31*
crib 1–2C*
cricket 2–3C*
cried 3–23, 4–25R*

crime 4–3
criminal 5–4CA, 6–17*
crisis 6–17
crisp 3–1C
critic 5–1C*, 6–23CA
criticize 6–22
crocodile 4–33SS
crook 2–22C*
crooked 3–31C, 4–19
crop 3–2, 4–4R*
crossing 2–13CA
crosswalk 4–13*, 5–15CA
crouch 4–9SS, 6–4
crow 4–4
crowd 3–9, 4–9R*
crowded 2–27C
crown 2–1CA, 3–9
crucial 6–17C*
cruel 5–17
cruise 5–4
cruising 4–16C*
crumb 3–2C, 4–7
crunchy 3–2C*
crush 5–1, 6–1R*
cry 1–23, 2–25R
crystal 5–26, 6–3R
cub 1–7*, 3–23CA
cube 2–8*, 3–3, 4–7R*
cucumber 6–4CA
cue 5–11CA
culture 5–23, 6–33R
cunning 5–7CA
cup 1–20
cupboard 4–7CA
cups 1–20, 2–20R
curb 6–5
cure 2–15CA, 4–11
curios 6–26C*
curious 4–11C*, 6–33
curl 3–14*, 4–11, 5–8R*
curlicue 5–4SS
curliest 5–28*
currency 5–8SS
current 3–28C*, 4–23, 5–33R
cursor 6–9C*
curtain 5–23
curve 4–11, 5–8R
cushion 4–8C*, 6–25
custom 6–11
customs 5–25CA
cut 1–7, 2–31R
cute 2–8, 3–3R*
cutter 4–31CA
cutting 2–34*
cycle 6–3
cyclone 6–3SS
cymbal 6–11SS
cymbals 6–26CA

D

daddy 2–26*
daily 4–17*
dairy 2–32CA, 4–10
daisy 2–13C*, 3–8CA, 4–26*
damage 4–20, 5–25R*
damaged 5–20
damp 3–13CA
dance 3–29, 4–20R*
dancing 4–16, 5–20R
danger 2–33C*, 3–27*, 4–23
dangerous 5–35, 6–33R
dare 3–19*
dared 4–16, 5–20R
dark 2–31*, 3–13, 4–19R*
darkness 4–28
darkroom 4–22CA
data 5–10CA
daughter 3–32, 4–14R
dawdle 6–4C*
dawn 4–9, 5–5R
daytime 5–9
dead end 6–7
deadline 4–33CA
deaf 5–1, 6–3R
deal 5–2, 6–2R
dear 2–23C*, 3–20*, 4–5,
  5–10R*
debate 6–34
debris 6–25CA
debt 4–34C
decade 6–16C
decathlon 5–35CA
decay 6–34
deceit 6–31C
deceive 6–31SS
December 3–33CA, 4–33*
decent 4–32C*
decided 2–35C, 5–20, 6–34R*
decimal 4–15C
decipher 6–34C*
decision 6–34
deck 4–14CA
declare 3–19C*, 4–29, 6–11R*
decline 4–29C*, 6–34
decorate 5–31, 6–28R
decoration 5–31
decrease 6–34
dedicate 6–34
deep 1–14*
deer 2–23C*, 3–20*, 4–5,
  5–10R*
defeat 6–34
defend 4–31
defended 5–20*
defense 6–34

defenseless 5–22C
deficient 6–34C
deft 6–1C
defy 6–3*
degree 4–29, 5–26R*, 6–34R*
dejected 6–14C*
delay 3–4C*, 4–31, 6–34R*
delete 6–16C
deliberate 6–34C
delicate 6–28C*
delicious 6–25*
delight 3–8C, 4–31*
delightful 5–22, 6–35R
deliver 4–33, 5–34R*, 6–34R*
delivered 5–20
delivery 6–2CA
demand 6–34
demerit 6–34*
democratic 6–33
Democrats 5–2CA
demonstrate 6–34
dentist 3–1SS, 3–31CA, 6–11
deny 6–3
department 4–33, 5–35R*,
  6–35R*
departure 5–23C, 6–33
depend 4–31, 6–34R*
deposit 4–15CA, 5–34, 6–34R
depreciate 6–32CA
depress 6–34*
depth 5–1SS, 6–1
deputy 5–4CA
derisive 6–34C*
descent 4–29C, 6–8C*
describe 6–34
descriptive 6–22
desert 4–4CA
deserve 6–16
deserved 5–20
design 4–34C*
designer 5–33CA
desire 4–3C*, 6–17
desk 4–2
desks 1–20SS
desperate 6–28
dessert 5–8C*
destination 6–13CA
destroy 3–15C, 5–26, 6–34R
detach 6–34*
detail 5–19, 6–34R
detective 5–25, 6–34R
determine 6–34
detour 6–34
develop 4–22CA
development 6–35
device 5–19C
devil 5–14
devote 5–29*
devotion 5–29*

devour 6–4C*
dew 5–4
diagnose 5–17C*
diagonal 6–10C*
diagram 5–34C*
dial 5–17
dialogue 5–11CA
diamond 5–14CA
diary 5–17
dictatorship 6–9CA
dictionaries 5–28C*
did 1–2, 2–3R
didn't 2–29, 3–20WOM*,
  3–35R*, 4–5WOM*,
  5–2WOM*, 6–13WOM*
die 3–8
died 4–5C*, 6–8
diesel 4–26C, 6–31
diet 2–22CA, 5–17
dietician 6–11CA
differ 6–15CA
difference 4–20C*, 6–28
different 3–35WOM*,
  4–10WOM*, 5–16WOM*,
  5–33, 6–15WOM*, 6–23R
difficult 5–35*, 6–17
dig 2–3
dilute 5–4C*
dime 1–11*
diminish 6–25C
dimmed 4–16, 5–21R
diner 4–32
dinner 4–32
dinosaur 6–29CA
diorama 6–29CA
dipped 2–34*
directing 5–20
direction 6–25
directions 3–34CA
director 6–9
dirt 3–14, 4–11R*
dirtier 5–28
dirty 2–26C*, 4–11, 5–31R
disable 6–27
disadvantage 6–27C*
disagree 4–21C*, 5–27, 6–27R
disagreement 6–35
disappear 5–8C*
disappointment 6–27C*
disaster 4–35CA, 5–27, 6–27R
disbelief 6–27*
disciplined 6–14C
discolor 4–21, 5–27R*
disconnect 4–21C*
discontinue 4–21C
discourage 6–27
discover 5–27, 6–3R*
discovery 6–27
discus 5–35CA

discuss 6–20
discussion 6–20
disease 4–28CA, 6–27
disgraceful 6–35
disguise 5–27C*, 6–27
dish 1–2C*, 2–16, 3–1R
dishes 2–20
dishonest 4–21C*, 6–27
disinfectant 6–27C
dislike 4–21, 5–27R
dismal 5–26*
dismay 5–2C*
dismiss 5–27, 6–27R*
disorder 4–21, 5–27R
display 4–1C*, 5–27
displease 4–21, 5–16R*
disposable 6–35C*
dispute 5–27, 6–27R*
disregard 5–27*
disrespect 6–27SS
disrupt 5–31SS, 6–19C*
disruption 5–31SS, 6–19C*
dissent 6–8C*
dissimilar 5–27SS
dissolvable 6–14SS
dissolve 6–27C*
distance 4–22C*, 5–26, 6–28R
distant 5–33*
distinction 6–35C
distort 6–5C*
distress 5–1C*, 6–27
district 5–16, 6–27R
distrust 4–21, 5–16R
disturb 4–22C, 6–27
ditch 5–1, 6–1R
dive 1–11*
divide 3–3C*, 4–32, 6–20R*
divided 6–14
dividend 6–16CA
divisible 5–33C*
division 5–35, 6–20R*
dizzier 4–25*
dizziness 5–28
dizzy 3–1C*, 4–17*
do 1–11SW, 2–21, 3–25R
dock 2–10C, 5–1
doctor 4–14, 5–11R
document 6–17
documentary 5–20CA
dodge 3–2C, 4–20
does 3–2, 4–35R*
doesn't 2–29C*, 3–35*
dog 2–15
doll 1–4C*, 2–4*
dollar 3–28, 4–14R
dolphin 4–19CA, 5–16
domestic 6–31CA
don't 2–29, 3–20WOM*,
3–35R*, 4–5WOM*,

5–2WOM*, 6–13WOM*
donate 6–28*
done 4–7
donkey 2–4C*
donor 4–35CA
door 3–13
doorbell 2–28C*
doorknob 3–21C*
dot 2–4
double 4–15, 5–14R
doubt 4–9C
dough 5–3
down 1–22SW, 2–4WOM*,
2–27, 3–9R*, 3–16WOM*
downstairs 2–28C*
dozen 5–26, 6–10R
drag 4–1
dragon 4–17CA
drain 4–1
dramatic 6–33
dramatized 5–20C
draw 2–15, 3–10R*
drawn 4–9, 5–5R*
dreadful 4–28C*, 5–22,
6–14R*
dream 4–2, 5–2R*
dreary 5–8C
dress 2–11
dresses 2–20
drew 3–31, 4–7R*
dribble 5–9CA
dried 3–23
driftwood 6–7
drill 4–3CA
drink 4–19
drip 2–3*
dripped 5–21
drive 1–11C*, 3–3*
driving 2–35*
droop 6–4
drop 1–4C*, 2–4*, 3–2, 4–4R
dropped 3–22, 4–16R*
drought 4–25CA
drown 5–5
drum 1–7C*, 2–5*, 3–2, 4–7R*
dry 1–23*, 2–25
dryer 3–19CA
duck 1–7C*
duckling 3–23CA
due 4–7
duke 5–4
dull 4–7, 5–1R*
dump 2–14CA
dune 6–7CA
dungarees 6–2C*
dungeon 4–17CA, 5–23*
durable 5–33C
dusk 4–7*
dust 1–16*

duties 4–25*, 5–28, 6–26R
duty 4–17
dwell 5–1
dye 4–35C*
dyed 4–5C*, 6–8
dynamic 6–3C

E

each 2–16
eager 4–32
eagerly 6–14*
eagle 4–15
ear 3–13
earlier 4–25
early 5–8
earn 2–20CA, 4–11
earnest 4–11C, 6–5
earth 6–5
earthquake 4–11C*
easel 3–4C
easier 4–25, 5–28R
east 4–2
easy 3–4C*
eat 2–14
ebb tide 6–7C
echo 4–2C*
echoes 6–26
eddy 4–23C
edge 3–1C*, 4–20
edition 4–33C, 6–25
editor 4–33CA, 6–9*
educate 5–34, 6–28R
education 6–20CA
eel 4–19CA
eerie 6–31C
effective 6–2CA
efficient 6–17C
effort 3–28C, 5–15, 6–11R
egg 1–5C*, 2–11
eight 3–4
eighth 6–32WOM*
eighty 4–17C*, 6–31
either 4–35
elaborate 6–28C
elastic 4–33C*
elbow 4–4*
elect 4–31C*, 5–29, 6–16R*
election 5–29, 6–25R*
electric 4–19, 5–35R*
electrician 6–25SS
elegant 5–33C
elementary 6–20CA
elephant 3–9CA
elevate 5–29C*
elevation 5–29C*
elevator 6–9
elf 4–17CA
eligible 5–33C*

elk 2–2C
else 6–1
elsewhere 5–9C*
emancipation 6–10CA
embassy 6–9CA
embroidery 4–21CA
emerald 5–14CA
emerge 5–8C
emergency 5–27CA
emotion 5–35
emphasize 6–2C
empire 5–15
employ 5–16, 6–11R
emptied 4–25
emptiness 5–28
empty 3–1C, 4–17, 5–16R
enactment 5–32C
enclose 5–32
encourage 5–25C*
encouragement 6–35
encyclopedia 5–32C*
end 2–19
endeavor 6–3C
endless 4–28
endorse 6–16CA
endure 5–32*
enemies 5–28, 6–26R
enemy 4–33, 5–34R
energy 4–16CA, 5–34
enforce 5–32
enforcement 6–35*
engage 5–32
engine 2–13CA, 4–23, 5–32R*
engineer 6–11CA
enhance 6–11C
enjoy 3–27, 4–23R, 5–32R*
enjoyable 6–23
enjoyment 5–22, 6–35R
enormous 4–11C
enough 3–32, 4–13WOM*,
4–32R, 5–27WOM*,
6–16WOM*
enter 4–14, 5–11R
entertaining 5–20C
enthusiastic 5–17C
entire 4–22*
entirely 6–14
entrance 3–29C, 6–28
entry 4–17*, 5–26
envelope 4–33C*
environment 5–31CA
envy 4–17C
epidemic 6–1C*, 6–27CA
episode 5–29CA
equal 4–26C*, 5–19
equaled 6–13
equator 4–4CA
equipped 6–13C

erasable 6–23SS
erasing 2–35C*
erode 6–25CA
error 6–10
escalator 5–11SS, 6–9C*
escape 3–3C, 4–22
essay 5–15
establish 6–25
ethical 6–17C
evacuate 6–19C*
evacuation 6–19C*
evade 6–20C*
evaluate 5–17C*, 6–23CA
evasion 6–20C*
event 4–31
eventually 5–17C
ever 2–33*, 3–33, 4–27R
Everglades 5–34CA
every 2–2C*, 3–35WOM*,
4–29WOM*, 5–25WOM*
everybody 3–21C,
4–29WOM*, 5–9,
5–34WOM*, 6–21WOM*
everyone 4–29WOM*,
5–25WOM*, 6–21WOM*
everything 4–13, 5–9R*,
5–25WOM*, 6–22WOM*
everywhere 4–13, 5–9R,
6–21WOM*
evidence 5–22CA
evident 6–23
evil 5–19
exact 4–27, 5–32R
exaggerate 6–28C
examination 6–19
examine 6–19
example 4–15C*, 6–17
excavate 6–19C
excavation 6–19C
exceed 5–15C
excelled 6–13C*
excellence 4–20C
excellent 6–23
except 6–20
exception 6–20
excess 6–27*
exchange 5–32, 6–27R*
excite 5–32, 6–27R*
excited 3–29C*
excitement 6–14
exclaim 6–11C*
exclude 6–20C
exclusion 6–20C
excuse 2–8C*, 5–32, 6–27R
executive 6–17CA
exercise 4–16CA, 6–22
exert 5–26C, 6–27*
exhaust 5–5C*, 6–27
exhausted 5–7CA

Complete Word List

exhibit 6–29CA
exist 5–32*
exit 2–4CA, 4–31, 5–32R
expand 6–27
expect 3–27C, 4–22*
expedition 6–25C
expenditure 5–23C*
expensive 6–27
experience 6–27
experiment 5–8CA, 6–27
expert 3–27C*, 4–22, 5–32R
expertise 6–27C
explain 3–4C*, 5–16, 6–27R
explanation 6–27C*
explode 3–3C, 6–20
exploration 6–19
explore 4–4CA, 6–19
explosion 6–20
export 6–27
expose 6–20*
exposition 6–20*
exposure 6–27C
express 5–31, 6–20R
expression 5–31, 6–20R
exquisite 6–27C*
extend 5–32, 6–27R*
extent 6–27
exterior 6–19CA
extraordinary 5–9C
extravagant 5–33C
extreme 5–16C, 6–27
eye 2–25, 3–20R
eyebrow 2–27SS, 4–9*
eyelash 3–21*
eyewitness 5–9C*

F

fable 3–28CA
fabric 2–1C, 5–33CA, 6–33*
face 2–7*, 3–29, 4–1R
fact 4–19*
factories 4–25C*
faculty 6–20CA
fad 5–33CA
fade 5–2*
fainted 4–16
fair 3–19
falcon 5–5CA
fall 2–15
false 3–10*, 4–9, 5–5R
familiar 6–9
families 4–25, 5–28R
family 2–25WOM*,
   3–27WOM*, 4–33*,
   4–35WOM*, 5–23WOM*,
   6–19WOM*
famous 4–32, 5–29R
fancier 5–28*

fancy 3–1C*, 4–32
fantastic 3–1C*, 6–33
fantasy 6–5CA
far 2–31
fare 5–7
far–fetched 6–7*
farm 2–31, 3–13R*
farmer 3–26, 4–29R
farther 4–14*, 5–16, 6–11R*
fascinate 5–29C
fascination 5–29C
fashionable 5–33, 6–23R*
fast 1–16, 2–31R
fasten 4–34*
father 2–33, 3–33R*, 4–29R*
fathom 6–1CA
fatigue 5–26C*
faucet 4–9C*
fault 5–5, 6–4R*
favor 4–14, 5–11R*
favored 6–13
favorite 3–35WOM*, 4–33*,
   5–35, 6–31WOM*
fawn 3–23CA, 4–9*, 5–5
faze 6–8SS
fear 3–13*
fearful 4–28, 5–22R
feast 2–19CA, 4–2
feat 4–5SS, 5–7CA
feather 2–33C*, 4–14
feature 4–26C, 5–23, 6–33R
February 3–33CA
fed 1–5*
feebleness 6–14C*
feed 1–14*
feel 2–14*, 3–4, 4–2R*
feet 1–14, 2–14R
feet 4–5SS
fellow 3–28C*, 4–22
female 4–26
fence 2–2C*, 3–29*, 4–20
fencing 5–35CA
Ferdinand Magellan 5–23CA
ferries 4–25
festival 5–35
festive 5–25*
fever 2–33C*, 4–26
few 4–7, 5–4R*
field 3–16CA, 4–2,
   5–17WOM*, 6–27WOM*,
   6–31R*
field trip 4–13C*
fierce 6–5
fiery 4–17C, 6–31
fifty 4–17
fight 2–25*, 3–8, 4–3R*
figure 4–31, 5–19R*
file 6–2

filibuster 5–32CA
filly 4–11CA
film 4–22CA, 6–1
filter 4–22C, 5–15*
final 4–15, 5–19R*
finalize 6–22*
finally 4–33*, 4–35WOM*,
   5–34WOM*, 6–19WOM*
financial 4–15C
find 2–25, 3–8R
fine 2–7
finger 2–33C*, 5–11
finish 2–16SS, 3–28CA, 4–27,
   5–17R
fir 6–8
firecracker 5–13
firefly 2–25C*
fireplace 4–13, 5–13R*
fireproof 6–7
firm 4–11, 5–8R
firmness 4–28*
first 1–16C*, 3–14, 4–11R
first aid 5–9, 6–7R
first–rate 5–9*
fish 1–19, 2–32R
fishing rod 3–2CA
fist 1–16*
fit 2–28CA
fitness 4–16CA
fitting 6–13
five 1–11, 2–7, 3–3R*
fix 2–3
fixing 3–22, 4–16R
fixture 5–23
fjord 6–25CA
flag 1–13, 2–28R
flair 3–19C, 5–7
flamboyant 6–4C*
flame 1–13SS
flamingo 5–5CA
flap 1–13*
flare 3–19C*, 5–7
flash 4–22CA
flashlight 5–13
flat 1–13, 2–9R
flavor 5–11
flaw 3–10C, 5–5*
flea 2–29CA, 5–10
flee 5–10
fleece 4–20C
fleet 4–31CA, 5–2
flesh 4–2*
flew 1–13C*, 3–31
flex 6–1*
flexible 5–33SS
flies 3–23, 4–25R*
flight 2–25C, 3–8*, 4–3
flip 1–13*
flipped 2–34C, 4–16, 5–21R

flippers 4–10CA
flirt 6–5*
float 3–5
flood 4–35
floor 1–13C*, 5–7
florist 6–11CA
floss 3–31CA
flour 3–1CA
flourish 6–16C
flow 2–10CA, 5–3
flower 2–33, 3–33R, 4–27R*
fluffy 3–2C*
fluid 5–17SS
flute 5–4
fly 1–23, 2–25
foam 3–5*
focus 5–8CA, 6–16*
fog 3–13CA
foil 3–15
fold 3–15CA
folded 4–16*
foliage 6–22C*
folk 4–4
folklore 5–7C
follow 2–4C*, 3–28, 4–23R
fond 5–1, 6–1R*
food 2–22
fool 3–31*, 4–8
foolish 3–31C*
foot 2–22, 3–31R*, 4–8R*
for 1–5SW, 2–19WOM*, 2–32,
   3–13R*, 3–21WOM*
forbid 5–26
forbidden (R) 4–22SS
force 3–29C*, 4–20*
forceful 6–14
forehead 6–7
foreign 4–11C, 6–31
forest 3–3CA, 4–27*
forever 4–13, 5–9R*
forfeit 6–5C
forget 3–27, 4–23R
forgetful 5–22
forgetting 6–13
forgiveness 5–22C*, 6–14
fork 2–10*, 2–32*
fort 2–32*
forth 6–8*
fortunate 6–28
fortune 4–23C*
forty 2–32C*
forty–four 5–9*
forward 5–9CA
fossil 2–8CA, 5–14
fought 3–32
foul 4–9C*, 5–9CA, 6–4
found 2–27, 3–9R*,
   3–16WOM*
foundation 6–19CA

fountain 5–23
four 2–32
fourth 3–13, 6–8*
fox 1–4*, 2–4
foxes 2–20*
fraction 4–1C*
fracture 5–23C*
fragile 5–26C*
fragrance 4–20C, 6–28*
fragrant 6–23
frail 4–1C*
frame 6–2
framed 3–22C
frantic 5–1C*, 6–11*
fraud 6–21CA
freckles 3–17C, 5–16*
free 1–14C*, 4–2, 5–2R
freedom 4–2C*, 5–26CA
freezing 3–22C*, 5–20
freight 6–31
freight train 5–13C*
frequency 6–17C*
fresh 4–2, 5–1R
fretted 5–21SS
fretting 5–21SS
Friday 2–25SS, 3–27CA
fried 3–23*
friend 2–9WOM*, 2–19C*,
   3–1, 3–11WOM*,
   4–27WOM*, 5–17WOM*,
   6–35WOM*
friendliness 4–28
friendly 3–26, 4–17R
fright 3–8*, 4–3, 5–3R*
frighten 6–10
frightening 3–8C*
fringe 4–20C
frog 1–20
frogs 1–20, 2–20R
from 1–11SW, 2–5, 2–9WOM*,
   3–11WOM*
front 3–2, 4–35R
frontier 4–32C, 6–5*
frost 4–25CA
frosting 3–10C*
frown 3–9*, 4–9, 5–5R*
frozen 4–26
fruit 4–7, 5–4R
fry 1–23*, 4–2CA
fudge 4–20*
fuel 5–17
fugitive 6–22C*
fulfill 4–8C*
full 4–8
fume 6–2
fumes 5–31CA
fun 1–7, 2–5
function 5–16C

fund 5–1, 6–1R*
funnel 5–14*
funnier 4–25
funny 2–26, 3–28R
fur 6–8
furious 6–33
furnish 5–15
furniture 5–23
furry 2–26C
furthermore 5–13
future 5–23, 6–33R

G

gadget 4–20SS
gain 4–1, 5–2R
galaxy 4–29CA
gallant 6–23
galleon 6–1CA
gallery 6–17C*
galley 4–14CA
galleys 6–35CA
gallon 6–10
galloped 5–21*
game 1–10, 2–32R
garage 6–17
garbage 4–23, 5–25R*, 5–31R
garden 2–31C*, 3–27, 4–22R
garlic 5–21CA, 6–33*
garment 5–33CA
gas 2–1*
gasoline 4–35
gate 1–10*
gather 2–33C, 4–29
gathering 5–21, 6–13R
gave 1–10, 2–7R
gaze 6–2
gear 2–9CA, 4–10
general 5–34
generous 5–35SS, 6–33
gentle 3–16C*, 5–14, 6–10R*
gentleman 6–7*
genuine 5–17*
geography 5–17C*
gerbil 3–16SS
germ 5–8
gesture 5–23C*, 6–2CA
get 1–5, 2–2R
getting 2–14WOM*, 2–34, 3–28WOM*, 4–4WOM*, 6–4WOM*
giant 3–16C*, 5–17
gift 2–3SS
gigantic 6–33
giggle 3–33*
ginkgo 6–8CA
giraffe 3–16, 4–31R
giraffes 2–20C*
girl 2–2WOM*, 3–14,

3–32WOM*, 4–11R*, 4–14WOM*
give 2–7, 3–15R
glacier 5–34CA, 6–25
glad 2–9, 3–7R
glance 4–20
glare 3–19*, 4–10*
glass 4–1
glide 2–23CA
glider 4–26CA
glimpse 6–1*
glitter 3–28C*, 4–14*
globe 2–8C, 4–4
gloom 6–4
gloomy 4–8C*
glorious 6–33SS
glory 5–7*
glove 1–20C*
gloves 1–20C*, 4–1CA
glow 4–4*
glue 4–7, 5–4R*
gnarled 6–5C*
gnaw 4–9C
go 1–8, 2–21
goal 2–34CA, 4–4, 5–3R
goat 3–5*
goes 2–8, 2–22WOM*, 3–15WOM*, 4–2WOM*
goggles 2–4C*, 3–5CA
going 2–22WOM*, 3–15WOM*, 4–2WOM*, 5–3WOM*, 5–21WOM*, 6–5WOM*
gold 3–5*, 4–4
goldfish 2–16C*
good 2–22, 3–31R
goodness 5–22
gorge 4–23CA, 5–7*
gorgeous 5–7C*
gossiped 5–21C*
got 1–4
government 5–22, 6–14R
governor 5–26CA
gown 2–1CA, 4–9
graceful 4–1C, 6–14
grade 3–3
gradual 6–10C*
graduate 6–20
graduation 6–20
grammar 6–9
grand 2–19C
Grand Canyon 5–34CA
grandchildren 6–7
grandfather 3–21, 4–14R*, 4–33R
grandmother 3–21, 4–13R*, 4–33R
grandparent 5–9
grapefruit 5–13

grapes 2–20*
graph 4–1C*, 5–10CA, 6–1*
grasp 5–1, 6–1R
grass 1–1C*, 2–11
grasshopper 2–28C*
grate 4–2CA
grateful 5–22C*
gravel 5–19*
gravity 4–29CA
gravy 4–32*
gray 4–1, 5–2R
graze 2–16CA
great 2–13
great–grandchild 5–13
greed 4–2
green 1–14, 2–14, 3–4R
greet 5–2, 6–2R
grew 3–31, 4–7R*
greyhound 4–9CA
grief 6–31
grieve 6–31*
grill 3–10CA, 6–1
grind 3–8*, 4–3
grinning 2–34SS, 3–22, 4–16R*, 5–21R*
groceries 4–25C*
grocery 5–35
groom 2–22CA
groove 5–4*, 6–4
ground 3–9
group 4–8, 5–4R
grouse 5–5C
grow 2–21, 3–5R*
growl 2–27*
grown 4–4, 5–3R*
growth 5–3, 6–2R*
grumpy 3–2C*
guarantee 4–35C
guard 4–35
guess 2–11C*, 4–8WOM*, 4–35, 5–35WOM*, 6–34WOM*
guest 4–35
guide 4–35
guilt 4–35
guilty 5–22CA
guitar 4–35*, 6–26CA
gums 3–31CA
guy 6–34WOM*
gym 2–7CA, 3–16, 4–35R
gymnasium 5–9CA
gymnastics 5–35CA

H

habit 4–27
habitat 6–1C
had 1–1

haiku 5–17CA
hail 4–25CA
hair 3–19, 4–10R*
haircut 6–7
hairy 4–10, 5–7R*
half 3–1C*, 4–34*
halfhearted 5–13C
hall 5–10
halves 6–26
hamburger 3–10CA, 4–33, 5–35R*
hammer 4–3CA
hamster 2–2CA
hand 1–1C*, 2–19
handkerchief 4–13C
handle 4–15
handled 5–20*
handsaw 4–3CA
handsome 4–34, 5–16R
handstand 2–28*
hang 4–1
hangar 4–26CA, 5–10SS, 6–8
hanger 5–10SS, 6–8
happen 3–28, 4–23R
happened 4–27WOM*, 5–29WOM*, 6–25WOM*
happiest 4–25
happily 5–35WOM*, 6–29WOM*
happiness 5–28, 6–14R*
happy 2–26, 3–28R*
harbor 4–14
hard 2–31, 3–13R
hardships 5–26CA
hare 3–28CA, 5–7
harm 4–10*
harp 2–11CA
harsh 5–7, 6–5R*
harshness 4–28C*
harvest 3–27C*, 4–22, 5–26R
has 1–17SW, 2–1
hasn't 2–29
hasten 4–34C*
hat 2–1
hatch 2–26CA
haul 5–10, 6–4R
haunt 5–5
have 1–5SW, 2–7, 2–21WOM*, 3–4WOM*, 3–25R
haven't 2–29SS, 4–5WOM*, 5–9WOM*, 6–28WOM*
hawk 2–15SS, 5–5, 6–4R
hay 1–17*, 2–13
hazard 4–27C, 6–27CA
hazier 4–25C
he 1–8, 2–14R
he'd 2–29C*
he's 3–35
head 3–1, 4–35R

headache 6–7
headband 4–13*
headline 4–33CA
headphones 5–13*
headquarters 5–4CA
heal 5–10, 6–8R*
health 4–35, 5–31R
healthy 2–15CA
hear 3–20, 4–5R*
heard 4–5*, 4–14WOM*, 5–31WOM*, 6–23WOM*
heart 4–10
hearth 4–20CA
heat 3–13CA
heaviest 4–25, 5–28R*
heavy 2–26C*, 5–19*
heavyweight 6–7SS
heel 5–10, 6–8R*
height 5–3, 6–31R*
heir 4–34C
heirloom 6–4C
helicopter 4–26CA
hello 1–8C*, 3–28, 4–22R
helmet 4–22
helmets 2–20C*
help 2–2
helper 3–26, 4–29R
helpless 4–28*
hen 1–5*
her 1–13SW, 3–14
herb 5–21CA
herd 2–16CA, 4–5*
here 2–8WOM*, 3–20, 3–32WOM*, 4–5R*, 4–14WOM*, 5–5WOM*, 6–2WOM*
here's 3–35*
heritage 5–25C, 6–22*
hero 6–5CA
heroes 6–26
heroine 6–5CA
herself 3–21, 4–13R*
hesitant 6–23
hesitation 5–29SS
hiccups 3–28SS
hid 2–3*
hidden 5–26
hide 1–11*, 2–7
hideout 3–21*
hiding 2–35
high 2–25, 3–8R*
high–pitched 5–13SS
high–spirited 5–13C
highway 2–13C*, 5–9
hike 2–10*
hiking 4–16, 5–20R*
hill 2–11
him 1–2, 2–3*
himself 3–21, 4–13R*

hinge 5–1*
hint 4–3
his 1–8SW, 2–3, 3–1WOM*
history 5–35
hit 2–3
hitting 5–21
hive 3–17CA
hoard 5–7C
hobbies 4–25
hobby 2–26*
hockey 4–17
hoe 2–33CA
hog 2–15*
hoist 6–4
hold 2–21*, 3–5, 4–4R*
hole 2–23, 3–3R*
holiday 1–17C*, 5–13
hollow 3–5C*, 4–23
home 2–8
home run 3–7CA, 4–13*
homemade 5–9, 6–7R
homesick 4–13, 5–13R
homestead 4–32CA
homework 2–28C*, 3–21*
honest 4–34, 5–26R
honey 3–17CA, 4–17, 5–19R*
honor 4–34, 5–11R
honorable 5–33
hood 2–31CA, 3–31*
hoof 2–22C, 4–8*
hook 3–2CA, 4–8
hoop 4–8*
hop 2–4
hope 2–8, 3–3R
hopeful 3–26, 4–28R
hopeless 4–28
hoping 2–35, 3–22R*
hopping 3–22*
horizon 5–35*
horizontal 5–14SS
horn 2–32, 3–13R*
horrible 3–13C*, 5–33, 6–23R*
horror 6–10
horse 2–32C*, 3–13*, 4–11, 5–7R
horseback 5–13*
hose 5–3
hospital 2–4C, 4–33, 5–35R
host 4–4
hot 1–4, 2–11R
hotel 3–29CA, 4–31*
hound 4–9*
hour 2–23*, 3–20, 4–34R
house 2–27, 3–29R
household 5–9
how 1–22SW, 2–3WOM*, 2–27, 3–5WOM*, 3–9R*
however 4–33, 5–13R

howl 3–9SS, 4–9, 5–5R
hug 1–7*, 2–5
huge 2–8CA, 3–3, 4–20R
hugging 2–34
hull 4–14CA
hum 1–7SS, 2–5*
human 4–26, 5–19R
humane 6–2C*
hummed 2–34C*
humor 5–11, 6–10R*
hundred 5–16
hungry 4–17, 5–16R
hunt 3–2
hurdle 4–11C
hurl 5–8
hurricane 4–25CA, 5–34*
hurried 3–23, 4–25R
hurt 3–14, 4–11R
husky 4–9CA
hygiene 6–31C
hymn 4–34C*

I

I 1–4SW, 2–3, 3–20R
I'd 3–35, 4–7WOM*, 5–21WOM*, 5–28WOM*
I'll 2–29, 3–26WOM*, 4–7WOM*
I'm 2–29*, 2–32WOM*, 3–26WOM*, 3–35, 4–7WOM*
I've 2–29, 3–35R*
iceberg 3–14C*, 5–27CA, 6–7
icicle 3–33C, 5–34*
iciest 4–25C
idea 5–17
identical 5–14C*
if 2–3
igloo 2–27CA
ignorant 6–23
ignore 5–15C*, 6–17
ill 2–15CA
illness 4–28, 5–16R
illuminate 6–28C
image 4–27C*, 5–17CA, 6–22
imaginary 4–17C
imagine 4–3C*, 5–35
imitate 5–31, 6–28R
imitation 5–31
immeasurable 6–15SS, 6–35C*
immediate 6–15
immense 6–15
immigrant 6–15
immortal 6–15*
immovable 6–15
immunize 6–27CA
impartial 6–15C
impassable 6–15*

impatient 6–15C*
imply 6–15C
impolite 6–15
import 6–15
importance 6–28
important 4–33, 5–33R
impose 6–15*
imposed 6–33CA
impossible 6–23
imprecise 6–15C*
impress 5–31, 6–15R
impression 5–31, 6–15R*
impressively 6–14C*
imprisonment 6–35
improbable 6–23C
improper 6–15
improve 5–16, 6–15R
improvement 6–35
improvise 6–28CA
in 1–2
inaccurate 5–27C*
inactive 6–15
inadequate 6–15C
inch 2–3C*, 4–3
inches 2–20SS
inclined 6–15
include 4–7C*, 6–15
incomplete 6–15
increase 5–27, 6–15R
incurable 6–35*
indefinite 6–15C*
indent 6–15
independence 5–28CA
indicate 6–17C*
indirect 6–15
individual 6–15
induce 6–15C*
industrial 4–15C
industry 5–34, 6–17R
inevitable 6–35C
infected 4–28CA
infection 6–15
infer 6–15C
infinite 6–15C*
inflate 5–27C
inflexible 6–15C
influence 6–28
inform 5–27, 6–15R*
informal 6–15
information 6–35
inhabitants 6–33CA
inhale 5–27*
inject 6–15*
injure 2–4CA
injury 4–17C*
inner 6–9
inning 5–3CA
innocent 6–15
inquire 6–15

inquiry 5–27C
insect 3–17C, 4–27CA
insert 4–32C*
inside 3–21, 4–13R
insist 5–27, 6–15R
inspect 4–3C, 5–31, 6–15R*, 6–19R
inspection 5–31, 6–19R, 6–35R*
inspiring 6–14C*
install 5–27, 6–15R*
instance 6–28
instant 5–16*, 6–11
instead 4–27WOM*, 5–31WOM*, 6–11*, 6–23WOM*
instruct 5–1C*, 6–20
instruction 6–20
instrument 6–15
insulate 6–19C
insulation 6–19C
insult 5–27, 6–15R
intact 6–1C
intelligent 6–23C*
intend 4–22*
intense 5–15*
interactive 6–29CA
interdependent 6–27C
interest 6–16CA
interfere 6–27
interior 6–19CA
interject 6–27*
intermediate 6–28SS
intermission 6–35
intern 6–11C
international 6–27
interpret 5–8C
interrupt 6–27
intersect 6–27*
intersection 5–15CA
intervene 6–27C
interview 4–33C, 6–27
into 1–20SW, 2–28, 3–14WOM*, 3–21R*, 4–28WOM*
intolerable 6–35C
introduce 6–20C*
introduction 6–20C*
intrude 5–4C, 6–15*
invade 6–20*
invasion 6–20*
invention 6–35
investment 6–16CA
invisible 5–27C*
invite 2–35CA, 3–27, 4–22R*, 6–15R*
invoice 6–32CA
involve 6–15
iron 4–5CA

irresistible 6–23C
irrigation 6–20SS
irritate 5–31C, 6–19*
irritation 5–31C, 6–19*
is 1–2SW, 2–3
island 4–10CA
isle 5–10C*
isn't 2–29, 3–35R
isolation 6–27CA
it 1–2, 2–29R, 2–33WOM*, 3–7WOM*
it's 2–29*, 2–33WOM*, 3–7WOM*, 3–20, 4–5R, 4–23WOM*, 5–13WOM*, 6–3WOM*
italics 6–35CA
itch 3–11*
item 6–16
its 3–7WOM*, 3–20, 4–5R, 4–23WOM*, 5–13WOM*, 6–3WOM*
ivy 4–20CA

J

jacket 4–19
jade 5–14CA
jagged 3–16C*
jail 4–1
jam 1–1SS, 2–1*
jammed 3–22C*
January 3–33CA
jar 3–16
javelin 5–35CA
jaw 3–10*, 4–9
jaws 2–15C*
jazz 6–14CA
jealous 4–27C, 6–33
jeans 3–16
jelly 3–16*
jellyfish 2–21CA
jerky 3–14C*
jet 1–20*, 2–2*
jets 1–20*
jetty 6–7CA
jewel 3–31C*, 5–14
job 1–4SS, 2–4, 3–16R
jog 2–28CA, 3–2*
jogging 2–34C
John Cabot 5–23CA
join 3–15
joint 3–15*, 5–5
joke 2–8*
joked 2–35*
joking 3–22, 4–16R
jolly 4–17*
journal 3–16C*
journalist 4–33C
journey 5–15C*, 6–11

joust 4–34CA
joy 3–15
judge 2–3CA, 3–16, 4–20R
judged 4–16*
juggler 3–9CA
juice 3–16C*, 4–7, 5–4R*
July 1–23C*, 2–25*, 3–33CA
jump 1–7C*, 2–5*, 3–16, 4–7R*
June 3–16, 4–7R
jungle 2–5C*, 4–4CA
junior 6–9
junior high school 5–9C
juniper 6–8CA
junk 3–16*, 4–19
juries 5–28*
just 1–16
justice 5–25
juvenile 5–35C*

K

kayak 5–35CA
keep 1–14, 2–14, 3–4R*
kelp 6–7CA
kennel 4–15*
kept 2–2SS, 4–2, 5–1R*
kernel 5–14C
kick 2–10, 3–17R*
kid 1–2*, 2–26CA
kilometers 6–3CA
kind 2–25, 3–8R*
kindergarten 4–10SS
kindling 4–8CA
kindness 4–28, 5–22R*
king 2–19, 3–17R*
kingdom 6–5CA
kiss 1–2C*, 2–11*
kisses 2–20*
kitchen 6–10
kite 1–20, 2–10R
kites 1–20
knapsack 5–1C
knead 4–2C
knee 3–11, 4–34R*
kneel 3–11*, 4–34
knew 2–27WOM*, 3–20, 3–29WOM*, 4–15WOM*, 4–26R, 5–5WOM*, 6–2WOM*
knickknack 6–1C*
knife 3–11, 4–34R
knight 3–11C*, 4–34
knit 3–11*, 4–34
knitting 6–13
knob 4–34
knock 2–10C*, 3–11, 4–34R
knoll 4–34C
knot 3–11, 4–34R*

know 2–26WOM*, 3–11, 3–29WOM*, 4–4R, 4–15WOM*, 5–5WOM*, 6–2WOM*
knowledge 5–25
knuckle 3–11C

L

label 5–14
labor 4–14
Labor Day 5–13CA
laboratory 5–8CA
ladder 3–22CA, 4–14
ladies 4–25*, 5–28
lady 2–26, 3–23R, 4–26R*
ladybug 2–28*
lagoon 4–10CA
laid 5–2
lair 5–7
lake 2–10, 3–17R*
lamb 4–34
lamppost 4–13SS
land 2–23CA
landed 4–16, 5–20R
landlord 5–13*
landmark 4–13C, 6–13CA
lane 3–5CA
language 5–25, 6–22R
lantern 4–8CA
lap 2–1*
lapel 6–16C*
large 2–31C, 3–16, 4–10R, 4–20R*
laser 5–19C
last 3–1, 4–1R
latch 4–20CA
late 1–10*, 2–7
lately 5–22, 6–14R*
later 2–33*, 3–33, 4–14R*
latitude 6–13CA
laugh 3–32, 4–35R*
laughable 5–33
laughter 5–16, 6–9R*
launch 4–23CA, 5–5
laundry 3–15CA, 6–11
law 3–10
lawn 2–15*, 3–10, 4–9R
lawyer 6–11
lay 1–17*, 3–4
layered 5–21C
lazy 4–17
lead 4–5
leaf 5–2, 6–2R*
league 5–3CA, 6–2
leap 4–2*
leapfrog 3–21SS
learn 3–26CA, 4–11, 5–8R
lease 5–2

leash 2–16*
least 2–14C*, 4–2, 5–2R
leather 6–3
leave 3–4, 4–2R*
lecture 5–23, 6–33R*
led 4–5
left 2–2*, 3–1, 4–2R
leg 1–5SS, 2–2
legal 5–14
legend 6–5CA
legible 6–23*
legislation 5–32CA
legislature 6–33C*
Leif Ericson 5–23CA
leisure 5–23C, 6–31
lemon 4–27*
length 6–1
lens 4–22CA
leotard 6–14CA
lesson 3–28, 4–22R
let 1–5
let's 3–35C
letter 2–23WOM*, 3–17WOM*, 3–28, 4–20WOM*, 4–23R*
lettuce 6–4CA
level 5–14, 6–10R*
levelheaded 6–7*
lever 6–3CA
levied 5–28C
liability 6–32CA
liar 5–17, 6–9R*
liberties 5–28
libraries 3–23C
library 4–33, 5–34R
license 4–26C
lie 3–8
life 3–3
lifeboat 5–27CA
lifeguard 5–9*
lifeless 6–14
lift 4–3
light 2–25, 3–8R*
light bulb 5–13*
lightning 3–8C*, 4–25CA
like 1–11, 2–22R, 3–10WOM*
liked 2–35
lilac 3–8C, 4–26*
lilies 3–23C*, 5–28, 6–26R
lily 4–27*
limb 4–34
limber 6–14CA
limelight 5–9C
limerick 5–17CA
limit 4–27
limited 6–13
limousine 6–3C*
line 1–11*, 2–7
linen 6–10

lion 5–17
liquid 4–27C*
listen 4–34, 5–17R
listener 3–26C
listening 6–13
litter 5–31CA, 6–10
litterbug 5–9*
little 1–23SW, 2–11WOM*, 3–17WOM*, 3–33, 4–15R
live 4–3
lizard 2–2CA
load 3–15CA
loaf 2–21SS, 5–3
loan 5–10
loaves 6–26
lobbyist 5–32CA
local 5–14
locate 4–26C*, 5–29, 6–19R, 6–28R*
location 5–29, 6–19R
lock 3–2*
locker 2–7CA
lodge 4–20
log 2–15, 3–10R*
logic 5–19C
logical 6–34CA
logo 6–22CA
loiter 5–5C
lone 5–10
lonely 4–17, 5–22R
long 2–19
longitude 4–4C, 6–13CA
look 1–19SW, 2–22, 3–31R*
loop 5–4
loose 3–31C, 5–4, 6–4R
loose–leaf 4–13C*
lord 4–34CA, 5–7
lose 5–4
losing 5–20*
lost 2–9
lot 3–2
lotion 5–19C*
loud 3–9, 4–9R
lounge 6–4*
lovable 6–23
love 3–3, 4–35R
loved 3–22*
low 2–21*
loyal 3–15C*, 5–5, 6–10R
luck 3–2, 4–19R
lucky 2–26
luggage 3–28C*, 5–25
lullaby 1–23C*
lumber 4–23
lump 3–2*
lunar 4–14C, 5–11
lunch 2–16C, 4–7
luncheon 5–23
luxury 5–27CA

M

macaroon 4–8SS
machine 4–29, 5–26R*, 6–3R*
machinery 4–17C*
made 1–10SS, 2–7, 3–3R*
Madison 4–13CA
maestros 6–26C
magazine 4–35, 5–35R
magic 4–27, 6–33R*
magnet 4–1C*
magnetic 6–1C
magnificent 6–23C
magnify 5–8CA
magnolia 6–8CA
mahogany 6–8CA
mail 2–13, 3–4R*
main 5–10
maintenance 6–3CA
majestic 5–34C
major 5–11, 6–10R
majority 5–32CA
make 1–10, 2–8R
make–believe 4–13, 5–13R
make–up 3–35CA
making 2–35, 3–22R
male 5–2
mallard 5–5CA
mammal 4–15*
man 1–1
manage 4–20, 5–25R
manageable 6–14*
management 6–17CA
mane 5–10
maneuver 6–10C
manner 6–8
manor 4–34CA, 6–8
manuscript 6–35CA
many 2–26, 4–17R*
map 1–1*, 4–4CA
maple 4–27CA
mapped 6–13
marathon 5–35CA
March 1–19C*, 2–31*, 3–13, 4–10R*
Marco Polo 5–23CA
mare 4–11CA
margin 3–27*
marine 4–31C, 6–3*
mark 3–13*
marker 3–4CA
market 2–31C*, 3–27, 4–32R
marooned 4–8C
marriage 4–20, 5–25R
married 3–23C*, 5–28*
marry 4–17, 5–10*
Mars 2–25CA
marshmallow 3–5C*

Martin Luther King Day 5–13CA
marvel 4–10C
marvelous 5–7C
mascot 5–1C
mask 2–1C, 4–10CA
mass 6–25CA
massive 5–1C*
mast 4–14CA
master 4–23
masterpiece 5–13
match 2–34CA, 3–11
material 4–15C*
math 2–17*
matinee 5–20CA
matter 5–11, 6–10R
May 1–17, 3–8CA
maybe 1–8C*, 2–28, 3–21R*
Mayflower 5–26CA
mayor 5–11, 6–9R
maze 2–7C*
me 1–8, 2–26R
meadow 6–3
mean 2–14
meant 6–3
meanwhile 4–13, 5–13R*
measure 4–2CA, 5–23, 6–3R
meat 4–5, 5–10R
mechanical 5–19CA
medal 3–16CA, 4–15, 5–14R*
media 6–22CA
medicine 4–28CA
medley 4–17C
meet 2–23SS, 3–5CA, 4–5, 5–10R
mellow 5–3SS
melodies 5–28C*
melodrama 6–28CA
melon 4–27C*
member 4–23
mementos 6–26C
memo 6–17CA
memorable 6–22CA
Memorial Day 5–13CA
memorized 5–20C*
memory 4–2C*, 5–34, 6–17R*
men 1–5, 2–19R
mental 6–10
mention 6–25
menu 4–2C
meow 2–27C*
merchandise 6–22C
merchant 5–33, 6–11R
merciless 5–22C*
mercury 4–5CA
mercy 4–17C
merit 6–16C*
Meriwether Lewis 5–23CA
merry 5–10*

mess 2–11*, 3–1*
message 4–20*, 5–25, 6–22R
messenger 6–9
met 1–5*
metal 4–15, 5–14R
meteor 5–17*
meter 6–9*
method 4–29C, 6–11
mezzanine 6–3C*
mice 1–11C*
microphone 6–2C
microscope 4–4SS, 5–8CA
middle 3–33C*, 4–15, 5–26R
might 3–8, 3–33WOM*, 4–28WOM*, 5–28WOM*, 6–32WOM*
migrant 5–33*
migrate 5–31, 6–28R*
migration 5–31, 6–25R
mild 3–8*, 5–3
mileage 6–14
milk 1–2C*, 2–3*, 3–1, 4–3R*
millimeter 5–35WOM*, 6–29WOM*
million 5–15
millionaire 4–10C*
mimic 6–1SS
mince 4–2CA
mind 2–25*, 3–8, 4–3R
mine 2–7*, 3–3
mineral 5–14C
minister 4–3C*, 6–9
minor 6–9
minus 6–16
minute 4–32, 5–29R
mirror 4–7CA, 5–11, 6–9R*
mischief 5–16, 6–31R
miser 5–19C*
miserable 6–23C*
missed 2–34
mission 6–25
misspell 6–11C*
mist 5–1
mistake 2–7C, 3–25CA, 4–19, 5–15R
mitt 3–7CA
mitten 2–3C*, 4–23*
mix 3–1, 4–3R
mixed 5–21
mixture 5–23
moan 5–3*
model 4–15, 5–19R
modeling 5–33CA, 6–13
moderator 6–34CA
modern 4–27
modernize 6–22
module 5–19C
moist 3–15C, 5–5, 6–4R
moisture 5–23, 6–33R*

mom 1–4*
moment 4–26, 5–33R
monarchy 6–9CA
Monday 3–27, 4–23R*
money 4–15CA
monitor 5–11C*
monkey 4–17
monologue 6–28CA
monopoly 6–31CA
monsoon 4–25CA
monster 3–2SS, 5–16
month 1–22C*, 4–35
monument 5–34
mood 5–4
moon 2–22
moose 2–22C
mop 1–4*, 2–4
moral 6–10
morale 6–17C
more 2–32
morning 2–32, 3–21WOM*, 4–16WOM*, 4–29R*, 5–31WOM*, 6–23WOM*
mortgage 6–16CA
mosaic 5–17C
mosquitoes 5–1CA, 6–26C*
most 2–21*, 3–5, 4–4R
moth 2–29CA
mother 2–33, 3–33R*, 3–34WOM*, 4–29R*
mother's 4–9WOM*, 5–32WOM*
motion 4–4C, 6–25
motivate 6–17CA
motive 5–22CA
motor 2–31CA, 4–14, 5–11R*
motorcycle 4–13C
mound 5–3CA, 6–4
mount 4–9
mountain 3–9C*, 5–23
mourn 6–5
mouse 2–27, 3–9R*
mouth 2–17C, 3–9, 4–9R*
move 4–8
movement 3–14CA, 4–28, 5–22R
movie 4–17, 5–29R
moving 3–22C*
much 1–19, 2–16, 3–2R
mud 2–5
muddy 2–26*
muffin 2–5C*, 4–7CA
mule 2–8C, 5–4
multiplies 4–25C*
multiply 1–23C*
mumble 5–14*
mural 5–14*
mural 4–15SS
murmur 5–8C*

muscles 2–28CA
muscular 5–35C
museum 4–33C*, 6–29CA
mushroom 3–31SS
music 3–14CA, 4–26, 5–17R
musician 6–25
mussel 6–7CA
must 1–16, 2–34R
mustang 4–11CA
mustard 4–7C*
mustn't 3–35C*
mute 6–2
my 1–23
myself 1–23SS, 2–28, 3–14WOM*, 3–21R*, 4–21WOM*
mystery 4–17C*, 5–22CA, 6–3*
myth 6–3

N

nail 2–13
name 1–10, 2–10WOM*, 2–27R
named 2–35
names 2–20
nap 1–1*
napkin 3–27, 4–22R*
napping 2–34*
narrate 4–22C
narrow 4–32
nation 5–19, 6–25R*
nationwide 4–13C
native 5–25
nature 4–32, 5–23R
naughty 3–32C, 6–4
navigate 6–13CA
navy 4–26
near 3–13, 4–10R
nearby 1–23C*, 5–9*
neat 3–4*
neatness 4–28*
neck 2–10*
need 2–14*, 3–4, 4–2R
needle 3–4C*, 5–14
needn't 3–35C*
negative 5–25SS, 6–22C*
neglect 5–26
neighbor 2–35CA, 3–4, 4–14R
neither 4–35*, 6–31
nephew 4–29C*
nerve 5–8
nervous 6–33
nest 1–16*, 2–9
network 5–29CA
neutral 5–14C, 6–34CA
never 3–33*, 4–27
nevertheless 6–7

new 2–27WOM*, 3–20
New Year's Day 5–13CA
newscast 4–7C, 5–9
newspaper 3–33SS, 4–33CA
next 1–5C*, 2–9, 3–1R*
nibble 3–2CA
nice 3–29, 4–20R
nickel 2–3C*, 4–15, 5–14R
nickname 2–10SS
niece 5–2, 6–31R
night 2–25, 3–8R
nightmare 2–25C*
nine 1–11, 2–7
ninety–nine 4–13, 5–9R
no 1–8, 2–21
no more 3–32C*
no one 4–13*
nobody 2–28C
nod 2–4
noise 3–15
noisier 4–25, 5–28R*
noisy 2–26C
nominate 5–2C
none 4–35*
noodle 3–31C*
noon 2–22*
normal 5–14, 6–10R*
north 2–32*, 3–13, 4–11R*
nose 2–8
not 1–4, 2–4
notch 3–11C*
note 2–8*, 3–3
nothing 3–21, 4–29R
notice 3–32CA, 5–25, 6–16R*
noticeable 6–23
noun 6–4
nourish 6–25*
novel 5–19, 6–10R
November 3–33, 4–33R
now 1–19SW, 2–3WOM*, 2–27, 3–5WOM*
nowhere 6–7
nuisance 5–19C
number 2–5C*, 4–22
numbness 4–28C, 5–22*
numerous 6–33
nurse 3–14*, 4–35CA
nurture 5–23*
nut 2–5

O

o'clock 3–35, 4–34WOM*, 5–19WOM*, 6–34WOM*
oar 4–5C
oatmeal 2–21C*
object 4–22C*, 5–15, 6–34R
obligation 6–34SS
oblige 6–34

oblong 6–34*
obnoxious 6–34C*
oboe 6–26CA
obscure 6–34C
observatory 6–34C*
observe 6–34
obsess 6–34*
obsolete 6–34C*
obstacle 6–34C
obstinate 6–34C
obstructed 6–33CA
obtain 6–34
obvious 5–34C, 6–34
occasion 6–34
occupy 6–34
occur 4–23C*, 6–34
ocean 2–21CA, 4–31, 5–31R
oceanographer 6–1CA
October 3–33, 4–33R
octopus 4–19CA
odd 4–4, 5–1R
odor 4–31*
of 1–2SW, 2–4, 3–26R
off 2–11, 3–2WOM*, 3–10R*, 4–33WOM*
offer 4–22
offered 5–20
office 4–32, 5–25R*
officer 5–4CA
official 6–25
often 3–10C*, 4–34
oil 3–15
old 2–21
old–fashioned 6–7
olive 4–27SS
Olympia 4–13CA
Olympics 5–35C
omitted 6–13C*
on 1–4, 2–4R, 2–19WOM*
once 3–29, 4–3WOM*, 4–20R*, 4–26R, 5–22WOM*, 6–7WOM*
one 1–7SW, 2–8, 3–20*
onion 4–35C*, 5–21CA
only 2–26, 4–17R*
onyx 5–14CA
ooze 5–4*
opal 5–14CA
open 4–31
operate 5–19CA
opinion 6–23CA
opponent 5–3C, 6–34CA
oppose 6–20
opposition 6–20
option 5–15C
or 1–14SW, 2–32
orange 3–16, 4–27R
orator 6–2CA
orbit 4–29CA, 6–5*

orchard 5–16
orchid 5–16*
ordeal 5–7C
order 2–32C*, 3–27, 4–14R*, 4–22R*
ordered 5–21, 6–13R
ordinary 5–7C*
ore 4–5C
organ 4–23
organize 6–22
original 6–16SS
orphan 5–16, 6–11R*
ostrich 5–5CA
other 1–16SW, 2–23WOM*, 3–34WOM*, 4–9WOM*, 4–29
ouch 3–9*
ought 3–32
ounce 4–9*, 5–5, 6–4R*
our 1–19SW, 2–4WOM*, 2–23*, 3–5WOM*, 3–20
ourselves 4–13, 5–9R*
out 1–10SW, 2–27, 3–9R
outfield 5–3CA
outside 2–27C*, 2–31WOM*, 3–21, 4–13R
outspoken 5–13C
oval 5–19SS
ovation 5–35C
oven 3–1CA, 4–27
over 1–20SW, 2–33, 3–33R*, 4–26R*
overjoyed 3–15SS
oversleep 3–25CA
owe 5–3
owl 3–9*, 4–27CA
own 3–5, 4–4R*
oxygen 6–3C
oyster 4–19CA

P

pace 6–2
pack 2–10*
package 4–29, 5–25R
paddle 4–23CA
page 2–19CA, 3–16, 4–20R
pageant 6–16C*
paid 2–13*, 3–4, 4–1R*
pail 1–20C*, 2–23*
pails 1–20C*
pain 3–4*, 4–1, 5–2R*
painful 4–28
painstaking 6–7C
paint 2–13SS, 3–4, 4–1R
paintbrushes 2–20C*
pair 3–19
pajamas 3–21CA
palace 2–27CA, 4–31
paleness 5–22

palm 4–34
pancake 2–28*
panda 2–1C*
panel 6–10
panic 6–16
panther 5–16*
pantomime 6–28CA
pants 1–1C*
paper 4–26
parachute 4–26CA, 5–35*
parade 4–32
parallel 5–14C*, 6–17
parcel 5–7C*
pardoned 6–13
parent 4–31, 5–33R
park 2–31*, 3–17
parka 4–1CA
parliament 6–9CA
parrot 2–2CA
parsley 5–16C*, 6–4CA
part 2–31
part of speech 5–13
part–time 5–13*
partial 6–25
participate 6–15CA
participating 5–20C*
particle 5–14C*
particular 6–9
parties 3–23, 4–25R*
partner 3–14CA, 5–16, 6–17R
party 2–31, 3–13R*, 5–2CA
pass 2–11*
passable 6–23
passage 5–25
passbook 4–15CA
passenger 6–9
passengers 5–27CA
passport 5–25CA
past 4–1, 5–1R*
paste 3–4CA
pasted 2–35C*
pastel 6–1C*
pasture 4–20CA, 5–23
patch 2–1C*, 3–11
path 1–22*
patience 5–10C*
patient 4–28CA
patients 5–10C*
patriot 5–28CA
patriotic 6–33
patrol 4–31CA
patted 3–22
pattern 4–23*, 5–15
pause 4–9*, 5–5, 6–4R*
pavement 4–28C*
paw 2–15, 3–10R*
pay 1–17*, 2–13
peace 4–5*, 5–10
peaceful 4–28, 5–22R*

peach 4–2
peak 4–5
peanut 2–14SS
pear 3–19
pearl 4–11*, 5–8, 6–5R
peasant 6–23*
peasants 4–34CA
pebble 4–15*
peculiar 4–19C
pedal 5–14
pedestrian 5–15CA
peek 4–5
peel 1–14*
peer 5–8
pelican 6–7CA
pen 1–5*, 2–2
penalty 4–33C*, 5–9CA
pencil 2–2C*, 3–29, 4–32R
penguin 2–2C, 5–5CA
pennies 3–23, 4–25R
penny 2–2C*
people 2–14, 3–17WOM*, 3–33R, 4–20WOM*, 5–32WOM*, 6–33WOM*
pepper 4–22*
perceive 6–31C*
percentage 5–10CA, 6–22
perception 6–29C
perch 2–22CA
perfect 3–14C, 4–22, 5–15R*, 6–29R*
perform 3–27C*, 4–22
performance 6–28
perfume 6–29
perhaps 5–15, 6–29R
peril 4–31C
perilous 6–5CA
period 5–34
perish 6–25C*
permanent 5–33C*, 6–29
permission 6–29
permit 5–15, 6–29R
permitting 6–13
perpendicular 6–9C*
perplexed 6–29SS
persecute 6–29C*
persevere 6–29C*
persist 6–29
person 3–14C*, 4–22, 5–15R
personal 5–35
personnel 6–17CA
perspective 6–29C
perspiration 6–29C*
persuade 6–29
pertain 6–2C
perturb 6–29*
pest 1–16*
pestering 6–13SS
pet 2–2

petal 4–32*
petals 2–33CA
pharmacist 6–11CA
phase 6–8SS
pheasant 4–27C
phoning 4–16, 5–20R*
photograph 4–33C
phrase 5–2C*
physical 6–17
physician 6–3C*
pianos 6–26
piccolos 6–26C
pick 2–10
picnic 2–3C, 3–17, 4–19R
picture 3–4CA, 4–22, 5–23R
pie 3–8
piece 4–5*, 5–10, 6–31R
pier 5–8, 6–31R
pierce 6–5
pig 1–2*, 2–3
piglet 2–26CA
pile 1–11*
pilgrim 5–26
pillar 5–11
pillow 2–21C*, 4–23
pilot 2–23CA, 3–8C*, 4–26
piloting 6–13
pin 1–2*, 2–3
pinnacle 6–10C*
pinned 2–34
pioneer 4–32CA, 5–35*
pirate 6–16
pistachios 6–26SS
pit 2–11CA
pitch 3–7CA, 6–1
pitcher 5–3CA
pitied 5–28
place 1–10C*, 3–29, 4–20R
plaid 4–35C*
plain 2–23
plan 3–22CA
plane 2–23
planet 2–25CA, 4–27
planetarium 6–29CA
plank 4–3CA
planned 5–21, 6–13R
plant 2–1C*, 4–1
plantations 6–10CA
plastic 4–23, 6–33R*
plate 1–10C*
platform 5–2CA
play 1–17, 2–13, 3–4R
player 1–17C*
playful 3–26*
playground 2–28C
playpen 2–13C*
playwright 5–11CA
plea 6–2*
pleasant 6–3

please 2–14, 3–4R*
pleased 2–35C*
pleasing 4–16, 5–20R*
pleasure 5–23, 6–3R*
pledge 6–1
plentiful 5–22*
plenty 4–17
pliers 4–3CA
plight 5–3C
plum 1–7C*
plumbing 6–19CA
plump 6–1
plunge 3–16C, 6–1
plus 2–5*
Pluto 2–25CA
Plymouth 5–26CA
poach 4–2CA
pocket 2–4C*, 4–29
podium 6–2CA
poem 5–17
poet 5–17CA
point 3–15
poise 5–5C, 6–2CA
poison 6–16
poison ivy 4–13C*, 5–1CA
polar 5–11
pole 5–10, 6–8R*
police 3–29C*, 4–31
policy 6–17
polish 4–3C, 6–25
polite 3–3C*, 4–31
poll 5–10, 6–8R*
pollute 4–7C*, 5–31, 6–20R*
pollution 5–31, 6–20R*
poncho 4–8CA
pond 1–4C*, 3–2, 4–4R*
ponies 3–23, 4–26R*
pony 2–21C*
poodle 4–9CA
pop 1–4*, 2–4*
popped 2–34*
popular 4–14C*, 5–34, 6–9R, 6–17R*
populate 5–29, 6–28R*
population 5–29
porch 3–13*
porcupine 4–27CA
pore 5–10
port 4–14CA
portable 6–23C*
porter 5–25CA
portion 4–11C*, 6–25
portrait 4–22CA
portraying 5–20C
pose 4–22CA
position 6–17
positive 5–25C*, 6–22
possible 4–4C*, 5–33
post office 5–13, 6–7R*

postage 5–25, 6–22R*
poster 2–21C*, 3–4CA
postscript 4–13C
posture 5–23C*, 6–14CA
pot 2–4
potato 5–34
potatoes 6–26
potential 6–17C
pottery 4–21CA
pounce 4–9C, 6–4*
pound 3–9*, 4–9
pour 5–10, 6–5R
powder 3–9C*, 5–11
power 2–33*
powerful 4–28, 5–22R
practice 3–29SS, 4–20C*, 5–25
prairie 4–32C, 6–31*
praise 5–2
prank 5–1CA
pray 3–4*, 4–1, 5–2R*, 6–8*
preach 6–2
preamble 5–32C
precious 6–25C*
precipitation 6–29C
precision 6–35C
predict 5–10CA, 6–29
predominant 6–23C
prefer 5–19, 6–29R*
preferred 6–13
prefix 5–32, 6–29R*
prehistoric 5–32C*, 6–29
prejudice 5–25C*, 6–29*
prelude 6–29*
prepaid 6–29
preparation 6–35
prepare 3–19C*, 6–29
prescription 4–28CA
presence 6–28*
present 2–2C*
preservation 6–29C
preserve 5–32, 6–29R
president 5–34, 6–17R
press 4–33CA
pressure 6–25
presume 5–4C
pretend 4–31C*
prettiest 4–25, 5–28R*
pretty 2–17WOM*, 3–13WOM*, 3–28, 4–17R, 4–31WOM*, 5–29WOM*, 6–25WOM*
pretzel 4–15C*
prevalent 6–29C*
prevent 5–32*
prevention 6–35
preview 6–29
previous 6–29
prey 6–8*
price 2–32CA, 4–3*

pride 4–3, 5–3R*
primitive 5–25C, 6–22*
prince 4–17CA
princess 4–17CA
principal 6–8
principle 6–8
prison 4–27, 5–19R*
private 5–3C*
privately 6–14
privilege 6–22C*
prize 1–11C*, 3–16CA
pro 6–34CA
probably 4–35WOM*, 5–23WOM*, 5–35C*, 6–31WOM*
probe 6–2*
problem 4–23C*, 6–17
procedure 5–32C
proceed 5–2C*, 6–29
process 6–29
procure 6–29C
prodded 5–21C*
prodigious 6–29C*
product 6–29
profession 6–29
professional 5–32SS
professor 6–11CA
profile 6–29*
profitable 5–33
profited 6–13C
profound 6–29*
program 3–5C, 5–26, 6–29R
programmer 6–11CA
progress 6–29
prohibit 6–29
project 6–29
projector 5–20CA
prominent 5–33C
promise 6–29
promote 5–31, 6–19R*
promotion 5–31, 6–19R*
prompt 6–1
pronoun 5–32
proof 5–4, 6–4R*
proofread 4–8C*, 6–35CA
prop 6–28CA
propelling 6–13C
proper 4–14
property 5–35
proposal 6–15CA
propose 5–32, 6–29R*
propped 3–22C
prospect 6–29
prosper 5–26CA
protect 5–31, 6–16R
protection 5–31
protective 6–22
protest 5–19*
proud 3–9*, 4–9, 5–5R*

proudly 3–26SS
prove 4–8
proverb 5–32, 6–29R*
providing 5–20, 6–29R
prowl 4–9C, 5–5
prune 4–7*
pry 1–23C*
public 4–19, 6–33R*
publish 5–15, 6–25R*
publisher 6–35CA
puddle 2–5C, 4–15*
pull 2–11C*, 4–8
pulse 6–1*
pump 4–7
pumpkin 3–2C*
punctual 6–17C
puncture 6–3CA
punish 4–27
pup 1–7*
pupil 2–7CA, 4–26
puppet 3–28*
puppies 3–23, 4–25R*
puppy 1–7C*, 2–26, 3–28R*
purchase 4–11C*
pure 4–11
Puritans 5–26CA
purple 3–33, 4–15R
purpose 5–26C*, 6–2CA
purposefully 5–22SS
purred 3–22C*
purse 6–5
pursuit 5–4C, 6–33CA
push 4–8
put 4–8
putting 4–16*
puzzle 3–33C*, 5–14
pyramid 5–35C*

quail 5–5CA
qualities 4–25C
quality 6–17
quarantine 4–35C
quarrel 3–25CA, 6–10
quart 3–17
quarter 4–15CA, 5–11, 6–9R*
quartered 6–13*
queen 3–17
quest 6–5CA
question 3–17C*, 4–19, 5–29R
questionnaire 5–10CA
quick 3–17, 4–19R
quick–witted 5–9C
quickly 3–26, 4–17R*, 5–16R*
quiet 5–17
quilt 2–3C
quilting 4–21CA

quintet 6–1C*
quirk 6–5SS
quit 3–17, 4–19R*
quite 4–3*
quiver 4–27C
quiz 3–17C*, 6–20CA
quizzed 4–16C*
quotation 5–3C*, 6–25*
quote 6–2

rabbit 2–1C*, 3–28, 4–23R*
raccoon 4–8C*
race 3–29*
raced 4–16, 5–20R*
radar 4–26C, 6–13CA
radiant 5–33C*
radio 4–7CA, 5–17
radioactive 6–7C*
radish 6–4CA
raft 4–23CA
railroad 2–13C, 4–13, 5–9R*
rain 2–13, 3–4R*
rainbow 2–21C, 3–21*
raise 5–2, 6–2R*
raisin 2–13C*
raising 2–35C*
rake 2–7*
ran 1–1*, 2–1
ranch 4–32CA
random 5–10CA
ranger 3–3CA
rapid 5–19
rapids 4–23CA
rare 4–10*, 5–7
rascal 4–22C, 6–17*
rather 4–29
rating 6–23CA
ratios 6–26
rattle 4–15*
rattlesnake 4–27CA
rave 6–23CA
ravine 6–3
raw 3–10, 4–9R*
ray 1–17*
razor 5–11*
reach 4–2, 5–2R*
react 5–29
reaction 5–29, 6–35R
read 2–14
readiness 4–28SS
ready 4–17
real 4–2
realize 5–17C*, 6–22
really 2–25WOM*, 3–13WOM*, 4–31WOM*, 5–23WOM*, 6–19WOM*
realm 6–3C

rear 5–8
rearrange 4–21C
reason 2–14C*, 4–26
reasonable 5–33
reasoning 6–13
rebel 5–28CA, 6–16
rebuild 4–21, 5–27R
rebuttal 6–34CA
receipt 6–31
receive 4–35, 6–31R*
received 6–27WOM*
recent 6–16
recess 3–26CA, 4–26*
recession 6–25C
recipe 5–34C*
recital 4–15C*, 6–14CA
reckless 4–19C*
recognize 4–3C, 6–22
recommend 6–23CA
record 5–19
recount 4–21, 5–27R*
recruit 5–4C*, 6–10CA
recurring 6–13C
recyclable 6–35*
recycle 4–21C*, 5–31CA
red 1–5, 2–2R
redecorate 4–21C
redo 4–21
reef 4–10CA
reel 5–20CA
referee 4–2SS, 5–9CA
reference 5–35C*
refill 4–21
refinement 6–14C
reflect 4–29C, 5–29*
reflection 5–29*
reflector 6–3CA
reflector 4–14SS
reflex 4–29C*
refold 4–21*
refresh 4–29*
refreshing 3–25SS
refuge 5–26C
refugee 5–2SS
refund 4–21C*, 6–21CA
refuse 2–8C*
refute 6–2C
regard 5–27
regardless 6–35
region 5–25CA
register 5–2CA
regret 4–29C*, 5–27*
regretful 6–17*
regretted 6–13C*
regular 5–34, 6–9R
regulate 5–29
regulation 5–29
rehearse 6–5
rehearsing 5–20C

reheat 4–21
reign 4–34C, 6–31
reins 4–11CA, 6–31*
rejected 5–20C*
rejoice 5–5C*, 6–4*
rejoin 3–25*
relate 4–31
relative 5–25, 6–22R*
relax 5–27
relay 4–1C
release 5–2C*, 6–16
relief 6–16
relieve 4–31C*, 6–31
relish 4–27C*
reluctance 6–28C*
rely 6–3
remake 3–25, 4–21R, 4–26R*
remarkable 5–33, 6–23R, 6–35R*
remember 4–33, 5–34R
remind 3–25C*, 5–27, 6–16R
remote 5–3C*
remote control 5–19CA
remove 5–27*
renew 3–25*
repaint 4–21, 5–27R*
repair 3–19C*, 5–26
repeat 3–34CA, 5–19
repetition 6–35
replace 4–21*
replacement 6–14
replay 3–25*
replies 5–28
reply 6–3
report 2–32C*, 5–27, 6–16R
reporter 4–33CA
represent 5–16CA
reprieve 6–31C*
reproach 5–3C
reptile 2–8CA, 4–23*
republic 6–9CA
Republicans 5–2CA
reputation 6–35C
request 4–19C*
require 6–16
reread 4–21
rescue 4–31CA, 5–4*, 6–11
research 6–27CA
resemblance 6–28C
resemble 5–27C*
resident 5–33, 6–23R*
resign 5–19C*
resolution 6–34CA
resourceful 4–28C
resources 6–31CA
respectful 6–35
respond 5–26, 6–17R*
responsible 5–27C, 6–23
rest 1–5C*, 2–2*

restaurant 4–2C
restless 4–28, 5–22R*
resulting 5–20
resume 6–4C*
retail 6–21CA
retell 3–25, 4–21R*
retirement 5–22, 6–14R, 6–35R*
retrieve 6–31C
reuse 3–25, 4–21R*
reveal 4–2C*
revenge 5–27
revenue 6–32CA
reverence 5–34C, 6–28*
reverse 5–8C*
reversible 5–33C
review 3–25C, 6–31
revise 6–35CA
revisit 3–25C*
revolution 5–28CA
reward 3–32CA, 4–32
rewind 4–21
rewrite 3–25, 4–21R
rhinoceros 4–34SS
rhyme 4–35C, 5–17CA, 6–3
rhythm 5–17CA, 6–3
ribbon 2–3CA, 3–28*
rich 1–19*
ride 1–11, 2–8R
ridge 4–20
riding 2–35
rigging 4–14CA
right 2–13WOM*, 2–25, 3–8R*, 3–33WOM*, 4–21WOM*, 5–4WOM*, 6–11WOM*
right of way 5–15CA
rigid 4–3C
ring 2–3CA, 4–5
rink 4–1CA
rinse 2–17CA
riot 5–17
ripe 4–3
ripped 3–22*
ripple 5–14*
rising 5–20
risk 4–19
rival 4–31C, 6–10*
rivalries 5–28C
river 3–2CA
river 4–27*
road 2–23, 3–5R*
roam 6–2
roar 3–9CA
rob 2–4*
robe 2–8*
Robert Peary 5–23CA
robin 2–4SS, 4–27
robot 5–19, 6–16R*

robots 2–20C*
rock 1–4C*, 2–10, 3–2R*
rocket 2–10C*, 4–29, 6–11R*
rod 1–4*
rode 2–23
rodeo 4–32CA, 5–17
role 5–11CA
romantic 5–34, 6–33R
roof 4–8
rookie 5–4CA
room 2–22, 3–31R*, 4–8R*
roost 6–4
rooster 2–22C*
roots 2–17CA
rope 2–8
rough 3–32*, 5–1
round 3–9
route 4–4CA, 5–4
routine 4–7CA, 6–3
row 3–5
rowboat 2–21C*
royal 3–15C*, 5–5
rub 3–2, 4–7R
rubbed 2–34*, 3–22, 4–16R*
rubbing 4–16, 5–21R
ruby 5–14CA
rude 5–4
rug 2–5
rugged 5–7CA
ruin 5–17
rule 4–7*, 5–4
rummage 5–25C*
rumor 4–26C*, 6–9*
run 1–7, 2–5R
runner–up 6–7
running 2–34, 3–22R*
runway 4–26CA
rupture 6–33C*
rural 6–10
rustic 5–1C

S

Sacramento 4–13CA
sacrifice 5–3C
sad 1–1*, 2–1
saddle 4–11CA
sadly 3–26, 4–17R
safe 3–3*, 4–1, 5–2R
safely 3–26C*, 5–22
said 1–13SW, 2–2, 2–21WOM*, 3–4WOM*, 3–26R
sail 2–13
sailor 4–14
Saint Bernard 4–9CA
salad 4–27
salary 6–17CA
sale 2–20CA, 4–1

salesperson 5–9
salt 3–10*
salute 5–26
salvage 6–1CA
same 1–10*, 2–7, 3–29R
sample 5–10CA, 6–10
sandbar 6–7CA
sandbox 2–28SS
sandwich 2–19C*, 5–16
sapphire 5–14CA
sassafras 6–8CA
sat 2–1
satellite 4–29CA, 5–34C*
satisfy 6–3C*
Saturday 3–27CA, 4–10WOM*, 5–33WOM*, 6–26WOM*
sauce 4–9
sausage 5–25C*, 6–22
save 3–3, 4–1R*
saved 2–35*
saving 3–22, 4–16R*
savings 4–15CA
saw 2–15, 3–10R
say 1–17, 2–21R
says 4–35
scald 3–10C
scale 5–2*
scallion 6–4CA
scalloped 5–21C
scamper 3–27*
scanned 6–13*
scar 4–10*, 5–7, 6–5R
scarce 4–10
scarcely 6–14
scare 3–19, 4–10R
scarf 2–31SS, 3–17*, 4–10
scariest 5–28
scaring 4–16*
scarlet 4–22C*
scarred 4–16C, 5–21*
scarves 6–26
scatter 3–28*
scene 3–20C, 6–8
scenic 5–25CA, 6–16*
scent 6–8
schedule 5–25CA
scheme 6–2*
scholar 5–11C
school 2–29WOM*, 3–17, 3–23WOM*, 4–8R, 4–20WOM*, 5–16WOM*, 6–10WOM*
schooner 4–14C
science 5–17, 6–28R
scientific 6–33
scissors 5–15*
scold 5–3*

scoop 3–31C*, 5–4, 6–4R
scooter 3–31C*
scorch 5–7*
score 2–34CA, 4–11, 5–7R*
scoreboard 3–5CA
scorekeeper 3–21C*
scorn 6–5
scornful 4–11C*
scoundrel 6–4C*
scout 4–9
scowl 4–9C*, 5–5
scramble 3–7C*
scrapbook 3–7SS
scrape 3–7*
scraped 4–16SS
scratch 3–11, 4–1R*
scrawny 4–9C
scream 3–7
screen 3–7
screenplay 5–20CA
screwdriver 4–3CA
script 5–11CA, 6–1*
scrub 6–1
scuba diver 4–10CA
scurried 3–23C*
sea gull 6–7
seal 5–2
search 3–32CA, 4–11, 5–8R*
seashore 2–32SS
season 2–5CA, 4–26
seat belt 4–13, 5–13R
seaweed 3–4SS
secede 6–10CA
second 2–19C*, 3–17, 4–27R
secondary 6–20CA
secret 4–29
secure 4–32C*, 6–16
see 1–14, 2–23R
seed 1–14*
seeking 5–20
seem 1–14SS, 3–4, 4–2R
seen 3–20C, 6–8
seesaw 2–15C*
seize 6–31
seizure 5–23C*
seldom 4–23, 5–26R*
select 4–31C*, 5–31*
selection 5–31*
self-assured 5–9C
self-confident 6–7C
self-defense 5–13C*
self-discipline 6–7C*
selfish 6–25
sell 2–11*
semester 5–11C*
Senate 5–16CA
senator 6–9
send 2–19*, 3–1, 4–2R*
senior 6–9

sensitive 5–35, 6–22R
sensors 5–19CA
sent 2–23C*, 6–8
sentence 6–28
separate 6–28
September 3–26CA, 4–33*
sequel 5–14C*, 6–23CA
series 5–29CA
serious 6–33
seriousness 5–22C
servant 5–33, 6–23R*
serve 3–14
service 5–25
session 5–16CA, 6–25
set 2–2
sets 5–11CA
settle 4–32CA
settlement 5–22
seven 2–2C*, 4–27
several 4–33, 5–34R*
sew 3–5
sewer 2–14CA
shade 1–10C*, 4–1*
shadow 5–19, 6–16R*
shake 3–3*
shall 4–1
shallow 3–5C, 6–25
shampoo 2–22SS, 3–19CA
shape 2–28CA, 4–1
share 2–35CA, 3–19, 4–10R*
shark 4–19
sharp 2–8CA, 4–10, 5–7R
she 1–8SS, 1–19, 2–16R
she'll 2–29*
she's 3–35
sheaves 6–26C*
shed 1–19*
sheep 2–16
sheet 2–16*
shelf 4–2*
shelter 4–32
sheltered 5–20
shelves 6–26
Shenandoah 5–34CA
sheriff 4–32C
shield 6–31
shine 1–11C*, 4–3
shiny 3–20CA
ship 1–19*, 2–16
shipped 5–21
shipwreck 4–10CA
shipyard 5–9
shirt 3–14*, 4–11
shiver 2–16C*, 6–16*
shock 4–4
shoe 1–19C*, 3–31, 4–35R
shoelace 2–28C*
shook 3–31, 4–8R
shoot 2–33CA, 4–8, 5–4R

shop 1–19, 2–33R
shopping 2–34
shore 2–10CA
short 2–32, 3–13R
shortage 5–25
shorts 1–19C*
shortstop 5–3CA
should 2–27
shoulder 5–15, 6–9R*
shouldn't 3–35
should've 3–35C*
shout 2–16C, 4–9
shove 6–3
shovel 4–27C*, 5–14
shoveling 6–13
show 2–21, 3–5R*
shower 2–16C*, 4–14
shown 4–4, 5–3R
shredded 5–21C
shrimp 2–21CA
shrink 4–3*
shrug 2–5C*, 5–1*
shuddered 6–13*
shut 3–2, 4–7R
shutter 4–22CA
shuttle 5–26*
shy 1–23*
sickness 4–28, 5–16R*
side 2–7, 3–3R
siege 6–31C*
sieve 6–31C*
sift 4–2CA
sigh 3–8C*, 4–3, 5–3R
sight 3–8, 4–3R
sightseer 5–25CA
sign 4–34C*, 5–3, 6–2R*
signature 5–23SS, 6–33
significance 6–28C
silence 6–28
silent 3–8C*, 4–26, 5–33R
silently 3–26C*
silhouetted 6–14C
silly 2–26, 3–28R*
silos 6–26*
silver 4–32
similar 6–9
simmer 4–2CA
simple 4–15, 5–14R
simply 5–16
since 4–20, 5–1R*
sincere 5–15C
sincerely 5–22C*, 6–14
sing 2–19
singer 3–26, 4–28R
single 5–14
sink 4–19
Sir Francis Drake 5–23CA
siren 2–25C*, 4–31
sister 2–33, 3–27R*, 3–33R*

sit 1–2
site 5–3C
sitting 2–34, 3–22R*
situate 6–19
situation 6–19
six 2–3
sixth 1–22C*
sizable 5–33*
skate 1–10C*, 4–1
skated 3–22SS
skeleton 4–19C*, 6–29CA
sketch 3–11C*
ski 4–1CA
skier 3–26C*
skies 3–23*
skill 2–11C, 3–17*, 4–3, 5–1R
skimmed 5–21
skin 3–17, 4–19R*
skip 3–14CA
skipped 4–16, 5–21R*
skipping 2–34C*
skirt 6–5
skit 3–35CA
skunk 2–19C*
sky 1–23, 2–25
skyscraper 3–29CA
slam 1–13*
slammed 5–21
sled 1–13, 2–2*
sledding 4–1CA
sleep 1–14, 2–35R
sleet 3–13CA
sleeve 6–2
sleigh 4–1CA
slender 5–11*
slept 5–1
slice 3–29*
slid 1–13*, 2–3*
slide 1–11C*, 5–8CA
slight 5–3
sling 3–11CA
slip 1–13, 2–9R
slipped 6–13
slippers 1–13C*, 3–21CA
slippery 5–35
sliver 5–11*
slogan 6–22CA
slope 4–4*, 5–3
slow 1–13C*, 2–21, 3–5R
slowly 3–26, 4–17R
slumber 4–7C
slur 6–5*
slurp 3–14SS
small 2–15, 3–10R
smart 2–31*, 3–13, 4–10R*
smear 5–8
smell 3–1, 4–2R*

smelling 4–16
smile 1–11C*, 3–3, 4–3R
smiled 3–22, 4–16R*
smog 3–10SS, 5–31CA
smoke 2–8SS, 3–3, 4–4R
smooth 2–17C*, 4–8
smuggle 6–31CA
snack 2–10C*
snail 2–2CA
snake 2–10C
snapped 2–34C*
snapping 4–16, 5–21R
snare 5–7
snarl 6–5
sneaker 3–33*
sneeze 2–14C*
snicker 4–29*
snore 2–32*
snow 3–5*, 4–4
snowflake 3–21*
snowmobile 4–1CA
snowplow 2–27C*
so 1–8, 2–21R
soak 3–15CA, 6–2
soap 2–21*, 3–5, 4–4R
soar 5–7, 6–8R
soccer 4–14*
sock 3–2, 4–19R
soda 4–32*
soft 3–10
soften 4–34*
softness 5–22
soil 2–33CA, 3–15
solar 4–14C, 5–19*
sold 3–5
soldier 6–10
sole 5–10
solid 5–26
solos 6–26
solve 4–4C*, 5–22CA
somber 5–26C
some 1–14SW, 2–5, 2–11WOM*, 3–11WOM*
somebody 6–7
someone 2–28, 3–21R, 4–32WOM*, 4–35R*, 5–14WOM*, 6–20WOM*
somersault 5–5C
something 2–31WOM*, 3–21, 4–13R*
sometimes 3–21, 4–13R, 5–14WOM*, 6–20WOM*
sonar 6–1CA
song 2–19*
soon 2–22, 3–31R
soot 4–8C
soothe 5–4C*
sopranos 6–26
sorcerer 6–5CA

sore 5–7, 6–8R
sorrow 5–15
sorry 2–26C*, 4–17
sought 3–32C, 6–4
soul 5–10
sound 3–9, 4–9R
soundtrack 5–20CA
soup 4–8
sour 2–27*, 3–20CA
source 6–5*
south 4–9, 5–5R
souvenir 5–4C*
space 2–25CA, 3–29, 4–20R*
space shuttle 4–29CA
spaghetti 5–35C*
spaniel 4–9CA
spare 3–19*, 4–10, 5–7R*
spark 3–3CA, 4–10*
sparkle 3–13C*, 5–14
sparkled 6–14*
sparse 6–5C
speak 3–4, 4–2R
speaker 3–26*
spear 4–10
special 4–15, 5–14R
species 6–31C*
specific 6–33
specimen 6–29CA
speck 5–1*
speckled 4–19C
spectator 5–35C
speech 5–2
speechless 5–22
speed 4–2, 5–2R*
speedometer 5–15CA
spend 1–5C*
spent 3–1*, 4–2
spicy 5–21CA
spider 4–26
spied 3–23*, 5–28
spinach 2–16C*, 5–26
spine 5–3*
spinning 5–21*
spiral 6–10*
spirit 6–16
splash 1–19C*
splendid 4–23SS
splint 3–11CA
split 5–1, 6–1R*
spoil 3–15
spoilage 5–25*
spoke 3–3*, 4–4, 5–3R*
sponge 4–19CA, 6–3
sponsor 5–29CA, 6–10*
spooky 2–26SS
spool 4–8*
spoon 2–22*, 3–31, 4–8R
sport 2–32*
spot 1–4C*, 2–4, 3–2R

spotted 5–21, 6–13R
sprawl 5–5C*
spray 3–7, 4–1R*
spread 3–7
spring 3–7
sprinkle 3–7C*
sprint 6–3CA
sprout 3–9C, 6–4
spruce 4–27CA
spy 1–23*, 2–25*
squad 5–4CA
squander 5–11C*
square 4–10, 5–7R
squawk 3–10C*, 6–4
squeak 2–10C*, 3–17*
squeaky 3–20CA
squeal 3–4C*, 6–2*
squeeze 3–17, 4–19R*
squeezing 5–20
squid 4–19C
squire 4–34CA
squirm 5–8
squirm 4–11SS
squirrel 4–19, 5–8R*
squirt 5–8
stack 4–1*
stadium 5–35
staff 5–1
staffs 6–26
stage 3–16, 4–1R
stagecoach 4–32CA
stain 5–2
stairs 3–19*, 4–10, 5–7R
stale 2–7C*
stalk 5–5
stall 2–15C
stamina 6–14CA
stamp 2–9*
stampede 4–32C
stamps 2–20*
stand 1–16SS
standard 4–32C*, 6–11
stanza 5–17CA
star 3–13
starch 6–5
stare 4–10, 5–7R*
starry–eyed 5–13C
start 2–31, 3–7R
started 2–20WOM*,
  3–15WOM*
startle 4–10C
starvation 6–25*
starve 4–10
statement 4–28, 5–22R*
station 6–25
stationary 5–10C
stationery 5–10C
stature 6–33C

statute 5–32CA
stay 1–17, 2–13R
steak 4–1
steal 4–5, 5–10R*
steel 4–5, 5–10R*
steep 4–2*
steeple 4–20CA
steer 4–23CA, 5–8
stellar 4–14C
stem 1–16*
stencil 5–15SS
stenciling 4–21CA
step 1–16, 2–9, 3–1R
stepped 2–34
stereos 6–26
stern 4–14CA, 5–8
stew 4–7*
stick 1–16C*, 3–1
sticky 2–26*
still 4–3
stimulate 5–34C
sting 1–16C*, 3–17CA, 4–3
stir 3–1CA, 4–11*, 5–8, 6–5R
stirrups 4–11CA
stitch 3–11*
stock 4–4
stole 5–3
stolen 4–26
stomach 4–19
stone 2–9
stood 4–8
stool 4–8
stoop 4–8*
stop 1–16, 2–28R
stopped 2–34, 3–22R,
  4–2WOM*, 5–15WOM*,
  6–22WOM*
storage 5–25*, 6–22
store 2–32
stories 3–23, 4–25R
storm 2–9C, 3–13, 4–11R
story 2–32, 3–13R*, 4–17R*
stove 1–16C*, 2–8*
straight 2–13C*, 3–7, 4–26R
strain 6–2
strange 3–7C*, 4–20
stranger 5–11*
strap 3–7*
strapped 2–34C*
strategic 6–33C
strategies 5–28C
straw 3–10
strawberry 2–15C*
stray 2–16CA, 4–1*, 5–2
stream 2–14C, 3–7
street 2–14C, 3–7, 4–2R*
strength 3–7C

strengthen 4–16CA
stretch 4–16CA, 5–1*,
  6–33WOM*
stretcher 3–11C
strict 3–7C*, 6–1
stride 5–3
strike 5–3
string 3–7
stripe 2–7C*
striped 4–16, 5–20R*
stripped 4–16, 5–21R
strive 6–2
striving 4–16C
stroke 5–3, 6–2R*
stroll 5–3
strong 3–7
struck 4–19
structure 6–11C
struggle 3–7C, 6–10
stubborn 3–28C, 4–23*,
  5–7CA
stuck 5–1, 6–1R*
student 5–33, 6–23R
students 3–26CA
studied 4–25, 5–28R
studios 6–26
study 2–26*
stuff 2–11SS, 3–2*
stumble 6–10
stung 6–1
stunned 5–21
stunt 5–20CA
stupid 6–16
sturdier 5–28*
sturdy 3–14C, 5–8*
style 3–19CA, 4–35
subdue 5–4C
subject 5–15
submarine 4–35C*, 6–1CA
submerge 4–23C
submerged 6–1CA
substitute 6–20C
substitution 6–20C
subway 2–13C, 3–29CA
succeed 5–2C
success 6–17
such 1–7C*, 2–16, 3–2R*
sudden 3–28, 4–23R
suffer 4–14
suffering 5–21
sugar 4–14, 5–11R*
suggest 4–23C*, 6–20
suggestion 6–20
suit 4–7, 5–4R*
suitable 5–33
suitcase 3–21C
sum 4–7
summary 6–23CA

summer 2–5CA, 3–33, 4–14R
summit 5–1C
summoned 6–13C*
sun 2–5
Sunday 3–27, 4–22R*
sunk 6–1
sunnier 4–25
sunshine 2–7C*
superb 4–8C
superhuman 5–7CA
superior 6–9
superlative 5–25C
supermarket 4–10C*
supervise 6–17CA
supper 4–22*
supplies 4–35CA
supply 6–11
support 4–22
supported 5–20
suppose 3–28C*, 4–22,
  5–15R*, 5–29WOM*,
  6–25WOM*
sure 2–16, 3–4WOM*,
  4–8WOM*
surface 5–26C*, 6–11
surgeon 5–23, 6–11R
surgery 4–28CA
surprise 6–17
surprised 2–35C*
surrender 6–9
surround 5–26*
survey 5–10CA
survive 3–27C*, 4–22, 5–15R*
survivors 5–27CA
suspect 5–22CA
suspenseful 5–22C
suspicion 6–25*
suspiciously 5–22C
swallow 2–9C*
swam 2–1C*
swan 2–9*
sway 1–17C*, 3–14CA, 5–2
sweat 6–3
sweater 3–33C*, 4–35*
sweatshirt 2–28C*
sweet 1–14C*, 3–4*, 4–2
sweetheart 5–13
sweetness 4–28*
swept 5–1
swerve 5–8*
swift 4–23CA, 5–1, 6–1R
swim 2–9
swimming 3–28WOM*,
  4–4WOM*, 5–3WOM*, 5–21,
  6–4WOM*
swirl 4–11*
switch 4–3SS, 5–1*, 6–1
swivel 4–31SS
swollen 6–10*

Complete Word List

sword 6–5
sycamore 6–8CA
symbolic 6–33C
symphony 6–3C*
system 6–11

T

table 3–10CA
tackle 3–33C*
tacks 6–8
taco 4–19*
tacos 6–26*
tadpole 2–26CA
tail 2–23, 3–20R*
tailor 5–33CA
take 1–10, 2–10R
taking 3–22*
tale 1–10*, 2–23, 3–20R*
talent 4–27
talk 3–10, 4–34R
tall 2–15*
tambourine 6–26CA
tame 2–22CA
tandem 6–3CA
tangerine 4–35C*, 6–3*
tank 4–10CA
tanning 4–16, 5–21R*
tape recorder 6–7*
taped 2–35*
tapered 6–13C*
tapping 3–22, 4–16R, 5–21R*
target 2–31C*, 3–27*
tariff 6–31CA
taught 3–32
taut 6–4C
tax 6–8
taxation 5–28CA
taxi 3–29CA
teach 2–16*
teacher 3–26, 4–29R
team 2–14*
teammate 5–9SS, 6–7
tear 3–19SS
tease 5–2*
teasing 2–35C, 6–14
technician 6–25C
teeth 2–17, 3–32R
telephone 4–4C*
telescope 3–3C*
televise 5–29, 6–22R
television 5–29
tell 2–11
teller 6–16CA
telling 2–34
temper 4–14
temperature 6–33
ten 1–5, 2–2

tender 4–22
tennis 6–11
tense 5–29, 6–1R
tension 5–29
tent 1–5C*, 4–8CA
tentacle 6–10SS
tepid 6–1C
term 5–8
terminal 4–26CA
tern 6–7CA
terrain 6–3CA
terrible 5–33, 6–23R
terrier 4–9CA
terrific 6–33
territory 6–5C*
terror 4–14*
test 2–9*, 3–26CA
test tube 5–9
textbook 6–20CA
texture 5–23C
than 2–17, 3–3WOM*, 4–1WOM*
thank 2–19, 3–1R*
thankful 3–26, 4–28R, 5–16R*
Thanksgiving Day 5–13CA
that 1–22, 2–33R
that's 2–29*, 2–32WOM*, 3–26WOM*, 4–34WOM*, 5–13WOM*, 6–3WOM*
thatched 4–20CA
thaw 2–17*
the 1–1SW, 2–14
theater 5–11
their 1–16SW, 2–28WOM*, 3–9WOM*, 3–20, 4–5R, 4–19WOM*, 5–11WOM*, 6–9WOM*
them 1–5C*, 2–17, 3–3WOM*
theme 6–2
then 1–22*, 2–17, 3–3WOM*, 4–1WOM*
there 1–8SW, 2–28WOM*, 3–9WOM*, 3–20, 4–5R, 4–19WOM*, 5–11WOM*, 6–9WOM*
there's 2–29C*, 3–35*, 4–34WOM*, 5–2WOM*, 6–27WOM*
thermometer 3–33C
these 1–22*, 2–8
they 1–5SW, 2–13, 3–9WOM*, 3–34R, 4–1WOM*, 5–26WOM*, 6–13WOM*
they're 2–29C, 3–20, 3–35*, 4–5R, 4–19WOM*, 5–11WOM*, 6–9WOM*
thick 2–17SS, 3–1, 4–3R*
thief 5–2, 6–31R
thigh 3–8SS, 5–3

thin 3–1
thing 1–22C*, 2–19
things 2–20
think 1–22C*, 2–19, 3–1R*
third 3–14, 4–11R
thirst 5–8, 6–5R*
thirsty 3–14C*
thirteen 4–11, 5–8R*
thirty 4–23
this 1–22, 2–34R
thorn 6–5
thoroughbred 4–11C
those 2–8
though 3–5, 4–35R*
thought 2–17C*, 3–23WOM*, 3–32, 4–13WOM*, 5–27WOM*, 6–16WOM*
thoughtfully 3–32SS
thousand 3–9C*, 5–5, 6–4R*
thread 3–7C*, 6–3
threat 6–3
threaten 4–35C
three 1–14C*, 2–14*, 3–7, 4–2R
threw 2–23C, 3–7*, 4–7
thrill 3–7*
throat 3–7*
throne 2–19CA, 6–2
throttle 5–26C*
through 2–23C, 2–29WOM*, 3–23WOM*, 3–32, 4–13WOM*, 4–26R, 5–27WOM*, 6–16WO
throughout 5–13, 6–7R*
throw 3–7
thrown 5–3
thumb 2–17C*, 4–34
thumbtack 5–13C*
thunder 2–5C, 4–25CA, 5–11
thunderstorm 3–21C*
Thursday 2–17C*, 3–27CA
ticket 4–29
tickle 3–17C*
tie 2–34CA, 3–8
tiger 2–25C*, 4–26
tight 3–8, 4–3R
tightrope 2–25C*
timber 5–15*
time 1–11, 2–10WOM*, 2–35R
tin 4–5CA
tiniest 5–28
tiny 2–25C*, 4–26
tiring 4–16C
tissue 4–7C
titanic 6–33C*
title 4–15, 5–17R
to 1–2SW, 2–23, 3–8WOM*, 3–20R*, 4–26WOM*, 5–1WOM*, 6–1WOM*

toad 2–21*
toast 2–9C*, 6–2
toboggan 4–1CA
today 1–17C*, 3–14WOM*, 4–31
toe 2–21
together 4–33, 5–35R
token 5–3C*
told 2–21, 3–5R*
tolerant 5–33C*
tomatoes 6–26*
tomorrow 4–33, 5–35R
tongue 6–3*
tongue–tied 6–7C*
tonight 4–3*, 4–28WOM*, 5–28WOM*, 6–32WOM*
too 2–23, 3–8WOM*, 3–20R*, 4–26WOM*, 5–1WOM*, 6–1WOM*
took 2–22, 3–31R*, 4–8R*
tool 4–8
tooth 3–31, 4–8R
toothache 4–13C*
toothbrush 2–17CA, 6–7
top 1–4, 2–4
topaz 5–14CA
Topeka 4–13CA
topic 3–2C*, 4–19
torch 5–7, 6–5R
tore 5–7, 6–5R*
torn 3–13*
tornado 3–13C
torrent 6–23*
tortoise 3–28CA
torture 5–23*, 6–33
total 4–15, 5–19R
touchdown 5–13, 6–7R*
tough 3–32*, 5–1
tournament 4–34CA, 5–34C*
towel 2–27C*, 4–15, 5–14R*
tower 2–27C*, 5–5
town 2–27, 3–9R
toxic 5–31CA, 6–33*
toy 3–15
trace 2–7C*, 3–4CA, 4–1*
traced 4–16, 5–20R
track 3–16CA, 4–19, 5–1R
tractor 5–11
trade 2–9*
traffic 2–31CA, 4–19*, 5–15
tragedies 5–28C*
tragedy 6–28CA
tragic 6–33
trail 2–13
trailer 2–27CA
train 2–13
trainer 3–9CA
trait 6–2
traitor 4–32C*

trampoline 6–3C
transfer 6–16CA
transmitted 6–13C
transportation 6–25C*
trapeze 2–9C*
trash 2–14CA
travel 3–33, 4–15R*, 4–27R
traveled 5–21*
tray 1–17*, 2–13*
treasure 5–23, 6–3R*
treatment 4–28
treaty 5–26CA
tree 1–14*, 2–14
trek 5–1C
tremble 4–15C*
tremendous 6–33C*
tremor 5–11C
Trenton 4–13CA
trespass 5–15C
trial 5–17
tried 2–26WOM*, 3–23, 3–31WOM*, 4–17WOM*, 4–25R*, 5–26WOM*
trifle 4–15C
trim 3–19CA
trip 2–9
triple 5–3CA
trombone 3–27SS, 6–26CA
troop 5–4
trophy 5–9CA, 6–11*
trot 2–4*
trouble 3–25CA, 4–15, 5–14R*
trough 3–32C*
trout 6–4
truce 6–4*
truck 2–10, 3–2R*
true 4–7, 5–4R
trumpet 2–9C*
trunk 2–31CA, 4–7, 5–1R
trust 2–5SS, 3–2*
truth 4–7
truthful 4–28*
try 1–23*, 2–25, 3–8R*
tuba 2–11CA
tube 4–7, 5–4R*
Tuesday 3–27CA
tug 2–5*
tulip 3–8CA, 5–19, 6–16R*
tuna 4–26
tune 2–11CA, 4–7
tunnel 5–15
turkey 4–17
turmoil 6–5C
turn 3–14, 4–11R*
turnip 4–23*
turnpike 5–9
turquoise 6–4C
turtle 3–14C*
tutor 5–11*

336   Complete Word List

tuxedos 6–26C
twice 4–20, 5–3R
twig 1–2C*
twilight 4–3C*
twins 2–3C*
twist 1–16C*, 3–1*
two 1–20SW, 2–23, 3–8WOM*,
  3–11R, 3–20R*, 4–26WOM*,
  5–1WOM*, 6–1WOM*
type 4–35
typical 5–35, 6–3R
tyrant 6–33CA

U

ugly 2–5C*, 4–17
umbrella 4–33C*
umpire 5–3CA
unable 3–25C*, 5–27
unanimous 6–33C
unaware 5–27
unbelievable 6–35
unbuckle 3–25C*
uncertain 4–21*
uncle 4–15, 5–14R*
unclear 3–25, 4–21R
under 2–33, 3–27R
underrated 6–7C*
understand 4–13, 5–9R*
understudy 6–28CA
uneven 4–21, 5–27R
unfair 3–25, 4–21R
unfamiliar 4–21C
unfold 3–25*
unfortunate 5–27C
unhappy 3–25, 4–33R
unhurt 3–25
unicorn 5–7C
unified 5–28C
uniform 4–31CA, 5–34
unimportant 3–25C, 5–27*
uninterested 5–27C*
unite 4–3C*, 6–16
unkind 3–25, 4–21R
unkindness 6–35
unknown 3–5C*, 5–27
unlawful 6–35*
unlike 3–25, 4–21R*
unload 4–21
unlock 3–25*
unlucky 4–21, 5–27R*
unnecessary 5–27C
unpack 4–21
unpaid 4–21
unravel 6–10C*
unready 3–25C*
unscramble 4–21SS
unsinkable 5–27CA
unskilled 5–27

unskillful 6–35
unsure 4–21, 5–27R
untidy 4–21, 5–27R*
untie 3–25, 4–21R*
until 3–27, 4–22R, 5–7WOM*
untrue 4–21*
unused 4–21*
unusual 4–21C
unwrap 3–25, 4–21R*
up 1–7, 2–5R
up–to–date 5–9
upon 2–28
uproar 6–7
upsetting 5–21C*, 6–13*
urban 5–8C*
urge 6–5
urged 4–16C
urgent 5–33*
us 1–7, 2–29R
usable 6–14
usage 6–22
use 2–8
useful 3–26, 4–28R
useless 4–28
using 2–35
usual 5–17
usually 4–31WOM*,
  5–34WOM*, 6–31WOM*

V

vacant 5–33, 6–23R*
vacation 5–34, 6–25R*
vaccine 4–35C
vain 4–5C, 6–8
Valentine's Day 5–13CA
valid 6–1C*
valley 4–17, 5–15R*
valor 6–10C
valuable 5–33, 6–14R
value 5–19, 6–16R
van 1–20*
vane 4–5C
vanish 5–19, 6–25R
vans 1–20*
variety 5–17C
various 6–33C*
vault 5–35CA, 6–4
vehicle 5–15CA
veil 6–31
vein 4–5C, 6–8
velvet 5–15
venture 4–23C, 6–33*
verb 5–8*
very 1–17SW, 2–17WOM*,
  2–26, 3–13WOM*, 3–23R,
  4–17R*
vessel 4–23C, 6–17*
vest 2–1CA

Veterans Day 5–13CA
veto 5–32CA
vetoes 6–26C
vibrant 5–26SS
vibrate 4–29C, 5–31*
vibration 5–31*
victims 4–35CA
victories 5–28
victory 4–33, 5–35R*
video 5–29CA
videos 6–26*
videotape 4–13C*
view 5–4, 6–31R*
viewpoint 6–15CA
vigor 6–16C
village 4–20, 5–25R
villain 5–23C
vinegar 5–21CA
violate 6–28C*
violence 6–28
violet 3–8CA, 5–35
violin 5–17C*, 6–26CA
virus 6–27CA
visible 6–23
visit 2–3C*, 3–21CA, 4–27
visiting 5–21, 6–13R*
visualize 6–22C
vital 5–14C, 6–16
vivid 4–27C
voice 3–15C*, 5–5*
volcano 4–19C*
volcanoes 6–26
volume 6–16*
volunteer 4–35CA, 5–34*
voted 2–35C*
voter 5–2CA
voyage 5–25, 6–22R*
vulture 5–23*

W

wade 2–10CA
wafer 4–26C*
wagon 1–20C*, 4–32
wagons 1–20C*
waist 3–20SS, 5–2
wait 4–5, 5–10R
walk 3–10, 4–9R
wall 3–10
wallpaper 2–15C*
wandered 5–21
want 2–1, 2–15WOM*,
  3–2WOM*, 3–34R
ware 4–5
warehouse 5–13
warm 2–31
warmly 3–26*
warn 5–7
warrant 5–4CA

warranty 6–21CA
was 1–4SW, 2–1, 2–15WOM*,
  3–2WOM*, 3–32R
wash 2–16
washable 6–23
washer 3–15CA
wasn't 2–29*, 3–35
waste 5–31CA
wasting 4–16
watch 3–11, 4–34R*
watches 2–20C*
watchful 5–22
water 2–33, 3–33R*
water–repellent 6–7C
waterfall 2–15C*
watermelon 5–13
waterproof 4–8CA
wave 1–10*
waver 4–26C
waving 2–35*
wax 2–1SS
way 1–17, 2–13
we 1–8, 2–14
we'll 2–29
we're 3–35*, 4–22WOM*,
  5–8WOM*, 6–8WOM*
we've 2–29, 3–35*
weak 2–23*
wealth 4–35, 6–3R*
weapon 5–22CA, 6–10
wear 3–19*, 4–5
weariest 5–28SS
weary 4–10C, 6–16*
weasel 4–26SS
weather 2–5CA, 4–14, 5–11R*
weaving 4–21CA
web 2–2*
webbed 5–21*
wedge 4–20C*
Wednesday 3–27CA
week 2–23*, 3–17, 4–19R
weekend 5–9, 6–7R
weigh 3–4
weight 4–5, 5–10R
weird 4–10, 5–17WOM*,
  6–35WOM*
welcome 2–35CA, 4–22
welfare 5–13
well 2–11
well–known 4–13*
went 2–2, 2–16WOM*, 3–1R*
were 1–10SW, 2–8WOM*,
  3–14
weren't 2–29C*, 3–35
west 4–2
wet 2–2
whale 4–19CA
what 1–13SW, 2–17
what's 3–35SS

wheat 4–2*
wheel 2–17, 3–11R*
wheelbarrow 2–17C*
wheelchair 5–9
when 1–22, 2–17, 3–11R*
whenever 4–13, 5–13R*
where 1–22C*, 2–20WOM*,
  3–19, 3–32WOM*,
  4–23WOM*
whereabouts 5–13
whereas 6–7
whether 4–29, 5–26R
which 1–22SS, 2–17, 3–11R*
while 1–22*, 2–17, 3–11R*
whimper 2–17C*
whine 2–17*
whining 6–14*
whip 1–22*, 2–17*
whipped 4–16C*, 5–21,
  6–13R*
whirl 3–14SS, 5–8*, 6–5
whirlpool 4–23CA
whirred 5–21C
whisker 1–22C*
whiskers 4–29*
whisper 4–14C*, 6–11
whistle 2–17C, 3–5CA, 5–14,
  6–10R*
white 1–22, 2–17R
whittling 4–21CA
who 1–23SW, 2–22
who's 3–35C, 6–8
whoever 5–9
whole 2–23, 3–11R*,
  3–29WOM*, 4–15WOM*,
  5–22WOM*, 6–7WOM*
wholeheartedly 5–13C*
wholesale 6–21CA
whose 6–8
why 1–23, 2–25R
wicked 4–17CA
wide 3–3
wield 6–31C
wife 3–3*
wild 2–25*, 3–8, 4–3R*
wilderness 5–34
wildlife 5–9, 6–7R
will 1–11SW, 2–11
win 1–2*, 2–3
wind 4–3
windier 4–25
window 3–27, 4–22R*
windowsill 2–11C*
windshield 5–9C*
wing 1–2C*
wink 2–19*
winning 5–21, 6–13R
winter 2–5CA, 3–33, 4–23R*

wiped 4–16*
wisdom 3–27C, 5–26
wish 1–19*, 2–16
wishes 2–20
with 1–22, 2–17
withdraw 4–15CA
wither 4–29SS
without 2–28, 3–21R*
witness 5–15
wizard 4–17CA
wolves 6–26
women 4–35
won 3–20*
wonder 2–33C*, 4–35
wonderful 3–26C*
wondering 6–13
won't 2–29C*, 3–35
wood 3–31*, 4–8
wool 4–8
word 3–14, 4–11R*
work 2–10C*, 3–14, 4–11R
workable 6–23
workout 4–16CA
world 4–11, 5–8R
worm 3–14*, 4–11
worn 4–11
worried 3–23C*, 4–25, 5–28R*
worry 3–32CA, 5–8*
worse 5–8
worship 5–26
worst 4–11*
worth 5–8
worthiness 5–28
worthless 4–28C*
worthwhile 5–13, 6–7R*
would 1–10SW, 2–5WOM*,
    3–9, 3–31WOM*,
    4–11WOM*, 4–27R,
    5–9WOM*, 6–28WOM*
wouldn't 2–29C, 3–35,
    4–11WOM*, 5–9WOM*,
    6–28WOM*
would've 3–35C*
wound 4–28CA
wrap 3–11, 4–34R*
wrapped 3–22, 4–16R, 5–21R*
wrapping 2–34C*
wreath 4–34*
wreck 3–11C*, 6–1
wrench 4–3CA
wrestle 4–34C
wring 3–11C*, 4–5
wrinkle 3–11*, 4–34
wrist 3–11SS, 4–34
write 2–7C, 2–13WOM*, 3–11,
    3–33WOM*, 4–21WOM*,
    4–34R*, 5–4WOM*,
    6–11WOM*
writing 5–4WOM*,

6–11WOM*
wrong 2–19C*, 3–11, 4–34R
wrote 2–8C*, 4–4, 5–17R

X

x–ray 3–31CA

Y

yard 2–31
yardage 5–25*
yarn 6–5
yawn 2–15*
year 1–23SW, 4–10, 5–8R
yearn 5–8C
yeast 4–2C
yellow 2–21C*, 3–28, 4–22R
Yellowstone 5–34CA
yes 1–5, 2–2
yesterday 4–33, 5–35R
yield 5–15CA, 6–31
yogurt 4–26*
yolk 4–4*
Yosemite 5–34CA
you 1–4SW, 2–1WOM*, 2–22,
    3–25WOM*
you'll 2–29, 3–35R*
you're 2–29, 3–25WOM*,
    4–5R*, 4–22WOM*,
    5–8WOM*, 6–8WOM*
young 2–19C
youngster 6–9
your 1–16SW, 2–1WOM*,
    2–32, 3–25WOM*, 4–5R*,
    4–22WOM*, 5–8WOM*,
    6–8WOM*
youth 5–4
yo–yo 1–8C*

Z

zero 1–8C*
zinc 4–5CA
zip 1–2SS
zipper 2–33*, 3–33*
zoo 2–22, 3–31R*
zucchini 6–4CA

This scope and sequence chart shows where specific skills and content are taught, practiced, and tested in Level 2 of *Houghton Mifflin Spelling and Vocabulary*. The chart references the student book, the Teacher's Edition, and the Teacher's Resource Book for this level. The following codes are used:

TE = Teacher's Edition

TRB = Teacher's Resource Book

A page number that is not preceded by one of the above labels refers to the student book page and the accompanying Teacher's Edition page. A page number that follows one of the above labels refers to the page in that component only.

Bold page numbers indicate that instruction in the skill occurs on that page. All other page numbers indicate that the skill is practiced on that page.

The following sections appear in this chart:

PHONICS

Auditory Discrimination	
Initial Consonants	16–18 **TE 16, 18**
Final Consonants	19 **TE 19**
Short Vowels	16, 20–21 **TE 20**
Long Vowels	17
Sound–Symbol Association	
Picture Clues	12–14, 16–17 **TE 16**
Consonants	16–19 **TE 18–19**
Short Vowels	16, 20–21 **TE 20**
Long Vowels	17

PHONICS/SPELLING PRINCIPLES

Phonics: Consonants	
Spellings for |b|	16, 18–19
Spellings for |d|	16, 18–19, 43, 45, 84, 92

PHONICS/SPELLING PRINCIPLES *(continued)*

Spellings for |f|	16, 18–19, 37, 45, **84–85**, 92, 211, 246 **TRB** 49 **TESTS: TE** 84A, 87 **TRB** 52
Spellings for |g|	16, 19, 84, 92
Spellings for |h|	17, 37, 45
Spellings for |j|	17–18, 45
Spellings for |k|	17, **78–79**, 82, 91, 245 **TRB** 45, 53 **TESTS: TE** 78A, 81 **TRB** 48
Spellings for |ks|	19
Spellings for |kw|	17
Spellings for |l|	16, 18–19, **84–85**, 88, 92, 246 **TRB** 49 **TESTS: TE** 84A, 87 **TRB** 52
Spellings for |m|	16, 18–19, 45, 61
Spellings for |n|	16, 18–19, 43, 45, 61
Spellings for |p|	17–19
Spellings for |r|	17–19
Spellings for |s|	17–19, 61, **84–85**, 92, 246 **TRB** 49 **TESTS: TE** 84A, 87 **TRB** 52
Spellings for |t|	17–19
Spellings for |v|	16
Spellings for |w|	17–18
Spellings for |y|	16, 31
Spellings for |z|	17
Consonant Clusters *(bl, br, cl, dr, fl, gl, gr, nd, sm, st, sw, tr, xt)*	**72–73**, 75, 79, 85, 91, 109, **132–133**, 162, 245, 250 **TRB** 41, 53, 91 **TESTS: TE** 72A, 75, 132A, 135 **TRB** 44, 94

Consonant Digraphs	
ch	114–115, 117–118, 127, 248 **TRB** 73, 81 **TESTS: TE** 114A, 117 **TRB** 76
ng	132–133, 136, 162, 250 **TRB** 91 **TESTS: TE** 132A, 135 **TRB** 94
nk	132–133, 162, 250 **TRB** 91 **TESTS: TE** 132A, 135 **TRB** 94
sh	114–115, 117, 127, 248 **TRB** 73, 81 **TESTS: TE** 114A, 117 **TRB** 76
th	120–121, 124, 128, 249 **TRB** 77, 81 **TESTS: TE** 120A, 123 **TRB** 80
wh	120–121, 124, 128, 249 **TRB** 77, 81 **TESTS: TE** 120A, 123 **TRB** 80
Double Consonants	84–85, 88, 92, 246 **TRB** 49 **TESTS: TE** 84A, 87 **TRB** 52
Phonics: Patterns for Short Vowels	
Spellings for |ă|	16, 20–21, **24**–25, 27, 28, 54, 241 **TRB** 5, 25, 28 **TESTS: TE** 24A, 27 **TRB** 8
Spellings for |ĕ|	16, 20–21, **30**–31, 34, 54, 241 **TRB** 9, 25, 28 **TESTS: TE** 30A, 33 **TRB** 12
Spellings for |ĭ|	16, 20–21, **36**–37, 40, 55, 242 **TRB** 13, 25, 28 **TESTS: TE** 36A, 39 **TRB** 16
Spellings for |ŏ|	16, 20–21, **42**–43, 55, 242 **TRB 17, 25, 28** **TESTS: TE** 42A, 45 **TRB** 20

PHONICS/SPELLING PRINCIPLES/Phonics: Patterns for Short Vowels *(continued)*

Spellings for |ŭ|	16, 20–21, **48**–49, 52, 56, 243 **TRB** 21, 25, 28 **TESTS: TE** 48A, 51 **TRB** 24
Phonics: Patterns for Long Vowels	
Spellings for |ā|	17, **60**–61, 64, 90, **96**–97, 126, 244, 247 **TRB** 33, 61, 81 **TESTS: TE** 60A, 63, 96A, 99 **TRB** 36, 64
Spellings for |ē|	17, **66**–67, 90, **102**–103, 106, 126, **174**–175, 178, 198, 244, 247, 253 **TRB** 37, 65, 81, 123 **TESTS: TE** 66A, 69, 102A, 105, 174A, 177 **TRB** 40, 68, 126
Spellings for |ī|	17, **60**–61, 90, **168**–169, 198, 244, 253 **TRB** 33, 119 **TESTS: TE** 60A, 63, 168A, 171 **TRB** 36, 122
Spellings for |ō|	17, **66**–67, 70, 90, **144**–145, 163, 244, 251 **TRB** 37, 99 **TESTS: TE** 66A, 69, 144A, 147 **TRB** 40, 102
Spellings for |yo͞o|	17, **66**–67, 90, 244 **TRB** 37 **TESTS: TE** 66A, 69 **TRB** 40
Phonics: Patterns for Vowel + *r*	
Spellings for |är|	**204**–205, 208, 234, 256 **TRB** 147 **TESTS: TE** 204A, 207 **TRB** 150
Spellings for |ôr|	**210**–211, 214, 234, 256 **TRB** 151 **TESTS: TE** 210A, 213 **TRB** 154
Spellings for |ər|	**216**–217, 235, 257 **TRB** 155 **TESTS: TE** 216A, 219 **TRB** 158

Phonics: Patterns for Schwa	
Spellings for |ər| (*See* SPELLING PRINCIPLES: Patterns for Vowel + *r*)	
Phonics: Patterns for Other Vowel Sounds	
Spellings for |ô|	**108**–109, 112, 127, 248 **TRB** 69, 81 **TESTS: TE** 108A, 111 **TRB** 72
Spellings for |ŏŏ|	**150**–151, 154, 163, 251 **TRB** 103 **TESTS: TE** 150A, 153 **TRB** 106
Spellings for |ōō|	**150**–151, 154, 163, 251 **TRB** 103 **TESTS: TE** 150A, 153 **TRB** 106
Spellings for |ou|	**180**–181, 184, 199, 254 **TRB** 127 **TESTS: TE** 180A, 183 **TRB** 130
Word Structure	
Configuration Clues	**TRB** 5
Inflected Forms (*-s, -ed, -ing*) Plurals	**138**–139, 162, 250 **TRB** 95 **TESTS: TE** 138A, 141 **TRB** 98
Dropping Final *e*	**228**–229, 236, 258 **TRB** 163 **TESTS: TE** 228A, 231 **TRB** 166
Doubling Final Consonant	**222**–223, 235, 257 **TRB** 159 **TESTS: TE** 222A, 225 **TRB** 162
Comparative Endings (*See* MECHANICS AND USAGE: Usage—Comparative Forms of Adjectives and Adverbs)	
Compound Words	**186**–187, 189, 190, 199, 254 **TRB** 131, 139 **TESTS: TE** 186A, 189 **TRB** 134

PHONICS/SPELLING PRINCIPLES/Word Structure *(continued)*

Contractions	**192**–193, 195–196, 200, 255 **TRB** 135–136, 139 **TESTS: TE** 192A, 195 **TRB** 138
Syllable Patterns Syllabication and Stress	**174**, 216–217
Spelling and Meaning	
Word Families/Word Forms	**57**, **93**, **129**, **165**, **201**, **237**, 272–275
Special Study Words	
Homographs	226
Homophones	**156**–160, 164, 196, 211, 252 **TRB** 107–109, 111 **TESTS: TE** 156A, 159 **TRB** 110

VOCABULARY SKILLS AND STRATEGIES	
Skills	
Antonyms	55, 73, 85, 91, 133, 145, 163, 169, 198, 200, 217, 220, 244, 256 **TE** 174A **TRB** 34, 120
Base Words *(See also* PHONICS/ SPELLING PRINCIPLES: Word Structure— Inflected Forms; DICTIONARY SKILLS)	57, 93, 129, 165, 201, 237, 272–275
Cloze Activities	29, 31, 32, 35, 41, 43, 44, 47, 49, 50, 53–57, 65, 68, 71, 73, 80, 83, 89, 90–93, 101, 103, 107, 109–110, 112, 115, 119, 121–122, 125–129, 134, 136–137, 143, 149, 151, 155, 157–158, 160–165, 173, 181, 188, 191, 197–201, 206, 208, 212, 215, 217–218, 221, 223, 227, 233–237, 241–258 **TRB** 5, 14–15, 17, 19, 21, 37, 43, 46, 49–51, 63, 65, 70, 75, 91, 103–104, 107, 109, 119, 135–137, 147–148, 156, 159, 161, 163
Compound Words	**186**–190, 191, 199, 254 **TE** 186A **TRB** 131–132 **TESTS: TE** 186A, 189 **TRB** 134

Definitions (*See also* VOCABULARY SKILLS AND STRATEGIES: Skills— Multiple Meanings; DICTIONARY SKILLS)	25, 62, 79, **110**, 146, 152, 170, 175, 182, 206, 211, 218, 251, 253, 257 **TE** 24A, 29, 35, 41, 42A, 47, 53, 60A, 65, 71, 77, 78A, 83, 89, 96A, 101, 102A, 107, 113, 119, 125, 137, 143, 144A, 149, 155, 161, 173, 174A, 179, 180A, 185, 191, 197, 204A, 209, 210A, 215, 221, 227, 233 **TRB** 7, 18, 42, 62, 96, 123, 151, 155, 157, 160, 164
Exact Words	**46**, 76, 95, 100, 131, 148, 167, 172, 202, 203, 239 **TE** 71, 75, 119 **TRB** 146
Homographs	226
Homophones (*See also* DICTIONARY SKILLS)	**156–160**, 164, 196, 252 **TE** 156A **TRB** 107–109, 111 **TESTS: TE** 156A, 159 **TRB** 110
Idioms	**TE** 222A
Multiple Meanings (*See also* DICTIONARY SKILLS: Definitions)	**146**, 170, 182, 206 **TE** 24A, 24, 30, 36, 42A, 42, 48, 60A, 60, 66, 72, 78A, 78, 84, 96A, 96, 102A, 102, 108, 114A, 114, 120, 132, 138, 144A, 144, 150, 156, 168, 174, 180, 186, 204A, 204, 210A, 210, 216, 222, 228
Phonograms/Rhyming Words	25, 28, 31, 33–34, 40, 43, 45, 49, 51–52, 54, 64, 67, 70, 75, 81–82, 85, 88, 90, 97, 103, 109, 111–112, 121, 123, 127, 133, 136, 139, 145, 151, 154, 159, 162, 178, 181, 184, 199, 205, 207–208, 211, 214, 219, 223, 236, 242, 246, 248, 250, 257 **TE** 48A, 66A, 84A, 108A, 132A, 139, 150A, 168A, 180A, 204A, 228A **TRB** 10, 13, 45, 61, 92, 99, 105, 124, 128
Suffixes	142, 232
Synonyms	25, 55, 76, 91, 100, 115, 157, 172, 187, 229 **TE** 204A **TRB** 111
Using a Thesaurus	**46**, 76, 95, 100, 131, 148, 167, 172, 202, 203, 239
Word Families/Word Forms (*See also* DICTIONARY SKILLS: Word Forms)	57, 93, 129, 160, 165, 201, 237
Content Area Vocabulary	
Art	29 **TE** 29 **TRB** 7
Careers	113, 125 **TE** 113, 125 **TRB** 71, 79

VOCABULARY SKILLS AND STRATEGY/Content Area Vocabulary *(continued)*

Health	47, 191 **TE** 47, 191 **TRB** 19, 133
Math	143 **TE** 143 **TRB** 97
Performing Arts	89 **TE** 89 **TRB** 51
Physical Education/Recreation	77, 227 **TE** 77, 227 **TRB** 43, 161
Science	35, 53, 71, 83, 107, 149, 155, 173, 179, 197, 221 **TE** 35, 53, 71, 83, 107, 149, 155, 173, 179, 197, 221 **TRB** 11, 23, 39, 47, 67, 101, 105, 121, 125, 137, 157
Social Studies	41, 65, 101, 119, 137, 170, 185, 209, 215, 233 **TE** 41, 65, 101, 119, 137, 170, 185, 209, 215, 233 **TRB** 15, 35, 63, 75, 93, 109, 129, 149, 153, 165

MECHANICS AND USAGE

Capitalization	
of First Word in a Sentence	**33, 45, 259**
in Greetings and Closings in Letters	**261**
of the Pronoun *I*	**259**
of Proper Nouns	**63, 77, 135, 141, 153, 259**
of Titles of Long and Short Works	**189, 260**
of Titles with Names	**177, 259**
Punctuation	
Apostrophes in Contractions	**192–193, 200, 255, 260** **TRB** 136

Commas	
with City and State	**213**, 260
with Dates	**195**, 260
after Greetings and Closings in Letters	**219**, **260**–261
Periods	**33**, **177**, 260
Question Marks	**45**, 260
Underlining	**189**, 260
Usage	
Comparative Forms of Adjectives and Adverbs	**117**
Pronouns	**99**

LITERATURE AND WRITING

Types of Literature	
Fiction (poem, story, tall tale)	58, 94, 130, 202
Nonfiction	166
Letter	238
Reading Comprehension Skills	
Following Written Directions	All pupil book pages
Identifying Details	58, 94, 130, 166, 202
Identifying Main Idea/Topic Sentence/ Supporting Details	94, 166
Identifying Point of View	58
Making Inferences/Drawing Conclusions	58, 94, 130, 202, 238
Predicting Outcomes	130
Reading for Information	29, 35, 40, 46, 52, 64, 70, 76, 82, 88, 100, 106, 112, 118, 124, 136, 142, 148, 154, 160, 166, 172, 178, 184, 190, 196, 208, 214, 220, 226, 232
Recognizing Sequence	130, 166
Using Context Clues	54, 55, 56, 57, 71, 86, 90, 91, 92, 93, 119, 126, 127, 128, 129, 134, 158, 162, 163, 164, 165, 182, 188, 198, 199, 200, 201, 212, 234, 235, 236, 241, 242, 243, 244, 245, 246, 247, 248, 249, 250, 251, 252, 253, 254, 255, 256, 257, 258 **TRB** 5, 14–15, 17, 19, 21, 37, 43, 46, 49–51, 63, 65, 70, 75, 91, 103–104, 107, 109, 119, 135–137, 147–148, 156, 159, 161, 163

LITERATURE AND WRITING *(continued)*

Types of Writing	
Ad	40, 75, 101, 141, 214 **TE** 33, 207 **TRB** 97, 129
Announcement/Notice/Message	**TRB** 67, 101
Book Titles	189
Brochure	**TE** 153
Bumper Stickers	207
Captions	76, 171, 226
Catalog	**TE** 141
Clues	190, 208 **TRB** 47
Commercial	**TE** 213
Comparison and Contrast	**TRB** 125
Creative Writing	33, 39, 69, 70, 88, 101, 123, 135, 141, 147, 153, 154, 159, 161, 171, 195, 219, 225, 233 **TRB** 7, 39, 42, 67, 70, 79, 121, 129, 133
Daily Plan	63
Dialogue	**TRB** 7
Description	33, 34, 117, 159, 203
Diary/Journal Entry	71, 195 **TE** 51, 225
Dictionary	**TE** 75
Expository Writing *(See also* LITERATURE AND WRITING: Types of Writing— Comparison and Contrast, Instructions, Report*)*	**TRB** 11, 71, 93, 153, 165
Fairy Tale	**TE** 135
Friendly Letter	53, 177, 219, 239 **TE** 81
Guidebook	**TE** 153
Instructions	111, 167 **TE** 189

Interview	**TE** 231
Invitation	27
Jingle	**TE** 213
Label	123 **TE** 39, 69, 207
List	51, 63, 87, 213
Message	161 **TE** 159
Personal Narrative	59, 95, 99, 183, 231
Play	233
Poem	70 **TE** 99, 147
Post Card	81
Program	147
Questions	**TE** 195
Riddles	153, 197
Safety Quiz	45
Safety Rules	**TE** 45
Science Fiction	**TE** 171
Sentences	34, 44, 80, 88, 98, 100, 122, 146, 148, 154, 170, 172, 212, 230
Speech	105, 225 **TE** 87
Story	39, 59, 69, 95, 99, 131, 183, 231 **TE** 123, 219
Titles/Headlines	**TRB** 121
Tongue Twisters	**TE** 117
Weekly Plan	135
Writing Process (prewriting, drafting, revising, proofreading, publishing)	
Class Story	59 **TRB** 31
Personal Narrative	95 **TRB** 59

LITERATURE AND WRITING/Writing Process *(continued)*

Instructions	167 **TRB** 118
Story	131 **TRB** 88
Description	203 **TE** 27, 63, 111, 177, 183 **TRB** 146
Friendly Letter	239 **TRB** 174
Composition Skills	
Selecting and Narrowing a Topic	59, 95, 167, 203, 239 **TRB** 31, 59, 88, 118, 146, 174
Purpose and Audience	239 **TRB** 31, 88, 146, 174
Main Idea/Topic Sentence/Supporting Details	95, 131, 167, 203, 239
Using Details	59, 95, 131, 167, 203, 239 **TRB** 174
Sequence of Steps/Order Words	59, 167 **TRB** 118
Plot	131 **TRB** 88
Exact Words	59, 95, 131, 167, 202, 203, 239 **TRB** 146
Sense Words	203 **TRB** 146
Letter Form Friendly Letter	239, 261
Handwriting	
Manuscript Models	316 **TRB** 185, 187, 189, 191
Cursive Models	316 **TRB** 186, 188, 190, 192

PROOFREADING

For Capitalization	
of First Word in Sentence	33, 45, 59, 167
of Proper Nouns	63, 75, 95, 134, 141, 153
of Titles of Long and Short Works	189
of Titles with Names	177, 203
For Punctuation	
Apostrophes in Contractions	195 **TRB** 136
Commas with City and State with Dates after Greetings and Closings in Letters	213 195 219, 239
Periods after Abbreviations at the End of a Sentence	177 33, 59, 167
Question Marks	45, 59, 167
Underlining	189
For Spelling	
Misspelled Words	27, 33, 39, 45, 51, 59, 63, 69, 75, 81, 87, 95, 99, 105, 111, 118, 123, 131, 135, 141, 147, 153, 159, 167, 171, 177, 183, 189, 195, 203, 207, 213, 219, 225, 231, 239 **TRB** 10, 22, 38, 46, 70, 78, 100, 108, 124, 136, 152, 164
For Correct Usage	
Comparative Forms of Adjectives and Adverbs	117, 131
Pronouns	99

THINKING SKILLS AND STRATEGIES

Analyzing	24–25, 30–31, 36–37, 42–43, 48–49, 57, 60–61, 66–67, 72–73, 78–79, 84–85, 93, 96–97, 102–103, 108–109, 114–115, 120–121, 129, 132–133, 138–139, 144–145, 150–151, 156–157, 165, 168–169, 174–175, 180–181, 186–187, 192–193, 201, 204–205, 210–211, 216–217, 222–223, 228–229, 237 **TRB** 93, 125, 153

THINKING SKILLS AND STRATEGIES *(continued)*

Brainstorming	59, 95, 131, 167, 203, 239 **TRB** 31, 59, 88, 118, 146, 174
Classifying/Categorizing	25, 31, 37, 43, 49, 57, 60–61, 66–67, 72–73, 77–79, 84–85, 93, 96–97, 102–103, 108–109, 114–115, 120–121, 129, 132–133, 138–139, 144–145, 150–151, 156–157, 165, 168–169, 175, 180–181, 187, 193, 201, 205, 211, 217, 222–223, 228–229, 237 **TRB** 9, 13, 33, 45, 53, 65, 69, 73, 77, 81, 91, 99, 103, 119, 127, 137, 151, 157
Comparing and Contrasting	**TRB** 125
Creative Thinking	33, 39, 69, 70, 88, 101, 123, 135, 141, 147, 153, 154, 159, 161, 171, 195, 219, 225, 233 **TRB** 7, 39, 42, 67, 70, 79, 121, 129, 133
Critical Thinking	29, 35, 41, 47, 65, 77, 83, 89, 107, 113, 125, 137, 143, 149, 155, 173, 179, 185, 191, 209, 215, 221, 226 **TRB** 93, 125, 153, 165
Evaluating	59, 95, 131, 167, 203, 239
Identifying Main Idea	166
Making Analogies	31, 49, 73, 109, 121, 151, 157, 181, 217 **TRB** 148
Making Generalizations	24, 30, 36, 42, 48, 60, 66, 72, 78, 84, 96, 102, 108, 114, 120, 132, 138, 144, 150, 156, 168, 174, 180, 186, 192, 204, 210, 216, 222, 228
Making Inferences/Drawing Conclusions	37, 50, 54, 57, 61, 85, 86, 92, 98, 103, 126, 139, 152, 162, 164, 187, 198, 223, 235, 241, 242, 243, 245, 247, 250, 254, 258 **TRB** 15, 23, 43, 46, 51, 67, 70, 75, 77, 91, 103, 109, 133, 137, 159, 161
Predicting Outcomes	130 **TRB** 133
Problem Solving	231 **TRB** 15, 43, 51, 75, 109, 161, 165
Sequencing	26, 38, 50, 68, 74, 110, 122, 130–131, 134, 135, 147, 158, 166–167, 170, 182, 218, 230 **TRB** 88, 118

Synthesizing	27, 33, 39, 40, 45, 51, 53, 59, 63, 69, 71, 72, 75, 81, 87, 95, 99, 101, 105, 111, 117, 123, 131, 135, 141, 147, 153, 159, 161, 167, 171, 177, 183, 189, 195, 197, 203, 207, 213, 219, 225, 231, 233, 239 **TE** 25, 31, 37, 43, 49, 61, 67, 73, 79, 85, 97, 103, 109, 115, 121, 133, 139, 145, 151, 157, 169, 175, 181, 187, 193, 205, 211, 217, 223, 229 **TRB** 129
Using Graphic Organizers	142, 232 **TRB** 31, 59, 88, 118, 146, 174

LISTENING AND SPEAKING SKILLS AND STRATEGIES

Listening	
in a Cooperative Learning Activity	33, 39, 45, 74, 75, 87, 105, 116, 146, 153, 159, 183, 197, 206, 225, 231 **TE** 74, 116, 146, 206
for Correct Pronunciation	24, 30, 36, 42, 48, 60, 66, 72, 78, 84, 96, 102, 108, 114, 120, 132, 138, 144, 150, 156, 168, 174, 180, 186, 192, 204, 210, 216, 222, 228
to Follow Directions (*See* LITERATURE AND WRITING: Reading Comprehension Skills)	
to Make Inferences/Draw Conclusions (*See also* THINKING SKILLS AND STRATEGIES)	**TE** 36A, 48A, 132A
for Meaning	**TE** 24A, 42A, 48A, 60A, 66A, 72A, 78A, 84A, 96A, 102A, 108A, 114A, 132A, 138A, 144A, 150A, 156A, 168A, 174A, 186A, 192A, 204A, 210A, 216A, 222A, 228A
to Recall Details	**TE** 24A, 30A, 36A, 60A, 66A, 72A, 78A, 84A, 96A, 102A, 108A, 114A, 120A, 132A, 138A, 144A, 150A, 156A, 168A, 174A, 186A, 192A, 204A, 210A, 216A, 222A, 228A
for Rhyme (*See also* VOCABULARY SKILLS AND STRATEGIES: Skills)	**TE** 36A, 42A, 48A, 66A, 96A, 108A, 132A, 150A, 168A, 180A, 204A, 228A
for Sequence (*See also* LITERATURE AND WRITING: Reading Comprehension Skills)	**TE** 120A
in a Writing Conference	59, 95, 131, 167, 203, 239

LISTENING AND SPEAKING SKILLS AND STRATEGIES *(continued)*

Speaking	
in a Cooperative Learning Activity	33, 39, 45, 75, 87, 95, 105, 131, 153, 159, 167, 183, 197, 203, 225, 231 **TE** 26, 68, 74, 140, 152, 176, 188, 206, 218 **TRB** 28, 56, 84, 114, 142–143, 170–171
Discussing to Revise Written Compositions	59, 95, 131, 167, 203, 239
Dramatizing	95 **TE** 233
Giving a Report/Speech	105, 225 **TE** 107, 215
Interviewing	**TE** 197
Participating in Discussions	58, 94, 130, 166, 202, 238
Pronouncing Words Correctly	24, 30, 36, 42, 48, 60, 66, 72, 78, 83–84, 96, 102, 108, 114, 120, 125, 132, 138, 144, 150, 156, 161, 168, 174, 180, 186, 192, 204, 210, 216, 222, 227–228
Responding to Literature	58, 94, 130, 166, 202, 238
Telling a Story	59

DICTIONARY SKILLS	
Alphabetical Order	26, 38, 50, 68, 80, 86, 104, 122, 276 **TRB** 9, 11, 49, 128
Base Words	224, 230, 276
Definitions	110, 146, 158, 170, 182, 206, 276
Entry Words	68, 80, 86, 104, 110, 122, 276
Guide Words	86, 104, 276
Homophones	156–160, 164, 196, 252
Parts of a Dictionary	50
Parts of an Entry	276
Sample Sentences/Phrases	110, 276
Word Forms	224, 230, 276

Teacher's Edition

For each of the selections listed below, grateful acknowledgment is made for permission to excerpt and/or reprint original or copyrighted material as follows:

UPWORDS®, SCRABBLE®, and BOGGLE® are registered trademarks of Hasbro Inc. Used by permission of Hasbro Inc. All rights reserved.

"Word Lists for Qualitative Spelling Inventory Table" from *Qualitative Inventory of Word Knowledge*, by Edmund Henderson and Marcia Invernizzi. Used by permission of Marcia Invernizzi, McGuffey Reading Center, University of Virginia.

Photography: Banta Digital Services—viii. Allan Landau—pp. iv, v, 28, 34, 76, 100, 178, 196. Steve Nelson—pp. 52, 116, 218, 226. Tony Scarpetta—pp. iii, vi, vii, viii, 40, 46, 50, 64, 68, 70, 82, 88, 104, 106, 118, 124, 136, 140, 142, 148, 154, 152, 172, 184, 190, 208, 214, 220. Katherine Templeton—iii.

Blackline Masters

The blackline masters in the following section can help you assess each student's level of word knowledge and reinforce students' development of word analysis skills and recognition of word relationships.

This section includes ten masters.

Qualitative Spelling Inventory Checklist This checklist is intended to be used with the Qualitative Spelling Inventory on page xvi of this Teacher's Edition. The inventory will reveal the types of spelling errors, or miscues, your students make. By identifying these error types, you will be able to confirm the developmental phase of spelling at which each student is functioning and help children focus on the particular patterns or principles with which they need further instruction or practice.

The checklist can be used throughout the year to document children's progress.

Graphic Organizers The graphic organizers provide charts where children can try out and record spellings of words they're working with as well as interesting visuals to help children work with common word parts and spelling patterns. Using the graphic organizers, children can see how word parts are combined to build words. This practice with word construction and analysis helps build a strong foundation of word knowledge.

Directions for using each master are included on the master along with suggested units where it could be appropriately used.

Qualitative Spelling Inventory Checklist

This checklist will help you identify the particular stage of spelling development for each student and whether the student is in the early, middle, or late phase of that stage. Using the list from the Qualitative Spelling Inventory, found on page xvi of the Teacher's Edition, that corresponds to the student's instructional level, check for the features below. The last feature for which you check "Often" corresponds to the student's stage of development.

Alphabetic Stage

Early
- Is there a vowel in each word?　　　　Yes_____　　Often _____　　No_____

Middle
- Are consonant blends and digraphs　　Yes_____　　Often _____　　No_____
  correct? (*track/shade*)

Late
- Are short vowels spelled correctly?　　Yes_____　　Often _____　　No_____
  (*hid, chop, such*)
- Are *m* and *n* included in front of other　Yes_____　　Often _____　　No_____
  consonants? (*bump, pink*)

Within-Word Pattern Stage

Early
- Are long-vowel spellings in single-　　Yes_____　　Often _____　　No_____
  syllable words "used but confused"?
  (*SLIED for slide, MAIK for make*)

Middle
- Are many long vowels in single-　　　Yes_____　　Often _____　　No_____
  syllable words spelled correctly but
  some long-vowel spellings still "used
  but confused"?

Late
- Are most *r*- and *l*-influenced vowels in　Yes_____　　Often _____　　No_____
  single-syllable words spelled correctly?
  (*start, milk*)

Syllables and Affixes Stage

Early
- Are inflectional endings added correctly to base words with short vowel patterns? (*hugging, pinned*)   Yes_____   Often _____   No_____

- Are consonant doublets spelled correctly? (*dollar, letter*)   Yes_____   Often _____   No_____

Middle
- Are inflectional endings added correctly to base words with long-vowel patterns? (*waving, striped*)   Yes_____   Often _____   No_____

Late
- Are less-frequent prefixes and suffixes spelled correctly? (*confession, production, capture, collar*)   Yes_____   Often _____   No_____

Derivational Patterns Stage

Early
- Are most polysyllabic words spelled correctly? (*expansion, community*)   Yes_____   Often _____   No_____

Middle
- Are unaccented vowels in derived words spelled correctly? (*prohibition, opposition*)   Yes_____   Often _____   No_____

Late
- Are absorbed prefixes spelled correctly? (*irrelevant, accomplish*)   Yes_____   Often _____   No_____

Adapted from *Words Their Way* by Donald R. Bear, Marcia Invernizzi, Shane Templeton, Francine Johnston (Englewood Cliffs, NJ: Prentice-Hall, 1996)

Have a Go!

First try	Second try	Correct

Instructions: Encourage children to use this chart to try out spellings of new words they want to spell, using any spelling patterns they have learned. Check their efforts, and show them the correct spellings, if necessary. Praise correct applications of spelling patterns. **Suggested for use anytime.**

Words I Can Spell

Date	Word

Instructions: Have children keep track of new words they have learned to spell by writing each Spelling Word and the date. **Suggested for use anytime.**

Word Building (1 Word Family)

Instructions: Choose a word family to be written on the mother duck's wings. For each duckling, choose a consonant or a cluster that can be combined with the word family to make a word. Then have children write rhyming words, using the consonants or clusters and the word family. **Suggested for use with Units 1, 2, 3, 4, 5, 7, 8, 10, 11, 13, 15, 19, 21, 22, 25, and 27.**

Word Building (2 Word Families)

Instructions: Choose two word families to be written on the kites, one on each kite. For each kite tail, choose a consonant or a cluster that can be combined with the word family to make a word. Then have children write rhyming words, using the consonants or clusters and the word families. **Suggested for use with Units 1, 2, 3, 4, 5, 7, 8, 10, 11, 13, 15, 19, 21, 22, 25, and 27.**

362 Teacher Resources

Word Building (3 Word Families)

Instructions: Choose three word families to be written on the dinosaurs, one word famly on each dinosaur. For the rocks and plants, choose consonants or clusters that can be combined with the word families to make words. Then have children write sets of rhyming words, using the consonants or clusters and the word families. Ask children to write the word sets in the boxes provided. **Suggested for use with Units 1, 2, 3, 4, 5, 7, 8, 10, 11, 13, 15, 19, 21, 22, and 27.**

Word Web

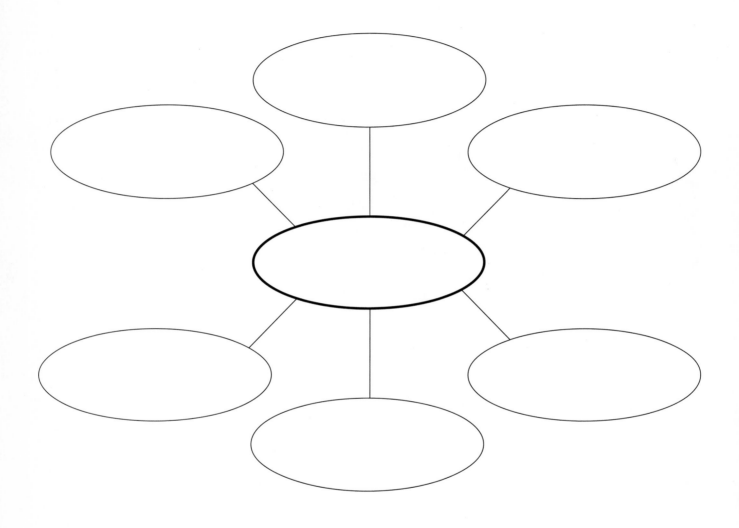

Instructions: Choose a phonogram to be written in the center oval. Then have children work in small groups to make rhyming words, using the word family. Ask children to write the words in the satellite ovals. **Suggested for use with Units 1, 2, 3, 4, 5, 7, 8, 10, 11, 13, 15, 19, 22, 25, and 27.**

Word Sort

Instructions: Write a word in each strip, one letter per box. Then cut out each word strip. Have children sort the words by vowel sound, alliteration, rhyme, concept, pattern, structure, or children's own logic. **Suggested for use anytime.**

Word Sort

Instructions: Write a word in each strip, one letter per box. Then cut out each word strip. Have children sort the words by vowel sound, alliteration, rhyme, concept, pattern, structure, or children's own logic.
Suggested for use anytime.